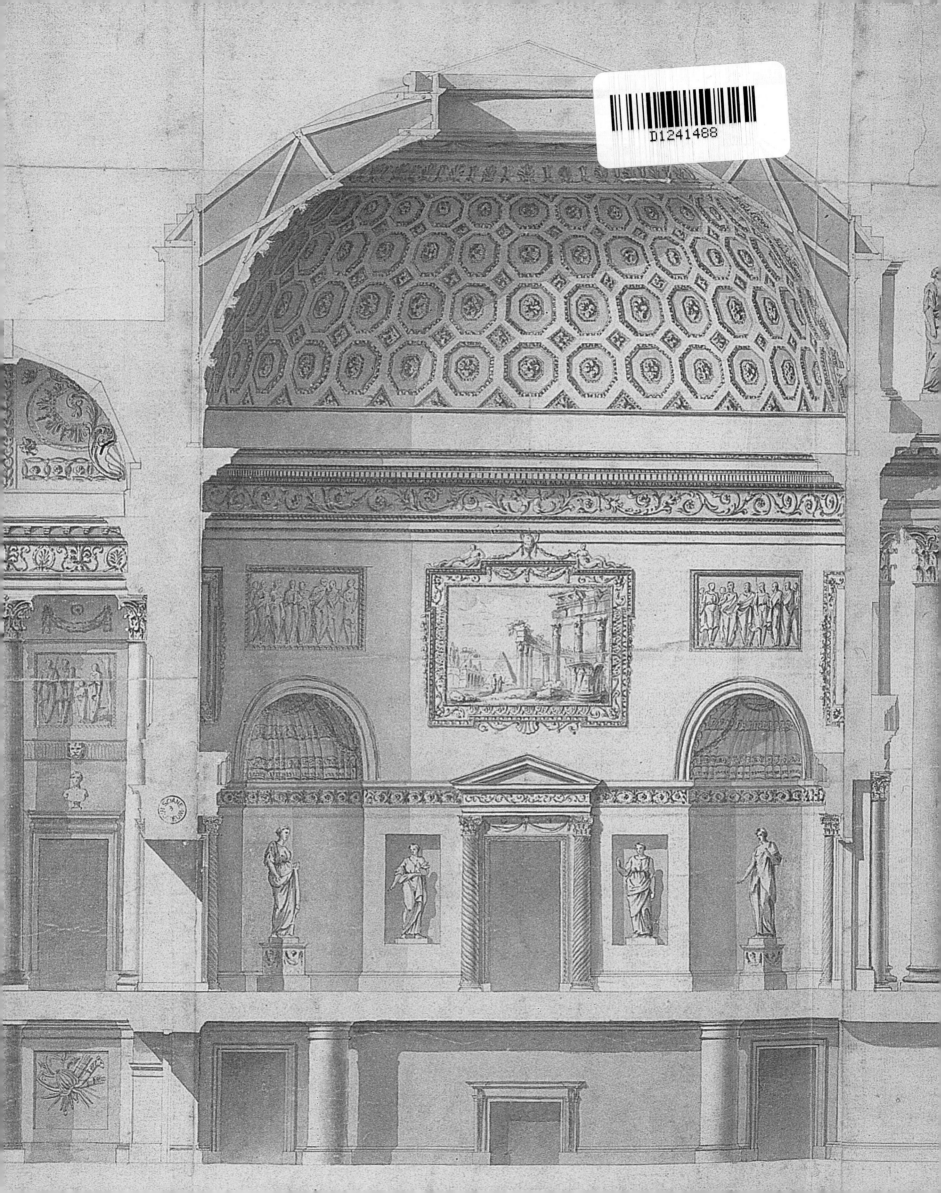

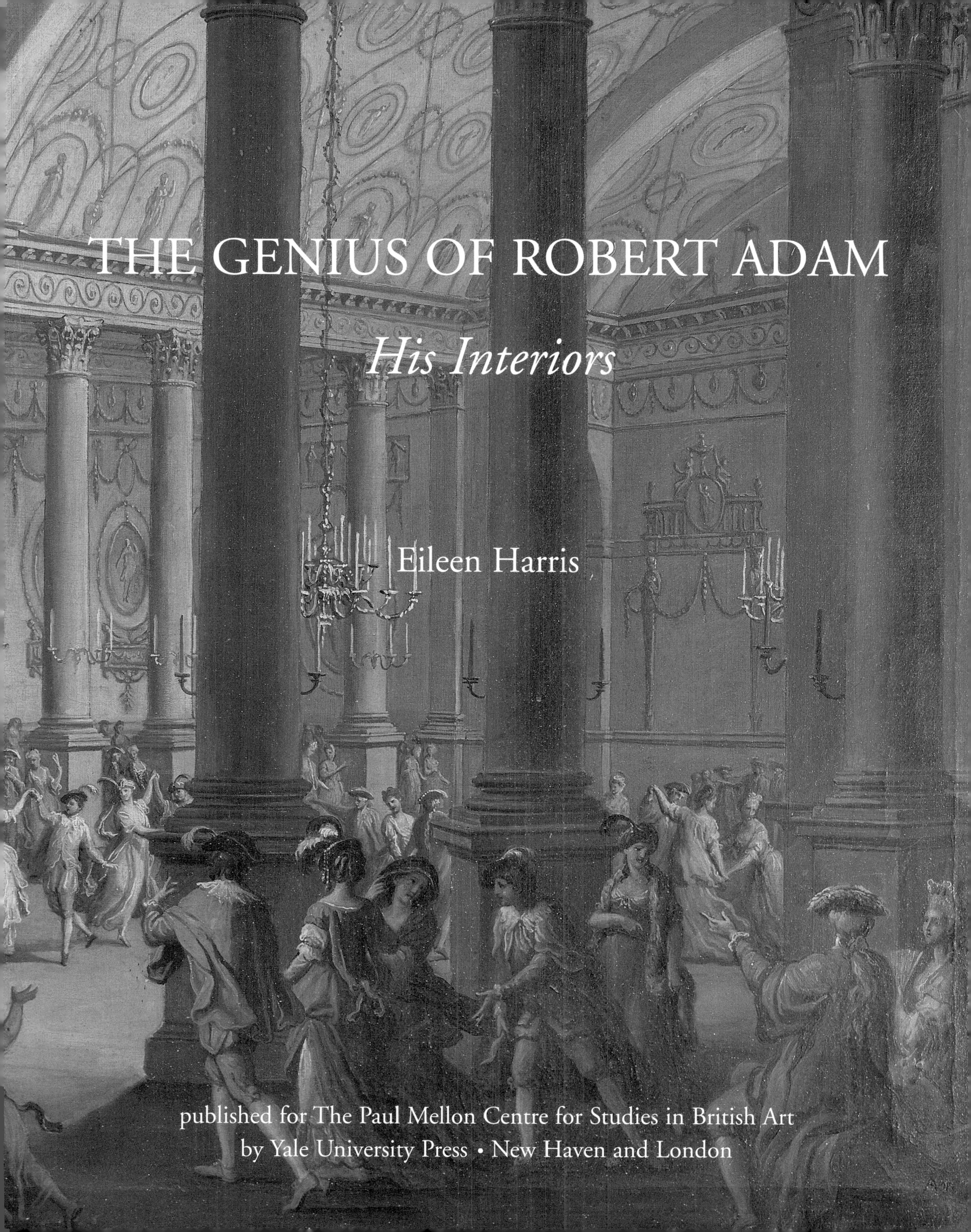

THE GENIUS OF ROBERT ADAM

His Interiors

Eileen Harris

published for The Paul Mellon Centre for Studies in British Art
by Yale University Press • New Haven and London

Typeset in Adobe Garamond by Best-set Typesetter Ltd, Hong Kong
Designed by Sally Salvesen
Printed in Singapore

Library of Congress Cataloging-in-Publication Data
Harris, Eileen.
The genius of Robert Adam : his interiors / Eileen Harris.
p. cm.
Includes bibliographical references and index.
ISBN 0-300-08129-4 (alk. paper)
1. Adam, Robert, 1728–1792 – Criticism and interpretation. 2. Interior architecture – Great Britain.
3. Architcture, Domestic – Great Britain. 4. Architecture – Great Britain – 18th century. I. Title.
NA997.A4 H368 2001
728.8´092–dc21
2001003036

ILLUSTRATIONS

HALF TITLE PAGE
Detail of a commode with a medallion depicting Venus explaining the torch of Hymen
to Cupid from an engraving after Angelica Kauffmann. Osterley Park.

TITLE PAGE
The ball-room in the pavilion erected for the Earl of Derby's *fête champêtre* at The Oaks, Surrey,
designed by Robert Adam, 1774. Collection of the Earl of Derby

PAGE VI
Design for a mirrored wall decoration in the Chinese style for an unspecified client, by Robert Adam, 1769
(Sir John Soane's Museum: Adam drawings, vol. 20:73)

PAGE X
Detail of a design for the ceiling of the library or 'Sanctuary', Home House, 20 Portman Square, London,
representing the triumph of wisdom with twelve cameos of the most celebrated poets and philosophers including Robert Adam,
by Robert Adam, c.1775 (Sir John Soane's Museum: Adam drawings, vol. 12:163)

For

JOHN FLEMING

A valued friend whose work on Robert Adam is my lodestar

CONTENTS

PREFACE

Robert Adam's name is so well known that it might be thought that nothing more need be written about him, or conversely that everything will be contained in my book. Both ideas are far from the truth and should be buried without delay.

Interiors were Adam's great achievement, his claim to fame. Yet architectural historians have on the whole shied away from his decorative work, fearing, it seems, that focus on this subject detracts from, and may even obscure, his importance as an architect. Quite the contrary; it enlarges it. The synthesis of architecture, planning and decoration is at the heart of Adam's achievement and only by considering these elements together and in depth can the breadth of his genius be properly appreciated.

The bulk of Adam's work was in pre-existing houses. In order to know exactly what he did and why, how much of his work was determined by circumstances and how much was left to invention, it is essential to set the scene at the time of his arrival: to identify the problems which he set out to rectify. It is equally important to know how much of what we see today has been affected by later alterations and renovations; by Adam-Revival additions and even by so-called accurate restorations undertaken during the past twenty-five years.

Though we are extremely fortunate in having a large corpus of drawings from the Adam office at the Soane Museum, they can be misleading, especially if considered in isolation. Close study of archival sources, other related drawings and above all the houses themselves often provided more accurate dates and identifications. The task was enormous and a great deal remains to be done.

I have concentrated on Adam's most complete and accomplished interiors. They are but a fraction of his total *œuvre*. To have attempted to submit all his interiors to the same detailed examination would not have been possible in my lifetime, nor would it have significantly altered the overall picture. The houses are arranged as nearly as possible in chronological order, broken on occasion in order to group the several commissions by a single patron together.

I hope that my efforts will open the way to a better understanding of the genius of Robert Adam.

ACKNOWLEDGEMENTS

The encouragement, advice and constructive criticism given me over the years by Professor Robin Middleton has been invaluable, not only in itself but also in setting a high standard which I have endeavoured to attain. I have also benefited from lengthy and stimulating dialogues with Ian Gow of the National Trust for Scotland and Nick Savage, Librarian of the Royal Academy, whom I frequently bombarded with difficult questions and who often posed others of equal import. Ptolemy Dean's professional architectural training and enthusiastic interest in historic buildings opened my eyes to aspects of Adam's work that might otherwise have escaped me.

A generous grant from the British Academy enabled me to make numerous visits to the surviving Adam houses I have written about and to archive offices up and down the country, from Edinburgh to Plymouth. The owners and custodians of these houses allowed me not only to examine their Adam rooms, but also to explore their basements, attics and roofs, to consult their archives and look at their drawings. I am grateful to Mr and Mrs Robin Compton, the Earl and Countess of Derby, Lady Victoria Fellowes, the Earl of Harewood, the Marquess of Lansdowne, the Duke of Northumberland, the Croome Estate Trust, Diageo (owners of 20 St James's Square), International House (once Coventry House), the Portman Estate (former owners of 20 Portman Square) and Mr Brian Clivaz, managing director of Home House. The largest single owner of Adam houses is the National Trust: many members of its staff have helped me, none more than Anthea Palmer, Tim Knox and the late Gervase Jackson-Stops. I should also like to thank Ian Angus, Jill Banks, Hugo Brown, Alexandra Coldham, Edward Gibbons, Geoffrey Haworth, Simon Jervis, Francesca Scoones, Lyndon Williams and Barry Williams.

Frequent access to the Adam drawings at the Soane Museum was, of course, essential and I am very grateful to Margaret Richardson, Peter Thornton, Susan Palmer, Christopher Woodward and Stephen Astley for making that possible. The Victoria and Albert Museum was my other mine of information. The staff of the Furniture and Woodwork Department were always helpful and encouraging: Frances Collard, Sarah Medlam, Tessa Murdoch, Christopher Wilk and not least James Yorke who responded generously to my numerous requests. Likewise, I wish to acknowledge Susan Lambert and Michael Snodin in the Department of Prints and Drawings, and Martin Durant in the Photographic Library.

I had the benefit of the special knowledge of Mary Mauchinline on Harewood, Francis Russell on the Earl of Bute and Michael Moss on the Kennedys of Culzean. I am grateful to them and to others who helped in various ways: W. H. Adams, Amy Barker, Patrick Baty, Geoffrey Beard, Roger Bowdler, Ian Bristow, Geremy Butler, Jonathan Cardale, Charles Cator, Martin Charles, Sir Howard Colvin, William Connor, Jonathan Cook, John Cornforth, Camilla Costello, Dan Cruickshank, Joan Davidson, Alan Dodd, Anna Eavis, Sebastian Edwards, Lynda Fairbairn, Kate Fielden, Geoffrey Fisher, Desmond Fitzgerald, Oliver Fairclough, Joseph Friedman, Richard Garnier, Jane George, Christopher Gibbs, Mark Girouard, Sir Nicholas and Lady Goodison, Nicholas Grindley, Ruth Guilding, Michael Hall, Ivan Hall, John Hardy, Jonathan Harris, Richard Hewlings, Kathy Hiesinger, Angelo Hornak, Cathy Houghton, Morris Howard, Helen Hughes, Mrs Hutchins, Peter Inskip, Royston Jones, Frank Kelsall, David King, Hugh Krall, Emma Lauze, Peter Leach, Phillipa Lewis, Martin Levy, James Lomax, Nick McCann, Andrew McLean, Edward McParland, James Macauley, James Methuen Campbell, Lee Hunt Miller, Leila Meinertas, Jeremy Musson, Richard Pailthorpe, William Rieder, Hugh Roberts, Isla Roberts, John Martin Robinson, Alistair Rowan, Alan Rubin, Jonathan Scott, Jane Sellars, Mark Slade, Veronica Steele, Lady Shaw Stewart, Lanto Singe, Veronica Steele, Alan Tait, Jill Tovey, Alison Turton, Jane Waddington, Nigel Wilkins, John Wilton-Ely, Philip Winterbottom, Lucy Wood, and Giles Worsley.

It is owing to the dedication and enthusiasm of John Nicoll and Sally Salvesen of Yale University Press and the generous support of The Paul Mellon Centre for British Art and its Director of Studies, Brian Allen that my book is published. *Furthermore*, the publication program of the J. M. Kaplan Fund, awarded me a grant which enabled me to have several plans expertly redrawn by Christopher H. Woodward.

Finally, my warmest thanks to my husband John for his constant encouragement, advice and patience.

RAPHAEL SANCTIVS VRBINAS

INTRODUCTION

... what a pity it is that such a genius (as myself) should be thrown away upon Scotland where scarce will ever happen an opportunity of putting one noble thought in execution.

(Robert Adam to his sister Nelly. Rome, 12 July 1755)[1]

A few months in the stimulating atmosphere of Rome in 1755 brought this truth home to Robert Adam and made him decide, then and there, to aim for an 'English establishment', a practice in London, when he returned from abroad. The importance of this decision cannot be overestimated. It put quite a different complexion on Adam's three years in Rome: it drove and directed his studies, enlarged them, gave them a practical motive – an urgency that they might not otherwise have had – and in the long run affected his whole career. Had he opted to practise in Edinburgh, he would not have needed so long in Rome.

His hard-headed calculation of the challenges posed by the London scheme and his determination to overcome them are spelled out at length in a letter to his brother, James, written on 18 June 1755:

When I came here and had my views confined to Scotland alone I imagined that it would be sufficient for me to enlarge my ideas, to pick up a set of new thoughts which, with some little instruction in drawing I imagined would be sufficient to make one who had seen as much carry all before him in a narrow country where the very name of a traveller acquires respect and veneration to no great geniuses. But with respect to England the affair is quite different. There you have rivals, and these not unformidable: you have people of real taste, and not few of them. The first will do all they can to destroy real merit and the others will judge and from that condemn or approve. For this reason it is evident that unless one can appear equal if not superior to these antagonists, so as to acquire the preference from the connoisseurs, all attempts to succeed, even with good interest, won't continue for any tract of time, so that after a little blaze you are sent home with little honour and less profit. These considerations made me determine to go to the bottom of things – to outdo Chambers in figures, in bas-reliefs and in ornaments, which, with any tolerable degree of taste so as to apply them properly, make a building appear as different as night from day.

You'll own the attempt was bold, but nevertheless I have attempted it. I am drawing hands and feet, from which I make the proper advances to full figures and from that to composing and putting any story or fancy together. My progress is as yet very trivial, though (Laurent) Pecheux, my instructor, gives me great encouragement and assures me in three or four months I shall do infinitely better than Chambers ever did or will do. Thus you see, my dear Jamie, *that* obstacle is not insurmountable. Ornaments come of themselves as I see and copy every day and have made some progress in sketching them – whilst I find my ideas of architecture are a good deal enlarged and my principles of the grand more fixed than ever they were before. Clérisseau preaches to me every day to forbear invention or composing either plans or elevations till I have a greater fund, that is, till I have made more progress in seeing things and my head more filled with proper ornaments and my hand more able to draw to purpose what I would incline, as he very justly says that inventing indifferently and drawing so-so ornaments is to fix these in your head and to prevent you getting into the taste of better ones.[2]

Being told by someone as highly regarded by connoisseurs as Piranesi that he had 'more genius for the true noble architecture than any other Englishman ever was in Italy' gave great encouragement to Adam's London ambitions and to his confidence of success as well.[3] And as if that was not enough, Piranesi declared that his plan of ancient Rome was to be dedicated to him with the title, 'Friend and Architect Dilectantissimo nella Antichità'.[4] He envisaged his name sailing before him in print, giving a 'vast notion' of him to all the connoisseurs in England and Scotland whose 'preference' he sought to acquire.[5] In the event, Piranesi's *Campus Martius* with the promised dedication did not appear until 1762, by which time Adam's career was gathering momentum. Meanwhile, and of more fundamental value, he had the benefit of Piranesi's 'amazing and ingenious fancies' which he described as 'the greatest fund for inspiring and instilling invention in any lover of architecture that can be imagined'.[6]

1   *Loggi di Rafaele nel Vaticano* (1772), title-plate showing groups of visitors studying Raphael's painted decorations in the Vatican loggia, engraved by Giovanni Volpato after a drawing by Pietro Camporesi (Sir John Soane's Museum, hand-coloured copy)

Enlarging his ideas of architecture, improving his draftsmanship and his taste were Adam's foremost concerns, but self-advertisement in the form of a publication as successful as Robert Wood's *Palmyra* (1753) and *Balbec* (1757) and as famous as Stuart and Revett's still-awaited *Antiquities of Athens* was never far behind. Knowing that such books were what the connoisseurs wanted, he feverishly embarked on two schemes – a revised edition of Antoine Desgodetz's *Les edifices antiques de Rome* (1682) and a monograph on the Roman baths – before he finally settled on recording the remains of the late-Roman ruins of the palace of Diocletian at Spalatro in Dalmatia, which he visited with Charles-Louis Clérisseau and two draftsmen, or 'Myrmidons' as he called them, Agostino Brunias and 'the Liégeois', Laurent-Benoît Dewez, on his way back to England.[7]

Robert Adam arrived in England in January 1758, bringing with him a vast trunk full of the precious drawings he and others had made – his Roman trophies – and his indispensable 'Myrmidons', Brunias and Dewez, without whom he admitted he 'would not have had the courage to settle in London'. They knew his manner of drawing, which he regarded as essential to the success of his practice and, in case he did not 'meet with sudden employment', they could be employed in 'preparing his works for publishing'.[8] Before long, he and his entourage (two 'Myrmidons', two sisters to keep house for him, and later his younger brothers, James and William) were established at a smart address in Lower Grosvenor Street, surrounded by all his drawings, his large collection of pictures, antique fragments, vases, figures, bas-reliefs and other ornaments 'to use in his architecture' (pl. 324).[9] This splendid set-up was intended to 'dazzle the eyes' of the rank and fashion – his prospective clients – who were invited to hear him hold forth on his notions of architecture.[10] Here, in the privacy of his own house, he could politely lead connoisseurs to chant his praises and praise themselves for being clever enough to do so.[11] Even more important, he could keep control over his ideas – reveal just enough of them to raise the desire for more and prevent them from being executed without his advice. The idea of exhibiting his designs was anathema to Adam, tantamount to throwing his distinctive 'manner' into the hands of the ignorant rabble.

THE LONDON OFFICE

. . . let the Adams be the sovereign architects of the United Kingdom.[12]

The whole of the close-knit Adam family was involved in Robert's 'English Establishment' and had been right from its Roman inception. And so it should have been, for it was the proceeds of the successful architectural practice built up by his father, William Adam (run in partnership with his older brother, John, following William's death) that kept him in Rome in style for three years, that enabled him to bring Dewez and Brunias back with him and helped to finance the purchase of a smart London house. He tried hard to convince his younger brother, James (1732–94), to join him in Rome and benefit from Clérisseau's tutelage, but that would have placed too great a burden upon the family business in Edinburgh.

James waited until Robert was settled in London before embarking on the Grand Tour in 1760 and returned in 1763 to become a junior partner in Robert's fast-growing practice. Though lacking his brother's inventive genius, his architectural experience and managerial skills were invaluable. In 1764, William, the youngest of the four Adam brothers, set up a parallel firm of developers and builders' merchants, William Adam & Co., which served both the London and Edinburgh establishments.

As theirs was a family firm with two masters, Robert and James had no real need to train apprentices or pupils as Sir Robert Taylor, James Paine and William Chambers did, and they were in any case extremely wary of imparting their special knowledge to anyone who might eventually become a competitor. They preferred instead to rely on a hand-picked team of experienced draftsmen: the cream of the Edinburgh office including, among others, George Richardson, who accompanied James on his Grand Tour, Robert Morrison and Robert Nasmith, and an unusual number of foreign artists, mainly Italians who had cut their teeth on antique and Renaissance grotesques under Clérisseau's supervision. Agostino Brunias, Laurent-Benoît Dewez, Michael Angelo Pergolesi, Giuseppe Sacco, Giuseppe Manocchi, Antonio Zucchi and Joseph Bonomi are the only ones who can be identified as draftsmen. There must have been several other drawing-hands as well as a large contingent of anonymous hacks and clerks, or 'drudges' and 'beagles' as Adam called them, who kept the machine in running order.[13] Some of the Italian draftsmen were also employed as decorative painters: Brunias in the painted breakfast-room in the family pavilion at Kedleston in 1760, Pergolesi in the gallery at Syon in 1765–7 and Zucchi in approximately twenty-five Adam houses in the fifteen years from 1766 to 1781 that he was in England.[14] Whether these artists had any influence on Adam's style is difficult to determine. Though Manocchi is said to have introduced a darker palette, there is no evidence that this ever went beyond his watercolour renderings.[15]

According to Bonomi, he – and no doubt all the others in the Adam office – was employed for a seven-year term during which he 'could do nothing, not even for (his) own use, under a penalty of paying them (Messrs. Adam) £200:0:0'.[16] Bonomi, Zucchi and Morrison agreed (or were persuaded) to stay on for another seven years, but the others all complained of exploitation and left after their first term. Dewez, thinking he had been taken into slavery, escaped in less than a year and returned to Belgium where he became the foremost architect.[17] Evidently these draconian conditions were specially devised by Robert and James for the London establishment and distinguished it from the family business run by their brother John in Edinburgh, as well as from other architectural practices. Though George Richardson claimed that he was employed by Messrs Adam 'in Drawing and Designing upwards of eighteen years',[18] over twelve were with John Adam in Edinburgh. After spending three years, from 1760 to 1763, as James's draughtsman in Italy, during which time he had to conceal any sketches he made in his own time, he joined the London office but left in 1765 (before his term was up) and started exhibiting architectural designs under his own name at the Society of Artists.

Adam was a hard taskmaster and a relentlessly hard-worker himself. Without an extremely efficient office, he could never have produced such an immense number and variety of finished drawings, many of them fully coloured and all of a consistently high standard. Not only were fair drawings made for the clients, but duplicates and in some cases triplicates of the same size and the same or variant colouring were also made for the office. These were used by Adam as samples to persuade and guide other patrons, new and old; and by craftsmen, like the plasterer, Joseph Rose, to make estimates. Most of the office material is now at the Soane Museum. Fair drawings, however, remained the property of the client who commissioned them and paid for them, regardless of whether they were executed or not. The Earl of Coventry's attempt to deduct the cost of designs he decided not to execute brought an interesting reply from Adam on 3 April 1764, explaining that he computed in his charges 'the Time employed by my Clerks, the high wages I pay them & the particular attention I have always & will continue to bestow on every thing . . . that it consumes the same Time, & requires the same money from me for Drawings, Executed or not Executed . . .'.[19] Between 1760 and 1779, Coventry spent £757.4.7 on designs for Croome Court and Coventry House, Piccadilly.

Adam's charges ranged from £16.16.0 for laid-out wall elevations for the drawing-room at Lansdowne House, Berkeley Square, coloured 'in the Stile of the Ancients' and £12.12.0 for a design for its painted ceiling in the same style, to £5 for a stove for the lobby of Sir Lawrence Dundas's house at 19 Arlington Street and £1 for 'Painting Patterns of Bed Carpet & Sewed Chairs for Lady Dundas at Moor Park'.[20] Clients wanting an Adam carpet had to pay for at least two and sometimes three drawings: a finished watercolour of the whole design and an accurate colour sample of one quarter of the pattern painted in oil or distemper to be given to the manufacturer. Lord Coventry paid Adam £10 for a design of a carpet for the great room at Coventry House and £5.5.0 for a quarter drawing to give to Zucchi who was paid £10 for a model painted in distemper for the carpet-maker, Thomas Moore of Moorfields.

If, having paid Adam for his designs, the client decided to employ him to oversee their execution, he then had to pay him the normal surveyor's fee of four or five per cent of the total expenditure. Though working drawings needed by the artificers were generally included in this fee, some 'drawings at large' for articles of furniture and ornamental items were separately billed: two designs for frames for Sir Lawrence and Lady Dundas costing £3.3.0 each were 'drawn at full size & given to the Carvers', a 'Design at large of 4 panels representing the Seasons' for the dining-room at Lansdowne House cost £4.4.0 and two 'drawings at large of a Dial Stand' for Bowood £1.1.0 each.[21] All this was standard practice. What made Adam's interiors expensive was not his charges, but rather the profusion of ornament in his schemes, his introduction of inset paintings on ceilings and walls and the reliance upon large, imported mirrors in gilt frames.

ADAM'S PATRONS

Adam was fortunate in having a circle of influential Scottish friends in London – Alexander Wedderburn, Gilbert Elliot of Minto, John Home, General Sir Charles Hay, Lady Lindores and others – who regarded him as a 'man of genius' and were pleased to recommend him to potential patrons. Rich and cultivated people excited by the antique flocked to his house to see his portfolios of Roman drawings and though all came away enchanted 'with his taste, his production, and his manners', few came back with firm commissions.[22] In his first two years in London, only a handful of 'small things . . . (was) cast up': a new drawing-room and greenhouse for General Bland at Gordon House, Isleworth, and ceilings and chimney-pieces for the principal rooms in Admiral Boscowan's house, Hatchlands in Surrey.[23] His most promising patrons, Sir Edwin Lascelles of Harewood and Sir Nathaniel Curzon (created first Lord Scarsdale) of Kedleston, were already committed to other architects – John Carr and Matthew Brettingham respectively – and to begin with, Adam had to be content to 'tickle up' their plans and design new garden buildings.

This did not deter him. The foundations of his practice were laid and he was confident that 'larger things' would soon follow. He was right. By July 1760 he was in full control of virtually everything at Kedleston, he had designed the Admiralty Screen in Whitehall and a monument to Lieutenant-Colonel Roger Townshend (d. 1759) in Westminster Abbey, and had new commissions from the Duke of Northumberland at Syon and the Earl of Coventry at Croome Court.[24] The opportunity given him by Northumberland to create a magnificent suite of rooms 'entirely in the antique style' at Syon was of the utmost importance to his development as an interior architect.

Gaining the support of his fellow countryman, the Earl of Bute, was more difficult than he expected and most rewarding when he finally achieved it. Not only did Bute, in his capacity as George III's prime minister, place Adam in one of the two newly created posts of Architect to the King's Works in 1761 (Chambers got the other position), but he also gave him his first commission in 1761 to build an entirely new house, Bute (later Lansdowne) House in Berkeley Square. A new country-house commission (his only one on a grand scale), Luton Hoo in Bedfordshire, followed in 1764.

During the two years that James was abroad, the number of men of taste and means wanting him to remodel their interiors increased dramatically. He was, he told Lord Scarsdale, 'so prodigiously teased by different persons in Town calling upon (him) every day for their Drawings' that he could not finish his drawings for Kedleston on time.[25] Among these pressing patrons were the Earl of Shelburne at Bowood, the Childs at Osterley, Sir Francis Dashwood at West Wycombe, William Beckford at Witham, William Drake at Shardeloes, Sir Wyndham Knatchbull at Mersham-le-Hatch, Lord Willoughby de Broke at Compton Verney and others. It must have been an enormous relief to Robert when James rejoined him in London in October 1763 to help with the running of the busy office.

In the course of thirty years of practice, the brothers attracted over three hundred clients, most of them wanting whole suites of neo-classical reception rooms, some, like Paul Methuen of Corsham Court, only one or two pieces of furniture, while for a few, the succès d'estime of having commissioned an impressive Adam design was enough in itself. These patrons do not form an homogeneous group. There were a host of fellow Scots, numerous noblemen and MPs, some members of the Society of Dilettanti, bankers, lawyers, military and naval men, several women (including Mrs Pitt, Lady Innes, Lady Mills, Mrs Montagu, Princess Lubomirsky of Poland, Catherine the Great of Russia) and craftsmen, like Joseph Rose the plasterer, John Devall the mason and John Hobcroft the carpenter, who grew rich executing Adam's works. The common denominator was wealth – new or old made little or no difference.

While most patrons were content to put themselves entirely in Adam's hands and accept his ideas subject to cost, as Robert Child did at Osterley and Sir Roland Winn did at Nostell, others had strong ideas of their own or large collections that had to be accommodated. Such 'directions and caprices' had a tendency, as General Robert Clerk observed, to 'spoil the whole'.[26] Clerk was probably thinking of Bute, who not only had fixed notions about privacy, stairs and water-closets, but also had staggering collections of books, pictures, vases, objects of *virtu* and scientific instruments, a monumental barrel organ and a substantial number of large cylinders all clamouring for space. Proper provision for the display and storage of these collections took precedence in the planning of his Berkeley Square house and Luton Hoo, cramping Adam's style. Bute's active participation in the architectural design of his houses further diminished Adam's freedom to exercise his inventive genius. Clerk was right: his demands, directions and indecision resulted in lame, unsatisfying compromises. Bute House was sold unfinished to the Earl of Shelburne (later Marquis of Lansdowne) and Luton Hoo was never finished as planned.

Lord Scarsdale was another patron with a large collection of pictures and firm ideas about their permanent arrangement recessed in the walls of the reception rooms at Kedleston. Hanging-plans sketched by him were the basis of Adam's finished wall elevations and a decisive influence upon his organ design.

ASPECTS OF STYLE

Looking back on the first fifteen years of their London practice, Adam could justly claim that he and his brother 'had been able to seize, with some degree of success, the beautiful spirit of antiquity, and to transfuse it, with novelty and variety, through all (their) numerous works';[27] above all, in the decoration of interiors, where he had brought about 'an almost total change'. Gone were the 'ponderous' ornaments of ancient Roman temples and public buildings which the Palladians had inappropriately and 'indiscriminately' imposed , as Soane said,[28] upon the insides of private dwellings in this country. Instead, Adam turned for inspiration to the remains of 'their private and bathing apartments'. There he found a lighter, more varied style of decoration, full of 'movement', 'delicacy, gaiety, grace and beauty', which was not only more appealing to his picturesque taste and more conducive to his inventive genius, but was also much better suited to the refinements of modern life.[29]

Adam was not the first to introduce the fanciful grotesque decorations employed by the ancient Romans and imitated 'in no inconsiderable degree' by Raphael, Giovanni da Udine, Pirro Ligorio and other Renaissance artists in the Vatican Loggie, Villa Madama and Caprarola, places that were known to him. William Kent preceded him with ceilings *alla grotesca* in the Presence Chamber at Kensington Palace (1724) and the parlour at Rousham (1738); stimulated by the republication of Pietro Santi Bartoli's *Picturae Antiquae* in 1750, other 'antique' ceilings

were executed in the red drawing-room at West Wycombe Park (*c.*1750) and in the library closet at Narford; the walls of the Earl of Strafford's dining-room at 5 St James's Square were painted in imitation of the Vatican Loggie (pl. 1) by the French painter, Jean-François de Clermont, and in 1758 and 1759, James 'Athenian' Stuart, Adam's 'Archipelagan' *bête noire*, was designing interiors in the *gusto greco* for Kedleston, Spencer House in London, Wimbledon House in Surrey and Nuneham Park in Oxfordshire.[30]

When Adam returned to England from his studies in Italy, he had recourse, as did his patrons, to the engravings of Pietro Santi Bartoli, the Comte de Caylus and Bernard de Montfaucon, and to Richard Topham's collection of coloured copies of antique paintings at Eton College.[31] He could also call on James, while the latter was in Rome, to supply his need for coloured drawings of antique ceilings.[32]

Everything Adam appropriated – whether from antique Roman sources, from the works of English Palladians, or from French architects – he reinterpreted ('translated' might suggest faithful reproduction, which was contradictory to his ideas of creative genius) in his own personal language. What distinguishes his interpretation of classical forms from that of his predecessors, his contemporaries and numerous followers is the picturesque qualities of 'movement' and variety with which it is transfused or synthesized.[33] Chambers's 'taste' was accurately described by Adam as 'more architectonic than Picturesque'.[34]

'Movement' was defined in Adam's *Works* in architecture as:

> the rise and fall, the advance and recess, with other diversity of form, in the different parts of a building, so as to add greatly to the picturesque of the composition. For the rising and falling, advancing and receding, with the convexity and concavity, and other forms of the great parts, have the same effect in architecture, that hill and dale, foreground and distance, swelling and sinking have in landscape. That is, they serve to produce an agreeable and diversified contour, that groups and contrasts like a picture, and creates a variety of light and shade, which gives great spirit, beauty and effect to the composition.[35]

His taste for picturesque effects was inspired by Sir John Vanbrugh (whom his father also admired) and applied not just to the silhouette and contour of exterior architecture, but equally to the planning, modelling and decoration of interior spaces. James, summarizing earlier discussions with Robert, wrote in 1762: 'A proper mixture of domes, vaults and coved ceilings and flat soffits over rooms of various shapes and sizes are capable of forming such a beautiful variety as cannot fail to delight and charm the instructed spectator. A movement in the section is likewise derived from steps in a great circular or long room . . .'.[36] The short flights of stairs which Adam introduced in the hall at Syon enabled him to 'increase the scenery and add to the movement' and, in so doing, to convert the 'apparent defect' of unequal levels 'into a real beauty'.[37] The sculpture gallery at Newby is a good example of variety and 'movement' in the section; Derby House and Wynn House at 20 St James's Square are others.

Domes, vaults and coves were more expensive and difficult to insert into pre-existing interiors. It was considerably easier to suggest the illusion of domes and vaults by two-dimensional circular and X-shaped patterns (as in the second drawing-room at Derby House and the ante-room at 20 St James's Square) and to vary the ceiling decorations of each room. Apses, niches and straight-sided recesses served not only to convey an 'antique' aura, but also to produce a 'diversified contour' and a lively play of light and shadow. They were used to give an illusion of depth to small spaces (like the ante-room at Derby House) and conversely to decrease the actual size of rooms (like the hall at Osterley, the dining-room at Syon and the library at Kenwood) so as to improve their proportions and bring them into 'proper relief' in the progressive sequence of apartments; in the case of the ante-room at Lansdowne House, 'to prevent it from appearing near so large as either of the rooms to which it gives access . . .'.[38] The great apse in the dining-room at Kedleston performed the function of a stage for Adam's sideboard display, distinctly set apart from the rest of the room. Picturesque effects were frequently achieved by the addition of screens of columns in the manner of the Roman baths, one of Adam's favourite scenic devices.

'Movement', in the widest sense, was also assisted by surface decorations: by ceilings, for instance, decorated with contiguous circles or octagons cut off incomplete at the edges as if caught in motion in an indefinite space in the music-room at Home House, the saloon at Nostell, and the dining-room at 20 St James's Square; and by a general diversity of stucco and painted ornaments, figurative subjects and lively, fanciful grotesques which, executed in different colours and occasionally picked-out in gold or highly japanned, added to the 'variety of light and shade'. Each room, apart from being varied in itself, was treated differently from its neighbour in accordance with its particular use and importance.

PLANNING

The skilful . . . will easily perceive within these few years, a remarkable improvement in the form, convenience, arrangement, and relief of apartments . . . and in the decoration of the inside an almost total change.

Works, I, i, 1773

Though Adam's name is associated almost exclusively with interior decoration, planning was, in fact, the field in which he had the greatest interest. The handling of spaces, the relation of one to another and the placement of elements within each space was Adam's genius. It was the vital underpinning of his interiors; the branch of architecture he esteemed 'above all the others the most essential to the splendour and convenience of life'.[39] The 'diversity of form as well as dimensions . . . to which the Ancients were extremely attentive' and the 'proper arrangement and relief of apartments . . . in which the French have excelled all other nations' were his twin touchstones.[40] Few other English architects, apart from James Paine and Sir Robert Taylor, ventured beyond the simple rectangular shapes of their Palladian predecessors.

The 'new art of distribution', or interior planning, was perfected in the first half of the eighteenth century by French architects like Jacques-François Blondel, Charles Etienne Briseux,

Germain Boffrand and others, whose books proudly proclaimed the importance of their achievement. Adam knew their *hôtels* from their published engravings and praised them as 'objects of universal imitation'.[41] But his own 'imitation' (if one dare foster such an abhorrent notion on Adam) was general rather than specific and, as usual, utterly unslavish, entirely personal and difficult to detect. He was an outspoken admirer of the elegance of French life, their nice attention to comfort, privacy and convenience in the provision of baths and water-closets as well as back stairs and corridors enabling servants to move about unnoticed, their differentiation between *appartements de parade* (formal rooms of reception), *appartements de société* (lesser rooms for informal gatherings) and *appartements de commodité* (private rooms), and their compact arrangements of moderate-sized rooms of different proportions and shapes.

For him, a 'proper arrangement and relief' also depended upon an ascending gradation or progression of spaces which, in the words of his friend, Lord Kames, 'gradually swells the mind' and culminates in a 'climax'.[42] The view back from the crypto-porticus to the interior of Diocletian's Palace at Spalatro is cited as a 'striking instance' of this climax.

Adam's eye for the picturesque encouraged him to regard rooms as scenery, best approached at an angle from which there is an incomplete view that stimulates the imagination and whets the appetite for more. The relationship between the hall and vestibule at Syon, the third drawing-room and Etruscan dressing-room at Derby House, and the long vista from the library (originally the dining-room) through to the far apse of the sculpture gallery at Newby are examples of picturesque planning. The reason Adam gave for not publishing his drawings in 1756 is applicable to many of his interiors '. . . the more you keep people from seeing the more their imaginations have occasion to work'.[43]

The structural problems involved in remodelling existing interiors was a powerful stimulus to his inventive genius – the more difficult the challenge, the better his response. He was a master at turning awkward situations to advantage, leaving no hint in his elegant, well-integrated solutions of the difficulties he surmounted. His initial scheme for a 'Great Apartment' at Syon (pl. 96) provides a rare opportunity to see his empirical procedure at work and to judge the extent to which the existing structure determined the size, the shape and the use of virtually every room in his final plan. By and large, the few new houses he built were not so free and imaginative.

While his remodelling of country-house interiors was normally confined to the principal reception and family rooms on one floor, the *piano nobile*, in narrow London houses it was spread over two floors. Each had a private apartment towards the back of the house – the gentleman's on the ground floor, the lady's above – with water-closets and back stairs at the very end and suites of reception rooms towards the front. The more important suite of drawing-rooms was arranged in a graduated sequence on the *piano nobile*; the eating-room and parlour were on the ground floor. These rooms were persuaded into varied shapes and ingeniously fitted together to form fluid circuits for 'the parade, the convenience and the social pleasures of life'.[44]

The positions, dimensions and uses of rooms in the pre-existing houses which Adam was called upon to refashion in the neo-

2 Design for the dressing-room ceiling at Mrs Montagu's house in Hill Street, by Robert Adam, 1766 (Sir John Soane's Museum: Adam drawings, vol. II:200). Into a classical framework Adam inserted eight roundels of chinoiserie scenes. He also designed a chinoiserie carpet to answer the ceiling

classical style were all established in the first half of the eighteenth century (and will be dealt with in detail in John Cornforth's forthcoming book on *The Grammar of Decoration*). A brief outline of the situation regarding principal apartments, especially those about which Adam had something significant to say or which are otherwise interesting, is sufficient here.

For magnificence – and frequently for size as well – the drawing-room, or great drawing-room if there were several, as at Harewood, Luton, Lansdowne House and Derby House, was the 'climax' of the parade, often preceded by a smaller anteroom. It was the room where guests were received before dinner and to which ladies withdrew afterwards in order to escape the noise of the gentlemen who remained in the dining-room to talk and drink. For the latter reason – and for the benefit of the ladies, it would seem – drawing-rooms and dining-rooms were placed on opposite sides of the house: the drawing-rooms on the garden front furthest from the entrance and the eating-rooms on the main front or the north side, as at Osterley. Above all, it was the 'manner of decoration' that distinguished the two rooms.

Adam was quite precise about the treatment of dining-rooms. 'Instead of being hung with damask, tapestry, etc. (as drawing-rooms were), they are always finished with stucco and adorned with statues and paintings, that they may not retain the smell of victuals'.[45] His dining-rooms at Lansdowne House and Syon

were treated like sculpture galleries, with statues in niches; most others, like Osterley and Newby, had panels of stucco grotesques. Similar restrictions regarding hangings were observed in common parlours used for everyday eating.

It is not surprising, given Adam's reputation as a 'man of genius' with a superior taste and knowledge of the antique freshly acquired in Rome, that the refurbishment of galleries surviving in Tudor houses like Syon and Osterley, or built for symmetry rather than necessity at Croome Court and Harewood, should be among his earliest commissions. The problem in these long, narrow, potentially dull spaces was how to diversify them and make them interesting and entertaining in themselves, regardless of their contents, and at the same time to give them some focus. A chapel and a sculpture gallery with statues in niches and a towering tabernacle chimney-piece were considered for the gallery at Harewood in 1759 and 1762 respectively, but were abandoned in favour of a picture gallery.

Spatially, galleries and libraries were interchangeable. A gallery modelled on the one at Holkham was designed in 1764 to house Bute's library in his house in Berkeley Square; though built, it was ultimately fitted out by Smirke in 1819 to a design by George Dance as a sculpture gallery. The idea of 'finishing (a) Gallery in the Manner of a Library' evidently appealed to Adam, for he proposed it in 1761 for Croome Court and Osterley, neither of which was executed.[46] Croome was treated like a sculpture gallery and Osterley remained as it was, a picture gallery which Adam later 'tickled up' with some novel girandoles and mirrors. On the other hand, at Syon his synthesis of 'library and museum' or 'columbarium', containing a mixture of books, statues and vases in niches, paintings, Etruscan urns, plaster bas-reliefs and medallions, was a complete triumph. The 'great variety and amusement' of his decorations made the room suitable, he claimed, for the reception of company before dinner and the retreat of ladies as far as possible from the dining-room afterwards. Being brighter and more cheerful than the north-facing family apartment and having two fireplaces and stairs to the garden at the south end, it must also have been used as an informal, daytime living-room in much the same way as Lady Louisa Conolly's gallery at Castletown, Co. Kildare.[47]

For the Duke of Northumberland's principal seat at Alnwick Castle, Adam designed a large gothic library 'in the form of a Gallery' which was described in 1790 as the best room in the house and 'the apartment in which the family generally reside'.[48] No doubt the library beyond the grand saloon at Saltram was used as a family room before it was converted to a formal dining-room and hardly used at all.[49] The Adam library at Kenwood was designed to double as a formal drawing-room, there being no other grand room in the earlier house. It is unlikely that the stony, 'dead' white, north-facing library at Osterley was ever used as a comfortable living-room in the way the gallery was. In the early nineteenth century it had a piano, a billiard table and a motley assortment of 'tables, sofas and chairs . . . studiously *derangés* about the fire-places . . .'.[50]

Ladies' dressing-rooms or boudoirs, especially in London, had come to be like jewel cabinets, containers of special furniture and decoration for public show on grand occasions and at other times for receiving personal friends. They were the most inventive rooms in Adam's houses. Mrs Montagu described the dressing-room (known as the Silver Room) that he designed for her house in Hill Street in 1766 as 'just the female of the great room, for sweet attractive grace, for winning softness, for delicacy, for le je ne scai quoi, it is incomparable'.[51] She did not exaggerate: as one of Adam's rare works in the Chinese style (pl. 2), her dressing-room was indeed 'incomparable'. So too were the Etruscan-style dressing-rooms he designed at Derby House, Apsley House, Home House and Osterley. These, he boasted, were 'unlike anything hitherto practised in Europe'.[52] The only comparable dressing-room in an Adam country house, Mr Lascelles's 'Circular Dressing Room' at Harewood, was removed by Barry in 1848.

Though on the whole Adam's staircases are not as inventive as those by Chambers and Paine, there are some exceptions that merit attention. The spectacular oval staircase ringed by superimposed colonnades at Culzean Castle, Ayrshire, is a masterpiece of scenic architecture. Designed in 1787, it is one of his last works and certainly one of his finest. Chambers's design for York House, Piccadilly (made in 1759 and exhibited in 1761) seems to have sparked Adam's interest in centralized, colonnaded stairs, which he developed (sadly to no avail) for Great Saxham, Suffolk, in 1763 and again in 1779, for a house for the Earl of Shelburne at Hyde Park Corner in 1764 and for John Robinson's house, Wyke Manor, Isleworth, in 1778.

3 Detail of the ironwork balusters at 20 St James's Square, made by William Kinman in 1774 to a design by Robert Adam

His London staircases, being the main route to his reception rooms, tend to be more imaginative and interesting than his country-house ones. Their confined space certainly taxed his ingenuity to advantage: 20 St James's Square and Home House are the outstanding examples. In the first – a new house built for Sir Watkin Williams-Wynn in 1772 – the typical long, rectangular hall, with stairs rising in three stages against the walls (pl. 3), was given a monumental 'antique' appearance by the ingenious formation of large, semi-circular exedras on the ground and first-floors. These cavernous recesses, accompanied by lower rectangular doors on either side and bas-reliefs in the upper register, form a classical triumphal-arch pattern which is repeated pictorially, in two dimensions, on the remaining walls. Here, as in the vestibule at Syon, exterior architecture is brought inside.

Home House, as built by James Wyatt in 1772, had a squarish rectangular staircase with the stair set against the walls. Into Wyatt's shell Adam squeezed a circular container articulated all round with variations upon the triumphal-arch theme and a symmetrical imperial stair rising to the *piano nobile*. The components are, perforce, more refined and tightly controlled than those at 20 St James's Square and the composition better integrated and more diverting.

4   Design for the chimney-piece in the Beauclerc Room at Horace Walpole's house, Strawberry Hill, Middlesex, by Robert Adam, 1767 (Sir John Soane's Museum: Adam drawings, vol. 22:229). Adam's chimney-piece and gothic ceiling (see pl.140) were both executed and are still in the house

5   'Design of a chimney-piece for the Great Drawing room at Bolton House', by Robert Adam, 1777 (Sir John Soane's Museum: Adam drawings, vol. 22:277). The chimney-piece was executed but the exquisite scagliola inlays were removed prior to the demolition of the house, 26 Southampton Row (later Russell Square), in 1913

In earlier seventeenth- and eighteenth-century staircases, the balusters were the most notable enrichment. The neo-classical cast-iron ones designed by Adam are not only a hallmark of his presence, but were also put to work – as every other element of decoration was – to define his architecture. Hence the different forms chosen for 20 St James's Square and Home House: the bottle-shaped balusters at Wynn House have horizontal bands dividing the neck and bowl, which run parallel to the line of the skirting on the opposite wall and carry the eye upwards on a steep incline. At Home House, where the balusters are tapered towards the base like classical terms, enriched inside with open guilloche and linked by curved festoons, the emphasis is more vertical. The ornaments were clearly chosen to suit the circular container and were originally painted grey and white to match.

DECORATION

Though Adam's decoration is usually regarded as little more than delicate surface embroidery, its purpose, in fact, was considerably broader and more architectonic. 'Arranged (by him) with propriety and skill', it served to articulate, focus and define a room, to relate the different elements within it, to achieve balance and symmetry, and to give character. Ceiling patterns, for instance, were put to a variety of uses: to mark out the subtle rhythm of the wall elevations in the dining-room at Lansdowne House, or to repeat it in the hall at Harewood; often to draw the attention to the centre of the room, and occasionally, as in the front parlour at Home House and the library (now the dining-room) at Saltram, to divert the eye away from asymmetrical walls; to emphasize the curve of the low segmental-arched ceiling in the drawing-room at 20 St James's Square; to suggest a shallow dome or a groin vault by a circle or cross on a flat ceiling. Baroque *quadratura* ceilings, though very different in appearance, may be cited as a precedent.

Regardless of whether Adam's ceilings were executed in stucco or painted in the 'Antique Style', whether they incorporated paintings by Zucchi of classical subjects or were purely decorative, they required no knowledge, understanding or effort on the part of the spectator. Their pleasing impact was immediate, being derived, in accordance with the aesthetic of Roger de Piles, from the arrangement and colour of the composition. From Adam's point of view, grotesques and geometrical patterns had the additional advantage of allowing him maximum artistic freedom. Similar reasons were given by James for his (and no doubt Robert's) preference for wall panels enriched with foliage or trophies: unlike the orders, 'one can vary the proportions at pleasure . . . and likewise the ornament within the panels may be changed to grotesques or any other composition as light as one chooses'.[53] In the course of thirty years' practice, Adam rang endless changes on his range of decorative works, conjuring ever lighter and more refined effects.[54]

After the ceiling, the most important feature of his interiors was the chimney-piece. As it was the traditional hub of a room and more often than not the first thing that was seen on entering, it naturally merited special attention. On most eighteenth-century chimney-pieces, this took the form of a carved tablet in the centre of a decorated frieze. Except, perhaps, for his use of enriched panels in place of pilasters or columns, which freed him from the rules of proportion, Adam did little or nothing to alter this basic model. He concentrated instead on employing his large vocabulary of classical motifs with grace and delicacy in all sorts of novel permutations. Piranesi's *Diversi maniere d'adornare i cammini* (1769) provided occasional inspiration, but on the whole his fantasies were too bizarre for English taste.

Colour was Adam's most distinctive contribution to chimney-piece decoration: not the broad bands of yellow or green marble or scagliola often set into a frieze, but small-scale inlaid scagliola ornaments in a wide range of colours, distributed over the entire white marble surround in the manner of the much sought-after neo-Renaissance mosaic table slabs that were produced in Florence in this period by Enrico Hugford and Lamberto Cristiano Gori. James was quite impressed by the versatility of scagliola when he saw it in Florence in 1760. It is 'curious', he wrote, 'and could be made to answer different purposes; for instance, for columns resembling different marbles, for tables resembling mosaic work, and for most elegant floors for baths and low (lower) apartments, or for linings to any place damp &c.; and likewise for imitating different marbles in cabinet work, and such like things.'[55] Evidently the idea of chimney-piece decoration had not yet occurred to him. The gothic chimney-piece designed in 1766–7 for the round drawing-room at Strawberry Hill (pl. 4), which Walpole described as being 'taken from the tomb of Edward the Confessor (in Westminster Abbey), improved by Mr Adam and beautifully executed in white marble inlaid with scagliola, by Richter', is the earliest documented example of its kind in Adam's *œuvre*.[56] It is also the earliest recorded work in England by Johann Augustus Richter, who arrived from Dresden in 1767 and set up in partnership with the Livornese craftsmen, Domenico and Giuseppe Bartoli.[57] As an attempt to reproduce Italian thirteenth-century Cosmati work (glass and stone mosaic) in a 1760s English drawing-room, it is a freak, an antiquarian curiosity dreamed up and directed by Horace Walpole.

Adam did not design another inlaid scagliola chimney-piece until six years later, in August 1772, prompted this time by Sir Watkin Williams-Wynn's decision to introduce Wedgwood tablets in the chimney-piece in Lady Wynn's dressing-room at 20 St James's Square. Two alternatives were offered to accompany the tablets: one with the frieze and pilasters embellished with 'antique' red cameos; the other with a frieze of ivy festoons and fluted Ionic columns.[58] Although the latter, as it harmonized with the wall frieze, was the preferred choice, the tablets, in the event, were in the Etruscan style – the central one with a multi-coloured classical subject and the two side blocks with red figures – all three on black grounds.

The decorative possibilities of inlaid scagliola were ideally suited to Adam's fanciful neo-classical style and he lost no time in putting them to use in his glamorous London houses: Ashburnham House, Northumberland House and Derby House in 1773, Home House in 1775, Roxburgh House and Bolton House in 1777 (pl. 5), Sir Abraham Hume's house in Hill Street in 1779, the Duke of Cumberland's house and Sir John Hussey Delaval's in 1780; and outside London in the tapestry drawing-room at Osterley in 1775 and the Etruscan drawing-room at Byram in 1780.

Colour had much the same effect on a statuary marble chimney-piece as it did on a ceiling – it took off the 'glare of the white and helped to create a harmony', an equilibrium with the wall decorations, particularly when they were as rich and overpowering as the Boucher–Neilson tapestries at Osterley or the red and green spangled-glass walls covered with gilded traceries in the drawing-room at Northumberland House. In the drawing-room at Syon, ormolu mounts were needed to tie the white marble chimney-piece and ivory door-cases in with the gorgeous three-coloured damask hangings and richly gilded ceiling.

The idea of applying the style of ornament and colouring found on ancient Greek and Etruscan vases to the decoration of late-eighteenth-century apartments was claimed by Adam to have been entirely his 'discovery'.[59] It is true, despite recent attempts to give the palm to Stuart.[60] He was the first to develop and carry into execution a new 'class of decoration and embel-

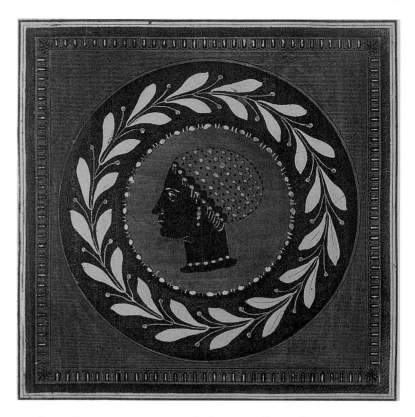

6   Pierre François Hugues, pseud. d'Hancarville, *Collection of Etruscan, Greek and Roman Antiquities from the cabinet of the Hon.*[ble] *W.*[m] *Hamilton* (1766), vol. 1, pl. 38

lishment' which was distinctly different from the grotesque style, though it shared the same classical vocabulary. However, there was nothing especially new about the principal features of this so-called Etruscan style – black and terracotta colouring and open compositions of small, abstracted, isolated ornaments linked by thin chains, containing no naturalistic rinceau. They were to be found in various combinations in the decorations of Nero's Domus Aurea, on Raphael's painted pilasters in the Vatican Loggia, Giovanni da Udine's decorations in the loggia of the Villa Madama and elsewhere.

The extent of Adam's hyperbole is even more apparent in the context of the contemporary efforts of Wedgwood and Bentley. Wedgwood's contribution to Lady Wynn's dressing-room chimney-piece has been briefly touched upon; attention should also be drawn to the resemblance between Wedgwood's black basalt wares and the black and gold pedestals incorporated in the decoration of the ceiling of the second drawing-room at 20 St James's Square, which followed close on the heels of the dressing-room chimney-piece. Sir Watkin Williams-Wynn was one of Wedgwood's earliest and most generous patrons: he presented him with the first volume of coloured engravings of the Etruscan vases in Sir William Hamilton's collection as soon as it was published in 1767 (pl. 6); he gave him the use of the vases he had acquired on his Grand Tour and lent him cameos and intaglios from his collection.[61] By September 1769, antique tablets, medallions and cameos were being manufactured by Wedgwood and Bentley in 'black Basalts with Etruscan red burnt-in Grounds, and in polished Biscuits, with brown and grey grounds'. In 1773 they published the first catalogue of their wares in which they recommended these Etruscan ornaments as 'fit either for inlay, as Medallions, in the Panels of Rooms, as Tablets for Chimney Pieces, or for hanging up, as Ornaments in

Libraries, &c. . . . as Pictures in Dressing-Rooms, or for ornamenting Writing-Tables, Book-Cases, Cabinets, and the walls of Apartments, in the richest Manner, and at a very moderate Expense'.[62]

1773 was also the decisive moment for Adam's Etruscan style. In that year Lady Derby decided to have his design for her dressing-room ceiling at Derby House painted 'in the colouring of the Etruscans' with fawn ornaments on a dark brown ground, and that set the tone for the rest of the room – its scagliola chimney-piece and mirror in a black frame picked out in gold, its curtain cornices, girandoles and splendid inlaid marquetry commode executed by Ince and Mayhew – and for her *en suite* bedroom as well, which had an extraordinary bed upholstered in Etruscan colours. Evidently the idea of painted wall decoration like that designed for Osterley in 1775 did not occur to Adam when he was working at Derby House in 1773 and 1774. However, he would have achieved something of the same effect in the countess's Etruscan dressing-room by using pairs of tall girandoles incorporating oval and circular medallions with terracotta figures on a black ground, painted by Zucchi but looking like Wedgwood, interspersed with carved and gilt urns with half-female branches for candles, sphinxes and pendant lamps.

Derby House had an immediate and compelling effect upon the Etruscan dressing-rooms at Osterley and Apsley House and the bedroom at Home House, all three designed in 1775. Horace Walpole's description of the Osterley room as 'painted all over like Wedgwood's ware, with black and yellow small grotesques' is well founded.[63] The similarity to Wedgwood ware and sixteenth-century grotesques is unmistakable; moreover, it was evidently what Adam intended and what his clients wanted. Piranesi's eclectic designs for wall decorations published in his *Diversi maniere* (1769), though generally cited as the source of inspiration for Adam's Etruscan wall decorations, were uncoloured and superfluous in the circumstances.[64] All the elements were in place, waiting for Adam's genius to assemble them in an entirely new mode of decoration which was truly different 'from anything hitherto practised in Europe'.

This is not to suggest that the exchange between Adam and Wedgwood flowed only in Adam's direction. Wedgwood evidently thought he had done well to employ one of Adam's former carvers, the little-known John Voyers (or Voyez), as a modeller in 1768;[65] he had high hopes (too high as it happened) of profiting from 'Mr Adam's power to introduce (his and Bentley's) things into use . . .';[66] and was no doubt aware of the potential benefits of access to the brothers' renowned store of antique models. In September 1771, John Freeman of Chute Lodge, Wiltshire (a house built *c.*1768 by Sir Robert Taylor) 'assured (him) that he knew Mr Adams kept Modelers at Rome employed in copying Bas reliefs & other things for them & he thought a connection with them would be of great use to (them)'.[67] By 1780, Etruscan decoration had taken root and branched out from ladies' dressing-rooms and bedrooms into

8   Design for lock furniture in the Etruscan style for the Duke of Cumberland at Cumberland House, by Robert Adam, *c.*1781 (Sir John Soane's Museum: Adam drawings, vol. 25:75)

larger, more important rooms, like the Duke of Cumberland's great dining-room at Cumberland House, Pall Mall (pls 7, 8) and Sir John Ramsden's drawing-room ceiling at Byram in Yorkshire.[68] The latter led Ramsden's sister, Mrs Weddell, to commission a suite of furniture painted in the Etruscan style for the dining-room at Newby which already had Adam's earliest black and terracotta ornaments on the ceiling, dating from 1768, and a pair of gilt side-tables with Etruscan-style scagliola slabs designed in 1775.

COLOUR

Adam's interiors have been restored more frequently and diligently than any other architect's; so much so that not a spot of their original paintwork survives untouched. What, then, do we really know about his use of colour? The watercolour drawings at the Soane are a prime source of information and in many cases the only one. However, as much as they reveal about the range of tints used and the various patterns of distribution,[69] they still cannot be relied upon as conclusive evidence of what was finally executed. One has only to compare the rose-coloured renderings of the Northumberland House drawing-room with the deep-red glass walls spangled to imitate porphyry to recognize the limitations of watercolour as a measure of the depth and intensity of another material or another medium like wall-paint.

There are other questions posed by the Soane watercolours, which, it must be remembered, are copies or samples made for office use. What conclusions, for example, are we to draw from duplicate renderings of a design, each with different colouring or with no colouring at all, which in the case of the library at Osterley was discovered to indicate white paint; and to what extent are these nuances and variations attributable to the different draftsmen employed? The colour annotations or keys inscribed on some drawings at the Soane, or communicated by letter, like the one from James Adam in the Nostell archive regarding the painting of the library there, are a somewhat safer guide. Painters' accounts can be even more informative, though expert knowledge may be needed to interpret them, and contemporary descriptions are also valuable evidence, but by far the most accurate data can be obtained by scientific colour analysis

7   Design (unexecuted) for the chimney side of the great dining-room at Cumberland House, Pall Mall, by Robert Adam, *c.*1781 (Sir John Soane's Museum: Adam drawings, vol. 14:138)

9   Design for the ceiling of Sir Edward Knatchbull's drawing-room at
Mersham-le-Hatch, Kent, by Robert Adam, *c.*1771–2 (Sir John Soane's
Museum: Adam drawings, vol. 11:182)

of a large number of samples. However, scientific investigations, undertaken as they are for the purposes of authentic restoration, are of little value when such utterly unsympathetic modern materials as acrylic latex paint are used (as they were in the case of the Lansdowne House drawing-room in the Philadelphia Museum of Art), or when (again in Philadelphia and more recently in the restoration of the Adam hall/dining-room at Kenwood) there is no understanding of Adam's vision of the room as a whole, his *toute ensemble* in which the colours of ceiling and walls were carefully balanced and pictures, mirrors and other decorations taken into account.

How painted elements – ceiling, frieze and dado – ought to be restored in relation to surviving hangings is another, more difficult, problem. At Newby, it was decided to repaint Adam's pink, green and white ceiling in anaemic tones to blend with the faded Boucher–Neilson tapestries. The alternative might have been to leave it alone.

In addition to the finished ceiling designs made for the client and the office copies, Adam also supplied coloured working drawings for the use of the painter, who was normally an experi-enced London craftsman chosen by him as he did 'not think any of the country hands could do (the work), as it ought to be'.[70]

Tinted grounds had been used for ceilings in England since the 1730s, though not as commonly as white, and have antique and Renaissance precedents.[71] A variety of grounds – especially pink and green, which were the prevailing fashion – were favoured by Adam in order, he wrote, 'to relieve the ornaments, remove the crudeness of the white, and create a harmony between the ceiling and the side walls'.[72] His dismissive comment about white led to the mistaken belief that he never designed a ceiling or a room of that colour. On the contrary, there are several monochromatic white and 'dead stone' (off-white) Adam interiors: the gallery at Croome Court (1760–4) in which the wall furniture was also painted 'dead stone' colour and which he described as being in the 'Antique Taste'; the white and gold dining-room with matching furniture at Syon; the pearl and white dining-room and white sideboard suite at Lansdowne House (now in the Metropolitan Museum of Art, New York), where there was also a 'dead' white and stone-colour library on the first-floor; the contemporary library at Osterley; and there were no doubt others. Derby House, for example, had an ante-room entirely painted – ceiling, walls, girandoles and other ornaments – in different tints of green, which, Adam claimed, 'had a simple and elegant effect', and a great dining-room all 'Blue of different tints'.[73]

It was not white in itself that Adam disliked, but rather the jarring and divisive contrast on a vertical plane of a white dado, skirting or frieze against a deep coloured wall, whether painted or hung. Thoughtful application of different colours to these architectural elements enabled him to achieve a finely tuned balance and great variety at the same time: a 'harmony of many contrasts', in Summerson's words, in which the ceiling and floor-covering were included.[74] Thus the drawing-room at Coventry House had red damask hangings, a green dado, rose-coloured skirting, a green frieze picked out in gold, seat furniture to match the frieze and an Adam carpet with a yellow ogee pattern on a rose ground and a maroon border with green interlaced circles. Kaleidoscopic yes, but unified none the less.[75]

Hangings, carpets and other attendant decorations – perhaps even the proportions of the room – should also be considered in the formula, as they evidently were by Adam and his patrons. Sir Edward Knatchbull wrote to him in February 1772,

I like the Painting (i.e. coloured design) of the (drawing-room) Ceiling only ye Colours are hardly strong enough to be seen and distinguished at a great Distance. You know the room is 18 feet high. I shod. be glad to know whether it will make any alteration in Yr. Painting as to what Colour the Curtains & hanging of the Room. For upon further consideration, it seems to be destined to have no Pictures in ye Drawing Room, but a full length over ye Chimney piece & to hang the family pictures in the Great Dining Parlour. I think the next month is the best time of the year for painting to avoid the flies. Mr Cole is therefore to send to the Painter he talked with in London to fix his time for coming down.[76]

What colour the hangings were and whether Adam made any alterations to his ceiling design (pl. 9) is not known.

Normally the decision to cover the walls of one or more rooms with fabric, paper or tapestry was made by the client, perhaps with the assistance of an upholsterer but without prior consultation with Adam, though he was certainly informed of the chosen colour and pattern in time to make any necessary adjustments to his designs. The state apartment at Osterley was an exception, where the sequence of colours – red in the tapestry drawing-room, green in the state bedroom and pale blue in the Etruscan dressing-room – and their allusions to the elements and seasons, with the windows and pier-glasses on the outer wall representing ice and winter, must have been orchestrated by Adam.

Some clients decided not to have any hangings, especially in their country houses: the Earl of Shelburne had none at Bowood or Lansdowne House; at Luton, all the rooms on the *piano nobile* were lined with light-green paper to show the pictures to advantage. On the other hand, most of Adam's splendid London drawing-rooms were hung with damask, and some, like Derby House and Home House, with lustrous satin, which was the latest fashion in the 1770s. Harewood was exceptional in having different-coloured damask hangings in each of the three main reception rooms in the state apartment. The Earl and Countess

of Coventry opted to have the ante-room, drawing-room and bedroom on the first-floor of their house in Piccadilly uniformly hung with red damask, relying upon Adam's ceiling, carpets and furniture to provide variety and novelty in an appropriate progression.

On the whole, Adam's use of architectural gilding was saved for the best drawing-room, where it was limited to selective picking-out of frieze and ceiling ornaments. The ostentatious Duke and Duchess of Northumberland demanded considerably more than that: every room in the state apartments at Syon was lavishly gilded and at Alnwick 1,480 books of gold were used to enrich the gothic decorations in the chapel. Expensive nineteenth- and twentieth-century refurbishments left most Adam interiors with a good deal more gilt than they had to begin with. The drawing-room ceiling at Osterley is said to be one of the few surviving examples of original gilding; solid gilding, hatched gilding and 'Party gilding' applied only to raised parts are specified in the accounts of the painter, David Adamson.[77] Whether the architectural gilding suggested on Adam's drawings by yellow paint was executed or rejected seems to have depended not so much upon the dictates of fashion as the number of gilt-framed pictures on the walls. This would explain the absence of architectural gilding in the dining-room at Kedleston and throughout Luton.

FURNITURE

How Adam's interiors were furnished was primarily up to their owners. Designs were only supplied by him on request and for a not inconsiderable fee – as much as seven guineas for a drawing of a clothes press for Lady Coventry's bedchamber. If accepted, they were given, either by him or by the client, to one or more London furniture-makers to execute, and sometimes to a craftsman already employed in the house. At Kedleston, for example, James Gravenor carved all the alabaster capitals as well as Adam's mirror-frames in the drawing-room and estate carpenters were responsible for the dining-room sideboard suite which, though not especially well executed, is extremely important as Adam's earliest furniture in the neo-classical style.

The saving of time as much as, if not more than, the saving of money, encouraged the majority of patrons to bypass Adam altogether and obtain pieces directly from Chippendale, Linnell or Ince and Mayhew – experienced craftsmen who were perfectly capable of making neo-classical designs themselves and did so at no extra cost. Chippendale supplied all the furniture for Harewood, Adam's largest commission, and for Mersham-le-Hatch, the first of his very few complete country houses.

Those clients who did commission furniture from Adam were persuaded by his attractive wall elevations to have at least something of what he proposed, something integral with his wall decorations: pier-glasses and *en suite* tables, curtain cornices, sideboards with flanking pedestals and urns, commodes, bookcases and other items of wall furniture. The rest – chairs, sofas, and other movables that were not depicted in his elevations – was normally obtained from specialist furniture-makers or brought from elsewhere in the house and did not necessarily agree with the neo-classical style of his decorations. The suite of rococo drawing-room seat furniture at Osterley is an example.

10 Pier-glass and table in the picture gallery at Corsham Court, Wiltshire. One of four made for Paul Methuen to a design by Robert Adam, 1767 (Collection James Methuen Campbell)

for her drawing-room at Mersham-le-Hatch, which was supplied by Chippendale.[79] It was on Adam's recommendation that Sir Rowland Winn employed Chippendale to furnish his (Adam's) rooms at Nostell Priory; it was with Adam's advice and consent that 'a Section of the Saloon with designs of the furniture' was drawn up (by Chippendale?) on 21 June 1774, and that decisions were made regarding the upholstery of Chippendale's chairs and sofas and the gilding of Adam's glass and picture-frames in oil gold and his table-frames and candle stands in burnished gold.[80]

Adam's position of authority was evidently accepted by Chippendale; the two men had a good working relationship and their collaboration at Nostell was more extensive than hitherto thought.[81] His relationships with the other fashionable craftsmen favoured by his clients – the furniture-makers John Linnell and Ince and Mayhew, the carpet-makers Thomas Moore of Moorfields, London, and Thomas Whittey of Axminster, the scagliola-makers Bartoli and Richter, and others – must have been much the same, for they all stood to benefit from his recommendation. In addition to these stars, a string of lesser-known tradesmen were employed on his interiors: carvers and gilders like John Gilbert, Sefferin Nelson and Sefferin Alken; locksmiths like Thomas Blockley and Edward Gascoigne; and William Bent, the ironmonger who made most of his door furniture.

Furniture arrived on Adam's agenda for the first time in 1760 at Kedleston, where he was expected to improve upon the advanced neo-classical designs made two or three years earlier by 'Athenian' Stuart. That he had no previous experience in the field made not the slightest difference; neither did Kent, Chambers, Stuart and many other architects before them. However, the paucity of antique or Renaissance models that could be adapted to the refinements of modern life was something of a challenge.

The only examples of neo-classical furniture available to him before 1763, when the end of the Seven Years War enabled Englishmen like the Earl of Coventry to make purchases in Paris, were the *goût grec* pieces shorn of all rococo frills included in Jean François Neufforge's *Recueil Elementaire d'architecture*, which appeared in parts starting in 1757 (Adam owned parts IV, 1761, and V, 1763), and 'Athenian' Stuart's Franco-Greek designs for Kedleston (1757–8) and Spencer House (1759).[82] Both were wholly at odds with his picturesque interpretation of antiquity and his zest for variety, novelty and movement. Though temporary exigency led him to rely on Stuart in his early furniture designs for Kedleston – notably his gold-and-white sideboard suite on which 'Mr Stuart's Tripod' was displayed – it was by experimenting with different combinations of antique ornaments applied to straight architectonic forms and curvaceous Kentian ones that he forged a personal style of neo-classical furniture which conformed and contributed to the decoration of his interiors.

Adam's decorative style was by nature remarkably versatile and open to infinite variation and refinement. In the mid-1760s, large pier-glasses and tables, cabinets and chairs were embellished with robust, naturalistic rinceaux, anthemia, sphinxes, rams' heads and other classical ornaments in high relief. The drawing-room furniture at Syon, the Earl of Coventry's clothes-press and the suite of seat furniture designed for Sir Lawrence Dundas at Moor Park, Hertfordshire and 19 Arlington Street are

Rarely was Adam responsible for all the furniture in his interiors. The first fully decorated and furnished Adam room was the gallery at Croome Court, completed in 1765. There are three others at Osterley: the dining-room (1767), the state bedroom and the Etruscan dressing-room, both of 1772. It was even more unusual for him to design furniture for houses in which he was not already employed in some other capacity. His splendid mirrors, tables and picture frames (1767–72) for Paul Methuen's gallery at Corsham Court are notable exceptions (pl. 10).

Whether furniture designs were commissioned from him or not, he was the *arbiter elegantiarum*. Lady Shelburne received his 'entire approbation' for her idea of upholstering the furniture in the ante-room at Lansdowne House in 'pea green satin spotted with white and trimmed with a pink fringe'[78] and Lady Knatchbull conferred with him in 1774 concerning the furniture examples. The furniture of the next decade, the late 1760s and 1770s, is more elegant and above all more inventive; it is enriched with a profusion of delicate, small-scale ornaments and is well integrated both in itself and in relation to the larger scheme of decoration.

Fully integrated Adam rooms – parodied as ones 'in which the cheese cakes and raspberry tarts, upon the ceiling, vie with, and seems to reflect those upon the floor with such wonderful precision; and where the insupportably gorgeous ceiling, and the fervently glowing carpet, cause the poor walls to be seemingly dissatisfied, uneasy and impatient to retire from such fine company, as if conscious of their meanness and poverty' – were not always his doing.[83] It was Chippendale who supplied the Knatchbulls with 'a design for an Axminster Carpet to Correspond with (the) Ceiling' in Adam's bow drawing-room at Mersham-le-Hatch in 1775 and he probably did the same for Edwin Lascelles's music-room and yellow drawing-room at Harewood, for which no Adam carpet designs are known.[84] While Adam did design carpets to answer his ceilings (there is one, for instance, in the drawing-room at Osterley), he also designed some that were deliberately discordant, so creating what Summerson called 'a harmony of many contrasts'.[85] The drawing-rooms at Syon, Coventry House and 20 St James's Square are examples.

But carpets were not the only furnishings used by Adam to unify his rooms. By reiterating certain key motifs, he created more extensive harmonies. Thus, in the drawing-room at Osterley, similar combinations of griffons, rams' heads, portrait medallions and rinceaux linked his pier-glasses, commodes, door-cases, chimney-piece and grate and clearly distinguished his contribution from Linnell's modified-rococo seat furniture. On the other hand, in the drawing-room at Coventry House, where Adam's ceiling and carpet were at odds, the seat furniture, though not designed by him, was painted green and picked-out in gold to match his wall frieze.

Large looking-glasses imported from France at great expense were *de rigueur* for the glamorous look of Adam interiors, especially drawing-rooms. Their usual placement above chimney-pieces, pier-tables and commodes to form vertical units follows French prototypes, the likes of which can be seen in Neufforge's *Receuil*. However, their use as wall coverings for shallow niches on which gilded ornaments were applied seems to have been Adam's invention, first employed in the library at Kenwood in 1767 and continuously elaborated.

Mirrors, by virtue of their reflection and in their design – whether treated like embroidered wall decorations or like Venetian windows divided into three unequal parts by term figures or filigree pilasters and raised in the centre as at Luton and Bolton House, Southampton Row – were a principal source of 'movement'. Moreover, the rising and falling of the three-part division was reflected in the spacing of table-legs, which, in themselves, were often multiform and complex like those at Osterley, Coventry House, Lansdowne House and Nostell. Enriched pilasters were similarly used to articulate semi-circular commodes at Osterley and Derby House.

Colour also contributed to the varied effect: table-slabs of white marble had Adam designs inlaid in scagliola, marquetry commodes were inlaid with stained woods; other pieces, like Sir

11 A pair of carved and gilt-wood torchères and candelabra designed by Robert Adam, 1778 for the great drawing-room at Apsley House. The torchères are based on a 2nd-century Roman candelabra from Santa Costanza, Rome, now in the Salle dei Candelabri II in the Vatican Museum

Watkin Williams-Wynn's organ-case and Lady Wynn's dressing-room bookcase at 20 St James's Square, were completely painted; medallions, cameos and tablets painted with classical figures or in imitation of Wedgwood ware were applied to mirror crests, table-frames, commodes and girandoles in the same way that real Sèvres porcelain and Wedgwood were used as mounts on French furniture.

Antique forms were cleverly adapted for modern use. Vases and pedestals transformed into lead-lined water cisterns and pot-cupboards became an essential part of the sideboard suite; Roman altars were use to support tall candelabra in the great drawing-room at Apsley House (pl. 11); lyres, as Horace Walpole observed, made a 'charming harmony' on the backs of the dining-room chairs at Osterley; tripods served as candlesticks and as ornaments for girandoles; the tomb of Agrippa in the Pantheon was remodelled as a hall stool for Lansdowne House and Bowood.

Gothic furniture for the church of St Mary Magdalene at Croome d'Abitot, near Croome Court, was among Adam's earliest commissions in 1761. He evidently found it easier to work the elements of ecclesiastical architecture – traceries, cusped pinnacles and clustered columns – into a chair than to create a chair in the antique style. His experience at Croome stood him in good stead for the white-and-gold gothic chair and reading desk he designed in the later 1770s for the chapel at Alnwick.

Adam's prestige as the most fashionable architect in England faded in the 1780s and James Wyatt took the limelight. What remained of his diminished practice shifted mainly to Scotland where his genius still commanded considerable respect and he had fewer critics and rivals, but where there was not so much money available for extravagant interior decorations, even less for furniture. 'Plain and elegant and not expensive' was evidently what Scottish clients like the Honourable George Baillie of Mellerstain wanted and that, it so happened, was the general direction in which his style was heading anyway.[86] His late furniture, whether for the Duke of Cumberland at Cumberland House, Pall Mall, or the Earl of Cassillis at Culzean in Ayrshire, is quite streamlined, linear and almost two-dimensional, depending, in the case of Cumberland House, more on painted decorations than carving in relief. This is demonstrated by a comparison of the tripartite mirror designed in 1772 for Luton and the one designed ten years later for the long drawing-room at Culzean, one of the very few Scottish houses for which he designed furniture.[87] There is little evidence of his earlier taste for movement and the picturesque, which towards the end of his life he lavished on drawings of romantic castles – a few intended to be built, but most flights of his fertile imagination.

THE REPUTATION OF THE ADAM STYLE

By 1773, when the first part of Adam's *Works in architecture* was published, the decoration and furniture of his interiors had already 'met with . . . the imitation of other artists to such a degree, as in some measure to have brought about in this country, a kind of revolution in the whole system of this useful and elegant art.'[88] The truth of his claim was never seriously contested and was indeed corroborated by Wyatt's statement that 'when He came from Italy (in 1768) He found the public taste corrupted by the Adams & He was obliged to comply with it'.[89] However, the cocky, self-congratulatory tone of the *Works* went against the grain and as a result his designs were censured along with his ill-chosen words. The reaction might soon have fizzled out; instead it was kept alive and exacerbated by the appearance year after year for the next six years of subsequent parts of the two volumes.

To coincide exactly with the publication in April 1779 of the second and final volume of the *Works*, 'Roger Shanhagan, Gent.' (a pseudonym for the painter, Robert Smirke, father of the architect, and William Porden, a pupil of Wyatt's) issued a satirical skit entitled *The Exhibition or a second anticipation; being remarks on the principal Works to be exhibited next Month at the Royal Academy*, containing a scathing attack on the Adam brothers, though they were not exhibitors. Their genius was described as 'irregular, elevated and magnificent. Like Michael Angelo,

they look down with contempt on all the inferior excellencies and, like him, astonish by a grandeur of style that can never be imitated'.[90] They were censured for 'adapting the same noble style to interior and exterior decoration'; for their shamelessly arrogant assertions of their originality and the comparative excellence of their manner; and for making architecture 'contemptible by decking her with the flutter of a Courtezan'.[91] Adam was the villain, Wyatt the hero.

Shanhagan's mischievous pamphlet was circulated far and wide; a copy was even sent to Soane in Rome in 1779, though, as we shall see, it had no effect on what he told his Royal Academy students about Adam thirty-five years later.[92] However, at the time it certainly damaged Adam's reputation and must have contributed to the decline of his English practice in the following decade.

His style of decoration being so distinctive and pervasive meant that it was an easy target. Horace Walpole, a former admirer and client, mocked it as 'all gingerbread, filigraine, and fan painting' and preferred Wyatt, whom he thought had 'as much taste, (was) grander, and more pure'.[93] In the third edition of his *Treatise* (1791), Chambers, who had tried unsuccessfully to block Adam's rise right from the outset, finally struck at the very heart of his famed 'revolution' by taking up the cudgels for the Palladian style that the brothers overthrew.

> That stile, though somewhat heavy, was great; calculated to strike at the instant; and although the ornaments were neither so varied, nor so numerous as now; they had a more powerful effect: because more boldly marked, less complicated in their forms, and less profusely applied. They were easily perceptible without a microscope, and could not be mistaken for filigrane toy work. Content with the stores, which the refined ages of antiquity had left them, the architects of that day ransacked not the works of barbarous times; nor the port-folios of whimsical composers; for boyish conceits, and trifling complicated ornaments.[94]

A more objective, even-handed assessment of Adam's achievements was made by Soane in his lecture on ornament at the Royal Academy in 1815. The brothers' failure to 'retain the favourable opinion of the Public to the extent expected' he blamed on the debased antique sources of their style and its indiscriminate use in 'Public and Private Buildings, internally and externally'.[95] He excused the occasional flights of fancy that led Adam to descend to trifles by summoning the great Kent – designer of everything from buildings and gardens to cradles – as a precedent. Unlike the 'hyper-fastidious' Chambers, he had great praise for Adam for 'breaking the talismanic charm, which the fashion of the day (Burlington's Palladianism) had imposed, and for the introduction from Ancient Works of a light and fanciful style of Decoration, better suited for Private Buildings, and the elegance of modern refinement'. His concluding tribute was: 'To Mr Adam's taste in the Ornaments of his Buildings, and Furniture, (to which) we stand indebted, in-as-much as Manufacturers of every kind felt, as it were, the electric power of this Revolution in Art'.[96]

Soane met Adam in the early 1770s, when he was working under Henry Holland at Claremont House, Surrey, and found him 'certainly a man of uncommon talents, of an amiable disposition, and of unassuming manners'.[97] He shared his picturesque taste, his interest in contrast and variety, and his penchant for spatial manipulation. Like Adam, Soane was at his best in the handling of interiors.[98]

Soane's influence can be detected in the appreciation of Adam published by Robert Stuart Meikleham (who was admitted into the Royal Academy Schools in 1813) in his *Dictionary of architecture* (1832):

His style . . . ought not in fairness, to be subjected to a scrutiny or comparison with that founded on the imitation of Greek buildings, of which little or nothing was then known, but with that of his contemporaries and his models. It will be found abounding in beauties of a high and original kind, and which, it is hoped, will long preserve them as examples of a style of arrangement and decoration to which we would give our unqualified admiration, had they been the production of an architect of the lower Roman empire.[99]

Such 'unqualified admiration' for Adam was rare. Most nineteenth-century writers on architecture condemned his designs for having too great a profusion of ornament of an excessively flimsy, trivial sort, but agreed that they were original, 'strikingly novel', full of ideas and imagination and preferable to the 'formal heaviness of his predecessors'. William Henry Leeds, 'setting aside . . . his vitiated taste in embellishment', gave him 'the merit of having effected very great improvements in domestic architecture, generally, as regards internal accommodation, convenience, and comfort'.[100] In Joseph Gwilt's opinion, there were no redeeming features at all in Adam's 'depraved compositions'.[101]

These love–hate pronouncements on Adam by professional architects had no effect whatsoever upon the Adam revival, or the Adam Style as it came to be called, which, though it bore the name of an architect – and was exceptional in that respect as no other architect, neither Jones, Wren, Chambers nor Pugin, had a style named after him – did not apply to architecture in the usual sense of plans and elevations, but rather to mainly interior embellishments: chimney-pieces, ceilings, wall decorations, furniture and the like. My book on *The Furniture of Robert Adam*, published in 1963 dealt briefly with this complex phenomenon. Since then, interest has grown, more information has emerged, especially regarding Scottish interiors, and the subject now deserves to be treated on its own in much greater depth than can be attempted here.

The onset of the Adam revival was brought about by a number of trends in the decorative arts: a preference for English, as opposed to foreign, design and workmanship; a reaction against rococo fashions of the 1830s and 1840s in favour of neo-classical and Louis XVI styles – in *The Cabinet Maker and Art Furnisher* of June 1881, Adam decoration was described as 'the English version of Louis Seize'; revived interest in Herculaneum and Pompeii and, most influential of all, an increase in the collecting of 'Old Wedgwood' and improvements in the factory's new products after a period in the doldrums.

At the 1862 International Exhibition in London, Wright and Mansfield, a London firm of cabinet-makers and decorators, exhibited several pieces of furniture inlaid with Wedgwood

medallions, including a 'large dwarf bookcase' which was described in the catalogue as 'in the style of the Adelphi Adams, or good Pompeian'.[102] These first Adam-revival pieces were made for one of the most esteemed Wedgwood collectors of the period, Dudley Coutts Marjoribanks, MP, later Baron Tweedmouth, for the library and drawing-room of his recently acquired Scottish sporting estate, Guisachan, near Inverness. They were intended to harmonize with the Adam-style chimney-pieces and wall decorations inlaid with Wedgwood panels which must also have been supplied by Wright and Mansfield. All that survives of the firm's extensive work for Marjoribanks, to whom they owed their rise in fame in the 1860s as 'high class and exclusive' Adam specialists, is the distinctly Adamesque piano painted with pale-pink-and-green grotesque cameos and medallions picked-out in gold. The illustration of the piano in J. B. *Waring's Masterpieces of industrial art and sculpture at the International Exhibition, 1862* was bound to have attracted a certain amount of attention.

But this was as nothing compared to the widespread publicity that greeted Wright and Mansfield's award-winning Adam-style cabinet inlaid with Wedgwood at the International Exhibition in Paris in 1867. With the V&A's prompt purchase of the piece for the nation, the Adam revival was well and truly launched. By 1880, the popularity of the style had become so great and copies of the 'prized' *Works* so scarce that B. T. Batsford was induced to publish *The architecture, decoration and furniture of Robert and James Adam*, containing photo-lithograph copies of twenty-six plates of ceilings, chimney-pieces, furniture and decoration which, they claimed, amounted to 'well nigh all of general interest or value', the façade of 20 St James's Square being the only representation of architecture *per se*. This sole architectural plate was omitted and five more plates of furniture were added in the second edition of the book, published in 1901.

Batsford, recalling the circumstances of his initial publication, gave an interesting account of the Adam phenomenon over the ensuing twenty years. 'In 1880', he wrote, 'few, if any, supposed that we were as yet only in the beginning of a revival destined to last for many years. But so it has proved, for there is as yet no sign that the work of the period is falling to disrepute; and of the talented brothers it safe to say that they have given their name to a style likely to become historic at least in their own country'.[103] By then, the Adam style had already spread beyond the British Isles to New York, where a selection of photo-lithographs from the *Works* was published by W. Helburn in the 1880s, and to Paris, where the first full-size facsimile was published by E. Thézard in 1900–2. Nor was the *Works* the only source for authentic Adam designs; the volumes of drawings at the Soane were also culled by John Alden Heaton for furniture designs which he published in 1892 in the first of his profusely illustrated three volumes on *Furniture and decoration in England during the 18th century*.

These books were not only used to make reproduction 'Adams' furniture for interiors of all sorts all over the world, but also to supply surviving genuine Adam houses, like Culzean and 5 Charlotte Square, Edinburgh, with authentic Adam ceilings and chimney-pieces which they did not have from Adam. By focusing attention upon Adam's interiors, they may have been responsible in some measure for their remarkable survival.

12   The south front of Kedleston, designed by Robert Adam, 1768

I

KEDLESTON HALL

Adam was introduced to Sir Nathaniel Curzon by his friend General Sir Charles Hay in December 1758, a month after he succeeded as fifth baronet. Had their meeting taken place a few months earlier, the job of building a new house at Kedleston in Derbyshire to rival Holkham might have gone to Adam instead of the sixty-year-old Matthew Brettingham. None the less, it was an occasion of momentous importance, which he reported at length to his brother James in Rome.

Curzon, on being shown the drawings that Adam had brought back with him from Italy in January of that year, was

> struck all of a heap with wonder and amaze. Everything he converted to his own house and every new drawing he saw made him grieve at his previous engagement with Brettingham. He carried me home (to Audley Square) in his chariot about three o'clock and kept me to four o'clock seeing all said Brettingham's designs, and asking my opinion. I proposed alterations and desired he might call them his own fancies. I went back on Saturday evening at six o'clock and sat two hours with him and his lady who is a daughter of Lord Portmore, Lady Caroline Collyear, . . . I revised all his plans and got the entire management of his grounds put into my hands, with full powers as to temples, bridges, seats and cascades, so that as it is seven miles round you may guess the play of genius and scope for invention . . .[1]

It seemed to him that he had found the perfect patron: 'a man resolved to spare no Expence, with £10,000 a Year, Good Temper'd & having taste himself for the Arts and little for Game', who, in addition, appreciated his genius.[2]

This was not his only triumph. Few things could have pleased him more than Curzon's showing him the rejected designs made in 1757 or 1758 by one of his most dreaded rivals, James Stuart, the 'Great Athenian'. These, he informed his brother, were

> so excessively and so ridiculously bad, that Mr Curzon immediately saw the folly of them and said so to some people which so offended the proud Grecian, that he has not seen Sir Nathaniel these 2 years and he says he keeps the Drawings Sacred in self defence. He made a Gallery only 5 feet high so that by that one would think the modern Greeks diminished in size as well as in spirit. But forgot that Brittains were taller. Then he advances his columns in his Great hall, so much as

only to leave 14 feet of space which you know was making a narrow passage of it. His ordinary Rooms beggar all description however ridiculous, I confess myself unequal to the task. Tables 2 foot sq. in a Room of 50 foot longer with belts of stone and great pannels and roses and festoons and figures all rammed in wherever there was a hole to be got for them, and he wanted to fitt frames for Sir Nat's. pictures but not having or rather I suppose, not being willing to confine his Genius to the sizes of the pictures, he cutts 3 foot off the length of the best pictures and 2 foot off the height of others to make them answer, and Draws all the Pictures and colours them in his Drawings. But they are so ill done that they move pity rather than contempt.[3]

Aiming squibs at Stuart was a favourite sport of Adam's; they pepper his correspondence and should not be taken too literally. It was not Stuart's work (of which there was precious little to be seen in 1758) that he despised, but rather the high esteem in which his 'Gusto Greco' was held by the *cognoscenti* eagerly awaiting the publication of his *Antiquities of Athens* in 1762. Though Adam never missed a chance to belittle the 'Proud Grecian', he had no qualms about using his neo-classical ideas.[4]

Stuart's 'Room of 50 foot long' was a five-bay, two-storey picture gallery, 30 feet high and 30 feet wide, with windows on ground- and first-floor levels and a glazed garden-door (pl. 13); his 'Great Hall' has not been traced.[5] These designs were probably made for the existing, c.1700 house by Smith of Warwick, but certainly not for the new house, as we know it, built from c.1759. Curzon, having bought a large number of pictures, statues and busts in 1756 and 1757, had to start thinking of how and where to display them. Evidently his first idea, probably influenced by his aged father, who was also a picture collector, was to adapt the pre-existing house. Designs for a two-storey entrance hall (52 × 28 × 28 feet or 15.8 × 8.5 × 8.5 metres) lit from one end and a gallery (50 × 30 × 30 feet or 15.2 × 9.15 × 9.15 metres) were obtained from three different architects, one after the other: the first unidentified, followed by the fashionable, but as yet unproven, Stuart, and finally Matthew Brettingham.[6]

This idea was promptly dropped when Curzon succeeded in November 1758. Brettingham was then engaged to build an entirely new house, consisting of a central block with four wings linked by quadrant corridors, following the configuration of

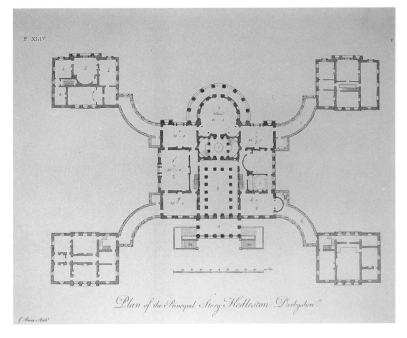

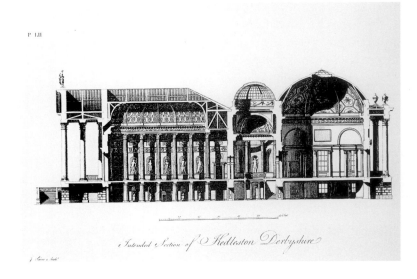

16 James Paine, 'Plan of the Principal Story Kedleston Derbyshire', *c.*1759–60 (*Plans, elevations and sections of noblemen and gentlemen's houses*, II, pl. XLIV)

17 James Paine, 'Intended Section, Kedleston Derbyshire', *c.*1759–60 (*Plans, elevations and sections of noblemen and gentlemen's houses*, II, pl. LII)

13 James 'Athenian' Stuart, design for a hall-picture gallery at Kedleston, *c.*1757 (Kedleston, The National Trust)

14 James 'Athenian' Stuart, design for an organ niche at Kedleston, *c.*1757 (Kedleston, The National Trust)

15 James 'Athenian' Stuart, design for a sideboard niche at Kedleston, *c.*1757 (Kedleston, The National Trust)

18   Section of Kedleston, by Robert Adam, 1760 (Sir John Soane's Museum: Adam drawings vol. 40:3)

Palladio's Villa Mocenigo, which was also the model for Nostell Priory, Yorkshire. Work started in 1759 with the demolition of the eastern part of the old house and the construction of the north-east wing, or family pavilion, and was to progress westwards in three stages. However, before the year was out, Brettingham left, attracted perhaps by the greater opportunities offered by the vastly rich Lord Lowther (the Earl of Bute's son-in-law) at Lowther Castle, Westmorland.[7]

James Paine, who had established a successful practice in the northern counties (having started at Nostell in 1736) and was currently working in Derbyshire at Chatsworth, was brought in to oversee the completion of the house.[8] Though he had to adhere to Brettingham's design in building the north-west, or kitchen, pavilion which was his first task, it was not too late for him to make alterations to the body of the house and corridors. Encouraged, no doubt, by Curzon, he devised a new plan in 1759, adding a Pantheon-like domed rotunda (42 feet in diameter) on the south front, which was separated from the columnar hall by a double staircase in two apsidal compartments screened by columns, with large semi-domed niches and a domed skylight.

But by far the most extraordinary feature of his scheme was its garden façade, with half the rotunda projecting as a monumental bow surrounded by a semi-circular, octastyle portico of giant, free-standing columns. Its source was almost certainly Robert Castell's reconstruction of Pliny's Villa Laurentinum, a copy of which was, conveniently, to be found in Curzon's library.[9]

Paine's plan, section (pls 16, 17) and south elevation have not survived and are known only from the engravings published by him in 1783.[10] It has recently been argued, however, that these do not represent his original designs but are enhanced versions

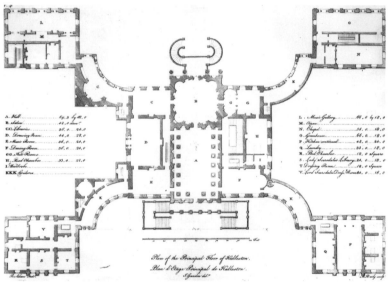

19   Plan of the principal floor of Kedleston, by Robert Adam, c.1764–65 (*Vitruvius Britannicus*, IV, pl. 46)

made to convince the public of his superiority to Adam, who had supplanted him.[11] That Paine should have gone to such trouble in search of revenge more than twenty years after the event seems extremely dubious.

Just as Adam's opinion had been sought on Brettingham's scheme, so it was on Paine's, where Curzon's principal concern must have been the enormous expense entailed by the bow, its colonnade and two domes. By May 1760, Adam had produced a more economic plan (pls 18, 19), with the main stairs on the west side and the rotunda set in a square and brought within the body of the house, leaving a reasonable projection of 3 metres (10 feet), as opposed to Paine's of 6.4 metres (21 feet), which he dressed with a readily recognizable 'antique' portico (pl. 12) modelled on the Arch of Constantine.[12] At about this time he also began drawing wall elevations for the nearly finished state rooms on the east front.

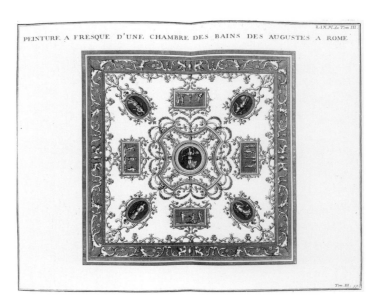

20   Design for the ceiling of the painted breakfast-room in the family pavilion, by Robert Adam, 1760 (Kedleston, The National Trust)

21   Bernard de Montfaucon, engraving of an antique Roman ceiling in the Baths of Augustus (*Supplèment au livre de l'antiquité expliquée*, Paris [1764], vol. III, pl. LIX)

Though Paine had reason to be resentful, there is no evidence that he was, or indeed that Adam harboured any competitive antagonism towards him. The employment of two architects at once expedited matters and was not so unusual as generally thought: Gibbs, Campbell and Kent all worked together at Houghton.

According to Paine, he was 'employed to make (i.e. to execute) the plans for the magnificent mansion in the year 1761, and the foundations were soon after accordingly laid'. Everything was ready for 'carrying on the buildings with all possible dispatch' when he suddenly departed, not because of the pressure of work elsewhere, as he stated, but owing, it seems, to a disagreement with Samuel Wyatt, the clerk of the works, over his charges.[13]

On 15 April 1761 Adam signed a contract with Lord Scarsdale specifying his responsibilities as 'Surveyor to the main body of his Lordship's house' and agreeing that he was to have 'no concern with the corridors leading to the wings or with the wings themselves'; the family and kitchen pavilions were finished by then and there was evidently no urgency for the southern wings.[14] On 9 May Paine exhibited his 'plan of the principal floor, garden front, and a section through the North rooms of a house designed in the year 1759, for a person of distinction, in the County of Derby'.[15]

Would Kedleston have been very different if Paine had stayed on? Probably not. Even during Paine's tenure, Adam was designing ceilings, wall decorations and other furnishings for the family pavilion as well as the state rooms and would doubtless have continued to do so. Moreover, Scarsdale, like Sir Thomas Coke of Holkham, took an active role in the design of the interiors.

The situation was reported by Robert to his brother James in Rome in July 1760:

We have had the greatest revolutions at Sr Nat^s that You ever heard of. Mr Swan the great, is dismissed & Mr Wyatt the Carpenter now fills his place which I think is mostly brought

about by me and now none of them Setts a Stone or Cutts a bit of Timber without my Positive Instructions'. Furthermore, 'Sir N. spoke to me . . . about publishing the Designs of His House, which I told him I certainly would do so soon as all is done & Executed.[16]

But, as we shall see, all was never 'done & Executed' and what was done took so long and was subject to so many alterations that in the end Adam never published any of his designs for Kedleston. Ironically, it was to John Woolfe, who had worked at the house under Paine, that Curzon entrusted Adam's latest (i.e. 1764–5) plans, section and elevations for publication in *Vitruvius Britannicus*, IV in 1767. Although what Curzon had in mind when he spoke to Adam in 1760 was almost certainly a monograph like the one Brettingham was then preparing on Holkham, Adam (despite his reluctance to make his 'Manner', 'Ornaments' and 'Studys' available for others to plagiarize) had bigger ideas. 'Sir Nat$^s.$ Fronts & Sections', he told James, 'may make near 10 plates including the painted room, & if you publish details of organ, Silver plate, Carpets &c many more. Then there is the Bridge, the Ruins, the Towers, the pheasant House (a new Contrivance) a new Gateway to his avenue and a new Temple'. In addition, 'there is M$^r.$ Lascelles's plans & fronts. General Bland's Room & Green House & Temple . . . my Lord Northumberland, my Lord Coventry, in short many others . . . which would make no bad publication already'. The idea soon fizzled out as others had done before.

The painted breakfast-room in the north-west corner of the family pavilion was Adam's first and most innovative room at Kedleston, the only one in which he had a free hand, unconstrained by Curzon's collections, and which was unaltered in execution. He described his scheme to James in July 1760 as 'quite in a new taste' which Agostino Brunais, a trusted Clérisseau-trained painter whom he brought back with him from Italy, was then 'employed in painting in size to learn that method as Oyl

22 Design for the decoration of one of the walls of the painted breakfast-room in the family pavilion, by Robert Adam, 1760 (Kedleston, The National Trust)

colours will by no means answer. They call that manner of painting in French, à la detrempe, and I think he (Brunais) succeeds wonderfully with it.'[17]

Composing decorative designs in the antique style was no problem for Adam: the ceiling was adapted from a Roman model published in Montfaucon's *Antiquité* and 'the paintings and antique ornaments' were said to be 'after the Baths of Diocletian' (pls 20, 21).[18] However, carrying them out in tempera to resemble frescos was a different matter which Brunais evidently had to learn. The ornaments were painted on paper, then cut out and pasted up around two large oval figure paintings and five rectangular scenes on canvas which were set into the walls in gilt-wood frames carved by Sefferin Alken in 1761 (pl. 22). When the room was dismantled in 1807, the five rectangular paintings and some of the original Adam furniture were saved. The paintings were sold to the V&A, but the Adam furniture designed for the room in 1760 and executed by Robert Robinson, a local craftsman, remains in the house. It consists of a pair of early neo-classical tables with spiral-fluted legs and scagliola armorial slabs, and two gilt-wood window-seats with lambrequin aprons inspired by the canopy over the organ in Stuart's design for a gallery (pl. 13).[19]

23 Sketches for neo-classical tables and accompanying mirror frames, by Robert Adam, *c*.1763. There are notes dated May 1763 pertaining to Kedleston on the verso (Sir John Soane's Museum: Adam drawings vol. 54, pt. i:93)

24 The music-room with the organ on the west wall, designed by Robert Adam, 1768

25 *Design for the West End of the Musick Room* showing the organ, by Robert Adam, 1760 (Kedleston, The National Trust)

26 Design for the organ case, by Robert Adam, 1762 (Sir John Soane's Museum: Adam drawings, vol. 25:2)

The house itself offered considerably less scope for Adam's inventive genius than the family pavilion or garden buildings. Scarsdale's collections – his pictures above all else – governed virtually everything. Indeed, it was partly with them in mind that Scarsdale conceived the idea of a suite of three state rooms on the east front, each devoted to a different art – music, painting and literature – and each with an appropriate architectural order: Corinthian for the withdrawing-room, the largest and most magnificent room (apart from the hall and saloon), Ionic for the music-room and the manly Doric for the library. He went to great pains to make the arrangement of the pictures as near perfect and as permanent as possible, having many of them set into the walls; excessive projection was a particular bugbear.

What part Paine played in all this, apart from establishing the proportions of the three rooms and the basic form and location of their doors and windows, remains unknown. It is tempting to attribute the pedimented, alabaster doorcases and Venetian window in the drawing-room to him rather than Adam, for whom they seem too heavy and old-fashioned. It is hard to disentangle the division of responsibility or the sequence of events from the set of finished wall elevations of the rooms that Adam worked-

up from Scarsdale's sketches, which are uniformly dated 1760 though they were demonstrably drawn at least a year later, after Paine had left and he was in full command.[20]

The circuit of the state rooms begins in the music-room, which Paine planned as a library, at the very end of a route that went down the main axis, through the hall and staircase to the rotunda, and then turned east to a drawing-room and saloon; he had no music room as such. It was in this moderate-sized room (10.9 × 7 × 6.7 metres, or 36 × 23 × 22 feet) that Scarsdale decided to display his two largest and most striking possessions: Luca Giordano's *Triumph of Bacchus* (an appropriate starter!) and the great Snetzler organ of church proportions which he bought in 1758.[21] They could only be accommodated on the end walls, and then only if the false doors that would normally have been introduced there for symmetry (and were included in Paine's plan) were omitted.

Pride of place was given to the Giordano on the east wall directly opposite the entrance to the room, where it had an immediate impact. The whole of the west wall – except for the door and one picture above it – was to be occupied by the organ, for which Adam designed a monumental case, approximately 5.4 metres tall, 3.6 metres wide and at least 1 metre deep (18 × 12 × 3½ feet), with four life-size Ionic caryatids in front of the pipes and musical trophies on the base (pl. 25).[22] By some oversight, no provision was made (as it had been in Stuart's gallery-design) for a recess in which to place the instrument, nor was it possible to introduce one, owing to the fact that the west wall was already eaten into by the niches in the hall.[23] It was obvious that the great Snetzler was too large for the room. Curzon considered placing it in the gallery of the chapel in the south-east pavilion, but nothing came of that idea and on 11 April 1762 he wrote asking Bute if he would offer the king an 'organ that Judges in musick tell me is very excellent'.[24] The response was presumably negative, for Adam's revised plan of *c.*1764–5 (pl. 19) introduced a music-gallery in the south-east pavilion with special provision for a large organ, flanked by a room for the organ bellows and a closet for music books. Finally, in March 1766, the organ was sold back to Snetzler.[25] By then, it had been replaced by an older instrument of considerably smaller size (approximately 2.7 × 1.6 × .9 metres, or 9 × 5½ × 3 feet) for which Adam designed a new case in July 1762 with a circular opening for the pipes (a fairly new element, first found on the Eton College organ of 1760) framed by Ionic pilasters and two winged female figures lifting a curtain (pl. 26).[26] There was now space on the west wall for three pictures in addition to the overdoor, one of them a recently purchased, putative Rembrandt.[27]

It must have been apparent by 1765, when the pictures were up and the organ was in place (still in its old painted-pine case), that Adam's new design was too elaborate and would detract from the pictures. A simplified version (pl. 24), without the figures but evidently with a bit more ornament than there is now, was executed by local craftsmen and fixed to the organ in December 1765.[28] The disappointing outcome of Adam's organ designs for Lord Scarsdale was offset in 1775 by the successful completion of a closely related organ for Sir Watkin Williams-Wynn at 20 St James's Square.

There were no such problems regarding the decoration of the music-room. By 27 August 1760, Adam had finished his designs

27 The drawing-room showing Adam's coved ceiling and caryatid chimney-piece

for the ceiling, entablature and plaster picture frames to be fixed in the walls and had given them to Joseph Rose for estimates. He was busy 'getting Mouldings ready' which, as he told Sir Nat., 'require both time & Study, else the Effect may be much hurt if not entirely lost by (their) disproportion . . .'.[29] The Ionic chimney-piece is not mentioned in the correspondence and there are no bills or designs for it; however, it is shown in Adam's wall-elevation, with its lyre and quiver frieze but without the tablet depicting an Epithalamium (Greek wedding-chorus) from Bartoli's *Admiranda Romanarum*.[30] The Danish sculptor, Michael Henry Spang, is credited with carving it as well as the drawing- room and dining-room chimney-pieces.[31] Apart from the organ-case, the room has no Adam furniture. Linnell is thought to have supplied the gilt-wood curtain cornices; the pair of eagle pier-tables was designed and carved by James Gravenor in 1765, together with a pair of oak-leaf pier-glass frames which were replaced in the nineteenth century by the present ones with eagle crests.[32]

The music-room is, in effect, a prelude to the magnificent withdrawing-room (pl. 27), hung with the cream of the picture collection on pale blue damask and furnished with splendid gilded sofas and pier-glasses. Architecturally, it is dominated by an exceedingly large Venetian window, with projecting Corinthian columns and pilasters and four pedimented Corinthian doorcases, all executed in pink-veined Derbyshire alabaster. Whether these heavy, old-fashioned elements are by Adam or Paine is uncertain.[33]

There is no question, however, that Adam was responsible for the decoration of the coved ceiling and caryatid chimney-piece (pls 28, 29); both were designed in 1760 and are related to contemporary work for Admiral Boscowan at Hatchlands in Surrey (pl. 30).[34] On the flat centre of the ceiling is an interlaced quatrefoil of antique origin, taken from Bartoli's *Pictorae Antiquae* (1750) and used in variant forms at Hatchlands (1759), the anteroom at Syon (1761), and other early houses.[35] The cove, on the other hand, has a nautical theme represented by sea-horses and merfolk, which may have been inspired by a design by Spang of 1758, for a painted ceiling depicting naval aspects of the Seven Years War. This, according to its scale, was for a larger room (14 × 8.5 metres, or 47 × 28 feet), possibly in the old house, but not in the new one.[36]

If the date 1759 inscribed on Adam's design for the drawing-

28 'Design of a Ceiling in the Antique Stile for the Venetian Wind^W. Drawing Room at Kedleston', by Robert Adam, 1759 (Kedleston, The National Trust)

29 One of the caryatids on the drawing-room chimney-piece

30 The drawing-room (originally the dining-room) at Hatchlands, Surrey with Adam's caryatid chimney-piece of 1760 on the back wall

31   One of four sofas carved with sea nymphs and dolphins, by John Linnell, 1765

32   'Design of a Sopha for Lord Scarsdale & also executed for Mrs. Montagu in Hill Street', by Robert Adam, 1762 (Sir John Soane's Museum: Adam drawings vol. 17:69)

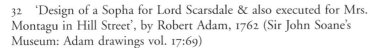

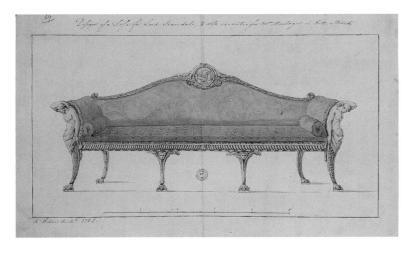

33   The window wall of the drawing-room showing Adam's flamboyant mirror frames with John Linnell's chaste neo-classical card-tables below them

room ceiling is correct, then it is one of his earliest interior designs for the new house, contemporary with two carpets (one 12.8 × 8.5 metres or 42 × 28 feet, the other 6.1 × 9.1 metres or 20 × 30 feet) which are the subject of a letter to Curzon of 31 July 1759 and may be identified with two undated and unscaled designs at the Soane.[37] The large carpet would only have fitted the drawing-room and the other might have been destined for the library or music-room, but neither is known to have been executed.[38]

Adam's role in the design of the two magnificent pairs of sofas (3.6 and 3.9 metres, or 12 and 13 feet long) supplied by John Linnell in 1765 is unclear (pl. 31). Their carved and gilt dolphins, sea-nymphs and tritons are more than an answer to his ceiling; they are a celebration of George III's accession as 'Monarch of the Ocean', which brought Curzon his eagerly awaited peerage as 1st Lord Scarsdale on 9 April 1761.[39] Horace Walpole was quick to recognize the similarity of the 'gilt fishes and Sea Gods' to the state coach designed for George III by Sir William Chambers.[40] Significantly, Linnell also competed for the commission with a design that was engraved in 1761 and dedicated to Lord Scarsdale. It was rumoured that designs for the coach were sought from Adam too, but none have been traced.[41] Nicola

Salvi's Trevi Fountain in Rome (1732–62) was not only the common source for Chambers and Linnell but was also a forerunner of Adam's triumphal arch on the south front of Kedleston.[42]

Among the Adam drawings at the Soane is one inscribed at a later date, 'Design for a Sofa for Lord Scarsdale & also executed for Mrs Montagu in Hill Street' (pl. 32), which lacks the baroque vigour of the Kedleston sofas and also differs in other respects.[43] Though signed and dated 'Robert Adam Archt 1762', it is probably earlier and may not be an original Adam design, but rather a record of a drawing by Linnell. Indeed, it is closely related to a Linnell drawing in the V&A for an armchair inscribed 'For Sir Nathl. Curzon'.[44]

Linnell's Kedleston sofas, upholstered in light-blue damask to match the walls and curtains, were delivered to the house in July and August 1765. The larger pair was placed on either side of the chimney-piece and the smaller one against the end wall, where there is a nice juxtaposition of a sensuous sea-nymph and a painting of *Sleeping Cupid* above it.

Nothing could be more different in style from the spectacular gilt sofas than the pair of neo-classical marquetry card-tables also designed by Linnell in 1765 (pl. 33). His inspiration in this case was the much admired *bureau à la grec* that the Earl of Coventry

34 The library showing the massive Doric door at the west end and the 'mosaic' ceiling

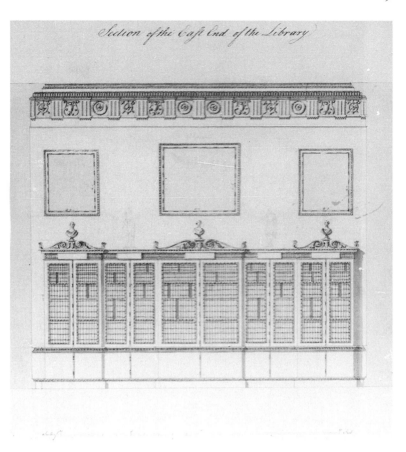

35 'Section of the East End of the Library', by Robert Adam, 1760 (Kedleston, The National Trust)

(another patron he shared with Adam) had purchased from Poirier in Paris in January 1765.[45] Hearing of Linnell's latest commission for Kedleston, Samuel Wyatt wrote to Lord Scarsdale in March 1765, 'I presume your Lordship intends the Card Tables for the Drawing Room to stand under the glasses. I hope they will not be made to project too far into the room'.[46] Oddly enough, it was not their projection that Adam objected to, but their propriety. 'Marble Tables', he told Scarsdale, 'are not so proper for a Withdrawing room as Card Tables, or Tables for Tea China'.[47] This puzzling advice was given well before the arrival in 1767 of his flamboyant pier-glasses under which the card-tables appear dwarfed and stylistically discordant. When the Duchess of Northumberland visited Kedleston in August 1766 the card-tables (which are similar to the pair Linnell made for Alnwick) were not standing against the piers, but in the deep window embrasures.

The glasses to which Wyatt referred seem to have been a pair of old mirrors. By May 1765, a decision had been made to replace them and Wyatt informed Lord Scarsdale that he would 'get a design and estimate made for the glass frame in the drawing room. I presume it must be so contrived as to use your Lordship's old plate glass', an understandable economy in view of the high

price of mirror-glass at that date. A month later, a design was received from Adam for oval glasses framed by bold acanthus scrolls and anthemia, echoing the ornaments in the cove of his ceiling, and fitted with swivelling candle-branches.[48] These frames were carved by James Gravenor, who was also responsible for carving the alabaster Corinthian capitals for the Venetian window and doorcases in 1760. They were still in the hands of Mr Smith, the gilder, on 5 January 1766 – 'delayed . . . by Mr Smith and (Wyatt) not agreeing about the prise of the gilding' – and were not noticed by the perceptive Duchess of Northumberland when she visited the house that summer.[49]

In 1767, Scarsdale obtained another design from Adam for a pair of long, narrow girandoles to match the mirrors (which must by then have been in place) and to hang opposite them on either side of the chimney-piece.[50] While these girandoles, each with five candle-branches, would have considerably improved the lighting of the room, they would also have cramped the carefully balanced arrangement of the pictures and competed with their gilded frames described by the Duchess of Northumberland as being 'immensely expensive'. This may explain why they were not executed. A crystal chandelier was the principal source of artificial light.[51]

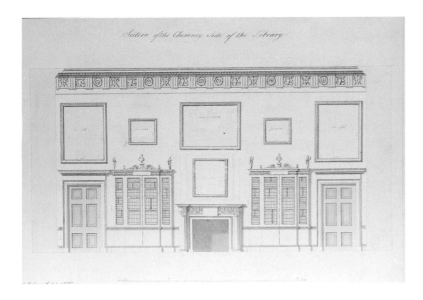

36 'Section of the Chimney Side of the Library', by Robert Adam, 1760 (Kedleston, The National Trust)

37 'Section of the Chimney Side of a Book Room for Kedleston House', by Robert Adam, 1768. This was proposed as an extension to the library, but was not executed (Kedleston, The National Trust)

38 The columnar screen between the ante-room and dressing-room. The capitals are derived from Diocletian's palace at Spalatro

In contrast to the festive music-room and drawing-room, the library, the last in the suite of state rooms, is a sober, predominantly male preserve in the masculine Doric order (pl. 34). There is hardly a trace here of the graceful arabesques and rinceaux seen in the preceding rooms. The repeat pattern of octagonal and circular coffers in the so-called 'mosaic ceiling' is almost identical to an unexecuted design made a year later for the library at Shardeloes and similar to the ceiling in the gallery at Croome Court, which is also of 1761 and was initially intended as a library.[52] Despite the distaste for the glare of white that Adam expressed a decade later in his *Works*, all three rooms (like the library at Osterley) were monochromatic white and dead-stone architectural compositions.[53]

There are two sets of wall elevations: one, at the Soane, which, though undated, is probably 1760 and almost certainly incorporates Curzon's ideas and perhaps some of Paine's as well; the other, at Kedleston, is a more finished drawing, dated 1760 but

drawn around 1765 after the proposed south pavilions were abandoned.[54] Scarsdale's indecision regarding the completion of the south front is reflected in the variant designs for the east wall of the library. While the Soane drawing has a door to the south-east corridor, a matching false door and a breakfront bookcase between them (pl. 35), the corresponding later elevation at Kedleston and an undated plan of the room at the Soane both show the whole of the wall closed off and occupied by a large three-part bookcase which would have unified the decoration had it been executed.[55] However, in the event, the two disruptive and unnecessary doors, which evidently were already in existence, having been made by Paine, were retained.[56] They were finally removed around 1830 and the bookcase was extended to its present size.

It is more difficult to explain the unsuitability of the two pedimented doors with Ionic pulvinated friezes in the unfinished Soane elevation of the chimney-side of this Doric room (pl.

39 Design for the window wall of
the proposed 'Book Room', by
Robert Adam, 1768 (Sir John Soane's
Museum: Adam drawings vol. 14:122)

36).[57] Were they also made by Paine when the library was a drawing-room, or are they merely errors communicated by Curzon? Whatever the case, the pediments were removed and the friezes corrected in the final, executed elevation.[58] And whose idea was it to have a giant, pedimented Doric doorcase dominating not just the west wall but the entire room? More likely Curzon's than Adam's, though he was responsible for its design.[59] Not surprisingly, there were thoughts of replacing it in 1775 with a more elegant, arched doorcase by George Richardson, who also designed refinements for the music-room ceiling.[60] Nothing came of either of these ideas, and in the 1830s the second Baron Scarsdale resorted to simplifying the bookcases by removing their outdated open-scroll pediments and octagonal glazed doors.

The library, built to Brettingham's and Paine's plans, did not lend itself to the integrated arrangement of bookcases that Adam achieved at Shardeloes in 1761. Free-standing pieces were the only alternative. His mahogany breakfront bookcase with drawers for clothes below, designed in August 1760 for Lady Curzon's dressing-room in the family pavilion and made in London by William Linnell, was the model for the library bookcases made at Kedleston by local craftsmen in 1765.[61]

The delicacy, harmony, novelty and variety lacking in the library are abundantly present in Adam's unexecuted designs of 1768 (pls 37, 39) for a mirrored 'Book Room' to be furnished and decorated in much the same manner as the library at Kenwood, designed the previous year.[62] It was suggested by Lord Scarsdale that access to the proposed eastern extension should be through 'folding Doors very Large or a Screen of Columns' in the centre of the problematic east wall of the library so that 'the View of the very broad part of the River may be taken from the Salloon Door or farther'.[63] A screen of columns in the library would have answered the columnar screen with capitals derived from Diocletian's palace at Spalatro which had recently been erected

between the ante-room and dressing-room in the 'Principal Apartment' on the west side of the house (pl. 38).

The corresponding western extension was to contain a circular painted breakfasting-room with a domed ceiling and four semi-domed alcoves, all painted with highly coloured grotesques in the style of the ancients (pls 40, 41).[64] It is very closely related to the circular dressing-room at Harewood, c.1767–9, which was executed but later destroyed.[65] These distinctive, Adamissimo rooms would have been an anomaly tacked on to the main body of the house conceived in the Holkham mould as a museum for Scarsdale's collections. They were not executed and the west wall of the dressing-room, instead of opening to the painted breakfasting-room and partaking of the extensive view from its tall window, was hung with a tripartite mirror framed by gilded palm trees and surmounted by the Scarsdale arms. This enormous mirror, seen from the saloon or further, increases the sense of space within the house. Like the state bed, with its gilded palm posts and the accompanying palm pier-glass and torchères, it was designed in 1764 by James Gravenor and carved by him and his assistant, Joseph Hall.[66] George III's coronation coach seems to have had almost as much influence upon these pieces as it did upon the slightly earlier drawing-room sofas.[67]

The principal apartment was conceived by Scarsdale himself in 1764 as an alternative to the apartment planned by Adam, which consisted of a rectangular ante-room and principal bed-chamber on the south front, leading to a great apsidal dressing-room with screens of Ionic columns at each end and a Venetian window on the west wall. Being in direct communication with the dining-room, the great dressing-room would have served as a withdrawing-room for the ladies to retire to after dinner and a general reception room of less formal character than the with-drawing-room in the state apartment. Moreover, Scarsdale would have been able to use the room to display statues in four niches and more of his pictures.[68]

40 Design (unexecuted) for the painted dome of the breakfasting-room, by Robert Adam, 1768 (Kedleston, The National Trust)

41 Design (unexecuted) for the chimney side of the painted breakfasting-room proposed to be added to the south-west corner but not built, by Robert Adam, 1768 (Kedleston, The National Trust)

Although Adam was 'sorry to lose so elegant a Room as the Dressing room', he agreed that communication with the south-west pavilion would be better through a small dressing-room as proposed by Scarsdale than a state bed chamber as he had planned. But, to render Scarsdale's idea of an apartment 'à la Français' more complete, he advised 'une petite Chambre à Coucher pour le Domestique . . . as also le Commoditez or Water Closet both of which I have got very Conveniently'.[69] Admittedly, the servant's room (presumably tucked in behind the back stairs) would have to make do with 'a small borrowed light' from the wardrobe, 'but that', he assured Scarsdale, 'is very common in French apartments & no great inconveniency as it is a night Room & serves at the same time as a passage Room to the Escalier Derobé, & gives the compleat apartment: viz. premier antichambre, Second antichambre (i.e. dressing room), Grand Chambre à coucher, Garderobe (ingeniously inserted in the angle between the wardrobe and dining room), Chambre à Coucher du Valet, un Commoditez, et l'Escalier Derobé'. Scarsdale's 'Grande Chambre' was no match either for Adam's great dressing-room or for his principal bedchamber, which was to have a star-shaped ceiling of antique origin similar to the one designed by Chambers for Augusta, Dowager Princess of Wales at the Alhambra at Kew in 1758 and published in 1763.[70] In order to give 'the Idea of grandeur to the apartment' and at the same time to make the room 'more regular', Adam recommended that the state bed be placed 'within a Screen of Columns'. His advice was not taken and he played no part in the furnishing of the apartment. In the event, the southern pavilions were abandoned and Scarsdale's revised plan was no improvement; the house would have been better built as Adam planned it.

The dining-room was not intended to be entered, as it is now, from the wardrobe, but rather from the hall, giving the visitor a full and striking view of the large niche on the end wall with its impressive display of the Scarsdale plate (pl. 42). A normal, rectangular sideboard placed against a flat wall would have been perfectly adequate for showing the silver; however, a recess of some description was required for the massive Sicilian jasper cistern, supplied by the sculptor, Richard Hayward.[71] Stuart (who may have been responsible for its design) provided a tall, arched alcove at one end of the two-storey gallery he designed for the old house, and within that a rectangular sideboard under which it sheltered.

It was Paine who introduced the great niche in the dining-room, intending to give it a screen of columns that would have resulted in a quite different and perhaps more focused composition. The columns were omitted, leaving a cavernous, semi-domed opening (3.6 metres, or 12 feet, in diameter) for the cistern, around which Adam designed a curved sideboard composed of three crescent-shaped tables separated by a pair of square pedestals, with lower, oval pedestals in front of them (pl. 43) – all painted white and picked out in gold.[72] Although the tables were admired by the Duchess of Northumberland for their 'very pretty shapes' and 'beautiful marble tops', and are of historical interest as early examples of Adam's work in this field, they are less notable as pieces of furniture than the related pier-tables and are wholly subservient to the *mise-en-scène*. Upon them Adam arranged a unified but picturesque ensemble of eight knife boxes supporting silver dishes, a pair of gun metal and

42 The sideboard niche at the west end of the dining-room with Adam's display of plate, etc. restored to its original appearance

43 'Design of the West End of the Dining Room with the Nich & Sideboard', by Robert Adam, 1762 (Kedleston, The National Trust)

44 James 'Athenian' Stuart, tripod perfume burner with candle-branches made for Sir Nathaniel Curzon probably by Diedrich Nicholas Anderson, *c.*1760

45 Two abutting doorcases in the south-west corner of the dining-room

46 A figure of Bacchus with a cup and thyrsus, one of the terms on the dining-room chimney-piece. The other term figure is of Ceres, goddess of fruitfulness, designed by Robert Adam and carved by Michael Henry Spang, *c.*1761–62

ormolu 'chestnut vases' with goat's-head handles, two late-seventeenth-century silver wine fountains and cisterns, 'done-up' in the latest fashion in January 1759, and – occupying centre-stage – 'Mr Stewart's Tripod' (pl. 44), an ormolu tripod perfume burner made by Diedrich Nicolaus Anderson to a design by 'Athenian' Stuart.[73] Stuart is also credited with the vase-shaped plate warmer of ormolu-mounted gun metal signed by Anderson and dated 1760.[74]

The sideboard put George Montagu in mind of an ancient altar 'set out for a sacrifice with numberless tripods, vases of crystal, lamps, *et cetera*, which has been fetched up from Herculaneum'.[75] Whether Adam was disgruntled or perversely pleased to design a grand Roman architectural setting for the small, fashionable Grecian creations of the 'Great Athenian', whose fame he feared and envied, is a matter of speculation. There is no doubt, however, that he was inspired by Stuart's earlier niche design (pl. 15). This is particularly apparent in his coloured design of 1762 which shows the semi-dome richly painted and gilded with a fan-shaped decoration similar to Stuart's, rather than the umbrella-pattern of white stucco ornament on a green ground that was ultimately executed.[76] On the wall below are pencil sketches of oval frames, festoons and swags. These ornaments would have integrated the semi-dome and the

47 'Design of the Ceiling of the Dining Room', by Robert Adam,
1762 (Kedleston, The National Trust)

sideboard composition far more effectively than the broad palmette and anthemion frieze that was added under the dome and
extended to the outer edges of the wall.

The jarring conflict between the frieze and the pediment of
the abutting doorcase on the south wall (pl. 45) is unworthy of
an architect of Adam's calibre and difficult to explain. A single-
minded determination on Scarsdale's part to display his family
silver, as he did his pictures, in a clear and uncluttered manner
may well have led him to prefer the frieze to Adam's painted decoration, regardless of its awkwardness. When the tables and cistern were placed in the niche in July 1765, it became apparent
that the expanse of blank wall between the frieze and the silver
ensemble was too great. Not only were the standing pedestals
promptly heightened, but the tripod and bases were also raised
on small pedestals of their own.[77] The cumbersome marble cistern, on the other hand, proved too high, and though its plinth
was removed, it still partly obscures the tables.[78] For all its novelty and originality, the Kedleston sideboard fails to rise to the
Roman niche. It is more effective on paper than in reality. The
Kenwood sideboard composition, conceived under less difficult
circumstances, is more successful.

En suite with the sideboard are two carved and gilt pier-tables
with additional pendant swags on the legs, which recall Stuart's

rejected design and are characteristic of French neo-classical furniture.[79] The accompanying pier-glasses with elaborate crests of
oak-leaf garlands and winged sphinxes were evidently made
*c.*1773 for the front drawing-room at Lord Scarsdale's house in
Mansfield Street and brought to Kedleston at a later date.[80]

Space for pictures is more limited here than in the reception
rooms on the west side of the house and did not lend itself to a
flexible arrangement. As a result, all the paintings (including the
Life of Porsenna and two landscapes illustrating scenes from
Milton's *Allegro* by Francesco Zuccarelli specially commissioned
for the room) were permanently set into the walls in gilded
stucco frames according to a scheme devised by Scarsdale and
drawn by Adam in April 1761.[81] They are presided over by the
statuary marble term figures of Ceres and Bacchus on the chimney-piece which was designed by Adam and carved by Spang (pl.
46).[82]

The ceiling was also inset with specially commissioned paintings (pl. 47): a central roundel of *Love Embracing Fortune* by
Henry Robert Morland, four corner roundels of the *Continents*
by Zucchi, and four oblongs of the *Seasons* by William
Hamilton. These were evidently put up in 1776 or 1777 (probably on the advice of George Richardson) instead of the nine
paintings by Zucchi of different subjects that were there in 1769.

48   The marble hall

49   Design for the hall pavement, Robert Adam, *c.*1760 (Kedleston, The National Trust)

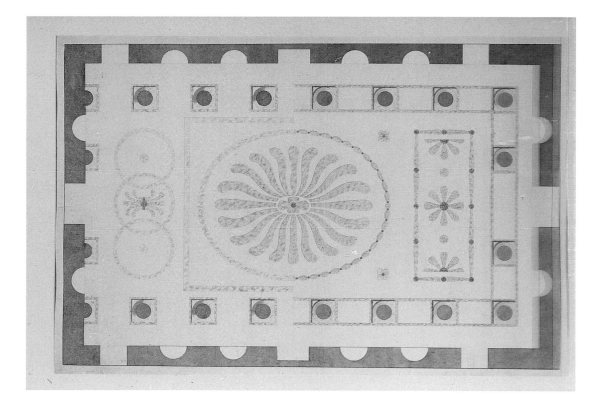

Adam's finished design, based on an antique prototype in the Palace of Augustus in the Farnese Gardens in Rome, was intended to have a deep-blue frame and gilded grotesque ornaments on a white ground.[83] Had it been executed as drawn, it would have been the richest, most ornate and colourful ceiling in the house. That, however, was not to be; the decorations undertaken in May 1765 were much subdued. 'The Ceiling is on a Pale Purple Ground & very pretty' is how the Duchess of Northumberland described it in 1766.[84]

Gilding was evidently considered superfluous and possibly too much of a distraction from the pictures and plate. That is not to say there was no gilding in the room. Apart from the gilt picture frames and furniture, all five doors had ormolu escutcheons and doorknobs designed by Adam and made by Matthew Boulton. The pattern sent to Boulton by Samuel Wyatt on 31 July 1765 was not only Adam's first design for door furniture but also Boulton's earliest recorded commission for such ornaments.[85] These particular acanthus-scroll escutcheons and knobs became a favourite Adam model which he used at Osterley and Saltram and illustrated in his *Works*, where, however, there is no reference to Kedleston.[86] Though the commission was probably triggered by Adam's introduction to Boulton in April that year, it is also in keeping with his determination to modernize even the most ordinary elements. This was displayed five years earlier when he contrived a 'new manner of Ornamenting the Mahogany Doors of (the) principal Rooms' and had a carved model of it sent to Kedleston in July 1760.[87]

Horace Walpole, having completed a tour of the house, proclaimed the dining-room to be 'in the best taste of all'.[88] His reference to it as the 'great parlour' suggests that it may have served as an informal reception room in lieu of Adam's abortive great dressing-room.

When he visited the house in September 1768, the hall and saloon, which he described as 'oblong and octagonal temples, sky-lighted', were unfinished, though the former had its twenty alabaster columns, each twenty-five feet high with Corinthian capitals of white marble, and an Adam pavement of local Hopton Wood stone inlaid with marble (pls 48, 49).[89] Had he arrived a year later, he would have had the benefit of the first edition of Lord Scarsdale's printed *Catalogue*, giving the antique sources of these two splendid interiors: 'The Hall and Salloon were after the Greek Hall and Dome of the Ancients, proportioned chiefly from the Pantheon at Rome and from Spalatra (*sic*). The Columns were proportioned from the three Columns in the Campo Vaccino at Rome, supposed to have belonged to the Temple of Jupiter Stator.'[90]

Palladio's *Quattro Libri* was in fact the immediate source. It was there that Adam found an illustration of the Corinthian capital from the Temple of Jupiter Stator as well as the glowing description of its beauty that he used to convince Lord Scarsdale of the value of the additional expense compared to the capital Paine had proposed.[91] Paine, probably inspired by Palladio's reconstruction of the Temple of Mars, articulated the walls with niches for statues and an upper register of panels which were filled, after his departure, with grisaille paintings from the antique and Homer's *Iliad*, in imitation of bas-reliefs.[92] Decorative details were left to Adam; so too were chimneypieces, which Paine had entirely omitted.

Adam's alterations to Paine's hall consisted mainly of a skylight instead of windows under the portico and a reversal of the free-standing and engaged columns on the end walls, moving the latter from the north to the south wall and thereby giving greater prominence to the entrance to the saloon and greater emphasis to the north–south axis, despite the fact that that was not the prescribed route through the house. The resulting succession of spaces is one of the grandest in England and comparable to the atrium and vestibulum (inverted) of the Palace of Diocletian at Spalatro, an account of which Adam was preparing for publication in 1764.

His introduction of a central skylight required a quite different design for the flat of the ceiling from the one he had sketched out for Paine's hall in 1759.[93] Although by 1760, when he drew

50 George Richardson, 'Design for Finishing the Sides of the Hall, Kedleston House', 1774 (Kedleston, The National Trust)

51 One of the mahogany doors in the hall with *papier mâché* panels painted with grotesque ornaments, *c.*1776–7

his revised section of the house, he had decided to divide the ceiling and cove into sections corresponding to the columns, he did not get down to making a finished design until 1763, by which time the columns were erected and it was found that one skylight was not enough: three were needed and even so Dr Johnson thought the hall 'ill lighted, and of no use but for dancing in'.[94] On 1 September 1763 Adam wrote to reassure his anxious patron: 'I have a great partiality to that Ceiling myself & Rose says it will be the finest Ceiling for a Hall He ever Saw, or had Conceived any Idea of'.[95] Indeed, he never designed another hall ceiling like it. Scarsdale's decision to defer the decoration of this room and the saloon for financial reasons must therefore have been a great disappointment to him; not so great, however, as having his favourite design modified in imitation of his style by his former pupil and draughtsman, George Richardson, in 1774, and a stunning watercolour of it exhibited at the Royal Academy in 1776 and published in Richardson's *Book of Ceilings* (dedicated to Lord Scarsdale) in the same year without any credit to him.[96]

Richardson's intervention in 1774 (pl. 50) was part of a very belated and somewhat desperate effort on Scarsdale's part to bring the ponderous 1760s interiors in line with the delicacy of the fashionable neo-classical style of Adam's designs for the painted book room and breakfasting-room that Scarsdale had rejected in 1768. To that end, the columns were fluted in 1775 and the mahogany doors embellished with grotesque ornaments painted on papier-mâché panels supplied by Henry Clay of Birmingham in 1776–7 (pl. 51). This 'minute decoration' was criticized by the historian William Mitford for being not only superfluous, but also inappropriate in an entrance hall where an air of noble simplicity and grandeur were required. If it 'could be anywhere desirable, it would be in the lady's dressingroom to the state-bedchamber'.[97] The same might be said of the pale pink and green colouring of Richardson's ceiling, which is a far cry from the white or dead-stone colour normally used in architectural halls. According to Richardson, these light tints were meant 'to create a harmony between the ceiling and the paintings on the side walls': not the upper range of Homeric grisailles executed in the 1760s under Adam's supervision, but the coloured circular paintings after Domenichino and Gravelot which were introduced by him above the two chimney-pieces.[98] The chimney-pieces themselves were thoroughly emasculated: their existing tablets depicting episodes of Roman history (*The Rape of the Sabines* and *The Continence of Scipio* after Michelangelo) were changed for new ones with Lord Scarsdale's arms; and the tall tabernacles planned by Adam in proportion to the columns were supplanted by more fashionable but unsuitably slight overmantels, with elegant female figures, tripods and vases in stucco, modelled on Adam's rejected design of 1768 for the painted breakfasting-room.[99]

Richardson's harmony of pale tints was evidently too bland for nineteenth-century taste. In order to bring out the figures in the niches, the colour of the columns was enhanced with varnish. Naturally, this grew darker with age and was removed by Francis Lenygon when his firm redecorated the interiors for George Nathaniel, first Earl (later first Marquess) Curzon of Kedleston, around 1912. Though Percy Macquoid briefly thought of highlighting the white figures by introducing strong colours on the walls, in the end he accepted the wisdom of Curzon's opinion that 'this cold classic style . . . rather suggests a charm of form and proportion than color'. The 'negative colors' (i.e. Richardson's pale tints) adopted by Curzon were deemed 'the safest style'.[100]

53 Detail of the stucco decorations surrounding the roof-light in the dome of the saloon

52 The saloon 1914. Note the hearth-rugs in front of the radiators, the bronzed pedestal and urn in the niche incorporated a stove

The only furniture in the 'Greek Hall' is a set of twelve carved and gilt stools described in the 1778 edition of the *Catalogue* as 'after the ancient Sarcophagus', meaning the so-called tomb of Agrippa in the Pantheon. These stools were evidently inspired by Adam's hall stools for Bowood and Lansdowne House, which were executed by Linnell in *c.*1765–6 and 1768 respectively. There can be little doubt that they were also made by Linnell, but to his own, rather than Adam's, design.[101] Linnell is also credited with the set of white-and-gold seat furniture, consisting of twelve armchairs and eight settees with cane seats and backs, made in the early 1780s for the saloon.[102]

The vanity of the grandiose hall and saloon were not to Dr Johnson's liking. The hall he thought would be better if the massive pillars were 'away'.[103] As it stood, it 'would do for the judges to sit in at the assizes; the circular room for a jury chamber, and the room above for the prisoners'.[104] The saloon was otherwise 'useless and therefore ill contrived'. His pronouncements, as Boswell admitted, were rather extreme, but they were not altogether unreasonable.

What *was* the purpose of this towering domed rotunda (pls 51, 52), 18.9 metres (62 feet) high (i.e. 6.7 metres, or 22 feet, taller than the hall), occupying a pivotal position between the state rooms and the principal apartment, yet totally unheated until 1789? In Scarsdale's mind it was evidently a symbol of Rome fol-lowing the 'Greek Hall', modelled on the Pantheon and embellished with elements taken from other ancient Roman temples illustrated by Palladio: octagonal coffering in the dome (pl. 52, 53) taken from the Temple of Peace (Basilica of Maxentius) and lozenge-shaped coffering in the apses from the Temples of the Sun and Moon.[105] Adam made it into a sculpture gallery with four large alcoves and eight rectangular niches, all filled with casts of antique statues.[106]

In 1787–9 the twelve statues were removed: four went to the great staircase and eight to the hall, which until then had only four statues on the end walls (*Antinuous* and *Mercury* on the north wall; *Apollo Belvedere* and *Meleager* on the south) and nothing in the niches on the long walls.[107] The rectangular niches were blocked up and the walls were inset with girandoles incorporating oblong stucco panels of playing putti possibly designed by Richardson but not by Adam. Large cast-iron 'altar' stoves in the form of antique pedestals and urns made by the Carron Works were placed in the alcoves.

William Hamilton, a protégé of Adam's and the son of one of his Scottish assistants, was commissioned to make four large paintings of Roman ruins to replace the less appropriate copies after Rubens by Henry Robert Moreland, which had been placed in elaborate frames designed by Adam and set into the walls above the pedimented doors. Between these are grisailles of scenes from English history by Biagio Rebecca. To add more colour to the predominantly white and gold decoration and to lighten the overall effect, the fluted composite columns on the doorcases were replaced by Ionic pilasters of verde antique scagliola supplied by Bartoli and Richter.

Contemporary visitors to Kedleston, while invariably struck by its splendour, were somewhat concerned by the extravagance displayed. Walpole's abbreviated dictum sums up the opinions of Doctor Johnson, George Montagu and others: 'magnificently furnished and finished; all designed by Adam in the best taste, but too expensive'.[108]

54   The south or garden front of Croome Court, built 1751–2 by
Lancelot 'Capability' Brown following designs by Sanderson Miller

2

CROOME COURT

The circumstances of Adam's introduction to George William, sixth Earl of Coventry (1722–1809) and his engagement at Croome in Worcestershire are obscure. On 24 July 1760 he wrote to his brother James, naming the earl as one of several patrons whose designs might be included in a future publication of his works.[1] His earliest finished drawings – an 'Elevation & Plan of a Greenhouse' and a 'Design of a Ceiling for the Gallery' – were made the following August and September respectively; only the greenhouse was executed.[2]

Lord Coventry was then a mature man of thirty-eight with an eminently beautiful wife, Maria Gunning, whom he married in 1752, and three young children. On succeeding to the title in March 1751, he relinquished his seat as Tory MP for Worcester and, through the influence of his godfather, the Duke of Newcastle, was given the post of Lord Lieutenant of the county (previously held by his father) and a secure place in the Royal Household as a Lord of the Bedchamber to George II and George III.[3] Despite his active social life in London and the ancestral hospitality he dutifully maintained at Croome, he was by nature a private, retiring person, noted and sometimes ridiculed for his excessive seriousness, scrupulousness and prudence bordering on prudery. Horace Walpole described him as a 'grave young lord of the remains of the patriot breed' and 'sillier in a wise way' than his 'very silly wife';[4] George III esteemed him 'the wisest, handsomest, prudentest of his subjects';[5] to Adam he was the most faithful of patrons, employing him in 1760 and acting as his pall bearer in 1792.

Paris was Coventry's mecca, not Rome. Though according to Walpole he was not fluent in the French language,[6] he was, none the less, a keen, well-informed follower of French fashion – rococo and neo-classical – and an astute buyer of the latest French furniture, ormolu, porcelain, tapestries, looking-glasses and clothing. By 1765 he was well known to the Paris *marchands-merciers*, Dulac, Simon-Philippe Poirier and others, for his remarkable taste and elegance.[7] 'Gilly' Williams 'told him that he and the Count Caylus were joined together as the standard of taste, which pleased him so much that he made (him) repeat it ten times'.[8]

Croome Court, the family seat near Worcester, was a double-pile house of the 1640s with eleven bays, two-and-a-half storeys and a hipped roof. Its main front, facing north, had a projecting porch and perron in the centre and two projecting bays at either end; the garden front had no forward projections, but two single-storey lateral pavilions, each of five bays articulated by giant Ionic pilasters.[9] Viscount Deerhurst, as he then was, found the old house too large and too much like an 'Inn' perpetually full of guests. In the summer of 1750, to the surprise of his friends (including Sanderson Miller, the gentleman architect on whom he relied for advice), he pulled down the two low pavilions on the garden front and began to think of other improvements, 'not . . . to be executed in a hurry'.[10]

Miller provided him with designs for new stables (1750), for a lodge where he could enjoy the company of his friends in peace, and no doubt for Palladianizing the old house itself (pls 54, 55).

55 Ground-floor plan of Croome Court (*Vitruvius Britannicus*, IV (1767), pl. XXIX)

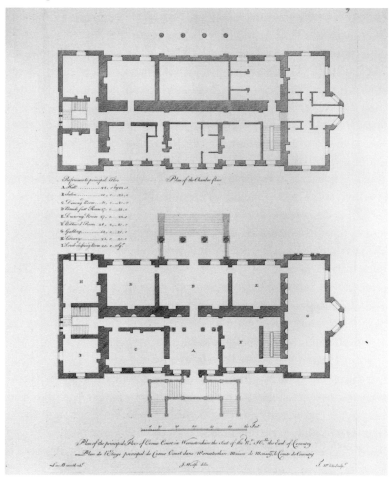

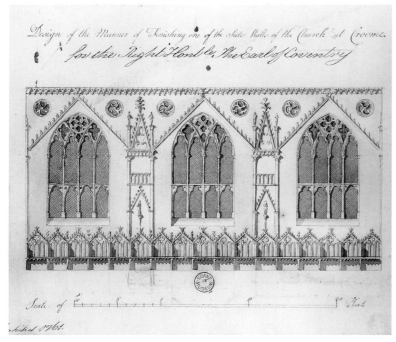

56 'Design of the Manner of Finishing one of the Side Walls of the Church at Croome', by Robert Adam, 1761 (Sir John Soane's Museum: Adam drawings, vol 50:15)

57 'Design of a Gothic window with painted Glass . . . (for the) Chapple at Croome', by Robert Adam, 1762 (Croome Estate Trust). Not executed

In 1752 Coventry wrote to Miller, 'Whatever merits it (Croome) may in future time boast, it will be ungrateful not to acknowledge you the primary Author';[11] moreover, its resemblance to Hagley Hall, Worcestershire, which Miller designed in 1754 for their mutual friend, George, first Lord Lyttelton, appears to confirm his authorship. The execution of Miller's proposals was entrusted to 'Capability' Brown, who, though he had no previous architectural experience, was conveniently on hand, landscaping the park.[12]

The structural remodelling of Croome was not as extensive as is often supposed. Instead of demolishing the old house and building an entirely new one at great expense and inconvenience, Coventry decided to retain the existing structure except for two bays at each end, which were taken down and rebuilt with corner towers to give it a Palladian look. The whole was refaced and balustraded, pediments were added on both fronts, and a tetrastyle, Ionic portico was created on the garden side (pl. 54).[13] These improvements to the fabric were completed by 1758 and work then began on the decoration of the interior.

John Hobcraft was the carpenter; most of the carving, including thirteen chimney-pieces, was done by William Linnell in collaboration with James Lovell, who had worked at Stowe and Hagley; Linnell was also responsible for upholstery and some furniture, though the principal suppliers at this stage were the royal cabinet-makers, William Vile and John Cobb.[14] Francesco Vassalli, the *stuccatore* at Hagley, was responsible for the stucco

decoration, of which some wall elements can still be identified, though ceilings cannot. In 1761 he submitted a bill for the 'Ceiling in ye Salon according to My designe 47:15:0 & That done before according M^r. Stuard designe 22:5:0'.[15]

'Athenian' Stuart's presence at Croome (noted by Geoffrey Beard but overlooked by architectural historians) can probably be dated to around 1759, when he was working at Hagley for Coventry's close friend and arbiter of taste, Lord Lyttelton.[16] Regardless of what he did and why it was redone by Vassalli, the fact of Stuart's being at Croome is important in itself as the first sign of Coventry's avant-garde interest in the rising neo-classical style. This new penchant did not bring about an abrupt rejection of the rococo furniture and decoration already in place or on order; evidently the two styles were not considered to be as incompatible as generally supposed, and, in any case, such whimsical behaviour was not in Coventry's character. What it did do, however, was prepare the way for Adam's employment in 1760.

Unlike Kedleston, the plans for Croome (pl. 55) were too recently fixed and the decoration of the principal rooms – in the old house and in the new east end – was too far advanced for any radical alterations to be contemplated. All that was left for Adam was the 65-foot (19.8-metre) long gallery occupying the whole of the new west end. However, his services were required elsewhere: to design a bridge over the river; to smarten up Coventry's London house at 3 Grosvenor Square; and, most important, to

59 Initial design (unexecuted) for the ceiling of the gallery, by Robert Adam, 1760 (Sir John Soane's Museum: Adam drawings: vol. 11:34)

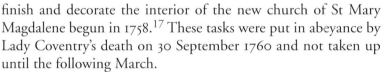

58 The canopy of the pulpit in Croome church, designed by Robert Adam c.1762

finish and decorate the interior of the new church of St Mary Magdalene begun in 1758.[17] These tasks were put in abeyance by Lady Coventry's death on 30 September 1760 and not taken up until the following March.

The church at Croome is Adam's earliest known essay in Gothic interior decoration and was to stand him in good stead eight years later when he replaced James Paine as architect at Alnwick Castle. The Georgian-gothic building, credited to Brown, has a tall tower at the west end, an unusually long chancel and a squarish body divided by slender clustered columns into a coved nave and lower, flat-ceiling aisles, each with three windows. Adam's first designs for the 'Inside finishing' (pl. 56) and ceiling (in May and July 1761 respectively) were in a 'Decorated' gothic style akin to the work of Henry Keene, Sanderson Miller and Horace Walpole.[18] It was much more elaborate than what was finally executed, with mock fan-vaulting on the ceiling, reticulated traceries in the windows, pinnacled canopies on the window-piers and a good deal of crocketing. Indeed, the delicate, embroidered effect is comparable to Adam's neo-classical style of decoration characterized by the exactly contemporary ceiling in the long gallery at Syon. He also made much simpler, alternative designs, but they were pared down in execution to crocketed ogee mouldings over the door, chancel-arch and windows, and decorated stucco ribs and circular bosses in the coved ceiling. Joseph Rose was responsible for the stucco-work and John Hobcraft for the carpentry and joinery.

Nothing came of his attractive watercolour designs for painted glass for the chancel window (pl. 57) or of the armorial hatchments he suggested for the aisle windows.[19] Instead, the windows were hung with green damask curtains supplied by William France and John Bradburn in 1765, depriving the interior of the convincing medieval appearance achieved on the exterior.[20] Furnishings turned out to be Adam's principal contribution: the gothic doors, the pews and the font, the pulpit (pl. 58), the Communion rail, probably the clerk's and reader's desks and a gothic armchair were all executed to his designs with only minor alterations.[21] In the Adam volumes at the Soane is a drawing inscribed 'Copy of one of the Chairs in the Church at Croome for the Earl of Coventry' and dated 1761,[22] which is identical to the gothic armchair made for the chapel at Alnwick in the late 1770s. The Croome chair, which has not been traced, must have been slightly different from the design, for according to Sefferin Alken's bill for making it in 1762, the '2 Boys heads & foliage' on the arms were 'not Us'd'.[23]

Decorating the inside of the church in the gothic style was a digression from the principal purpose of Adam's employment at Croome which was to finish the interior of the recently constructed long gallery – the largest room in the house – in the latest neo-classical fashion. He began in September 1760 with a ceiling design composed of three large octagonal compartments aligned on the projecting half-octagon bow-window in the centre of the west wall (pl. 59).[24] Six months later, he prepared a

60 View of the gallery, c.1918 showing the ceiling, the niches filled with statues, and the Adam side-tables and mirrors flanking the bow on the left

61 Laid-out wall elevations for finishing the gallery at Croome Court as a library, by Robert Adam, 1761 (Sir John Soane's Museum: Adam drawings, vol. 50:10)

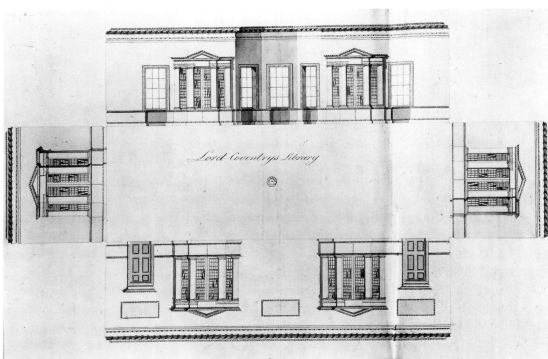

Lord Coventrys Library

new design for a coffered ceiling of elongated octagons and diamonds closely modelled on Palladio's illustration of the vaulted ceiling of the Temple of Peace in Rome, where Vespasian was said to have kept all the valuables and vases he brought from Jerusalem.[25] This approved design had a determining effect on the entire room and, as it turned out, on other rooms at Croome as well. Not only did it enhance the apparent length of the gallery, but it also gave it a Roman architectural character that called for monochromatic stone colours rather than gay tints (pl. 60).

The sobriety of the scheme, coupled with the fact that

Coventry did not have a large collection of pictures, seems to have suggested that the room should become a library. In November 1761, a 'Section for finishing the Gallery in the Manner of a Library' was duly drawn up (pl. 61) with six aedicule bookcases of the Ionic order: one at each end of the room closing off the existing windows, two flanking the bow-window on the west wall and two more on either side of the chimney-piece, where niches were later constructed.[26] For Adam, bookcases were evidently preferable to pictures as a means of diversifying the disproportionate length of the space and making it more visually entertaining. He proposed similar solutions that same

62 The mahogany bookcases in the library at Croome Court before they were dismantled and purchased by the V&A. Designed by Robert Adam, 1763 and executed by William Vile and John Cobb with specialist carving by Sefferin Alken, 1764

year, 1761, for the long galleries at Syon and Osterley; only the former was executed.[27]

The drawback of the Croome library–gallery design was that it would have rendered the library, which had recently been fitted-up in the east tower, redundant. Coventry therefore rejected it and decided instead to have niches constructed for statues, like those in the gallery at Holkham. However, he was now so obsessed by the antique that he commissioned Adam to remodel the existing library along the lines of the unused library–gallery scheme, and to design a ceiling for the adjacent breakfast-room, which he was determined to make into a tapestry room. The finishing of the gallery was left in abeyance for six months.

Adam's accounts for January 1763 include designs for a 'Ceiling for the Library' and a 'Ceiling for the Tapestry Room', costing £10.10.0 each. Only one of the ceiling designs survives; it is an office copy correctly dated January 1763 but mistakenly inscribed for the library.[28] Its dimensions (according to the given scale) are not those of the library, but of the tapestry room, which is where it was executed. There was no change of mind, as is often supposed. The surviving library ceiling has an Adamesque border of alternating anthemia and double calyces (a simplification of the gallery frieze derived from the Temple of Concord in Rome) and corner medallions containing heads in high relief, encircled by laurel wreaths and placed on thyrsi, which are normally associated with Bacchus and would be more suitable for an eating-room than a library. The central laurel wreath is uncharacteristic of Adam and indeed the whole composition is too weak to be his. Joseph Rose executed the ceiling in 1764 and may have designed it as well.

A 'Section of the 4 Sides of the Library & the manner of the

Bookcases' was also made in January 1763; that being approved, working drawings of 'all the mouldings at Large for Messrs. Cobb & Vyle & the Oranments for Mr. Alken for the Bookcases . . .' followed in June; and by the end of 1764 the 'Sett of Large Mahogany Book Cases' with their 'Pilasters' altered 'By the Order of the Surveyor' was complete.[29] Their pedimented Ionic fronts were adapted from the library–gallery scheme and updated by the addition of anthemion cresting derived from the Choragic Monument of Lysicrates which had just been published in Stuart and Revett's *Antiquities of Athens* (pl. 62).[30] Maria, Countess of Coventry was one of the subscribers. It took '2 Men at Croome 226 Days taking down the old Book Cases & putting up the new ones, taking them Down again and Cutting the old Dado & Brick work & Putting them up again'.[31] Finally, in May 1765, the wall above John Wildsmith's turtle-dove chimney-piece and other unshelved areas were lined with canvas and three layers of 'crown Elephant & stout Imperial paper' and painted with several coats of 'Dead Stone' colour 'to appear as Stucco';[32] and in June the Venetian windows were hung with crimson damask festoon-curtains.

The earl's decision to have a three-quarter-length portrait of himself in a crimson coat with his books at hand painted by Allan Ramsay in 1764, and to hang the picture over the library chimney-piece, is a measure of the importance he attached to this room.[33] It would have been his preserve at Croome, and was fitted with a jib door in one of the bookcases, which opened to a short passage under the main stairs leading directly to his dressing-room on the north front, an even more secluded place for gentlemen to retire to. The ladies presumably retired to the countess's dressing-room on the first floor.

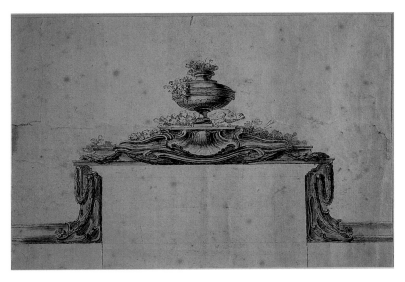

63 Unidentified French artist, design for the Gobelins tapestry above the chimney-piece in the tapestry-room, *c*.1763 (Croome Estate Trust)

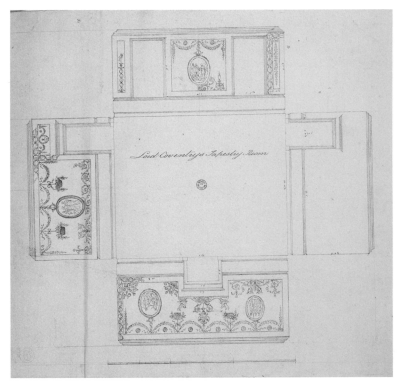

64 'Design for altering the French design for the tapestry room', by Robert Adam, *c*.1763–64 (Sir John Soane's Museum: Adam drawings, vol. 50:12)

The library's main communication was with the breakfast-room to the east, also known as the 'Tapestry Room', a name first used by Adam in connection with a ceiling design made in January 1763. Coventry must have decided to line the walls with tapestries in the previous autumn at the latest, and was presumably encouraged by Lord Lyttelton who had created a tapestry room at Hagley in 1758. The start of the peace negotiations with France in September 1762 would also have opened the prospect of his going to Paris in the not too distant future; a treaty was signed on 10 February 1763 and in August he left for Paris, 'determined to be as private as an upholsterer, and to pass his time in buying glasses and tapestry, for a place in which he never sees himself, but he wishes himself, and all belonging to it, at the devil'.[34] Whether he had any inkling of what was in store for him at the Gobelins factory we shall never know.

While the Seven Years War raged, extensive improvements were made to the *Manufacture Royale* under the direction of Mme de Pompadour's brother, the Marquis de Marigny, Surintendant et Directeur des Bâtimens du Roi, and the neo-classical architect, Jacques Germain Soufflot, Contrôleur des Bâtimens and Directeur des Manufactures. The *basse lisse* (horizontal) looms managed by Jacques Neilson (*c*.1718–88) were restructured so as to produce tapestries of the same quality as the *haute lisse* looms in less time and at lower cost; and in August 1758 a new composition was devised 'sur l'idée de M. Soufflot' with '*Tentures de Boucher*' in oval medallions suspended from '*une moûlure avec ses bordures très riches, peintes et feintes en or imitant la sculpture . . .*'.[35] The great advantage of Soufflot's '*idée*' over traditional narrative compositions was its flexibility: the arrangement of the medallions could be varied and their subjects changed, the ground colour was open to choice and the whole composition could be enlarged or reduced to meet the requirements of the purchaser, which was especially suited to the English custom of covering all four walls with tapestries, a taste not shared by the French.

On 10 September 1762, Maurice Jacques, the Gobelins' Peintre et Dessinateur, who was responsible for the oval frames and borders, prepared a coloured picture '*representant un Apartement tel qu'il doit être, avec les tentures de la tapisserie, le lit,*

le fauteuil, et le canapé. Ce projet a été fait pour disposer et faire décider les particuliers qui désiroient cet ouvrage énoncé'.[36] Lord Coventry was the first purchaser of the new Boucher–Neilson tapestries and his example was followed by four more Englishmen: William Weddell of Newby Hall, Yorkshire, Sir Henry Bridgeman of Weston Park, Staffordshire, Sir Lawrence Dundas of Moor Park, Hertfordshire and Robert Child of Osterley. Adam, who worked for all these men, may have helped to spread the word, but he did not initiate the idea.[37]

Measured or scaled elevations of the four sides of the tapestry room, like the 'Section' listed in Adam's accounts for November 1763 (but now lost), must have been sent to Paris for the medallion composition to be adjusted to Coventry's requirements. The Gobelins, in turn, sent Lord Coventry a design of the room as a whole (which has not been traced) and a detail of the tapestry above the chimney-piece, which is in the Croome archives (pl. 63). In January 1764 Adam billed the earl for 'Altering the French Design for the Tapestry Room in Colour' (pl. 64) and making a 'Design for finishing the sides of the Tapestry Room (Not finished)'.[38] There is a partly coloured drawing at the Soane showing three walls hung with Adam's alternative medallion tapestries, which are more distinctly neo-classical than those supplied by the Gobelins: instead of the large horizontal medallions on the end walls, he proposed smaller vertical ones the same size and shape as those on the chimney-piece and window walls, flanked by pendant flower baskets; and Maurice Jacques's elaborate flora and fauna at the base were to be replaced by neo-classical rinceaux (corresponding to Adam's ceiling) and sphinxes over the chimney-piece. Each panel was to be bordered by interlaced vines applied to the wall instead of the '*très riches*' imitation gilt-wood frames.[39]

The subjects chosen by Coventry for the oval medallions were

65　View of the tapestry-room from Croome Court with the suite of
furniture provided by Ince and Mayhew, 1769–70 (Metropolitan
Museum of Art, New York)

the four elements, two of which – Vetumnus and Pomona
(earth) and Aurora and Cephalus (air) – were painted by
Boucher in 1763. Neptune and Amymone (water) is dated 1764
and Venus and Vulcan (fire) is undated.[40] Some finished pieces
were sent to London through diplomatic channels in 1767, but it
was not until 1771 that the whole order was complete. In June of
that year, Ince and Mayhew were at Croome, putting up the tapestry hangings and fixing the tapestry covers to the suite of six
armchairs and two settees ('for Each side of the Chimney') which
they had made in London in October 1769 to their own design
(pl. 65).[41] They also supplied a carved and gilt pier-glass, two
curtain cornices and a pair of festoon curtains of 'Superfine
Crimson Tammy' (worsted) trimmed with rich crimson silk lace
and deep silk fringe. One would have expected the curtains to be
of the same red damask used in the other reception rooms, but
for some reason – a clash of colour or pattern, perhaps – this was

considered inappropriate in the presence of the *damas cramoisy*
imitation damask devised by Maurice Jacques in 1758 as a background for the medallion tapestries.

Croome's tapestry-covered chairs are the earliest known
English seats with oval backs characteristic of the neo-classical
style. Though their classicism may seem somewhat hesitant and
unconvincing to us, they were regarded by Ince and Mayhew as
'Antique', whereas the matching serpentine sofas were not. Like
the oval-back chairs in the tapestry rooms at Newby, Moor Park
and Osterley, which are slightly later and by different makers,
they are clearly related to the oval medallions of the
Boucher–Neilson hangings. Whether Maurice Jacques's lost 1762
painting of a furnished tapestry apartment included chairs of
this description may never be known. We can be quite certain,
however, that the idea was passed by the Gobelins in some form
to their English customers and did not emanate from Adam, as

Fiske Kimball maintained.[42] There are no Adam designs, or bills for designs for any of the tapestry furniture made for Croome, Newby, Moor Park or Osterley.

Along with the six armchairs that Ince and Mayhew sent to Croome on 18 November 1769 was a 'Tripod Bason Stand' (pl. 66) made by them in June 1767 to support a Sèvres basin and ewer bought by Coventry in Paris earlier that year.[43] This piece (now at Earls Croome) may have been executed from the 'french design for a Water Stand' which was 'altered' by Adam on 6 May 1767. Adam's alteration can be seen in a rough sketch at the Soane (pl. 67), inscribed 'Lord Coventry's (?) for', with the words 'Water Stand' boldly written over, and in two finished designs published in the *Works* (pl. 68).[44]

One of these is described as a 'tripod, designed for the Earl of Coventry, with a vase and branches for three candles, executed in or molu, for Sir Laurence Dundass, and afterwards for the Duke of Bolton'; but, unlike the vase design – from which a set of four candelabra was made before 1763 for Dundas's London house, 19 Arlington Street – no tripod of this description is known to have been executed.[45]

The other, 'a tripod, designed for the Earl of Coventry, with a vase for candles', is closer to the Soane sketch and was probably engraved from the finished design for a 'Tripod altered from a french Design for a Water Stand 1.1.0' included in Adam's bill; the water basin having been transformed into a decorative support for the vase-candelabra, and the water pitcher replaced by a carved urn. While Ince and Mayhew's tripod for the Sèvres basin and ewer may have been an appropriate ornament for the French tapestry room, this tripod was better suited to Coventry's London house. It has never been traced.[46]

In 1905, the medallion tapestries and tapestry-covered furni-ture were sold by the ninth Earl of Coventry to M. Fenaille, the great authority on tapestries, who was acting for Wildenstein in Paris, and the room was then redecorated as the 'green drawing room'.[47] After a short period of separation, the tapestries, the suite of furniture and its tapestry covers, the ceiling and the chimney-piece were all reunited in the Metropolitan Museum of Art in New York.[48]

Having ordered his tapestry room, Lord Coventry's interest turned, in December 1763, to a new bed (pls 69, 70). A design was made by Adam and given to the firm of William France and John Bradburn, who supplied a 'large Wainscott double screw'd bed^sd' with mahogany spiral-fluted posts and Corinthian capitals, a coved and fluted cornice and a large dome embellished inside and out with carved ornaments and topped by a central vase.[49] This domed architectural structure, which survives in a much altered state at Earls Croome, was Adam's earliest executed bed. It was upholstered in green silk damask and placed in the 'best bedroom' in an architectural alcove flanked by a small dressing-room and closet, designed by Adam in March 1764.[50]

Adam turned his attention back to the delayed long-gallery project (pl. 71), and in June 1763 presented a 'New Section of the Gallery finished in the Antique Taste with Statues Bas Reliefs &c.', conforming to the Horreum mentioned by Pliny 'as a repository for statues, bas reliefs, and other curious productions of art' and resembling the sculpture gallery at Holkham and his own contemporary design for the dining-room at Syon.[51]

The 'Antique Taste' consisted not just in the plaster replicas of antique statues by John Cheere placed in the ten niches with bas-reliefs above them (pls 72, 60), the coffered ceiling based on the Temple of Peace, the palmette frieze from the Temple of Concord and other ornaments from other Roman buildings,

66 Mahogany tripod made to support a Sèvres basin and ewer, by Ince and Mayhew (Croome Estate Trust)

67 Sketch for Lord Coventry of a 'Tripod altered from a French design for a Water Stand', by Robert Adam, 1767 (Sir John Soane's Museum; Adam drawings, vol. 6:177)

68 'Miscellaneous designs of various pieces of Furniture, done for different persons . . .' including two tripods for the Earl of Coventry, the one on the right with a vase candelabra. The vase on the left was executed in ormolu for Sir Lawrence Dundas and later for the Duke of Bolton, by Robert Adam, *c.*1767 (*The Works in architecture of Robert and James Adam*, vol. 1 (1778), pt. 1, pl. VIII)

69 Design for a bed, by Robert Adam, 1763 (Sir John Soane's Museum: Adam drawings, vol 17:152)

70 Detail of one of the mahogany footposts of the Coventry bed, executed by William France and John Bradburn, 1764 (Croome Estate Trust)

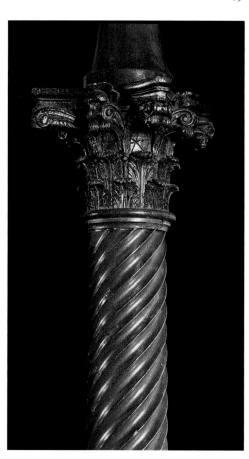

71 Laid-out wall elevations of the gallery 'finished in the Antique Taste with Statues and Bas Reliefs', by Robert Adam, 1763 (Croome Estate Trust)

72 View of the gallery chimney-piece and overmantel showing part of the ceiling, two of the chairs, and the grate designed by Adam. The latter has since disappeared

but also in the monochrome 'dead stone' colour of the ceiling, the walls and the wall-furniture.[52] Although the furniture has all been dispersed, some of the architectural decorations still remain intact. Joseph Wilton's 'large Statuary Chimney piece composed of Statues representing Nymphs of Flora, holding a Wreath, &ca.', for which he charged £300 in December 1766, is the focus of attention. It is shown in Adam's 1763 section of the gallery and is closely related to the caryatid chimney-pieces he

designed in 1759 for the great dining-room (now the salon) at Hatchlands in Surrey, for the drawing-room at Kedleston in 1760, and for the gallery at Harewood in 1777.[53] In June 1765 he designed a fire-grate and fender enriched with a variety of classical ornaments including the enclosed palmettes used elsewhere in the room (pl. 73). It was made in the following year by the firm of Hartley & Cooper and is said to be the earliest securely dated example of fireplace furniture by Adam. Though

73 'Design of a Grate & Fender for the gallery fireplace', by Robert Adam, 1765 (Sir John Soane's Museum: Adam drawings, vol. 17:121)

74 Side-table from the gallery with part of the *en suite* mirror above. One of a pair, carved pine, painted dead-stone colour; designed by Robert Adam, 1765 and made by Sefferin Alken (Philadelphia Museum of Art)

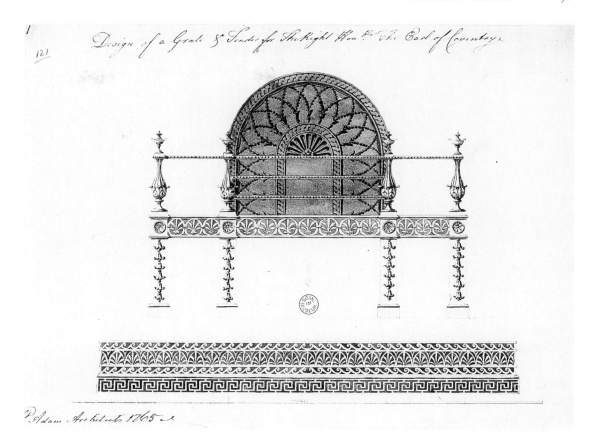

it was still in place in the 1920s, its present whereabouts are unknown.[54]

Above the chimney-piece was a *trompe l'oeil* painting of a Roman sacrifice in an Adam frame carved by Sefferin Alken to match the pair of pier-glasses flanking the bow-window on the opposite wall.[55] The grisaille painting and its stone-coloured frame were acquired by the Metropolitan Museum in 1960 and replaced by replicas. An appropriate new home for the painting

was found above the chimney-piece in the museum's installation of the Lansdowne House dining-room, but the frame is still in storage. One of the pair of related pier-glasses and tables is also at the Metropolitan; the other pair is in the Philadelphia Museum of Art (pl. 74).[56]

Adam's distinctive aedicule pier-glasses – with anthemion borders, profile female terms on consoles supporting Corinthian capitals at the sides, elaborate foliate friezes and scrolled pedi-

75 Mahogany scroll stool from the gallery, one of ten, designed by Robert Adam, 1765 and made by John Bradburn and Sefferin Alken (Croome Estate Trust)

76 Mahogany arm-chair from the gallery, one of a suite of eight, designed by Robert Adam, 1765, and made by William Vile with specialist carving by Sefferin Alken (Croome Estate Trust)

ments – were included in the section of the gallery which he submitted in June 1763, prior to Coventry's trip to Paris in August 'to talk of . . . glasses'. However, his finished design and 'Drawings at full size' for Alken to work from were not made until July 1765, by which time the glasses had been delivered. Alken's bill for £67.12.0 for carving the two frames, though fairly high, was probably a fraction of the cost of the silvered plates imported from France.[57]

The intention in 1763 was to have accompanying pier-tables with spiral fluted legs in the French style, similar to the scagliola tables (1761–2) in the painted breakfast-room at Kedleston (see pl. 23); James Adam was commissioned to obtain 7-foot (2.13-metre) long slabs for them in Rome.[58] In 1765, when it was time to supply Alken with working drawings, this model was abandoned in favour of a more innovative architectural design with tapered legs in the form of pilasters, having recessed panels of classical ornament on each face and capitals bearing female masks. Beneath the frieze was an apron of pendant anthemion and husk swags answering that on the overmantel-frame; these ornaments are described in Alken's bill but have since disappeared. Although the design of the table and drawing at large included in Adam's bill have also vanished, there is a drawing at the Soane inscribed 'for the Drawing Room at Sion', which is identical to the Croome tables. Having been rejected by the Duke of Northumberland because the row of female heads was 'much more like a family pew or a supper box for a ball' than a

table, it was offered to the Earl of Coventry, who quite rightly snapped it up.[59] It was well suited to the 'finishing' of the gallery at Croome in a 'dead stone', architectural, 'Antique Taste'.

Finally, in January 1766, after all the wall and seat furniture had been made to his design, Adam provided (or at least invoiced) drawings for 'Two Ornamental paintings in Chiaroscaro for two large pannels in the Gallery at Croome at £10 each' and 'Four dittos for smaller pannels in ditto Gallery at £4 each'. Why these drawing were left until last is not known. Judging from Adam's description of them and from his 1763 wall elevations, they must have been meant for the west wall: the two large panels at the ends and the four narrower ones flanking the pier-glasses and tables. What survives in the gallery now has been extensively over-painted. In the early nineteenth century, the extravagant seventh earl rid the room of its 'Antique' sobriety by painting it bright blue and used it as a 'morning family room'.[60]

The Croome Court gallery is one of the earliest rooms, if not the very first, wholly decorated and furnished by Adam. Apart from the fixed pier-glasses and tables, he provided a large suite of movable seat-furniture consisting of ten mahogany stools (pl. 75) (described as 'Scrole chairs' or 'Scrole sofas') covered with blue morocco and eight similarly upholstered armchairs with fluted seat rails and round fluted legs with block capitals (pl. 76). These are his first fully neo-classical pieces of seat-furniture. In the office copy of his 1763 wall elevations at the Soane, the stools are indicated in pencil under the niches, the four on the end walls being slightly larger than those on the chimney-piece wall. In the event, stools of three different sizes were supplied in January 1766 by John Bradburn in collaboration with Sefferin Alken: two large ones '8ft 2ins (2.4 metres) from out to out', four 6 feet 5 inches. (1.95 metres) long, and four at 4 feet 2 inches. (1.27 metres).[61] The two largest were probably placed against the west wall, either under the windows or the chiaroscuro panels; the four middle-sized ones may have stood between the niches on the chimney-piece wall, and the smaller ones under the niches on the end walls. Four armchairs could then have been placed on either side of the middle-sized stools and the other four flanking the pair of pier-tables.

A 'Design for a Sopha (i.e. stool) for the Gallery' was made in October 1764, but this evidently was not acceptable and in February 1765 Adam made 'another Design of a Sopha or Scrole Chair' as well as a 'Design of a Chair for the Gallery'. The only surviving drawing that corresponds to the Croome stools is an undated one in the Soane which is inscribed 'Sopha for Sir Lawrence Dundas' and is included in Adam's bill of 1766 for drawings made for Moor Park.[62] Dundas seems not have shared Coventry's taste for the *goût grec*.

Unlike the stools, the *en suite* armchairs with palmette splats were not made by France and Bradburn, but by their rival, John Cobb, the specialist carving of the splats and other enrichments again being done by Sefferin Alken.[63] Spreading the load amongst different craftsmen was an effective means of hastening the completion of the work. Pressure to finish Croome was stepped up in 1765, partly by the earl's marriage in September 1764 to Barbara St John, daughter of the 10th Baron St John of Bletso, but above all by his purchase in October 1764 of a new London house in need of refurbishment. Yet, despite the added drain on his purse, the perfection of the gallery was not compromised. It was Adam's most important work in the house.

77   Coventry House (later the St James's Club, now International House), 106 (formerly 29) Piccadilly, probably by Matthew Brettingham, c.1761

3

COVENTRY HOUSE

The London residence of the Earls of Coventry from 1735 to 1764 was an ample (too ample, according to the sixth earl) five-bay, three-storey house built around 1731 on the east side of Grosvenor Square. Though the sixth earl began refurbishing it as soon as he inherited in 1751 – and continued to do so until 1761, in which year he employed Adam to design a new bed-alcove and bed – his cosmetic improvements did not cure the inherent faults which the house evidently shared with its neighbours, erected by the same speculative builder, John Simmons, a carpenter by trade.[1]

Considering the well-being of his two young children by his deceased first wife, the comfort of his second wife, Barbara, daughter of the tenth Baron St John of Bletso, whom he married on 27 September 1764, and his own desire to display his fashionable neo-classical taste to London society, he decided to build himself a new house on Piccadilly, which was fast becoming 'a street of palaces'. His appetite must also have been whetted by the designs that Adam was then making for a new house at Hyde Park Corner for the Earl of Shelburne.[2]

In October 1764 Adam charged Coventry £26.5.0 for 'Time spent in examining a situation for a house in Piccadilly, making various sketches of Designs for ditto, treating with Messrs Garden & Carter for the Ground & Clerk's time and Expences in measuring & planning ditto'.[3] None of his 'various sketches' has been identified and nothing came of the project.

Two months later, Coventry bought Sir Henry Hunloke's house on the corner of Piccadilly and Brick Street (pl. 77): a house with an impressive stone façade overlooking Green Park, which had been completed in 1761, probably to designs by Matthew Brettingham, and only occupied for two years.[4] 'Various Designs of Alterations on the house in Piccadilly with Estimates 10.10.0', a 'Design of a Table frame . . . 3.3.0', a 'Design of a Cieling (sic) for the Bedroom . . . 7.7.0' with 'Drawings of the Ornaments at large for the Execution 1.11.6' and a 'Drawing of an ornamented frieze . . . 0.10.6' were supplied by Adam in February 1765, a month before Coventry took possession. It is tempting to associate the design for a table frame with William France and John Bradburn's bill dated 25 May 1765 'For a large Sideboard Table Frame richly carved, and gilt in burnishd Gold and Mens Time putting up Do in your Eating Room £41.10'.[5] Apart from that, only the bedroom ceiling was executed; it is still intact and will be discussed in the context of that room.

All that survives of the 'Various Designs of Alterations' is a rough sketch at the Soane of a first-floor plan inscribed 'Ld Coventry Piccadilly' (pl. 78).[6] It is an overly ambitious scheme for remodelling the interior to provide a grand imperial staircase in the centre of the house, leading to a pivotal ante-room and large dining-room on the Piccadilly front, and an *appartement de parade* or suite of public rooms on the east side, consisting of a drawing-room and two apsidal 'Assembly' rooms – an odd term in the context of a private house, presumably suggested by Coventry but never used by Adam. The offices at the rear were to be converted to an *appartement de commodité*, a suite of private or semi-private rooms, as the occasion demanded, containing an apsidal 'Ladys' Dressing room' or boudoir, followed by a circular bedchamber and a ladies' maid's room. Although the ground-floor rooms (about which nothing is known) would have been somewhat simpler, they still had to be rearranged in relation to the central staircase.

This plan demanded far more time and money than Coventry was prepared to spend (pl. 79), especially since his improvements at Croome were still unfinished after nearly thirteen years. Adam was therefore required to effect a compromise with the existing late-Palladian interiors, keeping the ground floor more or less as it was and focussing his attention on the first-floor reception rooms, the rooms of show: the ante-room and drawing-room at the front of the house, facing Green Park, and behind them the bedchamber and Lady Coventry's dressing-room.

By cleverly orchestrated decoration, he succeeded in investing this suite of conventional, rectangular spaces with variety, novelty and many contrasts, in the spirit of the ancients. The interconnecting ante-room, drawing-room and bedroom, referred to in the building accounts as 'the 3 rooms', were uniformly hung with crimson silk damask (the same colour as the hangings at Croome) and matching festoon curtains. Their dados were all painted green and their skirtings rose-colour; the carved friezes round the walls, doors and windows in the two front rooms were green, picked out in gold. Uniform colouring of the wall surfaces served to emphasize the originality and diversity of Adam's ceilings, chimney-pieces, carpets and wall-furniture.

Special attention was naturally given to the drawing-room, the so-called 'great room', for which he supplied a 'Design of a painted ceiling in the Antique Stile . . .' costing £20 in June 1765. This expensive drawing, now lost, can be identified with a

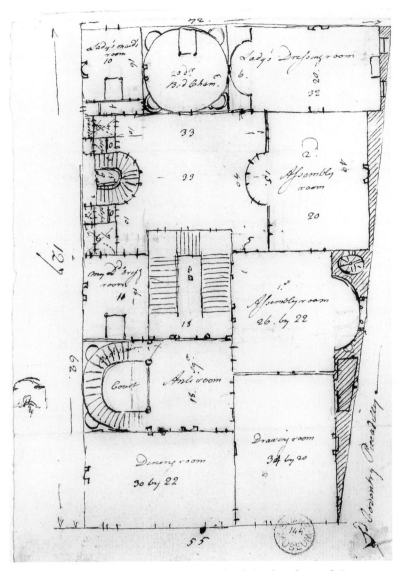

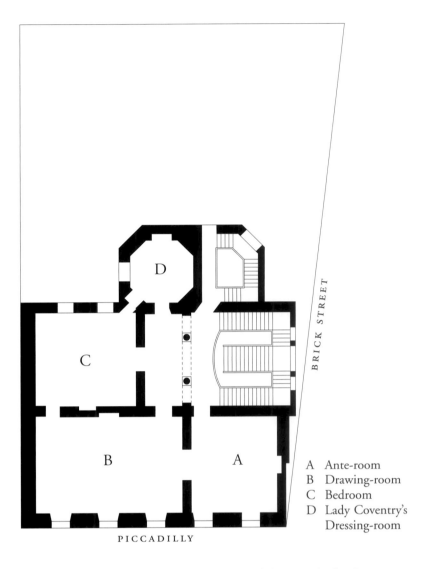

78   Preliminary sketch plan (unexecuted) of the first floor of Coventry House, by Robert Adam, 1765 (Sir John Soane's Museum: Adam drawings, vol. 7:144)

79   A reconstruction of the first-floor plan of the main body of Coventry House. The original configuration of the rooms and offices at the rear of the house is not known. The thin black line represents the perimeter of the site as shown in Adam's sketch plan, pl. 78

coloured office copy at the Soane (pl. 80) which, though correctly dated June 1765, is mistakenly inscribed for the dining-room.[7] His 'Alteration on the Design for the painted Ceiling of the great Room' made later that year for the small sum of £1.10.0 was evidently not very extensive and has not been identified. It is tempting to think that it increased the number of oval paintings in the rectangular panels on either side of the central square from two to six in anticipation of Antonio Zucchi's arrival in England in 1766. These ovals of classical subjects, the figured roundels in the four corners and the Aurora in the middle of the ceiling, were all painted by Zucchi before 17 June 1767 and are amongst his earliest works in this country (pl. 81).[8] He was also responsible for the central ring of twenty-four medallions of Coventry heraldic eagles alternating with musical trophies, and the outer border of smaller cameos of classical heads and vases in lozenge-shape frames enclosed in circular wreaths. The ceiling survives intact, but its present colour is questionable.

Adam's design for the drawing-room carpet (invoiced on 8 July 1767) was the rejected ogee-pattern on a rose-coloured ground which he had devised six months earlier for the gallery at Syon, and which had no relation whatsoever to the ceiling.[9] A full-size drawing of one section of it was made in December (pl.

82) and given to Zucchi who used it to made a 'Model peint en detempre, d'un quart de Tapy pour la Grand Chambre, pour donner au Manufacture des Tapy'.[10] When Lady Mary Coke visited Thomas Moore's carpet manufactory at Moorfields in April 1768, she 'saw one that was making for Lord Coventry that he had agreed to give a hundred and forty guineas for; it is indeed extremely fine'.[11] Moore also made 44 yards (41 metres) of 'fine Bruss Carpet Circle patt' for the ante-room in 1768, which may be related to the large-scale drawing at the Soane of a carpet, inscribed 'Carpet for the Earl of Coventry', with a pattern of interlaced circles enclosing lozenges and central rosettes.[12]

Had Adam wanted the drawing-room to be a fully integrated room of the sort with which his name has come to be associated, he would have given it this circle-pattern carpet, which related to the lozenge border of its ceiling and was virtually identical to the scagliola slabs he designed for his two side-tables. But an integrated interior was evidently not what was sought. The 'great room' is a deliberate and carefully considered combination of discordant elements, a 'harmony of contrasts', as Sir John Summerson elegantly put it.[13] This stimulating dissonance is also to be found in the contemporary drawing-room and gallery at Syon.

40. Design of a Cieling for the Dining Room at The Right Honble. The Earl of Coventry's House in Piccadilly, In the Style of the painted ornaments of the Ancients. 34 ft by 21 ft 7½ & 17 ft 9 high

80   Design for the drawing-room ceiling 'In the Style of the painted ornaments of the Ancients', by Robert Adam, 1765 (Sir John Soane's Museum: Adam drawings, vol. 11:40)

81   Detail of the drawing-room ceiling as executed

Two richly ornamented gilt-wood table frames (pl. 83) – each with eight legs of complex form, combining rectangular blocks and round tapering balusters, joined by concave platform stretchers in the French style, and pendant half-patera and swags of husks below the frieze – were carved to Adam's design by Sefferin Alken in 1768.[14] They were specially contrived to support scagliola 'Mosaic Tables' with red and blue interlaced circles on a cream-coloured ground that were supplied in the same year by Bartoli and Richter, the leading firm of scagliola makers (pl. 84).[15] These tables were sold at Christie's in 1986 and are now in a private collection.[16] Originally, they must have stood on either side of the main entrance from the ante-room (being too wide, at 5½ feet (1.6 metres), for the window piers) with mirrors above to reflect the colourful scagliola slabs. The '2 Glass frames' carved by Sefferin Alken in July 1768 were 9 × 4½ feet (2.7 × 1.3 metres) and had crests of female figures reclining on foliage and baskets of fruit amidst foliage at the base.[17] Adam's design was adapted from one initially intended for the drawing-room at Lansdowne House, which the Earl of Shelburne rejected.[18]

82 Record drawing of Adam's carpet designs for the drawing-room (right) and ante-room (left), Adam office, 1767 (Sir John Soane's Museum: Adam drawings, vol. 49:53)

83 Side table of carved and gilt wood, one of a pair designed by Robert Adam, 1768, and made by Sefferin Alken. The scagliola tops, also designed by Adam, were made by Bartoli and Richter (Private collection)

84 Design for the 'Mosaic' scagliola table top, by Robert Adam, 1767 (Sir John Soane's Museum: Adam drawings, vol. 5:78)

85 Design for a concave mirror and girandoles for the ante-room, by Robert Adam, 1769 (Sir John Soane's Museum: Adam drawings, vol. 20:59)

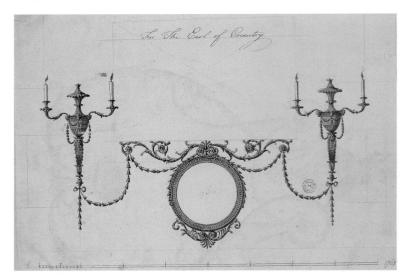

To complete the window-wall – here and in the ante-room – Adam designed 'Rich' curtain cornices which were executed by John Touzey in February 1768 and hung with festoon curtains of the same red silk damask as the wall hangings.[19] In the nineteenth century the windows were lowered to the floor so as to give access to the balcony which had been added to the front of the house. Before that, they would have held part of the suite of eight large arm-chairs 'Richly Carv'd in the Antique manner, and gilt in Burnish'd gold the Ground pick'd in green covered with his Lordships Crimson Silk Damask' supplied by the firm of Gordon and Taitt in July 1768 along with three large sofas to match.[20] Two of the sofas would have been placed on either side of the chimney-piece and the third in the centre of the west wall opposite the main entrance to the room, flanked by armchairs. Adam must have been consulted on the 'Antique manner' of the suite, though he was not responsible for its design.

A marble chimney-piece with swags of husks in the frieze and a tablet depicting Cupid and Psyche was carved by John Devall in July 1767 from drawings provided by Adam two years earlier.[21] Designs for a grate followed in November 1767 and were executed in 1768 by Hartley & Cooper, the firm of smiths who executed Adam's grate for the gallery at Croome.[22] It and the marble chimney-piece have long since left the house.

The ante-room, being a prelude to the great room, was perforce more restrained and harmonious, but it was by no means dull or lacking in novelty. Circles were the decorative theme here: they are found on the ceiling, on the frieze round the walls, over the doors and on the chimney-piece, on the green circular-pattern carpet with pink, yellow and brown ornaments made by Thomas Moore in 1768 and on the round concave mirror linked by garlands of husks to two girandoles (pl. 85) in the form of classical urns (the room's ancillary motif) for which Adam pro-

86 Mahogany clothes-press designed by Robert Adam c.1764–65 and made by John Cobb with specialist carving by Sefferin Alken, 1766 (Victoria and Albert Museum)

87 Detail of pl. 86 carved by Sefferin Alken

vided designs and working drawings in 1769 and 1770 respectively.[23]

Distorting mirrors were a current French fashion which was also taken up by the Duchess of Northumberland, for whom Adam incorporated both convex and concave forms in the decoration of the central bay of the gallery at Syon. Lord Coventry's combined mirror and girandoles must have been placed on the long wall opposite the windows where the return reflection from the pier-glass would have added to the amusement. Alken supplied the pier-glass frame, complete with an urn finial, in 1769, but who executed the 'rich moulding' of the convex glass and the urn girandoles is unrecorded. Nor do we know what other furniture the room contained. Adam's bill for 'taking dimentions of pictures' suggests that he was responsible for their frames as well as their hanging.

Behind the drawing-room was the bedchamber, the main entrance to which was from the vestibule or lobby at the top of the stairs. It was part of the new Countess of Coventry's apartment and was the first room in the house to be finished in September 1766.[24] Time was evidently saved on its ceiling by leaving the pre-existing Brettingham compartments and simply replacing their ornaments with new ones designed by Adam.[25] The result is patently hybrid and not entirely successful, even less so as recently painted and gilded.

Apart from the various architectural finishings, there was a large mahogany clothes press made in February 1766 by John Cobb and 'very painfully' carved by Sefferin Alken (pl. 86, 87), with scrolled foliage issuing from vases in the door panels, an anthemion and palmette frieze, four female terms, a Greek key cornice and four classical vases on top. Evidently this monumental structure (approximately 2.4 × 3.6 metres, or 8 × 12 feet), which may originally have been intended for Croome, proved too large for Lady Coventry's bedroom in town; in June 1767 it was taken by Cobb to his house, dismantled and divided into two, according to a new design by Adam. Finally, in February 1769, the two sections were put up in the lobby at the head of the stairs on either side of the entrance to the bedroom. The wardrobes passed by descent to Cornelia, Countess of Craven of Coombe Abbey, Warwickshire and were sold at auction by her son, the sixth Earl of Craven, in October 1965.[26] One is now at the V&A.

The pier-glass designed by Adam in June 1768 and made by Alken two years later has disappeared altogether. Instead of a normal carved frame, it had a pierced anthemion fret laid over the glass (which in this instance was supplied by Chippendale) and a crest 4½ feet (1.37 metres) tall of scrolled foliage surmounted by a figure of Cupid.[27] There are mirrors of the same date and similar description in the galleries at Osterley and Corsham Court.

Lady Coventry's bedchamber and dressing-room were primarily for show rather than use; as soon as their decoration was finished, a private apartment containing an additional bedroom, powdering room and water-closet was proposed in a rear extension. An elevation and a full set of plans with outline copies on 'stampt parchm[t].' were supplied by Adam in January 1767.[28] These have not survived and subsequent remodelling of the interiors at the back of the house make it difficult to determine how much of his scheme was executed.

88   Elevations of six of the eight walls of Lady Coventry's octagonal
dressing-room, by Robert Adam, 1765 (Sir John Soane's Museum: Adam
drawings, vol. 14:141–2, 145–8)

It was in the small compass of Lady Coventry's octagonal dressing-room that Adam made his most complete and distinctive contribution to the decoration of Coventry House (pl. 88). Every surface – walls, ceiling and even the floor – was embellished with a variety of small-scale ornaments in the 'antique stile'. There were guilloche pilasters joined by Greek key friezes and flanked by drops of husks; panels of carved strigillation in the dado and stucco ones bordering the fluted cove, where they served as pedestals for vases issuing from scrolled foliage and accompanied by winged griffons. Large-scale working drawings were provided by Adam in November 1765 and executed in the following year by Rose and Alken.[29]

All the ornaments were painted 'best dead white', picked-in rose and green and gilded by John Touzey in April 1767.[30] In addition, there were separate paintings by Zucchi (seventeen in all, costing £183.15.6) applied to the walls: four panels of multi-coloured arabesques of 'Rainceau' ornament each with a figured medallion, a large panel and medallion opposite the chimney-piece where Adam initially intended to place an oval mirror and eight oblong tablets of classical figures in the frieze. The long tablet intended to go above the chimney-piece was replaced by a stucco ornament like the one above the door, for which Adam made a separate design in May 1767. The latter presumably superseded the classical sarcophagus flanked by winged griffons shown in his 1765 wall elevations.[31]

Alken's modest charge of £4.7.7 for making a 'Moulded frame' of four richly carved members for the mirror over the chimney-piece suggests that the untraced mirror design supplied by Adam in August 1767 for £2.8.0 was considerably simpler than what he proposed in his wall elevation.[32] It is not clear whether John Hobcraft's bill for making and fitting up a frame and moulding for a glass in the octagon room on 9 November 1767 and John Cobb's bill for supplying a plate of silvered glass and fitting it into 'the blind frame in the Octagon Room' in February 1768 refer to Lady Coventry's dressing-room or the octagonal room on the ground-floor about which very little is known.

The statuary marble chimney-piece (pl. 89), with a tablet depicting a lion tamed by Cupid in an oval medallion and a frieze of antique torchères flanked by half-boys emerging from foliage, was carved by John Devall, junior in 1767 and is his first documented work.[33] When the rear of Coventry House was altered for the St James's Club in 1888, the chimney-flues were removed from the octagon rooms and replaced by the present windows; Devall's chimney-piece was re-erected in the back parlour on the ground floor, where it still stands.[34]

Some of the stucco wall decorations also survive, albeit overpainted and largely obscured, but Zucchi's inset paintings have vanished without a trace. The De Young Museum in San Francisco has the octagonal needlework carpet with a flowerhead medallion surrounded by floral swags on a pink ground and bands of blue-and-white Greek key pattern enclosing a border of scrolled foliage on a yellow ground, which was designed in 1767 to answer the ceiling (pl. 90). It is thought to have been worked by Lady Coventry herself, probably using Zucchi's '*Model d'un quart de Tapy pour chambre Octagone peint a l'huile, de la grandeur just, avec beaucoup d'ornaments de Girlandes et de Fleurs*'.[35]

An 'Oval Dressing Glass frame 2.4 by 1.8 (71.2 cm. × 40.7 cm.)

89 Marble chimney-piece from Lady Coventry's dressing-room, designed by Robert Adam, 1766 and carved by John Deval, junior, 1767. Removed to its present position on the ground floor in 1888

with Coat of Arms at top & bottom & supporters at Bottom standing on rock work 2 women & folege at sides & festoons of husks over glass &c' was made for Lady Coventry by Sefferin Alken in February 1770 from a drawing 'at large' of one of '2 Designs of two Dressing Glasses' provided by Adam in March 1769 (pl. 91).[36] The preferred design, now lost, seems to have evolved from two earlier designs at the Soane dated 1768 – one inscribed for Lady Coventry and the other for the earl.[37] A similar dressing-glass with a crest of entwined dolphins supporting Venus, female figures at the sides, festoons of husks over the glass and birds and foliage at the base, was designed in 1771 for Lady Colebrooke's dressing-room at 23 Arlington Street.[38] Lady Coventry's dressing-glass probably stood on the 'very neat Dressing Table with apparatus' made by Ince and Mayhew in 1769.[39]

The drawings 'at large' for the front and one end of an 'antique stool for the Octagon room' included in Adam's account for 20 March 1767 have not been identified, nor are there any surviving bills for their execution. However, there is a rough, uninscribed sketch at the Soane of one end of a stool formed of two scrolls and pendant palmettes loosely based on an antique sarcophagus, which is comparable to the back of a hall-chair designed for the Earl of Coventry in 1767 and presumably intended for his London house (pl. 92).[40] Whether there is any

90 Needlework carpet made for Lady Coventry's dressing-room from a design by Robert Adam, 1767 (De Young Memorial Museum, San Francisco, California)

relationship between this chair design and the design 'For a pattern Chair for the Hall left with Mr Adam for Determination' by John Bradburn in May 1765 remains uncertain.[41]

Lady Coventry's octagonal dressing-room was in essence an ornament to the unified suite of three reception rooms, but not an integral part of it. Though there may have been a jib door from the bedroom, the principal entrance was from the staircase-lobby, making the dressing-room, to all intents and purposes, a separate entity.[42] The octagon room on the ground-floor was similarly arranged, with a door from the staircase-hall, a window on the opposite wall and a fireplace to the left. Nothing more is known about its use or appearance.

When the principal reception rooms on the first floor were finished, attention was turned to the dining-room on the ground floor, beneath the drawing-room. This is not to say that the dining-room remained empty and unused for three years. On the contrary, the first recorded pieces of furniture to be made for the house were three window cornices 'carved . . . to a Drawing' by France and Bradburn in November 1765 and 'a large sideboard Table Frame neatly carved and gilt in burnish'd gold'.[43] It is tempting to relate the sideboard to Adam's bill for a 'Design of a Table frame for house in Town' in February 1765; the design has not been traced. Apart from that, the room was filled with a great deal of hired furniture while the redecoration was in progress.

If there were ever any thoughts of redecorating the dining-room ceiling in the 'Antique Stile', they came to nothing.[44] Lord Coventry evidently decided to leave the room more or less as it

was – with Brettingham's late-Palladian doorcases (which are still *in situ*) and a plain ceiling – and to rely instead on distinctive mirrors to dispel the old-fashioned blandness and introduce the spirit of antiquity in a novel form.

A 'Design of an Oval Glass for the Eating Room 2.2.0' is entered in Adam's accounts for August 1769. There is a finished watercolour drawing at the Soane of an oval pier-glass with a tall hanging device and an anthemion ornament at the bottom, which is inscribed 'Design for a Glass Frame for the Eating Room for the Earl of Coventry', but dated 1768.[45] Added to the drawing are faint pencil sketches suggesting female terms on the sides of the frame and a different hanging device. These ideas were worked up in a half elevation of an oval mirror inscribed 'for Lord Coventry' and dated 1770, which corresponds to Adam's bill of 30 June 1770 for 'another Design for the Glass frame in the Eating parlour 2.2.0'. A drawing of the 'moulding for Oval Glass at large for Dining Room -.5.-' was supplied on 27 June 1771.

The second design was an alternative to the first one, not a design for an additional mirror. It has a fluted oval frame of exactly the same description and dimensions as its predecessor and was also intended for the two piers (approximately 5 feet 2 inches, or 1.57 metres, wide) between the dining-room windows (pl. 93). The draped female terms reaching out to grasp tasselled ropes from which the frame appears to be suspended are the added ingredient that gave the mirrors their novel neo-classical character. In order to accommodate them in the restricted space,

91   Design for a 'Glass frame for Lady Coventry's Dressing room', by Robert Adam, 1769. The frame was carved by Sefferin Alken in 1770 (Sir John Soane's Museum: Adam drawings, vol. 20:62)

92   'Sketch of a Hall Chair for The Rt. Honble The Earl of Coventry', by Robert Adam, 1767 (Sir John Soane's Museum: Adam drawings, vol. 17:92)

93   Detail of the pier-glass of carved and gilt-wood from the dining-room at Coventry House, designed by Robert Adam, 1770 and carved by Sefferin Alken, 1772 (Victoria and Albert Museum)

Adam was forced to place the figures as near as possible to the narrow top of the oval and its foliate cresting; this, in turn, required a proportional reduction of approximately 2 feet (60.9 cm.) in the height of the hanging device. None of these adjustments was left to chance; Adam's painstaking arrangement of the various elements is demonstrated by the squaring of his design; and, lest there be any doubt that the mirror would fit the space, the line of the window is drawn in on the right.

In 1934, one of the mirrors, described as 'coming from an old Adam House in Devonshire Street, Portland Place . . .', was exhibited by the firm of Dawson Inc. at The First Annual Fine Arts Exposition in New York.[46] Having been released from the constraints of the window pier at Coventry House, a wider oval frame was substituted for the narrow original and the attached figures were lowered, thereby increasing the overall width from a maximum of 5 feet (1.52 metres) to a little over 6 feet (1.95 metres). At the same time, the two separate ornaments of the

hanging device (a rams'-head vase and a lion's-mask patera) were compressed into a single vertical unit, taking about 19 inches (48 cm.) off the height. These new proportions were much more suitable to modern American rooms, but they are not those of an eighteenth-century English pier-glass. The mirror (assuming it was the same one and not its pair) was subsequently acquired by the New York collector Benjamin Sonnenberg and sold with the rest of his collection in 1979 at Sotheby's Parke Bernet.[47] Ten years later, it appeared in Doyle's auction rooms in New York and was bought by Alan Rubin of Pelham Galleries, London, who was the first to link it not only to Adam's design at the Soane, but also to a receipt from Sefferin Alken dated 4 February 1772 for 'Eighty pounds in full for two carved oval Gilt Glass Frames & of all Demands'.[48] The superb quality of the carved figures makes this one of Alken's finest works. This, together with its full documentation, led to its purchase by the V&A in 1992.

94 View of Syon from the south-east

4

SYON HOUSE

Within the Jacobean shell of Syon House, Middlesex, Horace Walpole witnessed the emergence in 1764 of 'another Mount Palatine',[1] a suite of state apartments of varied geometrical shapes, planned and fitted up by Adam 'in a magnificent manner . . . entirely in the antique style', according to the wishes of Hugh Smithson, Earl (later first Duke) of Northumberland himself a person of extensive knowledge and correct taste in architecture . . . who possessed not only wealth to execute a great design but skill to judge of its merits'.[2] The earl's architectural judgment had been formed by travel and study as well as by experience gained from the extensive improvements he had been making since 1750 to Northumberland House in the Strand, Alnwick Castle in Northumberland and Syon, which he inherited, along with his titles, from his father-in-law, Algernon, seventh Duke of Somerset.[3]

The quadrangular house – built in 1547 by the Protector Somerset out of the remains of the dissolved Bridgettine monastery of Sion – was granted to Henry Percy, ninth Earl of Northumberland, by James I in 1604 (pl. 94, 95). Large sums of money were spent on it by the ninth and tenth Earls, and further alterations were made by the Proud Duke of Somerset around 1700. Yet, fifty years later, the new earl found it not merely old-fashioned, but also 'ruinous and inconvenient'.[4] Nothing, for example, had been done to eliminate the anomaly of unequal floor levels, particularly in the entrance hall, which was lower than the rest of the ground-floor rooms.

In 1751, Smithson began making 'many considerable alterations in the (principal bedroom) apartments of the east front over the long gallery' and improvements to the staircase, dining-room, drawing-room and 'green room' (probably an ante-room) on the north front.[5] It is not known who his architect was. The greatest improvements were to the garden, where by 1760 'the most beautiful piece of scenery imaginable' had been made by 'Capability' Brown on the east and west fronts and two bridges had been built (one in the Gothic style) by James Paine.[6] It must have come as a considerable shock to Paine to find his principal patron, for whom he had been working for the past six years at Northumberland House and Alnwick, turning to a newcomer like Adam to transform Syon into a magnificent neo-classical palace.

Adam was evidently working at Syon by the summer of 1760.[7]

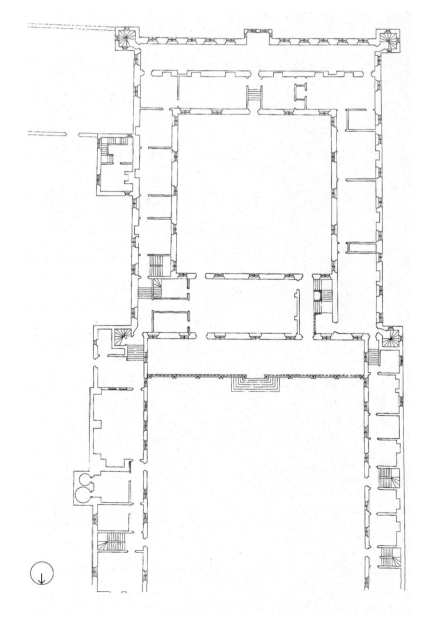

95 Plan of Syon *c.*1593. The service wings on the west front were later demolished

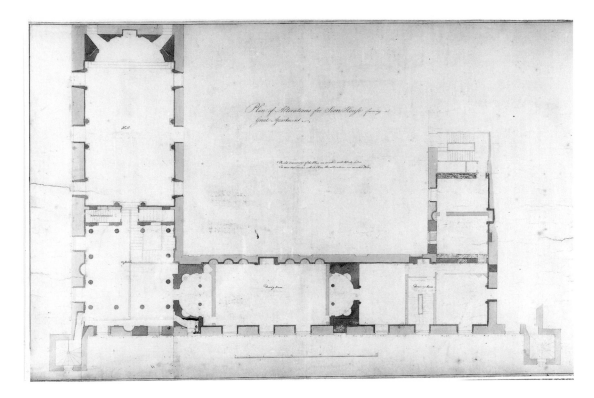

96 'Plan of Alterations for Sion House forming a Great Apartment', by Robert Adam, *c.*1760 (Collection of the Duke of Northumberland)

97 Preliminary (unexecuted) design for the hall, by Robert Adam, 1761 (Sir John Soane's Museum: Adam drawings, vol. 39:3)

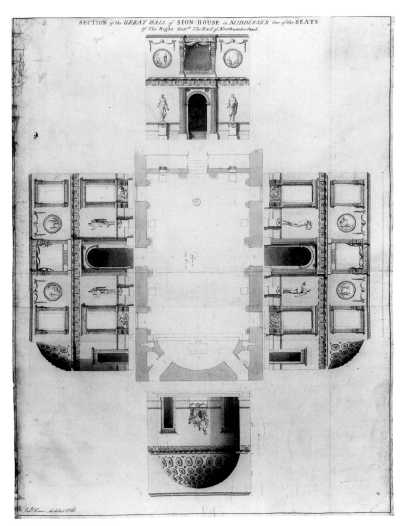

related elevations at the Soane, had an existing partition wall at the south end with a central door (matching those on the east and west walls) leading into the old screens passage where Adam intended to insert new stairs in place of the old ones which were to be removed to make way for his columnar vestibule or ante-room.[9] This was superseded in 1761 by a modified design in which the south wall was opened to form a square recess screened by two enriched Doric columns framing a superb bronze cast of the *Dying Gladiator* made by the leading Roman goldsmith and founder, Luigi Valadier. Whether the bronze precipitated the introduction of the square recess is hard to say, as the date of Valadier's commission is unknown.[10] The opposite end of the hall was formed into a cavernous semi-circular apse which, apart from concealing a short flight of stairs to the private apartment, also gave a basilica-like shape to the hall.[11]

In the *Works* the apse is shown containing a version of the famous *Laocoön* raised on a broad pedestal specially designed for it by Adam (pl. 98), rivalling the bronze cast in the great hall at Houghton.[12] Though the pedestal was executed, the statue, presumably another bronze cast commissioned from Valadier, never arrived and its place was filled instead by Joseph Wilton's marble copy of the *Apollo Belvedere* which was originally meant to stand opposite the main entrance, his outstretched arm directing visitors towards the state apartment. A bronze *Laocoön* would not only have been much more spectacular than the marble *Apollo*, but also better proportioned to the width of the apse and better balanced colour-wise with the *Dying Gladiator*. Northumberland's appeal to James Adam in 1761 to procure him a cast of a colossal consular figure also came to nothing.[13]

The old south block then contained four rooms and another staircase, all of which were removed, whereupon the space was divided into two very large rooms: the dining-room with screened apses at each end and niches on the inner wall, and beyond that the drawing-room taken all the way back to the gallery. Obviously, rooms of such length required proportional height, which was obtained by taking space from the bedroom

His earliest surviving design is a 'Plan of Alterations for Sion House, forming a Great Apartment' (pl. 96) on the remaining south, east and west fronts.[8] This shows the existing partition walls and stairs in grey, his proposed stairs superimposed in faint pencil and new work in black.

The initial scheme for the hall (pl. 97), for which there are floor above; the fenestration on the south front also needed adjustments to bring it into order.

The 'Great Apartment' with the revised hall, the long gallery and the private apartment on the north front completed the plan for the whole quadrangle in which Adam sought to combine the 'variety and gracefulness of form, so particularly courted by the ancients' with the 'proper arrangement and relief of apartments . . . in which the French have excelled'.[14]

It has always been believed that the engraved plan published in 1773 and retrospectively dated 1761 is entirely of the latter date (pl. 99). However, it seems clear from the absence of any direct communication between the south block and the proposed rotunda that this grandiose central feature was not part of Adam's original scheme, but rather an afterthought inspired by the spectacular temporary pavilion erected for the 'Grand fete' given for the King of Denmark in October 1768.[15] On that occasion the plain, open court was 'fitted up as a Grand Salon illuminated with many Thousand[d] lamps disposed in Festoons & various ornam[ts] in wch Bands of Music were dispos[d] in Niches admirably contrived with large niches in ye angles with Triumphal Arches adorn[d] wth Transparent Paintings & said to have cost upw[ds] of 3000£'.[16] This extravagant neo-classical *coup de théâtre* was presumably designed by Adam to equal if not upstage the pavilion erected by Chambers in Richmond Gardens for George III's reception in honour of his dim Danish son-in-law. Chambers's pavilion also had a domed central rotunda supported on eight columns; according to him, 'the Centre part (of the façade) had been contrived for the Queen some years before by Mr Adams but never used'.[17]

The domed, top-lit rotunda planned as a permanent addition to Syon would have been just as spectacular as the temporary 'Grand Salon' – its walls being lined with statues in niches and containing an inner circle of eight piers, each flanked by columns and adorned with more niches and statues. Indeed, its diverse forms and openings were likened by Adam to a theatrical decoration that 'apparently increases the extent, and leaves room for the imagination to play'.[18] Apart from serving as a 'general rendezvous', it was meant to fulfill the practical function of a *rond point* or junction leading north to the 'Grand Stair' (also an afterthought) in the private apartment, and east, through a 'circular back stair', into the centre of the long gallery for the 'reception of company before dinner and for ladies to retire to afterwards'.

Though the rotunda and 'Grand Stair' were both 'still intended' when the plan was published in 1773, there cannot have been any hope for the rotunda after the duchess's death in 1776. Had it been built, the circuit of the state rooms would have moved in the opposite direction, been shorter and made more sense than it does today.

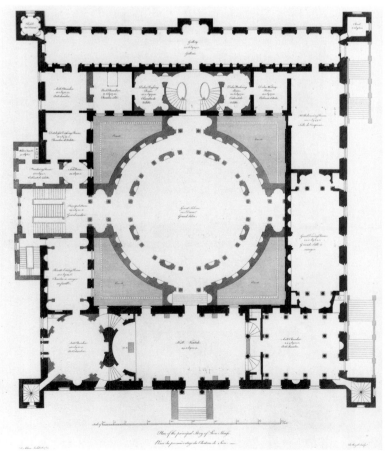

98 Elevations of north end of the hall towards the Dying Gladiator and the 'great Apartment' (top), and the south end towards the Laocoön and the 'private Apartment' (bottom), by Robert Adam, *c*.1761 (*The works in architecture of Robert and James Adam*, vol. I (1778), pt. I, pl. VI)

99 'Plan of the principal Story (ground-floor) of Sion House', by Robert Adam, *c*.1768 (*The works in architecture of Robert and James Adam*, vol. I (1778), pt. I, pl. V)

100 The entrance hall looking south, showing the ceiling and the related pavement

To begin with, Adam removed the old main staircase behind the hall, opened a large arch in the wall and used the space to create a square recess in which he placed two short, curved flights of stairs leading to the state rooms (pl. 99). The diversity of shapes here, coupled with the play of light and shadow, gave what he called 'an additional picturesque to the scene'. Added to this was the illusion of space gained by seeing the columnar screen across the great arch repeated at the end of the vestibule, a sight which he was at pains to depict in his *Works* (pl. 98).

No doubt he would have maintained that the liberty he took in ornamenting the hall with diverse and uncommon forms of the Doric order was entirely in the spirit of the ancients whose creative genius was not constrained by rules (pl. 100). Apart from the principal order – a fluted Doric considered 'very proper in Halls'[19] – there are mannerist Doric terms with lion masks on

the attic windows and spiral fluted Doric columns supported by scrolled consoles framing the lower windows (pl. 101), which are similar to those prominently featured in the frontispiece (pl. 102) to his book, *Ruins of the Palace of the Emperor Diocletian at Spalatro* (1764).[20]

The architectural hall was originally 'stucco'd & left white', its ornaments being considered bold enough not to require the picking-out introduced in the 1960s by John Fowler.[21] What its original pavement was like is less certain. Mary Anderson, who visited the house around 1770, simply described it as 'black and white'; yet the absence of any relation between Adam's 'antique' diapered design (pl. 103) and the ceiling raises the possibility that the present pavement echoing the ceiling dates from the nineteenth century.[22] Be that as it may, the hall, as already noted, was conceived as a repository for copies and

101 Scrolled consoles supporting the spiral-fluted Doric columns framing the four lower windows in the hall

102 Francesco Bartolozzi, a *capriccio* of Istrian and Dalmatian remains after a drawing by Charles-Louis Clérisseau (Robert Adam, *The ruins of the Palace of the Emperor Diocldetian at Spalatro in Dalmatia* (1764), frontis., pl. 1)

103 Design for a pavement for the hall as first designed (see pl. 97), by Robert Adam, *c.*1761 (Sir John Soane's Museum: Adam drawings, vol. 39:4)

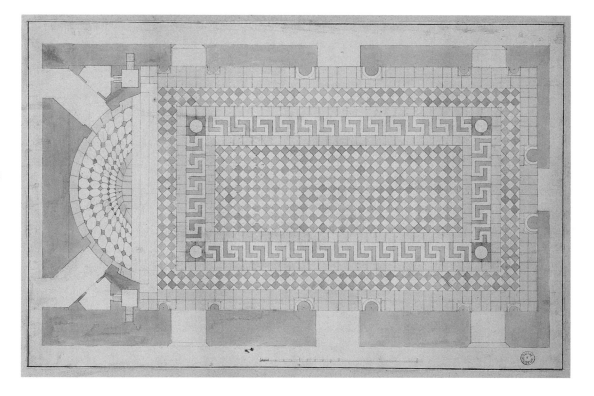

casts of antique sculpture placed on pedestals designed by Adam, and bas-reliefs (some of stucco by Joseph Rose, others *trompe l'oeil* paintings in grisaille by Giovanni Battista Cipriani) set into the upper region of the walls. This, however, was just a proem to the Northumberland sculpture collections which extended to the vestibule, dining-room and gallery and would have been centred in the rotunda had it been built. While Northumberland House had the bulk of the paintings, Syon had the sculpture. Its state rooms were comparable in this respect to the seventeenth-century royal apartment at the Alcazar in Madrid.[23]

The vestibule, or ante-room (pl. 104), though considerably smaller than the two-storey hall, is just as monumental and architectural. There, however, the similarity ends, for this corner room with its highly polished marble and scagliola columns,

scagliola floor, bronze casts and lavish gilding is one of Adam's most resplendent creations.

Through the agency of his brother James in Rome, columns and pilasters of dark-green verd-antique marble, said to have been rescued from the bed of the Tiber, were conveyed to Syon in September 1765.[24] They were used 'to form the room', or rather to transform it – after the removal of pre-existing partitions that had divided it into a staircase, a room on the west front and another at right angles extending into the south block – from a rectangle to a square in which a symmetrical arrangement of chimney-piece and doors could be achieved by the simple measure of bringing the four columns on the south side about six feet further forward than the others. This also created a colonnaded passage in front of the windows, leading in one direction to the stairs in the tower and in the other to a

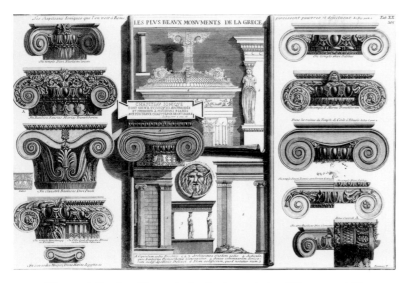

105 Giovanni Battista Piranesi, the Ionic capitals of Rome and Greece compared (*Della magnificenze ed architettura de' Romani* (1761), pl. xx, Wilton-Ely no. 790)

106 'The Ionic Order of the Anti-Room, with the rest of the Detail of that Room', designed by Robert Adam (*The works in architecture of Robert and James Adam*, vol. II, pt. IV, pl. v)

107 Detail of the statuary marble and verd-antique chimney-piece designed by Robert Adam in 1764 and carved by Joseph Wilton

104 A view of the brilliantly coloured ante-room looking back into the white hall, showing the ceiling and related scagliola floor

convenient water-closet alongside the door to the dining-room.

To these genuine Roman shafts – or at least partly genuine, as some were made to match in scagliola – Adam added white marble bases trimmed with gold and gilded Ionic capitals 'ornamented in the most splendid manner, of which this Order is susceptible', combining Greek and Roman prototypes.[25] The inspiration was quite clearly Piranesi's polemical plate in the *Magnificenza ed architettura de' Romani* (1761), which exposed the fallacy of Le Roy's dismissal of the Ionic capitals seen in Rome as poor and defective by comparing a variety of them with the Ionic capital of the Erectheion (pl. 105), depicted for the first time in Le Roy's *Ruines des plus beaux monumens de la Grèce* (1758).[26] Adam's employment of Piranesi to engrave the plate of the Ionic order at Syon (pl. 106) for the second volume of his *Works* published in 1779 could not have been more appropriate.[27]

The spirit of Piranesi is much in evidence in the vestibule. The two great panels of gilded trophies, exquisitely executed in stucco by Joseph Rose and set into the walls on either side of the entrance from the hall, may also owe something to him, though they are ultimately derived from the famous Roman trophies on the Campidoglio, of which Adam had first-hand knowledge.[28]

There was, no doubt, a certain pleasurable poignancy in Adam's recreating the rich variety and magnificence of ancient Rome in the small compass of the vestibule and making irreverent use of the palmette necking of the Erechtheum capital as a frieze decoration at the very moment that Stuart and Revett's

Antiquities of Athens was about to appear. It was a way of venting his annoyance at being forced to delay the publication of his *Ruins of the Palace of the Emperor Diocletian at Spaltro* for eighteen months lest it be eclipsed by the excitement surrounding Stuart's long awaited Grecian work.

The vestibule is a brilliant display of the opulence and taste of the Romans as much as that of the Northumberlands. It is the first English interior decorated in the manner of a classical triumphal-arch with projecting columns carrying free-standing figures. The triumphal-arch motif seems to have been of particular interest to Adam at this early stage, for he also used it in his design for the south front of Kedleston in 1760. Among the twelve gilded statues rather uncomfortably poised in the space between the columns and the ceiling (and serving to link the two) is one of Bacchus made in 1766 by Joseph Wilton, who was also responsible for the white statuary marble chimney-piece carved with robust rams' heads and enriched with panels of verd-antique marble (pl. 107) which tie in with the rest of the decorations and relieve the glare of the white.[29] In 1831, one of the original gilded figures was replaced by a copy of Canova's Hebe.[30]

In the niches between the windows are bronze casts by Valadier of the Belvedere *Antinous* and Borghese *Silenus*, and over the chimney-piece is a large stucco medallion painted to look like bronze, elaborately framed in gold and set into a blue-green panel of the same colour used in the friezes, in the rinceau panels above the entablature and in the trophies. Mary Anderson found it difficult to distinguish the real bronzes from the green-paint *tromperies*.[31]

Brilliant colour and lustre – the keynotes of this remarkable room – are fused in the highly polished pavement of yellow, blue, red, pale green and brown scagliola in a pattern similar to that of the white and gold ceiling. Nothing could be further from the delicate, pastel colours usually associated with the Adam style. Even A. T. Bolton, with his comprehensive knowledge of Adam's works, seemed somewhat jarred by its brilliance, and pleased to note in 1919 that it had 'faded to an extent sufficient to harmonise the whole in a blended colour effect, and that it has thus lost any original crudity that it might, perhaps, have had when it was new'.[32] In all probability it is not an overstatement of the showiness of the Roman empire at its height. Materially, however, the original was cruder than Bolton realized. Like many stucco floors made in this country in the eighteenth century, it did not wear well and in 1831 was replaced by William Croggan, successor to Mrs Coade, with a costly 'imperishable scagliola' floor of the same colours and pattern as Adam's design.[33]

This was part of a comprehensive refurbishment of the state apartment which involved recarving, repainting and regilding the entire vestibule and introducing more furniture from other rooms. It is difficult to reconstruct the original furnishing of the vestibule. Creative repairs as well as replicas made in the early 1830s, the arrival of most of the furniture from Northumberland

House after it was demolished in 1874, and the continuous moving of pieces all add to the problem, which affects all the state rooms (pl. 108).[34] The two tables under the trophies were designed by Adam in 1765 for the dining-room, and enriched in the 1830s by Thomas Ponsonby, who also made the slightly smaller replica placed under the niche on the west wall.[35]

Originally the vestibule had only one table, which is shown in Adam's engraving under the niche opposite the entrance and was described by Mary Anderson as having a gilt frame and purple marble top, though according to the 1847 inventory the slab was of verd-antique.[36] This table may be the 'Side Board Table in the Vestibule' for which Adam designed a classical vase with satyr masks and Bacchic putti which was 'proposed to be executed in Silver'; whether it was is not known.[37] As there was no suitable place for a sideboard in the dining-room, the columnar passage in the vestibule leading to the turret stairs going down to the kitchens was particularly convenient. The duke's rough list of things wanted for the room includes another table seven feet (2.13 metres) long which is nearly the size of the table now in the hall in front of the *Dying Gladiator*. Though this has been painted white and has an inlaid marble slab, it could conceivably have come from the vestibule.

Stools were also on the duke's list. Mary Anderson noted three gilt chairs upholstered in white floral needlework, which were probably placed against the walls where the three tables now stand and might be the three needlework settees in the 1847 inventory. These pieces have not yet been identified.

Visually, the vestibule is a colourful pivot between the stark white hall and the white and gold dining-room. But what was its real function? Adam called it the ante-room and said it was for 'the attendance of servants out of livery and tradesmen'.[38] However, it is extremely unlikely that unliveried servants and tradesmen on private business would be left waiting in the state apartment. It is referred to in the building accounts as the vestibule or grand vestibule and that is the name it retains, but unlike normal vestibules it has a fireplace and seats and was not just a room to pass through. Two contemporary visitors, Lady Shelburne in 1765 and Mary Anderson around 1770, described it as a saloon.[39] Though it is not as large as most saloons, it is magnificently decorated and is the only room, apart from the hall, that could have been used as a reception room before dinner, unless one crossed the open court to the gallery. The hall was probably used in the several ways recommended by Isaac Ware: as a reception room for larger parties, a waiting-room for people of second rank and a cool summer dining-room.[40]

In the normal arrangement of apartments, the dining-room was preceded by at least one drawing-room. Adam's reason for reversing the order at Syon is explained by a survey of the existing west and south blocks on which he drew his first 'Plan of Alterations . . . forming a Great Apartment' (pl. 96). The south block had one decent-sized three-bay room with a central fireplace on the inner wall. To the west was the residue of the room that had been incorporated in the vestibule. This remnant, being too small to be of any use on its own, was annexed to the large, three-bay room and transformed into a semi-circular apse screened by columns in the antique style.[41] A symmetrical apse was added at the opposite end by taking one bay from the next room whose fenestration was improved as a result. It was

108 The dining-room looking through into the drawing-room. The seat-furniture comes from elsewhere in the house (and probably from Northumberland House as well) and may reflect the use of the room as a ballroom in the 1920s

109 The dining-room chimney-piece with a Corinthian aedicule containing a marble relief of the *Three Graces* made for the Duke of Northumberland in Rome in 1762 by Luc-François Breton

also an improvement to have an unbroken central axis through the south block from the vestibule to the gallery instead of the old enfilade divided between the window side and the inner wall.

As the entire inner wall of the apsidal room (but only half the wall next door) was solid masonry, Adam was able to enliven that side by carving out niches for statues on either side of the chimney-piece (pl. 109). This mode of finish, ultimately derived from Palladio and perfected in the statue gallery at Holkham, militated against hangings which were *de rigueur* in a grand drawing-room; and so there could not be a drawing-room here.

Adam's account of Syon in the *Works* includes pertinent observations on the treatment of eating-rooms in France and England. He begins with a definition of French custom which, though recommended in most aspects of interior design, is not to be imitated in the case of dining-rooms.

> Their eating rooms seldom or never constitute a piece in their great apartments, but lie out of the suite, and in fitting them up, little attention is paid to beauty or decoration. The reason of this is obvious; the French meet there only at meals, when they trust to the display of the table for show and magnificence, not to the decoration of the apartment; . . . It is not so with us. . . . The eating rooms are considered as the apartments of conversation, in which we are to pass a great part of

our time. This renders it desirable to have them fitted up with elegance and splendor, but in a style different from that of other apartments. Instead of being hung with damask, tapestry &c. they are always finished with stucco, and adorned with statues and paintings, that they may not retain the smell of the victuals.[42]

Apart from the enriched architectural elements – the fluted Corinthian columns and foliate friezes, the semi-domes in the apses and the tripartite ceiling closely modelled on the library ceiling at Shardeloes[43] – sculpture is the principal adornment of the dining-room at Syon. A richly framed marble bas-relief of the *Three Graces*, carved in Rome in 1762 by Luc-François Breton, has pride of place in a pedimented Corinthian aedicule above the chimney-piece.[44] And immediately above that – in the upper region of the wall demarcated by a string-course – is a portrait medallion in stucco of the Duchess of Northumberland, as the fourth grace, matched on the opposite wall by a companion piece of the duke.

In the niches on either side are six full-length marble statues specially made for the room. Five are copies of antique models (including a figure of Mercury copied from a cast belonging to Lord Bateman) and one is a copy of Michelangelo's *Bacchus*, made in 1761 from a cast in the Duke of Richmond's academy at Whitehall by Joseph Wilton, one of the academy's directors.[45] The niches in the apses would either have held full-length statues as shown in Adam's sections and wall elevations, large vases, or busts on fairly tall pedestals.[46] The present busts on low socles are dwarfed by their surroundings. According to Mary Anderson, everything in the room – 'tables, glasses, ceiling, chimney etc. (was) all elegant & white & gold'. The dark reddish-brown marbling of the niches is later and too strong a contrast; though it emphasizes the statues, it disrupts the unity of the wall, detracts from the four long *trompe l'oeil* paintings of classical reliefs by Andrea Casali over the niches and windows, and generally spoils Adam's antique spirit.[47]

A pair of pier-glasses and tables are the only pieces of furniture that Adam designed for the room.[48] It is not known who executed them. William France, Sefferin Alken and John Linnell were all employed at Syon. In the early 1830s the tables (white and gold according to Adam's 1765 design and Mary Anderson's description) were enriched with uncharacteristic reeding in the frieze and entirely gilded, thereby destroying their eighteenth-century look.[49]

Though curtains (liable to 'retain the smell of victuals') were rendered unnecessary by the gilt enrichment of the splayed window reveals and shutters, there presumably was either an oil cloth or carpet to cover the floor. Northumberland's list of *desiderata* for this room included a carpet 31 feet 5 inches long and 14 feet 8 inches broad (9.5 metres × 4.4 metres).[50] In 1847 it had – in addition to the pair of Adam pier-glasses and tables – a Turkey carpet, a 'set of mahogany dining tables with 6 shifting flaps', thirty-four dining chairs and four mahogany side-tables.[51] Now, there is an assortment of large gilt-wood side-tables, but no floor covering, no visible dining-tables and no pier-tables of any description, those by Adam having long since been commandeered for the vestibule. It has the impersonal look of an assembly-room or ballroom, which is what it was used as in the

110 The drawing-room around 1900. While the black and white Batsford photograph captures the showiness of the decoration, the profusion of furniture introduced in the nineteenth century makes it difficult to appreciate Adam's finely tuned harmony of many contrasts. The damask was rewoven in 1829 and applied to the previously bare dado and to all the original seat-furniture as well as new pieces like the arm-chair and footstool in the foreground

111 The drawing-room photographed in 1992 for Gervase Jackson-Stops, with the original furniture removed from the Adam carpet made by Thomas Moore, and properly placed against the wall

112 Design for the drawing-room ceiling, by Robert Adam 1762 (Sir John Soane's Museum: Adam drawings, vol. 11:20)

113 The window wall of the drawing-room, *c.*1917, showing the two large pier-glasses and tables designed by Robert Adam, 1765. The curtain cornices were probably part of the 1829 refurbishment and replace those designed by Adam for festoon curtains

1920s. However, its principal function must always have been as a means of passage to the great drawing-room.

As if to justify the drawing-room's unusual position in relation to the eating-room, Adam, gave it two female-oriented functions: an after-dinner buffer which prevented the noise of the boisterous gentlemen who remained in the dining-room from disturbing the delicate ladies who retired to the gallery, and a quiet sanctuary for ladies wanting to withdraw from the buzz of social activities in the gallery before *and* after dinner.[52] Neither of his explanations (probably based on having the rotunda built) is convincing, nor was the decoration of the drawing-room in the least bit quiet or restful.

When Adam arrived at Syon, the end of the south block had a muddled arrangement of two rooms separated by a staircase, with a passage along the inner wall leading to the gallery. All this was cleared away to create a three-bay drawing-room of exactly the same dimensions as the main body of the dining-room (pls 110, 111). In a properly ordered apartment, the drawing-room ranked highest and was expected to be the most spectacular room of all, exceeding the splendid show in the vestibule. Adam's introduction of a deep coved ceiling was not sufficient in itself, though it did enhance the apparent height of the space (pl. 110). Northumberland, having great wealth and a commensurate desire to display it, decided to hang the walls with the newest and most sumptuous three-coloured silk damask with a bold pattern of silvery-white roses and green sprigs entwined by green and white ribbons on a crimson background (pl. 113).

The fashion for such material originated in Paris and was hardly known in England until after the Seven Years War, when it was imported for use in grand drawing-rooms in much the same way as contemporary Boucher–Neilson tapestries: as wall decorations which dispensed with the need for pictures and were only accompanied by large looking-glasses.[53] Its use at Syon was quite avant-garde. The fact that imports were still curtailed when it was decided upon in 1762 did not deter Northumberland; it was, as he said, 'the first of its kind ever executed in England', presumably by French weavers at Spitalfields.[54] A sample of the material would have been shown to Adam at an early stage, his task being to create a balanced relationship between the overwhelming upholstery and the rest of the furniture and decoration.

Starting in 1761, he made three designs for the ceiling before one was accepted in 1762. The first, with three large octagons on the flat part and figured medallions linked by floral swags in the cove, was too much like the adjacent dining-room. The second, dated December 1761, consisted of roundels in octagons, hexagons and squares in framed sections on the cove as well as the flat; a comparable pattern was used in 1763 in the gallery and after that in the drawing-room at Audley End. This was followed in 1762 by a simpler, more compact mosaic pattern of contiguous octagons and small diamonds, containing a greater number of roundels, which enabled it to stand up to the bold cabbage roses on the walls better than the previous designs (pl. 112).[55] It was executed with somewhat more elaborate paintings, but without the heavy partitioning proposed for the angles of the cove. The subjects of the figured roundels were evidently chosen by Northumberland himself, mainly from the first three volumes of *Le pitture antiche d'Ercolano* (1757, 1760, 1762), and were painted on paper by Cipriani.[56] Alternating with them are intri-

114 Detail of the ram's-head capitals on the drawing-room pier-tables, designed by Robert Adam, *c.*1765

pale pink or a subdued ivory colour to tie in with the ivory door cases. The drawing-room seems to have been the only reception room at Syon that was curtained; however, its original festoons were later dropped for paired drapes, and the curtain cornices, designed by Adam to answer the overmantel, replaced by new ones.[61] Exactly when these alterations were made is not clear: they are not included in the bills of the upholsterer in charge of the 1829 refurbishment, Robert Hughes, later of Morel and Hughes. Regardless of how the curtains worked, one must imagine them drawn for one of the duchess's 'pompous festinos', the room illuminated by the superabundance of candles for which she was renowned and the hundreds of silvery roses on every side flickering like little lamps.[62]

Unlike the three-coloured damask made for the first time in England, the large pier-glasses could only be obtained in France. George Selwyn, who was intimate with leaders of taste and fashion on both sides of the Channel and especially with Marie Leczinska, wife of Louis XV, bought two silvered plates costing £421.9.8 for Northumberland in Paris in 1763.[63] They were said by the duke to be 'two of the largest that then had ever been seen in England'.[64] Their frames were designed by Adam in 1765 (along with all the other furniture for the 'Grand Apartment') and executed later that year by Jean Bruno Guichard, a French carver and gilder working in London.[65]

For the accompanying pier-tables Northumberland purchased

cate rosettes and fan-patera on the same blue ground used for the figures and small red cameos with grisaille heads and urns in the diamonds.

Unlike Adam's other ceiling designs, this one was never repeated, not because of any dissatisfaction or disinclination on his part, but because of the high cost of executing it. As Cipriani was paid something in excess of £284 for the figured roundels alone, the total cost of the paintings must have been close to £400, added to which were Joseph Rose's charges for making the stucco frames to the compartments in 1764 and Thomas Davis's for gilding them in 1765. According to the duchess, £550 was paid for the drawing-room ceiling and £254 for stucco-work.[57] Though she and the duke were bound to be pleased with the ostentatious display, there were critics who misunderstood its *raison d'être*.[58]

Mary Anderson, who saw the room shortly after it was finished, had nothing but praise for the 'Mosaic' ceiling which she described as being 'very beautiful', the compartments 'prettily painted & very gay'. It was the 'magnificent' hangings that disturbed her: they robbed the ceiling of 'much of its beauty', made it 'rather confused & (did) not show either it, ye Cornice, Glasses etc to advantage . . .'[59] Her reaction is understandable, but she failed – just as A. T. Bolton did – to appreciate the finely tuned balance that Adam achieved here; a unity of diverse elements.

When Bolton saw the room in 1917 or thereabouts, the hangings were almost ninety years old, having been rewoven to the original colour and pattern in 1829 for the third Duke of Northumberland, who was even richer and more extravagant than Adam's patron.[60] It was he who applied the fabric to the dado which was previously painted in the normal way, perhaps

115 Detail of the Corinthian chimney-piece designed by Robert Adam *c.*1765 and carved by Thomas Carter with an 'overdress of brass lace thrown over [its] white marble form'

116   One of the two carved and gilded drawing-room doors with ivory panels in the pilasters overlaid with gilt metal ornaments by Mr Bermingham and ormolu medallions of classical heads attributed in Diedrich Nicolaus Anderson

'two noble pieces of antique mosaic found in Titus baths . . . from the Abbe (Filippo) Farsetti in Rome', doubtlessly through James Adam, who first met this congenial collector of antique sculpture at his villa outside Venice.[66] In 1765, a year after the antique mosaics arrived in London, Robert Adam designed a table frame with eight square tapered legs like pilasters capped by female masks and enriched with recessed panels of classical ornaments. In the eyes of the duke, the faces made it look too much 'like a family pew or supper box for a ball' and he rejected it.[67] The Earl of Coventry was happy to have it for the gallery at Croome Court (pl. 74) and a similar frame with ram's head capitals was made for Syon (pl. 114).[68]

In addition to the two mosaic tables, there was a mosaic hearth, which was presumably a piece of ancient paving obtained by James Adam in response to a request from Northumberland in February 1761.[69] Where it is now is not known, possibly on a table elsewhere in the house, waiting to be identified.

Amidst such a diversity of gaudy decorations, Adam's statuary marble chimney-piece with fluted Corinthian columns would have been quite obtrusive had it been left naked. In order to tie it into the scheme, it was embellished with ormolu, or as Bolton aptly put it, it had 'an overdress of brass lace thrown over (its) white marble form' (pl. 115).[70] Thomas Carter was paid a total of

£282.8.4 for the chimney-piece on 1 March 1766, which included the large sum of £144.6.6 for 'drawing and Modeling the ornaments for the Founder, Carving the Mouldings in reverse to receive the Brasswork (and) Carvers time in letting in, fitting and working the ornaments together . . .'[71] The founder, however, has not been firmly identified. Matthew Boulton, the name usually given, has been eliminated by Sir Nicholas Goodison, leaving as principal contenders Mr Bermingham (or Brimingham), who made the gilt lead ornaments for the shutters and doors, and the better-known Diederich Nicolaus Anderson, who made the edging for the precious mosaic tables and medals for the doors, both in ormolu, in 1766–7.[72]

To be on a par with the chimney-piece, the tall Corinthian door-surrounds dominating the end walls required even more lavish enrichment (pl. 116). Their capitals, frieze and cornice were carved and gilded and their pilaster panels, nearer the eye, were of ivory mounted with gilt metal arabesques and ormolu medals of profile heads. In the Duke of Northumberland's 'Memorandum Book of Work at Syon' are three significant words pertaining to the drawing-room: 'corniche too white'.[73] It was subsequently gilded, as were the glazing bars and the enriched mouldings on the shutters and door panels. Of course, ostentation played a large part, but so did aesthetic judgment.

Finally, to complete the *mélange*, Adam designed a carpet (pl. 111) that is totally and deliberately at odds in pattern and colour with everything else – the ceiling, the upholstery and the mosaics. Its resemblance to the dining-room ceiling has led to the suggestion that it was intended for that room (see pl. 108).[74] However, its measurements correspond to those given in Northumberland's 'Memorandum Book' for the drawing-room carpet, whereas a carpet 3 feet (90 centimetres) shorter and 1 foot (30 centimetres) broader was wanted for the dining-room;[75] its design at the Soane is inscribed for the drawing-room; and more important, as the inscriptions are not always reliable, it was seen in the drawing-room by Mary Anderson.[76] The carpet, signed by Thomas Moore and dated 1769, is the earliest surviving example of his work. For Northumberland to have commissioned such an important and no doubt costly Adam–Moore carpet for his dining-room but not the great drawing-room is inconceivable.[77] The red drawing-room is altogether different from the fully integrated compositions normally associated with Adam. There is nothing homogeneous or uniform about it. Instead, it is a carefully considered balance of dissonances – what Summerson called 'a harmony of many contrasts' – on which no expense was spared.[78]

The Jacobean long gallery and the great hall were the most challenging rooms that confronted Adam at Syon (pl. 117). The hall because of its unequal floor levels, and the gallery because of its great length – 136 feet (41.4 metres) – which was disproportionate to its meagre height and width of 14 feet (4.2 metres). The room was traditionally an indoor alternative to the garden path which in the eighteenth century was expected to 'afford great variety and amusement'. Thus, apart from being a place for parade, a place for the reception of company before dinner and

117   The long gallery looking north

118 Elevation of the inner wall of the gallery showing the bookcases, chimney-pieces and niches filled with vases and statues, designed by Robert Adam c.1762–63 (*The works in architecture of Robert and James Adam*, vol. III (1822), pl. III)

the retirement of ladies afterwards, it also served as a 'library and museum' or 'columbarium' which Walpole claimed was 'an idea that (he) proposed to my Lord Northumberland'.[79] Adam's decoration integrated the various functions of the room and increased its variety and novelty in such a way as to counteract its excessive length.

There were three pre-existing entrances to the room: one in the centre directly opposite the projecting bay on the east front, and two at the ends, which Adam moved a little further in. It was from the advantageous mid-point that his engraved view of the room was taken.[80] The two halves are identical; each has a chimney-piece in the middle and a door towards the end – one leading to the drawing-room, the other to the private apartment. The three doors are flanked by rectangular niches and the twin chimney-pieces by semi-circular ones with circular recesses in the frieze. It was these numerous and varied niches that created the columbarium-style museum noted by Walpole.

Between these tripartite units are bookcases – four in all – each subdivided by four Corinthian pilasters with subordinate Ionic pilasters framing the shelves (pl. 118). There is a smaller

119 Detail of the elevation of the window wall showing the oval mirrors originally on piers, designed by Robert Adam c.1762–63 (*The works in architecture of Robert and James Adam*, vol. III (1822), pl. III)

bookcase flanked by only two pilasters at the north end of the gallery; the corresponding one at the south end is a jib door concealing an exit to the garden. Evidently these cases had folding doors and were modelled on the library at Northumberland House, which was begun in 1749 by the duchess's father, the seventh Duke of Somerset, and completed by her husband, possibly to a design by Paine.[81] In order to avoid any 'superadded encumbrance' to the narrow gallery, the cases were 'formed in Recesses . . . (and) made part of the general finishing of the Room.'[82] Indeed, the only salient features of the decoration are the pediments over the doors, which make them easy to locate from a distance.

In 1828 the niches that were designed to break up the long wall and give it variety and movement were fitted with flush bookshelves which have quite the opposite effect.[83] According to a note in the duke's 'Memorandum Book', 'James Byers (was) to get (him) at Rome 4 Bronze Statues and 4 smaller ones gilt for the Gallery with pedestals and Six landscapes from the Antique'.[84] The gilt statues were for the niches on either side of the chimney-pieces, where they would have glittered in the firelight, and the bronze ones for the niches flanking the two end doors. The central door had shallower niches which are shown in Adam's engravings filled with vases on pedestals.

The six landscapes painted in Rome by William Marlow were wanted for the panels flanking the doors. They completed the decoration of the frieze, which included Francesco Zuccarelli's two semi-circular paintings over the chimney-pieces and F. Lindo's thirty-six medallion portraits of the descendants of the Percy family going back to Charlemagne.[85] These were commissioned to celebrate the elevation of the earl as Duke of Northumberland and Earl Percy in October 1766. Some of the portraits – including those of Henry VIII, Jane Seymour and Protector Somerset – were removed to the west corridor to make way for portraits of successive dukes and duchesses.

Naturally, the room's focal points are its fireplaces, which are shown in Adam's engravings and described by the duke as 'adorned with medallions after the most beautiful manner of the Antique finished in a remarkably light & elegant style & was the first Instance of Stucco work finished in England after the chaste

120 A corner of the projecting bay on the east wall showing one of the semi-circular 'pietra cotta' reliefs and one of the 'droll' convex mirrors set into the wall on the left. Above are three of the thirty-six portrait medallions of the ancestors of the Northumberlands by F. Lindo. The pier-table and its inlaid scagliola top are attributed to Adam, but the cane chairs, though made for the room, are not his

_____ of the Antique _____ at least equal if not superior to any of the finest remains of antiquity'.[86] This remarkable new stucco, patented on 6 March 1766 by Dennis McCarthy, was a cement composition called 'pietra cotta' which when polished (rather than painted, as it is now) was easily mistaken for marble.[87] Not only was it used for the chimney-piece medallions, which were tinted green to resemble bronze, but also for the six semi-circular bas-reliefs on the window piers (pl. 120) and the four round reliefs on the end walls.[88] There were two 'grates without fenders' costing 15 guineas each, which, being so expensive, must have been quite special, gilded perhaps and possibly designed by Adam.[89] Sadly, there is no trace of them.

The novel 'Antique' overmantels and the 'bat's wing' ornaments on the walls above them (which also appear on the stucco panels opposite) were replaced in 1828 by mirrors, thereby creat-

ing, with the attendant niches and circular recesses, a false 'triumphal arch' effect that was never intended (pl. 117).[90] Had mirrors been required here to attain the brilliant illumination so loved by the Northumberlands, they would doubtless have been introduced by Adam, but they were not. Evidently the six glasses on the alternate window piers and the concave and convex 'Drolle Ones' (yet another fashionable French import) in the projecting bay (pl. 120) were considered sufficient to reflect the candlelight, which was concentrated on that side of the room where there were pier-tables to support candle-branches and space for torchères in the uncurtained window embrasures.[91] The four large mirrors now filling the piers were put in at the same time as those over the chimney-pieces, replacing oval mirrors set into the walls amidst scrolls of stucco ornament, as shown in Adam's engraved elevation and resembling the two surviving circular mirrors on the end piers (pl. 119).

Compared to the stunning magnificence of the drawing-room, the decoration of the gallery is more 'pleasing & entertaining'. That is how it impressed Mary Anderson who attributed the effect to 'the variety & novelty of fitting it up which is very minute and delicate all the Antient Bass Relievos being either painted al Fresco or done with Papia Machee upon a very faint Sea Green Stucco & also a very faint Bloom colour, which gives and elegance & delicacy I cannot describe'.[92] The stucco ornaments were white, picked out in gold; the subordinate Ionic pilasters were pink and the sixty-two Corinthian pilasters were white, edged in gold and painted with naturalistic rinceaux in green, red and blue.[93] This was all the work of Michelangelo Pergolesi, an Italian designer and painter of 'antique' ornament who was brought to England by Adam in 1760. It evidently replaced earlier gilding of the panels and, regardless of the wasted expenditure, so pleased the duke that Pergolesi, in addition to being paid his bill of £130.4.0, was rewarded £20 more for a present.[94]

Pergolesi's charges also included alterations he made 'in colouring the Pannels in the Ceiling', possibly to match the wall panels. The stucco ceiling, executed to a design made by Adam in August 1763, is an intricate pattern of interlaced and subdivided octagons with alternating square and circular centres (the latter being predominant) and further enriched with small semi-circular paintings.[95]

Just as the outer wall was the chief source of light, so the inner wall was the principal sitting place, with four long stools alongside the chimney-pieces and six slightly longer ones beside the doors.[96] There are no Adam designs for any of the furniture in the gallery.[97] None the less, he can probably be credited with the pair of semi-circular tables on the central piers flanking the projecting bay, which have scagliola slabs and pendant anthemion finials repeating elements of the stucco decoration on the related wall panels.[98] And he may also have been responsible for the two pairs of marquetry card tables, one inlaid with rinceau ornament, the other with an ogee pattern matching his carpet designs.

The gallery carpet has a peculiar history. Adam made a design in 1766 or early 1767 offering variant ogee patterns that are totally unrelated to the geometric ceiling (pl. 121).[99] One is a continuous small-scale pattern with a projecting piece at the top to fit under the doors; the other is a large-scale version inter-

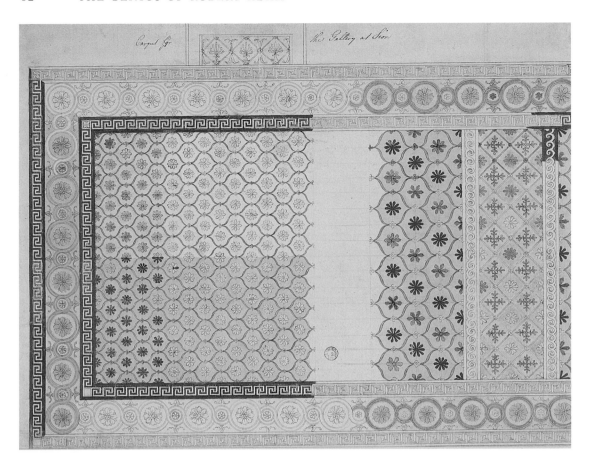

121 Design for the gallery carpet, by Robert Adam *c.*1766–67. Unexecuted at the time, but used by John Fowler in the 1970s to make the present carpet (Sir John Soane's Museum: Adam drawings, vol. 17:172)

122 The round closet in the north-east tower, showing the earlier carpet made to accord with the gallery ceiling. The chairs are probably from Northumberland House

rupted by a broad horizontal band of lozenges. While the latter was clearly intended to break up and diversify the excessive length, it is not absolutely clear whether it was meant to be an alternative to the continuous pattern strip-carpet or a separate design for the oil cloth or chimney carpets that were on the duke's list of *desiderata*.[100] In the event, Northumberland rejected the ogee carpet design and it was offered instead to the Earl of Coventry, who had it executed for his drawing-room at Coventry House, Piccadilly.[101]

Notwithstanding, the ogee pattern was used by John Fowler in the early 1970s to make the present uninterrupted full-length strip-carpet with a dusty pink border and pale green ground. Ironically, the carpet which this replaced had a pattern of octagons and crosses (not unlike the squares and lozenges shown in Adam's engraved view of the room) which matched the ceiling. This was presumably the carpet laid down in December 1770, in place of earlier Indian matting.[102]

The 'Designs for the Carpet & Tapestry at Syon House' made by Pergolesi in 1765 were not for the gallery, but rather for the square closet in the south tower.[103] They were preceded by Adam's design for the coved ceiling of the little cabinet dated 1765 and more particularly by a visit in September of that year 'to Mr. Moor to see his Tapestry'.[104] The tapestry in question is identified in the duke's 'Memorandum Book' as a furnishing fabric: 'Settee Tappestry White of Flowers Mr Moor'. His list of furnishings also includes a carpet, a 'Spring Curtain', 'Hangings 7:11 high' and 'Painted Silk Naples'.[105] The surviving silk hangings are painted with chinoiserie trees and birds.

According to Adam, the square cabinet was for miniatures and its circular counterpart in the north tower for china, which must have included some of 'that immense quantity of old china vases, of different forms and sizes' that Dodsley noticed 'crowded together in almost every apartment' at Syon in 1761.[106] The cir-

123 Elevation of one wall of the small closet decorated in the antique taste at the top of one of the towers, by Robert Adam *c*.1760. There is now no trace of this decoration in the surviving tower rooms (Sir John Soane's Museum: Adam drawings, vol. 27:74)

cular cabinet (pl. 122) is formed of four niches (one containing the entrance) flanked by columns on round pedestals and surmounted by a dome. Like the gallery, it is wholly encrusted with delicate stucco arabesques, anthemia and other such ornaments in low relief which, according to Mary Anderson, were painted the same faint sea-green and bloom colour.[107] The decoration and contents of these cabinets contributed 'an additional amusement' to the gallery. Wherever one looks in this room, there is something to divert the eye – sculpture, paintings, fine china and books – drawn together in a web of extremely delicate and varied stucco decoration in the antique style. Here, for the first time, is the quintessence of the Adam style which, as Summerson remarked, 'was to make the later interiors possible'.[108]

At the top of one of the towers, approached 'from ye leads of ye house (and) com[ding] a beautiful Prospect' was another small 'closet' which has disappeared without trace and without notice (pl. 123). According to the duke, it was 'fitted, painted & ornamented after ye antique being the first thing in that Taste executed in Eng[ld] w[ch] has since so universally prevailed in this kingdom'.[109] There is, in fact, a wall elevation at the Soane of a squarish room decorated in the antique taste, which is inscribed in pencil 'Sion' (pl. 123).[110] Its style is comparable to the painted breakfast-room at Kedleston which was Adam's first work for Nathaniel Curzon in 1760. It may also have been his first work for Lord Northumberland at Syon.

124   William Watts, view of Alnwick Castle and the Lion Bridge,
engraving after a drawing by Lord Duncannon, 1783 (British Museum).
The castle-style bridge is attributed to Robert Adam

5

ALNWICK CASTLE

The restoration of Alnwick Castle in Northumberland (pls 124, 125) as the northern seat of the Percys was well on the way towards completion when Adam succeeded James Paine as architect in 1769. It was begun in 1750 by the new Earl of Northumberland, Sir Hugh Smithson, who had recently succeeded to the title and taken the name and arms of Percy by Act of Parliament, and whose wife, Lady Elizabeth Seymour, had inherited the Percy barony and estates in her own right through her maternal grandmother.

Quite a lot had been achieved by spring 1759 when John Adam, the eldest of the four brothers, went to Alnwick to see the 'Reparation and additions' for himself.

> The dining room & drawing room . . . are all extremely noble & elegant in the Gothick taste but the drawing room pleased me most, at least it struck me with that idea. The ornaments of both these rooms on walls & ceiling are done in very good Gothic stile, of stucco. My Lady's Bed Chamber, Dressing Room &c. are very suitably finished. These all in the old building.[1]

That 'old building' was the medieval shell-keep whose plan was aptly likened to 'a section of the clustered Saxon pillar in our Cathedrals'.[2]

One of the first rooms to be renovated was the dining-room on the east side, where the medieval great hall had been. A wall elevation in the Adam collection at the Soane (possibly drawn by Henry Keene or John Adam, but not by Robert) shows most of the decorations noted in later descriptions: flat Gothic arcading round the walls, 'large Embossments' hanging from the ceiling, 'the niches and other compartments', and the deep window recess formed in one of the round towers at the upper end of the room, matched by a shallower recess which was added to give the wall a semblance of symmetry.[3] There was also an elaborate Gothic chimney-piece, which has been associated with a separate drawing of a Batty Langley-style surround, incorrectly labelled 'Drawing Room Chimney Piece for Alnwick Castle' and almost certainly predating Robert Adam's involvement there.[4]

There are no known drawings or detailed descriptions of the Gothic drawing-room admired by John Adam. After Robert created the 'great' drawing-room north of the dining-room, this became the breakfast-room. From it, a short passage led to an oval stair and, beyond that, on the western side of the castle, the

private apartment consisting of two bedchambers with dressing-rooms and closets.[5]

Who was responsible for this early work? Payments made to Joseph Rose for stucco-work starting in April 1755 would rule out

125 Plan of the principal floor of Alnwick Castle, 1817. From *Castles of Alnwick & Warkworth, &c. from sketches by C. F. Duchess of Northumberland, 1823*, London (privately printed for the Duchess by J. W. Nicol (1824))

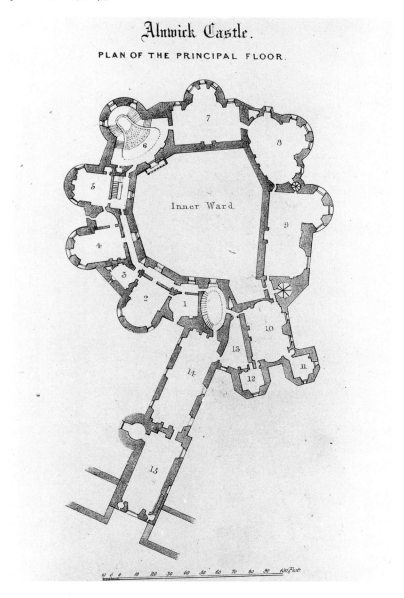

126 The window recess in the saloon, lithograph after a drawing by Charlotte Florentina, Duchess of Northumberland, 1823. From *Castles of Alnwick & Warkworth, &c. from sketches by C. F. Duchess of Northumberland, 1823.* London (privately printed for the Duchess by J. W. Nicol (1824))

James Paine, who is not recorded at Alnwick until June of that year.[6] The most likely candidate – suggested by Giles Worsley – is Henry Keene, surveyor both to the Dean and Chapter and to the Fabric of Westminster Abbey and one of the pioneers of the Gothick fashion in architecture, who was employed by Northumberland from December 1750 to November 1759.[7] The 'great' staircase in the north-west corner, much admired for its 'very singular, yet pleasing form, expanding like a fan', was certainly Paine's work.[8] Presumably he was also responsible for its white stucco decorations on a blue ground and the 'Iron Railing of Netlike Form painted green, the connecting parts richly gilt', which were probably finished in 1764 when the completion of the castle was commemorated in a note placed in a bottle and buried in the wall.[9] The 'chain of escutcheons round the cornice' was added after Paine's departure and will be discussed later.

Furniture for the reconstructed rooms was sent to Alnwick by the upholsterers, Walle and Reilly, in 1768 and 1769.[10] It consisted of a suite of two chairs and six cabriolets with padded backs, probably destined for the Gothic drawing-room, painted white with gilt flowers and 'ridges' and covered with extravagant three-coloured silk damask, presumably the same as the red damask with silvery white flowers and green sprigs used in the drawing-room at Syon and later in Adam's 'great' drawing-room at Alnwick; a 'bed a la Polonaise' carved and gilt with two colours of gold and upholstered with crimson damask, probably for the duke's bedchamber; and a bed with an 'imperial dome' carved and painted in natural flowers (now at Syon) for the duchess, with eight cabriolets, eight chairs and four stools to match, all upholstered in red, green and white striped material.

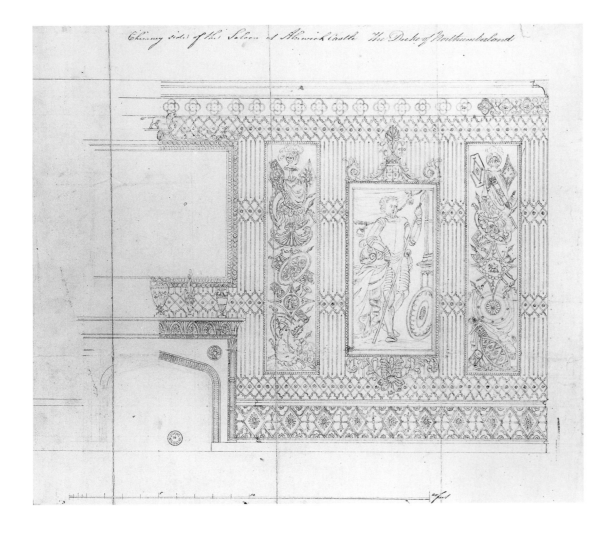

127 Design of the *Chimney side of the Saloon at Alnwick Castle*, by Robert Adam, *c.*1769 (Sir John Soane's Museum: Adam drawings, vol. 39:16)

These pieces, none of which had a trace of Gothick, were evidently ordered by the duchess without the architectural advice either of Paine, who had ceased working at Alnwick after 1767, or of Adam, who took his place in 1769 just after completing the state rooms at Syon.

Under Adam's direction, the Gothick style set in the 1750s was maintained and the quantity of heraldic ornament greatly increased in response to the earl's elevation on 22 October 1766 to the titles of Duke of Northumberland and Earl Percy. In June 1769, one hundred and ten escutcheons of the Percy family, painted in 'Oil on Paper' by Joseph Edmondson, were sent to Alnwick as an additional decoration for the cornice of the 'great' staircase.[11] The idea was presumably the duke's and is doubtless related to the frieze of ancestral portraits put up in the gallery at Syon in 1767.

1769 is the year of Adam's earliest dated designs for chimney-pieces for the saloon and library (pl. 127). The saloon, being the first reception room reached from the great staircase, may well have been planned by Paine, but it was fitted up 'in the gayest and most elegant style of Gothic architecture' by Adam.[12] The walls were painted blue and covered with white stucco tracery and straw-coloured compartments filled with 'Helmets and other warlike Trophies'. In the centre of the window wall was a large fan-vaulted recess with its front corners cut back to form subsidiary recesses in which clustered pillars were placed, making a Gothic variation upon a classical screen (pl. 126); inside was a pair of tall pier-glasses (8 feet 10 inches × 2 feet 4 inches, or 2.6 × 0.7 metres) with ormolu-mounted Pembroke tables of inlaid wood, supplied by John Linnell in c.1770, under them.[13]

129   The saloon chimney-piece combining classical anthemia and gothic tracery, now in the housekeeper's room at Alnwick Castle

Opposite this recess was a chimney-piece of local Denwick stone 'executed after a design by Mr. Adam' (pl. 129), with Gothic pilasters at the sides, a frieze composed of 'ten elegant Gothic brackets' alternating with honeysuckle, and two roundels 'richly adorned by the crest of the Percy family encircled by the Garter'.[14] The flanking walls were hung with full-length family portraits and over the doors were 'square Frames with circular Tablets, having thereon the Figure of St. George slaying the

128   Design for the library ceiling, by Robert Adam, c.1769 (Sir John Soane's Museum: Adam drawings, vol. 39:13)

130 Preliminary design for the end walls of the library, by Robert Adam, *c.*1769 (Sir John Soane's Museum: Adam drawings, vol. 24:214)

131 Alternative design for the end walls of the library, by Robert Adam, *c.*1769 (Sir John Soane's Museum: Adam drawings, vol. 39:12)

Dragon'. A flat ceiling with white stucco ornaments in blue and straw-coloured compartments covered the main part of the room.

By 1785, there were two suites of seat furniture: one carved and gilt, upholstered in Gobelins tapestry; the other with cane seats painted white with blue and gold ornaments. Adam was not responsible for any of these pieces, nor can he be credited with the pair of gilt neo-classical tripods, $5^{3}/_{4}$ feet (1.7 metres) tall, with goats' feet and heads and 'serpents twining up the center', on which were placed a pair of four branch vases.[15]

His decorations for the adjacent 'great' drawing-room are known only from Peter Waddell's description in 1785. The room had three curved recesses: one containing a bow window opposite the chimney-piece and two on the end walls. Arches, which sprang from Gothic pilasters flanking the chimney-piece and the bow window, divided the ceiling into three parts. The central part was flat and decorated with a rose of eight segments painted green and pink, with white stucco ornaments and delicate ribs in the corners. Over each recess was a semi-dome 'formed into the shape of a Shell, having Rays and Ornaments of the same kind with those in the central part'. The two doors were also in small recesses with Gothic arched surrounds.[16]

Adam's design for the chimney-piece was almost certainly made in 1769, at the same time as his designs for the saloon and

Chimney Piece for the Library at Alnwick Castle

132 Design of the 'Chimney Piece for the Library at Alnwick Castle' with the Percy lions passant and a Gothic temple containing a clock, by Robert Adam, 1769 (Sir John Soane's Museum: Adam drawings, vol. 22:54). The chimney-piece was executed in Denwick stone

library chimney-pieces, and was executed with modifications to the frieze.[17] Above it was a large mirror (9⅓ feet × 5⅓ feet or 2.8 × 1.6 metres) in a 'white Frame highly enriched with Gold Ornaments'. Like the drawing-room at Syon, the walls and the seat furniture – consisting of two large carved and gilt wood sofas and eighteen 'French arm chairs' – were covered with magnificent crimson, green and white silk damask.[18] This was matched in colour by a close-fitting carpet 'of an elegant Pattern manufactured by Mr Moore of Chiswell Street London'. In addition, there were two marquetry card-tables with ormolu mounts, which were supplied by Linnell probably in 1770 and nearly replicate the pair noted by the duchess in the drawing-room at Kedleston in August 1766.[19]

The drawing-room was brilliantly lit to the high Northumberland standard by a pair of four-branch girandoles in front of the overmantel mirror and an eighteen-branch crystal chandelier whose cost – £126 – was high enough to be recorded in the duchess's list of 'Alnwick Prices'.[20] The duchess also noted that the room was 'finished and first used on (her) Wedding day (i.e. anniversary)', 9 July 1770, to receive John Egerton, Bishop of Durham.[21]

Diagonally opposite the saloon and 'great' drawing-room, in a projecting wing near the Middle Gate, was the library, the largest of the state apartments (64 × 23 × 16 feet or 19.5 × 7 × 4.8 metres), conceived 'in the form of a gallery', as at Syon and Croome Court. Waddell's description of its flat ceiling, divided

into twenty-seven framed compartments of light straw-colour containing blue and white ornaments, corresponds to a design of a 'Ceiling for Alnwick Castle' at the Soane (pl. 128).[22] The design at Alnwick for 'Finishing the Library Ceiling . . .' with two large octagons is attributed to Paine, which dates it before 1768, at which time the library wing was probably under construction.[23] On the end walls were two chimney-pieces (pls 130–132) of Denwick stone, each of which had placed over its centre 'a Model of the Front of a Gothic Temple having within it a Dial, one a Time Piece, the other a Wind Dial'. Flanking the temples were statuettes of lions passant, the Percy crest, and bishops on small pedestals.[24]

By 1773, the room was 'properly fitted up for books', having on each side 'four cases richly ornamented in the Gothic Stile and well filled with books on various Branches of polite and useful Literature . . .'[25] A decade later, it had a mummy brought from Cairo by Lord Algernon Percy, two American flags taken during the Revolution by Earl Percy, two superb ormolu-mounted neo-classical writing tables and a small marquetry billiard table in the same style, both by Linnell.[26] This 'large and handsome room' was in James Plumptre's opinion, 'the best in the house'.[27] Like the present library at Alnwick, it was 'the apartment in which the Family generally reside(d)'.

From the library, a short passage with 'richly pannelled and gilded' walls and ceiling gave the only access to the chapel, another long, narrow room, generally agreed to be the most magnificent of all the state rooms. Its white walls were decorated

133 'Design for finishing the Pannells in the Chapel at Alnwick containing the Pedigrees of the Family proposed to be partly done in Stucco & partly in Painting', by Robert Adam, 1777 (Sir John Soane's Museum: Adam drawings, vol. 39:19)

134   Design for painting the east window of the chapel, by Robert Adam, 1773 (Sir John Soane's Museum: Adam drawings, vol. 39:18)

135   Design of the 'Carpet for the Circular Recess or Pew in the Chapel', by Robert Adam, 1780 (Sir John Soane's Museum: Adam drawings, vol. 17:201)

136   Gothic arm-chair of carved, gilded and painted wood, designed by Robert Adam for the chapel, c.1780 (The Duke of Northumberland, Alnwick Castle)

with cusped panels, 'bordered with light green and purple, and each surmounted with pyramids (i.e. pinnacles) of purple and gold; the mouldings and other projecting Parts being enriched with Gilding . . .' Near the top of each panel was a coat of arms plainly labelled 'for the information of those unacquainted with Heraldry'.[28] In the centre of the long walls were larger 'pedigree' panels 'shewing the Descent of this illustrious Family in direct line from Charlemagne, and their Intermarriages with some of the most honourable and noble Houses in Europe' (pl. 133).[29] The antiquarian Francis Grose saw the chapel in 1773, before the heraldic enrichments were introduced, and described it as being 'painted after the great church in Milan'.[30] This was not to say that the cusped panels had been copied from Milan cathedral, but rather that Adam, by using the Gothic rather than classical style to refurbish the medieval castle at Alnwick, had followed boyant foliate ornament, painted in shades of yellow, purple and green, more nearly approaches *art nouveau* than medieval Gothic. All were emblazoned with heraldic crests and placed in splayed recesses 'enriched with a Variety of gold Ornaments on light purple Grounds and bordered by green and gold pannels'.[33] Equally rich decoration was applied to the four doors, one of which, at the south end, opened on to a grate for a fire.

The fan-vaulted stucco ceiling, painted light green with the ribs picked out in gold, was taken from King's College Chapel, 'regarded as the crowning glory of Gothic'.[34] Though no designs have yet been identified, it is safe to assume that they were not much different from the surviving designs for a green, purple, red and yellow carpet made by Adam in 1780.[35] In the event, the chapel floor was 'covered with a curious Floorcloth', which may well have had Adam's design painted on it.[36] However, the circular pew had a 'carpet of exquisite workmanship', presumably made from the design supplied by Adam in August 1780 (pl. 135).[37] This design may have been related to the fan-vaulted ceiling of 'transcendent beauty' supported by 'six Gothic columns'.[38]

In 1785, Peter Waddell noted 'three chandeliers, each holding twelve candles . . . of beautiful, light and elegant forms, made in composition by Mr Smith of Bond Street and richly gilt', a lantern enclosing four lights, twenty-four stools with white and gold frames and green silk seats, nine gold and white wheel-back chairs with cane seats and green velvet cushions in the family pew, and 'a Reading Desk and chair of an antique Form, painted white with gold Ornaments and Crimson Velvet Seat and Cushion . . .'[39] Only the Gothick lectern and chair, both of which survive at Alnwick, can be firmly credited to Adam (pls

137 Lectern of carved, gilded and painted wood, designed by Robert Adam for the chapel, *c.*1780 (The Duke of Northumberland, Alnwick Castle)

138 Design for the ceiling of the circular banqueting-room in the Record Tower at Alnwick Castle, by Robert Adam, 1770 (Sir John Soane's Museum: Adam drawings, vol. 11:30)

the example of the several seventeenth- and eighteenth-century architects who, though normally working in a classical style, had used Gothic designs to complete the façade of the famous cathedral.[31]

Francis Grose was evidently shown the designs for the windows that Adam had made in December 1773 (pl. 134), before they were sent to the painter, James Pearson, to execute, and could thus assure his discriminating readers that they would be 'in a stile superior to any thing that has yet been attempted and worthy of the present more improved state of the arts'.[32] The three windows – the largest at the south end, modelled on the Five Sisters at York Minster; another on the east wall 'near the Door and immediately behind the Reading Desk'; and the third in the circular family pew in a projecting round tower on the north-west corner – were only completed in 1780. Their flam-

139 'Part of the Section of the Circular Room' showing a Gothic stove on a classical ram's-head pedestal, by Robert Adam, *c.*1770 (Sir John Soane's Museum: Adam drawings, vol. 30:10)

140 Design of a 'Ceiling for the Honorable Horace Walpole Esq'. in the Beauclerc Room at Strawberry Hill, Middlesex, by Robert Adam, 1766 (Sir John Soane's Museum: Adam drawings, vol. 11:234). The ceiling was executed and still survives

136, 137). The latter corresponds with a design of 1761 for one of the chairs in the church at Croome for the Earl of Coventry. The desk is clearly *en suite*, but no designs have been traced.[40]

Few private places of worship in England could vie with the colourful, glittering magnificence of the chapel at Alnwick. Here, 'expense' – which included the cost of nearly 1,480 books of gold leaf, £691.8.6 for painting and gilding by the London craftsman John Wateridge and £345.13.0 for James Pearson's painted windows – had 'reached its utmost limits', and was thought by some to be too great and too conspicuous 'for so serious a place'.[41] Joseph Farington and other visitors questioned the propriety of 'recording the "boa(s)t of heraldry"' in the presence of the 'humility of the Creator'.[42] 'To see the *House of prayers*, turned into the *House of ostentation of the Percy family*' filled James Plumptre with such indignation that he promptly left the castle.[43]

Puritan sensibilities were offended too by the duchess's cenotaph 'inscribed with her thousand titles, (and) serving as *an altar*.[44] The sarcophagus, placed in a recess under the main window, was executed in 1778–9 by Nicholas Read, 'agreeable to Mr Adam's design'.[45] No design has yet been found, the sarcophagus no longer exists and all we have is Waddell's description of it as

> resembling an antique sarcophagus of Statuary Marble 9 feet long, 3 feet 7 inches deep, 4 feet 2½ inches wide (2.7 × 1 × 1.8 metres), most superbly decorated having in its Front a Miniature Bust of the late Duchess in a circular Recess and two Statues in Niches near the end. On the top are two figures, the one of a Lion the other an Unicorn, and a Tablet with the following inscription having a Ducal Coronet over it. Sacred to the Memory of Elizabeth Percy . . . d. Decr. 5 1776.

It was not just the sarcophagus, but the entire chapel that was dedicated to the memory of the duchess. Its decoration was conceived after her death and the great expense lavished on it by the duke, who owed everything to his wife, was intended as a grateful tribute and not an ostentatious display of noble pride and wealth, as it seemed to appear.

The chapel was the last room at Alnwick to be furnished. One of the first was the circular banqueting-room – 29 feet (8.8 metres) in diameter and 24½ feet (7.4 metres) high – over the evidence (or archive) room in the restored Record Tower on the eastern perimeter of the curtain wall. More Adam drawings have survived for this room than any other at Alnwick. The earliest, dated January 1770, is for a pale-green ceiling decorated with pink traceried ovals or vesica, overlaid with a chain of quatrefoils painted with putti (pl. 138).[46] Wall elevations show the room ringed by six round-headed niches containing three Tudor-arched windows on the east side and a stove flanked by two doors on the west (pl. 139).[47] On the intervening walls were mirrors treated like ogee-arched windows, overlaid with gilded tracery and fitted with candle branches. Bordering the pale-green walls were a pink dado and frieze, the latter ornamented with green and gold squares and lozenges enclosing maroon medallions of urns and putti.[48] The combination of classical and Gothic motifs is noticeable in all the designs, most particularly in the curious hybrid stove in the form of a tall Gothic casket resting on a classical Roman pedestal complete with rams' heads and sphinxes.

Decorating the circular banqueting-room in 1770 must have reminded Adam of his experiences two or three years earlier, designing a chimney-piece based on the Shrine of Edward the Confessor at Westminster Abbey and a ceiling from a circular window in old St Paul's for the round drawing-room in the Round Tower at Strawberry Hill (pl. 140).[49] However, unlike Walpole, who furnished him with engravings of the monuments that he was to adapt and 'improve' for execution, the Duke of Northumberland left him to interpret the style as he wished, and – if Syon and Northumberland House are anything to judge by – would doubtlessly have approved of the classical undertones of his 'pretty' Gothic pastiche at Alnwick. However, he did not accept the classical–Gothic ceiling design that Adam made in 1770 for the glass drawing-room at Northumberland House.[50]

The duke's 'consummate taste and judgement' in restoring Alnwick 'as much as possible in the Gothic style' made it, in the opinion of Francis Grose, 'one of the most magnificent models of a great baronial castle'.[51] On the contrary, Thomas Pennant, though equally well disposed to the Gothic style, was not at all pleased by his visit to the house in 1769. To him, the tame elegance of the eighteenth-century restoration was incompatible with the 'grandeur of the feudal age' and its 'military prowess, deeds of chivalry and spoils of the chase'.[52] C. R. Cockerell dismissed all Adam's 'mock gothic' at Alnwick in one fell sweep as 'Wretched "colefichets meschine" taste totally devoid of character'.[53]

The fourth duke, who succeeded in 1847, was equally contemptuous of what his ancestor had done to make the dilapidated castle habitable. Its reduction in size had robbed it of 'much of its original beauty and variety of effect' and its pastel, pastiche Gothick interiors were not only insipid and wholly inaccurate, but also lacked 'the domestic comfort and modern conveniences requisite in the residence of a nobleman of his Grace's rank'. In no way did Alnwick accord with romantic mid-nineteenth-century notions of 'a great baronial castle'.[54] Believing it to be his duty to himself and his successors as well as to the noble line from which he descended 'to surround himself with noble and imposing associations', the fourth duke determined to sweep out the eighteenth-century restorations and to replace them with interiors in the Italian Renaissance style. His architect, Anthony Salvin, did as he was told, though his own wish, he said, would have been to 'devise Medieval decorations to a plan consistent with modern requirements'.[55] In Sir Giles Gilbert Scott's opinion, the duke had made 'one of the greatest and most lamentable mistakes which has been made in the present day.'[56]

South View of Northumberland House.

141   Charles Grignion, view of the south front of Northumberland
House overlooking the garden and the Thames, engraving after a
drawing by Samuel Wale. The three first-floor windows to the left of the
portico belonged to the glass drawing-room (Guildhall Library)

6

NORTHUMBERLAND HOUSE

Until 1768, Adam's work for the first Duke of Northumberland was confined to the magnificent new suite of state rooms at Syon. Once that had been accomplished, he was promptly given James Paine's job as architect at Alnwick Castle and Northumberland House in the Strand, in London.

A programme of extensive alterations to the early seventeenth-century quadrangular house in the Strand was already in progress in February 1750 when Hugh Smithson succeeded his father-in-law, Algernon Seymour, seventh Duke of Somerset, as eighteenth Earl of Northumberland. It had been started in the early 1740s by Charles Seymour, sixth Duke of Somerset, who acquired the property through his marriage to the twice-widowed Lady Elizabeth Percy, and after his death in December 1748 was continued on a larger scale by his son, Algernon, who died just over a year later.

Algernon's ambitious plans, which included altering the Strand front to make it 'appear less like a prison' and adding a 'new wing on the right hand (west) side of the garden . . . (to) contain a library, bed chamber, dressing-room, and a waiting-room', were completed by the new earl.[1] He also extended the opposite wing to form a large, two-storey picture-gallery-cum-ballroom which was 'finished and opend' in May 1757, and created a tapestry room hung with Soho tapestries in the projecting south-west corner of the quadrangle, adjacent to the drawing-room.[2] His architect was one of Lord Burlington's disciples, Daniel Garrett, who died early in 1753 and was succeeded by James Paine.

By the time Adam arrived on the scene in 1769, the first phase of new building was finished and Northumberland, created a duke in October 1766, was ready to turn his attention to the principal reception rooms – the great dining-room and drawing-room in the centre of the garden front (pls 141, 142). Although the decoration of these rooms was evidently splendid enough for the 'embroidered dinners' and vast assemblies of the nobility for which the Northumberlands were renowned, it might have been quite old-fashioned, for as far as we know there had been no major alterations to this part of the house since Edward Marshall built the great stone stairs to the garden in 1655–7 and John Webb made designs for the dining-room and drawing-room chimney-pieces in 1657.

The earliest indication of projected improvements are three ceiling designs by Adam – one for the dining-room and two for the drawing-room – dated June 1770 (pl. 143).[3] Wall elevations and designs for wall furniture and chimney-pieces would normally have been supplied later that year or early the next. For some unknown reason, however, all new designs, including those for the decoration of the chapel being constructed at Alnwick, were held in abeyance while plans and surveys were made of Syon, Alnwick, Northumberland House and other Percy properties.[4]

The scheme for redecorating the drawing-room was resumed in 1773, but the dining-room was dropped or shelved, probably for want of time rather than money.[5] Adam's accounts for twenty-three new designs – many of them 'at large' and 'for the execution' – made in the short period between 9 June and 15 July and including everything except a carpet and slabs for the chimney-piece and tables, suggest a certain degree of urgency on the part of the duke to execute this extraordinary room, which was to be entirely lined from dado to cornice with mirrors and plate-glass walls.[6]

The measurements of the eight huge mirrors were immediately given to Peter Reilly, 'Upholsterer, Dealer, Chapman', who had an excellent, though undeserved, reputation as an importer of French furniture and glasses at reduced Customs duties.[7] On 29 June, Reilly sent the duke a 'Memorandum' agreeing to 'procure and deliver' the specified looking-glasses for the sum of £1,465.16.0. The duke protested in a letter to his steward, Thomas Butler, on 6 July that Reilly's price was 'greatly beyond what he first mentioned . . . and is full as much as if I entered them myself at the Custom House and paid the whole Duty, which is 75 pr. ct. upon the first Cost, whereas he adds 20 pr. ct. for silvering Duty at Paris, package, and freight, and then expects 60 pr. ct. upon the whole, which it is by no means worth my while to give, and unless he will take 60 pr. ct. upon the price of the Glasses at Paris according to the printed Tariff I will not take them, and he must immediately write to forbid the Glasses from being sent.'[8] Rather than lose the profitable commission, Reilly dropped the surcharge and on 12 July sent the duke a revised 'Estimate Charging 60 per cent only on the prime Cost of the Glasses'.[9] As will be seen, there would be an ironic outcome to this looking-glass deal, but first there is the question of the duke's sudden urgency after three-years delay.

Having imported two of the largest and most expensive looking-glasses ever seen in England for the drawing-room at Syon in

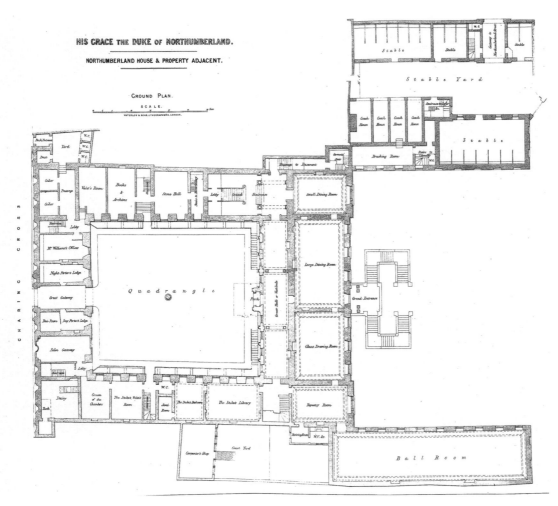

142 Plan of the principal floor of Northumberland House, 1819

143 Design (unexecuted) for the drawing-room ceiling, by Robert Adam, 1770 (Sir John Soane's Museum: Adam drawings, vol. II:32). The Gothic style is a carry-over from the ceilings which Adam designed for Alnwick around 1769

144 'Inside View of the Theatre Royal Drury Lane as it appears from the Stage altered & decorated in the year 1774', by Robert Adam (*The works in architecture of Robert and James Adam*, vol. II (1779), pt. v, pl. VII. Hand-coloured copy at Sir John Soane's Museum)

1763, and being an active member of the Society for the Encouragement of Arts, Manufactures and Commerce, Northumberland was very well aware of the considerable advantages of establishing a plate-glass manufactory in England capable of producing sheets of the size and quality that was only available in France at that time. He was persuaded to invest in just such a venture and on 10 April 1770 inserted anonymous advertisements in the *Daily Advertiser* and *Gazetteer* informing 'Any Person inclinable to establish a Manufacture of Plate Glass, upon an extensive plan . . . of a situation the most advantageous in all respects, that can be desired, by applying to Mr Lodge, attorney-at-law, in Gray's Inn.'[10]

By 1773 the promoters of 'the British Cast Plate Glass Manufactory' had 'formed themselves into a Society' and 'already engaged several Persons of Skill and Knowledge in the Business', foremost amongst them Philip Besnard, who had worked in the principal factories in Picardy and Burgundy before coming to England in 1771.[11] They had also discovered, however, that the vast sums needed to establish and maintain the manufactory safely and on a permanent foundation could only be raised by forming a company whose joint stock, and not their private fortunes, would pay their debts. A petition for authority to incorporate themselves was submitted to Parliament on 20 January 1773 and given royal assent in April. The Company of British Cast-Plate Glass manufacture was duly established at Ravenhead, St Helen's, Lancashire; £12,000 was invested by David Garrick and an unknown sum by the Duke of Northumberland.[12]

While the duke might have hoped in 1770 that the manufacture he was actively promoting would provide the glass for the new drawing-room at Northumberland House, in which case he would have had an English glass-room and an English tapestry-room side by side, he clearly had no such delusions by 1773.[13] The company did not begin production until 1776 and was unable to supply the large plates that he required or the smaller but similarly foiled green and crimson glass pilasters employed by Adam in the decoration of Garrick's Theatre Royal, Drury Lane, which opened on 30 September 1775 (pl. 144).[14]

145 Elevation of the chimney side of the drawing-room, by Robert Adam, 1773 (Sir John Soane's Museum: Adam drawings, vol. 39:6). The chimney-piece is generic, the first design for it followed a few weeks later (see pl. 151)

146 Elevation of the window wall of the drawing-room including the pier-glasses, a pier-table and a pair of unusual commodes, by Robert Adam, 1773 (Sir John Soane's Museum: Adam drawings, vol. 39:5)

Nevertheless, these two unique interiors by Adam, like their proprietors, shared links with the founding of the Cast-Plate-Glass Manufactory. As William Rieder and David Owsley suggested, the drawing-room and theatre were probably intended to create a fashion for plate-glass panelling, and thus to attract customers, in much the same way as the model tapestry-room prepared by the Gobelins Manufactory in 1762, which

Northumberland would almost certainly have seen on one of his tapestry-buying sprees in Paris.[15]

How much these extravagant advertisements contributed to the success of the manufactory is hard to say. Most critics were favourably impressed by the 'rich and brilliant' decoration of the Theatre Royal, though William Nicholson, editor of the *Critical review of the public buildings . . . in and about London* (1783) pro-

147 Design for the interior of Lloyd's Coffee House, by Robert Adam, 1772 (Sir John Soane's Museum: Adam drawings, vol. 30:59). The coffee house is thought to have been intended for a new building at the bottom of Freeman's Court opening off Cornhill, London, which was never executed

148 A section of one of the walls of the glass drawing-room at Northumberland House as reconstructed by the Victoria and Albert Museum in 1953. A more accurate reconstruction is presently being made for the V&A's new British Galleries

nounced the ornaments 'frippery and unmeaning. Slender columns of glass may strike the vulgar as very fine, but the judicious would wish to see propriety consulted as well as the rage of gaudy decoration'.[16] This, however, was in 1783, the year the glass-fronted pilasters were removed. Evidently they were immaterial to Soane's praise for the theatre as perhaps the fullest manifestation of 'Adam's wonderful versatility of invention'.[17]

The death of the Duchess of Northumberland after a long illness in December 1776, coupled with the American Revolution, put a damper on the glittering entertainments that were expected to launch the taste for spangled glass rooms. Hardly anyone followed the lead, nor was it ever repeated by Adam.[18]

Reilly's attempt to have the French looking-glasses (cast at St Gobain, Picardy) sent over in the name of the Venetian ambassador was intercepted by Customs and in the end the duke was forced to pay the 75 per cent duty he was so eager to avoid.[19] The arched mirrors were evidently delivered by August 1774, when workmen began drilling holes in them and the plain plates before fixing them to the baize-lined walls. The overmantel mirror was the last to be drilled, in January 1775.[20]

Initially, the plan was for all the mirrors, except the two on the narrow end piers on the window wall, to be raised in the centre and divided into three parts by thin, overlaid balusters. In the event, however, only the mirrors on the central window pier and over the chimney-piece were tripartite (pls 145, 146). The latter was treated like a Venetian window, with a high central arch and lower rectangular sides framed by female terms.[21] No matter whether the balusters or other ornaments were applied in full on the mirrors or halved at the edges, they were invariably continued on to the plate-glass walls above and were the source of two tiers of arched and scrolled branches: one used to frame the looking-glass and the other to frame the panel over it. Thus the mirrors and walls, apart from being made of the same material, were also integrated decoratively.

149 Design for the ceiling of the glass drawing-room as executed, by Robert Adam, 1770 (Sir John Soane's Museum: Adam drawings, vol. II:33)

Adam had first used mirrors as large-scale wall decorations partitioned by applied ornaments in 1767, in the library at Kenwood. A similar arrangement proposed for the book-room at Kedleston in 1768 was not executed, and nor was the large apse, lined all round with an arcade of mirrors resembling windows with balconies of applied ornament in the lower parts, designed in 1772 for Lloyd's Coffee House (pl. 147).[22] The Venetian window form also entered his repertoire in 1772, starting with a pier-glass made for the drawing-room at Luton Hoo and several designs for mirrors for Bolton House, Southampton Row.[23]

All the mirrors in the drawing-room of Northumberland House, except those on the window piers, were flanked by pairs of Corinthian pilasters with capitals and bases of carved and gilt wood. The central wooden strips were lined with varnished cloth, which was then covered with glass panels painted green and flecked with gilt copper spangles on the back, and edged with lead and copper borders painted brown and gold. Placed over the glass were delicate gilt filigrees of husks and palmettes stamped in copper. At first, painted ornament was proposed for the pilasters; however, while saving money, it would have spoiled the unity of the decoration and was wisely rejected.[24]

Every inch of the remaining wall space was covered with plate-glass panels foiled in a deep crimson colour to resemble highly polished Egyptian porphyry (pl. 148). Gilded swags of husks and bell flowers, tripods and pedestals, anthemia, paterae, female terms and other antique ornaments cast in lead were applied to the surface, in some cases to conceal the joints, but mainly for decorative enrichment. The founder was G. Collett, of the firm of Jack and Collett, who also supplied lead embellishments for the red drawing-room at Syon; the gilder was Dominique Jean.[25]

Above the mirrors and on the flanking walls were sixteen oval medallions of classical subjects painted in oil on paper. Only two of these survive; however, greater care was taken to save the larger and more valuable overdoor roundels designed by Angelica Kauffman and painted by Antonio Zucchi.[26]

Those parts of the walls that were not glazed – the dado, entablature, doorcases and doors – were painted green. Though their embellishments, including elaborate grotesques on the door panels, are shown in Adam's design painted deep pink, they were evidently gilded in execution.[27]

Pale green and pink were also the predominant colours of the ceiling, whose tripartite divisions, semicircular motifs, round and oval inset paintings on blue grounds and other ornaments picked out in gold further reflect the treatment of the walls (pl. 149).[28] The central cruciform pattern, its arms radiating from a circle within an octagon and ending in large semicircles, may be traced back to early Christian ceiling decorations of the type found in the third-century crypt of Lucina in the cemetery of St Calixtus outside Rome, though the immediate inspiration is more likely to have been the loggia ceiling by Baldassare Peruzzi and Giovanni da Udine in the Villa Madama.[29] It is a recurrent theme in Adam's work of the late 1760s and early 1770s; varia-

150 Design of an inlaid scagliola slab for a pair of pier-tables in the drawing-room, by Robert Adam, 1774 (Sir John Soane's Museum: Adam drawings, vol. 39:8). The tables and slabs are now at Syon

151 Inlaid scagliola chimney-piece and hearth-slab formerly in the glass-drawing-room, designed by Robert Adam, 1774 and probably made by Bartoli and Richter. Now in the green drawing-room at Syon

tions are to be found in the Lansdowne House drawing-room ceiling of 1767, the ceiling designed for the Duchess of Bolton's dressing-room in 1770 and the carpet for the great drawing-room at Derby House.[30]

Articles of furniture like tables and seats which normally stood against the dado were designed to partake in the wall decorations. Adam's sections show two large *confidentes* (a new French fashion) on either side of the chimney-piece, two large sofas between the doors on the end walls, and eight flanking armchairs – all gilded, their seat-rails corresponding to the frieze round the walls, their scrolled backs (the height of the gilded dado rail) crested with palmettes and covered in red fabric with a pattern of gold vases and foliage related to the gilt metal enrichments of the mirrors and glass panels under which they were to stand.[31] Although pairs of *confidentes* and sofas were executed by James Cullen (an 'Upholder and Cabinet-maker' who had worked at Hopetoun House in the late 1760s) for the positions Adam proposed, they were not made to his design and were too large to receive accompanying armchairs; hence, instead of eight chairs there were only four, one in each window bay.[32] The entire suite was covered in crimson, green and white silk damask supplied in October 1778 by the firm of King and Padget, which presumably had the same pattern of large cabbage roses and sprigs entwined with ribbons that was used at Syon and Alnwick and also for the furniture in the tapestry-room at Northumberland House. Four matching festoon curtains and gilt curtain-cornices are also listed in the 1786 inventory.[33]

Adam's scheme for the window wall called for a central pier-table with a scrolled apron and eight straight, spiral-fluted legs in pairs aligned on the vertical divisions of the accompanying pier-glass, and two flanking double-bowed commode-tables of bizarre Piranesian description supported either by columnar legs or foliate scrolls. In the event, a modified version of the pier-table was executed with the same baluster legs as the chairs, a shaped stretcher and an antique mosaic top; but the curious

commodes were rejected in favour of normal semicircular pier-tables *en suite* with the rectangular one.

Designs for the table frames do not survive and are not recorded in Adam's bills. There is, however, a design dated 6 May 1774 for the semicircular inlaid scagliola slabs with cameo heads suspended from bell-flower festoons within a broad frame of interlaced floral wreaths bordered by Etruscan-style bands of black and terracotta anthemia (pl. 150).[34] As we shall see, the Etruscan colouring compensated for the duke's forfeiture of the Etruscan-style chimney-piece first proposed by Adam. All the table tops, rectangular and semicircular alike, are enriched with ormolu borders in much the same manner as the pier-tables in the red drawing-room at Syon, where, as it happens, Adam's three Northumberland House tables have come to rest.

Designing a chimney-piece – a focal element – that would work with the extraordinary spangled glass and mirrored walls was a challenge of the kind Adam had met almost a decade earlier in the red drawing-room at Syon. He must have known from that experience that a plain white statuary marble chimney-piece with carved terms, like the one shown in his section, would have been far too prominent and intrusive. This conventional chimney-piece was a generic model rather than a design. The first proper design – full-sized and coloured – was made on 29 June 1773, three weeks after the section, and was for a white marble surround with panels of inlaid scagliola ornaments in the Etruscan style.[35] However, as he soon realized, a room as singular as the glass drawing-room did not require and would not benefit from his novel adaptation of Etruscan vase painting nearly as much as the Countess of Derby's Etruscan dressing-room.[36]

In March 1774 he made a new design (keeping the mirror which could not be altered at this late stage) for a more colourful and ornate scagliola chimney-piece with recessed Ionic columns reminiscent of the Corinthian ones at Syon (but fluted with blue-green

152 Design for a 'Carpet for the Drawing Room Northumberland House', by Robert Adam 1774 (Sir John Soane's Museum: Adam drawings, vol. 17:173)

scagliola instead of ormolu) and a tablet consisting of an oval painting of Diana in her chariot flanked by rectangular pictures of dancing nymphs (pl. 151). The added profusion was altogether appropriate to the room and agreeable to Northumberland; an inlaid scagliola hearth slab was designed in June and the chimneypiece ensemble was probably executed by Bartoli and Richter, though there are no surviving bills.[37] It is now installed in the green (private) drawing-room at Syon. In 1786 it had a garniture of '7 Ornaml Vases and 2 standing (candle) Branches', from which the pair of covered bronze vases with ormolu medallions of classical figures currently at Syon may have derived.[38]

What became of the 'large carpet to cover the Room 36 f by 22 . . .' (10.9 × 6.7 metres) listed in the 1786 inventory remains a complete mystery: we do not know what it looked like or whether it was in any way related to the slightly smaller carpet (approximately 34 × 20 feet, 9.27 × 6.09 metres) for which Adam made a large-scale coloured drawing of a quarter of the pattern – the kind of drawing normally intended for execution – in June 1774 (pl. 152).[39] Although this design repeats the three-part division of the ceiling, the similarity ends there; it has an altogether different pattern of circular and semi-circular motifs in a greater variety of colours: purple, brown and yellow as well as pink and green.

A harmonious and fully integrated composition of similar elements would have been wasted and unavailing in a room entirely lined with glass, which multiplied and divided everything many times over. What was wanted here was a different sort of harmony, a harmony of carefully contrived divergences.

Brilliant light, for which the Northumberlands were renowned, was vital for the full effect of the glass drawing-room and was obtained with fewer candles than it took to illuminate the less reflecting surface of a hung room. Adam's sections call for fifteen urn-shaped girandoles to be incorporated in the gilt-metal traceries applied to the glass panels and mirrors, providing a total of thirty-two candle branches. Full-size drawings of the girandoles were made in July 1773, but the number executed was fewer than planned.[40] In 1786 the room had provision for only twenty-five candles: a sixteen-branch lustre chandelier; '2 standing Branches on the Chimney piece' probably with three branches each as shown in Adam's section; and a 'Tripod Vase and Lamp with three Branches gilt', which must originally have stood on the rectangular, mosaic table in front of the mirror on the central window pier. Presumably the large crystal lustre,

153 Unknown artist, watercolour of the glass drawing-room at Northumberland House, c.1870 (Collection of the Duke of Northumberland)

154   Photograph of the glass drawing-room shortly before the demolition of Northumberland House in 1874

which was more costly and no doubt larger than the one in Adam's 'great' drawing-room at Alnwick, compensated for the omission of the girandoles and provided more evenly diffused light and a great deal more sparkle.[41]

The glittering drawing-room was probably first used on 8 June 1775 for the marriage of Lord Algernon Percy to Isabella Susanna Burrel 'with the utmost privacy because of the ill health of the Duchess and Mr Burrel's father'.[42] Six months later, the jovial duchess was dead.

In 1820, the south or river front, which had been found to be structurally unsound, was rebuilt by Thomas Cundy further forward, towards the garden, and with fewer windows. As a result, the drawing-room had to be dismantled and widened, the ceiling raised on a cove in order to fit the larger space and the piers adjusted for three rather than four windows (pls 153, 154). The original three-coloured silk damask upholstery was replaced by mossy green satin with pink rosettes and the floor was covered with a carpet of similar pattern. When the room was opened to the public during the Great Exhibition in 1851, it was described as

a very antique and seemingly old looking chamber. It is of the

most magnificent description, though the ornaments are quaint, and, in many respects overdone . . . The gilding and carving are of the most profuse order – perhaps carried to excess, wall and roof being literally one mass of intricate and involved workmanship, the numerous details of which, however perfect and beautiful individually, detract from the harmony of the whole . . . The effect . . . though elaborate in the highest degree, is perhaps too intricate and discordant, wanting that simplicity and harmony of arrangement which are necessary for the production of great designs.[43]

Though Adam's brilliant 'harmony of many contrasts' was no longer appreciated, at least its uniqueness was recognized.[44] When Northumberland House was demolished in 1874, the room was dismantled and stored at Syon. A few small pieces are still there, but after the Second World War the remainder was sold to Bert Crowther of Syon Lodge, who hired it out for party decoration. Finally, in 1953, it was purchased for the V&A, whereupon the large areas of crimson foil were insensitively restored and have since faded. Only one section is to be exhibited in the new installation of the British Galleries.

155   John Buckler, view of Bowood House, Wiltshire from the south-west. Watercolour, 1806 (Wiltshire Archaeological Society, Devizes, Wiltshire). The house was demolished in 1956

7

BOWOOD HOUSE

It was said of William Petty, Viscount Fitzmaurice, second Earl of Shelburne and later first Marquess of Lansdowne (1737–1805) that 'he was never satisfied with what anyone did, or even with what he did himself, but altered and changed without end'.[1] Such characteristics were bound to strain his relationship with his architects, Robert and James Adam, and to have a detrimental effect upon his building projects. Neither Bowood in Wiltshire nor Shelburne (later Lansdowne) House in Berkeley Square was completed according to plan. Posterity was not kind to either building: the great house at Bowood was demolished in 1955 and Lansdowne House was altered beyond recognition in 1930.

When his father died on 14 May 1761 and he 'came to the estate', Fitzmaurice was twenty-four years old and had only just returned to England the previous December after three years of military service abroad. He had 'no person employed in (his) affairs but such as serve to mislead . . . no agent in the habit of accounting regularly . . . (and) . . . neither house in town or country except Wycombe (Loaks, now Wycombe Abbey), which was barely habitable and without a tablecloth'.[2] Bowood and a house in Hanover Square had been left to his mother.

With characteristic impetuosity, but without much thought, he promptly 'ordered Mr Adam to look out for space to build a hotel upon' in London.[3] A month or so later, his mother sold him Bowood by a family arrangement at a valuation of £15,000 – half of what his father had laid out on the property – and returned to live in Ireland.[4] Now his plans to house himself in a style appropriate to his rank as colonel and aide-de-camp to George II and MP for Chipping Wycombe were in a real quandary. Should he build in town or in the country? The advice given him by General Robert Clerk, under whom he had served in the army and by whom he was treated like a son, was that with 'not more than 2,000 a year to lay out in buildings', the

principal point of building at present, . . . must be Bowood park. The house and offices may and ought to be finished first, together with the mausoleum, (which his mother had com-

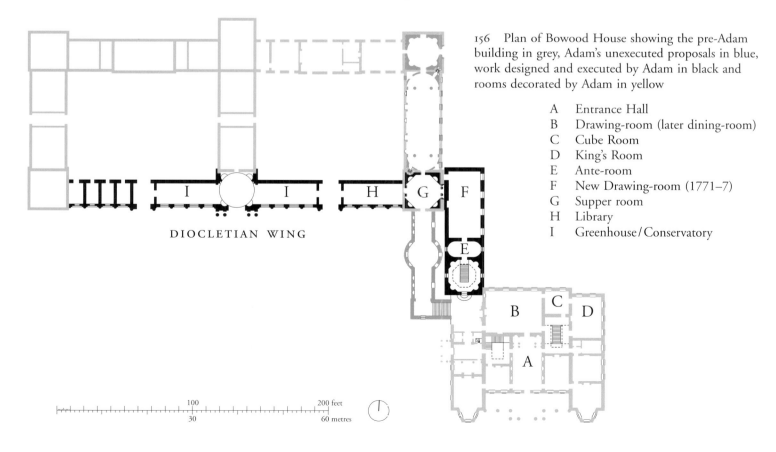

156   Plan of Bowood House showing the pre-Adam building in grey, Adam's unexecuted proposals in blue, work designed and executed by Adam in black and rooms decorated by Adam in yellow

A   Entrance Hall
B   Drawing-room (later dining-room)
C   Cube Room
D   King's Room
E   Ante-room
F   New Drawing-room (1771–7)
G   Supper room
H   Library
I   Greenhouse/Conservatory

DIOCLETIAN WING

100   200 feet
30   60 metres

157 The entrance hall at Bowood, designed by Robert Adam

missioned Adam to design and build in 1761), before the Park wall is begun. The house and offices may be done in such a manner as to live well with perhaps 4 or 5,000 pound. When the annuities for lives fall in, or deaths of people to whom he succeeds should happen, or if My Lord follows John Bull's advice, or if Townshend finds out mines in Carey, great sums are found of course for building a great Palace in London, finishing Bowood and even gradually building a noble house there.[5]

Bowood was bought by John Petty, first Earl of Shelburne, in January 1754 from Sir Orlando Bridgeman, who had begun building the house around 1725 but had not quite finished it (pls 155, 156). Shelburne employed Henry Keene to add a range of rooms on the north front and projecting bows on the south, and to build stable and kitchen courts to the north-west of the house. Keene also made designs and working drawings for 'Finishing . . . Hall &c. Do. for Arcades, front Piers, & finishing Stable &

Kitchen Courts, with the Drawings & Directions for the Workmen'; these were 'not yet executed' when he left for Ireland in April 1761 in the service of the new Lord Lieutenant, the Earl of Halifax.[6]

The south portico and the decoration of the entrance hall, the staircase hall to the east and the three rooms on the north front were Adam's first tasks (pls 155, 156). He started in December 1761 with the hall, which he heightened by taking in the room above (pl. 157).[7] This required the addition of quadrant balconies to replace the lost communication between the two sides of the house. It was an awkward solution that interfered with the simplicity of the arched Doric screen across the north wall, which supported a linking passage or gallery on the first-floor.

Round the room were seven niches: two under the screen flanking the central door into the drawing-room (later the dining-room), two on either side of the chimney-piece and three on the opposite wall between the doors at each end. The young earl is known to have commissioned James Adam to buy antique statues for him in Rome early in 1762 and these were presumably

Stool for the Hall at Shelburne House

1768

158 Design for hall stools for Bowood and Shelburne House (later Lansdowne House), Berkeley Square, by Robert Adam. 1764 and 1768 respectively (Sir John Soane's Museum: Adam drawings, vol. 17:76). The stools were made by John Linnell

159 Giovanni Battista Piranesi, dedication to Robert Adam of *Il campo marzio dell'antica*, Rome (1762), with an engraved vignette of the Egyptian porphyry sarcophagus found in the ruins of the baths of Agrippa and moved to the basilica of St John Lateran to receive the ashes of Pope Clement XII (Wilton-Ely, no. 564)

160 The interior of the first Earl of Shelburne's mausoleum at Bowood, by Robert Adam 1761–64 showing two stools removed from the hall of the house

Labrum aegyptiacum porphyreticum, repertum inter rudera thermarum M. Agrippae, nunc uria sepulchralis Clementis S.M. Clementis XII in Basilica S. Ioannis Lateranensis. Operculum hand effossutum est, quod recens factum, cum Labrum pro urna usurpatum est

AL CHIARISSIMO SIGNORE

IL SIG. ROBERTO ADAM

GIOVAN BATTISTA PIRANESI

S Omigliantissima, anzi gemella, io giudico, *CHIARISSIMO SIGNORE*, che sia la condizione di chi da altri in altri paesi va trasferendosi non men per diporto, che per apprendere più agevolmente, dopo aver osservati i costumi de' popoli, il maneggio de' pubblici e privati affari; e di chi s'applica per sì fatta maniera ad investigare gli antichi monumenti, che come se vivesse ne' trapassati secoli, diligentemente ricerca, qual cosa sia stata fatta di que' tempi, quale sia stata la maniera di fabbricare, quale la pulitezza, quale l'uso di trattare i pubblici ed i privati interessi. E da tale studio, e, per così dire, pellegrinaggio, non v'è chi non vegga, quanto piacere ne ritraggono quelli, che lo intraprendono, quanto utile gli altri. Per la qual cosa, se cotanto da Omero vien commendato Ulisse, per aver osservati i paesi, che allora erano in

a 2 no in

161 Detail of the Palmyrene ceiling in the great drawing-room at Bowood, reconstructed in the boardroom of Lloyds of London in 1983

162 Soffit of a Roman sepulchre from Robert Wood, *Ruins of Palmyra*, London (1753), pl. XXXVII

163 Elevation of the chimney side of the great drawing-room, by Robert Adam, *c*.1762 detail (Sir John Soane's Museum: Adam drawings, vol. 39:68). The 'mosaic' ceiling shown here was rejected in favour of the 'Palmyrene' one (see pl. 161)

intended to adorn the stone-coloured hall.[8] Between the niches were six white-painted stools made by John Linnell on 9 August 1764 to an Adam design which was closely modelled upon the antique porphyry bath that appeared on Piranesi's dedication to him of *Il Campo Marzo dell Antica Roma* in 1762 (pls 158, 159).[9] At about the same time, Linnell also carved and painted four terms with mahogany tops to support '4 glass lanthorns with carved & gilt Pedestals in the shape of Vases . . . with 4 brass cast lamps & lights each'. Like the stools, these were done 'by Drawing' probably by Adam, and were most likely destined for the hall. They have not been traced.

Of all the rooms at Bowood, including the three behind the hall which were designed by Adam in 1763 (the north-east corner room or 'King's Room', the 'Cube Room' and the 'Great Room' or drawing-room), the drawing-room was by all accounts the most 'spacious and rather noble'.[10] In the late 1770s, when a new drawing-room was inserted between the house and the offices, the 1763 'Great Room' became the principal dining-room. As we are concerned here with its genesis, we shall call it by its original name, the 'Great Room' or drawing-room. The ceiling, composed of recessed circular coffers or dishes with central bosses (pls 161, 162), was taken from Robert Wood's *Ruins of Palmyra* (1753) and the walls were decorated with panels of grotesque ornament (pl. 165) of the type found at the Villa Pamphili and used by Adam for the first time a year or so earlier in the dining-room at Shardeloes.[11] There were panels with simple mouldings for paintings over each of the six doors; a large panel in the centre of the south wall; and more elaborately carved panels with scrolled pediments, profile terms at the sides and swags of husks at the bottom on the east and west walls. The one above the chimney-piece contained a Van Dyck of Henrietta Maria (pls 163, 164).[12] The carving of all the panels, doorcases, shutters and other architectural elements was done by John Linnell and completed by April 1765.

Two 'highly wrought and expensive' chimney-pieces of statuary marble and variegated brocatella with engaged Corinthian columns were made for the room in 1764 by Benjamin Carter 'according to the Design of Robert Adam Esq'.[13] Both were sent

164　The chimney-piece in the great drawing-room at Bowood before the demolition of the house in 1956

165   One of the panels of stucco decoration flanking the great drawing-room chimney-piece

to Bowood in May 1765, but it was decided to put up only one on the west wall and to extend the architectural frame on the opposite side by three feet (0.9 metres) bringing it down to the chair rail. The second chimney-piece remained in storage for about three years until it was put up in the drawing-room at Lansdowne House.[14]

The description of the room in a 1767 inventory as the 'Green Drawing Room' must refer to the colour of the walls.[15] Ian Bristow's investigations of the surviving fragments that were re-erected in the boardroom on top of the Lloyds building in the City of London in 1983 found a 'deep blue-green' colour on the grounds of the grotesque wall panels and the ceiling dishes and lozenges, and a 'dull pink' on the remainder of the ceiling and the ground of the frieze.[16] Presumably the ornaments, architectural frames and mouldings were picked out in white; the door and window surrounds were white, the dado was deep pink and the skirting darker green, a combination of colours found at Lansdowne House and elsewhere at this time. However, the bright colours chosen by Adam to create a room in the antique style at Bowood were deemed inappropriate for the high-tech atmosphere of Richard Rogers's Lloyds building. The paler hues of straw-colour and green that were favoured twenty years later, in the 1780s, were recommended as a legitimate compromise and accepted. Monochromatic pearl and white – the colours of Shelburne's London dining-room, finished in 1767 – would have been even more in keeping with

modern taste and much more authentic as well, given the fact that the room from Bowood had also functioned as a dining-room from the 1770s. Perhaps grey was too modern and not 'Adam' enough for Rogers and Bristow.

Pier-glasses for the drawing-room were the only articles of furniture, apart from the hall stools, known to have been designed by Adam for Bowood (pl. 166). An oval pier-glass was added by another hand to his elevation of the window wall made around 1763. This was superseded in 1765 by his own design for rectangular frames for glasses a little over 8 by 4 feet (2.4 by 1.2 metres) with crests and bases of scrolled foliage, anthemion, palmette and shell motifs exactly like those on an oval glass he designed in 1764 for the Earl of Thanet's house in Grosvenor Square.[17] Although there were three glasses of these dimensions in 'gilt glass bordered frame(s)' at Bowood in 1805, when the first Marquess of Lansdowne died and the contents of the house were sold, they were not in the original drawing-room but in the new one.[18] Whether these were the mirrors designed by Adam and where they are now is not known.

Ince and Mayhew were the principal suppliers of important furniture for Bowood. On 14 March 1765 Ince was given 'plans from Herculaneum & Palmyra for ornaments for a Comode of Yew Tree wood inlaid with Holly & Ebony' which was most likely intended for the drawing-room with its Palmyra ceiling.[19] Unfortunately, this intriguing neo-classical piece has not been traced. In June, the Earl of Shelburne and his young wife, Lady Sophia Carteret, (daughter of John, second Earl of Granville) whom he married on 5 February 1765, went again to 'Ince the cabinet Maker to see (their) furniture for the drawing room and (Lady Shelburne's) dressing room at Bowood'.

Bowood was unusual in not having any of its reception rooms hung with damask. Shelburne's preference for stucco or painted grotesque ornament can be seen as a manifestation of his deep interest in antiquity and above all in sculpture. Pictures, which were essential for most hung rooms, were not the strong point of his collection.

By the end of May 1765, the house, according to Lady Shelburne, was 'habitable & beautiful'; paving was all that was needed at the mausoleum (pl. 160); and 'only the offices remained to be finished'. At that stage, however, her husband's interests shifted to London and building work in the country was suspended. On 1 October he bought the unfinished house in Berkeley Square that Adam was erecting for the Earl of Bute, and in the following July he accepted the high office of Secretary of State for the Southern Department under Pitt, which he held until October 1768, leaving his tradesmen and neighbours at Bowood 'all in the Dumps'.[20]

In January 1768, when the bulk of Adam's design work for the London house was finished, but a good half year before the place was habitable, Shelburne evidently began to turn his mind to creating another 'Great Room' at Bowood at the east end of the office block. Adam began by preparing a 'Drawing of part of the Great Room Ceiling . . . with Coloured Grounds' on 7 January, and by 25 August had more 'plans of building and of joyning the house and offices by an additional apartment' to discuss with his patron at Bowood.[21] Being extremely indecisive and difficult to please, Shelburne required repeated alterations to the scheme over the next two years. Although his wife recorded in her diary

166 Elevation of the window wall of the great drawing-room showing the pier-glass and curtain cornices, by Robert Adam, *c.*1762, detail (Sir John Soane's Museum: Adam drawings, vol. 39:68)

Section of a Room for The Earl of Shelburne at Bowood

in June 1769 that 'the offices are now shutting up with a screen of buildings Mr Adam designed for that purpose', the final 'plan of the Ground Story of the Offices for execution' was not made until 15 June 1770.[22]

Sadly, Lady Shelburne did not live to see Bowood finished. Work on what later became known as the Diocletian Wing was interrupted by her unexpected death at the age of twenty-five on 5 January 1771. Four months later, relations with Adam were severed when Shelburne joined Lords King and Tankerville in a public protest against the Act of Parliament, which had been given royal assent on 8 May, authorizing the Adam brothers to embank the Thames at Durham Gate and use the reclaimed ground to their own private advantage in their Adelphi development.[23] On that quite decisive, outspoken note, the widowed earl set off with his close friend, Isaac Barré, for an extended tour of France and Italy.

When he returned in January 1772, his first concern was whether to build a library or a sculpture gallery at Shelburne House. The completion of the offices at Bowood took second place and was entrusted to a local builder, James White, who had worked there under Adam after Henry Holland, Sr was dismissed in 1766.[24]

To what extent White's Adamesque interiors were dependant upon designs that Shelburne had received from Adam is impossible to determine. The partly coloured drawing of the 'Great Room' ceiling made in 1768 and the sections of the dining-room (or supper-room?) and library made in April 1769 and June 1770,

which are listed in Adam's accounts, are all lost. Only one of his rejected schemes survives – an elevation and plan of greenhouses on either side of a central entrance, and a long gallery on the east front in what became the 'little house' for Lord Fitzmaurice. This gallery, with niches for sculpture, columnar screens and apsidal ends opening to a circular room at the north end and an octagonal one at the south, is reminiscent of the proposed library at Lansdowne House.[25]

Adam's executed scheme – consisting of an octagonal staircase hall leading up from the house to an oval ante-room, followed by the large new drawing-room with an apse at the far end and an interconnecting supper-room and library in the eastern part of the Diocletian Wing – was recorded in survey plans drawn by George Dance in 1792, before the extensive alterations made by C. R. Cockerell in 1821 and Charles Barry between 1833 and 1860 for the third Marquess of Lansdowne.[26] The latter's regeneration of Bowood followed the sales of most of the contents of this and Lansdowne House by his half-brother, the second Marquess, following their father's death on 7 May 1805. In the four years he possessed Bowood (1805–9), the second marquess left the house unoccupied, preferring to live in his Gothic castle at Southampton.[27]

The deaths of three sons of the sixth Marquess of Lansdowne in the Second World War and the complex division of the settled estates and contents of Bowood, added to other pressures, finally resulted in the sale of the fittings and fixtures of the house in June 1955, prior to its demolition.

167   The front of Lansdowne House facing Berkeley Square in 1921

8

LANSDOWNE HOUSE

In 1935, the mutilated remains of Lansdowne House (pl. 167), the private palace off Berkeley Square in London begun by Adam in 1762 for the third Earl of Bute and completed for the second Earl of Shelburne, were reconstructed as the headquarters of what is now the Lansdowne Club.[1] Adam's drawing-room and dining-room had been purchased and removed five years earlier by the Philadelphia Museum of Art and the Metropolitan Museum in New York respectively; and though parts of his ante-room were incorporated in what is now the Lansdowne Club bar, his other interiors were destroyed. The original furniture, pictures, sculpture, china, books and so forth had long since been dispersed at auction sales following the death of the first Marquess of Lansdowne in 1805.

From Adam's point of view, the history of Lansdowne House must have been rather disappointing, especially as it began in 1761 with the promise of being the very first house that would be entirely his, inside and out.

When William Petty, Viscount Fitzmaurice succeeded his father as second Earl of Shelburne on 14 May 1761, he immediately 'ordered Mr Adam to look out for space to build a hotel upon.'[2] His friend, Henry Fox (later Lord Holland) wrote to him on 29 June, recommending 'a fine piece of ground for that purpose, still to be had, the garden of which, or the court before which may extend all along the bottom of Devonshire Garden, though no house must be built there: the house must be where some paltry old stables stand at the end of Bolton Row.'[3] This desirable site in a tranquil spot off the main thoroughfare came on the market after the death of its owner, Thomas Coke, Earl of Leicester in April 1759. Plans for a new house had been made by Lord Leicester in collaboration with his builder, Matthew Brettingham, who intended to engrave them after publishing the *Plans, elevations and sections of Holkham* in 1761, but never did so.[4]

Shelburne was all set to embark on a great new palace in London, when Bowood, the family seat in Wiltshire, came his way. Finishing the improvements started by his father took precedence over his personal ambitions, and that was all he could afford, having no more than £2,000 a year to spend on building.[5]

The Berkeley Square site had also been recommended – over a year earlier, in February 1760 – to John Stuart, third Earl of Bute, by his great friend, Thomas Worsley, Surveyor of the

Office of Works.[6] Bute finally bought it on 3 December 1761, by which time Adam had made him a survey and four variant plans for a square or rectangular house with a library extension to the north.[7] The entrance was tried on the south side, in a large semi-circular bow; on the west, in the slightly projecting centre of a seven-bay front; and on the east, in a portico in antis. Various

168 Plan of the principal floor of Bute House, by Robert Adam, 1764 (RIBA Drawings Collection)

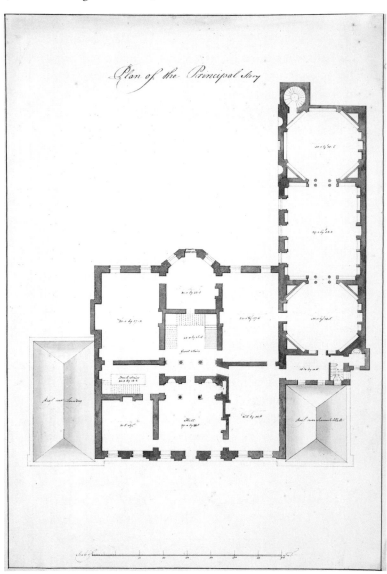

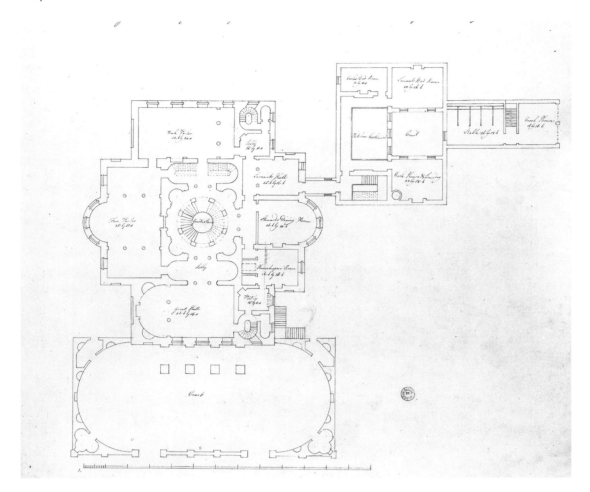

169 'Parlour Story of a house for The Right Honor^{ble} Earl of Shelburne fronting Piccadilly', by Robert Adam, 1764 (Sir John Soane's Museum: Adam drawings, vol. 43:89)

spatial shapes were introduced: circular stairs; a hall with one or two apsidal ends and columnar screens; a large cruciform library, and so forth. At least half a dozen other plans, including two with a library extension on the west front, were produced in the course of the following year.[8] Evidently these not only had to satisfy Bute's requirements, but were also passed to Thomas Worsley for his advice and approval.[9]

In the summer of 1762, before anything was settled, word spread that Bute had 'laid aside (his) intention of building on that spot of ground'.[10] His sudden change of mind was almost certainly due to discontent: not with Adam's proposals, but rather with the location of the spot bordering on the garden of the Duke of Devonshire, who was at that moment his most feared and hated enemy. Other building sites were suggested, as were houses for sale, including Lord Robert Manners's house in Grosvenor Square which Adam himself recommended.[11] Devonshire's dismissal as Chamberlain on 28 October 1762 may have eased Bute's mind somewhat, but it was not until he himself resigned as prime minister in April 1763 that he returned whole-heartedly to the building of his Berkeley Square house. As soon as he did so, he was lampooned by the popular press for selling out to the French in the Treaty of Paris and using the gains to build himself a grand palace.[12]

> This is the House that JACK is building.
> As I pass'd by the Quagmire near Berkley Square,
> I beheld such a Sight as oblig'd me to stare;
> The Sons of cold *Hebron* with Trowel and Hodd,
> Were raising a Temple to GISBAL their *God*.

> *English* bricks on each other were laying by Scores,
> All strongly cemented by *French Louis-d'Ores*.
> *Unhappy Britannia!* This grand stately Roof
> Of *Bondage* to come is too glaring Proof;
> In Time then awake, and instead of a Palace,
> To the Joy of *Old England, erect him a Gallows*.

After numerous alterations and refinements, mainly to the principal floor, which was at ground level rather than the first floor as the elevation would lead one to believe and as was the norm in London, a definitive plan was finally achieved, consisting of a seven-bay, three-storey block with the principal entrance on the east front, flanked by slightly projecting three-bay two-storey wings, a canted bow in the centre of the west or garden front, and a library extension on the north-west side (pl. 168).[13] This was quite restrained, compared to the earlier schemes, and had little of the spatial ingenuity at which Adam excelled, except in the great library which, as we shall see, was indebted to the gallery at Holkham. The main block was divided into three parts. In the centre were the entrance hall, the great staircase and the bow-windowed room. To the left were the principal reception rooms: the ante-room and 'Organ Drawing Room' separated by back stairs, and the 'Great Dining Room' in the south wing. To the right were Bute's rooms: his ante-room, dressing-room, powdering-room and water-closet, a private drawing-room, the great library and a staircase which was exclusively for his use and top-lit like all the others stairs.

While Bute's house was going up, Shelburne found himself a somewhat smaller plot at Hyde Park Corner. Here, in the words of his close friend General Robert Clerk, Adam had the rare

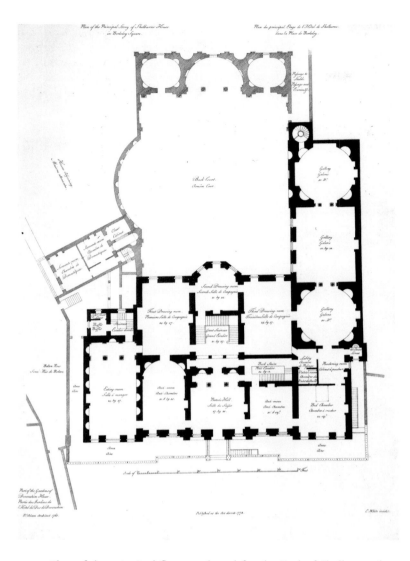

170   Plan of the principal floor as altered for the Earl of Shelburne, by Robert Adam, *c*.1765 (*The works in architecture of Robert and James Adam*, vol. II (1779), pt. III, pl. I)

'opportunity to think up a house at leisure and do what he plans without directions and caprices, which often spoil the whole.'[14] On 19 February 1765, a little over a fortnight after Shelburne's marriage to Lady Sophia Carteret, Adam went to Bowood, bringing 'ye plan of Ld Shelburne's new house' (pl. 169), which was much more varied and innovative than that for Bute House.[15] However, Clerk thought it was too small, 'Lord Bute's house is worth ten of it upon that account', nor was he impressed by its situation which lacked ground and privacy.

> Tranquility, quietness, retirement when one pleases, with real dignity are the proper qualities in a house . . . Burlington-house gives an idea of it . . . Go beyond Portman Square, Middlesex hospital, or where you like . . . take a piece of ground with a wall round it 30 feet high & road round it, you have all within yourself . . . your mind to yourself to your friends & to mankind, without trifling, dissipated, momentary, & in a short while tiresome, pleasures of the eyes.[16]

Six months later, on 16 September 1765, Clerk came to Shelburne with news that 'Lord Bute was going to sell ye House he is building in Berkeley Square', whereupon Shelburne commissioned him to buy it for him. On 1 October contracts were exchanged for Shelburne to purchase the house for £22,000 'to be begun to be paid in eight years till wch time he is to pay 900

p^ds a year interest to commense from the time he gets into it.'[17] According to the agreement, 'Messrs Robert & James Adam architects were to compleately Finish the said Mansion House . . . according to & as the same as specified more particularly in a description thereof . . . and all Bills Changes & Expences attending such finishing & compleating' should be paid for by the Earl of Bute.[18] What enabled Shelburne to strike such a favourable and unusual bargain remains a mystery. Evidently Bute was far from pleased: he thought 'it very hard to borrow money to build for (Shelburne)', and felt 'as if he had been driven to it and not as if it had been an action of his own doing.'[19]

Fear of the mob drove Bute more than anything else; added to that was another mishap which may have been the last straw. By some oversight, the carefully worked-out plan – which gave him all the stairs and water-closets he required, a bedroom adjoining his libraries, a basement room for his collection of scientific instruments and a drawing-room with a very large recess for his vastly expensive mechanical organ – made no provision for his fifty-eight outsize organ barrels or cylinders, each 4½ feet (1.3 metres) long.

Having agreed that the house was to be completed exactly as 'specified', Lord and Lady Shelburne promptly and quite wisely decided that it would be considerably improved if, instead of two secondary stairs, the back stair to the left was removed and another service stair built in a rear extension behind the dining-room.[20] This was very much to Adam's liking, for it enabled him not only to create a more fluid suite of interconnecting reception rooms, but also to introduce, by way of contrast, one of his 'antique' apses at the end of the ante-room (pl. 170).

James Adam's reply to Lord Shelburne's comments on the revised plan is a measure of the extent of Shelburne's architectural interest, and more especially of the Adam brothers' attention to the relative importance of rooms and their different uses: for evening entertainment, for daytime business and for the continual necessities of private domestic life.

> . . . the nich or Circular part at the end of the Anteroom will prevent it from appearing near so large as either of the rooms to which it gives access (dining-room and drawing-room), and tho upper servants do wait there, we should imagine there could arise no inconvenience from thence since the Room for Company before dinner (the drawing-room), will never probably be us'd by Your Lordship for private business, as there is the Bow window room, the room to the right of it and the Library for that purpose: and as one in the suite of Levee rooms it is infinitely better to go first into the anteroom and from there directly into the room for Company before dinner, without any passages or back stairs intervening, which it was not in the power of art to make clever. The back stairs next Your Lordship's appartment (on the right) go to the top of the house and will be lighted by a skylight. The water closets in the atticks will make it perfectly unnecessary that anything disagreeable should be conveyed by those stairs, and if Your Lordship should even incline that servants should not be seen in that part of them leading from Your room to My Lady (on the first floor) they may in that case pass through two rooms in the principal story (i.e. the drawing- room and dining-room) (which never will be used by My Lady but in the

171 The hall in 1921 showing the stone chimney-piece designed by Robert Adam, *c*.1766. The relief of Aesculepius in an Adam frame over the mantel was not part of the original design, but was acquired later in the 1770s. An impression of depth and movement is created by Adam's placement of the chimney-piece in front of the large wall panel

evenings) and from thence can go down the attic back stairs (behind the dining-room) to the offices.'[21]

By January 1766, the house was roofed, the main stair was built and its niches were filled with busts. Except for the revised ante-room, all the rooms were formed with their recesses and niches according to the designs that Adam had made for Bute.[22] In the summer of 1766 Adam was commissioned to make new designs for ceilings, chimney-pieces and wall elevations for the secondary reception rooms and the library on the first floor. These, according to his accounts, were supplied in August 1766; others followed in 1767.

The Shelburnes moved in in August 1768, 'very much pleased' with the house but conscious of the fact that 'few people wou'd have come to live in it, in so unfinished a state'.[23] The 'state' as described by Lady Shelburne was that

on the ground floor . . . the Hall, Antechamber, & Dining Room . . . (were) quite finished except for the glasses, the window curtains, & chairs which makes it very doubtful if we can ask the King of Denmark to dinner. The attics (were) all complete, the middle floor we have the Library and three other rooms, all to the Square (not modelled by Adam), which Royle is now busy in papering, but the masons who are cleaning down the staircase and the bell hangers make it as yet impossible for us to see any but people of business & very intimates.[24]

Though advice on curtain material and some designs for mirrors, tables and carpets were sought from Adam in the following year, his contribution to the furnishing of Shelburne House was not as extensive as it was at Coventry House in Piccadilly, where he was currently refurbishing the interiors. His input in this field might have been much greater and almost certainly more fully implemented had Lord Shelburne not diverted his attention in August 1768 to building the new wing at Bowood. Adam's speculative venture at the Adelphi was an additional distraction and one to which Shelburne publicly objected in May 1771, thereby severing their relationship.[25]

Work had in any case been suspended by Lady Shelburne's death on 5 January 1771, and remained so during the disconsolate earl's seven-month trip to Italy. There he was exposed to the influence of Gavin Hamilton, his appetite as a collector of antiquities was whetted and his indecisiveness exacerbated. Nevertheless, apart from the decoration of a few rooms completed in the late 1770s and the gallery built by Robert Smirke in 1819, the interiors at Lansdowne House were Adam's creation.

Entering the severe Doric hall (pl. 171) – with no hint of the elaborately embellished apartments around it – must have roused the imagination in much the same way as the bizarre perspective view of the hall table alone in an empty space, which Adam chose to publish in the second volume of his *Works* (1778).[26] The table frame, supporting an inlaid marble slab a little over 4 feet (1.2 metres) wide, was carved by John Gilbert in 1768 and painted 'dead White', with the Vitruvian scrolls and foliage in the frieze and the bell-flowers on the legs picked out in gold.[27] Against the remaining walls were eight white-painted stools like those at Bowood, based upon an antique sarcophagus and carved by John Linnell.[28] They were sold with the contents of Lansdowne House in 1806, as was the table, which has not been seen since.[29]

An elevation of the columnar screen is the only one of Adam's designs for the four sides of the hall to survive. Comparison with the room as executed confirms Lord Shelburne's observation that the design was 'reduced', the Shelburne armorial centaurs

172 Laid-out wall elevations of the ante-room, by Robert Adam, 1766 (Sir John Soane's Museum: Adam drawings, vol. 39:58)

173 The east end of the ante-room in the 1920s when it had become the front drawing-room

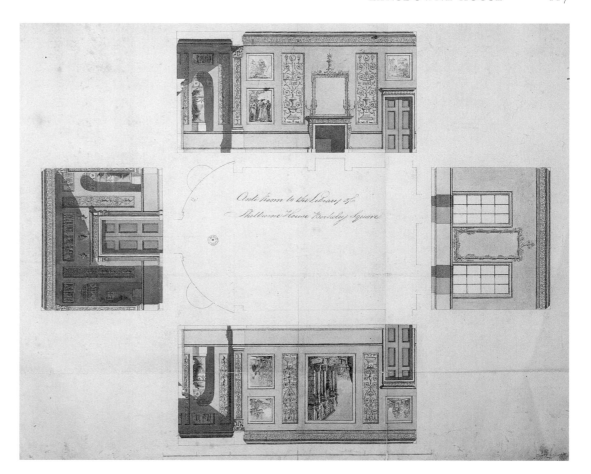

intended for the metopes being the most notable omission.[30] There were no significant alterations to his bold ceiling design of 1766 or to the chimney-piece.[31]

To the left of the entrance was the suite of state rooms, starting with the ante-room (pls 172, 173) which, according to James Adam, was a waiting-room for the upper servants of invited company who proceeded from there directly into the drawing-

room before dinner. The ante-room was originally planned as a square space of 21½ feet (6.5 metres), matching that in the private apartment to the right of the entrance and separated from the drawing-room by the back stairs. Shelburne's decision to remove these stairs added an extra 14 feet (4.2 metres) to the length of the ante-room, which Adam formed into a large semicircular apse in order, he said, to make it appear smaller and

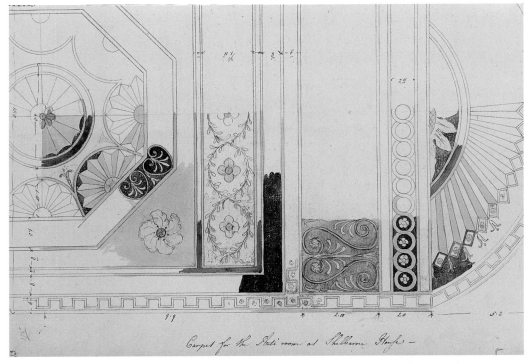

174 Design for a carpet for the ante-room, by Robert Adam, *c.*1769 (Sir John Soane's Museum: Adam drawings, vol. 17:175, detail)

175 Design for a pier-glass and table for the ante-room, by Robert Adam, 1768 (Sir John Soane's Museum: Adam drawings, vol. 20:25)

176 Console for Sir Lawrence Dundas at 19 Arlington Street, designed by Robert Adam, 1765

properly subservient to the more important drawing-room and dining-room. As ante-rooms go, it was quite large; larger, for example, than the one at Syon.

Green and pink were the predominant colours here: 'fine green' on the walls with white mouldings, the frieze picked-in in pink, the dado pink, the skirting green, the ceiling pink and green with white stucco ornaments. The only exception was the 'two Nitch heads with frames, Mouldings and Ornaments (of stucco, painted) in Various colours', making a background for the statues.[32] Set into the walls were eight tall panels of stucco arabesques, rather more intricate than those designed in 1763 for the Great Room at Bowood: four were in the apse flanking the two niches on either side of the door into the drawing-room; the other four were on the long walls, flanking the chimney-piece and the large painting of ancient ruins by Antonio Zucchi opposite it.[33]

The intervening spaces (near the apse and over the two doors leading to the hall and dining-room) were panelled to receive pictures in gilt frames. In the upper region were four square paintings of scenes in the life of Achilles by Giovanni Battista Cipriani, which were described by Lord Shelburne in 1777 as 'just finished'.[34] The two lower panels on either side of the apse, being the 'largest and nearest to the eye', Shelburne reserved for Gavin Hamilton, to whom he left the choice of subject, though suggesting sacrifices of Iphigenia and Polyxena as most suitable to the 'antique . . . which is the character of the room'. However, Hamilton admitted that owing to other commitments he was likely to be 'the cause of the room remaining too long imperfect' and in any case would rather provide paintings for a room hung with damask than be restricted in size and shape by panels.[35] The spaces reserved for him were never filled. The only paintings put up before Adam's departure were Zucchi's large architecture picture opposite the chimney-piece, his three oblong bacchanals in the apse and eight lunettes of putti in the circular compartment of the ceiling.[36]

Adam's design for the ceiling is not known, nor is it recorded in his accounts. It is possible that the main part – consisting of a central overlapping lozenge and diamond in a large square surrounded by an octagonal border incorporating eight arcs – was originally designed for Bute and later enlarged. In 1769 he designed a carpet (pl. 174) which echoes the geometry of the ceiling but has different ornaments, coloured yellow, pink, blue and brown on a green ground with a pink border of yellow rosettes. His provision of detailed measurements as well as a large-scale drawing of one quarter of the pattern in colour suggests that the carpet was executed. Whether this was the 'large and excellent Axminster carpet' sold in 1806 is impossible to tell.[37]

His designs for a pier-glass and semicircular pier-table were executed by John Gilbert in 1768 (pl. 175).[38] The gilt mirror frame is almost identical to one made in the same year for Coventry House, Piccadilly; the table, supported by three curved legs with rams' heads and paw feet and with an apron of pendant anthemia and swags of husks, is reminiscent of the console-table designed and executed in 1765 for Sir Lawrence Dundas at 19 Arlington Street (pl. 176).[39] Lady Shelburne's ecstatic visit to Dundas's house in March 1768 may well account for the similarity.[40] Both pieces were sold in 1806.[41] In addition to the pier-glass, there was a chimney-glass in a white fluted frame with a crest of scrolled foliage.[42]

Nothing is known about the seat furniture in the ante-room apart from the fact that it was originally upholstered in pea-green satin 'spotted with white and trimmed with a pink & white fringe', which was Lady Shelburne's 'own thought and met with (Adam's) entire approbation'.[43] The only green satin furniture in Lansdowne House at the time of the first marquess's death was in the drawing-room and consisted of a suite of twenty-five pieces.[44] The ante-room (then called the front drawing-room) had a pair of green silk damask festoon curtains and twelve gilt cabriole chairs covered in the same material.[45] Without a more detailed description of the two suites, it is impossible to determine whether they were in any way related. Though Adam approved the upholstery fabric for the ante-room

177 The drawing-room in 1914 showing the organ recess filled with a mirror and canapé and the walls hung with damask of a fairly bold pattern

and made two coloured designs in the antique style 'intended by My Lady Shelburne to be workt for the back of the Chairs in the Drawing Room at Shelburne House', he is not known to have been responsible for either suite.[46]

Visitors went from the apse end of the ante-room directly into the somewhat larger drawing-room which had been built for Bute as an 'Organ Drawing Room' with a capacious organ recess in the centre of the south wall (pls 177, 178).[47] Bute's instrument was one of the largest, most costly and celebrated mechanical barrel organs of the period.[48] Its construction was begun in 1762 and in 1763 Adam made a design for a pedimented case with term figures of Apollo and Marsyas, holding a lyre and pipes respectively, flanking an oval opening for the pipes. Although this is much more restrained than the case he had designed a year earlier for Nathaniel Curzon at Kedleston, he still saw fit to supply Bute with an even simpler alternative.[49] It is highly unlikely that either of these designs was used when the organ was eventually installed at Luton Hoo almost ten years later.

Designs for a 'Section of 4 sides of the Drawing Room, coloured in the stile of the Ancients (£)16.16.0' and a 'painted Cieling (sic) for Ditto room in the same stile (£)12.12.0' were invoiced in August 1766 (pl. 179), and on 28 February 1767 a 'General Estimate' was made of work to be finished that year, nearly all of it in the drawing-room.[50] It was, of course, wildly

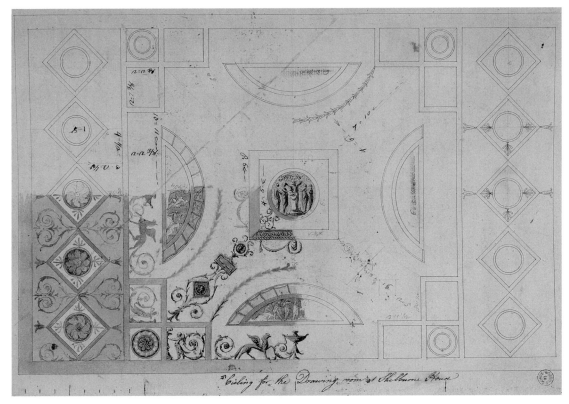

178 The drawing-room showing the chimney-piece and part of the ceiling, 1921

179 Design for the drawing-room ceiling, by Robert Adam, 1766 (Sir John Soane's Museum: Adam drawings, vol. 11:83)

181 Thomas Chippendale, design for a caryatid table, c.1760 (*The gentleman & Cabinet maker's director*, 3rd ed. (1762), pl. CLXXVI)

180 Design for a pier-glass and table frame for the drawing-room, by Robert Adam, 1768 (Sir John Soane's Museum: Adam drawings, vol. 20:24)

optimistic to think that a room elaborately decorated in the 'stile of the Ancients' could be entirely finished in just one year. When the accounts were delivered to Lord Shelburne on 21 April 1769, all but five of the fifteen items on the 'Estimate' had been finished. Twelve squares of plate glass were added to the two windows, making them into french windows with eighteen panes each; 'Joiners work' was finished; fourteen pilasters were in place with their stucco Corinthian capitals executed by Joseph Rose, who was also responsible for the enriched Corinthian cornice and other stucco work. Sefferin Nelson did the 'Carving in Wood', including '7 Circular frames', a jib door and three mahogany doors which had not yet been gilded but were fitted with locks by the locksmith, Timothy Marshall.[51]

A note subjoined to the 'Estimate' made clear that 'the Earl of Shelburne (had) a Chimney Piece ready prepar'd for this Room'. It was one of the two with Corinthian columns that was designed by Adam in 1763 for the drawing-room at Bowood and carved by Benjamin Carter in the following year. Though the two chimney-pieces were sent to Bowood in May 1765, only one was erected there.[52]

Francis Pitsala painted the shutters, dado and skirting pink and green; the 'frieze pickt in a pink'; and 'On face of Cieling (sic) Enrichd 3 times Distemper and pickt in Various Colours'. He also painted the '1 Frame over the Chimney' listed in the 'Estimate'. Whether this was intended to contain mirror glass, as he stated in his account, is not clear. In any case, it was probably

similar in design to the mirror frame over the chimney-piece in the ante-room, which Pitsala painted at the same time.[53]

The 'Great Glass & Great Table Frame' (pl. 180), estimated at £100, were intended for the window pier and can be identified with a design at the Soane inscribed 'for the Earl of Shelburne', but dated 1768, a year after the 'Estimate'. This is for a semicircular table approximately 6 feet (1.8 metres) wide supported by four full-length female figures holding swags of husks; and a mirror a little over 4 feet (1.2 metres) wide and 6 feet (1.8 metres) tall, with an pierced anthemion and bell-flower border and a 3 foot (0.9 metre) tall crest featuring a central medallion flanked by two seated female figures.[54]

Classical caryatids were first used as table supports by Chippendale in a design of 1760 published in the third edition of the *Director* in 1762 (pl. 181), two years before Stuart and Revett's *Antiquities of Athens*. His armless female figures were literal copies from the engraving of the Erectheion caryatids in *The ruins of Athens* (1759), Robert Sayer's English version of J.-D. Le Roy's *Ruines des plus beaux monumens de la Grèce* (1758). What prompted Adam to take up the idea in 1767 is not known. He tried it again in 1785 in a design for a semicircular pier-table for the second drawing-room at Cumberland House, Pall Mall.[55]

The first pier-glass design for Shelburne's London drawing-room was clearly no match for the caryatid table and was superseded in 1769 by another design for a larger but simpler frame, the same width as the table and 9 feet 9 inches (2.9 metres) tall,

182 The drawing-room installed in the Philadelphia Museum of Art. Flanking the niche are two pedestals by Robert Adam from Croome Court. The sofa is part of a suite of furniture originally upholstered in Gobelins tapestry, made *c.*1770 for Sir Lawrence Dundas for the tapestry room at Moor Park, Hertfordshire. Adam was not the designer who remains unknown

surmounted by a crest of half putti in foliage.[56] Not only would the 'Great Glass & Great Table Frame' have made a striking termination to the room, but they were also needed to balance the large alcove. Though a French plate-glass in a gilt frame of the same dimensions as Adam's design was in the room at the time of the 1806 sale, there was no caryatid table; only an 'Oriental granite slab on a gilt frame'.[57]

The most expensive items on the 1767 'Estimate' – 'Gilding in Burnish'd Gold Ceiling & Pilasters (£)1000.00.00' and 'Paintings (£)500.00.00' – were still unexecuted in 1769. At Shelburne's request, Cipriani submitted a bill on 6 February 1771 for 'the five Pinting in the Celing' (i.e. the central roundel and four lunettes), the 'five betwixt the Pilaster' and 'the three not yet Pintea't'. We shall return to the last eight paintings later. On 2 April 1773, Zucchi was paid £320 for the arabesques in the

pilasters and the ornaments in the alcove and ceiling, all of which were painted in numerous sections on sheets of paper and then fixed to the painted plaster.[58] The procedure was much the same as that employed by Adam in 1760 and 1761 in the painted breakfast-room at Kedleston, his first room painted in the 'stile of the Ancients'. In September 1775, after Cipriani's paintings and Zucchi's ornaments had been put up, 'all the stucco work of the Cieling, Cornish, Pillaster, Base and Sur Base, Doors and Window Shutters Alcove &c' were gilded by Joseph Perfetti for just £63.10.0, a fraction of the £1,000 originally estimated for gilding.[59] He also painted the 'stuco, Carving and Joiners Work, in white & Grounded out in different Colours &c', and did the 'Carving and Gilding (of) two additional Pieces for a Glass Frame'.

Though much of the work planned by Adam before he was

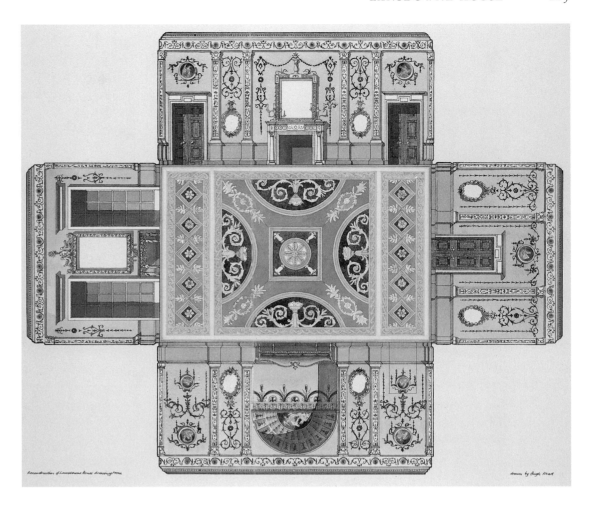

183 A reconstruction of Robert Adam's lost 'Design of a Section of 4 sides of the Drawing Room, coloured in the stile of the Ancients', 1766, also including his design for a 'Carpet for the Drawing Room at Shelburne House', 1769

released in 1771 is known to have been finished by 1776, it is by no means certain that all of it was executed. Had the four sides of the room been 'coloured in the stile of the Ancients' according to his designs? And what about the '6 Oval Glass frames' that were on the 'Estimate' of work to be completed in 1767: were they ever executed, and where were they meant to go? What, for that matter, happened to the '7 Circular frames' that Sefferin Nelson made; where were they put? Adam's coloured 'Section of 4 sides of the Drawing Room' would have answered most of these questions and been a treat to see, but unfortunately it is lost. Nevertheless, from the 'Estimate' of works to be finished, the bills for what was executed and his few designs for furniture, it is possible to reconstruct the room as it was intended to be (pl. 183), which is rather different from the way it has been reconstructed at the Philadelphia Museum of Art (pls 182).[60]

Each of the two long side walls was divided into five bays by painted pilasters. The north wall had the chimney-piece and chimney-glass in the centre and two doors at either end: one leading to the bow-window room, the other to the main staircase. The opposite wall (with a jib door into the dining-room at the east end) was dominated by the organ recess, which was decorated with a colourful lunette in the form of a 'Pavillion' or tent painted by Zucchi and a semicircular painting of the *Toilet of Venus* by Cipriani. The latter was correctly identified by Fiske Kimball as one of the 'five (paintings) betwixt the Pilaster'.[61]

Zucchi described the alcove in 1773 as containing '*le canappé*', and this can be identified with an Adam design dated 1769 for a sofa of exactly the same width (11 feet, or 3.3 metres) as Bute's organ, with a central medallion of the Shelburne centaur (a

motif also incorporated in the decoration of the pilasters), surmounted by an earl's coronet. If it was executed, it was not in the house at the time of the 1806 sale, when the alcove had a gilt cabriole sofa covered with green satin, which may have been similar to the pea-green satin with white spots bespoke by Lady Charlotte Shelburne for the ante-room in 1768.[62]

Before speculating on what might have been intended for the wall above the *canappé*, it is best to remain on firm ground and consider the decoration of the other walls. According to the 'Estimate', the room was to have '6 Oval Glass frames' of fairly elaborate design, to cost £30 each. As it is unlikely that the jib door would have been encumbered with a heavy mirror, they must have been intended to flank the alcove, the chimney-piece and the door to the ante-room.

The '7 Circular frames' made by Nelson were to receive four of Cipriani's five paintings 'betwixt the Pilaster' (the fifth being the semicircular canvas in the alcove) and the 'three not yet Pintea't'. The latter, which were a bit more expensive (£60 for three as opposed to £80 for five paintings) and presumably somewhat larger, must have been destined to go over the three doors. This leaves the two end bays 'betwixt the Pilaster' on the alcove wall as the logical places for the four remaining paintings. Adam's antique-style decoration of Lady Coventry's octagonal dressing-room at Piccadilly in 1765 is a good indication of what he is likely to have produced on a much grander scale at Shelburne House in 1767.

Though mirrored alcoves overlaid with elaborate gilded ornaments are to be found in Adam interiors of this period (e.g. the library/drawing-room at Kenwood, 1767, and the unexecuted

184 'Section of a Room for Sir George Colebrooke', by Robert Adam, *c.*1771 (Sir John Soane's Museum: Adam drawings, vol. 50:54)

185 'Section of the Great Eating Room', by Robert Adam, 1766 (Sir John Soane's Museum: Adam drawings, vol. 39:56)

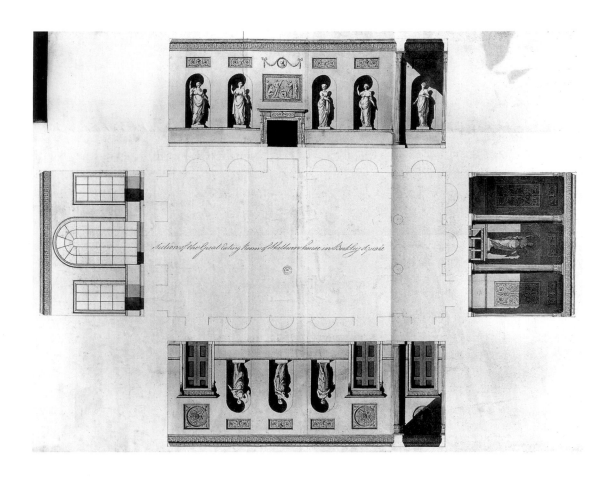

186   The dining-room in the early 1900s showing the statue of Dionysus in the niche behind the screen of columns. The white, semi-circular console table partly visible at the far right is one of a pair designed by Robert Adam in 1768 for the first ante-room or breakfast-room on the first floor

design for a book-room at Kedleston, 1768), neither the 1767 'Estimate' nor the 1806 sale catalogue mentions a mirror here. The absence of one is further confirmed by the 'drapery curtain' on the alcove in 1806.[63] It is reasonable, therefore, to suppose that the alcove wall was intended to be painted in a manner consistent with Zucchi's 'Pavillion' lunette, possibly with swags like those in the sofa-niche designed *c*.1771 for Sir George Colebrooke's house in Arlington Street (pl. 184).[64]

The decoration of the drawing-room was incomplete at the time of Lady Shelburne's death and Adam's departure, and was evidently abandoned. But what was done in its place? It is difficult to imagine anything more at variance with the 'stile of the Ancients', Adam's decorative style, or indeed eighteenth-century custom than the semi-nude walls erected at Philadelphia, now improved by being hung with pictures. Gavin Hamilton, replying in August 1776 to a request from Lord Shelburne for a suitable picture to go over the chimney-piece, wrote 'I take it for granted that the intermediate spaces (between the painted

pilasters) are to be hung with silk, pictures in particular require something of this sort & marbles perhaps doe (*sic*) better with stucco ornaments & a little guilding.'[65] Among Shelburne's papers pertaining to Lansdowne House is an undated 'Calculation of Genoa Damask' for hangings, window curtains, chairs and sofas in the 'Bow Window Room', the 'large Drawing Room', 'Other large Drawing Room' (on the north side), and 'Other bow window Room' (on the first floor).[66] However, there were no hangings at Bowood and Shelburne would have none at Berkeley Square. Apart from being expensive, they would not go with the antique look. Though '2 Curtain Cornices' were included in the 1767 'Estimate', the drawing-room was the only reception room without either paired or festoon curtains when the contents of the house were sold in 1806.

The first marquess's distaste for hangings was not shared by his son, Henry, second Marquess of Lansdowne. In 1826, Karl Friedrich Schinkel described the room as having:

Golden-yellow wall-covering and curtains, the walls hung with pictures, a yellow carpet with simple brown pattern, white pilasters painted with colourful arabesques and pictures, old paintings in gold frames on the golden-yellow wall-coverings. Sumptuous mirror behind the sofa niche, furniture arranged all around in the room, mahogany doors, pleasing arrangement.[67]

The room looked more or less the same when it was photographed in 1910 and still had yellow silk damask hangings (possibly rewoven) when it was purchased by the Philadelphia Museum of Art in 1930. Fiske Kimball, the director of the museum, seems to have known that the fabric fixed on to wooden battens covered with canvas and felt was not of the Adam period, but had the good sense to preserve it until 1949, when it was beyond repair. He then decided to 'paint the surfaces as they evidently were originally before there was any gold damask', and chose 'neutral tan', a colour utterly uncharacteristic of Adam.[68]

The most recent scientific restoration was unable to determine 'whether the canvas-covered wood was used in the first installation (in the early nineteenth century) and only later plastered over and covered with wall cloth (possibly when the damask was removed and the walls repainted about 1949) or whether it was not used at all after it was brought to Philadelphia'.[69] The original wall surfaces and any architectural elements under the wood on which the damask was hung were left in the house. Since the wood battens were destroyed, all the museum now has is 'large undecorated expanses of wall between chair rail and frieze' made of new 'plaster supported by wire-mesh lath'. These vacant expanses have been painted blue-green, following the discovery of flecks of that colour at the edges of several pilasters, which the museum concluded were the result of the walls having been painted after the pilasters. But were these flecks the first or last coat of paint?

Though the bright colour is bound to jar modern viewers who naturally expect and indeed enjoy seeing signs of mellowing in a place of some age, it may not be chromatically incorrect. Adam's unexecuted design for a carpet in 1769 has a similar background colour, with brown, red, yellow, pink and green ornaments.[70] However, instead of the oil- and water-based paints used in the eighteenth century, the restorers opted for long-lasting acrylic latex and gouache, which, applied to the new precision-made walls, gives a thoroughly modern, mechanical appearance to the whole room.

Nothing could be more different from the richly coloured and gilded drawing-room than the monochromatic, dead-white and pearl-colour eating-room lined with statues in niches (pls 185, 186). Yet both are equally 'antique'. Here, as at Syon, striking tonal contrasts were used by Adam to achieve the variety upon which the spirit, beauty and effect of his interiors depended. The 'particular' feature of the dining-room, in his words, was its 'great dimension': 47 feet 2 inches long, 24½ feet wide, and 18 feet high (14.8 metres by 7.4 metres by 5.4 metres). It was the largest single room in Lansdowne House. By introducing a screen of 'Composed Doric' columns with 'antique' capitals derived from Spalatro at the far end of the room,[71] Adam managed not only to reduce the length, diversify the contour and

increase the play of light and shadow, but also to create a special place, a kind of temple or sanctuary for the large sideboard and its attendant vase-shaped coopers on round pedestals. In the circumstances, this suite, made in 1768 by John Linnell 'after Mr Adam's design' and painted 'flake white', became a veritable altar to Dionysus whose giant figure (7 feet 9 inches (2.3 metres) tall) occupied the niche behind it.[72] There were practical advantages too: a convenient jib door in one of the arabesque panels led to a buffet and the back stairs going down to the kitchens; a door to the drawing-room provided a service route from the basement offices to the back stair in the private apartment, which went up to the attics. An amateurish elevational drawing of this end of the dining-room in the Bowood archives is the only surviving visual record of the sideboard composition: Adam's design is lost and the suite was sold in 1806.

Having finished the ante-room with stucco arabesques and paintings of classical subjects, and the drawing-room with a painted ceiling and pilasters 'in the stile of the Ancients', the dining-room, to be different as well as elegant and splendid and impervious to 'the smell of the Victuals', had to be adorned with statues.[73] The dining-room at Syon was a model; but there, where Adam was challenged by a difficult pre-existing space, he was typically more inventive than he was in the new house he designed on Berkeley Square.

Apart from Dionysus, who rules the room, there were eight full-size casts of antique statues: three on the north wall flanked by two doors (one blank, the other to the ante-room); four on the opposite wall on either side of the chimney-piece; and the eighth, separated from the rest, on the south wall of the screened area, facing the door to the drawing-room. (When installed in the Metropolitan Museum, the two side walls were reversed.) The statues were in place in 1768, having been supplied with fig leaves by John Gilbert at a cost of five shillings each.[74] Their niches were not arranged in strict symmetry, but rather in carefully balanced units which coincide with the three-part division of the ceiling.[75] In terms of decoration, the emphasis, as Bolton observed, is on the elaborate stucco ceiling. The tall arabesque panels flanking the end niche and the smaller ones in the upper register of the walls are the only other ornaments in this chill architectural room.[76] Unlike the dining-room at Syon, there was not a glimmer of gold here. Were it not for the dining-room furniture, which included two smaller white-painted sideboard tables made by Linnell (not to Adam's design), three mahogany '2 flapt' dining-tables, and fourteen Chippendale chairs with 'antique' backs, the room might be mistaken for a gallery or hall.[77] Three crimson silk damask drapery curtains on the windows, a 'Turkey carpet 11½ yards by 8 cut to the fireplace' and a painted floor cloth were the sole sources of colour.[78]

Although the dining-room appeared to Lady Shelburne to be 'quite finished except for the glasses, the window curtains & chairs' in August 1768, her husband was more demanding, especially when it came to checking the accounts delivered on 21 April 1769 against the designs, the estimates and the completed work.[79] 'The dining room', he complained, 'remains to be fin-

187 Design for the 'South Side of the Great Stair Case', by Robert Adam, 1766 (Sir John Soane's Museum: Adam drawings, vol. 39:66)

Nº. 4 or South Side of the Great Staircase in Shelburne House Berkely Square

188 The staircase hall in 1921 with a statue of Diana on an Adam pedestal, two bas-reliefs against the back wall and another set into the wall above, continuing the pattern of Adam's panels of stucco ornament

ished according to the first design there being no ornament as yet done in the panel over the chimney'; and the £180 that the carver, John Devall, charged him for the chimney-piece was £30 over the estimate.[80] However, he failed to notice that the ornament on the chimney-piece and door cases had been placed upside-down on the frieze round the wall. This ornament was illustrated in the *Works* and described by Adam as 'new' in contrast to the 'antique' capital; Devall called it 'Gothic'.[81] Adam's 'Section of the Great Eating Room' shows what looks like a bas-relief in the panel over the chimney-piece. Bolton's photograph of the room in 1921 shows the space empty; it is now appropriately filled in the Metropolitan installation by the *trompe l'oeil* relief of a Roman sacrifice made for the overmantel in the gallery at Croome Court.[82]

Very little is known about the lighting of Lansdowne House. But if the dining-room is anything to go by, it must have been almost as brilliant as Northumberland House. In 1806 there were two '6 light cut-glass lustres, ornamented with drops, brass chain &c.', probably placed in the screened area, and three pairs of '3 light cut-glass lustres ornamented with drops' – one pair must have stood on the chimney-piece and the other two on Linnell's sideboards.[83] The pearl and white stucco walls would have reflected more light than any of the other rooms.

The dining-room completed the circuit of grand reception rooms, the *appartement de parade*. The remaining ground-floor rooms (the bow-window room and third drawing-room on the

west front and the ante-room and bedroom on the east) were Lord Shelburne's domain and presumably were intended to be addressed by Adam after Lady Shelburne's rooms and the library on the first floor were finished. However, by that time, Adam was gone.

Like the rest of Lansdowne House, the grand, top-lit staircase (pls 187, 188) became a repository for busts, bas-reliefs and other pieces of sculpture introduced by Shelburne in preference to the classical ruinscapes proposed by Adam in 1766 to show off his new Italian painter, Antonio Zucchi, whom he had just brought to England.[84]

Chimney-pieces were designed for all the upper rooms, but only the library at the south end and Lady Shelburne's bedroom in the north-east corner above Lord Shelburne's room merited Adam ceilings.[85] Having a large library (pl. 189) on the first floor was most likely Bute's idea and may explain the exceptionally great dimensions of the dining-room immediately below it. The ceiling here was coved and boldly decorated with three large interlaced circles which are quite restrained, almost static compared to the circular pattern designed in the same year for the saloon at Nostell.[86] All the walls, except for the window side, were lined with breakfront bookcases articulated by ornamented pilasters carved by Sefferin Nelson, the bookcase in the north-west corner being formed as a jib door to the back stairs.[87] Alternating with the usual busts were stucco medallions set into the walls and bas-reliefs (presumably of plaster) over the two doors. It was evidently intended to set another relief in a panel over the chimney-piece, but Shelburne changed his mind and the panel was removed to make way for a picture.[88] An architectural effect was intended here just as it was in the exactly contemporary library at Osterley. Everything was painted dead white and stone-colour.[89]

Next to the library was the 'second Ante Room', corresponding to the apsidal state ante-room below and preceded by a smaller first ante-room (also known as the breakfast-room) in the centre over the entrance hall. Chimney-pieces and wall furniture were Adam's only contribution to these rooms. In March 1770 he designed a pair of 'Cabinets for the Room over the Anti Room' (pl. 190), each 10 feet 9 inches (3.2 metres) wide and 9 feet (2.7 metres) high, flanking a central door.[90] These imposing cases, raised on stands with tapering fluted legs, were evidently intended to display Shelburne's large collection of Chinese and Japanese porcelain behind arched openings protected by wire-mesh, ornamented with figured medallions and swags of husks, and framed by Ionic pilasters which answered those used elsewhere in the room.[91] The only wall long enough to accommodate both cases was the curved apse, which had a central door leading to Lord Shelburne's dressing-room (or study) over the drawing-room. This was one of the last designs Adam made for Lord Shelburne before he left, and there is no record of its being executed.

A pair of semicircular console tables with aprons of pendant anthemia and baluster legs with lotus capitals of the type used on the Osterley sideboard in 1767 was executed for the first ante-room, though its design, dated 1768, is inscribed for the '2d Anti Room 1 pair at Shelburne House'.[92] There was no obvious place in the apsidal room for two tables with accompanying mirrors, but in the first ante-room (or breakfast-room) they could have

189 Design for the chimney-side of the first-floor library, detail, by Robert Adam, 1767 (Sir John Soane's Museum: Adam drawings, vol. 39:57)

190 'Design for Cabinets for the Room over the Anti Room', intended for the large collection of Chinese and Japanese porcelain, by Robert Adam, 1770 (Sir John Soane's Museum: Adam drawings, vol. 17:216)

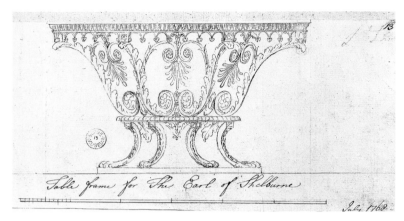

191 Design for a table frame, by Robert Adam, 1768 (Sir John Soane's Museum: Adam drawings, vol. 17:113)

ror frame of interlaced branches terminating in a tall palm crest which seems to have been executed by Mr Royle; and an extraordinary Piranesian table frame of scrolled branches of foliage and anthemia, raised on concave legs with paw feet (pl. 191).[95] The table may have been inspired by an antique bronze and intended to be executed in metal. Whether it was executed at all is not known, nor do we know whether these pieces were designed for the apsidal ante-room or the ante-room (also called the second ante-room) to Lady Shelburne's bedroom on the north side of the house.

The three upper rooms on the west front – Lord Shelburne's dressing-room, Lady Shelburne's bow-windowed picture room and her dressing-room – had no Adam decorations.

In 1771 Gavin Hamilton made a design for the bow-window room (also known as the second drawing-room or breakfast-parlour) on the ground floor, and it may have been on the basis of this that it was formed into a rotunda with two niches and a shallow dome.[96] A sky was painted on the dome by Cipriani and Giovanni Borgnis in 1776; the walls were painted straw-colour; there was a bronze copy of the *Three Graces* in the Villa Borghese; and statues of Narcissus and Paris were moved here from the ante-room and placed on pedestals.[97] Adam intended the bow-window room to command a wide view of a Roman courtyard with an imposing screened exedra opposite and a curved wall lined with niches to the left. Smirke built the exedra in a simplified form, but the wall of niches came to nothing.

The third drawing-room, corresponding in size and shape to the first drawing-room, was painted with 'Party Colours on (the) Ceiling', blue on the walls and dead white on the cornice with ornaments picked out in blue and gold.[98] Under the direction of Gavin Hamilton, the 'Blue Room' became the 'Statuary Room': the repository of seventeen or more antique sculptures and

stood in the piers between the three windows. It was from that centre room that they were sold in 1806. One table was bought back by the family (it can be seen on the far right of the photograph of the dining-room taken in the early 1900s, pl. 186) and is now at Bowood, the other is untraced. Sold with them was a pair of 'excellent French plate(s) of glass 82 inches by 48 inches in . . . gilt frame(s)', about which nothing more is known.[93] Their proportions are quite different from Adam's mirror design which had a glass 5 feet by 3 feet 3 inches (1.5 metres by 1.1 metres) in a frame with a broad pierced border, sphinxes at the base, and a tall crest of scrolled foliage centring a medallion with a putti finial.[94]

Adam's account includes only two other designs for furniture for the first floor: a mirror and a table frame for an ante-room. They can be identified with designs at the Soane for an oval mir-

192 Section of the great library, by Robert Adam, *c.*1764 (Sir John Soane's Museum: Adam drawings, vol. 39:61)

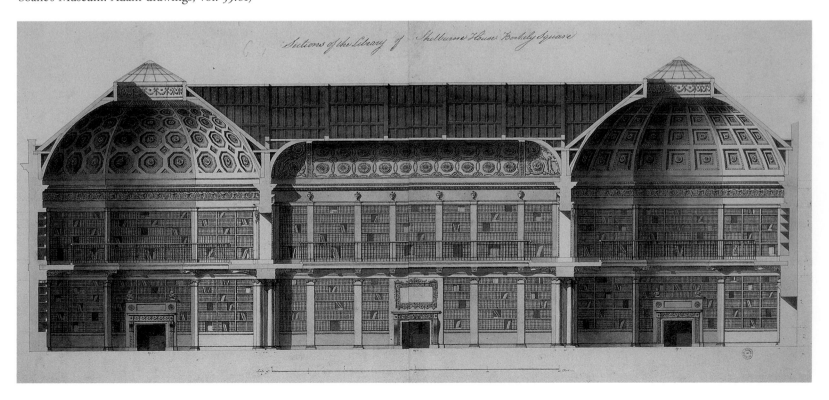

numerous urns and vases. A 'Memorandum by Lord Shelburne on his collection of Sculpture', probably drawn up in February 1777, lists more than twenty figures, busts, urns and vases in the 'Blue Room': several he had acquired from Adam and now considered indifferent. Over the chimney-piece was a bas-relief designed by Clérisseau, which he thought 'much too slight for the room as now fitted up, and particularly for the Basso Relievo above'. An 'idea of Cipriani's' was sent 'for M^r H(amilton)'s consideration and advice – to be afterward executed in Rome if a good design can be had and (any) fragments (can be found) to compose it.'[99]

The third, or blue, drawing-room was the principal entrance into the great library (or gallery, as it turned out) extending westwards on the northern perimeter of the garden and rising the full height of the house. The library extension first appeared in this position in about 1762 or 1763 in two of Adam's preliminary schemes for Bute House.[100] By 1764 it had been transformed into three interconnecting rooms: a central coved oblong space flanked by two domed octagonal ones, reminiscent of the sculpture gallery and tribunes at Holkham. While Bute was conferring with Adam over the library that was to be the crowning glory of his London palace, he was also involved with Sir William Chambers on George III's library at Buckingham House, which owes the inspiration for its famous octagonal library to Adam's design for Bute House.[101]

Adam's splendid set of wall elevations (pl. 192) was cherished by Bute and copies were made (presumably at his expense) for Shelburne.[102] These show the two-storey rooms with galleries all round, completely lined with books: even on the window piers in the main room and above and alongside the chimney-pieces in the octagons. Everything was done to achieve the 'rise and fall, the advance and recess, with other diversity of form . . . so as to add greatly to the picturesque of the composition'.[103] One

entered from a dark recess into the top-lit domed octagon. On the opposite wall, in another recess, was a chimney-piece with a bas-relief set into its high lintel. Proceeding under a columnar screen at the west end (the east end connected with the private apartment of Lord Bute and later Lord Shelburne), one emerged into the large main room which, though better lit by six windows on the ground floor and gallery, had a lower coved ceiling decorated with Palmyrene interlaced circles.[104] Behind the columnar screen at the end of this room was the door to the second octagonal room, just like the first but with a different coffering pattern and chimney-piece, and a concealed door to a circular stair.

Nothing had been done to the empty shell when the widowed earl went to Italy to drown his sorrows in the study and acquisition of antiquities. There he was encouraged by Gavin Hamilton to abandon the idea of a library and use the space instead for a great sculpture gallery 'that would make Shelburne House famous not only in England but all over Europe'.[105] After ambitious designs based on the Farnese Gallery had been prepared by Francesco Pannini, Shelburne decided not to have a gallery, but a library to house his newly acquired collection of important manuscripts. The designs made in 1774 by Clérisseau for a large subdivided room had none of the 'movement' and 'picturesque effects' of Adam's scheme, though in any case Shelburne changed his mind again and commissioned designs for a gallery from François Belanger in 1779. In 1786 he settled at last on a library and had designs made by Joseph Bonomi, an architect trained in the Adam office. These were superseded in 1792 by another library scheme by George Dance, which was unexecuted when the first Marquess died in 1805. Finally, in 1819, after the collection of books had been sold, Dance's designs were revised by Robert Smirke as a gallery for the third Marquess of Lansdowne.

193   The north front of Harewood House

9

HAREWOOD HOUSE

Adam's attempt, in June 1758, to 'dazzle the Eyes' of the wealthy Yorkshire squire, Edwin Lascelles, with a 'tickled up' version of John Carr's Palladian designs for his new £30,000 house at Gawthorpe, or Harewood (pl. 193) as it came to be called, was not the instant success he had hoped for.[1] He had to wait a full seven years – until 1765, when the house was finished – before he was commissioned to design its interiors. By then he was a rising star, employed at Syon, Croome Court, Bowood, Lansdowne House, Kedleston and Kenwood.

Though Lascelles was willing to consider Adam – fresh from his Italian studies – on the recommendation of Lady Lindores, he was too cautious with his Barbadian fortune and too uncertain of himself as a builder to risk employing a Scottish innovator with little practical experience when he already had Carr, a perfectly reliable local architect and third-generation stone mason, in his employ.[2]

There had also been other contenders. The first, in 1755, was William Jones, architect of the Rotunda at Ranelagh Gardens (1742) and Surveyor to the East India Company (1754), of which Lascelles's father was a former director. He was regarded by Carr as a serious competitor and his design might have been executed had he not died in 1757.[3] Early in 1756, William Chambers submitted an advanced neo-classical scheme and two general plans were subsequently made by 'Capability' Brown. Chambers's drawings are the only ones prior to Adam's that survive.[4]

Adam was more fortunate than his predecessors in having a few of his suggestions incorporated in the already approved scheme. Though the 'well advanced' designs by Carr that he saw in June 1758 do not survive, their general appearance can be deduced from his account of his alterations to them. Carr's plan was for an extended villa comparable to Campbell's Wanstead III or Ware's Wrotham, consisting of a two-storey main block over a rusticated basement, with a hall and saloon on the central axis and two rooms separated by staircases on each side, flanked on both fronts by low wings linked to slightly taller, single-bay pavilions enclosing open courts. There is no knowing what shapes Carr's rooms were, but his façades were evidently fairly plain, with pedimented centres and an applied portico on the south or garden front.

According to Adam,

the plan did not admit of a great many (alterations, and) that has prevented the fronts from being much Changed likewise: The portico I made projecting, & bold dressings round the windows, the pavilion fronts are quite different & the Collonades (on the links) also & look well; Statues, etc. adorn the whole, an enriched frieze, & being done to a large Scale, it is magnificent . . . I have thrown in Large Semi-circular Back Courts with columns betwixt the House & Wings.[5]

There are plans (pl. 194) and elevations answering this description at the Soane Museum which show other features that can be credited to Adam: a large Venetian window in the centre of the west front directly opposite the entrance to the 'Great Gallery'; square recesses with Venetian windows and columnar screens at either end of the gallery, flanked by small oval and rectangular closets

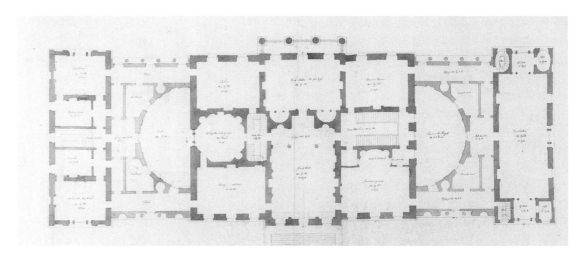

194   Plan of the principal floor (i.e. the ground floor) of Harewood House, by Robert Adam, 1758 (Sir John Soane's Museum: Adam drawings, vol. 35:8)

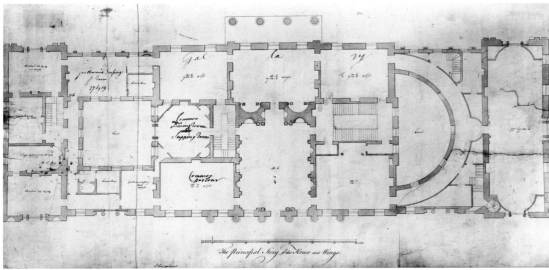

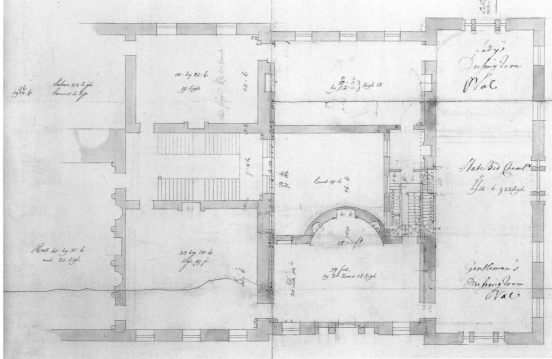

195   John Carr, revised plan of the ground floor of Harewood House, *c.*1759 (Present whereabouts unknown)

196   Revised ground floor plan of the west side Harewood House, by Robert Adam, 1762 (The Earl of Harewood)

197   Ground floor plan of Harewood House as executed (*Vitruvius Britannicus*, v (1771), pl. 24)

and stairs; a large semicircular sideboard niche in the dining-room: and a columnar screen across the hall, creating a 'passage' at the south end.[6] The idea of a circular or octagonal room in lieu of a symmetrical staircase on the left side of the hall is quite likely to have been his, and knowing his penchant for antique shapes it is tempting to attribute the two screened apses in the saloon to him as well.[7] In his own mind, 'Lascelles's plans & fronts' were more his than Carr's and he included them in the list of works that he contemplated publishing in July 1760.[8] This, however, is largely speculative: Adam's contribution cannot be proven and Carr still has to be considered, with the influence of Burlington's York Assembly Rooms and *Fabbriche antiche* in mind.

As presumptuous as Adam was in expecting Lascelles's immediate approval for his proposals, he had good reason to be annoyed at being kept waiting for over two months without any response whatsoever. Seething with indignation, he wrote to James on 5 September, 'While Lascelles is silent I shall be so But Lady Lindores & all the people there think him prodigiously to blame I have enough ado to keep them in Temper they are in such a passion For as they say if the Man likes it, It is very Cruel

not to say so, & if he does not why wou'd he keep one in Suspence or propose his Alterations, or a new Plan'.[9] Little did he know that his drawings, like those of all the other competitors, had first to be shown to Lord Leicester for his advice and then to Carr for estimates before Lascelles could make any decision. His semicircular courts must also have contributed to the delay. Their novelty, which was evidently quite appealing, had to be weighed against the extravagance of the additional cost of building curved walls and the impractical loss of accommodation. The answer was a compromise which underlined the distinction between the private and public apartments on the east and west sides of the house respectively.

While Carr's conventional square court (pl. 195) was to be retained for the private apartments, visitors parading the state apartment were to be treated to the *coup de théâtre* of a large semicircular court – comparable to an antique amphitheatre – ringed by the curved corridors that Adam had initially planned only for the ground floor. Evidently Lascelles also decided that the dining-room was to have a plain rectangular sideboard-recess screened by two columns rather than the semicircular one pro-

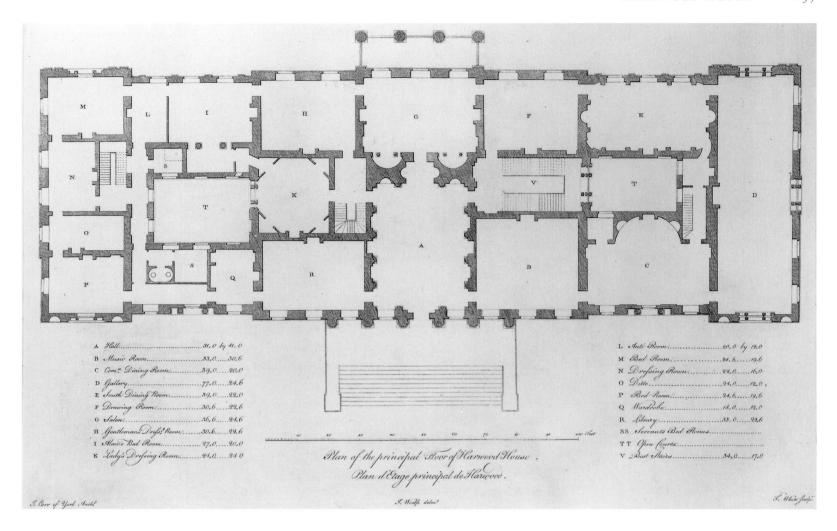

A	*Hall*	31.0 by 41.0
B	*Music Room*	33.0....30.6
C	*Com: Dining Room*	39.0....20.0
D	*Gallery*	77.0....24.6
E	*South Dining Room*	39.0....22.0
F	*Drawing Room*	30.6....22.6
G	*Salon*	36.6....24.6
H	*Gentleman's Dress. Room*	30.6....22.6
I	*Above Bed Room*	27.0....20.0
K	*Lady's Dressing Room*	24.0....24.0

L	*Anti Room*	20.0 by 12.0
M	*Bed Room*	24.6....19.6
N	*Dressing Room*	22.0....16.0
O	*Ditto*	24.0....12.0
P	*Bed Room*	24.6....19.6
Q	*Wardrobe*	18.0....12.0
R	*Library*	33.0....22.6
SS	*Servants Bed Rooms*	
TT	*Open Courts*	
V	*Best Stairs*	34.0....17.0

Plan of the principal Floor of Harewood House.
Plan d'Etage principal de Harewood.

J. Carr of York Archt.

J. Woolfe delint.

J. White Sculpt.

posed by Adam; the gallery was to have semicircular ends, with simple arched windows instead of Venetian ones, though the latter were to be expressed on the façades; a hexastyle portico was to be applied to the main front; and there were minor alterations to Adam's colonnades and pavilions.

Revised plans were requested from both architects. The three that survive are all undated and different: one is signed by Carr and the other two are attributable to Adam.[10] Carr's plan is singular in naming the rooms and especially in allocating the entire south front of the main block to a three-room gallery apartment, leaving the use of the west pavilion undetermined. The octagonal room was to be a 'Common Dining room or Supping Room' entered from one of the gallery rooms, with an additional door to the gentleman's dressing-room on the north front.

Bolton published an 'Intermediate Plan' which he saw at Carr's old office at York and 'believed to be by Adam in 1759'.[11] This differs from Carr's plan in having an imperial staircase, no columns at all in the hall and saloon, a ring of columns forming a circular vestibule to the gallery on the west front and a screen of columns at the north end of the gallery. The circular room east of the hall, which Adam initially conceived as a dressing-room for Mr Lascelles, linked to his library, was now a lady's dressing-room also open to the parlour on the south front.

The third plan has an octagonal room in place of the circular dressing-room, which is inscribed in a different hand 'Q Billiard room or Chappell' and does not open directly into the library but rather into an interconnecting wardrobe. In relation to this plan, and possibly in response to Carr's idea of placing the gallery on the south front, Adam supplied Lascelles with a 'Plan of a Chapel & Window' to occupy the west pavilion.[12]

There was no immediate urgency to decide upon these internal variations. The overall plan was clear enough for the foundations to be laid in March 1759 under the direction of Carr as architect. In April, Adam was asked to provide the church with 'a finishing to the top of the Steeple in the Gothick taste', but apart from that his services were no longer required.[13] Lascelles had no need to retain him as a consultant and is unlikely at this early stage to have made any firm commitments regarding the interiors.

Three years later, there was an unexpected crisis. In May 1762, when the building was quite well advanced, a fault was found which necessitated the demolition of the curved walls of Adam's court. The wall of the main body of the house was unaffected and somehow had to be incorporated into a new court (pl. 196). Adam was bound to be consulted and it was most likely he who suggested reproducing the remaining east wall on the west side and joining the two on the south by another straight wall and on the north by a projecting bow belonging to a room quite like the dining-room he had planned in 1758.[14]

The bow was a bone of contention. Carr objected to it and wanted it left out, but was overruled by Sir Thomas Robinson of Rokeby, who replaced Lord Leicester after his death in 1759 as Lascelles's guru. Evidently Robinson sent Lascelles a plan of the alterations and wrote him a letter in which 'he fully answers Carr's objections, and explains his own Sentiments & ammendments', which Lascelles saw 'no reason to vary from'.[15] His argument in favour smacks very much of Adam: the bow, he wrote, 'certainly makes a great alteration in the Elegance & variety of the Rooms Otherways the 2 Rooms resemble each other'.[16] In the event, another compromise was effected (pl. 197). The bow remained, but was walled in, and the problem of the three exist-

ing windows on the east side was solved by eliminating one of them and combining the other two in a large Venetian window, lighting the principal staircase.

These alterations resulted in the creation of an unusually long parade of state rooms which Adam was keen to divide into two alternative suites on the north and south fronts, each consisting of a drawing-room (or ante-room, as the music-room was called) and a dining-room opening to the gallery, which instead of being set to one side was now an integral part of the state apartment.[17] To balance the plan, adjustments were also made to the private apartment: its court was reduced and a state bedroom (roughly corresponding to the new south-west dining-room) was created on the south-east, *en suite* with an ante-room and a state dressing-room.

In February 1765 the house was roofed and a 'rearing' party was held to mark the occasion. Lascelles was then fifty-two years old and a childless widower – his wife having died the previous August – but that did not prevent him from keeping apace if not one step ahead of his building programme. In June, before Carr even had time to order the plastering to begin, his thoughts were already on the decoration of the interiors. On 12 June he had his steward, Samuel Popplewell, send a plan down to London of the principal floor as it stood after all amendments, which he promptly showed to Adam.[18] Popplewell's letter of 22 June, promising to send plans of the music-room and dining-room to clarify what 'Mr Adams (had) misapprehended' in the measurements, provides a precise date for the beginning of Adam's involvement with the interiors of Harewood. Having put that in motion, Lascelles set off on 13 July for a month in Paris.[19]

By the end of the year, Adam had made ceiling designs and laid out wall elevations for all the reception rooms. Drawings for most of the chimney-pieces and the remaining ceilings followed

198 Plan and laid-out wall elevations of the hall, by Robert Adam, *c.*1766 (Sir John Soane's Museum: Adam drawings, vol. 35:13)

199 View of the hall in 1914

in 1766 and 1767, and by 1771 his task was completed, except for the gallery chimney-piece, which was delayed until 1777. The decoration of a total of seventeen rooms on the ground floor makes Harewood Adam's biggest job. It also makes the complete absence of furniture from his brief all the more surprising, if not unique. There is no other major Adam house in which this was the case. The commission went exclusively to Chippendale, whose firm is reckoned to have been paid over £10,000 between 1767 and 1777 and continued supplying pieces until Lascelles's death in 1795.[20] Though much of their furniture is in the Adam style, none of it is integrated with Adam's decoration.

Lascelles's approach to building was quite rigid and businesslike, perhaps another sign of his lack of self-confidence in such matters. His negotiations with Adam (unlike those with Carr, Chippendale and other craftsmen) did not go through his steward, Popplewell, but were evidently conducted directly in

London. This may account for the absence of Adam correspondence and bills in the Harewood archives, but the absence of any recorded payments from Lascelles to Adam's account in Drummond's bank is inexplicable.

Fortunately, there is a complete set of designs for the interiors at the Soane Museum, supplemented by plans and archival material belonging to the Earl of Harewood, most of which are deposited in the West Yorkshire Archives in Leeds. Even so, Adam's achievement is difficult to appreciate. The house was extensively remodelled by Sir Charles Barry in the 1840s, spruced-up and Adamized in 1929 by Sir Herbert Baker for the Princess Royal, and partially redecorated and restored by her son, the present Earl of Harewood. Chimney-pieces have been moved or replaced, furniture sold and pictures acquired. It is not only the decoration of the rooms that has changed, but also their uses and their names. The old library and music-room are the

200 Plan and laid-out wall elevations of the saloon, by Robert Adam, *c.*1767 (Sir John Soane's Museum: Adam drawings, vol. 35:14)

only relatively unadulterated Adam rooms left. The rest can only properly be judged from his designs.

The plan published by Carr in *Vitruvius Britannicus* in 1771 suggests a counter-clockwise circuit of the state apartment, starting with the music-room, and this was followed by eighteenth-century tourists.[21] However, the logical route, which was the original one before the amendments of 1762 and the one taken here, is clockwise, going from the hall into the saloon, through the first and second drawing-rooms to the gallery and returning via the music-room.

The hall as planned by Carr was a large rectangular space (41 × 31 feet; 12.4 × 9.4 metres) lined with engaged columns and semicircular niches for statues.[22] Wentworth Woodhouse, the Yorkshire seat of the second Marquess of Rockingham, Lascelles's political supporter, where Carr was employed from about 1760, is the likely model. Adam, determined to alter Carr's plan in any way he could and no doubt eager to make as bold a mark on the entrance hall as he did on the portico, proposed various schemes to enliven the space and give it variety and 'movement' in the spirit of the ancients. His first plan (*c.*1758) introduced a columnar screen cutting off about a quarter of the space and forming a 'passage' between the private and state apartments at the far end, which was articulated with pilasters, as distinct from the main body of the hall which had only two engaged columns flanking each of the two chimney-pieces; a screened hall of similar plan was executed in the 1760s at Lansdowne House. (See pl. 171)

Another proposal was to create a basilica-like hall with a large apse screened by columns (pl. 198).[23] Both schemes were rejected. His alternative was to 'tickle up' the wall elevations by enlarging the profile of the engaged columns from half to three-quarters and replacing the semicircular niches on the sides by more unusual square recesses fitted with unorthodox pedestals that projected from the dado into the central space. The diversity of round and square projections and recessions was intended to produce a lively play of light and shadow, giving an additional picturesque to the scene, as Adam would say. In addition, he carefully arranged the various elements in such a way as to give the long walls a focal centrepiece suggestive of a triumphal arch, with four engaged Doric columns, a chimney-piece surmounted by a tall overmantel in the middle and two square recesses of exactly the same height on either side. There were to be two lesser units at each end containing doors with circular reliefs above them. This three-part subdivision was also applied to the ceiling design.[24]

Lascelles, having received Adam's designs for finishing the hall and staircase, wrote to him on 19 November 1766 to say that he approved of both, but wanted to be informed of the cost of executing them, adding, 'I woud (*sic*) not exceed the limits of expence that I always propose to myself. Let us do every thing properly & well, mais pas trop'.[25] Diversity does not come cheap. The estimate evidently did exceed Lascelles's limits and as a result the lively design was watered down to a bland composi-

201 The ceiling of the saloon, designed by Robert Adam 1767

tion of columns of lesser projection (pl. 199); smaller oblong stucco reliefs by William Collins, depicting *Mars tamed by Peace* and the *Triumph of Neptune* above the chimney-pieces; and six large trophy medallions (also by Collins) punctuating the upper register in tandem with long panels of rinceaux, like dots and dashes.

What the original colour scheme was is not known; probably stony-white, like the hall at Syon.[26] By 1819 the room had been audaciously redecorated in the 'Egyptian Style': the walls were painted to resemble Siena marble (grey or ochre?), the six statues – Euterpe and Bacchante on the side of the music-room and dining-room, Night and Minerva on the side of the library and bedrooms (where Peace tamed Mars), and Iris and Flora in the semicircular niches on the south wall towards the garden – were bronzed and, to add to the antique atmosphere, there were Grecian stools and chairs, eight Chippendale armchairs painted with the family crest and an 'exceedingly large' gilt brass lantern with eight winged cupids by Chippendale, under which was a large slab of dove marble on a Grecian frame.[27] Some of this furniture is still in the hall; others pieces are elsewhere in the house.

Since 1819 there have been more drastic alterations: one of the chimney-pieces has been removed, likewise the dado rail; Barry replaced the square recesses with rounded niches lowered to the floor and filled with busts instead of standing statues. What remained of Adam's scheme was further vitiated in the 1960s when the columns, capitals and bases, and even the frieze, were painted in imitation brown marble, the walls light blue and the ceiling pink and terracotta. A more sensitive and intelligent restoration is hoped for the future.

As designed by Adam, the entrance from the hall into the saloon through a low passage with niches each side would have been a varied and interesting spatial experience. However, its position in the centre of the long wall of the saloon made for an awkward division of the space, demanding duplicate chimney-pieces on each side, but prohibiting an immediate view of the two apses screened by Corinthian columns that flank the pedimented door (pl. 200). These important features can only properly be seen from the south side, which suggests a possible correlation with the portico added by Adam.

Reconciling the height of the saloon (22 feet or 6.7 metres,

202 One of the two tabernacle chimney-pieces in the saloon, designed by Robert Adam, 1768. The lower part is of statuary marble carved by John Devall; the upper part of wood and plaster attributed to William Collins

203 Pietro Santi Bartoli, engraving of an antique Roman vaulted ceiling (*Gli antichi sepolchri, ovvero mausolei Romani, ed Etruschi trovati in Roma* (1697), pl. XVI)

compared to 20 feet or 6 metres in the hall and 19 feet or 5.7 metres in the adjacent rooms) with the size of the windows posed an even more difficult problem. Adam's solution was to lower the cornice and the height of the walls by introducing a deep cove, and to divide the flat of the ceiling into three compartments corresponding to the principal entrance and two apses (pl. 201).[28]

Two-storey tabernacle chimney-pieces (pl. 202) were a matter of efficacy here and not, as has been suggested, a residue of Palladian taste.[29] The spaces might have been filled with large overmantel pictures had Lascelles been a collector or a younger man with time to commission canvases of the required size, but he was not; and swagger mirrors virtually the same height as the doorcases in elaborate gold frames would have been out of place in this prelude to the highly ornate drawing-room. The chimney-pieces designed in 1768 are reminiscent of the one made six years earlier for the dining-room at Syon. Their lower parts of white marble with griffon tablets and urn and palmette friezes, like those over the doors, were supplied by John Devall in

September 1769.[30] The architectural overmantels of painted wood and plaster contain circular stucco reliefs of sacrifices which are attributed to William Collins.[31] These were formerly bronzed and would then have been comparable to the framed medallion above the chimney-piece in the ante-room at Syon. Whether this was Adam's intention is not known.

Each chimney-piece was originally flanked by two doors, over which hung views of Harewood Castle, Aysgarth, Knaresborough and Richmond (all family properties) painted by Nicholas Dall before his death in 1776. At a later date the two false doors (nearest the apses) were removed to make way for additional paintings and the entire north wall was fitted by Barry with bookcases. These not only conform to the curve of the apses, but also preserve Adam's decoration of the semi-domes. Though the colour of the decoration is not recorded, it presumably included sufficient green to prompt Chippendale's green and gold furniture. When Joseph Farington visited Harewood in August 1801, the saloon was a 'sitting room for Ladies'.[32]

204 Design for the ceiling of the first drawing-room (now the Yellow Drawing Room), by Robert Adam, 1768 (Sir John Soane's Museum: Adam drawings, vol. 11:161)

Initially, the room to the right of the saloon (now the Yellow Drawing Room, previously the Rose Drawing Room) was the only drawing-room in the state apartment and was decorated with appropriate richness. Wall elevations do not survive, but were presumably supplied in 1765 along with the first ceiling design.[33] The latter – an unusual composition of concentric rings of circles of decreasing size, like a two-dimensional coffered dome – was cast aside in 1768 for a new, star-shaped design (pl. 204) with a central rosette inspired by an engraving of an ancient Roman vaulted ceiling in the latest edition of Bartoli's *Antichi Sepolchri* published that year (pl. 203).[34] Adam must also have been familiar with Chambers's adaptation of the vault (from an earlier edition of Bartoli) for the flat ceiling of the Alhambra included in his book on *Kew* in 1763. There are several drawings for the Harewood ceiling, ranging from a rough sketch to the definitive design on which the colours are not only painted but also spelled out: lilac, purple, yellow, light and dark green.[35] The corresponding Axminster carpet has a straw-coloured ground

and rose, green and blue ornaments (pl. 205). When Bolton saw it in 1914, it had 'barely survived' seventy years' use of the room for billiards and smoking; it has since been repaired.[36]

Adam made five designs for the chimney-piece between 1770 and 1771, before one, with ram's-head consoles and a frieze containing three circular medallions of putti alternating with candelabra, was executed. Nollekens's name is inscribed on the first version of this design, but does not appear in the accounts. The chimney-piece was put up in August 1773 by Henry Gill, Devall's man, which suggests that Devall may have been responsible for it.[37]

The first chimney-piece design was an exact replication of the doorcases. They had friezes with cameos of putti riding seahorses (also repeated on the wall frieze) and pilasters with unconventional capitals and enriched panels of three-quarter patera and diamonds. These elaborate, pilastered surrounds, which do not survive, were quite similar to those in the saloon at Saltram, designed a year or two earlier. Originally, there were four doors:

205 View of the Yellow Drawing Room showing part of the star ceiling and the corresponding Axminster carpet. The chimney-glass by Thomas Chippendale, c.1779 was originally in the second (white) drawing-room or the gallery (Reproduced by kind permission of the Earl and Countess of Harewood and Trustees of the Harewood House Trust)

206 First design (unexecuted) for the ceiling of the second drawing-room (now the Cinnamon Drawing Room), by Robert Adam, 1765 (Sir John Soane's Museum: Adam drawings, vol. 11:165)

207 Plan and laid-out wall elevations of the second drawing-room (now the Cinnamon Drawing Room), by Robert Adam, c.1767 (Sir John Soane's Museum: Adam drawings, vol. 35:11)

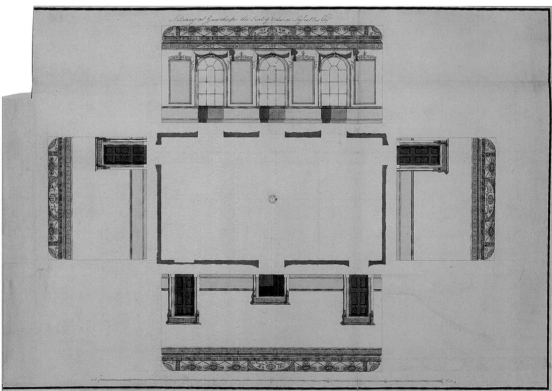

one at either end and, flanking the chimney-piece, a door opening to the staircase on the right and a false door on the left.

In October 1776 the walls and windows were hung with Lascelles's own yellow silk damask and the room was ready to receive Chippendale's matching suite of yellow and silver furniture: a pier-glass, chimney-glass and a pair of mirrored girandoles all 'highly finished in Burnished Silver'.[38] An anonymous tourist entering the 'lesser' drawing-room from the second or 'great' drawing-room at the end of his counterclockwise tour of the state apartment in 1787 found himself utterly surfeited: 'here, as if fancy and art had exhausted all their choice treasures, are exhibited colours and mixtures the most odd and disagreeable.'[39] Like it or not, the effect was certainly distinctive, which is no longer the case with only two of the four doors remaining and those incompletely decorated, the mirrors gilded and the rare silvered furniture dispersed elsewhere.

Even less of Adam's decoration survives in the second drawing-room (now the Cinnamon Drawing Room). This, as already noted, was formed by necessity in 1762 out of the corridor between the drawing-room and the gallery. Its proportions, as a result, are not ideal. To begin with, it was designated as the 'South Dining Room' and with that in mind Adam supplied two alternative ceiling designs in 1765: one divided into three units conforming to the treatment of the walls, the other a delicate refinement of his design for the din-

208 Design for the ceiling of the second drawing-room (now the Cinnamon Drawing Room) as executed, by Robert Adam, 1767 (Sir John Soane's Museum: Adam drawings, vol. 11:167)

ing-room ceilings at Shardeloes (1761) and Osterley (c.1763–4) (pl. 206), and both appropriately ornamented with wreaths of grapevines.[40]

His wall elevations are missing, but were evidently used by Carr for the final plan that was given to Woolfe and Gandon before 1769 for publication in the second volume of their *Vitruvius Britannicus* in 1771. This shows the room articulated with twelve pilasters, two apses on the end walls and four concave corners fitted with curved doors – an arrangement enabling Adam not only to improve the balance between length and width and bring the room together, but also to invest it with a lively diversity of shapes and contours.

When the north dining-room was finished in 1769, Lascelles decided not to proceed with the south dining-room. The door to the west stairs going down to the basement kitchen was walled up and Adam was requested to supply a new ceiling design and wall elevations for a 'great drawing room' (pls 207, 208).[41] Wanting greater splendour and variety, he sacrificed a little height and introduced a shallow cove. This was to be decorated with the same quatrefoil pattern of palmettes in heart-shaped frames (a motif also used on the friezes) as he used on the flat part of the ceiling, with the addition of lunettes containing classical ornaments in the centre of each side. The grounds were very pale pink in the frieze, white in the lunettes, with a hint of yellow in the ceiling; the ornaments were picked out in parti-

colours. Pink was the unifying colour, repeated on all the friezes and the dado; the skirting was green.[42]

Nothing is known about the marble chimney-piece supplied by Christopher Theakstone in September 1770.[43] It was replaced by the present 'French Chimney Piece with statuary ornaments and Green Ground' made by Thomas Atkinson of York in 1785.[44] In the following year Chippendale finished the room with white silk damask hangings bordered in gold and 'seven elegant glasses ornamented with festoons, particularly light and beautiful, also tables with the same', creating an effect 'as handsome as designs and gilding can make it'.[45] Adam's limited contribution was further reduced in 1852 by Alfred Stevens's redecoration of the cove and the central panel of the ceiling.

The gallery, though required for symmetry, was just as superfluous to Lascelles's needs as the second drawing-room and subject to even more vacillation. Regardless of whether the room was to be a 'great gallery', as it was called on Adam's first plan in 1758, or a chapel, as proposed in 1759, one thing was certain, the space had to be shortened and made as intimate, as varied and as entertaining as possible. By placing the entrance in the centre, with chimney-pieces either side, two focal points were created and the need to parade from one end to the other was removed. Apses were planned at both ends to reduce the length, and for variety's sake they were to be differently screened or framed by columns.[46]

All this was turned on its head by the rebuilding of the semi-

209   Design for the ceiling of the gallery, by Robert Adam, 1769 (Sir
John Soane's Museum: Adam drawings, vol. 11:170)

210   Plan and laid-out wall elevations of the gallery, by Robert Adam,
c.1765 (Sir John Soane's Museum: Adam drawings, vol. 35:10)

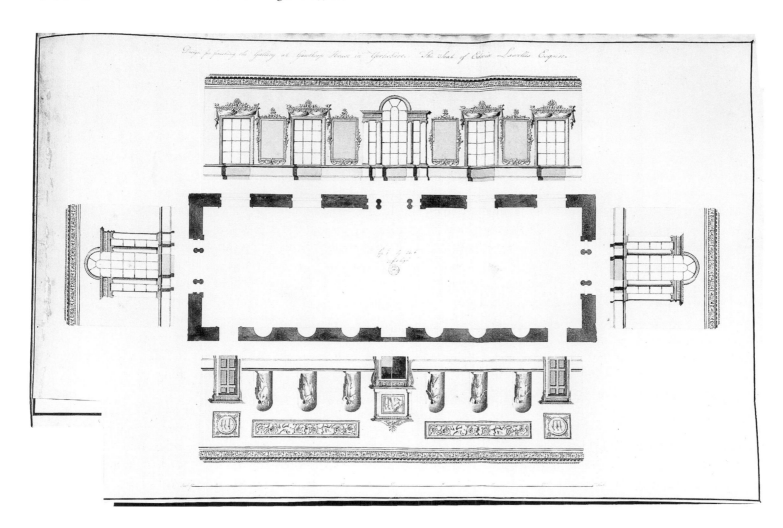

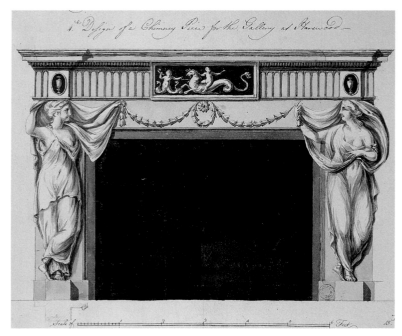

211 Design for the chimney-piece in the gallery, by Robert Adam, 1777 (Sir John Soane's Museum: Adam drawings, vol. 22:203)

212 John Scarlett Davis, View of the gallery at Harewood House. Watercolour, c.1827 (Reproduced by kind permission of the Earl and Countess of Harewood and Trustees of the Harewood House Trust)

circular court in 1762. The gallery now replaced the circular corridors as the link between the north and south apartments and had to be entered at the ends, thus prohibiting the formation of apses. While it would still have been possible to have two chimney-pieces, and indeed two were introduced by Barry in the 1840s, that was unnecessary and much less important to Adam than having a distinctive central feature facing the Venetian window on the west wall.[47]

His design for finishing the room treats it like a sculpture gallery – with a tabernacle chimney-piece containing a large bas-relief, three niches holding statues on either side, oblong bas-reliefs over the niches and square ones over the doors (pl. 210).[48] There are certain similarities to the gallery designed for Croome Court in 1763 and especially to the dining-room of 1761 at Syon. The sober architectural effect may not have appealed to Lascelles's showy taste, and though the niches did much to diversify the wall, the difficulty of aligning them with the window piers, which had been built at slightly irregular intervals, may have been cause for concern. For whatever reason, the scheme was not executed. Nor were the two alternative ceiling designs offered in 1765: one of three large circles with octagonal centres, the other an all-over pattern of large and small interlaced circles.[49] The definitive design of 1769 is of the type made for the Lansdowne House drawing-room two years earlier, incorporating inset oval and oblong paintings attributed to Biagio Rebecca (pl. 209).[50]

Five years later, the ceiling finished, thoughts finally turned to the chimney-piece. Adam made a drawing offering alternative

213 Plan and laid-out wall elevations of the dining-room, by Robert Adam, *c*.1765 (Sir John Soane's Museum: Adam drawings, vol. 35:12)

214 Plan and laid-out wall elevations of the music-room, by Robert Adam, *c*.1765 (Sir John Soane's Museum: Adam drawings, vol. 14:118)

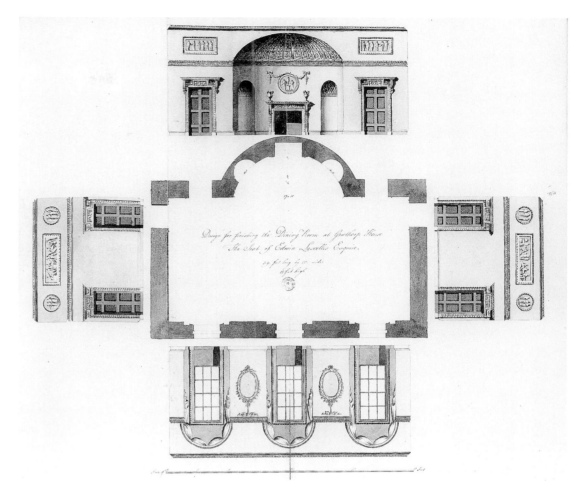

schemes in 1774, but Lascelles put off making a decision until June 1776. The chosen design had rams' heads and festoons on the pilasters and an elaborate arcade and palmette frieze, all intended to be of ormolu mounted on white marble.[51] This may have been related to the wallpaper of 'Antique Ornament with Palms &c . . . with a pink Ground', designed and hung by Chippendale in September 1776.[52] Nevertheless, it came to nothing. A little less gaudy and much more robust statement was what was required here, and as Lascelles had already decided against a tall tabernacle structure, it had to be a monumental caryatid chimney-piece like the one Lascelles's friend, Lord Coventry, had in the gallery at Croome Court.

Adam's final design was rapidly worked-up in June 1777 from staid beginnings to a showy spectacle with ormolu mounts and a porphyry-coloured tablet and cameos (pl. 211).[53] In the event, the chimney-piece was executed of plain statuary marble with a variant tablet depicting the triumph of Venus and cameos of putti riding sea-horses. Vangelder and Nollekens have been credited with the work, but neither is mentioned in the accounts. The caryatids, accompanied by busts of Homer, Faustina, Caracalla and Commodus on pedestals, resuscitated something of Adam's original idea of a sculpture gallery. But it was Chippendale's spectacular gilt-framed mirrors and pier-tables that made the most impressive 'show of magnificence and art'.[54]

Later owners of Harewood wanted less show, more comfort and sufficient space to accommodate their growing collection of pictures. The second Earl of Harewood, who succeeded in 1820, began by replacing the mirrors on the inner wall with paintings (pl. 212); the third Earl, who succeeded in 1841, had Barry make the room more habitable by installing two smaller chimney-pieces in place of the imposing caryatid one, which was moved next door to the remodelled dining-room. It has recently been returned to the gallery.

The principal feature of Adam's dining-room was an unusually large apse containing a chimney-piece executed by Devall from a design made in 1766, with a relief of Venus and Cupid above it and tall niches on either side (pl. 213).[55] Apart from contributing to the width, variety and elegance of the long room, the apse, by virtue of its size, also determined the arrangement of the other elements of wall decoration. In order to accommodate its height (18 feet, or 5.4 metres), the entablature was reduced to a simple moulding and the frieze lowered to the top of the windows so as to form a string course binding the room together and defining an upper register decorated with stucco reliefs in round and oblong panels. This line was also taken for the springing of the semi-dome within the apse as well as the arched pelmets over the three windows. To the left of the apse was a small closet and to the right a door leading to the back stairs – a much more convenient arrangement than the original one, when the dining-room was where the music-room is now. Chippendale's dining-room chairs and two ormolu-mounted sideboards, one with flanking pedestals and urns and the other with a wine

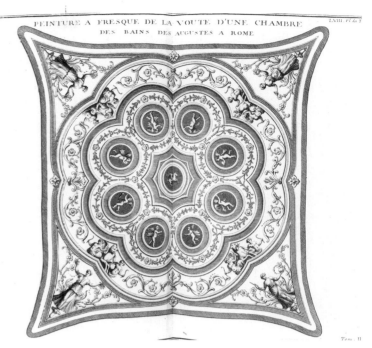

216 Bernard de Montfaucon, engraving of a vault discovered in Rome in 1721 in the Palace of Augustus (*Supplément au livre de l'antiquité expliquée* (1724), pl. LVIII)

cooler, are virtually all that remains from Adam's time.

Architecture and music share the stage in the music-room (pl. 214). Architecture – or to be precise, classical ruins depicted on four large canvases by Zucchi in 1771 – plays the leading role.[56] Musical themes are mainly on the ceiling, where there is a ring of ten roundels depicting the nine muses and Minerva from Ovid, with *Midas judging a musical contest between Apollo and Pan* in the centre (pl. 215). Adam intended the space between the central roundel and its ten satellites to be decorated with lyres and laurel branches, but this ornament – like the rinceaux meant to encircle the four corner roundels – was either omitted in execution or removed at a later date. The configuration of the ceiling was inspired by the painted vault in a bath in the palace of Augustus, which was discovered in 1721 and published by Montfaucon in 1724 (pl. 216).[57] It is echoed in the carpet by patera and rosettes.[58] The lyre is the keynote of the chimney-piece, for which Adam made two different designs: the first in 1766 was slightly modified and executed by Devall in 1768;[59] the second, in 1770, was probably made at the request of Lady Fleming, the widow of Sir John Fleming, whom Lascelles married in March of that year. It was rejected and offered instead to Sir Rowland Winn for the tapestry-room at Newby.[60] Two years later, Devall replaced the first chimney-piece with another – presumably the present one, with the head of Apollo in the centre flanked by putti and lyres – for which there is no known Adam design. The original chimney-piece is now in the state bedchamber (Princess Mary's Sitting Room).[61]

Reynolds's portrait of *Mrs Hale as Euphrosyne*, accompanied by music-making nymphs, is now appropriately hung in an Adam-style frame above the chimney-piece (see pl. 215). However, contrary to received opinion, it was not painted for this or any other room at Harewood, but was brought there by

215 View of the music-room showing Adam's ceiling, the related Axminster carpet, Antonio Zucchi's ruinscapes and Joshua Reynolds's portrait of *Mrs Hale as Euphrosnye* over the chimney-piece

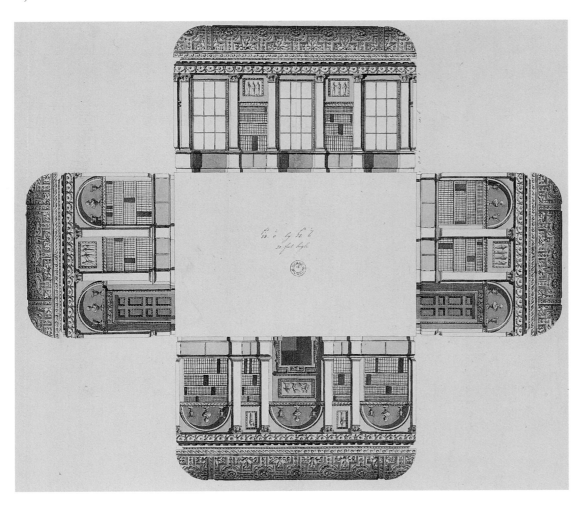

217 Plan and laid-out wall elevations of the library (now the Old Library), by Robert Adam, c.1765 (Sir John Soane's Museum: Adam drawings, vol. 35:15)

218 View of the Old Library as recently restored (Reproduced by kind permission of the Earl and Countess of Harewood and Trustees of the Harewood House Trust)

Edward Lascelles, first Earl of Harewood, whose wife was Mrs Hale's sister. It was not in the house when Farington visited in 1801, and in the 1820s it was hanging in a simpler frame in the gallery.[62] When the music-room was photographed in 1914, there was a portrait of the first Earl in the Adam-style frame where his sister-in-law's picture now hangs. Reynolds's portrait of Edwin Lascelles had pride of place in 1798, and was presumably lit by two of Chippendale's '4 Exceeding rich Carved Gerandoles with 3 branches each highly finished in Burnished Gold'.[63] The other two girandoles would have been placed at either end of the window wall.

Though in plan Harewood appears to be neatly divided by the hall and saloon into a state apartment on the west and a private apartment on the east, in reality the division was not so precise. The splendid state dressing-room and alcove bedroom on the south-east front were decorated by Adam and opulently furnished by Chippendale for public view, not for informal use. Informal gatherings probably took place in the library; business was conducted in the study; and privacy, at least on this floor, was only to be had in the bedrooms in the east wing. When Lascelles was not in residence, all the rooms were open to tourists, as they are today.

The library (now known as the Old Library) was restored by the seventh earl and is now much as Adam designed it in 1765, with recessed bookcases integrated into a decorative scheme of pilasters and arches, and an upper range containing busts and

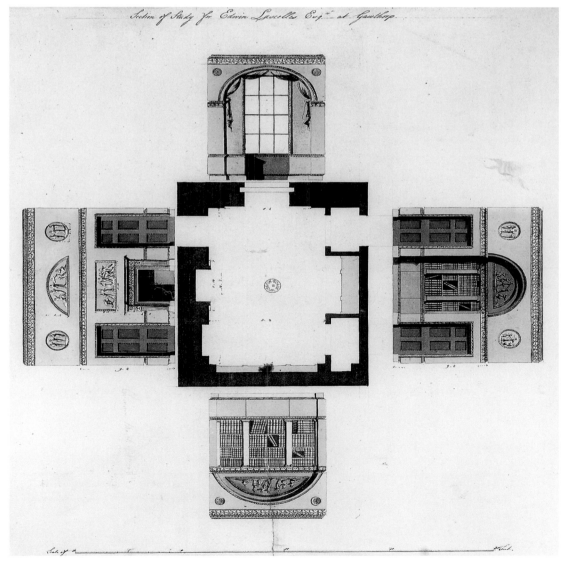

219 Princess Mary's Sitting Room (originally the state bedroom) showing Chippendale's Diana and Minerva commode in Adam's reduced bed-alcove. The commode has recently been replaced by Chippendale's restored state bed (Reproduced by kind permission of the Earl and Countess of Harewood and Trustees of the Harewood House Trust)

220 Plan and laid-out wall elevations of Edwin Lascelles's study, by Robert Adam, c.1766 (Sir John Soane's Museum: Adam drawings, vol. 35:18)

221   Design (unexecuted) for the circular dressing-room ceiling 'Painted
in the Style of the Ancients', by Robert Adam, 1767 (Sir John Soane's
Museum: Adam drawings, vol. 11:148)

222 Design for the circular dressing-room as executed, by Robert Adam, 1767 (Sir John Soane's Museum: Adam drawings, vol. 11:149)

painted panels attributed to Biagio Rebecca and Angelica Kauffman (pls 217, 218).[64] This arrangement depended on the introduction of a deep cove, which lowered the 20 foot- (6 metre) tall walls to the height of the windows and still left ample space for Lascelles's collection of books, part of which was shelved in the adjacent study or 'Little Library'. Barry's conversion of the saloon and state dressing-room into libraries rendered the Adam book rooms superfluous. The library had its bookcases neatly covered over and became a sitting- and smoking-room;[65] and the study (pl. 220) – a miniature Palmyrene room with a ceiling from Robert Wood's book and a stucco relief of the *Aldobrandini Wedding* over the chimney-piece – was made into a bathroom and water-closet; now it is the 'China Room'.[66]

It is hardly surprising that the state dressing-room and bedroom should have been adapted for practical use; the extravagance of such showpieces over and above a large state apartment was excessive. The two rooms were designed by Adam in 1767 as a unit with related (but not identical) ceilings composed of semi-circles. That in the dressing-room (now called The Spanish Library) is coved and quite like the ceiling designed in the following year for the saloon at Nostell. Drawings at the Soane

Museum and Harewood show it painted pale green, pink and straw-colour. The frieze of winged griffons, urns and tripods, which is now picked out in gold on a deep red ground, was intended to be 'Dark Straw Colour'.[67] Here, as elsewhere at Harewood, Adam provided the setting for Chippendale's finest and most expensive piece of cabinet furniture, the 'very large rich' Diana and Minerva commode, an accompanying pier-glass, an overmantel-mirror and two large girandoles with looking glasses all elaborately framed with antique ornaments, richly carved and highly finished in burnished gold.[68]

The space occupied by the state bedroom (now Princess Mary's Sitting Room) was planned by Carr as a passage between the main block and the east wing (pl. 219). It was extended into part of the court to form a deep bed-alcove screened by Ionic columns, and a small closet. Until the 1840s, the alcove housed a large, domed state bed by Chippendale.[69] This was removed when the Countess of Harewood took the room as her private sitting-room and had the alcove reduced to create an inner corridor.[70] For many years, the Diana and Minerva commode had pride of place in the alcove; now, however, the bed has been restored and reinstated.[71] The present chimney-piece is a replacement brought from the music-room. What the original

223   Elevation of the window wall of the circular dressing-room, by
Robert Adam, *c.*1767 (Sir John Soane's Museum: Adam drawings, vol.
14: 121)

chimney-piece (set up in October 1769) was like is not
known.[72] There are three drawings: two dated 1767 and
inscribed for the 'State Bed Chamber' but with inappropriate
sacrificial emblems in the frieze, and a third for a slightly larger
chimney-piece with a broad tablet containing a central head
and scrolled foliage, inscribed 'for the Bed Chamber at
Harewood' and dated 1768.[73]

Sadly, the most complete and distinctive Adam room at
Harewood, the 'Circular Dressing Room' (pl. 223) – a domed
octagon located behind the secondary staircase overlooking the
east court – was sacrificed in the creation of the Countess's corridor. Whether the room was included in Carr's plan from the outset or introduced by Adam in 1758 remains uncertain. Several
different uses were proposed for it: a dressing-room for Mr
Lascelles communicating with his library and adjacent
wardrobe-study but not with the room on the south front; a
'Billiard room or Chappel'; and a 'Common Dining Room or
Supping Room' with doors to the rooms north and south.[74]
Initially, there was a tall arched window (Venetian on the exterior) and two smaller windows each side which lit the triangular

closets formed by the octagon. When the court was reduced, the
flanking windows were suppressed.

In 1767, Adam supplied two alternative sets of coloured
designs for the dome and the window wall: one for a quite elaborate dome 'proposed to be Painted in the Style of the Ancients'
(pl. 221), and a simplified version to be executed in stucco with
very pale blue, green and pink grounds picked out in white (pl.
222).[75] Lascelles chose the latter and in the following year Adam
offered Lord Scarsdale a slightly modified version of the painted
scheme for the circular breakfasting-room in an intended extension to the south front of Kedleston.[76]

Meanwhile, eight pairs of Ionic pilasters were set up in the
angles of the octagon and Joseph Rose proceeded with the
stucco decoration of the shallow dome. Zucchi is said to have
painted eight inset roundels depicting 'Jupiter, Juno and
Neptune with a group of Muses, Milo petitioning a Roman
emperor, the rape of Proserpine, an antique marriage' and four
alternating paintings of boys playing.[77] In 1769 Adam made
designs for an oval chimney-glass in an elaborate stucco surround incorporating candle branches (pl. 224), and a large tri-

224 Design for a chimney-glass for the circular dressing-room, by Robert Adam, 1769 (Sir John Soane's Museum: Adam drawings, vol. 20:71)

225 Design for a tripartite mirror for the wall opposite the chimney-piece in the circular dressing-room, by Robert Adam, 1769 (Sir John Soane's Museum: Adam drawings, vol. 20:72)

partite mirror arched in the centre like a Venetian window 'so placed (on the opposite wall) that on it each single object appear(ed) three distinct representations' (pl. 225).[78] Though his design for the marble chimney-piece, executed by Christopher Richardson in 1769, has not been traced, there is a full-size detail in the Harewood archives of a shaped capital with a peltoid shield suspended from bell-flower festoons relating to the decoration of the dome.[79]

All in all, Harewood was not Adam's most successful work. With Carr as architect, he did not have the freedom or the degree of control he had elsewhere. Nor does he seem to have had the close rapport with his patron that is vital in the designing of interiors. Though the commission was prestigious and no doubt financially rewarding, it cannot have given him the same satisfaction as nearby Newby and Nostell, not to mention Syon, Bowood, Osterley and Kedleston.

226   The east front of Osterley Park

OSTERLEY PARK

Osterley, Middlesex, was a botched Elizabethan pile when Adam came there in 1761; when he left in 1778 it was 'a palace of palaces . . . so improved and enriched that all the Percies and Seymours of Sion must die of envy.' (pls 226, 227)[1]

The original house was erected in 1577 by Sir Thomas Gresham, 'Citizen and Merchant Adventurer of London', financial advisor to Queen Elizabeth I and founder of the Royal Exchange. A survey of Isleworth drawn by Moses Glover in 1635 contains the earliest known depiction of Gresham's 'faire and stately building of bricke'.[2] It shows a quadrangular house of two storeys and an attic, with projecting bays on the principal front, facing east, and four tall structures, probably chimneys, rising above the roof. There were lower stair turrets – like those on the stable block – in the internal angles of the courtyard. The entrance is not shown and was presumably in the side of the northern bay, as at Chastleton in Oxfordshire.

As Gresham's only heir of his own blood predeceased him, the property passed to his wife, Dame Anne, and her children by a previous marriage, who sold it in 1655 to Sir William Waller, the Parliamentary General. On Waller's death in 1668, an inventory of his goods and chattels at Osterley was made by four valuers, one of them Francis Child, then an assistant to the goldsmith and banker, Robert Blanchard. Forty-four rooms were listed and several others referred to: among them a hall, kitchen and chapel probably on the ground floor; a 'painted gallery', dining-room and bedrooms hung with tapestries on the first floor; and an 'Upper Gallery' and more bedrooms on the second floor.[3]

This, in essence, was the house bought in 1684 by Dr Nicholas Barbon, financier, building speculator and entrepreneur, whose great ambition was to live in the kind of 'mercantile magnificence' that Gresham, his hero, did. Barbon immediately raised a mortgage on Osterley from Francis Child (by then head of the bank) and two others, which he made no effort to repay.[4] In 1690 his creditors took legal action to eject him and recover the property, only to be informed that 'Barbon had pulled down part of Osterley dwelling house and was making considerable alterations in the house which was not fit to be inhabited unless Barbon went on to finish'.[5] It is assumed that he had demolished the stair turrets in the courtyard and built two square towers on the angles of the west front, one of which still retains a wooden staircase of his period. Whether he made or intended making any other alterations to the house is unknown, though some

work in the stables can be credited to him. In any event, he ran out of money and died in debt in August 1698.

Sir Francis Child, having been involved with Osterley for thirty years as a banker, was now in a position to acquire the property as his own and in so doing to aggrandize himself socially at a time when his prestige in the City had reached a peak with his appointment in 1698 as Lord Mayor of London and Jeweller in Ordinary to William III.[6] However, it took until 1713 for Child to gain full possession and in October of that year he died. He was succeeded by his three surviving sons, one richer than the others: Sir Robert (1674–1721), followed by Sir Francis, the younger (1684–1740) – both directors of the East India Company and presidents of Christ's Hospital – and finally Samuel (1693–1752), the only one of his eleven sons who married.

Osterley, having stood empty for fifteen years with Barbon's alterations unfinished, must have required a great deal of attention before Sir Robert was able to move in in 1720. However, the only surviving record of the work done by him is a bill for a marble chimney-piece made in 1720 by Edward Stanton, Master Mason at Westminster Abbey.[7]

Improvements and repairs were carried on by Sir Francis, the younger and Samuel almost without stop, with no comprehensive plan and quite conservative taste. One family of carpenters, the Hillyards, were employed by the Childs for over half a century at all their properties: their business premises in the City and their private houses at Parson's Green, 42 Lincoln's Inn Fields, Ham and Osterley.[8] In 1726 and 1727, Sir Francis paid Benjamin Hillyard a total of £2471.17.0 for work at Osterley. Exactly what this major building operation consisted of and what other works were done by other craftsmen – bricklayers, glaziers, masons and the like – is not known.

The evolution of the pre-Adam house is extremely perplexing: the surviving building accounts are fragmentary and evidence provided by the fabric itself is difficult to interpret, partly owing to the constant reuse of old materials. A plan of Osterley Park drawn by John Rocque in 1741 as part of his large map of London and the surrounding country, an anonymous survey of the south front of the house made around 1760 and Adam's longitudinal section through the existing west block in his 1761 design for rebuilding the rest of the house are the only depictions of the early Georgian mansion.[9] In such circumstances,

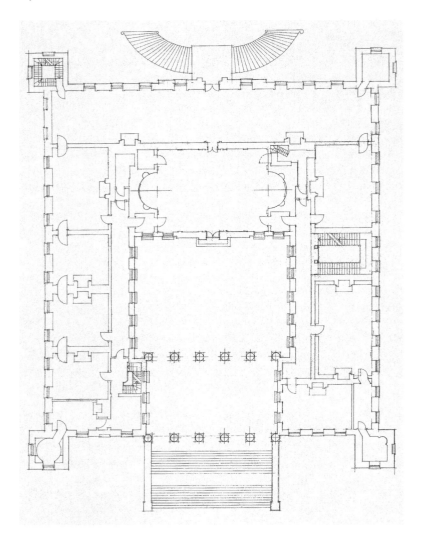

227   Plan of the principal floor of Osterley Park

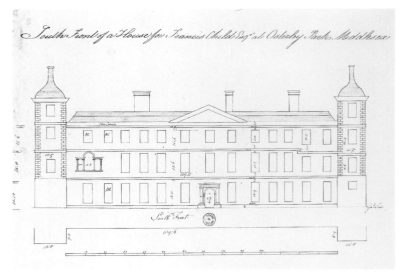

228   Unidentified draughtsman, survey of the south front of Osterley drawn for Francis Child, *c.*1760 (Sir John Soane's Museum: Adam drawings, vol. 43:94)

229   Plan for making Osterley into a regular U-shaped house with the entire east front removed and the north and south fronts reduced to the length of the west front, 'The Faint Shadowing Shows what is already Built & the Dark Colour the proposed Addition', by Robert Adam, 1761 (Sir John Soane's Museum: Adam drawings, vol. 43:97)

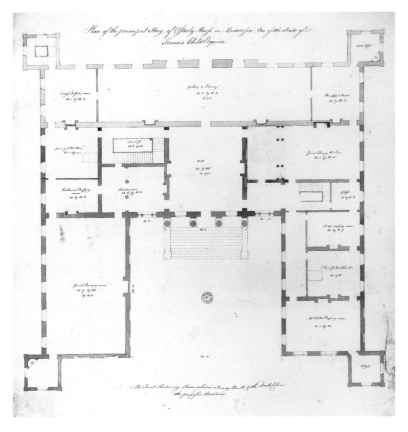

the historian, as Gibbon said, is 'reduced to collect, to compare, to conjecture . . . (but) never to place his conjectures in the rank of facts'.[10]

Rocque's survey outlines the work of the first two Child brothers: it shows the quadrangular house with Barbon's angle turrets on the west front and two short projecting wings – possibly Gresham's – on the east front aligned on the central avenue of a great *patte d'oie* modelled on nearby Hampton Court. One would expect some of the grandeur and formality of the garden to be reflected on the exterior of the house, which was presumably heightened by the Childs to create a proper third storey in place of the hipped roof with dormers shown in 1635 by Glover. Any other improvements Robert and Francis may have made to the house before 1740 are impossible to ascertain. However, there is some evidence of their work in the stables, including grandiose stalls based on a design by Inigo Jones for Holland House published by Isaac Ware in 1731.[11]

Samuel Child's contribution is better documented (though certainly not fully) by the *c.*1760 survey of the south front (pl. 228). It was he who brought the east front into line with the west one by adding matching turrets to the angles, thereby regularizing the shape of the house. To accomplish this, the existing wings were either demolished or, much more likely, the space between them was brought into the house and faced with a flat façade. It was probably at this juncture that the main entrance was brought up to the first-floor level, which became the *piano nobile*, leaving the ground floor to be used as a basement for services.[12] Dressing the angle turrets with quoins on the upper floors, but not below, served to reinforce the distinction.

Like the garden front, the main front must have had stone stairs rising to a first-floor hall. What form this stair took – whether it had landings and half turns or was a narrower version of the straight stair introduced by Adam – is not known.[13] The 1740s hall is slightly easier to reconstruct from the vaulting under the three central bays (where Adam's columnar portico is), which

230 'Section through Osterley House from West to East', by Robert Adam, c.1761 (Osterley Park, The National Trust)

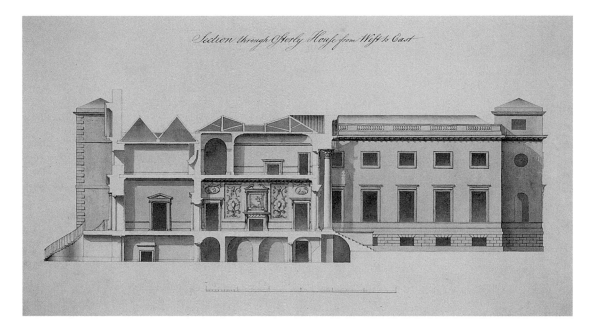

was constructed to support its stone-paved floor.[14] The stage when the hall was brought up to the first floor would also have been the logical time to raise the courtyard; it was evidently raised again by Adam in 1763 or 1764.[15]

Exactly how much Samuel Child achieved before his death in 1752 is impossible to tell. He was succeeded by his seventeen-year-old son, Francis, who, during the brief period from his coming of age in 1756 until 1760, proceeded with his father's piecemeal improvements. His first priority, however, was to accommodate the 'Entire and Valuable Library of the Honourable Bryan Fairfax, Esq. one of the Commissioners of His Majesty's Customs, Deceased' which he had purchased *en bloc* for £2,000 prior to auction set for 26 August 1756.[16] Not only was Bryan Fairfax (1676–1749) one of the most distinguished book collectors of the period, whose name thrilled 'bibliomaniacal nerves', he was also related to the Childs and, perhaps more important, was a cousin by marriage to the great Duke of Buckingham in whom Sir Francis Child had a particular interest.[17]

The Fairfax library – which was enlarged by Francis Child and later by his brother Robert – was one of the principal treasures of Osterley. The room set aside for it was a sizeable space of 1,167 square feet (108.4 square metres), presumably located in the centre of the east front above the hall. No time was lost in fitting it with bookcases framed by Ionic pilasters – part old, part new.[18] It was the demolition of this relatively recent addition to the house to make way for Adam's open portico that necessitated the relocation of the prized collection of books in a new library designed by Adam on the north front.[19] Some of the bookcases from the earlier room were re-erected in a passage behind the new library, where they still stand.

By 1760, large, white-painted timber pediments had been fixed to the cornice in the centre of each front; Venetian windows were inserted in the north and south ends of the gallery, which occupied the whole of the west front;[20] the second-floor bedroom windows were shortened; there was quite a bit of re-roofing; water-closets were installed in some of the turrets; old doors and shutters, cornices and architraves, mouldings and panels were adjusted and new ones made. Francis Child's bed-

room and the billiard room were finished and hung with pictures. The 'Yellow Taffety Bedchamber' was ready and so too was the gallery, except for its chimney-pieces.

The man responsible for all this work was Matthew Hillyard, who, like many experienced carpenters, did not require the intervention of an architect. Boulton Manwaring, a practising surveyor trained as a joiner, seems to have acted as clerk of the works and intermediary between Child and his employees, ordering work from specialist craftsmen, examining and paying their accounts. He was still serving Robert Child in this capacity in 1777.[21] It would have been Manwaring's job to contract with a sculptor to supply the marble chimney-pieces for the entrance hall on the east front and the gallery. The commission went to Joseph Wilton, who evidently procured designs from his close friend, William Chambers, who was working nearby at Kew and probably at Gunnersbury as well. This might explain the presence of Wilton's signature on Chambers's design for the hall chimney-piece, which is amongst the Adam drawings at the Soane.[22] Wilton was directly involved with Osterley, but Chambers was not.[23] Whether the hall chimney-piece was executed to his design is not known; if it was, it would have been removed when Adam opened the centre of the east front.

The two marble chimney-pieces in the gallery were adapted from a design by Chambers and installed by the bricklayer, Richard Norris, in 1764, by which time Adam was in full command.[24] Though designs by Chambers for the chimney-pieces in the 'Yellow Taffety Bedchamber' and Francis Child's bedroom may also have been obtained through Wilton, he did not execute them. They were the work of a specialist woodcarver, possibly William Linnell or his son John, who supplied the chimney-piece in Mrs Child's dressing-room. There is no conclusive evidence of any other work at Osterley by Chambers; nor was Francis Child a subscriber to his *Treatise on civil architecture*, published in the spring of 1759. The mishmash of remodelling done in the first half of the eighteenth century reveals the hand of an artisan architect like Manwaring, Hillyard or Norris, but certainly no one of the calibre of Chambers. Professional direction was sorely needed to bring the botched Elizabethan pile in line with fashionable neo-classical taste.

231 Furniture at Osterley, designed by Robert Adam 1767–*c.*1772, mistakenly published in 1822 as 'furniture at Sion-house' (*The works in architecture of Robert and James Adam*, vol. III (1822), pl. VIII)

232 Laid-out wall elevations of the dining-room, by Robert Adam, *c.*1763 (Osterley Park, The National Trust)

Why Francis Child chose Adam rather than Chambers can only be guessed. The Duke of Northumberland, who was employing Adam nearby at Syon, may have had some sway, but his opinion counted for little compared to the influence of Sir Francis Dashwood, later Lord Le Despenser. Dashwood was also an Adam patron: he got him the job of rebuilding the Shambles at High Wycombe in Buckinghamshire in 1761 and at the same time commissioned designs for his own houses in Hanover Square and at West Wycombe Park. More to the point, he was in control of the affairs of John and Charles Walcot (his brother-in-law and nephew) who were heavily in debt to Child's Bank. In consideration, the Walcots arranged Francis Child's uncontested return as Tory MP for Bishop's Castle, Shropshire in March 1761, as they had done for his father, Samuel, in 1747.

Adam was called upon in 1761 to modernize Osterley inside and out and to reduce its size, retaining the west range with its quoined turrets and newly finished gallery. That Francis Child was willing to sacrifice the library he had installed five years previously is remarkable. It is quite possible that the 1750s infill of the east range was faulty and that its removal was a matter of necessity which precipitated Adam's employment in the first place.

Be that as it may, Adam's proposal – set out in a section, plans and elevations (pl. 229, 230) – was to demolish the entire east range, cut back the north and south sides, give them new angle turrets to make them the same length as the west side and thereby transform the quadrangular house into a regular U-shaped one.[25] Its fenestration was methodically ordered, with tall windows on the *piano nobile* and square ones on the top floor, all in moulded surrounds. The ground floor was treated as a half-sunk basement and rusticated, while the rest of the exterior was rendered or refaced in stone. Probably at Child's request, the two old turrets were to retain their quoins, but the new ones were plain. Pyramidal roofs gave them all a Palladian look.

The inner wall of the west range was brought forward into the area of the courtyard, which remained at the level to which it was first raised by Samuel Child. This became the principal entrance front, distinguished by a tetrastyle Corinthian portico reached by a short flight of stairs and flanked by large Palladian windows.

Behind the portico was a hall of equal width leading to a library–gallery (87 feet, or 26.5 metres, long) like the one he designed for Croome Court in 1761, which occupied two-thirds of the pre-existing gallery and was considerably larger than the demolished library on the east front. The smaller rooms at each end were to be a ladies' dressing-room (or informal drawing-room) belonging to the state apartment on the south front and a breakfast-room (or informal eating-room) on the north side leading to a great dining-room with a double screen of columns at one end. The pre-existing main stair on this side of the house was demoted to a service stair for the dining-room and private apartment. A new grand staircase was to be formed on the south side of the hall, behind a screened ante-room where company could foregather before entering the 'great drawing room' in the south wing. This two-storey room, a little larger than the hall at Syon, must have been intended to receive the large and important pictures, notably Rubens's equestrian portrait of the Duke of Buckingham, still at 42 Lincoln's Inn Fields.

Adam's proposed disposition of the public reception rooms on the south side, with dining and private or semi-private rooms on the north, was maintained in his final plan and may reflect a pre-existing arrangement. On the whole, his first scheme is poorly integrated and has none of Syon's spatial variety; nor, indeed, does it have fundamental necessities like a kitchen. That, however, was not the reason for its rejection. It was far too radical and would have taken longer to accomplish than the impetuous young Francis was prepare to wait, especially with marriage in the offing.

What Francis Child favoured was a much simpler, more expeditious solution, which only removed the troublesome central section of the east front and left it open to form a U-shaped house. The rest of the building, including the four angle turrets, was to remain intact, with improved fenestration and a proper balustraded cornice to mask the roof.[26] There was no need to alter the existing layout of the interior, except for the space between the north and south ranges in front of the gallery where the new entrance hall had to be located. This space was enlarged as previously proposed, but left undivided. As Alistair Rowan has demonstrated, the second scheme was executed without an open, columnar portico filling the gap on the east front and with no thoughts of introducing one.[27] The portico was an afterthought, designed by Adam for Robert Child some years later. It was 'not quite finished' when Mrs Agneta Yorke visited the house in 1772.[28] Exactly what work was done or begun for Francis Child in 1762 and 1763 and what else he intended is not known. The surviving building accounts for this period are incomplete and unspecified, and the only design by Adam is for the Doric orangery in 1763.[29]

Osterley was 'all prepared for a wedding and posterity' when suddenly, on 22 September 1763, Francis Child died.[30] His bride-to-be was Maria Constantia Hampden, daughter of Robert Trevor Hampden (later 4th Baron Hampden), an old family friend and an able amateur architect, who was bound to have encouraged and advised his prospective son-in-law on the remodelling of Osterley.[31]

Francis Child was succeeded by his twenty-four-year-old brother, Robert, who, a fortnight later, on 6 October 1763, married Sarah, daughter of Gilbert Jodrell of Ankerwycke House, Wraysbury, Buckinghamshire. An illness that caused him to withdraw as candidate for Aylesbury in the by-election in January 1764 and the death of his mother in that month may briefly have delayed the progress of work at Osterley. However, by May 1764 the centre of the east front was demolished. Richard Norris, the bricklayer, then made a 'footing to the new front' in the forecourt and 'stopt up' the door from the 'attic into library'.[32]

Adam's improvements to the exterior, though by no means insignificant, are as nothing compared to his neo-classical interiors. They are an achievement that is unmistakably his and make

the house a 'palace of palaces'. Osterley can best be understood by examining the rooms in the order in which they were conceived, which is different from the order in which they were meant to be seen. Normally, Adam would have started with the entrance hall, but as this was in the process of being constructed, he began instead with the two reception rooms on either side of it – the dining-room to the north and the drawing-room to the south. The decoration of these rooms seems to have been undertaken in two or more stages and is not as refined or well integrated as other Adam rooms of the period.

1766 is the earliest date we have for the dining-room. It appears on a design for a vase-shaped cooper which, though uninscribed, is identical to the pair of spiral-fluted mahogany vases made for Osterley by John Linnell and referred to in a bill sent by him to William Drake of Shardeloes on 2 October 1767 for carving 'two coopers, the tops in the form of vases and large brass handles like Mr Child's one lin'd with lead to hold water and the other Top sham and a pot cupboard underneath and painting the same all compleat £30'.[33] Adam's designs for the sideboard (pl. 231) and pier-glasses are dated 1767, as are Antonio Zucchi's two large paintings of classical ruins.[34] These furnishings suggest a date of 1765 at the latest – more likely 1763 – for Adam's wall elevations (pl. 232), and a slightly earlier date – 1762 or 1763 – before Francis's death for his ceiling design, which does not survive.[35]

The ceiling, decorated with grape vines, wine ewers, thyrsi and other Bacchic motifs appropriate for an eating-room (pl. 233), is virtually identical to the one designed in 1761 for the dining-room at Shardeloes and executed in the following year by Joseph Rose.[36] It is exceedingly rare for Adam to repeat designs as exactly as he did in these two houses and also surprising to find the Osterley ceiling more robust than its model. The variation and refinement at which he excelled are demonstrated by a comparison of the Shardeloes ceiling with a similar one designed in 1765 for the green drawing-room at Harewood.[37] The reversal of his normal practice in his first room at Osterley may reflect the taste of the Childs and the style of the craftsman who executed the stucco-work. Like most of the other craftsmen habitually employed by the family, the unidentified stuccatore was presumably working at Osterley before Adam's arrival and may well have been responsible for the dining-room's cavetto cornice decorated with intertwined grape vines, which is not included in Adam's wall elevations (usually signifying pre-existence), is not a neo-classical profile and does not correspond in the normal way with the vine decoration of his door architraves and curtain cornices.[38]

His unconventional use of an enriched Doric order, normally reserved for halls, on the dining-room chimney-piece is much more difficult to explain, as is its large size (approximately 6¼ × 7½ feet, or 1.9 × 2.2 metres). There is as yet no evidence of its having been made for a different room, and as it appears in a simplified form in Adam's wall elevation, there is no reason to believe that it was designed by someone else.

The similarity to the drawing-room at Bowood (pl. 163) designed in 1763, with its arrangement of large paintings (though not as large as those at Osterley) in stucco frames flanked by arabesque panels is worth noting, and might have been more obvious had the Osterley arabesques been executed as shown in

233   View of the dining-room showing the ceiling, wall decorations and furniture

234   One of a suite of twelve mahogany lyre-back chairs for the dining-room, designed by Robert Adam *c*.1767 and made by John Linnell

Adam's drawing, with stucco tablets and roundels rather than painted ones. The dining-room was served by the old stairs behind the apse at the north end of the hall, the kitchen being quite far removed in the south-east corner of the house.

Visitors were meant to enter the room from the gallery and in so doing to be dazzled – as Mrs Agneta Yorke was when she visited the house in 1772 – by the theatrical display of the carved and gilt sideboard 'Magnificently furnished with plate', with a 'Massy & large silver Cistern' under it, a pair of white and gold mahogany pedestals and vases mounted with ormolu on either side, and set against a large backdrop of classical ruins with dancing figures painted by Zucchi.[39]

The table has a Greek key frieze incorporating paterae and bucrania related to the Doric chimney-piece and identical to the frieze around the hall at Harewood, designed a year earlier in 1766. Its unusually complex legs – tapered and spiral-fluted,

235 The drawing-room showing the Palmyra ceiling and related carpet, designed by Robert Adam c.1763–68

with alternating convex, concave and straight profiles – also appear on a contemporary table made for Coventry House.[40] The simpler legs on the pair of *en suite* pier-tables were not only suited to their subsidiary role but may also have been needed to support the weight of their 'antique' marble mosaic slabs. Unlike the mahogany top of the sideboard, these slabs rest on the chair-rail for additional support. A bill from the firm of Ravald and Morland for 'taking the Ornaments off the slab frames' on 24 December 1788 indicates that the frames were originally enriched with pendant anthemia, like the side-board.[41] The accompanying oval pier-glasses, with plates approximately 4⅔ × 3 feet (1.4 × 0.9 metres) in gilded frames overlaid with husk festoons and surmounted by ornamental hanging devices over 7½ feet (2 metres) tall, were designed in 1767.[42] Their robustness was presumably intended to balance the very large paintings, the outsize chimney-piece and the

prominent stucco arabesques. Adam's wall elevation shows much simpler oval frames.

It was the 'charming harmony' of the twelve mahogany chairs with backs 'taken from antique lyres' (pl. 234) and the scrolled foliage of the arabesque wall panels against which they were placed that struck a chord with Walpole.[43] These were designed by Adam and almost certainly made by Linnell, together with the rest of the dining-room furniture. They are contemporary with '2 Mahogany harp back chairs' made for Shardeloes in October 1767 and listed in the same bill as the vases 'like Mr Child's', but without Adam's participation. French interest in the ancient lyre both as a musical instrument and as a decorative motif in the early 1760s may have given rise to the English development of the lyre-back chair, which later became popular in France.[44]

The drawing-room (pl. 235) was probably begun for Francis

236 Soffit of the Temple of the Sun, Palmyra (Robert Wood, *The ruins of Palmyra* (1753), pl. XIXB)

237 Detail of the drawing-room frieze and cornice designed by Robert Adam and put up in 1772

238 The drawing-room chimney-piece

Child at about the same time as the dining-room, around 1763, and by 1767 work was sufficiently advanced for Adam to supply a design (not executed) for a pier-glass.[45] Neither his wall elevations nor his coloured design for the ceiling is dated.[46] The ceiling is modelled on the Temple of the Sun (pl. 236) published in Robert Wood's *Ruins of Palmyra* (1753).[47] By the early 1760s, Palmyra decorations had become quite fashionable and another plate in Wood's book was used by Adam in 1763 for the circular-coffered ceiling in the drawing-room at Bowood. However, the immediate inspiration for Osterley was the *trompe l'oeil* Temple of the Sun ceiling in the nave of West Wycombe Church, painted for Sir Francis Dashwood, Lord Le Despenser in 1763 by Giovanni Borgnis, whose son, Pietro, was responsible for Mrs Child's Etruscan dressing-room. Borgnis's ceiling in the hall at Dashwood's house, West Wycombe Park, is even more closely

related to Osterley, but its date is uncertain and may be as late as 1770.[48] Though there is no evidence of Adam's involvement with these ceilings, he did supply designs (none of which were executed) for West Wycombe Park as well as for Dashwood's town house in Hanover Square in the early 1760s, and was working at that time at High Wycombe, where he rebuilt the Shambles in 1761, and at Shardeloes, five or six miles away.[49]

Adam was not alone in having Buckinghamshire interests. The Childs did too. The father of Francis Child's fiancée, Robert Trevor (afterwards Hampden), inherited the Hampdens's Buckinghamshire estates and was joint postmaster-general with his friend, Sir Francis Dashwood. And it was, of course, to Dashwood and his nephew, Charles Walcot, that Francis Child owed his seat as MP for Bishop's Castle. The banker's connections with Dashwood doubtless increased in 1762 when the lat-

bold for the room; even the smaller coffering that was executed is somewhat heavy and overbearing in relation to the lighter treatment of the frieze, the door-cases and the chimney-piece.

Adam's undated design for the four walls shows a frieze of scrolled foliage – a standard classical motif that was also used in West Wycombe church, the drawing-room at Shardeloes and in many other places.[51] This motif is repeated in the friezes over the doors, where it is interrupted by a central tablet containing a profile medallion flanked by griffons. The chimney-piece is oddly disparate and was redesigned to match the doors, though in execution the griffons were superseded by sphinxes (pl. 238).[52]

In 1772, when the room was painted by David Adamson, the 'old Frize' was 'taken down' and replaced by the present one (pl. 237), which has a repeating pattern of arcades incorporating anthemia and bell-flowers picked out in gold on a dark crimson ground.[53] This frieze bears no relation to any of the other architectural elements in the room. However, there is an almost identical frieze in the hall at West Wycombe Park; again, the similarity cannot be mere coincidence.

Dark crimson seems to have been an uncommon colour for a frieze and Walpole made special note of the 'admirable effect' it had with the 'pale green damask' hangings.[54] The need for a bold and distinctive accent here may well have arisen in 1772 in relation to the novel plans for decorating the adjacent state apartment. A fashionable neo-classical boost was even more essential for the furniture, which consisted, at that date, of a suite of eight gilt armchairs and two large sofas in a modified rococo style (comparable to the suite made by John Linnell for Shardeloes around 1768) and a carpet designed by Adam to answer the ceiling, which, according to Agneta Yorke, was 'from Mr Moore's Manufactory'.[55] Instead of octagons with floral bosses modelled on the Temple of the Sun, the carpet has a pattern of circles and diamonds inspired by another Palmyra soffit in Wood's book, which Adam used on the ceilings of the drawing-room at Bowood and the study (now the china-room) at Harewood.

In January 1773, Adam designed a pair of bow-fronted commodes with figured roundels in the centre and sides (pl. 239), a

239 One of a pair of bow-fronted commodes and pier-glasses in the drawing-room, designed by Robert Adam, 1773

ter became Chancellor of the Exchequer. Robert Child had Trevor Hampden's support for his abortive candidacy in the Aylesbury by-election and was married to a Buckinghamshire heiress, Sarah Joddrell.[50] Thus, the idea of having a Shardeloes ceiling in the dining-room and a West Wycombe one in the drawing-room could just as well have come from the Childs as from Adam, who, it is worth noting, was never again tempted to use this particular Palmyra model in any form.

In order to fit the Temple of the Sun ceiling to the rectangular shape of the drawing-room, Adam replaced the circular centre with an oval and added a single row of octagonal coffers all round. This addition does not appear in his design, which adheres exactly to the coffering pattern of the original engraved model, increasing the size of the coffers rather than their number to fill the space. The large coffers would certainly have been too

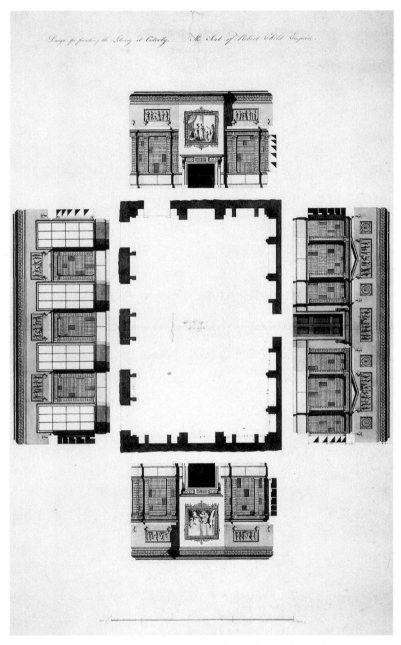

241 Plan and laid-out wall elevations of the library, by Robert Adam, 1766 (Osterley Park, The National Trust)

242 View of the library showing the carved enrichments on the front and sides of the Ionic pilasters on the bookcases as well as on the window embrasure and shutter-panels. The Vitruvian scroll frieze on the marquetry pedestal-desk designed by John Linnell, *c.*1768–69 may have been intended to answer Adam's bookcases

frieze to match the door architraves and an arcaded base corresponding to the frieze round the room. These commodes are strictly ornamental wall decorations; they have no function. Linnell is thought to have supplied the hollow cases and Christopher Fürlohg the marquetry roundels.[56] An alternative attribution to Ince and Mayhew has been suggested on the basis of the Derby House commode.[57] The central roundels depicting *Diana and her hounds* and *Venus explaining the torch of Hymen to Cupid* were taken from engravings after paintings by Angelica Kauffmann (pl. 240); the oval medallions on the sides have Bacchantes inspired by antique gems and wall paintings.

Adam's design for the entire commode does not survive, but must have been made before his detailed drawings, one of which is dated 30 January 1773.[58] Together with his unexecuted designs for a similar bow-fronted commode for the Duke of Bolton, also dated January 1773, this was the first of several such pieces in Adam's work of the 1770s and 80s, and both designs were a

source of inspiration for all manner of variations by other designers.[59]

The accompanying pier-glasses were designed on 21 July 1773 and have crests of seated female figures first used in 1771 in a design for a chimney-glass for the back drawing-room of Robert Child's house in Berkeley Square.[60] Contrary to normal practice, the bases of these frames were omitted and the tops and sides made narrower than usual so as to enhance the continuity and add to the apparent height of the decoration of the piers. Evidently this novel arrangement was not entirely satisfactory; in August 1783, Linnell supplied '2 Pieces of fine Brass Wirework in brass Molding frames to stand before the Glasses.'[61]

Adam's gold-coloured paktong grate and fender, which repeat the scrolled foliage on the chimney-piece and the arcaded enrichment of the wall frieze, were also part of the 1772–3 smartening-up of the room. Its semicircular cast-iron fire-back with arcaded edging was intended to have a figured medallion like the one proposed for the sides of the commodes, but was modified in execution.[62] This has the distinction of being the only documented Adam grate that remains in the place for which it was designed.

Chronologically, the dining-room and drawing-room were followed by the new library on the north front (pl. 241), designed in 1766.[63] The previous function of this room is uncertain. It is smaller than the earlier library (897 square feet, or 7 × 11.8 metres, as compared to 1,167 square feet), but over twice the size of the library designed by Adam at the same time and in much the same style at Nostell Priory. Its walls are lined with a run of projecting bookcases interrupted only by the door, four windows and two chimney breasts. Ionic pilasters with double wave or heart-scroll enrichments on the front and sides are used to frame and subdivide the bays, the two largest of which are accented by applied Ionic porticos with pediments and fluted engaged columns (pl. 242). The frieze, instead of being fluted as shown in the design, is ornamented with a more lively pattern of circles, bell-flowers and rosettes, which is repeated round the walls, on the chimney-pieces and over the doors. The bookcase in the north-east corner is fitted as a jib door opening to a passage behind the breakfast-room, where some of the Ionic fittings from the old library were placed before 1777.[64]

Above the bookcases are ten long paintings by Zucchi of classical subjects related to the arts and sciences, and four square panels containing stucco medallions of Greek and Roman writers: Homer and Hesiod, Horace and Cicero. Large paintings attributed to Giovanni Battista Cipriani of *Anacron sacrificing to the Graces* and *Sappho writing the Odes dictated by Love* are placed over the chimney-pieces in stucco frames designed by Adam.[65] The paintings, books, four green lustring window curtains, green-painted Venetian blinds with lines and tassels, green cloth covering the desk and green leather chair cushions are the principal sources of colour.[66] The rest of the room was stony white. Two copies of Adam's design for the ceiling – one coloured, the other uncoloured – were given to Child to choose from and are still at Osterley; a third copy with different colouring is among the Adam drawings at the Soane.[67] As a matter of course, late nineteenth- and early twentieth-century revivalist taste decided on 'Adam' green; recognizing the inaccuracy of this, the V&A restored the ceiling according to the coloured design at Osterley. However, a 'plain white' ceiling is what Agneta Yorke saw in 1772 and recent paint analysis has confirmed this. Adam's stated preference for ceilings 'coloured with various tints to take off the crudeness of the white' has led to the mistaken belief that there are no white ceilings in his *œuvre*; hence the impulse to colour Adam ceilings.[68] In fact, there are similar monochromatic white or 'dead stone'-colour schemes in the hall at Syon, the gallery at Croome Court and the library at Kedleston; they have a thoroughly architectural impact, like a classical building turned inside out. The Osterley library ceiling, with its small-scale ornaments and low relief, is more characteristic of Adam's work in the late 1760s than the robust dining-room and drawing-room ceilings.

John Linnell is thought to have supplied the superb suite of ormolu-mounted marquetry furniture in 1768 or 1769. Its remarkably sophisticated French neo-classical style can be credited to the two young Swedish cabinet-makers in his employ at

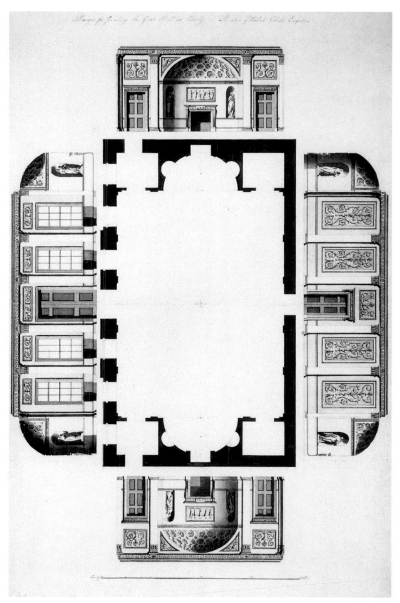

243   Plan and laid-out wall elevations of the entrance hall, by Robert Adam, 1767 (Osterley Park, The National Trust)

that time, Christopher Fürlohg and his brother-in-law, George Haupt.[69] The pedestal-desk was clearly meant to stand in the centre of the room; the two library tables were placed in front of the pedimented bookcases, with armchairs on each side, and the other four chairs in the suite were placed in the window embrasures.[70] The high quality of the furniture greatly impressed Agneta Yorke, as did all the taste lavished by Adam on ornamenting every part of the room. It is a measure of the value attached by Robert Child to the distinguished Fairfax library secured by his brother. Unlike other country-house libraries, this one does not seem to have been used as a family living-room; the gallery was where the family always sat.[71]

Adam's next task, and perhaps his most difficult one at Osterley, was to create a hall in the awkwardly proportioned space between the eating-room and drawing-room, which was too low in relation to its length and not long enough to divide into three separate rooms as he proposed in 1761. His solution, set forth in 1767, was to construct large semi-domed exedra at both ends, each containing a fireplace and niches for statues, like the alcoves he designed a year or so earlier for the dining-room at Harewood (pl. 243, 244).[72] These served not only to reduce the

244 View of the hall showing the ceiling and related pavement. The pedestals and urns predate Adam's involvement at Osterley

245 Sketch of a ram's-head stool, by Robert Adam, c.1764 (Sir John Soane's Museum: Adam drawings, vol. 54:66)

length of the room and thereby to increase its apparent height, but also to give it a Roman basilica effect and at the same time to provide 'movement' – that diversity of shapes and play of light and shadow upon which he set great store. In a further attempt to stress the vertical aspect, he reduced the entablature to a shallow Greek-key frieze and elongated the pilasters, which he modelled on those found in Diocletian's palace at Spalatro. For all his efforts, however, the lowness of the room has always been noted.[73]

It is hard to explain why his finished wall elevations retained the arabesque panels that he had proposed for the first hall six years earlier, in 1761, especially since the adjacent dining-room had been decorated with similar arabesque stucco work. For the sake of variety and also for stronger vertical emphasis, the arabesques between the pilasters (but not the ones over the doors and windows) were replaced by trophies of armour similar to those executed a few years before in the vestibule at Syon.

All the stucco ornaments, mouldings and architectural components are painted white and the grounds French grey, a colour more explicitly described by Agneta Yorke as 'greenish light grey'.[74] The marble floor answers the ceiling in reverse, with a black pattern on a white ground. It could be by Adam, but there

246   A carved and gilt-wood armchair upholstered in modern blue leather to match the original, designed by Robert Adam in 1764 and made by James Lawson for Sir Lawrence Dundas at Moor Park, Hertfordshire. The suite originally consisted of six arm-chairs, two sofas and two scroll stools. Two chairs, two sofas and two stools are now at Kenwood

247   One of a set of four hall stools at Osterley, painted white and upholstered in modern blue leather. Attributed to Robert Adam, c.1768–70

are no known designs, nor are there any bills prior to one for repairs by James Kerr in October 1778.[75] There are designs for the pair of carved-wood brackets and vase-shaped girandoles fixed to the pilasters between the windows, and for the scroll-end stools under the trophies (pl. 245).[76] The latter, a rough, uninscribed sketch probably dating from the early 1760s, suggests alternative ways of adding antique rams' heads to what is in essence a straightforward Kentian stool: either at the corners of the seat-rail, as was done on the suite of stools, chairs and settees made in 1764 for Sir Lawrence Dundas at Moor Park (pl. 246), or integrated with the legs as at Osterley.[77] The Osterley stools (pl. 247) cannot be precisely dated, nor can the brackets and vases, but they could have been made at any time between 1768 and the early 1770s. Though their robust naturalism is uncharacteristic of Adam's work of this period, it would be acceptable for hall furniture and can be compared to the hall stools designed in 1768 for the Earl of Shelburne at Bowood, and indeed to the pair of pedestals with rams' heads and paw feet in the great staircase at Osterley. Adam was not responsible for the hall pedestals.[78]

The decoration of the staircase (pl. 248) was undertaken in two stages. The first, for which there are no designs, probably dates from 1765 or 1766 and includes the screens of Corinthian columns on the *piano nobile* and Ionic ones on the floor above, as well as the friezes, oval medallions and square panels of large-scale stucco ornaments incorporating ewers and vases emblematic of hospitality. What the ceiling was like at this date is not known. In any case, it had to be adjusted in 1768 to accommo-

date Rubens's *Glorification of the Duke of Buckingham*, the Childs' great hero and distant relation.[79] This painting and Rubens's swagger equestrian portrait were commissioned by Buckingham for his London residence, York House, where they remained until the house was demolished in 1672, whereupon they were sent to Holland. Both canvases were purchased by Sir Francis Child the elder in 1697, while he was travelling in the Low Countries, and installed in his house at 42 Lincoln's Inn Fields. In 1767, Robert Child purchased a new house in fashionable Berkeley Square and the paintings were removed to Osterley. Unfortunately, the originals, together with other large paintings from Osterley, were destroyed by fire in Jersey in 1949. The *Glorification* has been replaced by a modern copy.

With the arrival of Rubens's ceiling painting, the staircase became a focus of attention requiring more varied and impressive decorations. Two novel designs for glass lanterns containing 'antique' oil lamps were made: one to hang between the Corinthian columns; the other to stand on a pair of ram's-head tripod pedestals in the north passage and on a landing. The standing lanterns incorporate ormolu dolphins derived from 'Athenian' Stuart's reconstruction of the lost tripod on the Choragic Monument of Lysicrates.[80] They were presumably made (possibly by Matthew Boulton) by 1772, when the tripod pedestals were painted green and white to match the walls. There was another pair of 'green and white painted Terms with bell glasses and lamps' in the small hall on the ground floor.[81]

Adam's design for the wrought-iron balusters decorated with classical anthemia and painted 'fair blue' does not survive, but was most likely of the same date as the identical balusters made in 1769 for the great stair at Kenwood. As a further, distinctive enhancement, the sides of the mahogany hand-rail were carved with Vitruvian scrolls to match the wall moulding.

Ideally the staircase should be viewed from the first floor, through the screen of giant Corinthian columns. The normal approach from the ground floor, where there was a family entrance and small hall, is rather disappointing, for it deposits the visitor in the north passage in a confusing and awkward position in relation to the hall and other reception rooms. However, Adam's plan was almost certainly determined to some extent by an earlier stair more or less in this place.

248 The staircase with three glass lanterns between the Corinthian columns on the first floor and a screen of Ionic columns on the floor above, designed by Robert Adam, *c.*1765–68

249 The Boucher–Neilson tapestry room showing Adam's ceiling (1772) and related carpet (1775)

250 One of six carved and gilt-wood girandoles on the alternate piers between the windows in the gallery, designed by Robert Adam, 1770. The carving is attributed to John Linnell

Like the staircase, the gallery also gained new importance from the arrival of Rubens's monumental equestrian portrait of the Duke of Buckingham. Prior to that, it was not Adam's concern and his work there was limited to removing the Venetian windows that had been inserted in the end walls before his arrival. In 1769 or 1770 he was commissioned to enliven the ten window piers with large mirrors and glass girandoles in neo-classical frames as distinctive and innovative as those he designed during the same period for Child's new house in Berkeley Square. A rejected design made for the drawing-room at Lansdowne House was used to frame 'four very large plates of Glass (6 feet 7 inches × 3 feet 4 inches, or 2 × 1 metres) . . . purchased at Gunnersbury', which, according to Agneta Yorke, were 'larger than those in his House in Town'.[82] Evidently the even larger girandoles (7½ feet, or 3.1 metres tall) with extraordinary heart-shaped mirrors (pl. 250), designed in 1770 to alternate with the pier-glasses, were not put up by 1772 or Mrs Yorke would doubtless have commented on them. Their carved and gilt

frames formed of foliate branches with female terms at the sides and husk festoons criss-crossed over the glasses are closely related to the oval pier-glasses shown in Adam's engraved elevation of the gallery at Syon, and to the dressing-room and dining-room mirrors designed in 1768 for Coventry House, Piccadilly.[83] They were almost certainly made by Linnell, who is also credited with the earlier suite of twelve mahogany armchairs and six large settees with seat-rails matching the dado and straight fluted legs echoing motifs found on Chambers's chimney-pieces.[84] Whether their design was by him or Chambers remains a matter of speculation. Adam had nothing to do with the suite.

251   The south-east corner of the tapestry room showing the pier-glass and table designed by Robert Adam, 1775

252   Detail of the crest of the pier-glass designed by Adam in 1775 to accord with the *trompe l'oeil* tapestry frame

253   Unidentified French artist, a watercolour drawing of the two medallions on the north wall of the tapestry room sent to Robert Child *c*.1774–75 by the Gobelins factory (Formerly in the possession of the Earl of Jersey, present whereabouts unknown)

254   Tripod pedestal of carved and gilt-wood with painted medallions; one of a pair designed by Robert Adam in 1776. The wing-figured candle vase is one of a pair supplied by Matthew Boulton in 1772 probably for the drawing-room

By 1809, the gallery had a profusion of 'tables, sofas and chairs . . . studiously *derangès* about the fire-place and in the middle of the room, as if the family had just left them, such is the modern fashion of placing furniture carried to an extreme'.[85] Henry James, writing in 1888, summed it up as 'a cheerful upholstered avenue into another century'.[86] The Palmyra drawing-room, on the other hand, remained a formal reception room associated with the state apartment, consisting of a tapestry drawing-room, state bedroom and Etruscan dressing-room.

These three very different rooms were conceived more or less simultaneously, starting in 1772 with designs for their ceilings. The tapestry-room ceiling is the only one that was executed without modifications (pl. 249). It is a variation upon a pattern consisting of a shaped cross in a circular frame and a central roundel in an octagonal frame, which was favoured by Adam in the early 1770s, the closest parallel being the Duchess of Bolton's dressing-room ceiling, designed in 1770.[87] The choice of pattern and colour were not determined by the French tapestry hangings, which most likely had only just been decided upon and not yet ordered.[88]

Robert Child was the last of five Adam patrons to commission medallion *tentures de Boucher* from Jacques Neilson, entrepreneur of the Gobelins factory.[89] The idea was almost certainly proposed by Adam and prompted by the installation of the Croome Court tapestry-room with its matching furniture in June 1771. The medallions of Child's set have the same theme as Lord Coventry's: the *Four Elements as personified by the Loves of Gods*. However, whereas Coventry had a medallion of *Neptune and Amymone* representing water, pier-glasses were used instead at Osterley. Over the chimney-piece is a medallion depicting *Cupid and Psyche*, prominently signed and dated 'Neilson ex 1775'; flanking it are smaller medallions of cupids; *Venus and Vulcan* (fire) are on the opposite wall; and on the inner wall facing the windows are two medallions, one of *Vetumnus and Pomona* (earth), the other *Aurora and Cephalus* (air). All are on a rose *damas cramoisy* ground. Their oval medallion frames are more distinctly neo-classical than earlier sets, as are the new, Louis XVI architectural borders, which support a variety of birds and animals appropriate to Mrs Child's celebrated menagerie at Osterley.

Pieces of tapestry of the same design were used to cover a fire-screen and chimney-board. The sofa and eight armchairs have matching rose *damas cramoisy* tapestry covers with Boucher's *Jeux d'enfants* in oval frames on the backs and floral compositions designed by Maurice Jacques and Louis Tessier on the seats and arm rests. John Linnell is believed to have designed and executed the suite around 1775.[90]

During that year, no effort was spared to make the room ready to receive the tapestries. All the painting and gilding was done, protective window blinds were put up and the chimney-piece was installed.[91] Its frieze of cameo heads and vases inlaid in coloured scagliola echoes the painted stucco frieze over the doors and is also related to the lozenge frieze with gilt cameos on the walls. Walpole was evidently thinking of the latter when he railed against the 'diminutive heads in bronze no bigger than a half-crown, (stuck) into the chimney-piece's hair'.[92]

A semi-circular pier-table was designed in March 1775, quite like the one made in 1774 for Northumberland House. It has painted plaques in the frieze corresponding to the inlaid scagliola ones on the chimney-piece, and a statuary marble slab with coloured scagliola ornaments related to both the ceiling and the carpet.[93] However, the design for the accompanying pier-glass had to wait eight months until Adam had seen a detailed sketch of the tapestry at the top of the pier – or even the piece itself (pls 251, 252). Only then would he have been able to design a compatible crest consisting of a pedestal and *tazza* of flowers flanked by two standing female figures holding garlands that appear to emerge from the tapestry.[94] Neilson supplied Child with a drawing of the principal *tenture* containing two medallions (pl. 253) and this must have been used by Adam in July 1775 when he made a design for the carpet, which is mainly related to the ceiling but also incorporates large baskets of flowers corresponding to the flower-vases in the tapestries.[95] It was executed by Thomas Moore (see pl. 249).

The tapestries arrived at Osterley in July 1776 and were put up that summer. Finally, in November, when all the fittings and furniture were in place, Adam designed a pair of unusual tripod pedestals combining pierced, painted, carved and gilded panels enriched with sphinxes, garlands, vases and other ornaments seen in the room (pl. 254).[96] These are an elaborated version of the pedestals designed in 1773 for Sir Watkin Williams-Wynn's house at 20 St James's Square. Curtains and curtain cornices are not listed in the 1782 inventory and, as at Croome Court, may have been considered excessive and unnecessary given the enriched window surrounds, shutters and protective blinds.

Writers about Osterley in the 1920s were able, and indeed bound, to compare the brilliantly coloured tapestry-room with the very much larger drawing-room at Syon where the red damask hangings still retained their bold, three-coloured pattern. Though both were overwhelming and unsuitable to dwell in, the tapestry-room was considered 'more entirely tasteful and satisfying' owing to the better relationship between the scale of the architectural enrichments and the wall coverings. The 'feast of many dishes, most richly concocted' by Adam in the tapestry-room was likened by H. Avray Tipping to a 'Brillat Savarin that has been at work with exquisite delicacy of touch and harmony of material'.[97]

In a formal sense, the French tapestry-room is the antechamber to the state bedchamber which, when Mrs Lybbe Powys saw it in 1788, was 'call'd the English bed-chamber, as all the furniture is English'.[98] Furniture is certainly the focus of attention, and the ceiling and wall decorations that dominate other rooms are subservient here. It is, nevertheless, to the ceiling that one must look for the overall theme – the pleasures of love and nature – depicted in five oval paintings from Tasso's *Gerusaleme Liberata*.[99]

Though the bed is the principal object (pl. 255), it did not have priority in the design sequence. Pier-glass frames to receive the very large and costly plates that were imported from France for this room and the adjacent dressing-room were evidently considered more urgent. Designs were made on 15 May 1775, with similar crests of mirror glass in the shape of concave rams'-headed pedestals incorporating painted roundels.[100] There was no such urgency for the chimney-glass, which was not only a smaller plate, but also one of the first to be made in England, adding substance to the room's 'English' sobriquet. Its design

255 The state bed showing the gilded headboard surrounded by putti and dolphins, designed by Robert Adam in 1776, and the bed carpet designed in 1778

waited until April 1777 and then was simply taken from the centre part of the chimney-glass in the Etruscan dressing-room at Derby House, designed in 1774 and published in the *Works* in 1779.[101]

The final design for the bed was produced exactly a year after the pier-glass, on 16 May 1776.[102] It is an improved version of an earlier, uninscribed design, dated 11 October 1775, for a canopied bed of the same plan, with pairs of columns projecting from the four corners so as to add movement to the composition, and with the same pedestal-shaped headboard surrounded by putti

and dolphins. This design has griffons at the corners of the entablature, and blue hangings that could not have been intended for the predominantly green bedroom presided over by sphinxes at Osterley.[103] It must have been made either for Child's London house, or for a different client (perhaps the Duke of Bolton or the Countess of Home), who rejected it.

The fluid plan of the Osterley bed – a rectangle with corner projections enclosing a circle representing the dome – can be seen in relation to the central feature of many Adam ceilings of this period (including those in the tapestry-room and dressing-

256 One of the four winged sphinxes symbolic of the *soleil nocturn* or eternal light on the projecting cornices of the entablature of the state bed

257 A gilt-wood arm-chair with winged sphinxes supporting the medallion back; one of a set of six designed by Robert Adam for the state bedroom in 1777

258 Design for the counterpane for the state bed. The panel with the eagle of the Child family crest in the centre is a simplified version of the ceiling pattern, by Robert Adam, 1776 (Sir John Soane's Museum: Adam drawings, vol. 17:159)

259 Design for the canopy for George III's box at the Italian Theatre, Haymarket, by Robert Adam, *c*.1775 (Sir John Soane's Museum: Adam drawings, vol. 27:83)

260   The Etruscan dressing-room, designed by Robert Adam, 1775

261   Design for the painted decoration of the east wall of the Etruscan dressing-room, by Robert Adam, 1775 (Sir John Soane's Museum: Adam drawings, vol. 14:131)

room), a circle with arcs cut out of each side containing a painted roundel, and to the supposed plan of the Temple of the Sun at Baalbec.

While its eight-poster canopied structure readily invites comparison with a temple dedicated to Venus, Pomona and the posterity of the Child family, a great deal of zealous source-mongering is needed to forge a weak and unconvincing link with the Choragic Monument of Lysicrates.[104] There is an abundance of painted, stuccoed, carved and embroidered flowers, including classical anthemion and palmette, which are also used on the wall and door friezes; rosettes and bell-flowers, which are repeated on the bed-carpet made by Thomas Moore from a design of February 1779;[105] marigolds, emblematic of Child's Bank, alternating in the valance with the eagles of the family crest and on the curtain cornice with poppy-heads, referring to sleep.

The predominance of green, a colour allied with fertility and traditionally preferred for beds, is also appropriate, though the velvet originally used to cover the walls was perceived by Walpole as an attribute of winter rather than spring.[106] While it was not uncommon for beds and mirror frames to be ornamented with loving putti and winged sphinxes (pl. 256) emblematic of the *soleil nocturn* and thus of eternal light, chair-backs supported by sphinxes were a novelty, first introduced here in 1777 and repeated only once more, in a more elaborate form, on a chair designed for Sir Abraham Hume's house in Hill Street in 1779 (pl. 257).[107] As the Osterley chairs were meant to stand against the dado, the sphinxes are carved only on the front.

Four-poster beds (in this case, eight-poster) lend themselves to architectural treatment, but nowhere is this more fully and successfully exploited than at Osterley. Even the valance and pelmet, drapes and counterpane (pl. 258) are designed to contribute to the baldachino effect in a way that Adam's other designs – the twin beds under one great dome designed in 1774 for Derby

House and the *lit à la polonnaise* designed for Lady Home around 1776 – did not.[108] The incongruity of dressing such a distinctly architectural structure in flowers made the bed an object of ridicule for Walpole. It is, he wrote, 'too theatric and too like a modern head-dress, for round the outside of the dome are festoons of artificial flowers. What would Vitruvius think of a dome decorated by a milliner.'[109] Walpole may not have been aware of the actual theatrical analogy between the dome of the bed and the canopied box designed by Adam at about this time for George III's box at the Italian Theatre in Haymarket (pl. 259).[110]

In relation to the overall scheme of decoration, the painted chimney-board designed by Adam in August 1778 is also incongruous, for although it contains appropriate motifs found elsewhere in the bedroom, its colour and composition are in the Etruscan style of the dressing-room. There are no known designs for the black and gold japanned commode with carved wood ram's-head capitals corresponding to the decoration on Adam's chimney-piece. It may have been supplied by Chippendale and is comparable to one he made in 1775 for Harewood.

Adam's first design for the dressing-room ceiling in 1772 had nothing Etruscan about it.[111] His final revised version, also dated 1772, is the same in all details except for a pale-blue rather than pink ground and the introduction of black and terracotta figured medallions suspended from the arms of the central cross and on the corner pedestals.[112] There were no plans to decorate the rest of the room in that style until 1775 (pl. 260), after the Etruscan dressing-room at Derby House was finished.[113]

The mode of decoration attempted at Derby House was, Adam claimed, unlike

anything hitherto practiced in Europe, for, although the style of the ornament, and the colouring of the Countess of Derby's dressing-room, are both evidently imitated from the vases and

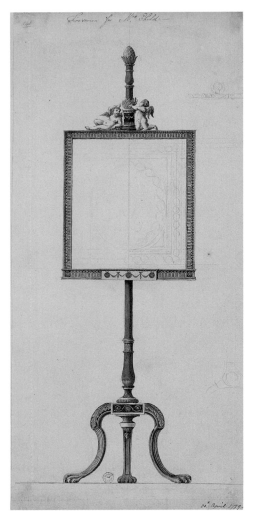

262   A 'Design of a Chair for the Etruscan Dressing Room at Osterly', by Robert Adam, 1776 (Sir John Soane's Museum: Adam drawings, vol. 17:96)

263   Arm-chair painted in the Etruscan style. One of a set of eight made for the Etruscan dressing-room; designed by Robert Adam, 1776

264   Design for a tripod firescreen in the Etruscan style for Mrs Child, by Robert Adam, 1779 (Sir John Soane's Museum: Adam drawings, vol. 17:148)

265   Design for an embroidered firescreen in the Etruscan style featuring the eagle of the Child family crest, by Robert Adam, 1776 (Sir John Soane's Museum: Adam drawings, vol. 17:141)

urns of the Etruscans, yet we have not been able to discover, either in our researches into antiquity, or the works of modern artists, any idea of applying this taste to the decoration of apartments.[114]

However, the Osterley ceiling designs clearly show that the taste was not distinguished by ornament, but rather by black and terracotta colours which were, as he said, inspired by the Etruscan vases in Sir William Hamilton's collection, published by D'Hancarville in four volumes, starting in 1767.[115] He must also have known of the imitation 'antique' tablets and medallions in 'black basaltes with Etruscan red burnt-in ground' that were being manufactured by Josiah Wedgwood as early as 1769. These were advertised in 1773 as being suitable for 'inlaying . . . in the Pannels of Rooms (and) Chimney Pieces, or for hanging up as ornaments in libraries . . . or as Pictures for Dressing Rooms'.[116] In 1778, Walpole described the Etruscan dressing-room at Osterley as being 'painted all over like Wedgwood's ware, with black and yellow small grotesques . . . It is like going out of a palace into a potter's field.'[117]

Piranesi's *Diversi maniere d'adornare i camini* (1769) was another precedent and possible model for the general pattern of the wall decoration with its thin vertical lines of strung-together ornaments linked by delicate arches and horizontal bands from which tablets, medallions, cameos and other ornaments are suspended.[118] The walls of the glass drawing-room at Northumberland House, designed in 1773, were also covered with delicate arched tracery incorporating urns, dancing nymphs, sphinxes and painted medallions. Adam evidently did not consider *that* decoration to be Etruscan. Yet it is interesting to note that his first design for the chimney-piece in the Northumberland House drawing-room, made in June 1773, had side panels in the Etruscan style, with terracotta ornaments on a black ground.[119] It was withdrawn and used instead for the Etruscan dressing-room at Derby House.

Adam's preference for pale bluish-grey as a ground for his Etruscan decorations here, at Derby House and at Home House is difficult to explain.[120] Was he trying to obtain a glass or an open-air effect? At Derby House the painted papier-mâché panels in the doors between the third drawing-room and the Etruscan dressing-room were said by Adam to have been 'so highly japanned as to appear like glass'.[121] Walpole saw the dressing-room at Osterley as a kind of pergola and thought 'it would be a pretty waiting room in a garden'. But as a termination to the two 'proud rooms' preceding it, it was inexcusably chilling and a 'profound tumble into the bathos'.[122] The vaulted garden-room under the stairs on the west front was also decorated in the Etruscan style in 1779.[123] Perhaps the sequence of French, English and Italian rooms was intended to reiterate the representation of the elements in Boucher's *tentures*: fire in the red tapestry-room, earth in the green bed-chamber and air in the dressing-room, with mirrors taking the place of water.

Finished coloured designs for the wall decorations, showing the chimney-piece, pier-glass and curtain cornices more or less as executed, were made on 11 October 1775 (pl. 261).[124] Pietro Mario Borgnis (?1742–c.1810), a figure and ornament painter who had worked with his father, Giuseppe Mattia Borgnis, at West Wycombe Park and church, painted the ornaments on sheets of paper which were then pasted onto canvas and fixed to the ceiling and walls.[125] The painted canvas chimney-board designed by Adam on 2 June 1777 can also be credited to Borgnis.[126] In lieu of painted decoration, the window wall has a pier-glass with a crest consisting of a painted medallion, repeating those on the other walls, and seated female figures flanking a basket of flowers, corresponding to the figures above the mantelpiece. Its black and gold frame harmonizes with the accompanying commode, incorporating panels of oriental lacquer and embellished with carved and gilt lions' heads. Like the commode in the state bedroom, this was probably supplied by Chippendale.

For the sake of completeness, a finished design for a carpet to answer the ceiling was made at the same time as the wall decorations.[127] It is unlikely to have been executed; no carpet is listed in the 1782 inventory, nor was one mentioned by Mrs Lybbe Powys in 1788.

Chairs were Adam's next task. His first design, dated 25 January 1776, had a black frame with terracotta ornaments, a vase-shaped splat and arms in the shape of winged griffons (pls 262, 263).[128] Apart from harmonizing with the black and gold pier-glass frame and japanned commode, these chairs might also have provided a much-needed counterbalance to the dark tablets and medallions on the upper part of the walls. But fearsome griffons were considered unsuitable companions for the festive female figures under which the chairs were to stand, and too masculine for a lady's dressing-room. A revised design was made on 6 March for a more conventional chair, painted grey with black and terracotta ornaments to match the walls.[129]

Few Adam rooms were furnished and decorated as completely and uniformly as this one. Not only did he design the tripod firescreen (pl. 264), with black and terracotta ornaments on a grey ground and lion's feet and masks relating to those on the japanned commode, but also the needlework panel embroidered by Mrs Child (pl. 265).[130] The survival of the Etruscan dressing-room unaltered is remarkable, especially after its occasional use as a schoolroom in the late nineteenth and early twentieth centuries.[131]

Osterley is one of the few houses in which Adam designed furniture for rooms where he was not otherwise involved. Apart from his girandoles and pier-glasses in the gallery, there is a pair of arched pier-glasses subdivided by slender female terms, with even more streamlined pier-tables (both designed in 1777) in the breakfast-room, and a bed (designed in 1779) with a fairly simple cornice of inlaid satinwood veneer surmounted by carved and gilt putti flanking a wreathed vase and anthemion, in the yellow taffeta bedroom on the second-floor.[132]

266   The south front of Kenwood House, designed by Robert Adam,
1764 (*The works in architecture of Robert and James Adam*, vol. 1 (1778),
pt. 11, pl. 11)

II

KENWOOD HOUSE

The house at Kenwood on the outskirts of London, in Hampstead (pl. 266), that the Hon. William Murray bought from the third Earl of Bute in 1754 was a modest villa of two storeys and seven bays, with a pedimented three-bay centre on the south front, a hipped roof and dormers. Its building history is uncertain.[1] The first house was probably built in the early seventeenth century by John Bill, printer to Charles I. There were later additions and improvements, principally to the south front, which could be seen from Hampstead Pond and which commanded a spectacular view over the Thames and the City of London.

Although the high offices that Murray held in the legal profession (solicitor-general, 1742–52; attorney-general, 1754–6) would have enabled him to afford a somewhat larger house in a more fashionable suburb, he had no need for one. He and his wife, Elizabeth (sixth daughter of Daniel Finch, seventh Earl of Winchelsea), both turned fifty in 1754; they had no children, their life-style was comfortable and generous but not lavish. According to the first Marquis of Lansdowne, William Murray (fourth son of David, fifth Viscount Stormont) 'was by nature a very eminent man, bred like all the great families of Scotland an intriguing aristocrat, poor and indefatigable, very friendly and very timid'.[2]

Though he did not share his father's and eldest brother, the Hon. James Murray's overt allegiance to the Jacobite cause, he was none the less tainted and plagued by it. In 1753 he was the victim of an insidious witch-hunt which culminated in formal charges of Jacobitism being brought against him.[3] The charges were proven baseless, but the unpleasant affair must have been a decisive factor in choosing a house outside London and away from political intrigue, yet within easy reach of the law courts and his rented house in Bloomsbury Square.[4] Neither Richmond nor Twickenham would have given Murray the independence he sought.

As Scots in England tended to band together, especially in the face of prejudice against them, it is not surprising that Murray should choose Kenwood, which had been in Scottish ownership since 1712, when it was bought by the second Duke of Argyll, who in 1715 conveyed the property to his brother, Archibald Campbell, Earl of Ilay and his brother-in-law, John Stuart, second Earl of Bute. In 1746, Ilay conveyed his half-share to his nephew, John Stuart, third Earl of Bute, who repaired and fitted

up the house, installed his library and instruments there and used the place as a retreat from town.[5]

Bute's chief interest was the garden, which he started in 1750, 'filling (it) with every exotic our climate will protect'. Of all the inhabitants of Kenwood, he is the one most likely to have built the greenhouse or orangery to the west of the house in front of the unsightly domestic offices. It certainly would have been within his abilities as an amateur architect to have designed the building himself, possibly with some advice from his friend Thomas Worsley. Though he might well have built a symmetrical building to the east had he remained at Kenwood, there is no evidence that he had formulated any plans before he left or that he encouraged Murray to do so later.

Murray – who was raised to the peerage, as Lord Mansfield, on 8 November 1756, the same day he was appointed Lord Chief Justice – was not as keen or as demanding a builder as Bute. Few people were. His only recorded improvements to Kenwood in his first ten years there were the papering of five rooms with painted Chinese-rail borders in 1757, and some work in and around the cold bath along the terrace to the east of the house in 1762.[6] These were straightforward builders' jobs.

The need for an architect did not arise until 1764, when Mansfield began to think of matching the greenhouse with a symmetrical eastern extension to house his library and generally tidy up the south front. He did not have to think hard about which architect to choose. The Adam brothers, apart from being fellow Scots, were already known to him. Robert had been introduced by his principal Scottish patron, John, Lord Hope, second Earl of Hopetoun, in June 1758 when he was setting up practice in London, and had visited Kenwood a few times in 1760 to pay his respects to Mansfield. The latter evidently gave him encouragement in his career as well as commissions for porphyry and sculpture to be obtained by James in Italy.[7]

James returned to England in 1763, and in 1764 launched his career as Robert's partner with designs for the interior of Mansfield's new library and for the ante-room linking it to the old house. These were accompanied by an exterior elevation of the south front designed by Robert. An undated and unsigned plan with attached alternatives also belongs to this initial scheme (pl. 267).[8] It shows the existing house with an entrance hall in the recessed centre of the north front; the main stairs, secondary stairs and breakfast-room to the east; the principal servants'

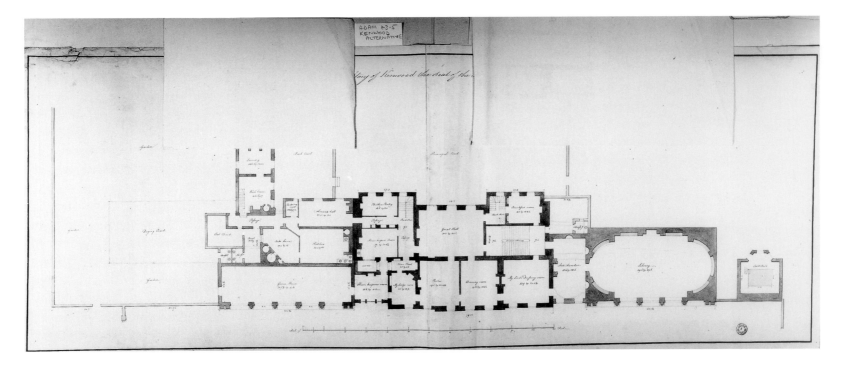

267 Ground-floor plan (unexecuted) for additions and alterations to Kenwood House, by Robert Adam, *c*.1764 (Sir John Soane's Museum: Adam drawings vol. 43:5)

268 Alternative ground-floor plan (unexecuted) for additions and alterations to Kenwood House, by Robert Adam, *c*.1764 (Sir John Soane's Museum: Adam drawings vol. 43:5)

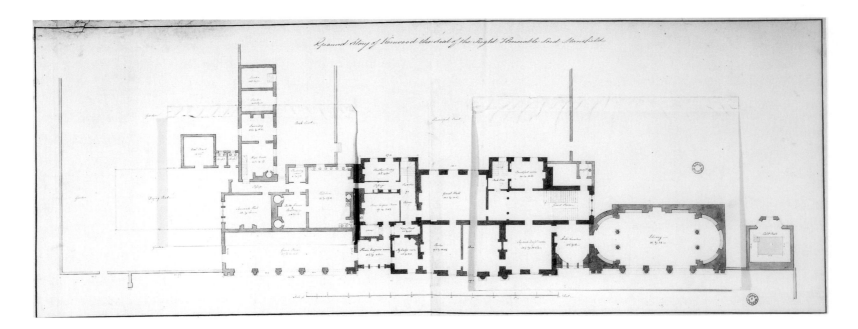

rooms and back or servants' stairs to the west; and four rooms on the south front. To this the Adam brothers proposed to add a wing the same length and height as the greenhouse – but 13 feet (3.9 metres) wider – containing an undivided book-room with semicircular ends, linked to the house by an ante-room with a Venetian window on the south front. There was to be a matching link with the greenhouse and the domestic offices behind it were to be rebuilt.

The chief objective of the alternative plan (pl. 268) was to improve the great staircase hall – through which visitors had to pass to reach the library – by extending it eastward, adding a columnar screen at the entrance and a spectacular Venetian window at the opposite end. Not only did this greatly reduce the size of the ante-room, but it also required a reduction in the width of the library, which, instead of being one large space, was to have

columnar screens separating the central part from the apsidal ends.

James Adam's section of the new wing (pl. 270) shows the north wall of the ante-room with a central niche according to the base plan, and the library according to the alternative plan: with a segmental vault decorated with long panels of figures suggestive of classical bas-reliefs over the main room and lower, flat ceilings on the screened apses. Despite the spatial contrasts, his design is quite static, heavy and monotonous compared to the interior as executed by Robert.

The same could be said of Robert's first design for the south front, which envisaged giant Corinthian columns and pilasters applied to the existing two-storey house. Evidently there was no thought at that date of adding an attic storey in the roof. Nor does there seem to have been any urgency to proceed with the

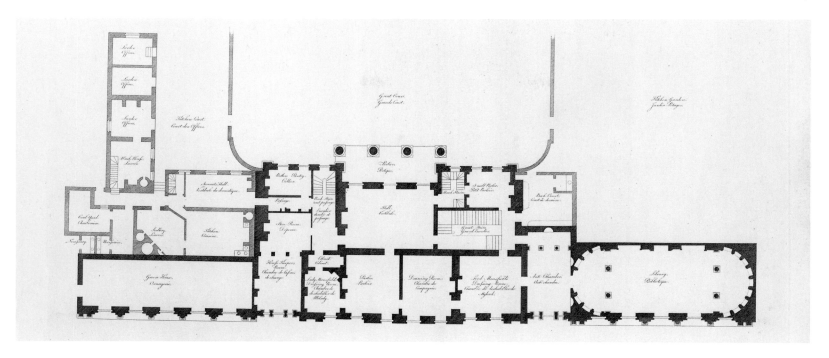

269 Final plan of the ground floor of Kenwood House, designed by Robert Adam, *c.*1767 (*The works in architecture of Robert and James Adam*, vol. I (1778), pt. II, pl. I)

270 James Adam, section showing the north wall of the library and ante-room, 1764 (Sir John Soane's Museum: Adam drawings vol. 43:3)

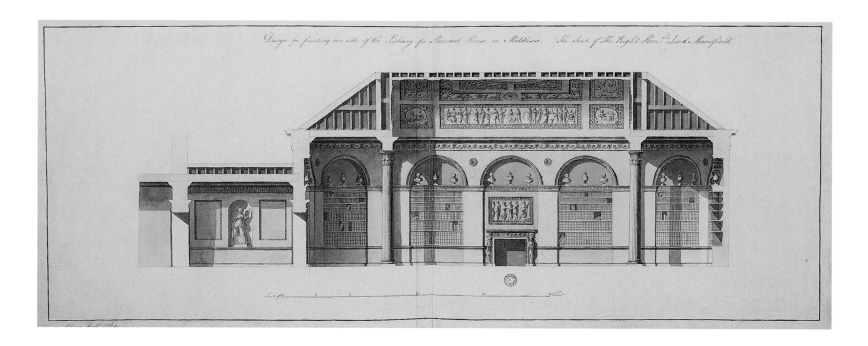

Adam brothers' proposed improvements. Their designs were shelved until 1767, when an unexpected change in circumstances suddenly demanded revised designs and prompt action.

In March 1766, Lord Mansfield's nephew and heir, David Murray, seventh Viscount Stormont, then ambassador to Vienna, lost his wife and it was decided that his six-year-old daughter, Elizabeth, should return to England to live at Kenwood in the company of her father's sister, the Hon. Anne Murray, and Elizabeth Dido Belle, a young mulatto who was the natural daughter of another of Mansfield's nephews, Sir John Lindsay. Additional bedrooms were urgently needed and the quickest and least disruptive means of providing them was to raise the walls and cover them with a new roof before removing the old one.[9]

In order to accommodate the attic, the south front had to be

redesigned (pl. 266); and before work could be commenced on the new buildings, the general plan had to be decided upon. The plan published in Adam's *Works* in 1774 (pl. 269) is to all intents and purposes the executed version which was probably finalized in 1767. It is fairly close to the earlier base plan, with minor modifications to the housekeeper's room in the west link.

By the end of 1767, the shell of the east wing was up and roofed. The ante-room was then decorated more or less as originally planned: with three niches filled with large plaster casts of 'Antyke figures viz. Flora Teis and a Muse' supplied in 1771 by James Hoskins and Samuel Oliver.[10] The niche on the north wall (shown in James Adam's section) was replaced by tall folding doors to the new lobby and dining-room built in 1793–6. In order for Adam to be able to centre the doors into the 'Great Room' or library to the east and Lord Mansfield's dressing-room

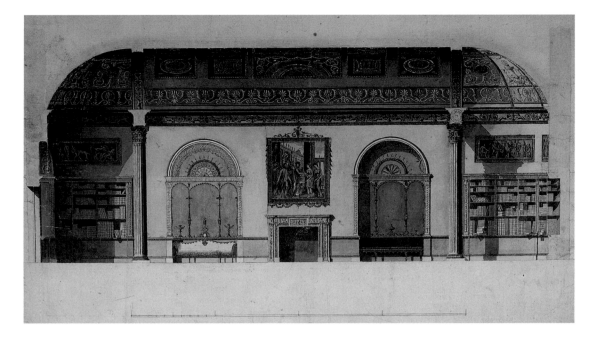

271 Section through the library showing the north wall, by Robert Adam, *c*.1767 (Sir John Soane's Museum: Adam drawings vol. 14:114)

272 Section through the library showing the south wall, by Robert Adam, *c*.1767 (Sir John Soane's Museum: Adam drawings vol. 14:115)

to the west, both of which were about 5 feet (1.5 metres) narrower than the ante-room, the width of the latter had to be proportionally reduced. This was accomplished by screening off part of the north end with a pair of Ionic columns and pilasters; in addition, necessity was turned to advantage by giving this part a low, flat ceiling that contrasts with the higher coved ceilings in the main part of the room and in the two-storey staircase hall preceding it.[11]

Little is known about the decoration of the ante-room apart from bills for stucco work and carving done in 1768 and 1769 by Joseph Rose and John Minshull respectively.[12] Accounts of the 1815–17 redecoration describe the ceiling as 'coloured' and the walls 'painted in oil', but do not specify the colours used.[13] The columns and pilasters were 'painted in imitation of red porphyry (and) Window Shutters, Doors &c. painted in imitation of Oak'. Red porphyry seems to have been the colour originally used by

Adam. The oak graining, however, was a new taste – a veritable rage at Kenwood – that was also applied to four long, white-painted stools covered with red leather.[14] These were probably placed on each side of the doors to the library and Lord Mansfield's dressing-room. It has been suggested that they were 'the sarcophagus shaped stools that stood in the entrance hall'; however, there is no evidence to corroborate this, nor is there any to suggest that the original ante-room stools were designed by Adam.[15]

The ante-room is a modest prelude to the library, which in scale and magnificence exceeds all the other rooms at Kenwood and is generally agreed to be one of Adam's finest interiors. According to Adam, it 'was intended both for a library and a room for receiving company. The circular recesses were therefore fitted up for the former purpose, and the square part, or body of the room, was made suitable to the latter.'[16]

273 Sections through the library showing the apses at the west end
(left) and east end (right), by Robert Adam, c.1767 (Sir John Soane's
Museum: Adam drawings vol. 14:113)

Despite its dual function, its design (pls 271–273) is altogether
more unified than James's earlier library scheme.[17] The height is
the same throughout, with half-domed apses at the ends
screened by Corinthian columns. The whole is bound together
not only by a frieze of lions and deer heads – 'the former being
the supporters, and the latter the crest of the family' – but also
by a continuous, broad anthemion band round the base of the
vaulted ceiling as well as the half-domes.

The proportions of the room – very nearly a double cube –
were claimed by Adam to have been 'reckoned elegant . . . and
the cieling (sic) in particular, which is a segment of a circle has
been generally admired'. He had quite a lot to say about the merits of this ancient form:

'It is an imitation of a flat arch, which is extremely beautiful,
and much more perfect than that which is commonly called
the coved ceiling, when there is height sufficient to admit of
it, as in the present case. The coved ceiling, which is a portion
or quadrant of a circle around the room, and rising to a flat in
the center, seems to be altogether of modern invention, and

admits of some elegance in the decoration. It is a sort of middle way, between the flat or horizontal ceiling, and the various
forms of arched ones practised by the ancients. As it does not
require so much height as the latter mode, it has been found
of great use in the finishing of modern apartments; but, neither is it's form so grand, nor does it admit of so much beauty
of decoration, as the ancient arched cielings; which consist of
three kinds, the dome, the groin, and the plain trunk arch,
such as that now before us, with their various combinations.[18]

Though a novelty in grand domestic apartments, flat or segmental arches had long been used in the roof construction of
vernacular buildings in south-west France, and in the eighteenth
century were perfected for wider use in gentlemen's houses as a
means of fireproofing. Count d'Espie's Manière de rendre toutes
sortes d'edifices incombustibles, published in Paris in 1754, was
promptly brought to the attention of Alderman William
Beckford, whose house at Fonthill had recently been destroyed
by fire. Beckford's keen interest in employing d'Espie's method
to rebuild himself a new fireproof house was made known to the

274 Design for the library ceiling, by Robert Adam, 1767 (*The works in architecture of Robert and James Adam*, vol. I (1778), pt. II, pl. VII. Hand-coloured copy in Sir John Soane's Museum)

275 The south wall of the library showing the curtain cornices and pier-glass frames designed by Robert Adam and carved by William France, 1769. The carved and gilt-wood pier-tables were designed by Robert Adam in 1765 for Sir Lawrence Dundas. They have been attributed either to France and Bradburn or to Fell and Turton

public with a view to promoting Louis Dutens's English translation of the book published in 1758. As it happened, his new house at Witham Park, Somerset was designed by Adam in 1762 and included a large saloon the same shape as the library at Kenwood, with apsidal ends and columnar screens.[19] It was probably also intended to have a similar vaulted ceiling, but no corroborative drawings survive and the unfinished house was demolished after Beckford's death in 1770. The ceiling in the second drawing-room at 20 St James's Square, designed in 1772, was of this type, and the house in Duchess Street built in 1779 for General Robert Clerk and later occupied by Thomas Hope had segmental vaults of bricks or tiles throughout.

Low-rising segmental arches, quite apart from their specialized interest to d'Espie and Beckford, were a very topical subject in the early 1760s, when the competition for the new bridge over the Thames at Blackfriars was won by a fellow Scot, Robert Mylne, with a design for unusual elliptical arches. Adam's own bridge designs often have segmental arches.[20]

The decoration of the ceiling is not as unusual as its shape, nor is it any more elaborate than other Adam ceilings of the late 1760s (pl. 274). Joseph Rose was responsible for all the stucco work here and elsewhere in the house.[21] Antonio Zucchi supplied the inset paintings of *Hercules between Glory and the Passions* for the central oval, *Justice embracing Peace, Commerce, Navigation,* and *Agriculture* for the four lunettes, figures representing *Religion, Jurisprudence, Mathematics* and *Philosophy* for the four flanking panels, and the four seasons for the corner roundels. On the walls of the apses are his oblong paintings of

276 One of the mirrored niches flanking the chimney-piece on the north wall. To the left is the antique bust of Homer, which Pope bequeathed to Lord Mansfield, on a pedestal designed by Robert Adam in 1765 for Sir Lawrence Dundas at 19 Arlington Street. The sofa is part of a suite designed by James 'Athenian' Stuart for Spencer House, Green Park where it is now

The Aldobrandini Wedding, an *Epithalamium* (marriage song), *The Rape of Europa*, a *Bacchanal* and *Minerva among the Arts*; and over the door is a semi-circular lunette of *The infant Hercules strangling two serpents*.[22]

According to Adam,

the grounds of the panels and freeses (were) coloured with light tints of pink and green, so as to take off the glare of white, so common in every ceiling, till of late. This always appeared to me so cold and unfinished, that I ventured to introduce this variety of grounds, at once to relieve the ornaments, remove the crudeness of the white, and create a harmony between the ceiling and the side walls . . .

Like other statements in his *Works*, this has to be treated with some caution. The impression he gives of being responsible for the introduction of coloured ceilings is demonstrably untrue.[23] His description of the colours used here is much more problematic. On the one hand, it is confirmed by his ceiling designs at the Soane, by contemporary hand-coloured copies of the engrav-

ing in the *Works* and by pencil notes on one of the ceiling designs, referring to the 'Soffit of the Collumns White, the Frieze Picked in Red Darker than the Red for Ceiling, the sides of the Room light Green, The Fans of the Recesses Blue'.[24] On the other hand, paint scrapes made in 1969 found no traces of green, only a distinct blue, pink, white and gold – an unusually limited palette for an Adam room of this grandeur and date. Whether these investigations were as comprehensive and systematic as present standards would demand is questionable; so too is the static homogeneity of the pink and blue throughout the room.

It is difficult to explain Adam's inaccuracy in describing his recent work, if that was indeed the case. Evidently, as the plan of Syon showed, he did not regard the *Works* as a topographical publication and was primarily concerned that the public should know and judge him by his designs, rather than by what was executed in accordance with the wishes of his clients. The Mansfields' preference for blue rather than Adam's proposed green would not necessarily have required the making of another coloured design for the use of workmen. Written instructions would have sufficed. Nor is it conceivable that Adam's finished coloured designs, which were quite expensive and highly regarded, were used by common workmen and then discarded, as Julius Bryant maintains.[25] It is far more likely that copies of the designs presented to Mansfield were destroyed by the Gordon rioters who set fire to his house in Bloomsbury Square in 1780.

There was not much scope for differing ideas about the decoration of the south wall (pl. 275). The window piers clearly called for a pair of large mirrors and in November 1768 these arrived from France, already fitted with plain wood-back frames as well as gilt moulded frames. William France's bill describes in detail his unpacking the cases; meeting Adam at Kenwood to decide how to put the glasses up; agreeing that the walls should be cut away, fixing very stout oak frames into the cavities; screwing the plates of glass with the back-frames 'very safe' on to the oak frames; 'finishing the Gilt mouldings &c . . . the Mitres & joints of the french frames being very ill done'; and finally 'Repairing & new gilding where wanting the 2 large pier frames the Gilding had been a good deal hurt by Unpacking & by Salt water'.[26] The oval medallion crests flanked by winged griffons and the foliate ornaments at the bases were Adam's additions to the French frames. They are not included in William France's bill and were probably made and put on later.

It was not the frames that attracted attention, but rather the size of the glasses: 8 feet 4 inches by 4 feet 2 inches (2.5 by 1.2 metres) – about 1 foot (30 centimetres) smaller in each direction than the glasses in the drawing-room at Syon.[27] Yet, despite its large French mirrors, the library at Kenwood does not have or even aspire to the fashionable French look of Syon. It is a distinctly Adam creation, his first and possibly his most successful in the grand manner.

Accompanying the pier-glasses were two richly carved and gilt pier-tables each with eight legs, 'sweep'd stretching rails' and pendant ornaments under the frieze, designed by Adam and made by William France in 1769 at a total cost of £67.12.0. The 'large square' tables with 'green marble tops 3 ft. by 2 ft. 6 in.' (90 by 70 cm) were last noted in the 1841 inventory, but have since disappeared and there are no designs that can be associated with them, nor do they appear in any of the early photographs of the interior.[28] The two pier-glasses, three carved and gilt curtain cornices (also designed by Adam and made by France in 1769) and the statuary marble chimney-piece are the only original furnishings remaining in the room. The chimney-piece, which was carved by John Devall, has Corinthian pilasters and a tablet like the one in the library at Osterley, with a sphere flanked by two half-boys and foliage.[29]

As designed by James Adam in 1764, the inner wall and the apses were to have uniform arched recesses, square in plan: one containing the chimney-piece and all the others fitted with bookcases (pl. 270). According to Robert's revised scheme (pl. 273), the apses were completely ringed with flat-topped bookcases articulated by Corinthian pilasters, and only two arched recesses were built in the north wall on either side of the chimney-piece. For these, Adam conceived a novel form of mirrored wall decoration (pls 271, 276) consisting of plates of different widths – the widest in the centre and the narrowest in the reveals – in arched frames supported by baluster-shaped colonettes and ornamented at the bottom with antique urns and scrolled foliage, all elaborately carved and gilt in burnished gold by William France.

The ten plates of French glass were supplied by Thomas Chippendale, who signed a formal agreement with Adam on 14 June 1769 to deliver the glasses 'in London Silver'd & ready to put up' at a cost of £340 'in about Two Months from this Date'.[30] The task of seeing that the agreement was properly observed fell to the cabinet-maker in charge, William France, who had to negotiate directly with Lord Mansfield on 25 August (when the two months was up) for £170, half the cost, to be paid to Chippendale in advance and an extension of three months to the delivery date, taking upon himself the responsibility of repaying the sum should there be any neglect on Chippendale's part.

The large plates were duly delivered to France and put in by him in November 1769, at which time smaller pieces of glass, easily obtained from an English maker, were placed in the bellflower frieze just above the arched mirrors. Unfortunately, these were omitted in the 1969 restoration of the recesses, which had been converted into bookcases between 1815 and 1817 (pl. 277).

Under the mirrors were '2 Sopha's made (by William France) to Mr Adams Design carv'd & gilt in burnish'd Gold the carving all finished in a very Elaborate Manner' and upholstered in the same crimson India silk damask used by France to make festoon window-curtains for the room. France also provided 'three Scrole headed Sopha frames for the windows . . . on the same principal as the Sopha's' and similarly upholstered. The suite was conceived by Adam as in integral part of the wall decoration, along with the mirrors, pier-glasses and tables, curtain cornices, the chimney-piece and the frame for David Martin's portrait of Lord Mansfield above it.[31]

Eight gilt cabriole elbow-chairs of an earlier date, covered with green silk, were brought from elsewhere in the house and reupholstered with crimson damask to match Adam's suite. They were probably placed in the two apses on either side of the door and flanking Nollekens's bust of Mansfield at the far end of the room. Other library furniture, notably the 'large Mahogany

Reading Stand on a Stout Pillar and Claw' and two red damask screens on carved and gilt mahogany poles, was made by William France to his own design, in a transitional rococo style.[32]

A needlework carpet, presumably worked by the several ladies residing at Kenwood, was in the room in 1796. By 1831 it had been replaced by a crimson fitted carpet with a gold border corresponding to the band of anthemia in the ceiling.[33] This was assumed by English Heritage to replicate the original carpet that was in the room in Adam's time and was therefore used as the model for a new carpet made in 1990. To explain and justify the plainness of this latest carpet, it was argued that 'the ceiling is so extraordinarily elaborate that a mirror image underfoot would have been quite overwhelming' and that the simple solution could also account for the absence of any Adam designs.[34] The evidence, however, is quite the contrary. There are several rooms of this period – the gallery at Syon and the drawing-room and octagonal dressing-room at Coventry House, Piccadilly, to name a few – with equally if not more elaborate ceilings for which Adam designed multicoloured floral or repeat-pattern carpets. But there are no known designs or examples of plain, bordered carpets, nor are there designs for borders specifically for carpets other than bed-carpets. The simple solution is atypical of Adam, but it is just what one would expect in 1815, when the house was extensively refurbished and every room was fitted with close carpets.

The library, with its vast pier-glasses and mirrored recesses, was surely intended by Adam to be 'quite overwhelming', and indeed ought to be more so than it is now, and more varied and scintillating too: with the small pieces of glass restored to the friezes above the mirrors, more gradations in the colouring of the walls and ceiling, and with the glaring, bathroom-white columns toned down to a dead-stone colour or even painted to imitate porphyry, as they were in 1950.[35]

While the library extension and attic storey were going up, Adam was at work on the interiors of the old house, starting with the 'great stair', an important space through which visitors had to pass in order to reach the 'great room'. This probably superseded a more modest stair, about which nothing is known, not even its exact location. Adam's stair was lit by a large window on the landing, which was filled in in 1796 when the north-east wing was built. As a result, his earlier ceiling (containing a rosette boss in a large diamond-shaped compartment) was removed and the present skylight put in in its place.[36] It is the cast-iron anthemion balusters more than anything else that mark the staircase as Adam's. They were made in February 1769 and are identical to those on the great stair at Osterley which were painted 'fair blue'.[37] It is likely that the Kenwood balusters were originally blue too; black, as they now are, seems too severe for a domestic interior. In 1815 they were gilt and bronzed, the woodwork and doors were painted oak, and the staircase was renamed the 'Oak Stair' to distinguish it from the lesser 'Deal Stairs' on the west side of the house.[38]

There is an Adam design for a term pedestal and glass lantern on which is written instructions that '(Sefferin) Nelson is to

277 A view into the library

278   The hall–dining-room. On the left, filled with plants, is the wine-cooler designed by Adam for the sideboard. The designer of the stools is not known

279   Designs of miscellaneous furniture for Kenwood House, by Robert Adam. The oval mirror on the right was for the hall–dining-room (*The works in architecture of Robert and James Adam*, vol. I (1778), pt. II, pl. VIII)

make one complete & if that is liked he is to do 3 more.'[39] One pedestal made from the design can be seen in a 1913 *Country Life* photograph of the staircase,[40] but the fact that there is no mention of the other three in any of the inventories suggests that it was not to Mansfield's liking.

Under Adam's supervision, improvements were made in every room of the old house; however, few of these were to his design and those that were consisted of friezes, chimney-pieces and furniture. The only rooms for which he also designed ceilings were the great stair and the hall, both of which were largely his creation. As part of the remodelling, an Ionic portico and pediment were added to the main entrance on the north front in 1772. At the same time, a decision was taken to decorate and furnish the hall as a dining-room (pl. 278) – an informal, colourful place for hospitality in sharp contrast to the imposing formality of the portico.

There was no room at Kenwood set aside exclusively for eating: the parlour on the south front was described by the craftsmen working in it in 1772 as the dining-room; and the small parlour on the east side of the north front was known as the breakfast-room.[41] The hall – being near the kitchens on the west side – must always have been used for large dinner parties; the upper hall (or Chinese room) might also have served that purpose.

Bacchus is the overriding theme of Adam's hall ceiling; slightly more so in execution than in his design dated 18 January 1773.[42] In the centre is a large roundel of *Bacchus and Ceres* painted by Zucchi '*en clair-obscur en forme de camée*', and around it is a stucco wreath of grapevines.[43] There are more bacchic figures in the four stucco medallions on the outer ring of corn husks, and six painted oval cameos of dancing Bacchantes by Zucchi in the two side panels.

The statuary marble chimney-piece carved by George Burns in May 1773 'from a Design of Mess.rs Adam' (now lost) has a head of Bacchus with a garland of grapes, swags of vine leaves and husks in the tablet and deer heads in the capitals. The deer head, which is Mansfield's crest, is also to be found in the metopes of the Doric frieze alternating with rams' heads. Originally, the architraves of the five doors had stucco tablets executed by Joseph Rose, flanked by carved-wood buchrania (sacrificial ox-skulls) supplied by Sefferin Nelson. These were removed in 1815 when the central door to the drawing-room was replaced by a tall niche and two new doors were introduced on either side of it. Zucchi's circular overmantel painting of *Diana and her muses resting after the hunt* and its carved and painted frame made by Nelson also vanished in the 1815 replastering of the walls.

Oval mirrors with flower baskets and winged griffons in the crest, Bacchus-head paterae at the base and novel side projections supporting urns and pendant garlands were designed 'for the hall' in March 1773.[44] The total width of the frames suggests that they were initially intended to be hung opposite the entrance, on either side of the door to the dining-parlour, where they would have reflected and enhanced the light from the north-facing windows. In the event, the lateral projections were omitted and the frames were made to fit the piers between the two windows and the glazed front door. The result was a veritable wall of glass. Sefferin Nelson was paid £200 on 17 August 1773 for carving and painting the two oval frames, supplying 'the glasses to both . . . with the borders', which were also of glass, and putting them up.[45] They too were victims of the 1815 restoration.

All that survives of Nelson's work in the hall is the sideboard suite, consisting of a table with a mahogany top, eight fluted legs and a fluted frieze; a pair of zinc-lined vases supported on ram's-head pedestals fitted as pot cupboards; and a mahogany wine cooler. This was 'done under the Direction of Messrs. Robᵗ and Jaˢ Adam' in 1773, painted white to match the pier-glasses and placed on the east wall between the doors to the principal and secondary stairs.[46] A year later, the brothers published the suite and their other Kenwood furniture in the second number of their *Works* (pl. 279), 'in order', they said, 'to give more utility and diversity to the work'. The table now in San Francisco's Legion of Honor Museum, which was presumably made from the engraving, is proof of the utility of their publication.[47] In 1815, David William Murray (1777–1840), 3rd Earl of Mansfield, had the sideboard, pedestals and urns 'painted oak' to match the woodwork.[48] By 1922, when the contents of the house were sold, the table and pedestals were white again, but the vases were mahogany.[49]

'Two tables of jet-black marble of a most excellent polish' were noted by Samuel Curwen, an American visitor, in April 1776 in what he called 'the great Hall'.[50] These are thought to be the pair of c.1760 gilt-wood side-tables with marble tops (possibly made by William France) which were recorded in the upper hall in 1796, where they were accompanied by oval mirrors in elaborate foliate frames of a similar date.[51] The upper hall, which had other black and gold furniture and a gilded chimney-piece, is a far more likely place for them than the hall, where nearly all the furniture was painted and there was no gilding. Had they been in the hall, they could only have been on the south wall opposite the front door, where Adam's oval mirrors were intended to go. There would then have been no place left for stools, or indeed for seats of any description. By 1796 the walls were lined with

LORD MANSFIELD,
Chief Justice of England, 1775.

280 David Martin, *William Murray, 1st Earl of Mansfield*, a replica of the original in the Mansfield collection at Scone Palace, Perthshire. The bust of Homer is shown on an Adam pedestal which has not been

chairs: twelve rosewood Chinese pattern armchairs and two mahogany splat-back chairs.[52]

According to Curwen, the 'Hall saloon Chambers &c (were) covered with paper of India or Chinese figures'.[53] We know from the accounts of the painter, George Steuart, that the hall doors were painted blue with white mouldings, the plinth was also blue, the 'Enrichd Mouldings to Pannels (of paper?) done flat white and afterwards blue' and the ceiling 'Two Greens purple & ornaments white'.[54] Purple was not only fashionable at the time, especially in combination with green, but was also associated with Bacchus. These colours would have blended well with the original patterned India paper, which is not the case in the recent restoration, where the walls and dado (not of Adam's time, having been entirely replastered in 1815) were painted plain duck-egg blue. Despite the scientific accuracy of the recently restored ceiling and its improvement upon past restorations, the room as a whole is devoid of the finely tuned balance and *élan* characteristic of Adam interiors. It is a safe, stereotyped 'Adam' compromise that only succeeds in misinforming the public.

Four white marble busts on black pedestals were recorded in the hall in 1796. The one that attracted the attention of Daniel Lysons was 'the antique bust of Homer . . . that was bequeathed to Lord Mansfield by Pope'.[55] This treasured antiquity was included in the portrait of Mansfield painted by David Martin in 1773, where it is shown standing on a carved and gilt Adam pedestal with ram's-head corners (pl. 280). A pedestal of similar

281 The chimney-piece in the upper hall with inset, painted Chinese tiles and carved and gilt-wood mounts, designed by Robert Adam, *c.*1772

282 Detail of a Chinese merman from whose tail a festoon of classical bellflowers is suspended

283 Detail of the palm frieze behind a Chinese fretwork fence

284 Detail of a putto in a scallop shell being drawn by two seahorses

description was in the hall at the time of the sale in 1922, but neither it nor any related Adam design has been traced.[56]

When Kenwood was built, the four bay centre of the south front was one large room, as it is now. At some stage before Adam's time, it was divided into a parlour and drawing-room. After the creation of the new dining-room in 1794, the parlour ceased to be used for dining; it and the drawing-room were then converted to libraries. Finally, in 1815, the third Earl of Mansfield had the partition wall removed so as to make one long 'Book Room' which became known as a 'Breakfast Room' in 1831.

Adam was not required to do anything in the drawing-room. The parlour, on the other hand, was completely refurbished by him in 1772 for use as a family dining-room. The accounts of the carver, George Burns, and the carpenter, John Phillips, provide the fullest record of what was done; the only surviving Adam designs being for the frieze and the oval pier-glass engraved in the *Works*. Round the room was a frieze of leaves and anthemion ornament which was repeated on the architraves of the four doors: one false door (mistakenly described as a gib) to match the door to the hall, another opening to the drawing-room and the fourth leading to Lady Mansfield's small dressing-room or boudoir.[57]

On the pier between the two windows was a large oval mirror, carved and gilded by Burns, with winged sphinxes on projecting shelves and scrolled foliage issuing from an anthemion base. This novel design was originally made in about 1772 for the dining-parlour at the Honourable Frederick Thynne's house at 30 Curzon Street, which was remodelled by Adam in

285 Cabinet with inlaid decorations and gilt bronze mounts framing *pietre dure* panels of Italian landscape made in Florence by Baccio Capelli, 1709. Designed by Robert Adam for the Duchess of Manchester at Kimbolton Castle, Huntingdonshire, 1771 (Victoria and Albert Museum)

1771–3.[58] The pier-glass seems to have left Kenwood when the parlour and drawing-room were amalgamated. Whether the mirror sold by Mallett & Sons in the early 1900s was the original or a copy made from the engraving in the *Works* is not known, nor is its present ownership. It was originally accompanied by a semicircular table with a mahogany top, tapered legs and a frieze echoing the one round the walls, 'Gilded in Oil Gold, and . . . painted blue colour'.[59] This was illustrated by John Swarbrick before it was sold in 1922, since when it has not been traced.[60]

The statuary marble chimney-piece has also vanished, as has Adam's design for it. According to the carver, George Burns, it had sphinxes and a vase in the tablet and trusses enriched with double guilloche and rosettes corresponding to the ornaments on the pier-glass. A 'Chimney Blind' was made for it in 1772 by the carpenter, John Phillips.[61] It is tempting to associate this with Adam's design for a chimney-board inscribed 'first Drawing room at Kenwood' (possibly meaning the parlour preceding the drawing-room) and with the 'chimney board, painted by Zoochi (*sic*)' which is recorded in the 1796 inventory as being in Lady Mansfield's dressing-room on the first-floor, above the parlour.[62]

Lord Mansfield's dressing-room is the only other ground-floor room with which Adam was involved – a bit later, after the library and main reception rooms were finished. There are

designs at the Soane for the chimney-piece dated 11 June 1779, and for the frieze; only the former remains *in situ*.[63] This room at the east end of the old house had previously been the library and was used as a reading-room by the first Earl of Mansfield. However, the learned second earl moved his large library into the two adjacent rooms and had it redecorated as a yellow drawing-room furnished with black and gold Japan furniture.

Lady Mansfield's small dressing-room or boudoir at the opposite end of the house was set aside for the ladies, of whom there were several in residence. They seem to have been better provided for on the first floor. The middle room on the south front was Lady Mansfield's bedroom; she had a sitting- or dressing-room to the west, which opened to a small, end room (known in 1796 as the white room and in 1815 as the blue room), and to the upper hall or drawing-room on the north front.[64] East of Lady Mansfield's bedroom was the so-called 'alcove room', with a bed-alcove and a small closet attached, and a separate entrance from the principal staircase. This was presumably Lord Mansfield's bedroom.

Adam designed two chimney-pieces for the private apartment in 1783. The one made for Lady Mansfield's bedroom has pairs of fluted Ionic pilasters, oval medallions in the blocks and a rosette frieze instead of the more severe flutes initially proposed.[65] The other design is for a slightly larger, more elaborate and more

feminine 'Painted Chimney', with a basket of flowers in the tablet and vases of flowers between widely spaced pairs of Ionic pilasters. It may have been intended for Lady Mansfield's sitting-room. Though large-scale coloured drawings of details were made, the chimney-piece was not executed, possibly owing to Lady Mansfield's death on 10 April 1784.[66]

The room on the north front, now known as the upper hall, was called the north drawing-room in 1796 and the billiard room in 1815. In Adam's time, it was referred to as the 'Chinese Room', not so much for its chinoiserie wallpaper, which was also used in several other rooms and was removed in 1815 when the north wall was taken down and rebuilt, but rather from its extraordinary chimney-piece (pls 281–4). This Piranesian composition was specially designed to display nine painted Chinese tiles in gilt frames, surmounted by gilded mermen and griffons, putti and sea-horses. In that respect it is comparable to the *pietre dure* cabinet designed by Adam in 1771 for the Duchess of Manchester at Kimbolton Castle (pl. 285). Above the tiled frieze is a deep palm-leaf cornice, which is fenced, as it were, by Chinese paling and broken in the centre to admit an arched panel of mirror glass. There is a rough sketch by Adam for the chimney-piece and a bill from Sefferin Nelson for 'Four Freezes to Chy Piece in the Chinese Room with Gilding ye Same' in 1772–3, which presumably refers to the sea-horses and putti over the four oblong panels in the frieze.[67] When the rest of the carving was done and by whom is not known.

Had Adam kept his promise and published another number of his *Works* containing the 'many alterations (he) made, and many inside decorations (he) added, in the apartments of the old house', this and other questions pertaining to his work at Kenwood might have been answered. As it is, much remains open to speculation.

Not least among them is the *raison d'être* and fate of his extraordinary designs for a grandiose epergne or table-centre for Lord Mansfield (pl. 286), fitted up as three garden pavilions with chinoiserie tented bows, a classical central dome quite like the state bed at Osterley (1775–6) and two gazebo turrets, supported on a multitude of palm-tree columns (at least sixty-four, some resting on winged sphinxes) linked by floral arches draped with festoons from which fifty or so glass lanterns were suspended.[68] The 'plateau' or floor of this long structure was 'paved' with *faux porphyry* and malachite or foiled glass or japanned papier mâché (pl. 287). Such a colourful extravaganza could only have been designed for a special occasion and there were two in 1776: Lord Mansfield's elevation to an earldom on 31 October and the marriage on 5 May of his nephew and heir, David Murray, seventh Viscount Stormont, to Lady Louisa Cathcart, which was celebrated at Kenwood.[69] The large scale and highly coloured finish of Adam's designs suggest that they were executed, but probably as a temporary structure, a party piece made not of precious materials like silver, but rather of painted and gilded metal. In that respect, it is comparable to the full-size *fête* pavilions erected in the central court at Syon in 1768 and at The Oaks in 1774.

286   Design for an épergne for Lord Mansfield, by Robert Adam, *c.*1776 (Sir John Soane's Museum: Adam drawings vol. 49:29)

287   Design for a 'Plateau for Lord Mansfield', being the base of the épergne, by Robert Adam, *c.*1776 (Sir John Soane's Museum: Adam drawings vol. 49:30)

288   The east front of Nostell Priory with the wing added by Adam to
the right

12

NOSTELL PRIORY

According to contemporary sources, Colonel James Moyser of Beverley designed the large new house that Sir Rowland Winn, fourth baronet (1706–65), began building around 1736 to replace the medieval priory at Nostell in Yorkshire.[1] Its plan – a central block with four pavilions linked by quadrants, inspired by Palladio's Villa Mocenigo – had evidently been fixed before 1731, when it was shown in outline on a survey of the park drawn by Joseph Perfect.[2] The similarity of the scheme to a design by Colen Campbell raises the possibility that he was the first architect consulted by Winn, some time between his coming of age in 1727 and his marriage in August 1729 to Susannah Henshaw, a descendant of Sir Thomas More.[3] During this period, Campbell was working in Yorkshire for Thomas Robinson at Baldersby and John Aislabie at Studley Royal. Campbell died in September 1729, which may account for the long delay between the conception of the design and its execution.

Winn, needing a sympathetic replacement, is likely to have sought the advice of Moyser: a local gentleman–architect, Lord Burlington's friend and disciple, who was doubtlessly known to him personally and was, moreover, a kinsman of Sir Charles

Hotham, Campbell's first Yorkshire patron, for whom he built a house at Eastgate in Beverley in 1716–17.[4] The precise date of Moyser's involvement at Nostell is not known, nor in the absence of any drawings by him is it possible to determine the extent to which his design was amended by James Paine, who in 1736, at the 'age of nineteen was entrusted to conduct' the building.[5] Paine continued working at Nostell until the fourth baronet's death in 1765.

When Bishop Pococke visited Nostell in 1750, the main block and the two pavilions on the south side (containing the kitchen and brew-house) were finished (pls 288, 289). The house was not yet habitable; nevertheless, he was greatly impressed by its plan, 'the most convenient I have ever seen, there are two great staircases, one (north) leading to the apartements in the attick story for the family, the other (south) for strangers'.[6] The principal private and state apartments are on the *piano nobile*, symmetrically arranged on either side of a central hall and saloon. Their interior decoration was begun in 1747 and left entirely to Paine, who introduced, here and at the Doncaster Mansion House, the fashionable rococo style which was still relatively unknown in the north of England. Though he made designs for most of the

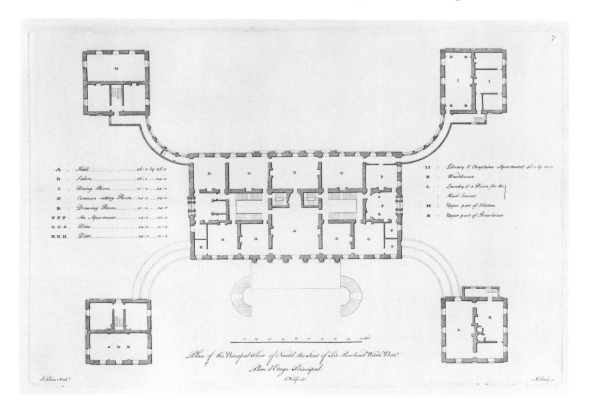

289   James Paine, plan of the principal floor of Nostell Priory (*Vitruvius Britannicus*, IV (1767), pl. 71)

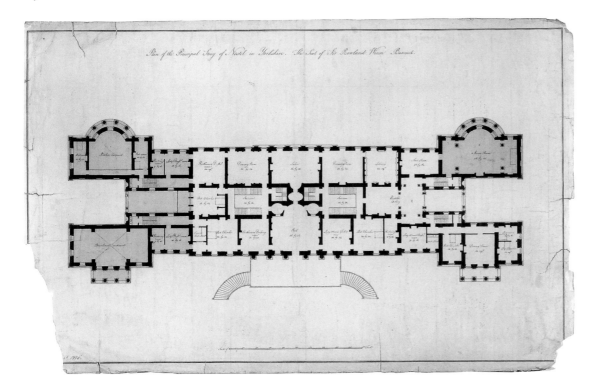

290 Plan of the principal floor of Nostell Priory, by Robert Adam, 1766. The shaded areas were not executed (Nostell Priory, The National Trust)

291 View of the library designed by Robert Adam in 1766, with the furniture by Thomas Chippendale, 1767. The maple-wood graining by Thomas Ward dates from the early 1820s

first-floor rooms, only those in the southern half and the two staircases were executed. The hall and saloon and the rooms to the north were simply finished off, but had still not been decorated in 1765; nor had their functions been finally decided.

Why the building of Nostell was so protracted is difficult to explain. Paine's preoccupation after 1745 with other commissions (notably Doncaster Mansion House) and a trip to Italy in 1755 may have contributed to the delay. But probably the magnitude

of Sir Rowland's ambition compared to his wealth – and he was quite a rich man – was more to blame.

The Winns were prosperous London merchants of Welsh origin. George Wynne (*c*.1560–1610) became Draper to Queen Elizabeth; his grandsons, George (1607–67) and Rowland (1609–76), were able to buy large coal-producing estates in the north of England during the Commonwealth, including Thornton Curtis in Lincolnshire in 1627 and Nostell Priory in

1654, and thereby established the family as gentry. At the Restoration, George was knighted.

The fourth baronet was High Sheriff of Yorkshire in 1731–2 (just when Lord Burlington was building the Assembly Rooms at York), but otherwise took no part in politics. While it is possible that the death of his wife in 1742 thoroughly disheartened him, one would still expect the completion of his new house to have been a matter of some urgency, given the fact that he was left with a large family of eight children. That was evidently not the case and after nearly thirty years only half the house was habitable and the two northern pavilions – one of which was to contain a billiard room and an octagonal cold bath, and the other a dairy, library and chaplain's apartment – remained unbuilt (pl. 290).

The course of action taken by his son, Sir Rowland Winn, fifth baronet (1739–85), is much better documented. Though just as ambitious, he was more impatient and demanding than his father, with whom he had a somewhat uneasy relationship. In 1756, at the age of seventeen, he was sent to Lausanne to learn French and complete his education. Though the customary trip to Italy was contemplated, his tutor, Isaac Dulon, thought the lifestyle of young Englishmen there too extravagant and recommended instead that he take a course in experimental physics at the Academy of Geneva.[7] Winn was described by Dulon as a high-spirited youth with grandiose aspirations and some talent, who needed direction and control to make him think and act seriously.[8] During his first year in Switzerland, he formed an attachment to Mrs Sabine Louise May, the estranged wife of Colonel Gabriel May and only daughter of Jacques-Philippe, Baron d'Hewart.[9] A foreign match was clearly not what the Winn family had been hoping for. Despite these misgivings, the couple married at Vevay in November 1761. Just over a year later, Sir Rowland wrote to inform the Baron of his 'regret that Sabine Winn (had) made so little effort to learn the English language that she is unable to speak it, and is cut off from much society.'[10]

The fourth baronet died on 28 August 1765 and was succeeded by the young Rowland, who promptly turned his thoughts to the completion of Nostell. At the end of October he wrote to Joseph Rose in London about finishing the sections of the hall and saloon that had evidently been drawn by Paine. Rose replied on 7 November, suggesting that if Winn was coming to London in the winter he should bring the sections with him.[11] However, nothing could be done in the winter months and in the spring Winn's attention was temporarily diverted by the purchase of a smart London house, 11 St James's Square, which he employed Chippendale to furnish.[12]

Returning to Nostell, the fifth baronet decided not to proceed with Paine's outmoded rococo designs, but rather to have the interiors finished in the latest neo-classical style by Robert Adam, who was then working nearby for Edwin Lascelles at Harewood. This was the third time, after Syon in 1760 and Kedleston in 1761, that Adam supplanted Paine. By 26 August 1766 he was in full control and able to inform Winn that he had engaged Benjamin Ware to superintend his works and would be sending him to Nostell the following week with drawings of the library, Sir Rowland's dressing-room and an 'Ornament for the Chimney that is to be put up in the Anti Chamber left side of the Hall as you enter'.[13] The chimney-piece completed the Paine room, which subsequently became the breakfast-room.[14]

292   The gilt door with sham books 'neatly Gilt and letterd' supplied by Thomas Chippendale, 1767, and an oval mirror in a stucco frame designed by Robert Adam, 1767 (Christopher Gilbert collection, Temple Newsam, Leeds)

Before Adam's arrival at Nostell, the central room on the north front, with a Venetian window corresponding to the one on the south front, had been planned first as an alcove bedchamber for Lady Winn and later as a library in lieu of the one intended for the north-west pavilion.[15] While the room itself had the advantage of three inner walls for bookshelves, in planning terms a library in that position would have interrupted the private apartment and isolated the north-west corner room. It was more sensible, as Adam saw it, to create a dressing-room for Sir Rowland here which communicated with an existing powdering-room and bedroom to the east and the new library to the west. The room was simply decorated and painted 'a light stone colour'.[16] Sir Rowland was dissuaded by Adam from his idea of making the dressing-room and library floors of plaster, which was unlikely to withstand the weight of a library table and chairs and would require dust-collecting mats or carpets 'not at all good in a Book room'.[17]

Maximum wall space for bookcases and a symmetrical arrangement were the prime requirements for the library. To that end, the two windows on the north side were filled in and the whole length of the wall, up to the height of the two remaining west-facing windows, was formed into a five-bay architectural bookcase with Ionic pilasters enriched with panels of double guilloche and a large pediment (pls 291).[18] Most of this was executed in stucco; only the frieze and capitals were entirely of

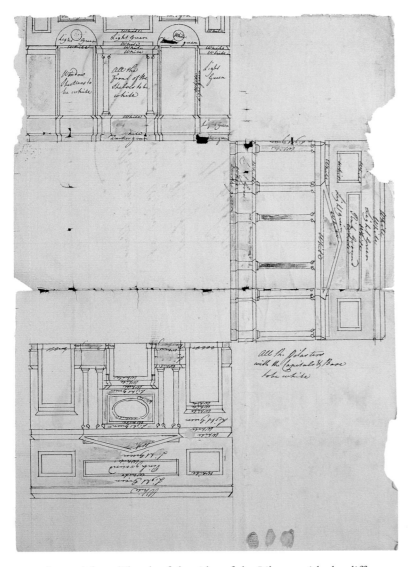

293 James Adam, 'Sketch of the sides of the Library with the different Colours markt on it', sent to Sir Rowland Winn with a covering letter, 1767 (Nostell Priory, The National Trust)

wood, and the pilasters were made according to Adam's instructions 'in the same Manner as those at Lord Thanet's with the Margin and Moulding of Wood and the Ornament in the Pannell of Stucco'.[19] The opposite wall is treated in exactly the same manner, the last bay being shelved with sham books supplied by Chippendale to disguise the jib door to the drawing-room (pl. 292).[20] A Chippendale medal cabinet was fitted into a recess behind one of the two doors on the chimney-piece side;[21] the other door opened to the dressing-room, now the library–billiard room. Between these two doors is a broad pediment embracing the chimney-breast and a narrow bay of shelves on either side. Adam initially proposed to recess the flue and introduce shelves above the chimney-piece itself, as he intended doing in the great library at Lansdowne House in 1766.[22] However, this novel idea was too risky for Sir Rowland, who decided to have a large oval painting by Zucchi instead.

Zucchi's oval and nine rectangular paintings to go above the bookcases and windows were sent to Nostell in August 1767. Meanwhile, designs had been received from Adam for elaborate stucco surrounds for two oval mirrors at either end of the window wall.[23] The choice of *Minerva presenting the arts of painting sculpture and architecture to Britannia* as the subject of the overmantel in April 1767 evidently caused Adam to change the sub-

ject of his design for the chimney-piece tablet from sphinxes to putti, representing the arts.[24] This more appropriate but complicated subject seems, in turn, to have resulted in a change of materials and a great deal of unforeseen trouble.

Unlike the sphinx tablet, which was 'to be of Wood and carv'd in town', the putti one was to be made as a 'bas-relief' in a composition that required special firing. William Collins, who had worked for Adam at Kedleston and Harewood, took longer than expected to carve the mould and when he finished there were difficulties in finding anyone 'to undertake to fire it for fear of its breaking'. After months of repeated complaints from Sir Rowland and as many promises and excuses from the Adam brothers, the firing took place and, as feared, the tablet warped and cracked in the process. At the end of November 1767, two plaster casts, 'one white & the other in a Tint resembling Terra Cotta' were sent to Sir Rowland to choose from. However, plaster was not what he wanted in such a prominent position and the tablet had to be carved in wood.[25] Evidently, this was not installed until December 1770, when the mouldings of the chimney-piece were ordered 'to be cut out the whole length of the tablet'. Two years later, there were further problems, requiring a drawing of the 'Cornice for the Library Chimney with the upper Moulding altered'.[26]

The library at Nostell has many features in common with the contemporary one at Osterley, but it is considerably smaller and hence was unsuited to the same severe, classical treatment in pure white. What was wanted here was a more intimate, varied and lively effect and that depended on colour: light-green walls, pink dado and darker-green skirting; white mouldings, friezes, doorcases, pilasters and pediments; pink tympana; pink picking-in of the friezes above the doors and the panels of stucco ornament above the pediments.[27] A similar colour scheme was applied to the ceiling, which is related to two earlier designs: one made in January 1763 for the tapestry-room at Croome Court and the other a rejected design of 1765 for the 'old library' at Harewood.[28]

Fortunately, we not only have a diagram by James Adam giving detailed instructions for the painting of the bookcases, but also a conversation piece painted around 1769 by Hugh Douglas Hamilton (pls 293, 294), showing Sir Rowland and Lady Winn in the library, which, though not entirely accurate, still gives a good general idea of the appearance of the room before Adam's distinctive gay colouring was neutralized by uniform maple-wood graining of the bookcases.[29] This transformation was most likely made around 1822 by Thomas Ward, the London decorator and upholsterer employed by Charles Winn, and was presumably intended to contrast with and focus attention on Ward's highly coloured redecoration of the adjacent drawing-room as a tapestry-room. Graining was the fashion of the time and was applied by Ward to Adam's white-painted tables with term figures in the upper hall. The 1815–19 refurbishment of Kenwood was another example of its application in an Adam interior.

Chippendale's furniture has fared far better than Adam's decoration and become the principal attraction of the library if not of the house. The large writing-table, which was finished by the end of December 1766, well before the bookcases, is considered his finest piece of mahogany furniture.[30] There is also a mahogany drawing-table, a library stool that opens to a step lad-

294   Hugh Douglas Hamilton, *Sir Rowland and Lady Winn in the Library at Nostell*, c.1769. Oil on canvas (Nostell Priory, The National Trust)

295   'Section of the Great Drawing Room (later the tapestry drawing-room) at Nostel', by James Adam after a design by Robert Adam, 1767 (Nostell Priory, The National Trust)

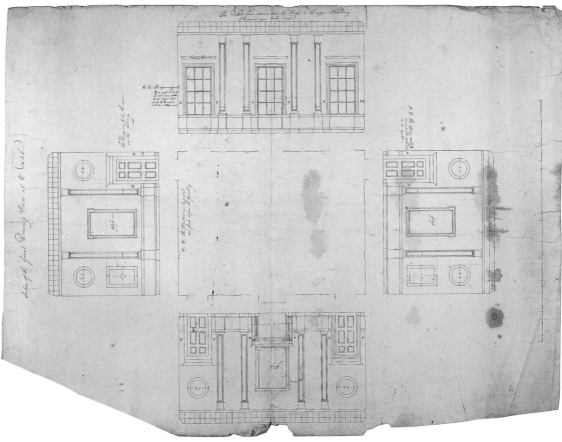

der, '4 Mahogany carvd library antique elbow chairs covered with black leather', six others covered with green hair cloth to match the lustring curtains and sunblinds, and two pedestals for globes made around 1770.[31] One of these pedestals features prominently in the portrait of Sir Rowland and Lady Winn, where it is shown supporting the bust of Venus de Medici bought for Winn in 1769 by the painter, Hugh Douglas Hamilton.[32]

Unlike the library, the drawing-room (now the tapestry-room; pls 295, 296) was still unfinished and without furniture when Sir Rowland died in 1785. This was no fault of Adam's. His designs (resembling those he had recently made for the Lansdowne House drawing-room) were sent to Nostell in April 1767 and promptly taken in hand. In August, Zucchi was reported to be 'going on briskly with the pilasters', doubtlessly painting arabesques for them, just as he was doing for Lansdowne House.

297 Detail of the statuary marble chimney-piece in the tapestry-drawing-room showing the frieze with winged sphinxes and the Composite capital of one of the pilasters with a peltoid shield above it. Designed by Robert Adam, 1767 and carved by John Devall

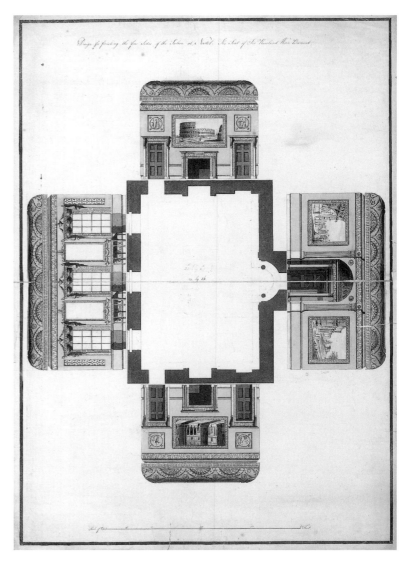

298 'Design for finishing the four Sides of the Saloon at Nostel', by Robert Adam, c.1767 (Nostell Priory, The National Trust)

By October, the plaster work of the ceiling was sufficiently far advanced for a paper pattern of the central panel to be made from the work and sent to James Adam before the painter could proceed with the ornaments.[33] However, Zucchi's paintings of *Cupid and Psyche* in the central roundel and the *Liberal Arts* in the eight lunettes took a little longer, which is hardly surprising, considering the enormous amount of work he did at Nostell (besides all his work at other Adam houses), for which he was paid the large sum of £1,276.19.0 in 1776. The last of the lunettes was installed in September 1771 and the six overdoor roundels in 1773.[34] Only two of these survive and are now placed above the pier-glasses; above the doors to the library and saloon are Zucchi's two rectangular paintings which originally hung on the opposite end of these walls to balance the doors.

It was not until 1772 that the floor was laid and the marble for the chimney-piece was received (pl. 297).[35] In December 1773, a message was relayed to Ware from John Devall that Sir Rowland's chimney-piece had 'come down', which can only refer to the one in the drawing-room.[36] Just as its tablet with an oval medallion of Cupid and Psyche echoes Zucchi's ceiling roundel, so its pilasters with composite capitals and panels of arabesque ornament would have been related to the twelve pilasters on the walls, which were removed in 1822 to make way for Charles Winn's Brussels tapestries.[37] On this occasion, the entire ceiling – except for Zucchi's insets – was repainted by Thomas Ward in 'Naples Yellow, Green and crimson' and the frieze in 'gold colour scrolage . . . and marone colour grounds'.[38] The present colour scheme is the result of a restoration undertaken in the 1920s.

The drawing-room was originally intended to be hung with damask and to have two large mirrors 'with head plates and borders in rich Carved & Gilt frames' on the end walls, a large

296 View of the tapestry drawing-room showing the ceiling and chimney-piece designed by Robert Adam, 1767–73, and the Brussels tapestries introduced in 1822

chimney-glass similarly framed, and four 'Rich Girandoles' to match, with large oval glass backs and three candle branches, two to go on either side of the chimney-piece and the other two on the window piers with carved and gilt pier-tables under them.[39] All this (except for the girandoles and two pier-tables) was planned by Adam in 1767 and entrusted to Chippendale to design and execute. On 5 March 1774, Chippendale replied to a query from Winn: 'with regard to the section of the Drawing Room, I took it when at Nostell, gave it you the same time & have not since – if you have mislaid it – it must be taken very Correct and all the dimensions very exactly measured and figur'd'.[40] Chippendale's graceless, commanding tone did not endear him to his patron.

After this flurry of activity, there was no further sign of urgency about the drawing-room. Winn's interests evidently shifted to the other reception rooms as well as to accommodation for his young family (Esther, born in 1768, and Rowland, in 1775); his finances were overstretched and craftsmen pressed for payment of their bills. On 30 June 1781, Haig and Chippendale sent him a list of the drawing-room and saloon furniture 'made upwards of two years and waiting for your Orders to finish them', and '13 Patterns of very rich Silks' in hopes that a choice would soon be made for hanging the drawing-room walls and covering the chairs and sofas that were to be moved over from

299 The saloon, view to the north-east with the door to the upper hall in the apse, designed by Robert Adam, 1767

the saloon. They had no reply and great difficulty in retrieving their valuable silk patterns.[41]

The saloon was the next task to which Adam turned, in August 1767 (pl. 298).[42] Here, not content simply to decorate its surfaces, he recast its plan in conjunction with the top hall and in so doing succeeded in transforming the conventional rectangular and square shapes of both rooms into much livelier, more diversified, interesting and unusual spaces based on classical prototypes.

In the centre of the inner wall of the saloon, he hollowed out a large apse, or niche, as he called it, which he framed with pilasters derived from Spalatro and which he intended to screen with two columns. This would have given 'an additional picturesque to the scene' and enhanced its Roman aura. Though detailed drawings of the capitals and bases of the columns were sent to Nostell on 2 May 1770, in July 1771 Sir Rowland decided, partly perhaps for reasons of economy, to omit the screen and

only have the pilasters, which he wanted as flat and inconspicuous as possible.[43]

Finishing the saloon was not smooth sailing. In December 1769, Adam discovered that the height of the cornice, cove and ceiling shown on the section he had sent a year earlier had been misinterpreted. After discussing the matter with Sir Rowland, it was decided that the cornice was to be lowered forthwith and the flat part of the ceiling, meaning the ornament within the central square, was to be altered, but the cove and frame, on which Rose had already done a great deal of work, were to remain.[44] A new ceiling design was duly made, with a simpler pattern of ovals and lozenges in the outer panels and in the centre a fan patera enclosed in a rhombus with peltoid shields on the sides and looped corners containing small rosettes.[45] This was not a significant improvement and it was finally agreed that the ceiling should be executed from the original design of 1767 (pl. 299), which is very similar to one made at the same date for the prin-

these can all be regarded as descendants of the Palmyra ceiling (which he closely followed in the study, now the China room, at Harewood in 1766), infused with movement.[47]

The present colour scheme of pink and blue picked out in white and edged in gold dates from the 1920s. Adam's design, with the colours of every part noted in French, calls for quite a bit of green, a different distribution of pink and blue, '*porphir claire*' cameo medallions on a green ground (instead of the present Wedgwood blue ones on a pink ground), and the central medallion of *Apollo's horses watered by the Hours* '*coleur de pierre*'.[48] The original pea-green walls, deep-pink frieze and white dado are now a bland and uniform beige, picked out in gold.

Zucchi, apart from designing all the ceiling medallions, also supplied four round overdoors and four large ruinscapes to hang on either side of the niche and over the two chimney-pieces. These were forwarded to Nostell in August 1776.[49] By then, the two chimney-pieces designed in 1772 and probably executed by Devall must have been up. They have unusual capitals, composed of elements from the Erectheion and Diocletian's Palace at Spalatro and friezes of anthemia and tazze corresponding to the frieze in the niche and on the doorcases (pl. 300).[50]

Adam was responsible for all the wall furniture, including picture frames. The two pier-glasses were designed first in 1770 (pl. 301). Their wooden frames are enriched with classical medallions, sphinxes and tazze above, and Apollo heads and husk fes-

cipal dressing-room at Harewood.[46] Winn's hesitation about this first scheme is perfectly understandable. Its pattern of contiguous circles, larger in the cove than the flat and all cut in half or quartered, is extremely restless and tense, which is no doubt just what Adam intended. His ceiling for the great drawing-room at Bowood in 1763 with whole and half circles and a coffered cove is calm by comparison, as is the composition of circles designed in 1775 for the music-room at Home House. Perhaps

300   Detail of the statuary marble chimney-piece in the saloon showing the enriched Corinthian capital and frieze with lion's heads in the cornice, designed by Robert Adam, 1772, carved by John Devall. Adam can also be credited with the anthemion and calyx picture-frame above, designed for a classical ruinscape by Antonio Zucchi

301   The window wall of the saloon showing the gilt pier-glasses with winged sphinxes on top answering those on the chimney-piece, the accompanying pier-tables, and the curtain-cornices all designed by Robert Adam, 1770–72

302 Detail of the wall frieze and one of the curtain cornices designed by Robert Adam, 1772 (Christopher Gilbert collection, Temple Newsam, Leeds)

303 'Plan and elevation of two tables for the Salon the tops to be of Scagliola', by Robert Adam, 1775 (Sir John Soane's Museum: Adam drawings, vol. 17:28)

toons below, all made in stucco by Rose. Three curtain cornices, with more tazze finials, were executed in 1772 by Sefferin Nelson 'from designs of Mr Adam' (pl. 302).[51]

Chippendale was commissioned to supply the rest of the furniture in 1774. A measured section of the room was made in March of that year and was sent to Sir Rowland in June:

> with designs of the furniture which has been settled by Mr Adams and myself & he totally approved of every thing therein sketched in our opinion the Chairs & Sofa should be coverd with silk Damask & the window Curtains of Lustring. As to the top of the Tables between the Peers I suppose Mr Adams will make a design himself of which you will please to remind him off, the Glass & picture frames must be oil Gold & the Table frames & Candle stands may be gilt in Burnished Gold. As to the Chairs & Sofas they may be painted or finishd Green & Gold which in my opinion will be the most Elegant way of finishing this Room You signifyd when in London that you would chuse the furniture as soon as possible, therefore you will please to favour us with you order soon as convenient as such furniture requires time for execution.[52]

It would seem from this that the tables for which Adam was expected to design a top were to be provided by Chippendale (pl. 303). In the event, however, they were designed by Adam in 1775. Their highly unusual legs, with square capitals and oval medallions, were adapted from a rejected sideboard design made in 1773 for Sir Watkin Williams-Wynn at 20 St James's Square.[53] The friezes are overlaid with central medallions, bearing the Winn eagle, flanked by portrait medallions; a combination of motifs which is repeated on the semicircular inlaid scagliola slabs supplied in 1777 by Richter and Bartoli.[54] The maker of the frames is unknown. Though Chippendale was not involved, he evidently stored the slabs, which were still in his warehouse in 1785, together with the mirror plates he had obtained for Adam's pier-glasses and the suite of seat furniture that he made in 1778.[55] Sir Rowland had ordered more than he could afford and died without seeing his newly decorated saloon furnished as Adam and Chippendale had planned.

Furniture made little difference to the 'antique' spirit of the architectural hall (pl. 304). What mattered here was the unexpected and entertaining succession of spaces of different shapes and sizes, some well lit, others dark, their surfaces variously modelled and minutely decorated with the utmost control. This is Adam's masterpiece at Nostell. He himself regarded it as 'different from anything yet executed' and was keen to see it engraved 'under his own Eye'.[56] That, however, did not happen.

The room as built by Paine was 36 feet (10.9 metres) square, with a short, apse-ended passage in the centre of the west wall containing a door to the saloon.[57] Adam changed the shape by taking 10 feet (3 metres) off the west side and used the intermediate space to create the appearance of a monumental Roman portico, consisting of a large central apse flanked by two enclosed oval lobbies with coved ceilings, giving access to the principal stairs.[58] Daylight for the lobbies is brought from the hall though tall openings corresponding to the windows in the outer wall, which are framed by Doric aedicules and intended to be filled with casts of antique statues. Advice on additional artificial lighting was sought from Adam in September 1776, when the room was finished, and on the basis of that '4 Antique Lamps for the Hall, with Ballance weights, Silk Lines and Tossells (and) 2 Lamps with Lines & Tassells for the Lobbies' were ordered from Chippendale. However, these had not been begun in 1781 and are not known to have been executed.[59] No matter how the

304 Plan and laid-out elevations of the four sides of the upper hall, by Robert Adam, *c.*1767 (Nostell Priory, The National Trust)

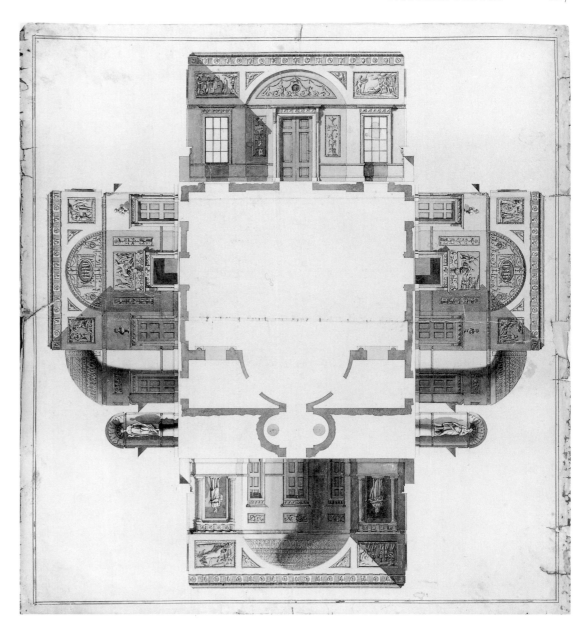

lobbies were illuminated, the play of light and shadow there was bound to have a lively and dramatic effect in the hall.

The vaulted passage linking the hall and saloon is not only much smaller and lower than those rooms, but also has no source of natural light. Nor evidently was any needed, for the passage would only have been used when the saloon was open for reception and its light could be borrowed. Two painted terms were to have been supplied by Chippendale, probably to support busts or statues as shown in Adam's design.

The articulation of the apse wall in the manner of a Roman portico or triumphal arch (pl. 305) set the basic pattern for the three-part division of the remaining walls into broad, arched bays flanked by doors or windows with square or rectangular panels above them. To answer the three doors in the apse, each arched bay was subdivided in three, with a central chimney-piece or door and two tall panels of stucco grotesques on either side.

The symmetry of Adam's scheme depended, right from the outset in 1767, on moving the chimneys built by Paine and shifting the flues on the floor below.[60] It was only after the feasibility of these alterations was determined in the spring of 1772 that detailed drawings of all the decorations could be made by Adam and sent to Nostell for Rose to execute. These included an amended version of his 1771 ceiling design, with trophies introduced in the corners to answer those in the spandrels.[61]

While the grotesque ornaments in the lunettes and panels were Adam's responsibility, Zucchi was meant to provide drawings for the bas-reliefs over the chimney-pieces, in the oval compartments in the lunettes above them and in the eight panels flanking the lunettes. However, these were still not done in August 1776, owing, Zucchi claimed, to his

not having heard a word mentioned of it, perhaps Mr Adam forgot them, but this ought to make so Sort of alteration, as Mr Adam may bring me the exact dimensions taken on the spot, according to which I shall make the drawings and forward to you (i.e. Winn) immediately, from the same, he that is to execute them in Basso rilevo may see all the possible Effect.[62]

Sir Rowland evidently decided to save time and money and do without the reliefs, spoiling the effect of a sculpture hall intended by Adam and making the hall his only room in which Zucchi played no part.

The same fate befell the brown and white geometric pavement designed by Adam in August 1776 to correspond with his ceiling pattern.[63] What his colour scheme was for the ceiling and walls is unknown. Could it have been all white? In 1819–20, Thomas Ward 'pick(ed) out Arabesques, scrolages etc. in the panels of the ceilings and of the walls (with) tints of cinnamon coloured

305 View of the upper hall showing the great apse on the west wall and one of the two chimney-pieces on the north wall

306 One of a pair of pier-tables supported by male terms, designed by Robert Adam in 1775 and probably made by Thomas Chippendale. The tables were originally painted white and grained by Thomas Ward around 1822 (Nostell Priory, The National Trust)

307 Thomas Chippendale, design for a cabinet supported by term figures, *c.*1760 (*The gentleman and cabinet-maker's director*, 3rd ed. (1762), pl. CXXII, detail)

308 The state dressing-room showing the bed alcove designed by Robert Adam, c.1768

brown'.[64] More common 'Adam' tints of pale green and biscuit were used in the latest redecoration. White, nevertheless, has always been predominant, and was more so before Ward grained the two painted Adam pier-tables and eight hall chairs attributed to Chippendale. The tables (pl. 306), supported by four muscular male terms, Atlantes, holding husk festoons suspended from medallions on the frieze (the central one with the Winn eagle), were designed in 1775 and are clearly indebted to the design for a cabinet supported by term figures published by Chippendale in the third edition of his *Director* (1762) (pl. 307).[65] They are also related to a sketch made by Adam around 1775 for an iron balustrade for Home House.[66] Though not very elegant or pleasing, they are completely novel and were evidently what Sir Rowland wanted.

Adam's responsibilities at Nostell were by no means confined to the completion of the unfinished rooms. Sir Rowland consulted him about every alteration he wanted, no matter how small or where it was. Paine's alcove bedroom (now called the State Dressing Room) had its alcove reduced and refronted by Adam in 1768 and a new, carved wood chimney-piece as well (pl. 308).[67]

Numerous changes were made in the dining-room in 1772–3 which were intended to dilute, but not to destroy, its distinctive rococo character. The trusses over the doors, and the cornices and pediments over the windows were taken down. A few stucco palm branches were removed from the circular overdoors to allow a better view of the paintings commissioned from Zucchi. The stucco frames to the pier-glasses were redone 'like the other sunk Pannells of the Room' which Zucchi enriched with arabesques. These were overpainted by Ward in 1819 and restored for the National Trust by John Fowler in 1971. Though Sir Rowland had described some of these changes to Rose and Ware on the spot, they could not be carried out until approved and

ordered by Adam.[68] Adam's own contribution centred around Paine's rococo sideboards, for which he provided brass rails and four accompanying round pedestals and vases. These were carved in wood by Sefferin Nelson in June 1773 and would have been painted white like the sideboards, probably with the ornaments picked out in gold. In about 1820 they were overpainted in imitation *verde antico* and porphyry to match the four additional pedestals and candelabra supplied by Thomas Ward.[69]

By 1776, the interior decoration of Nostell was very nearly finished and Sir Rowland's town house was ready with a fresh rendering of Liardet's newly invented cement. There would have been no further need for Adam were it not for the birth in 1775 of the Winns's second child, a son and heir also named Rowland. This important event created new demands and aroused new interest in Nostell. On 7 March 1776, Sir Rowland wrote to Adam, asking him to 'slip down' to Yorkshire for a few days:

> We are in great want of a Sett of Appartments for our young family . . . and are at a loss tho we have so large a House of how to find them. We are likewise in want of offices before we can pull down the old Building which I much wish to do this year so that the ground about it may be levelled & lay'd out.[70]

Demolition of the 'old Building' (meaning the south-east pavilion containing the brewery) was in progress in May and plans were made for four large wings to be added to the north and south ends of the main block (see pl. 290): the two flanking the entrance front, with Ionic porticos echoing Paine's larger frontispiece, and the pair on the garden front with segmental porticos.[71] Almost all the rooms planned for, or existing in the pavilions, were transferred to the new wings: a two-storey kitchen and brewhouse at the south end, and on the ground floor, to the north-west, a bow-fronted cold bath with ancillary dressing-rooms overlooking the garden and lake, and a laundry

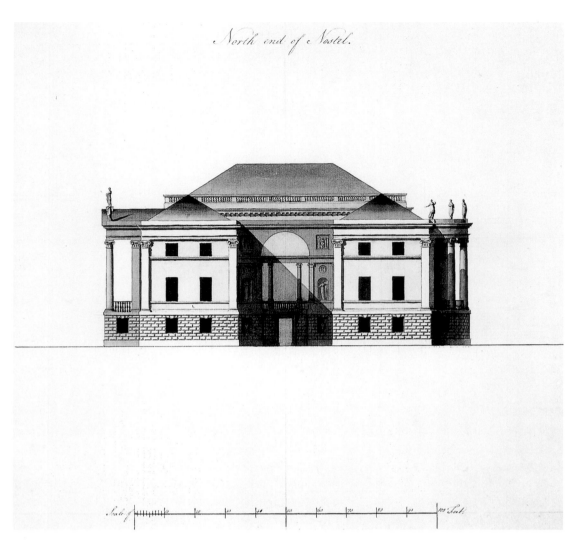

North end of Nostel.

309 Elevation of the proposed north front of Nostell showing the executed portico on the east front (left) and the proposed but unexecuted wing on the west front (right), designed by Robert Adam, 1776 (Nostell Priory, The National Trust)

310 The incomplete north front of Nostell

and dairy on the north-east side. Above the bath, there was to be a vast music-room (56 by 25 feet, or 17 by 7.6) divided in three by columnar screens with an organ at the north end, preceded by an ante-room. The east side was the family wing, containing a moderate-sized dining-room behind the portico, flanked by a water-closet, bedrooms and a dressing-room for Lady Winn with direct access to her private apartment in the main block.

The centre of the north front was brought forward on the ground and first floors to form a columnar vestibule or tribune linking the two wings to each other and to the rest of the house (pl. 309). It was also essential for the two pairs of service and domestic wings to have separate stairs, independent of the principal reception rooms. Only by placing these on the sides of the courts formed by the new wings could Adam gain light without sacrificing precious interior accommodation. This, however, reduced the width of the courts to just fifteen feet and would have had a detrimental, tunnel-like effect on the north and south façades. Adam's solution was to erect screens the full height of the house, each with a door and square niches on the ground floor and a large, open Venetian window flanked by arched niches, roundels and square panels on the *piano nobile*.[72]

Construction of the north-east wing was undertaken first (pl. 310), in order to provide the Winns with the 'Sett of Appartments' they wanted for their young family. In March 1780 the roof was slated, but there seems to have been no urgency to complete the interiors. Despite the death of Baroness d'Hervart in that year, leaving her daughter, Lady Winn, sole heiress to the family's Swiss estates, Sir Rowland was in financial difficulties

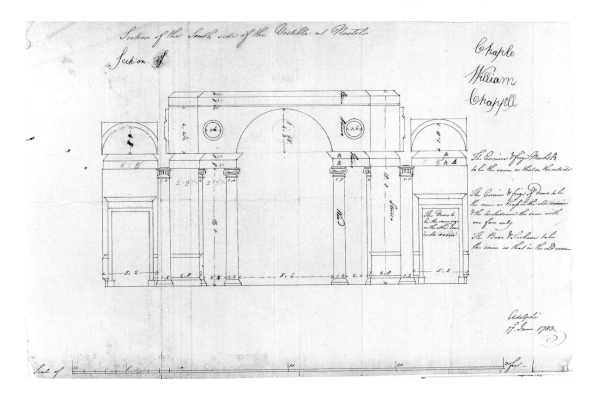

311 'Section of the South side of the Vestibule', by Robert Adam, 1783 (Nostell Priory, The National Trust)

and a poor state of health to boot.[73] Though the basic design for the vestibule had been worked out in 1776, measured and full-size drawings were not made until 1783.[74]

The large Venetian window in the dressing-room that Adam had created for Sir Rowland when he first arrived at Nostell in 1766 became the junction between the two parts of the T-shaped vestibule, and a new Venetian window was inserted in the centre of the north wall, overlooking the court. The Venetian window motif was repeated in the columnar screens at either end of the tribune, making all four sides alike (pl. 311). Behind the columns, there were to be doors to the east and west stairs and to the ante-room preceding the music-room, but there was no direct access to the family wing. The leg of the T, being within the main block, was evidently intended to serve as a vestibule or ante-room to the rooms located there. In the event, it became an over-spill for the library.

At the time of Sir Rowland's death in November 1785, the family wing was still a shell and thus it remained until Rowland Winn, created first Baron St Oswald, succeeded in 1875. The other three wings were never begun; nor was the south-west pavilion demolished. Sir Rowland's grandson, Charles Winn,

had the house expensively redecorated and furnished by the fashionable London upholsterer, Thomas Ward, in 1819, on the occasion of his marriage to Priscella, daughter of Sir William Strickland. However, he had no wish or need to complete Adam's plan. On the contrary, he considered pulling Nostell down, as it was 'so overgrown a house' and 'a place that has always been a burden since it was built'.[75]

The relationship between Adam and Winn was more than that of architect and client; they were trusting friends. Winn relied on Adam's advice for absolutely everything at Nostell, even the furniture-makers he was to choose, and in return encouraged him from the outset to apply to him for money whenever he wanted it.[76] Zucchi, whom he favoured to excess, never had that assurance; neither did Rose and certainly not Chippendale. Winn's showering Adam with sides of venison was as nothing compared to his promise to stand security for the brothers when the great run on the Scottish banks in June 1772 threatened the very survival of their firm. There was no one on whom Adam could 'more thoroughly rely for Relief', no one else he could ask 'frankly and boldly' for assistance and expect a frank reply. That, he said 'is the true footing of friendship'.[77]

312   The east front of Newby Hall, Ripon

13

NEWBY HALL

The convoluted architectural history of Newby Hall near Ripon in Yorkshire (pl. 312) is difficult to disentangle, though great headway has been made by Jill Low.[1] Not only is there another house called Newby – Newby Park (renamed Baldersby) – approximately twelve miles away, but its owners, the Robinsons, Barons Grantham, were related by marriage to the Weddells of Newby Hall and succeeded to that house in 1792 when William Weddell died without an heir. The third Baron Grantham, who became Earl de Grey and was a professional architect, brought with him to Newby Hall the architectural designs for Newby Park and Grantham House, Whitehall, made by Sir William Chambers around 1765; some designs by his father, Thomas Robinson, second Baron Grantham, an able amateur architect; and others by William Belwood of York, a carpenter turned

architect who had worked under Adam at Harewood, Syon, Nostell and Newby Hall and adopted his style.[2] These Newby Park drawings joined the large collection of designs for Newby Hall by Carr, Chambers, Adam, Belwood, William Weddell and Earl de Grey. Though the combined collections at Newby Hall have been sorted by Mrs Low, there is still some confusion of houses.[3] In addition, there is the corpus of Adam drawings for Newby Hall at the Soane Museum.

While Newby is fortunate in having such a full visual record of the complicated architectural patronage of its owners, this is sadly lacking in archival support. The sequence of events must therefore be deduced from a careful comparison of the drawings, one to another as well as to the fabric of the house itself.

Newby Hall in 1682 was an undistinguished two-storey, five-

313 Plan for alterations to the ground floor of the existing seventeenth-century house, c.1758–62 (West Yorkshire Archive Service, Leeds, NH/I/3/2)

314 Plan of the ground floor of Newby Hall. The pre-existing building is indicated in grey; the alterations made by Adam are in black

A Entrance Hall
B Tapestry Drawing-room
C Ante-room
D Dining-room (later Library)
E Sculpture Gallery
F Mr Weddell's Dressing-room
   (present Boudoir)

G Library or study
   (present Drawing-rom
H Parlour
I Evidence room
J Kitchen

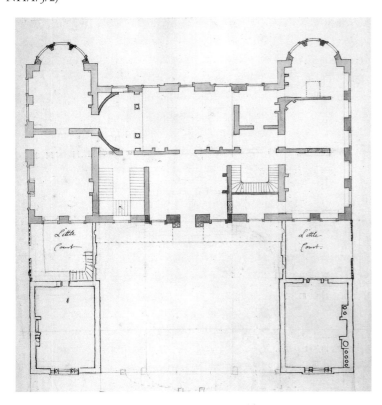

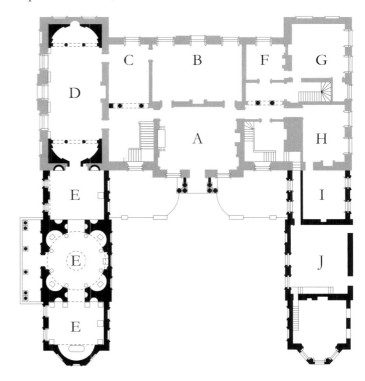

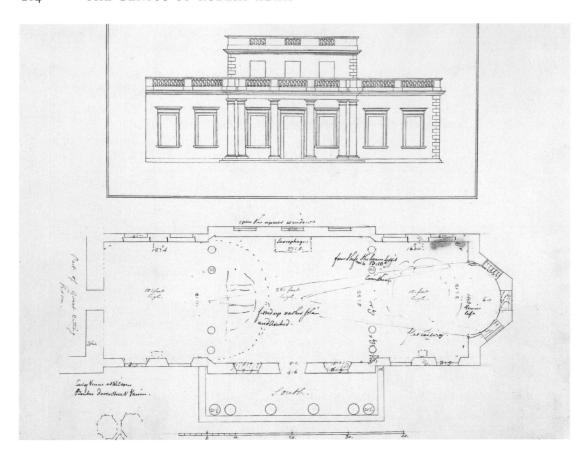

315 John Carr, plan and elevation of the sculpture gallery with annotations by William Chambers, c.1765 (West Yorkshire Archive Service, Leeds, NH/I/6/2)

316 The entrance to the sculpture gallery on the south front of Newby Hall

bay house with dormer windows.[4] It had been bought a few years previously by Sir Edward Blackett of Newcastle, MP for Ripon, who aggrandized it over the next two decades, adding two slightly projecting bays to each side and raising the dormers to a proper third storey, finished with a balustrade and a belvedere from which to view the gardens laid out by London and Wise. Celia Fiennes described it in 1697 as 'the finest house I saw in Yorkshire'.[5] The view of it drawn by Leonard Knyff at about this time and published in *Britannia Illustrata* in 1707 shows the west front (then the main entrance, but now the garden front) and a walled enclosure to the east with a small detached outbuilding on the south side.[6]

In 1748, Newby was sold by the Blacketts for £9,530 to Richard Elcock, a York grocer's son whose bachelor uncle, Thomas Weddell, had died the previous year, leaving him approximately £70,000 of his South Sea fortune for the express purpose of acquiring land. This, together with the acquisition of other properties in the area and in the city of York, a house in Pall Mall and chambers in Grays Inn inherited from his uncle, enabled Elcock to establish his family as landed gentry. Similar aspirations led him to change his name to Weddell.

It was only natural that Richard Weddell should wish to improve his newly acquired seat to accommodate his wife, Barbara Tomlinson, daughter of a York apothecary, and their three children, Thomas (born 1734), William (born 1736) and Margaret (died 1805). A payment of £12.1.0 to Daniel Garrett in June 1748 suggests that he started immediately.[7]

Improvements were evidently visible by August 1757, when the young Thomas Robinson of Newby Park visited Newby Hall, though to his eyes it was 'still a staring red & white house'.[8] The most obvious alterations at that date must have been on the east front, where there were two single-storey symmetrical pavilions with Venetian windows at the ends, separated from the

house by 'Little Court(s)'. These are shown as already executed on an undated plan made for Richard Weddell some time between 1758 and 1762 (pl. 313), which included proposals for moving the entrance hall to the east front, creating a large drawing-room with a screened apse at one end on the west front and adding semicircular bows to the corner projections on this side.[9] Only the revised entrance was carried out. The north-east pavilion was clearly the kitchen; it is shown in this position in later plans and remains of it can still be seen in the basement. The south-east pavilion must also have been ancillary to the house, possibly a laundry or dairy. These two mid-eighteenth-century blocks evolved from the late-seventeenth-century outbuildings depicted by Knyff at the back of the house, and were further developed in the late 1760s and early 1770s by William Weddell.

In December 1762, Richard Weddell died, leaving his entire estate to his only surviving son, William.[10] Eight months later, the twenty-six-year-old inheritor of Newby Hall set off for the Continent 'all alone', but no doubt well equipped by Thomas Robinson with useful advice and introductions.[11] Travelling through the Netherlands, he arrived at Paris on 24 September 1763 and remained there for the next four months. During this time, he is bound to have encountered some of the many Englishmen who had flocked there after the Treaty of Paris to buy tapestries, glasses, furniture and pictures. At the hub of it all was George Selwyn, a great friend of his neighbour at Castle Howard, Lord Carlisle, who might well have informed him of the new offers at the Gobelins, which Lord Coventry was the first to purchase and of the huge glasses destined for Syon, which he was negotiating for the Duke of Northumberland. Though it is doubtful that Weddell bought or even ordered anything for Newby at this early date, he would have been exposed to the raging *goût grec* and his appetite was whetted.

He would probably have travelled on to Italy, but his sister's illness required him to return to England in February 1764.[12] The need for improvements to the old-fashioned interiors and formal gardens at Newby must have been all too apparent, but they had to wait. First on the agenda was to get to Italy; he departed in August with his great friend, the Reverend William Palgrave, with whom he had been at Cambridge, and his servant, J'anson. Introductions from Thomas Robinson preceded them and instructions from the poet Thomas Gray as to what they should see followed by post.[13]

Travelling through France to Geneva (where they tried, but failed, to see Rousseau) and Turin, they finally reached Rome on Christmas Eve. In March, they went south to Naples and were enraptured; they climbed Vesuvius, puzzled over Pompeii and Herculaneum and were thrown into ecstasy by Pozzuoli and Baiae. At the end of the month they returned to Rome, where they stayed until May, when they set off for Venice, after which they would return home.[14] In this relatively short time, Weddell managed not only to have himself portrayed three times by Batoni and once with his companions by Nathaniel Dance, but also to buy pictures from Gavin Hamilton and enough marbles from the notorious Thomas Jenkins, the sculptor, Joseph Nollekens, Piranesi and the restorer, Bartolomeo Cavaceppi, to fill nineteen chests which were exported with

lettere di passo from the papal chamberlain's office and the assistance of the British Consul in Genoa on 27 March, 15 April and 17 May 1765.[15]

Weddell was back in England in August 1765 and by September improvements to Newby were going ahead at full steam. Thomas Robinson found himself 'amongst workmen of all sorts' when he visited the house on 23 September. 'We approve of the Alterations', he wrote, but, apart from the removal of the cupola, he did not specify what they were or who was responsible for them.[16]

Creating a home for the nineteen cases of antiquities was a matter of some urgency; the expedient solution was to join the existing service pavilions to the house and make the whole of the south wing a gallery (pls 313, 315). While this was to be finished with stone balustrades and quoins to harmonize with the house, it was also required to have a distinct architectural character of its own, and thus was raised to two storeys in the centre and provided with a Tuscan portico facing the garden.[17]

The idea was probably Weddell's, but the basic plan and elevation are attributed to John Carr, who was currently working at Wentworth Woodhouse for the Marquis of Rockingham, Weddell's valued friend and political patron. There is a preliminary design in his hand for the south front of the gallery, showing a portico in antis and doors at each end.[18] A revised version

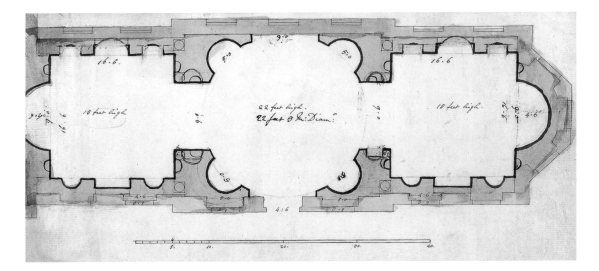

317 William Weddell and Robert Adam, plan of the sculpture gallery, c.1766–67 (West Yorkshire Archive Service, Leeds, NH/I/6/4)

pushed the portico forward, replaced the end doors with windows, introduced screens of columns to divide the space into three areas, created a canted bow at the east end where the c.1757 Venetian window was, and opened a door into the eating-room.[19]

The conventional arrangement of the interior did not satisfy Weddell's desire for an evocative antique setting for his marbles.[20] Later in 1765, or early the following year, he sought the advice of Sir William Chambers, Thomas Robinson's architect at Newby Park. Chambers's extemporaneous suggestions (pl. 315) – hastily made on a copy of Carr's plan – were that the central space should be 'fitted up rather plain and arched' so as to distinguish it from the small flat-ceiled spaces each side, that the three windows in the bow be blocked and a semicircular apse formed where *Venus life* (the statue discovered in the Palazzo Barberini by Gavin Hamilton and bought by Thomas Jenkins who, having restored it, sold it on for a vast sum to Weddell and also gave a cast of it to Thomas Robinson at Newby Park) could stand.[21] Weddell's huge sarcophagus, placed opposite the main entrance from the garden, was the axial focus; the upper windows in the raised wall above it were to be opened and Diocletians inserted at the sides.[22] This, apart from the large apse at the east end, was still not entirely what Weddell wanted.

There is another copy of Carr's plan, with tentative pencil suggestions of large apses in the corners of the central space and niches on the walls of the secondary areas, which, unlike previous plans, would provide individual settings for Weddell's major pieces.[23] This new turn was initiated by Adam; so too was the boldly articulated plan consisting of a domed central space with four apses flanked by two exactly symmetrical square rooms, each with an apsidal end and niches on the walls (pl. 317).[24] Of course, the ruins of ancient Rome were the underlying inspiration, but the most likely model for the linked domed and rectangular spaces has been identified by Robin Middleton as George Dance's design for 'A public gallery for statues, pictures, etc.' which was awarded the Gold Medal of the Accademia de Parma in May 1763 (pls 318, 319).[25] There can be no doubt that this extraordinary design, which Dance had been working on since November 1762, was known to James Adam, who was in Rome at the time, living quite near the Dance brothers, and who in fact left for Bologna and Parma in May 1763 on his way back to England.[26] James, having been profitably employed negotiat-

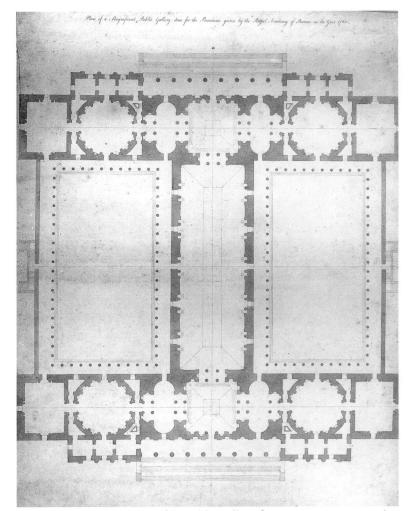

318 George Dance, plan of 'A public gallery for statues, pictures, etc.', 1763 (Sir John Soane's Museum: Dance drawings, D/4/II/3)

319 George Dance, section and elevation of the principal front of 'A public gallery for statues, pictures, etc.', 1763 (Sir John Soane's Museum: Dance drawings, D/4/II/2)

320 Section of the north wall of the sculpture gallery, by Robert Adam, c.1767 (West Yorkshire Archive Service, Leeds, NH/I/6/12)

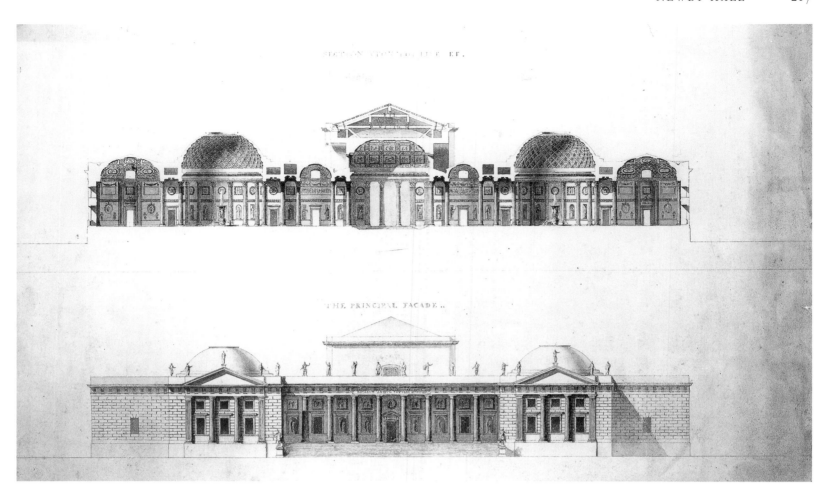

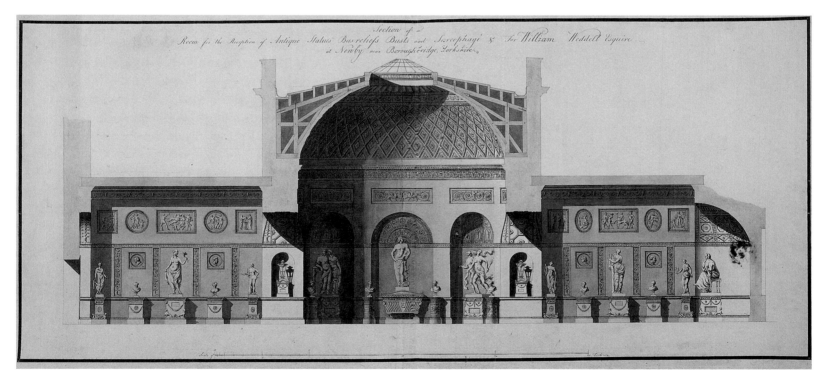

ing the purchase of antique sculpture for Robert's patrons, would certainly have taken careful note of a design for a sculpture gallery by one of his countrymen.

Why Weddell, fresh from Rome, did not approach Adam in the first place remains a mystery. That he did so in 1766 – when the shell of the gallery was finished – was probably connected with Adam's presence in Yorkshire at Harewood and Nostell. Weddell's return to Parliament as member for Hull in March 1766 and his election to the Society of Dilettanti in the following

month may also have encouraged a desire to be more in the swim of neo-classical fashion.

Weddell's attempt to impose Dance's grandiose scheme on his own small gallery at Newby failed, owing to the demand for exact symmetry, which, as it required an apse at the west end to answer the existing one at the opposite end, considerably reduced the size of the two side rooms. However, the concept was evidently appealing and only wanted some ingenious adjustment by Adam.

Section of the End next the Dining Room,
upon the Dotted Line A.B, Mark'd on the Plan.

322 View into the central rotunda from the room at the east end of the sculpture gallery

What Adam did was to abandon symmetry altogether and concentrate instead on creating the utmost variety and movement in an extended sequence of differently shaped rooms – all modelled with niches and apses enlivened by light and shadow – occupying the entire south front.[27] He must also at this stage have thought of the suite on the south front in relation to the entrance hall and the rest of the house. The two earlier rooms on the south front were thrown together into one large dining-room with screened apses at each end, which was entered from a small screened ante-room on the west front. Visitors were steered along the long axis of the dining-room into the gallery. While the eastern apse containing the great sarcophagus was the focus, the domed area was the spatial climax both of the parade and of the direct entrance from the garden. Carr's portico, however, lost much of its original significance and became a sheltered place to take tea and an exit, as it is today.

The precise date of Adam's intervention at Newby is not known, 1766 or 1767. His earliest dated designs are of 1767 for the gallery and dining-room ceilings.[28] But his preliminary 'Plan of the Alterations of (the) House' is earlier and it, in turn, was only made *after* his plans for the gallery had been fully worked out.[29] The sections and wall elevations of the gallery must date from about the same time as the ceiling, if not slightly earlier (pl. 320, 321).[30] The gallery, at least in execution, had priority over the dining-room.

Despite the differences in the sizes and shapes of the three interconnecting gallery rooms, their decoration is symmetrical and unified. Furthermore, it is carefully contrived for an ordered arrangement of Weddell's collection of busts and figures on pedestals (pls 322, 323). Continuous bands that run in and out of the recesses just above eye level and below the dado rail serve on the one hand to tie the three spaces together and on the other to divide their walls horizontally into three sections (pl. 320): the

323 The room at the east end of the gallery with the great apse and sarcophagus

middle one for antiquities, with Adam's antique-style decorations and pedestals above and below. Slender vertical panels of stucco grotesques complete the settings for the individual pieces placed against the north wall in the two small rooms, where there are no recesses. Evidently the colour of the walls and ceiling was also chosen with regard to the sculpture. According to the Reverend Warner, writing in 1802, 'the brightness of the Parian and Pentilican marbles is softened down by a pale strawberry ground', less plummy than the present colour.[31] Towneley, on the other hand, found the decoration objectionable: on 15 July 1779 he wrote to Jenkins in Rome, 'It's a Pity Mr Weddell should have been induced to overcharge his Gallery with Ornaments, but the Adams I am told have done it every where.'[32]

Though Adam's wall elevations depict fanciful sculptures in an ideal arrangement, which he presumably worked out with Weddell, they are in all other respects so detailed that large-scale working drawings for the craftsmen could be made directly from them by William Belwood, whom he brought to Newby from Harewood and Nostell to oversee the work. Belwood's working drawing of a pedestal with rams' heads at the corners of the frieze and winged sphinxes at the base is a case in point.[33] Bypassing Adam (or his London office) in this manner was certainly a saving for Weddell.

Economy might also account for Weddell's decision not to carry out either of Adam's two designs for pavements to answer the gallery ceiling, and for the very marked differences between those designs. The first (pl. 325), which is undated, is an intricate geometrical pattern, reminiscent of Roman mosaics and meant to be executed in small stones of pink, white and grey marble. It would have drawn the three sections together, enhanced the exquisite antique spirit of the whole and clearly distinguished it from the adjoining dining-room; but its estimated cost was

324 James Adam, sketch proposal for a domed sculpture gallery at the rear of 75 (later 76) Lower Grosvenor Street, the house occupied by the Adam brothers from 1758 to 1772. The date of the sketch is uncertain, but it is clearly related to Robert Adam's designs of c.1767 for the sculpture gallery at Newby. It is not known to have been executed (Sir John Soane's Museum: Adam drawings, vol. 7:223)

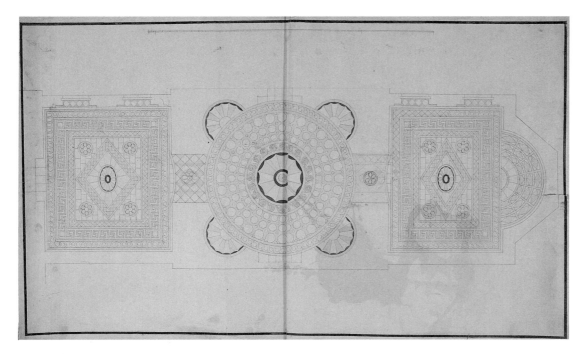

325 Design for a pavement for the sculpture gallery, by Robert Adam, *c.*1772 (West Yorkshire Archive Service, Leeds, NH/I/6/23)

326 A view from the entrance to the sculpture gallery into the dining-room (now the library), designed by Robert Adam, 1767–69

327 A view from the dining-room (now the library) into the sculpture gallery

probably prohibitive.[34] The second design, dated 10 April 1772, is a simplified, outline version of the same basic pattern, coloured red, yellow and green, most likely for cheaper scagliola.[35] This would certainly not have cost less than the £900 paid in 1831 to remake Adam's scagliola floor at Syon, and may also have been considered too bright and distracting. Weddell opted instead for plain wood, covered with mats.[36]

It was in order to facilitate his plan for the gallery that Adam created the great apse-ended eating-room in 1767, which the third Lord Grantham made into the present library in 1807 (pls 326, 327). As far as Adam was concerned, the room was finished in 1769 when the ceiling, wall elevations and chimney-piece had all been designed.[37] By the early 1770s (1775 at the latest) the apses and niches had been constructed by Belwood (pl. 328) and fluted Corinthian columns erected in front of them;[38] Joseph Rose had executed the stucco ornaments in the ceiling, the frieze and the panels flanking the chimney-piece;[39] Zucchi's five inset paintings – a *Triumph of Bacchus* in the ceiling, two overdoors

and two panels between the windows of Bacchant youths and maidens – were in place and his *Sacrifice of Ceres* put up in the overmantel. The chimney-piece itself was probably executed by John Devall, who was working at Harewood (pl. 329).[40] Its curious bacchic terms are reminiscent of Piranesi's chimney-piece for John Hope of Amsterdam, published in the *Diverse Maniere* in 1769 (pl. 330). [41]

Presumably the niches in the two apses were filled either with statues, as shown on Adam's laid-out wall elevations, or with other objects in the antique style, but not left empty. Whatever they contained in the 1770s was removed in the early 1780s, when Adam was requested to design a suite of furniture that would give the dining-room at Newby something of the fashionable Etruscan look that he had created at Byram, Yorkshire in 1780 for Mrs Weddell's brother, Sir John Ramsden, fourth Baronet.[42]

Though the original scheme of decoration has no ornaments that can be identified as Etruscan (pl. 331), the colours of the ceil-

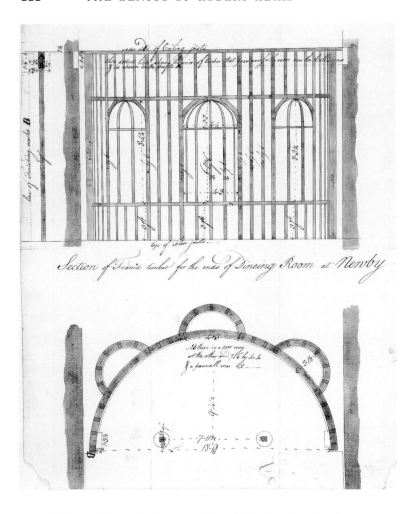

Section of Framis timber for the ends of Dineing Room at Newby

328 William Belwood, drawing of the timber framing for the construction of the apse and three niches at the west end of the dining-room (now the library), c.1770 (West Yorkshire Archive Service, Leeds, NH/I/7/3)

329 Detail of the statuary marble chimney-piece in the dining-room (now the library) with a head of Bacchus wreathed in grape-vines, crossed thrysii and a wine vessel. Designed by Robert Adam, c.1769; the carving attributed to John Devall

ing – black and terracotta or buff on a French grey ground – are what came to be known as the 'Etruscan style'. The fact that these colours are shown on a large-scale drawing of 1767 or early 1768 makes the Newby dining-room the earliest attempt, albeit a tentative one, to apply the Etruscan taste to the decoration of domestic interiors: close on the heels of the publication of Sir William Hamilton's *Collection of Etruscan and Roman antiquities* in 1767 and a year before Wedgwood began manufacturing imitation antique medallions in 'black Basaltes with Etruscan red burnt-in Grounds, and in polished Biscuits, with brown and grey grounds'.[43]

Adam took the opportunity to make more of the Etruscan tone of his ceiling in December 1775 in a design for gilt pier-tables with distinctive 'Etruscan style' scagliola tops.[44] Full-size

330 Giovanni Battista Piranesi, design of a chimney-piece for John Hope of Amsterdam (*Diversi Maniere d'adornari i cammini* (1769), detail, pl. 2, Wilton-Ely no. 823). Piranesi's wall decoration has been suggested as a possible source for Adam's Etruscan dressing-room at Osterley

Le Cariatidi l'architrave e gli altri pezzi di marmo sono avanzi di opere antiche dal Cavaliere Piranesi uniti insieme a formare il presente camino, che si vede in Olanda nel gabinetto del Cavaliere Giovanni Hope

Cavaliere Piranesi inven. ed incise

drawings for the slabs suggest that the tables were executed, most likely as a pair to be placed between the windows. They were removed in 1783, possibly to Weddell's London house, 6 Upper Brook Street, which he bought in 1772. The griffon candlesticks designed by Adam on 13 May 1776 were almost certainly intended for these tables, where their light would have been reflected in the pier-glasses.[45] Weddell's purchase of a perfume burner from Matthew Boulton on 30 March does not necessarily mean that Boulton was the maker of the candlesticks. However, it does raise the more interesting possibility that the candlesticks were inspired by Boulton's piece, which, though unidentified and untraced, could well have been a 'Griffon' vase, chosen by Weddell to match Adam's frieze round the walls.[46] It is likely that the 'French Grey Lutestring (drapery) Window Curtains . . . with Black & Buff Silk fringe' and 'Japann'd Cornices' included in the 1792 inventory also belong to the 1770s phase of decoration.[47]

The new suite of Etruscan furniture, painted grey, black and terracotta, included an elegant sideboard curved to fit the apse (pl. 332) and a matching ormolu-mounted wine cooler designed in 1783. which was presumably the date of the other pieces as well.[48] In the central niche above the table was an *Athénienne*

331 Design for the ceiling of the dining-room (now the library), by Robert Adam, 1767 (West Yorkshire Archive Service, Leeds, NH/I/7/6)

332 'Design of a Sideboard Table for the Dining room at Newby for William Weddell Esqʳ.', by Robert Adam, 1783 (Sir John Soane's Museum: Adam drawings, vol. 6:140)

333 Design for a griffon pedestal and alabaster vase for lights in the dining-room, by Robert Adam, c.1783 (West Yorkshire Archive Service, Leeds, NH/I/7/10)

334 'Design of a Plate warmer for William Weddell Esq*. The ornaments to be gilt upon a Bronze ground', by Robert Adam, 1784 (West Yorkshire Archive Service, Leeds, NH/I/7/9)

335 Commode table, one of a pair designed by Robert Adam, c.1783, for the piers between the windows in the dining-room (now the library) and later removed to the first-floor landing. The candlestick was designed by Robert Adam in 1776, presumably also for the dining-room which has winged griffons in its frieze

supported on a tripod with terracotta rams' heads, slender black legs and two candle-branches, raised on a pedestal with winged griffons at its base.[49] The four remaining niches held circular versions of the same pedestals surmounted by tall, translucent alabaster vases (pl. 333) with candles inside, which 'cast "a dim religious light" over this apartment, and assist the magic effect with which the mind is impressed when we look through the door in the recess at the opposite extremity of the room . . . into the *penetralia* of the temple – the museum, or gallery of statues' (see pl. 327).[50] If, as Mrs Low maintains, the four vases were in the niches in 1769, they would certainly have been on different pedestals or no pedestals at all: And what was in the central niche? The krater shape, though perhaps less popular amongst neo-classicists than narrow necked amphora, can hardly be called 'old fashioned' and was, in fact, far better suited to their use as lanterns.[51] There is probably an antique precedent for the use of the alabaster vases as lanterns; the Marquess of Rockingham, Weddell's close friend and political ally, had two pairs at Wentworth Woodhouse, which he bought from the sculptor, Richard Hayward, but at what date is not known.[52] One of the Newby vases and pedestals now has pride of place in the central niche of the present library. The others are in niches in the new dining-room designed by Earl de Grey in 1808, their pedestals having been repainted to match a pair of satinwood pedestals that may have come from Newby Park.[53]

Ancillary to the sideboard was a 'Large Pedestal with Carv'd Goats heads & Lyons feet and a figure in front with swags of husks &c Painted Grey Black & Buff fitted up as a Plate

Warmer'.[54] This was probably related to a design dated 1784 for a two-foot-tall (60 centimetre) circular 'Plate warmer for William Weddell Esq* The ornaments to be gilt upon a Bronze ground' (pl. 334).[55] It has not survived. Indeed, all that remains of the Etruscan suite, apart from the alabaster vases, is a pair of unusual 'Commode Tables' (pl. 335) with bowed centres in the form of tripods and *Athéniennes* answering the *Athénienne* with candle-branches in the central niche.[56] These tables have been repainted and removed to the first-floor landing, where they flank the door to the circular dressing-room. Originally, they

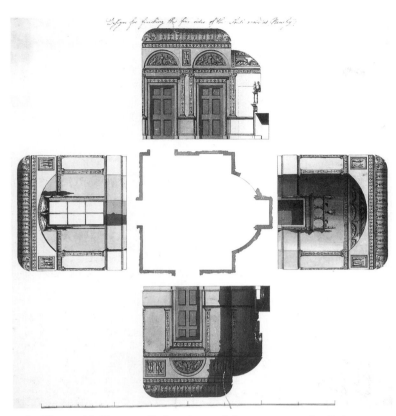

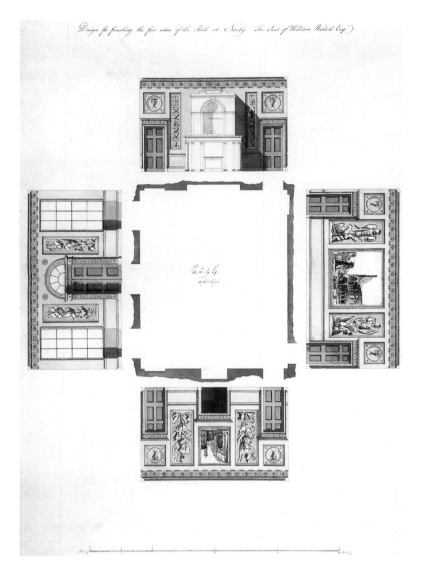

336 Plan and laid-out wall elevations of the ante-room, by Robert Adam, *c.*1769 (West Yorkshire Archive Service, Leeds, NH/I/11/1)

337 Plan and laid-out wall elevations of the hall, by Robert Adam, *c.*1769 (West Yorkshire Archive Service, Leeds, NH/I/8/1). The organ shown in outline was presumably not by Adam

were placed against the window piers with '2 Vause Shape Peir Glasses Richeley Carv'd and Painted' above them.[57] The mirrors may have been the oval ones with simple fluted frames, female masks in the crests and swags of husks at the bases designed by Adam in 1770.[58] A suite of eighteen mahogany chairs, probably by Chippendale, was placed against the remaining walls when the room was not in use.[59] Dining-tables and a 'Mahogany Dumb Waiter' (a stand with revolving trays) were stored in the staircase hall, where there is a secondary stair to the basement corridor which led to the kitchen on the opposite side of the house.

Though the third Lord Grantham's conversion of the south-facing dining-room into a sunny library–living-room in 1807 did not alter Adam's plan or decorations, it nevertheless spoiled the perception of his carefully contrived sequence of spaces from the hall to the gallery by blocking the preferred entrance from the ante-room, which provided the most complete and picturesque vista through the sculpture gallery to the great apse and sarcophagus at the far end.

Much more unfortunate was the destruction of the ante-room itself (pl. 336). This small, 'singularly beautiful, chaste, and classical' room, entered from the Gobelins tapestry drawing-room, constituted the proem to the antique sequence of dining-room and gallery and was the only other room at Newby that was modelled as well as embellished by Adam. It was 'fitted up with stuccoed Etruscan ornaments, and admirable *clair-oscuras*, in different compartments'.[60]

In plan, it was a miniature of the dining-room at Harewood designed in 1766, with virtually the entire wall opposite the window curved in a large apse containing a gib door into the staircase hall and a grey marble chimney-piece over which were 'a Convex and 2 Circular plates' in a 'frame Carv'd and Painted white'.[61] Adam's 'Design for finishing the four sides of the Anti-room' shows an overmantel of just this description which is almost identical to one designed for General Burgoyne.[62] Convex glasses imported from France, like the 'drolle' ones in the gallery at Syon, were a fashionable source of amusement appropriate to the use of the ante-room for cards.[63] There is a separate, undated and probably later design for a chimney-piece with inset tablets in the frieze which is inscribed for the ante-room, but evidently refers to the ante-room adjoining the principal bedroom on the first-floor, formerly known as the Satin Room and now called the Homer Room, where it still stands, executed in marble and scagliola.[64]

As in the small rooms in the gallery, the walls of the ante-room were articulated with decorated stucco pilasters joined at the top by a continuous horizontal band demarcating an upper register where there were the '*clair oscuras*, in different compartments': three arched ones over the doors and four rectangular ones over the pilastered bays, all painted by Zucchi.[65] According to the colour notes on the 'Design for finishing the four sides', these grisailles had a 'light Purple Ground/ Figures White upon a Darker purple Ground. (The) Pilaster Grounds dark purple & white ornaments'. The walls were said by Warner to be 'a pale

338 The Ionic organ attributed to James 'Athenian' Stuart in the Doric hall

339 Giovanni Battista Piranesi, engraving of an antique marble tripod owned by Piranesi, sold by him to William Weddell and still at Newby Hall (*Vasi, candelabri, cippi, sarcophogi* (1775), pl. 28a, Wilton-Ely no. 980)

340 View of the hall showing part of the ceiling and the related pavement. Adam's uncoloured ceiling design suggests that the room was originally painted dead-stone colour which was the norm for halls

341 The Gobelins tapestry drawing-room. Only the borders of the Axminster carpet designed by Adam in 1775 are related to his ceiling of 1769

green, relieved by light purple mouldings'.[66] Similar colours were applied to the coved ceiling and the semi-dome in the niche.[67]

Adam's control over the rest of the public rooms on the ground-floor was neither as comprehensive nor as finely tuned as it was in the 'antique' sequence on the south side. His detailed presentation 'Design for finishing the four sides of the Hall' (pl. 337) – presumably made in 1769, the date of his ceiling design – shows the prominent architectural organ case on the north wall only in outline, which suggests that it had already been made or at least designed by someone else.[68] John Cornforth has noted the resemblance between the unusual combination of paired pilasters and free-standing Ionic columns in the lower half of the organ to a design for a chimney-piece by 'Athenian' Stuart. Weddell's documented acquaintance with Stuart adds weight to the attribution.[69] Notwithstanding, there is something awkward and amateurish about the organ (pl. 338) – the absence of a base,

for instance, which one would expect on a piece of furniture of this description – which suggests that it might be by Weddell himself, compiled from various sources, including Stuart. The ornamental tripods between its pilasters are loosely based on a marble tripod that Weddell bought from Piranesi (pl. 339).[70] The raised plinth at the top of the organ originally supported a 'lion with a cupid seated on his back, playing upon a lyre; the harmony of which, seems to divest the royal beast of his natural ferocity'.[71] Perhaps these figures, reaching almost to the ceiling, precluded a proper base. A 'faun', presenting his syrinx', possibly the dancing faun that was in the gallery when Nollekens made his inventory in 1794, was appropriately placed in front of the organ.[72]

Adam decorated the remaining walls with a Doric frieze, paintings of classical ruins similar to those in the music-room at Harewood and panels of martial trophies in stucco (pl. 340). Trophies are also found on the ceiling, one of them bearing the

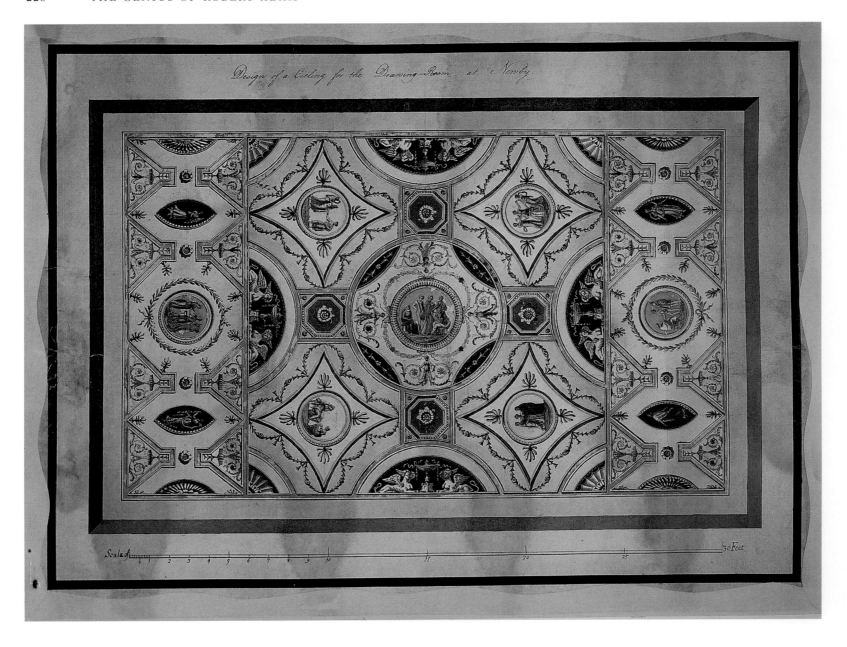

Design of a Cieling for the Drawing-Room at Newby.

342 Design for the tapestry drawing-room ceiling, by Robert Adam, 1769 (Cumbria Record Office, Carlyle)

343 Design for the drawing-room carpet, by Robert Adam, 1775 (Sir John Soane's Museum: Adam drawings, vol. 17:194)

date 1771, the year of Weddell's marriage to Elizabeth Ramsden, daughter of Sir John Ramsden and half-sister to the Marchioness of Rockingham.[73] He seems to have intended a more chaste architectural setting than the present scheme, perhaps painted white like the hall at Syon, or pale grey and white, like Osterley.

The black and white geometrical pavement composed of small stones (which he designed in April 1772) would have contributed to the ancient Roman look.[74] However, it was not executed; instead the outline of the ceiling with its circles at the corners and oval centre was repeated in black bands on a grey and white marble floor.[75]

The frieze of the stone chimney-piece was initially intended to correspond to the architraves of the six doors (three of them false). However, when the design was made in 1772, Weddell evidently decided that something bolder and more classical was needed and a central tablet with a tazza and sphinxes was incorporated in a revised design.[76]

From the chaste Doric hall, visitors entered directly into the drawing-room – the richest, most colourful and exuberant room in the house (pl. 341), hung with mauve pink (now faded to mushroom-colour) Boucher–Neilson medallion tapestries accompanied by a suite of tapestry-covered chairs and sofas. This was the second weaving of Boucher's *teintures*, the first being for

344 Plan and laid-out wall elevations of the study or library (now the family drawing-room), by Robert Adam, c.1769 (West Yorkshire Archive Service, Leeds, NH/I/10/1)

345 William Belwood, elevation of the west wall of the study or library (now the family drawing-room), 1771 (West Yorkshire Archive Service, Leeds, NH/I/10/5)

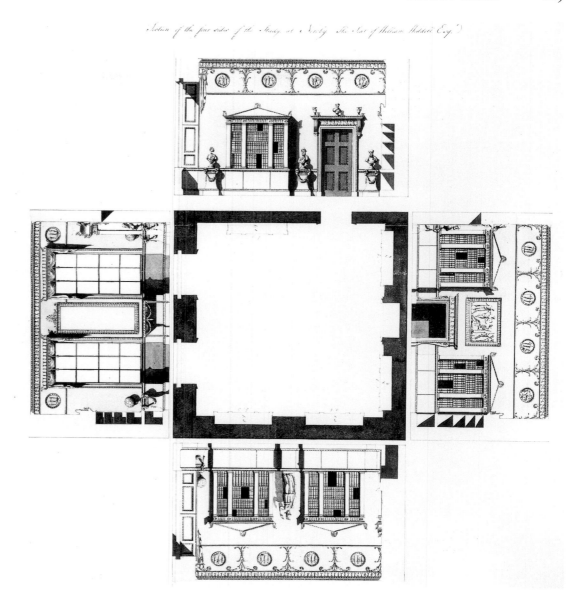

346 The early eighteenth-century staircase on the south side of the house embellished by Robert Adam in 1771 with new balusters like those at Osterley and a screen of Ionic columns by Belwood behind which is the enlarged ante-room

Lord Coventry at Croome Court. The subjects of the medallions, with one exception, are the same as Lord Coventry's: *Venus and Vulcan* (fire) appropriately placed over the chimney-piece, *Vertumnus and Pomona* (earth) and *Aurora and Cephalus* (air) on the north wall, and the *Birth of Venus*, from a new Boucher painting dated 1766, on the south wall, instead of *Neptune and Amymone* representing water. In addition, there are three over-doors and two narrow panels.

Weddell must have visited the Gobelins manufactory and seen the new medallion composition before August 1765, when he returned from his travels in Italy, and possibly as early as autumn 1763, on his first visit to Paris. Exactly when he decided to create a tapestry-room at Newby is not known, but it was certainly prior to Adam's arrival on the scene in 1766. Presumably Carr (who was last recorded at Newby in 1768) provided the Gobelins

with the required wall elevations, giving the precise measurements and locations of the chimney-piece and doors.[77] Part of Weddell's order had been completed and despatched by July 1767: the rest was made in 1768 and delivered later.[78] The '*petit pacquet*' of tapestries sent in July 1769 with Sir Lawrence Dundas's order was probably the last.[79] In that same month Adam made a preliminary sketch for the drawing-room ceiling which was subsequently modified at the sides to align with the windows and the doors opposite them.[80] Pink and pale green were the predominant ground colours, with blue circles and brown lozenges and quadrants containing eleven paintings by Zucchi, rose octagons, parti-coloured grotesques and purple bands edged in gold (pl. 342).[81] The repainting of the ceiling in 1978 in subtle shades of mushroom and white to accord with the faded ground of the tapestries, though understandable, has resulted in an uncharacteristic blandness and overemphasis on the geometrical pattern and inset paintings. For the floor, Adam designed an octagon and diamond pattern carpet in December 1775, with red and brown ornaments on green and gold grounds, which is related to the end panels of the ceiling but not to the main part (pl. 343). It was made at Axminster and has fared better colour-wise than his ceiling and the French tapestries.[82]

The fluted frieze around the room must have been designed and executed at about the same time as the ceiling. Unlike the matching architraves over the doors, it has a convex profile that repeats the shape of the woven raffle-leaf frames of the tapestries, which, though not yet in place, had evidently been seen by Adam. His frieze was presumably the model for the similar friezes on the pier-glasses, which normally would not have been designed until after the room was complete. Their crests, composed of vases, flowers and sheaths of arrows, are related to the floral trophies in the centre of the large tapestry panels. The massy neo-classical style of the mirrors and especially the tables suggests a French origin.[83] Chippendale, whose presence at Newby was recorded 1772 and 1776, is credited with a pair of flower-basket girandoles and the suite of twelve medallion-back armchairs and two sofas, the 'only known seat furniture which preserves its original upholstery'.[84]

The design for the chimney-piece, which had to fit under the wide and rather elaborate gilt tapestry overmantel, took an inexplicably long time to decide upon. Two designs were submitted to Weddell in 1770, both with a fluted frieze corresponding to the frieze on the wall and door cases, but incorporating incongruous lyre ornaments that first appeared in the music-room chimney-piece at Harewood, also designed in 1770.[85] The first drawing offered a choice of profile terms or ornamented pilasters at the sides.[86] Terms were evidently preferred and a second design was made accordingly.[87] This too was rejected by Weddell and was executed instead for the Duchess of Bolton's dressing-room at Bolton House, Russell Square. Four years later, in 1774, a third design was made with the same frieze and the pilasters, which was approved and executed.[88]

North of the drawing-room was the private apartment, entered from a passage off the hall and consisting of Mr Weddell's dressing-room and library, a parlour, evidence-room and kitchen on the north front. The dressing-room (now Mrs Compton's boudoir) had a chimney-piece of yellow Sienna and white marble designed by Adam in 1780.[89] The library (now the drawing-room) (pl. 344) was a newly formed room in the north-west corner of the house and required considerably more work. This was done in 1769 at the same time as the hall and drawing-room.[90]

As in the gallery, the walls were divided into three horizontal areas.[91] In the upper register were large medallions between paired calyces. The lower register, of exactly the same height, contained the dado and the bases of five architectural bookcases, each with Tuscan pilasters, and pediments complete with acrote-

ria. Flanking the cases were busts and globes – the traditional paraphernalia of libraries – on characteristic Adam pedestals; and, presiding over all, a life-size statue of Athena. The window pier was to have a fairly restrained pier-table and glass. A separate design for the mirror with female terms, festoons of husks and an anthemion crest and base was made in 1770, but no design has been identified for the table.[92]

One would have thought that this elegant neo-classical room, painted pale green and pink, would have been just what the avid collector of antiquities wanted. However, Weddell was evidently displeased with the asymmetrical arrangement of bookcase and door on the east wall, and revised, outline wall elevations were drawn up with a false door in place of the fifth bookcase.[93] For some reason – cost perhaps, or insufficient space for books, or the intervention of Mrs Weddell in 1771 – the design of the bookcases was passed to Belwood, who increased their height, made the two cases on the west wall into one and replaced Adam's classical pediments with cramped, old-fashioned, scrolled ones (pl. 345).[94] Judging from the inventory listing three bookcases, Belwood's design was executed.[95]

Adam's high opinion of Belwood was evidently shared by Weddell, who seemed prepared to entrust him with the execution of his more idiosyncratic wishes that might have been anathema to Adam.[96] The design of the staircase hall is a case in point. Adam's 'Plan of alterations', c.1766–7 proposed to replace the existing stair round the walls with an imperial stair rising directly in front of a screen of green Cippolino marble columns. Not surprisingly, this grandiose scheme was rejected and Weddell decided that embellishments in Adam's fashionable neo-classical style would suffice. In 1771, Adam made a design for the ceiling; friezes for the columnar screen and the walls followed, along with carved strings and new iron balusters like those at Osterley (pl. 346).[97] The area behind the screen was like an extension or overspill of the gallery, with bas-reliefs and busts and a sarcophagus between the columns.[98]

In the mid-1770s, after Adam's decorations had been executed, Belwood was given the task of providing a screen for the upper landing and the window on the half-landing.[99] His arcades, consisting of a broad central arch on slender Ionic columns aligned on the large columns below, flanked by two smaller arches, are a weak imitation of Chambers's grand staircase at Gower House, Whitehall, which Weddell and Belwood could have seen when the design was exhibited at the Royal Academy in 1770.[100] Chambers's patron, Thomas Robinson of Newby Park, would have approved.

Chambers may also have inspired Belwood's entrance porch on the east front, which Weddell preferred to the design made by Adam in November 1776 for a curved columnar portico with pedimented arms extending the whole width of the three-bay centre and projecting into the forecourt.[101] This was the only design Adam made for the exterior of Newby and would have made a noble introduction to his interiors.

347   The east front of Saltram

14

SALTRAM

While in some houses, like Syon and Osterley, Adam was able to display his genius in overcoming the irregularities of the earlier fabric by creating whole suites of grand reception rooms, elsewhere he was merely required to design one or two interiors, or even just a ceiling, table or mirror frame that would give a fashionable fillip to what the previous generation had done. Saltram in Devon is a case in point, where John Parker (1734–88), on succeeding in April 1768, promptly commissioned him to fit up two existing rooms as a saloon and library.

The original house was built in the sixteenth century for the Bagg family, who sold it in 1661 to Sir (later Lord) George Carteret. He is thought to have made some improvements to its west front before selling it in 1712 to the neighbouring landowner, George Parker of North Molton and Boringdon, who continued to reside a few miles away at the family seat at Boringdon until his death in 1743. His son, John, together with his wife, Lady Catherine, daughter of the first Earl Poulett of Hinton St George, Somerset, and their two sons, John (born 1734) and Montagu Edmund (born 1737) were the first Parkers to live at Saltram.

In about 1746, Lady Catherine, inspired perhaps by the Palladian house built by Roger Morris for Lord Clinton at Castle Hill, also in Devon, initiated a piecemeal programme of building activity at Saltram (pl. 347, 348) which proceeded clockwise from west to east, until her death in 1758. The west and south fronts were rebuilt on the old foundations; then the staircase hall and saloon were added in the centre of the east front above a new brick-vaulted cellar, the only dry cellar in the house. The architect is not known; Matthew Brettingham has been suggested, as he was being consulted at about this time by Lady Catherine's brother, the second Earl Poulett, for unspecified work at Hinton St George.[1] This might explain similarities between the saloon at Saltram and the drawing-room at Kedleston, where Brettingham had also preceded Adam.

Lady Catherine had been the driving force, and though work on the interior continued without her, it was evidently still unfinished when John Parker died on 18 April 1768. Work was in progress on the new double-cube saloon, 25 feet (7.6 metres) tall, the same height as the staircase hall. Its large Venetian window and deep cove (also comparable to the staircase hall) were in place and the chimney-piece may already have been made by Thomas Carter the younger, whose bill was one of the last paid

by John Parker senior in 1768.[2] What had been accomplished in the low, bow-fronted room next door (now the eating-room) is unknown.

John Parker the younger (created first Lord Boringdon in 1784) must have been quite keen to have the rooms finished and was persuaded by his close friend, the second Earl of Shelburne, to do so in the latest style by employing Adam, who was then working for him at Bowood and Lansdowne House. Shelburne's influence upon Parker, whom he met at Oxford in the 1750s, was very considerable.[3] Not only did he secure him a seat in Parliament for Bodmin in 1761 and Devon in 1762, but he also had a hand in his two marriages: the first, in 1764, to his cousin

348 Reconstruction of the ground-floor plan of Saltram as improved by Robert Adam, 1768–9

A Entrance Hall
B Morning Room
C Velvet Drawing-room
D Saloon
E Library (later dining room)

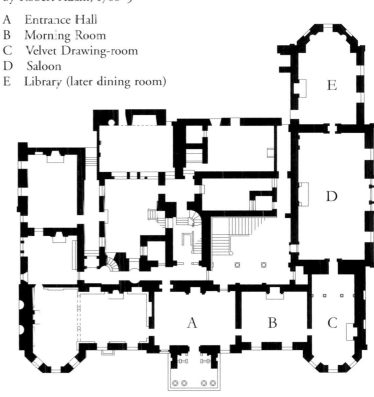

349   Preliminary design (unexecuted) for the drawing-room ceiling, by Robert Adam, 1768 (Sir John Soane's Museum: Adam drawings vol. II:253)

Frances, daughter of Josiah Hort, Archbishop of Tuam, who tragically died that same year, and the second, on 19 May 1769, to the Hon. Therese Robinson (with a dowry of £12,000), sister of his former foreign secretary, the Hon. Thomas Robinson, later second Baron Grantham of Newby (now Baldersby) Park, Yorkshire.[4]

Robinson, a connoisseur and architect, a Fellow of the Society of Antiquaries from 1763 and member of the Society of Dilettanti from 1761, became the Parkers' *arbiter elegantiarum*, as he had been for another relation, William Weddell of Newby Hall. While he was in Madrid as ambassador from 1770 to 1779, Therese, herself a woman of 'skill and exact judgment in the fine arts', kept him informed of every improvement at Saltram.[5] He was asked not just to give opinions and advice, but also to make designs for garden buildings and to procure 'any thing abroad of pictures bronzes &c that is valuable in itself, beautiful, and proper for any part of Saltram'.[6] In short, Lord Grantham – and to a lesser extent his younger brother, Frederick, who kept an eye on things ordered from London as well as the Parkers's house at 29 Sackville Street, for which Adam designed a drawing-room ceiling in 1770 – had as much influence upon the younger John Parker's building activities at Saltram as Shelburne had on his politics.[7]

Towards the end of 1768, some months before Parker remarried, Adam produced a full set of drawings – wall elevations, ceiling and chimney-piece designs – for the 'Great Drawing Room' and library.[8] As far as we know, his library designs were fully approved and executed; however, those for the saloon required revision. There can be little doubt that Therese and Thomas Robinson had some say, even at this early stage.

Adams design for the saloon chimney-piece, with an anthemion frieze, double guilloche pilaster panels and capitals from Diocletian's palace at Spalatro, corresponds exactly to the surrounds on doors and Venetian window, but was evidently made without knowledge of the chimney-piece recently supplied by Carter and was therefore redundant.[9]

His first design for the ceiling (pl. 349) – of which there is a finished version at Saltram and an unfinished one at the Soane – was a repeat pattern of connected ovals divided into three compartments, with an oval painting in the centre and eight smaller painted roundels in the intervening lozenges. This was replaced later in 1768 by a much simpler, bolder and more centralized composition of just three ovals, the largest in the centre flanked by two smaller ones at right angles, each enclosing a lozenge and roundel.[10]

In September 1769 the 'two new Rooms' were described by Thomas Robinson as 'very forward, they are highly finished . . . the Stucco in the other parts of the house is not in a good taste but still much too good to destroy'.[11] Joseph Rose is credited with the plaster work in the two rooms, for which he was paid a total of £434 in 1770 and 1772.[12] Antonio Zucchi supplied the inset paintings depicting *Diana* in the centre, the *Seasons* in the corner roundels, *Venus and Adonis* on one side, the *Death of Procris* on the other, and the *Triumphs of Neptune* and *Thetis* opposite one another in the cove.[13]

Adam's revised ceiling design was followed in 1769 by a related design for a carpet with a large central lozenge as the dominant figure, but no ovals (pl. 350).[14] This was woven at the local Axminster manufactory of Thomas Whitty, a specialist in large, seamless carpets of high quality and moderate price for which he had been awarded three premiums by the Society of Arts.[15] Thomas Robinson's visit to the manufactory on 22 August 1769 was probably related to the commission.[16] On the morning of 23 September 1770, the carpet, measuring 46 by 22 feet (14 by 6.7 metres) and costing £126, arrived at Saltram and was immediately 'spread upon the lawn' and admired as 'very beautiful indeed'.[17] Spread upon the floor of the saloon, with all the furniture placed against the walls in the normal way, its brilliant colours – red, green, yellow, pink and blue on a rich brown ground – are in sharp contrast to the light-blue damask walls. That, to judge from Adam's coloured design, is just what he intended. Interestingly enough, the entire central section of the carpet was reused in October 1770 in a ceiling design inscribed for 'Mr Farmer', probably one of the Fermors of Easton Neston, the maternal family of Lord Shelburne's second wife, Lady Sophia Carteret.[18]

The 'Section of the Great Drawing Room' at the Soane is a

350   View of the drawing-room showing Adam's ceiling and the related Axminster carpet

351 Elevation of the window wall of the drawing-room at Saltram, by Robert Adam, 1768 (Sir John Soane's Museum: Adam drawings vol. 11:253, detail)

352 One of four pier-glasses designed by Robert Adam in 1769 for the window wall of the drawing-room. In the event, two of the mirrors were placed on the inner wall flanking the chimney-piece. The two tables accompanying the pier-glasses were made by Joseph Perfetti in 1771

preliminary design, dated 1768, offering an alternative on the window wall (pl. 351): either oval pier-glasses in novel frames with delicate festoons suspended from the tops and held at the sides by female terms, which may be regarded as precursors of the girandoles made for the gallery at Osterley in 1770, or tall rectangular ones, which, while more conventional, would have been considerably more expensive, owing to the high cost of large sheets of imported glass.[19] Evidently the oval mirrors were Parker's first choice and four of these are shown in the finished client's drawing at Saltram. In the event, however, he changed his mind, preferring, as he did in the case of the ceiling design, a bolder, simpler look.

A design was made in 1769 for rectangular frames for '4 glasses 4ft. 6in. wide 8ft. high' (1.3 by 2.4 metres), with mermaids in the crest and Neptune at the base (pl. 352).[20] The nautical ornaments, though related to Zucchi's *Triumph of Neptune* in the cove above the windows, did not suit Parker, who decided instead to have crests of urns flanked by female figures seated on acanthus scrolls. This particular arrangement first appeared in Adam's work in 1771 in mirror designs for Paul Methuen at Corsham Court and General Burgoyne at Hertford Street (see pl. 10).[21] No design specifically inscribed for Parker has been traced, and the date, though also unknown, cannot be before 1771.

Instead of all the mirrors being placed on the window piers as originally planned, two were hung on the opposite wall, on either side of the chimney-piece, in lieu of pictures. Adam's wall elevation of 1768 called for a pair of large paintings (each 9 feet 4 inches, or 2.8 metres square) in this position. They had not yet

353 'Design of a Table Frame for His Grace the Archbishop of York', by Robert Adam, 1768 (Sir John Soane's Museum: Adam drawings vol. 17:11)

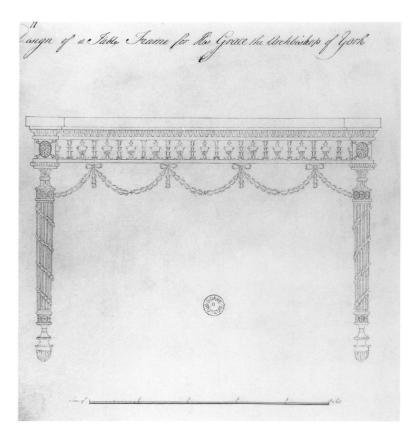

been found in April 1772, when Therese Parker wrote to Lord Grantham in Madrid, asking him to look out for 'two good Landscapes' for the saloon and a companion to the Van Dyck over the door to the library to hang over the door to the Red Velvet Room.[22] Evidently Mr Parker had tried unsuccessfully to buy a pair of Claude landscapes for £1,000, from Sir Joshua Reynolds, his lifelong friend and advisor, who was born in the neighbouring village of Plympton St Maurice. Under these mirrors stand two large gilt sofas which were supplied (together with eighteen *en suite* armchairs) by Chippendale in 1771 or 1772 and were always intended for that place.[23]

The pier-glasses on either side of the Venetian window are accompanied by distinctive gilt tables with bell-flower festoons suspended from their friezes and wrapped around their legs. They were made by Joseph Perfetti, a London carver and gilder later employed by Shelburne at Bowood, who was paid £41.1.0

354 One of a pair of carved and gilt-wood mirrors and console-tables in the Red Velvet Room flanking the door to the drawing-room, designed by Robert Adam, *c*.1772

on 29 January 1771.[24] Perfetti did not have an Adam design to work from as he did later that year when making the pair of related tables for the Red Velvet Room (pl. 353). What he probably did have was an inaccurate copy, possibly drawn from memory, of an Adam design made in May 1768 for the Hon. Robert Hay Drummond, Archbishop of York, at Brodsworth, Yorkshire, or a sketch of the table itself.[25] The obvious source was Thomas Robinson, who was a friend of the archbishop's and is known to have stayed with him at Brodsworth.[26]

This was not the only useful 'little Drawing' that Therese received from her elder brother: there are others recorded in her correspondence and preserved at Newby Hall.[27] Perfetti may also have been responsible for the poorly integrated addition of half-patera and buchrania to the friezes of the tables, which were presumably intended to reflect motifs on the picture frame over the mantelpiece, thought to be by Chippendale.

Lord Grantham was directly involved with the set of four 'King's' candle-vases ordered by Therese from Boulton and Fothergill in November 1771 and completed in March 1772.[28] Boulton, on receiving the commission, immediately sent a drawing showing the size of the plinth of the vases to his London agent, William Matthews, to deliver to Adam, presumably to enable him to design suitable pedestals. However, there is no evidence that the four ram's-head pedestals made for them were designed by Adam. They may well have been adapted, as the pier-tables were, from another design by him; they bear some resemblance to the tripod pedestals designed on 27 October 1772 for the Earl of Bute at Luton.[29]

It was part of Adam's original proposal that the walls should be hung with light-blue damask. In September 1769, Therese wrote to Frederick in London, asking him to 'send some patterns of Blue Damask, as we shall soon write to Genoa and wish to fix upon the best Blue for setting off the Pictures'.[30] A year later, the room was pronounced 'ready for the Damask though the windows (were) not put in'.[31] The Parkers, having paid £300 for the fabric and taken the trouble to get just the right colour, were bound to have provided adequate protection against the damaging effects of daylight. Adam's wall elevation shows gilt curtain cornices and crimson festoon curtains drawn up to clear the window surrounds. When the house was restored by the National Trust in 1960, his design was interpreted at face value and the drapes, instead of being allowed to drop, were fixed as pelmets. Originally there would also have been internal shutters either of the sliding type, like those on the Venetian windows in 20 St James's Square, or completely removable rigid panels. Shutters have now been fixed to the exterior of the house.

Adam's business at Saltram, at least as far as the house was concerned, was limited to fitting up the two new rooms; the last designs he made for that purpose were in 1769 for the saloon carpet and mirrors. However, two years later, as an afterthought, he was requested to provide an additional design for console-tables and mirrors for the earlier Red Velvet Room (pl. 354).[32] These pieces were strategically placed in the narrow spaces between the pilasters on either side of the door to the saloon as heralds of the fashionable new creation. The tables are much the same as those in the saloon, though better for being designed by Adam himself, and the mirrors are more elaborate despite their narrowness.[33]

Design for finishing the Library at Saltram. The Seat of John Parker Esquire.

Plan of the Library

355 Plan and laid-out wall elevations of the library (later the dining-room), by Robert Adam, 1768 (Sir John Soane's Museum: Adam drawings vol. 50:67)

The Red Velvet Room was probably the principal drawing-room before the great drawing-room was added. Whether it then became an ante-room is not certain. Adam, considering it in the context of an *appartement de parade*, described it as the first drawing-room and the room preceding it, now the Morning Room, as the ante-room.[34] The Parkers, instead of replacing the rococo decorations of these rooms, repainted them in 1770. In the Red Velvet Room, 'the ground of the Ceiling lightest of Greens & the Cornice Pink. They had painted the shutters & doors &c pink but not liking that they turnd it to white & Therese with her usual taste orderd all the mouldings, & parts of the Capitals of the Columns to be Gilt, which makes the Room

much chearfuller & handsommer'.[35] Adam's mirrors gave some much-needed light and sparkle to the dark end of the room behind the screen of columns.

The library was the first of the two new rooms to be finished, though both were designed at the same date, 1768. On 11 September 1770, when the saloon was still unglazed and only just ready for the damask, Frederick Robinson wrote to Lord Grantham, 'There is no describing the library, it is fitted up like a snuff box, they do not live in yet because of the noise of the workmen in the next room. there are more books than I thought.'[36] Exactly when the room was built is not known. It is certainly earlier than the saloon, much lower (14 feet, or 4.2

356 View of the dining-room (originally the library) showing the ceiling and related Axminster carpet as well as the sideboard, pedestals and urns designed by Robert Adam in *c*.1780 and somewhat uncomfortably fitted into the bow

metres, as compared to 25 feet, or 7.6 metres high), and quite irregular. Adam was confronted here with the difficult task of tailoring his bookcases and wall decorations to the asymmetrical spaces between the doors and windows in such a way as to give an apparently unified appearance to the whole room. Unfortunately, his finely tuned solution was spoilt when the room was remodelled as a dining-room and can now only be appreciated from his original design (pls 355, 356).

The bookcases with simple fluted friezes and Ionic guilloche pilasters were quite like those he had designed a year or so earlier for Lord Clifford's library at Ugbrooke Park, Chudleigh, about thirty miles north-east of Saltram and just two miles from Whiteway, where John Parker's brother Montagu lived.[37] Stucco medallions of *Socrates*, *Zeno*, *Cicero* and *Thales Milesius*, shown by Adam painted blue and white like Wedgwood ware, were set into the walls above the cases; over the chimney-piece is a classical landscape by Zuccarelli in a frame very similar to the one made in 1760 for the great room at Bowood (later the eating-room; now at Lloyds); and over the doors are paintings by Zucchi of episodes from ancient history, though Adam's design humorously suggested a shooting scene over the door to the passage, to please Mr Parker. Zucchi was also responsible for the

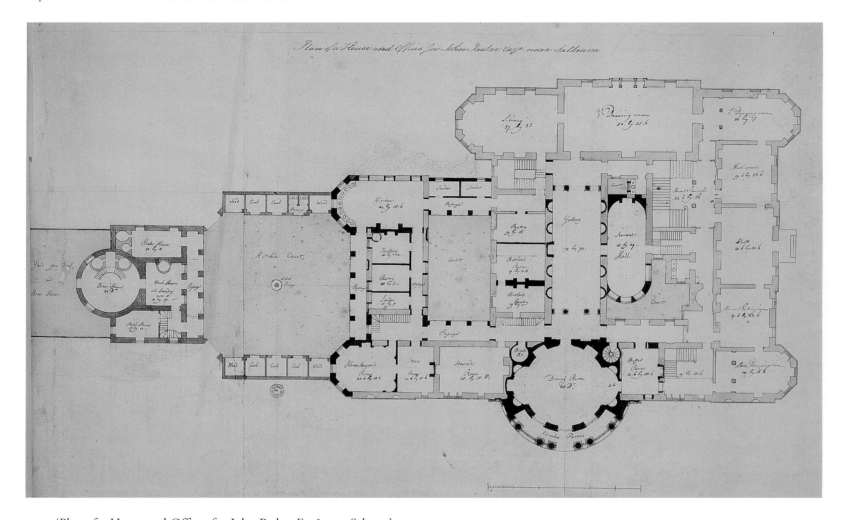

357 'Plan of a House and Offices for John Parker Esqr near Saltram',
by Robert Adam, 1779. The existing house is shown in pink, the
proposed but unexecuted additions and alterations in black (Sir John
Soane's Museum: Adam drawings vol. 50:66)

four segmental paintings of classical literary subjects in the ceiling.[38] The paintings for the library were finished by September
1769, when Therese asked Frederick to look at them in Zucchi's
studio in London and give his opinion.[39]

It was presumably to draw attention away from the asymmetrical arrangement of the walls that Adam provided a bold, distinctly unrelated, centralized design for the ceiling, instead of a
repeat pattern like the Palmyrene one designed in 1766 for the
study at Harewood.[40] The carpet supplied by Thomas Whitty of
Axminster is too exact a replica of the ceiling, in colour as well as
composition, to have been designed by Adam and was almost
certainly made from a drawing of the finished ceiling.[41] Its date
is unknown, but it is later than the saloon carpet.

On 8 November 1772, Therese wrote to Frederick:

All our Building draws very near a conclusion a new Eating
Room which will of course draw us in to build new Offices, as
it will oblige us to pull down Old ones, is thought of at a distance but if we leave nothing for the little Boy to do, he will
certainly pull to pieces what we have done or perhaps wonder
how money could be laid out at Saltram, & go & build at
Boringdon.[42]

Adam must also have been party to these thoughts for the future,
if not their originator, and would doubtlessly have agreed that
his grandiose saloon called for something more spacious and

conveniently placed than the comparatively small eating-room
quite a distance away on the west side of the entrance hall, where
the present library is. Notwithstanding, the Parkers put the idea
aside and had the pleasure for the first time since they came to
Saltram of living in their house without builders. Their pleasure,
however, did not last long. In December 1775, five weeks after
the birth of a daughter, Therese died and her sister Anne,
'Nanny', Robinson came to live at Saltram to look after the children. Then, in November 1778, some of the outbuildings on the
north side of the house were damaged by fire and John Parker
decided not just to make repairs, but also 'to alter for the better
by building a new Laundry and Brew house and turning the old
one into a Kitchen'.[43] Though Anne Robinson would have liked
Lord Grantham 'to plan and contrive it for the best', the job was
given to Mr Stockman, the estate carpenter, and Mr Parlby, chief
builder of the Plymouth docks.[44]

Parker's decision to build new offices revived the old idea of
making a larger dining-room. Adam was consulted again and
promptly drew up a comprehensive plan, rationalizing and
extending the north side for services and adding a grand circular
dining-room complete with apses, niches and a circular portico
in the centre of the west front (pl. 357).[45] A gallery, 71 feet (21.6
metres) long and 19 feet (5.7 metres) wide, with columnar
screens at either end and niches lining the walls, linked the dining-room to the saloon and its satellites – the first (Red Velvet)

358 The dining-room pier-glass and table in the Adam style, probably designed and executed by Mr Stockman, the estate carpenter

drawing-room, the ante-room (Morning Room) and library – to form a proper *appartement de parade*. The servants' hall, a large room (15 by 39 feet, or 4.5 by 11.8 metres) with apsidal ends, was conveniently located at the heart of the house, between the gallery and the back stairs. Normally this essential room would have been in the basement, but there is none to speak of at Saltram.

Adam's ingenious scheme was evidently more than Parker had contemplated or could afford and certainly more than his estate carpenter could handle. The simplest solution was to remodel the library as a formal dining-room and move the books and

bookcases into the old eating-room. This did not require Adam's costly expertise. However, had his scheme been adopted, the unity of the room would not have been destroyed, as John Cornforth rightly observed, nor would the necessary suggestion of height provided by the vertical bookcases have been lost.[46] Tall panels of painted or stucco grotesques of the sort found in almost every Adam interior might have served the purpose better than Zucchi's paintings, which do not fill the spaces occupied by the bookcases, but rather float between the now-meaningless medallions and the prominent dado. The horizontal lines that Adam did his best to play down are repeatedly emphasized, making the room seem even lower than it is.

Blocking two of the three windows of the canted bay in order to create a sideboard alcove would have been inconceivable to Adam. He would either have blocked the whole bay and formed a semicircular apse in the antique style, like the ones at Kedleston and later, in 1783, at Newby Hall, or at least screened the space with columns as he did in the Lansdowne House dining-room and elsewhere. The awkward position of the window behind the sideboard and the static, ungainly shape of the semicircular table are unthinkable in an Adam composition, where variety and movement are paramount.

Mr Stockman was perfectly capable of running up a streamlined Adam-style sideboard and pier-table without an Adam design (pl. 358). Pedestals and vases and a fancy pier-glass were another matter. Adam was asked to make designs for these pieces, which he did in November 1780.[47] The pedestals and vases were executed by a more sophisticated craftsman than Stockman, probably in London. Though painted green and white, to match the walls and ceiling, they have no ornaments in common with the rest of the room. The proposed 'Glass frame for the pier opposite the Chimney' – an oval 3¼ feet (1 metre) tall and 2½ feet (76 centimetres) wide suspended on long chains from a figured roundel (probably the existing one) with an oval medallion crest and anthemion base – was evidently thought to be too small in relation to Stockman's pier-table, which is over 5 feet (1.5 metres) wide, with a frieze copied from the one round the walls. Adam's second, approved design, dated 5 April 1781, was for a mirror 5 feet 9 inches (1.7 metres) wide and 8 feet (2.4 metres) tall with a crest of sphinxes flanking a painted medallion reminiscent of that on the Red Velvet Room mirrors.[48] It was probably made by Stockman, who did the frames for Zucchi's paintings, and was painted white to match.

Adam's final contributions did not really save his original room or significantly improve the remodelled one. In the end, Saltram lost both the opportunity of a grand unified plan and one of its two Adam rooms. Fortunately, Adam's magnificent saloon survives intact and his elegant console tables and mirrors remain *in situ* in the Red Velvet Room.

359 Elevation of the east front of Luton Hoo, designed by Robert Adam, 1771–72. Executed as shown except for the right-hand wing (*The works in architecture of Robert and James Adam*, vol. 1 (1778), pt. III, pl. IV)

15

LUTON HOO

In 1764 John, third Earl of Bute (1712–92) gave Adam the only opportunity he ever had to build an entirely new country house on a grand scale, at Luton Hoo in Bedfordshire.[1] Unfortunately, it turned out to be a blighted commission. Bute had his own particular requirements and ideas about architecture, and the design of the house was controlled by him; most inefficiently, as it happened, for he could never decide exactly what he wanted and always wanted more than he could afford. Adam's role was mainly to correct and complete his plans and to design elevations for them. Though he had greater independence in designing the interior decorations, Bute's important collections were always a conditioning factor.

Nevertheless, it was to his advantage – and evidently agreeable to Bute – to publish the preferred plans and elevations of Luton in the third number of the *Works* in 1775 (pls 359, 364, 365). The two previous numbers, on Syon and Kenwood, had demonstrated his skills in remodelling earlier houses; the fourth number was to be devoted to public buildings and the fifth to designs for the royal family. A new country house was urgently needed to complete his impressive display of commissioned architectural works. However, unlike Sir William Chambers, John Carr, James Paine and Sir Robert Taylor, who had several country houses and villas to their credit, he had only two houses in England to choose from: Sir Wyndham Knatchbull's at Mersham-le-Hatch in Kent and Luton. Witham Priory, Somerset, though it was abandoned after William Beckford's death in 1770, would have been another possibility had it not been published by Woolfe and Gandon in *Vitruvius Britannicus* in 1771. Luton was the obvious choice.

It did not matter how limited Adam's contribution had been, since he was Bute's chosen architect; Bute had secured him the post of Joint Architect to the King's Works in 1761 and had commissioned him to build a new town house at Berkeley Square (which he sold unfinished to the Earl of Shelburne) as well as Luton Hoo. Having his work approved by a noble patron 'so justly esteemed for his great taste and discerning judgment in the celebrated works of the ancients and in every branch of the arts' flattered Adam's vanity. There can be no doubt that he also saw Bute's patronage as crucial to establishing his reputation as a country-house architect. While the example of Luton may have attracted some patrons in Scotland, where Bute held considerable sway, it had virtually no effect in England.[2] Why Bute chose

Adam rather than Chambers is hard to say. The Scottish tie was bound to be an important factor, besides which Chambers was already well placed in the profession and not in as much need of encouragement as Adam was at that stage.

When the designs for Luton were engraved in 1774, Bute and his family were still living in the old house which he had bought in 1763. The new mansion that was to replace it was only half-finished; the principal front and north wing had not even been started, nor would they be in Bute's lifetime. Building work had come to a full stop and was not to be resumed until after 1825, when the second Marquess of Bute employed Robert Smirke to complete the house. Thus, apart from its other functions, the third number of the *Works* was meant to serve as a record of the house as it was intended to be built; in other words, to put a gloss on a bungled project.

The full story of Luton Hoo and its genesis is not told by the few designs selected for publication in the *Works*, but rather by the numerous rejected plans among the recently discovered drawings in the Bute collection and Adam's drawings at the Soane.[3]

The death of Lady Bute's father, Edward Wortley-Montagu, in February 1761, leaving her a life interest in his Yorkshire estates said to be worth £17,000 a year, transformed Bute from 'a poor Scot' to an English magnate and prompted him to seek a country estate of his own within reach of London. Several places were considered in the course of the next two years, but it was not until October 1763, when his political career collapsed and retirement from London became imperative, that he hastily purchased Luton from Francis Herne, MP for £94,000.[4] The existing late seventeenth-century house, though old-fashioned, was evidently in a good state of repair and large enough to house the earl and his family in comfort for at least twenty years (pl. 360a). It had two storeys and an attic, with a main west-facing front of eleven bays, comprised of a five-bay centre flanked by two tall three-bay canted bows and a shorter south range of seven bays. Behind this L-shaped arrangement was an irregular court.[5]

Bute began in 1764 with a fairly realistic idea of retaining the old house and making its L-shaped plan into an impressive quadrangle (pl. 360b). Adam's problem was to reconcile a symmetrical front incorporating the existing canted bows with a reasonable-sized court. His solution (pl. 360c) was to add lateral wings punctuated by square corner towers and to use the old

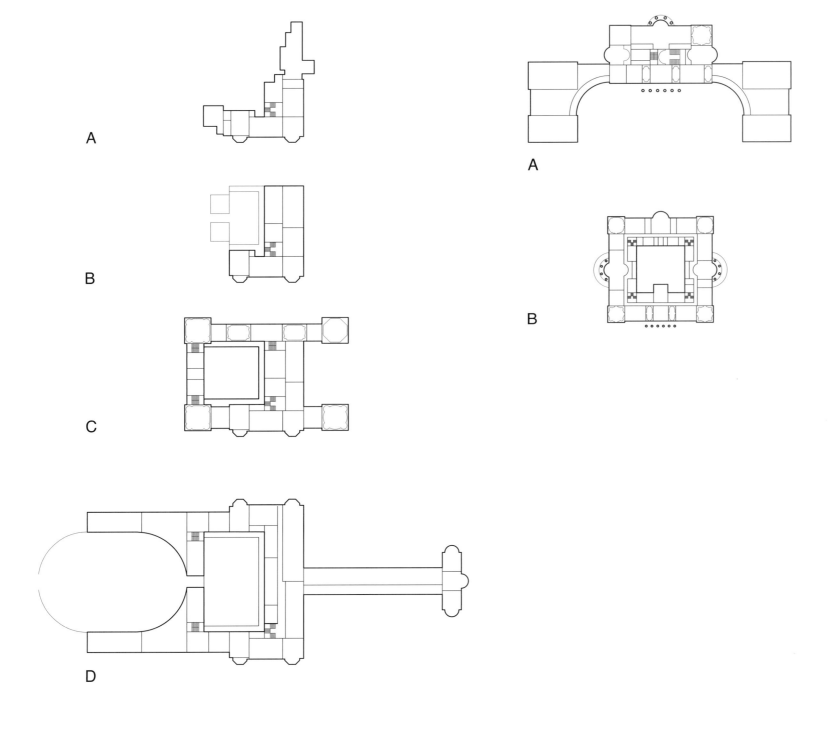

A

B

C

D

A

B

360 Plan of the existing house and three plans by Robert Adam for enlarging it: a. existing seventeenth-century house; b. first court-yard plan, 1764; c. enlarged quadrangle with projecting wings on south front, 1764; d. quadrangular plan with long T-shaped wing on south front, 1765–66

361 Plans for an entirely new house: a. 'New Design' for a house with quadrant wings, 27 December 1766; b. new design for a quadrangular house, February 1767

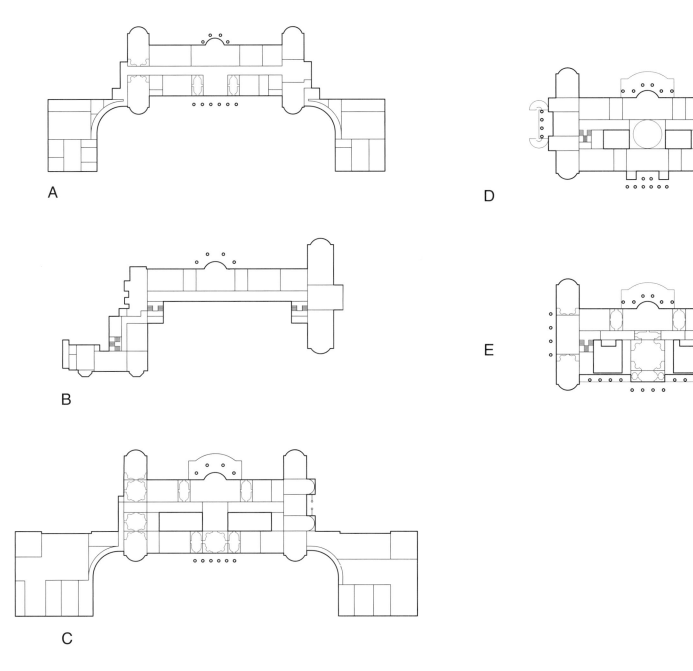

A

B

C

D

E

362 Revised plans for an entirely new house: a. improved 'New
Design', April 1767; b. plan of a new addition to the old house, 1767; c.
improved version of the second 'New Design' introducing court-yards
on either side of the main east-west axis, by Bute's son, Captain Charles
Stuart, 1769; d. corrected version of Captain Stuart's plan by Robert
Adam, 1771; e. the final plan by Robert Adam, 1772

100   200 feet
20   40   60 metres

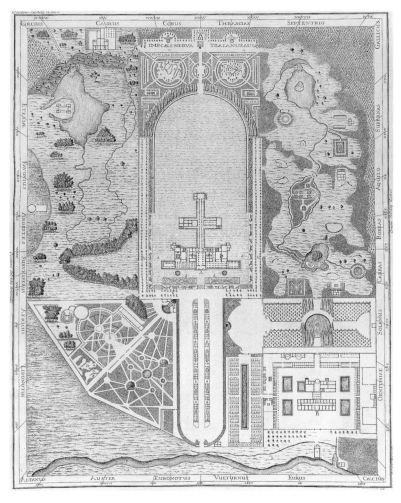

363 Robert Castell, reconstruction of the plan of Pliny's Tuscum Villa (*Villas of the ancients illustrated* (1728), detail)

house and the northern wing as the basis for a large quadrangle with four symmetrical but different fronts, the south front having two projecting wings. Though his 'Castle Style' façades may be dismissed as 'monotonous and unconvincing', his plan deserves more credit.[6] It answered the purpose and worked better than any of the subsequent schemes conceived by Bute.

There were three apartments: a grand guest suite consisting of a bedroom and circular dressing-room set apart in the projecting south-west wing, a library suite of just two rooms (one of them octagonal) in the corresponding south-east wing, with a pivotal vestibule linking it to the principal suite of reception rooms – a gallery and dining-room on the south front and a drawing-room, ante-room, dressing-room and bedroom on the east or garden front. While Luton was to be a showcase for Bute's large collection of pictures, the main repository for his famous library was to be in a separate wing of his new London house, then under construction.

With all Bute's particular requirements apparently fulfilled, the scheme was suddenly dropped; but not, as one might think, for reasons of cost. The two main causes of the *volte-face* were fear of the mob and an oversight in the provision of storage space at Bute House for the fifty-eight outsize cylinders, each 4½ feet (1.3 metres) long and 1½ feet (38 centimetres) in diameter, made for the vast and expensive mechanical organ that was to occupy a special recess in the London drawing-room.[7] This omission may also have been a determining factor in the sale of Bute

House in an unfinished state in October 1765. In any event, adequate accommodation for the organ and its cylinders became an essential requirement of all subsequent plans for Luton.

Bute's initial response was to proceed with the idea of incorporating the old house in a quadrangle, but to replace Adam's two short wings by a single 200 foot (68 metre)-long arm shooting out from the centre of the south front in a manner reminiscent of the long T-shaped wing of Pliny's Tuscum Villa (pl. 363) and not unlike the asymmetrical library wing attached to one side of Bute House.[8] Despite its eccentricity, the T-shaped extension, with an organ drawing-room and an enfilade of four smaller rooms backing on to a long corridor where the organ barrels (cylinders) were to be kept, provided just what Bute wanted for his collections and was the embryo of the house as finally built. But Adam never had to deal with this odd scheme, for Bute suddenly decided to demolish the old house and start afresh. His radical change of mind coincided with (and was surely precipitated by) George III's complete break with him in the summer of 1766, sending him unequivocally into retirement from public life.

A 'New Design' for a large Palladian house with a three-storey, thirteen-bay central block and two five-bay pavilions linked by quadrant wings was completed by Adam on 27 December 1766 (pl. 361a).[9] The principal front was to have an hexastyle portico raised on rusticated arches, and the garden front a large central bow with an Ionic tetrastyle portico. Its elevations, modelled on Paine's *c.*1759 designs for Kedleston, may not have been very original, but they were none the less acceptable. The plan, though it has much more variety, is poorly integrated, owing not to Adam's inability but rather to Bute's 'fixed ideas' about having a private stair for himself in addition to the principal and service stairs.[10]

The core of the house was largely given over to staircases (later altered to admit water-closets, another of Bute's fixations), with the parade and private apartments ranged round the perimeter: parade to the right (south), private to the left (north). Visitors were evidently expected to proceed from the ground-floor entrance hall up the principal stair to a 'great' ante-room (above the hall) and thence, counter-clockwise, to the first drawing-room, with screened apses at either end, through two lesser, differently shaped drawing-rooms and finally to the 'Picture and Music Gallery' – 80 feet (24.3 metres) long and 22 feet (7.4 metres) wide, with a great bow window in the centre – which was the climax of the parade. This oddly shaped and peculiarly proportioned space, with the inner wall partitioned to form a large organ recess answering the bow window and two 30 foot (9 metre)-long corridors for the cylinders on either side, was the main feature of all subsequent plans of Luton.[11]

Bute's desire for more book-space, combined with his lack of resolve and excess of ambition, led to another set of designs for a larger quadrangular house (183 feet, or 55.7 metres, square) being prepared less than two months later, on 7 February 1767 (pl. 361b).[12] This, in effect, was the 'New Design' opened out around a courtyard and combined with the Palladianized corner towers and long low façades of the 1764 scheme. The array of rooms is impressive: there were to be five book rooms occupying virtually the whole of the east front and part of the south, three drawing-rooms and a '4th Great Drawing Room as Picture and Music Gallery' with two separate rooms for the organ barrels, a chapel,

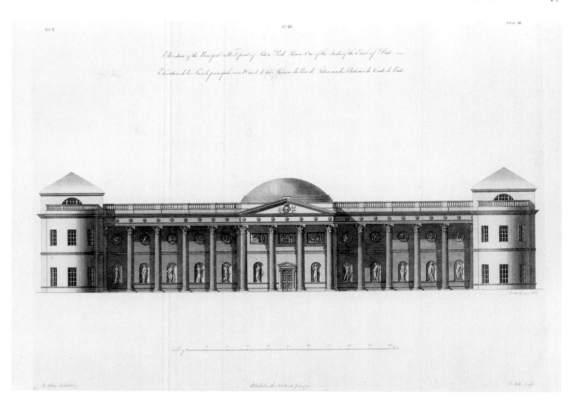

364 Elevation (unexecuted) of the west front of Luton Hoo, by Robert Adam, 1772. The absence of windows behind the colonnade of giant columns makes this look more like a public building than a country house (*The works in architecture of Robert and James Adam*, vol. I (1778), pt. III, pl. III)

365 Elevations of the north and south fronts of Luton Hoo, by Robert Adam, 1771. The north front was never executed; the south front was completed as designed (*The works in architecture of Robert and James Adam*, vol. I (1778), pt. III, pl. V)

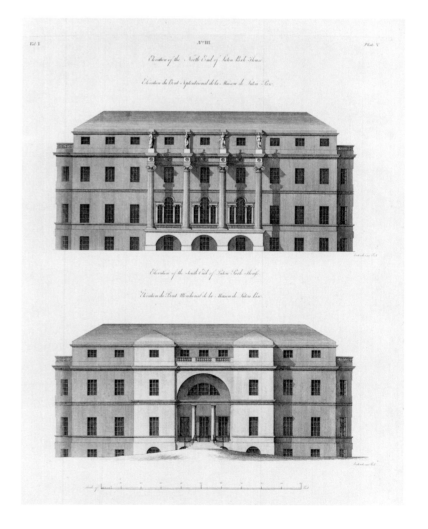

a billiard-room, stairs with columnar screens in the four corners of the court, bedrooms, dressing-rooms and more than the usual complement of water-closets. The provision of a continuous passage behind the rooms removed some of the inconvenience of the quadrangular plan. However, there is no rational explanation for the presence of semicircular columnar porticos on the north and south fronts but not on the garden front. The location of the two-storey kitchen in the south bow, between the library apartment and the guest bedroom suite, is bizarre. This palatial scheme may have been a reaction to the designs for George III's palace at Richmond made by Chambers in 1765 without Bute's involvement.[13] It cannot have been taken very seriously and only succeeded in convincing Bute to return to his previous idea of a central block and linked pavilions.

Finished plans and elevations for a revised version of the 'New Design' were duly drawn up by Adam on 15 April 1767 (pl. 362a).[14] The pavilions were little altered, but the house was lowered and stretched out to thirteen bays with taller projecting wings at either end, forming an elongated H or double T-shaped plan reminiscent of the curious T-shaped organ extension conceived by Bute a few years earlier.[15] The central staircase area in the 'New Design' was replaced by a spinal corridor over 200 feet (60 metres) long, running almost the whole length of the house and bisecting the east and west ranges of rooms. Though this was not a feature of English houses of the period, it is found in several Scottish houses, including Mellerstain and Bute's own family seat, Mount Stuart.[16] It introduced a strong north–south axis which was further developed in the later stages of the plan as well as in the end elevations.

Provision for Bute's collections of pictures and scientific instruments had priority. They occupied the entire south wing and two adjacent rooms on the east front. The north wing was the family's private apartment, consisting of a large drawing-room with an apse at one end and a bow window at the other and a 'Stewards Dining Room' of the same size and shape, entered only from the servants' wing and back stairs. There was an apsidal ante-room and formal dining-room to the left of the entrance hall, matched on the right by the principal guest apartment, consisting of a state bedroom flanked by two dressing-rooms. This reduced the suite of reception rooms to the first drawing-room, the organ drawing-room and the bow-windowed saloon. The parade evidently began at the north end of the corridor, in the organ drawing-room. At either end of the corridor

366 Design for the drawing-room ceiling, by Robert Adam, 1770 (Sir John Soane's Museum: Adam drawings, vol. 12:24)

house in stages, and to that end Adam supplied a 'Plan of the Principal Story of an Addition to connect with the Present House at Luton in Bedforshire. A new Addition being contrived to Answer as part of a compleat Design with Offices when the Old part of the House is pulled down' (pl. 362b).[17] His spelling-out of what was intended on the drawing itself reads like an informal contract which, knowing his patron as he did, he must have realized was unlikely to be fulfilled. Bute's cousin, Lady Mary Coke, had her doubts when she saw the work in progress in July 1769:

> The Place is very fine, & the House will be so if it is ever finished, but I think that part which is now going on will not do well without the rest; if you remember, no front will be compleat: in that respect what is built of Worksop looks more like an intire House. Ask Lord Strafford if he does not think it will look lame.[18]

But the truth is that 'the rest' was not needed; the range of reception rooms and book rooms on the east front, the library wing on the south and the long corridor nobly housed Bute's collections and that is what mattered most.

Building began late in 1767 on a modified version of the partial plan, of which a complete set of reduced copies was made, presumably to enable Bute to continue perfecting the remainder whilst he was in Italy for his health.[19] An 'Improved' version of the 1767 'New Design' (pl. 362c) was indeed 'Begun at Rome . . . (and) Finish'd at Genoa, April 1st 1769' by his sixteen-year-old son, Captain Charles Stuart, no doubt with Bute's encouragement.[20] This brought the west front forward and added a middle range between it and the corridor, containing a hall leading directly into the saloon and two open courts on either side. While the courts succeeded in lighting the corridor (which was the main purpose of the arrangement), the hall created an asymmetrical division owing to the fact that the north end of the corridor remained directly linked to the kitchen pavilion on that side. Instead of resolving the asymmetry, Stuart (just to add

were staircase halls screened by columns – as the main hall was – and behind these were secondary stairs. In addition, there were service stairs communicating with the pavilions. Instead of the corner towers that had featured in the two quadrangular schemes, the projecting wings of the H were given an additional, third storey and finished with lower bows at the ends. A little movement was thereby added to the otherwise static elevations which were the least satisfactory aspects of the scheme.

Having spent three years considering four different schemes and several variations upon them, Bute finally fixed on this one, though somewhat hesitantly and without committing himself to the whole. Ill health no doubt exacerbated his chronic indecision. To keep his options open, he decided to build the new

367 Design for the library ceiling, by Robert Adam, 1769 (Sir John Soane's Museum: Adam drawings, vol. 12:20)

368 The library at Mellerstain, Berwickshire, designed by Roberet Adam, 1770. The centre of the ceiling is taken from the unexecuted design for the library at Luton Hoo

more variety to the plan) exacerbated the differences between the informal north wing and the library apartment by giving the former two matching suites of round- and bow-fronted rooms. These shortcomings were rectified by Adam after discussion with Bute while he was in England from July to November 1769. The linked pavilions were abandoned and the family wing recast to mirror the library, with a recessed central vestibule and a grand entrance of its own modelled on the south front of Kedleston.

Adam's corrected version of Stuart's plan was published in the *Works* (pl. 362d), where it is described as 'Luton House as originally designed' and dated 1771, the date of Bute's final return, when minor alterations were made before it was approved.[21] It is ironic that the only known drawing of the penultimate plan should be amongst Chambers's drawings at the Soane Museum,[22] because of the similarity it bears to Chambers's rejected plan of 1756 for Harewood House, which Adam undoubtedly knew and which also has a circular tribune placed between the entrance hall and saloon, two flanking courts and long passages.[23] The idea of a central circular tribune was much in Adam's mind in 1770–1 for the Edinburgh Registry Office (1771) as well as Luton and these projects are likely to have influ-

enced his addition of a central rotunda to the undated plan of Syon published in the *Works* in 1773.[24] The colonnaded tribune was Adam's most significant contribution to Luton. It was intended to serve both as a ceremonial vestibule and as a music-room, with Bute's famous organ placed against the north wall and the barrels stored in the triangular closets and corridors.

Bute must have been pleased to see the architectural efforts of his favourite son so much improved by Adam, but he evidently had no intention of completing the 'Addition' in such a magnificent and expensive manner, especially not after the damaging fire at Luton in 1771. In fact, all that was needed to finish the house was a north wing to match the south one, a principal front and proper entrance. This is what the final scheme of 1772 provided, with disappointing results (pl. 362e). The private apartment is prosaic compared to the library and inconvenient too: its excessively large 'Great Anti-Room' is out of all proportion to the adjoining drawing-room and dining-room, and the latter, which is the only dining-room in the house, is quite difficult to reach. Linking the two wings was a windowless wall, a literal façade or screen for the two open courts behind, which, given a colonnade and niches, resembled 'a public work rather than a private build-

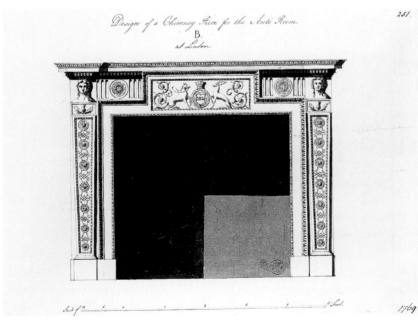

369   Design of the ceiling of Lady Bute's dressing-room on the first floor, by Robert Adam, 1769 (*The works in architecture of Robert and James Adam*, vol. 1 (1778), pt. III, pl. VII. Hand-coloured copy at Sir John Soane's Museum)

370   Design of an armorial chimney-piece for the ante-room, by Robert Adam, 1769 (Sir John Soane's Museum: Adam drawings, vol. 22:251)

371   Cornice, frieze and capital for the screens in the saloon, by Robert Adam (*The works in architecture of Robert and James Adam*, vol. 1 (1778), pt. III, pl. VI)

372 Miscellaneous furniture for Luton Hoo, designed by Roberet Adam (*The works in architecture of Robert and James Adam*, vol. I (1778), pt. III, pl. VIII)

373 Early seventeenth-century Venetian bronze andiron (one of a pair) attributed to Nicolo Roccatagliata, for which Adam supplied candle-branches and pedestals (Private collection)

ing'.[25] Such a compromised plan cannot have been what Adam wanted, nor is it surprising that the penultimate design was the one preferred by the second marquess, who employed Smirke to finish the house.[26]

By August 1774, the incomplete house was 'intirely finished & furnished' and ready to show to discerning friends and relations like Lady Mark Coke, Mrs Delany, the Duchess of Portland and Louis Dutens.[27] If the outside was still wanting, the interior, by all accounts, was perfection: magnificent without ostentation or 'extravagance of fancy'.[28] Bute's staggering collection of fine pictures, vases, marble tables, objects of vertu, books, scientific apparatus 'and a long et cetera of curiosities' was the principal attraction – indeed, the whole *raison d'être* of the building – to which all else was subservient.

There was little scope here for Adam's decorative flair; no space for his 'antique' wall panels or pilasters of stucco grotesques and painted rinceaux. All the rooms on the *piano nobile* were uniformly hung with plain light-green paper to show the pictures to advantage, the ceilings were 'elegant, and not loaded with ornament' and there was 'very little guilding' apart from Adam's curtain cornices (published in the *Works*; pl. 371) and the picture frames, of which there were an enormous number.[29] Evidently this was not just a matter of taste and balance, but also of economy. According to Lady Mary Coke, the coved drawing-room ceiling 'intended to be painted in small compartments remains unfinish'd as Mr Adams ask'd eight hundred pounds for the painting only' (pl. 366).[30] It was the simplest and cheapest of Adam's two designs for the library ceiling – the one without inset paintings and stucco tablets – that was carried out, leaving Adam free to use the end section of the rejected design (pl. 367) for the central part of the library ceiling at Mellerstain in 1770 (pl. 368).[31] In contrast to the simplicity preferred for the principal reception rooms, the most elaborate, most 'antique' alternative was chosen for the ceiling of Lady Bute's first-floor dressing-

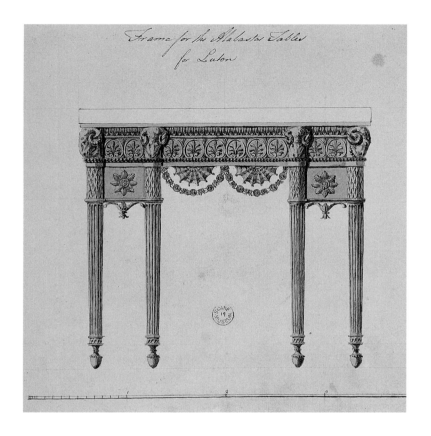

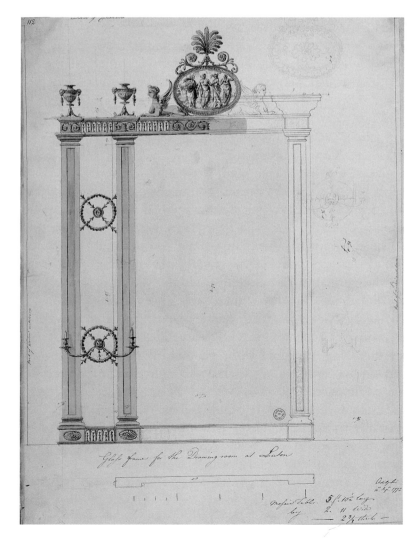

374   Design for armorial table frames with alabaster slabs in the saloon, by Robert Adam, 1772 (Sir John Soane's Museum: Adam drawings, vol. 17:19)

375   Pier-glass, table and torchères for the drawing-room at Luton Hoo, designed by Robert Adam, 1772, and all executed (*The works in architecture of Robert and James Adam*, vol. III (1822), pl. VIII, incorrectly labelled as 'Furniture at Sion House')

376   Preliminary design (unexecuted) for the drawing-room mirror with a 'mosaic' table indicated below, by Robert Adam, 1772 (Sir John Soane's Museum: Adam drawings, vol. 20:112)

room (pl. 369).[32] This design was the model for the Countess of Derby's Etruscan dressing-room designed four years later, in 1773.[33]

Adam's chimney-piece designs for the drawing-room, saloon and two flanking ante-rooms are more problematical.[34] There is no reason to assume that they were used for the five marble chimney-pieces sent from Rome in 1771 and 1772 by James Byres, who was perfectly capable of making his own designs. Nor is there any indication of where these costly Italian imports were placed, though they were certainly conspicuous.[35]

The saloon, instead of having two chimney-pieces at either end as planned, had only one opposite the bow window, where there was meant to be an entrance from the hall. An unusual

377   Carved and gilt-wood torchères from the drawing-room at Luton, designed by Robert Adam, *c*.1772 (Private collection)

378   Design of a cabinet for the Earl of Bute, possibly for the storage of music manuscripts, by Robert Adam, *c*.1763 (Sir John Soane's Museum: Adam drawings, vol. 25:5)

heraldic design was made by Adam in 1769 (pl. 370), bearing Bute's arms and supporters in the tablet, Garter stars in the metopes, Garter chains on the posts and the Thistles of his former order as dentils under busts of ancient heroes.[36] Thistles were repeated in the capitals of the two columnar screens subdividing the room (pl. 371). These capitals, 'altered from an antique one, the drawing of which his Lordship brought from abroad', and the ones on the screen of columns on the great stair were presented in the *Works* as examples of Adam's originality in interpreting the ancients, which was 'approved by men of taste' and 'imitated in various places, particularly in the Pantheon in Oxford Street'.[37] Presumably his design dated 17 November 1772 for a 'Frame for the Alabaster Tables' with Garter stars in the frieze and pendant Garter chains was also destined for the saloon (pl. 374).[38] It is not known to have been executed.

The only Adam furniture made (or at least agreed upon) for Luton was engraved in the *Works* (pl. 372). Most of it was for the great 'Withdrawing Room' or '*Salle d'Assemblée*'. In the four niches on the north and south walls were two pairs of Venetian late-sixteenth or early seventeenth-century bronze andirons – one by Andrea di Alessandro Baruzzi, Il Bresciano (1530–69), the other attributed to Niccolo Roccatagliata – for which Adam sup-

plied candle-branches and pedestals (pl. 373).[39] The pedestals (now lost) had a guilloche and rosette frieze, ram's-head mounts, winged animal feet, an enriched apron and other ornaments designed to harmonize with the 'busy and the picturesque' style of the sculpture. Between the windows was a pair of gilt wood pier-tables, designed in October 1772 (pl. 375), with antique mosaic tops set in marble surrounds, round fluted legs and guilloche friezes corresponding to those on the accompanying torchères depicted in the engraving in the *Works*, the bronze pedestals and the chimney-piece.[40] The pier-tables are now at Mount Stuart and since 1990 two pairs of torchères have passed through Christie's (pl. 377).[41]

There is no trace, however, of the large tripartite pier-glasses with draped female terms, medallions, urns, winged griffons and seated figures that were designed in 1772 to accompany the tables.[42] When Lady Coke visited the house on 30 August 1774, she found 'Fine glasses . . . only in one of the drawing rooms; the rest are to be brought here, as soon as the new project for casting larger plates here then (*sic*) they do at Paris is brought to perfection'.[43] That, however, was some years off. The new Company of British Cast Plate Manufacturers established in Lancashire in 1773 did not begin production until 1776, by which time Bute had lost interest in Luton and 'Capability' Brown and Henry Holland had

Organ Case for The Earl of Bute

1763.

replaced Adam at his London house, No. 75 South Audley Street, and probably at Highcliffe, his seaside villa in Hampshire, as well.[44] Though the Luton pier-glasses may well have been abandoned, a term mirror of much the same design was made for the chimney-piece in the dining-room at 20 St James's Square.[45]

One is left to guess where the great organ that had so influenced the plan of Luton was finally placed and what it looked like. Unfortunately, Mrs Delany omitted to say in her vivid account of the 'extraordinary piece of mechanism' and its entertaining music;[46] but the choices are limited. It could only have been at the north end of the drawing-room or in one of the screened spaces in the saloon and is unlikely to have had either of the two organ cases that Adam designed for Bute, one of which is dated 1763 and was intended for Bute House (pls 378, 379).[47]

The circuit of the new house – entered from the old house, up some stairs into the long corridor – began in the drawing-room and finished in the library, the most 'noble and extensive apartment' of all, consisting of three (or five) rooms: one in the centre divided into three sections by columns supporting segmental arches, and two square rooms with large bow windows at either end. When the doors were thrown open, it appeared 'like one large room or gallery', 144 feet (43.8 metres) long and 20 feet (6 metres) high.[48] This was considerably larger than the library wing designed around 1761 for Bute House (but shorter than the library at Blenheim) and much more varied in the configuration and modelling of the spaces. Its recessed centre and projecting rooms with semicircular window bays recall George Dance's prize-winning Parma Academy design for a 'Public Gallery' which Adam seems to have consulted when planning the sculpture gallery at Newby in 1766, a year or so before his final plan for the Luton 'Addition' in which the layout of the library was determined once and for all.[49]

Walls, window piers and apses were lined with bookcases in which there were 30,000 volumes 'locked up and seen through wires'.[50] In addition, the central room had a collection of maps and models; more models (cork ones of Roman ruins), manuscripts and a 'cabinet of mathematical instruments, and astronomical and philosophical apparatus . . . reckoned the most complete of the kind in Europe' filled the two small adjoining rooms on the garden front.[51] Space-consuming chimney-pieces were excluded from the library in preference for smaller but equally effective brass and steel stove-grates designed by Adam and executed in 1768.[52] These were puffed up in the *Works* as the first to be decorated in the neo-classical manner and thus the origin of the idea for the prevailing form in public and private buildings. How the idea could have been so widely transmitted is difficult to imagine, as access to Luton was quite limited. Moreover, the novel decoration would hardly have been visible if the inner walls of the library were as poorly lit as C. R. Cockerell found them.[53] Cockerell, who evidently examined the house in 1821 (possibly in connection with a plan to complete it) also found fault with the absence of any direct way to reach the end rooms without going through the central one.

It was to the library and scientific cabinets that Bute retired, 'more like a philosopher than a man of the world: applying his mind wholly to contemplation; and to the study of the arts and sciences'.[54] His family, meanwhile, lived under a blanket of 'ennui' in what Lady Louisa Stuart described as 'a scene of inconvenient melancholy magnificence'.[55]

'Melancholy magnificence' perfectly describes the present state of the house as completed by Sir Robert Smirke, c.1825–30, reconstructed by Sydney Smirke after a fire in 1843 and remodelled for Sir Julius Wernher by Mewes & Davis in 1903.

379 Design for an organ case for Bute House (later Lansdowne House), by Robert Adam, 1763 (Sir John Soane's Museum: Adam drawings, vol. 25:4)

380 The front of 20 St James's Square before 1936 when an attic storey
and mansard were added by Mewès and Davis

16

20 ST JAMES'S SQUARE

The 'Welsh Maecenas' Sir Watkin Williams-Wynn (1749–89) was only five months old when he succeeded as fourth Baronet of Wynnstay in Denbighshire on 26 September 1749. His father, the 'Great Sir Watkin', third Baronet, having inherited the large estates of his kinsman, Sir John Wynn, whose name he added to his own, was one of the richest and most powerful landowners in Wales: a veritable prince of Wales, a notorious Jacobite and unchallenged leader of the Welsh Tories.[1] A long minority of twenty years swelled the young Sir Watkin's accumulated fortune far above his father's, but it also eroded the family's political influence, which he made no effort to restore. Instead, he devoted himself wholeheartedly to the arts – architecture, painting, the theatre and above all music – and was one of the greatest patrons of the last quarter of the eighteenth century. However, the lavishness of his patronage was as much a foible as a virtue. While his annual income from rents alone trebled to over £27,000 in the first thirty years of his life, his disbursements on building projects, musicians and instruments, painters and silversmiths, scenery and costumes for his private theatre, works of art, benevolence and hospitality increased at an even greater rate, drawing him deeper and deeper into debt.[2]

On reaching the age of nineteen, he left Oriel College, Oxford, before taking his degree and set off in June 1768 on the Grand Tour with his steward, Samuel Sidebotham, and two companions, Captain Edward Hamilton and Thomas Apperley (father of 'Nimrod'), an Oxford friend and neighbour at Plas Gronw. The surviving account books for the eight-month tour record expenditures amounting in all to nearly £10,000 on pictures, intaglios, marble slabs, earthenware and other works of art, a group portrait by Batoni, a complete set of Piranesi's etchings, music books, masters to teach him drawing and music, the services of James Byres as a private antiquarian, and much else.[3]

Prior to the tour, plans had been laid for his marriage to Lady Henrietta Somerset, daughter of the fourth Duke of Beaufort, one of his father's Jacobite allies.[4] It was probably this important union that first led him to Adam, from whom 'Plans' were ordered to be sent to him in Rome or Naples. All we know about these drawings is that they had not arrived in Rome by 5 November 1768.[5] Though it is assumed that they were for Wynnstay, it is equally possible that they were for Sir Watkin's London house at 2 Grosvenor Square, which was being refurbished in his absence.[6] By no mere coincidence, Adam was mak-

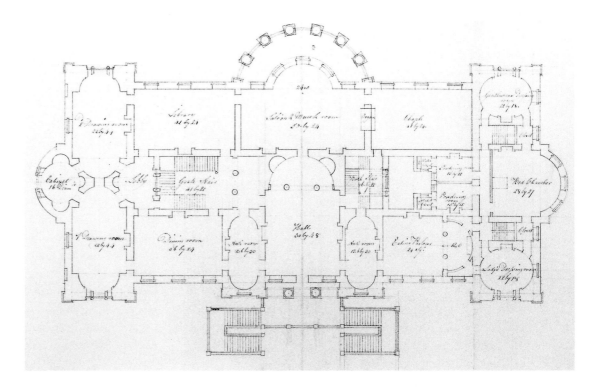

381 Plan of the ground-floor of a new house at Wynnstay, Denbighshire, by Robert Adam, 1771 (Sir John Soane's Museum: Adam drawings, vol. 40:63)

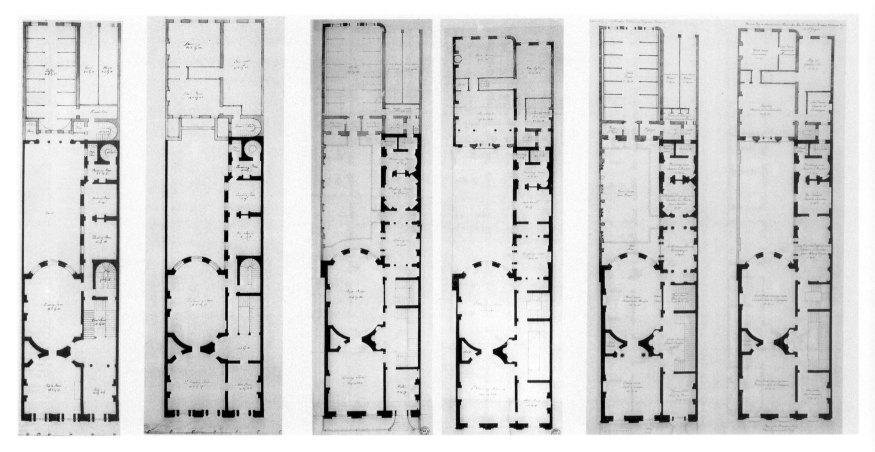

382   Ground and first-floor plans of 20 St James's Square showing the three stages of development (a. RIBA Drawings Collection; b. Sir John Soane's Museum: Adam drawings, vol. 40:65,66; c. *The works in architecture of Robert and James Adam*, vol. II (1779), pt. II, pl. I)

ing chimney-piece designs in 1768 for Lady Henrietta's brother, the fifth Duke of Beaufort, three doors away at 5 Grosvenor Square.[7]

Sir Watkin and Lady Henrietta Somerset were married on 11 April 1769. Three months later, he was widowed, whereupon Wynnstay became the focus of his extravagance. For his coming-of-age party in April 1770, he built a single-storey wing containing a 'fine handsome room of great dimentions (with) a bow at each end', invited 'at least 15,000 (to) dinner . . . all at the same time' and provided a bill of fare so extraordinary that the *Gentleman's Magazine* printed it for all to see.[8] The architect of the great new room is unknown. Thomas Farnolls Pritchard, who was working for Sir Watkin at Ruabon Church, has been suggested, but Adam must also be considered in view of his ceiling designs for the dining-room, drawing-room and dressing-room at Wynnstay, dated 1770.[9]

These designs, whether executed or not, clearly infected the impressionable Sir Watkin with an irrepressible building bug which led him later that year to commission Adam and Byres to make designs for a large neo-classical palace (pl. 381) to replace the unfinished house built for his father by Francis and William Smith of Warwick. To prepare himself for the rôle of architectural patron, he employed James Gandon to give him lessons in architecture, starting on 26 January 1771.[10] It was probably Gandon's design for a mausoleum in memory of Handel erected in a wood belonging to Sir Samuel Hillier in Staffordshire, which was exhibited at the Society of Artists in 1768, that attracted him to the young architect.

Before anything was done at Wynnstay, Sir Watkin's attention was diverted to 20 St James's Square. Having had a survey and valuation made by Gandon on 26 April 1771, he agreed to buy the house for £18,500 from the octogenarian Lord Bathurst, who covenanted to obtain a private Act of Parliament permitting the entailed freehold not only to be sold, but also, 'being very ancient and out of repair', to be demolished and rebuilt.[11] The opportunity to build himself an entirely new house (pl. 380), finished inside and out in the latest style by the most fashionable architect of the day, in one of the most sought-after squares in London was irresistible. All the more so since he was now engaged to marry Charlotte Grenville, the seventeen-year-old daughter of the recently deceased statesman, the Rt. Hon. George Grenville.[12]

Gandon's survey of the existing house was accompanied by 'five different Plans for a New House with an Elevation & Two Sections.'[13] These drawings were paid for, but not used and are now lost. By contrast, three different sets of Adam's plans survive, including the definitive one published in the *Works* (pl. 382).[14] All have one feature in common: an unusual configuration of large segmental apses set back to back in the principal reception rooms, which he carried over from his plan for Wynnstay.[15] He had seen this arrangement a decade earlier in Chambers's unexecuted designs for York House, Pall Mall, which was exhibited at the Society of Artists in 1761, and must also have known its antique source: the conjoined antique Temples of the Sun and the Moon near the Arch of Titus in Rome, published by Palladio.[16]

383 View of the staircase hall showing the triumphal-arch composition on the first floor, the open loggia above, and the domed sky-light

Novelty, variety and magnificence were what he was after here, notwithstanding the constraints of the long, narrow site. His first plan, though already an advance on Chandos House (1771), needed considerable revision to make it more fluid and better integrated, while preserving, or even strengthening, its main east–west axis. Lack of width was the principal problem in the top-lit staircase hall and the private apartments in the rear wing. One of the great advantages of the configuration of apsidal reception rooms, apart from its novelty and Roman pedigree, was the recesses it formed in the staircase hall (pl. 383). Developed as monumental exedra, modelled inside with niches and incorporated in a triumphal-arch composition with flanking architraved doors and panels of stucco decoration above the imposts, these recesses gave the impression of spaciousness without taking an inch from the principal room behind. Against this architectural background, Adam's delicate copper stair-rail makes an agreeable contrast.[17]

Above the stairs on the opposite wall is a corresponding triumphal-arch arrangement consisting of a large arched copy of Raphael's *Transfiguration* painted by William Parry (son of John Parry, the blind harpist of Ruabon) who was sent to Rome by Sir Watkin for five years in 1770; vertical landscapes by Thomas

Roberts of Dublin on either side; and enriched stucco panels above.[18] The blind arcading and railed openings on the top floor (reached by the secondary stair) add to the overall effect of an inner court. The staircase hall might thus be regarded as a counterpart to the exterior court, which Adam made into 'an object of some beauty and elegance' to be admired from the apartments by erecting a Venetian-windowed façade to conceal the offices, and by screening the party wall with an arcade executed in Liardet's new patent stucco.[19]

Entertainment was what the house was for and the *piano nobile* the stage on which it took place, in an *appartement de parade* ingeniously contrived to provide a variety of scenes of increasing size and elaboration. By treating this apartment of three reception rooms as a unit, uniformly hung and upholstered with pea-green silk damask, Adam made the diversity of its parts even more apparent and diverting.

The ante-room at the far end of the landing, past the prominent doors to the drawing-room, was the starting-point of the parade. It is a relatively small room, with a groined ceiling and large tympana, both painted pale green with white stucco grotesques linked by delicate chains of husks and bell-flowers in very low relief.[20] The marble chimney-piece, with a frieze of

384   The first drawing-room showing the chimney-piece wall and apsidal end

385   The first drawing-room chimney-piece, designed by Robert Adam, 1772

386   Giovanni Battista Piranesi, design for a chimney-piece (*Diverse maniere d'adornare i cammini* (1769), pl. 9A, Wilton-Ely, no. 848)

vases, festoons and paterae corresponding to the entablature and doorcases, was designed in August 1772 and supplied by John Hinchcliff in December 1773.[21] Above it is a mirror in its original carved and gilt frame, but lacking the medallion cresting shown in Adam's design.[22]

On entering the first drawing-room (pl. 384), the visitor is immediately struck by the chimney-piece, which is the largest and best in the house and was inspired by a plate in Piranesi's *Diversi maniere d'adornare i cammini* (pls 385, 386).[23] In addition to Adam's design made in October 1772, there were drawings by Zucchi for the long bas-relief representing *Aurora going before the Sun and the different Hours* and for the panels on the jambs containing standing figures of the muses Euterpe and Terpsichore.[24] The carver is unknown. A 'curiously embossed' grate with rams' heads on the legs was supplied by William Hopkins 'to Mr. Adam's Design' in November 1774.[25] Its present whereabouts is unknown.

Notes inscribed on Adam's designs for the overmantel-mirror and the pier-glass express concern about the heaviness and expense of their crests, though they are certainly no heavier than others of the period. Alterations were made to both designs, but the crests do not survive and may never have been executed.[26] The carved and gilt frames remain *in situ*; however, the one over the chimney-piece is flanked by pilasters painted with rinceaux, which are not called for in Adam's design but are identical to those in the second drawing-room. Exact repetition is so rare in Adam's work as to suggest that these were copied from the second drawing-room and added at a later date.

A scagliola table was proposed to accompany the pier-glass (pl. 387), but what it was like is not known. The pair of tables with scagliola slabs, an enriched Doric frieze, anthemion metopes, pendant swags and tapering fluted legs with ram's-head capitals and hoof feet – made to an Adam design of 24 August 1773 – were presumably intended for the walls on either side of

387 Pier-table from the first drawing-room, designed by Robert Adam, 1773. One of a pair (present whereabouts unknown)

the chimney-piece. They were noticed by Bolton in the first drawing-room in 1922, but were later in the possession of C. F. Kinderman. Their present ownership is unknown. Four 'gilt mettle Tripods to stand upon the Scagliola Tables' were supplied by Joseph Cresswell in May 1776.[27] Nothing is known about the other furniture; some of the chairs shown in early photographs belong to the suite attributed to John Linnell in the second drawing-room.[28]

There were six girandoles, with cameos of boys painted by Zucchi to answer the stucco medallions with classical figures on the ceiling and apse. The medallions were described by Bolton as having a blue ground; the rest of the ceiling is predominantly pink and green with some gilding indicated on the frames of the inner ovals.[29] Zucchi also painted eighteen figures in two colours with ornamental surrounds for the three folding doors.[30] Only the figures survive; the rest has been painted out.

The doors in the apse of the first drawing-room open into the broader, semi-domed apse of the second drawing-room (pl. 388), which has a corresponding bow with three windows at the opposite end.[31] This is the so-called 'Great Room', the climax of the parade. Its grandeur, beauty and novelty emanate from the segmental arched ceiling, an antique form rarely used in domestic apartments, which Adam had introduced in the library at Kenwood in 1767. Here, the rise of the arch is lower than at Kenwood and for that reason the initial idea of decorating the ceiling with an arbitrary repeat pattern (pl. 389) was quickly replaced by a banded design which appears in execution to repeat the curve and thus to emphasize it (pl. 390).[32] Broad painted strips of interlaced wreaths and anthemia, edged with gilt stucco mouldings, were used to divide the squarish central area (excluding the half-domed apse and bow) into three distinct sections. Each of these sections is subdivided into seven units: the central one has large ovals and rosettes; on either side are long, narrow paintings of classical subjects surrounded by a thin line of gilded husks; next, there are lunettes containing monochrome paintings of seated female figures and festooned tripods; and finally, long panels of scrolled acanthus issuing from half-figures of boys (corresponding to the friezes round the walls and over the doors) with intervening square panels in the form of black and gold ram's-head pedestals ornamented with tazze in low relief which appear to act as supports for the cross bands. The resemblance to Wedgwood's black basaltware must have pleased Sir Watkin, who was one of the firm's earliest and most liberal patrons.[33] All the ceiling paintings and the roundels in the semi-domes were supplied by Zucchi and placed on a predominantly pink and green ground in accordance with Adam's design.[34]

As a deliberate contrast to the ceiling, Adam designed a carpet (pl. 391) with a discrepant three-part division and an unrelated pattern of linked circles (akin to the ceiling of the eating-room on the ground-floor and comparable to Pinturicchio's ceiling in the Sale della Sibelle in the Torre Borgia at the Vatican) in bright green, blue, yellow, purple and pink on a brown ground. The carpet was designed in August 1774, a year after the ceiling, and made by Thomas Moore in December of that year from a model painted by Zucchi.[35] To add to the gay and exhilarating profusion of dissimilar elements, the door panels were painted by Zucchi with more colours than those in the preceding room; the

388 View of the second or 'great' drawing-room

389 Preliminary design (unexecuted) for the ceiling of the second drawing-room, by Robert Adam, 1772 (Sir John Soane's Museum: Adam drawings, vol. 12:52)

390 Design for the ceiling of the second drawing-room as executed, by Robert Adam, 1772 (Sir John Soane's Museum: Adam drawings, vol. 12:53)

391 Design for a carpet for the second drawing-room with the floor left uncovered round the perimeter 'where the Chairs & Sophas are placed', by Robert Adam, 1773 (Sir John Soane's Museum: Adam drawings, vol. 17:181)

392 A pair of carved and gilt-wood pedestals from the second drawing-room, designed by Robert Adam, 1773 (Private collection)

393 Laid-out wall elevations of Lady Wynn's dressing-room, by Robert Adam, c.1772 (Sir John Soane's Museum: Adam drawings, vol. 40:70)

walls were lined with pea-green silk damask and hung with gilt-framed pictures; there were panels of ornaments on the window piers and two pairs of elaborate, three-branch girandoles with *trompe-l'œil* cameos and small medallions painted by Zucchi on the long walls. Though the latter were described in Zucchi's accounts and referred to in a note in the Adam volumes, their design has not been identified.[36]

A pair of six-branch candelabra on tall tripod pedestals, with dancing muses in low relief on their concave sides, ram's-head capitals, lion's-paw feet, and free-standing winged sphinxes on the shaped base, were designed in 1773, probably to stand in the apse.[37] The fate of the candelabra is unknown, but the pedestals were executed and are now at Kenwood (pl. 392). Evidently this model found favour with other Adam patrons: an almost identical pair were made for the Duke of Northumberland and are now at Alnwick, and a variant with lion's masks and griffons at the base was designed in 1778 for the Countess of Home.[38]

This sparkling *mélange* was reflected in four large mirrors: two in the apse, one over the chimney-piece, and another on the opposite wall. The surviving mirror frames lack the crests shown in Adam's designs, with half-boys and scrolled foliage flanking a low altar on the chimney-glass and oval medallions on the other three mirrors.[39] Pilasters identical to the ones in the first drawing-room (and quite like those introduced by Adam in October 1772 in his designs for the drawing-rooms at Bolton House) frame the chimney-glass.[40] Though these do not appear in

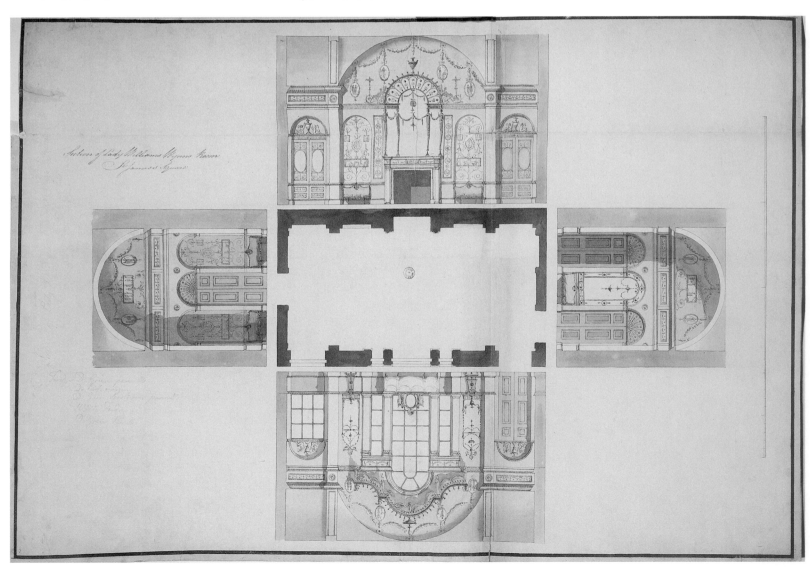

394   View of Lady Wynn's dressing-room *c.*1918

395   View of Lady Wynn's dressing-room. The door to the left leading
to the bedroom was originally in the centre of the wall

Adam's design, a note giving 'The size of ye Slips of glass 6 ft 5 in
(1.9 metres) high 13 in (33 centimetres) wide' suggests that side
panels were intended here.[41] Whether the present painted
pilasters (which have been in place at least since 1918) belong to
a revised Adam scheme or are later replacements of the glass slips
is not known.

The chimney-piece has fluted Ionic columns, a frieze of
scrolled foliage corresponding to that round the walls, and a central tablet representing the *Triumph of Venus* for which a drawing
was made by Zucchi. The executed design, dated 27 August
1772, was chosen in preference to one with a *Triumph of Bacchus*
in the centre and 'two Bacchanalian figures at the Sides' (also
drawn by Zucchi) and vine-wreathed columns reminiscent of
the carved columns in the round closet at Syon.[42]

To the rear of the house were the private apartments: Sir
Watkin's on the ground-floor and Lady Williams-Wynn's above,
containing his library and her dressing-room, their separate bedrooms, powdering-rooms, water-closets and a back stair linking
the two. These were initially planned as identical sequences of
conventional geometrical boxes approached by a narrow passage
alongside the secondary stair. A reduction in the size of the secondary stair gave some extra space within the main body of the
house to the library and dressing-room and in so doing opened
the way to a more varied and fluid plan.

Lady Wynn's dressing-room (pls 393, 394) was entered directly
from the great drawing-room, to which it became an appendage:
a coda to the parade of grand reception rooms, thrown open to

the public at big assemblies and expected to be as glamorous as
the rest, yet different. Adam's first task here was to create a symmetrical interior with asymmetrical windows, which he did by
introducing columnar screens to define a distinct central area
dominated by a large Venetian window and by balancing the
window at the far end of the room with a door towards the front.
This solution was initially proposed for the dressing-room as
well as the library. However, the final plan made a greater distinction between the ground- and first-floor rooms in the private
as well as public apartments. The dressing-room, being a sequel
to the grandest room on the *piano nobile*, naturally had to be
made to appear larger and more splendid than its ground-floor
equivalent of exactly the same size, 15 by 30 feet (4.5 by 9.1
metres).

Columnar screens were omitted and, instead, different forms
of ceiling and wall decorations were used to subdivide the long
space into three distinct units (pl. 395).[43] At the two ends are
shallow, barrel-vaulted spaces decorated with blind arches.
Adam's design shows a tall, arched mirror flanked by two doors
(one to the secondary stairs, the other false) on the front wall,
and a central door to the bedroom flanked by arched panels of
grotesque ornaments on the opposite wall. This arrangement
was subsequently altered so as to make the back wall the same as
the front.[44] As for the return arches, those on the chimney-piece
wall were meant to hold cabinets with glazed (possibly mirrored)
oval openings in their doors.

A groin vault and large Venetian window rising into the tym-

396 Josiah Wedgwood, a basalt tablet with the *Triumph of Venus* painted in encaustic colours after a design by Antonio Zucchi. The ivy festoons are of inlaid scagliola executed by Bartoli. The chimney-piece was designed by Robert Adam in 1772

397 Design for a pair of painted bookcases for Lady Wynn's dressing-room, by Robert Adam, 1776 (Sir John Soane's Museum: Adam drawings, vol. 17:222)

panum are the distinguishing features of the central space. Adam's proposal was to finish the inner wall like the outer one, with stucco medallions suspended from bell-flower festoons in the tympanum and an elaborate gilded chimney-glass in the form of a Venetian window articulated by female terms and capped by an arched band of glass trimmed with anthemion finials answering the curtain cornice. His use of surface decorations to define, focus and vary the space, and to give what he would call 'an added picturesque' to this cramped, asymmetrical room, was ingenious and original. The effect of so much glass in so small a space would have been sparkling and jewel-like and perfectly suited to a lady's boudoir. But it was evidently too extravagant even for Sir Watkin.

The chimney-glass designed in August 1773 shed its gilded female terms and shrank from a Venetian window to a 4 foot (1.2 metre) square mirror in a simple carved frame with a medallion cresting.[45] When the room was photographed in 1910, even this had been replaced. The walls, including the central arch at the front end, were hung with flock paper down to the dado and if there had ever been any panels of stucco arabesques, they were removed.

The ceiling, on the other hand, was faithfully executed from Adam's design, though what is there now is a second version reconstructed by G. Jackson & Sons to replace the original, damaged during the war.[46] Its groined vault is covered with delicate stucco ornaments in an incongruous flat pattern of concentric oval bands: the outer one incorporating half-boys emerging from scrolled acanthus, interspersed with tazze and pedestals supporting vases and elaborate candelabra. The tympana on each side of the room have a wide upper border of arched motif and, except for the one over the Venetian window, are decorated with a central figured roundel flanked by festooned pedestals and candelabra.[47] Instead of the usual continuous frieze, there are long panels filled with ivy festoons and rosettes which reiterate the articulation of the walls.

The chimney-piece also has ivy festoons and rosettes of coloured scagliola inlaid in its frieze. John Hinchcliff supplied the statuary marble surround and fluted Ionic columns; the scagliola inlay was carried out by Bartoli, who added further decoration between the flutes.[48] Sir Watkin himself seems to have been responsible for the idea of introducing one of Wedgwood and Bentley's new encaustic basalt tablets (pl. 396). A design for the chimney-piece was made by Adam on 27 August 1772 and on 6 September Wedgwood received the order. This was a prestigious commission and Wedgwood's response was ecstatic: 'The Tablets shall be put in hand tomorrow', he told Bentley, 'I wish us success in this new vein. I shall drink Lady Wynn & Sᵣ Watkin for Ever today.'[49]

Paintings in distemper by Zucchi representing the *Triumph of Venus* and cupids riding dolphins (Venus's attribute) were copied by Wedgwood in encaustic pigments of several colours. The new method of encaustic painting, which Wedgwood initially developed for vases but soon extended to tablets, was intended not only 'to imitate the Paintings upon the Etruscan Vases, but to *do much more*; to give the Beauty of Design, the Advantages of Light and Shade in various Colours; and to render Paintings durable without the Defect of a varnished or glassy Surface.'[50]

Sir Watkin's encaustic chimney ornaments were the first of

398 View of the eating-room in 1910 showing the ram's-head chimney-piece from which the original frieze – matching the frieze on the walls – was removed probably in the nineteenth century. The mirror is virtually identical to one designed in 1772 for the Earl of Bute at Luton

their kind. Adam immediately suggested them to the Earl of Ashburnham for his drawing-room chimney-piece at Dover Street and a few other patrons followed suite, but they remained a novelty rather than a serious alternative to coloured scagliola.[51]

The original colour scheme of Lady Wynn's dressing-room is not known. The walls have never been scraped to discover what, if anything, preceded the flock paper and the painting of the reconstructed ceiling was presumably based on surviving fragments, as there are no coloured designs. Colour-notes on Adam's elevations call for a 'white dado' (making the present white walls and skirting highly unlikely), 'D(ark) Green Plinth', 'Frieze D(ark) Green panels', 'Green scroll over panels' and a 'pink margin' in the frieze. The 1989 redecoration is bland by comparison and uncharacteristic of Adam.

Pink or red was the colour proposed for the festoon curtains and upholstery. There is a bill for rose Mantua silk for the petticoat of the dressing-table, which was trimmed with lace and tassels and placed in front of the Venetian window.[52] Curtains may have been rendered unnecessary by the sliding shutters that were fitted to the window (and the one in the library), especially if the shutter panels were decorated with grotesques as suggested by a design made in February 1775 which was 'To be sketched out at large'.[53]

Vase-shaped girandoles with detachable festoons and branches 'only to be joined when the Room is to be lighted up' were also designed in February 1775 and were to be placed on brackets on the four pilasters.[54] If these were executed, they have long since disappeared. The only surviving furniture is the pair of painted bookcases now in the Carnegie Institute of Fine Arts, Pittsburgh. They were designed by Adam in February 1776 (pl. 397), executed in mahogany by the carpenter and clerk of the works, Richard Collins, and painted by Zucchi with pale-green grotesques (not unlike those designed for the shutter panels) on the doors and coloured tablets depicting *Bacchus and Ariadne* and a *Triumph of Venus* similar to the chimney-piece tablet.[55] Their laurel frieze and ivy festoons on the drawers are also related to the chimney-piece. The bookcases must have been placed in the return arches on the chimney-piece wall, as shown in Adam's elevation. Lady Wynn's choice of the elegant cabinet form on slender fluted legs in preference to Adam's alternative design for an open breakfront bookcase is understandable in view of the small size of the room and its feminine character.[56]

Beyond the dressing-room was a square bedroom half the size, with a domed ceiling and a shallow, arched bed recess facing the window. Its decoration was simple in comparison with the preceding rooms, and was painted green with purple and white ornaments. A jib door gave access to an oval powdering-room leading to a water-closet and back stair, none of which survive.[57]

Visitors never penetrated beyond Lady Wynn's dressing-room. Having paraded the principal reception rooms, they descended to the eating-room (pl. 398) and music-room. Unlike the rooms on the *piano nobile*, those on the ground-floor were not hung,

have flat ceilings and the same mahogany doors furnished with chased gilt brass knobs and festooned escutcheons made by Edward Gascoigne to Adam's design.[58]

The eating-room is the same size and shape as the first drawing-room, but has a screen of fluted Corinthian columns and antae across its apse. Although Adam's dining-rooms often have a screened end, this one was evidently an afterthought associated with his decision to augment the distinction between the first- and ground-floor rooms.[59] Its effect is to make the dining-room look not only different from, but also slightly smaller than the first drawing-room. There is, however, a noticeable tension between this apparent reduction and the indefinite space suggested by the repeat pattern of octagons on the ceiling which is abruptly interrupted at the edges and left incomplete.[60]

The entrance is from the staircase hall into the rear of the room, with a corresponding false door towards the front. Rams' heads are the leitmotiv here: repeated in the entablature, at the sides of the doors, on the capitals of the columns instead of volutes, on the sideboard pedestal, the torchères, the chimney-piece and even on the grate (pl. 399).[61] The chimney-piece originally had a frieze of interlaced chains of husks and rosettes, matching the frieze round the walls and on the doorcases. This was probably removed in the nineteenth century.[62] Above was a large tripartite mirror articulated by four draped female terms,

399 Detail of the ram's-head console on the eating-room chimney-piece

400 Silver-gilt punch bowl made for Sir Watkin Williams-Wynn by Thomas Heming, 1771–72, after a design by Robert Adam

401 Design for a ram's-head candelabrum for Sir Watkin Williams-Wynn, by Robert Adam, 1773 (Sir John Soane's Museum: Adam drawings, vol. 25:125)

402 Candlestand of carved wood painted white on a pale blue ground. One of a pair designed by Robert Adam, c.1777. The candlestand can be seen in the corner of the room in the 1910 photograph (pl. 19)

403 View of the music-room *c.*1918, after it was converted to a dining-room. The shaped sideboards flanking the door to the original eating-room may date from this period. Panels of stucco decoration copied from others in the room replace Joshua Reynolds's *St Cecilia* and Nathaniel Dance's *Orpheus*

with a raised centre framed by urns and female figures seated on scrolled foliage on either side. Although the Adam volumes contain no drawings whatsoever of a chimney-glass for Sir Watkin's eating-room, there is a design dated October 1772 for the Earl of Bute's drawing-room at Luton Hoo which is virtually identical to the mirror that was at 20 St James's Square.[63] It is not certain whether the design was executed with minor variations for both patrons, or only for Sir Watkin. Nor do we know the maker of Sir Watkin's mirror. The high quality of the carving of the terms – judged only from old photographs, as the piece has not been traced since it left 20 St James's Square in the 1920s – is comparable to the oval mirrors with flanking figures made by Sefferin Alken in 1772 for Coventry House, Piccadilly and now in the V&A.[64] Female terms were introduced by Adam in several mirror frames designed in the early 1770s: for Robert Child's house in Berkeley Square (1771), Bolton House (1773), Derby House (1774) and Home House (1777).

Seated female figures were also favoured as crests in this period. Adam proposed to use them on the eating-room pier-glass as well as the chimney-glass; however, his design (made in August 1773) bears the countermand, 'this Glass without any top'.[65] According to Bolton, the pier-glass had an 'elaborately gilded framework' and was accompanied by a 'large console table'; but there is no evidence that the latter was by Adam.[66]

The sideboard and accompanying wine cooler, pedestals and urns (all now in the National Museum and Gallery of Wales) were designed by him and made around 1773–4. They stood in the centre of the long wall facing the chimney-piece and were painted pale green with blue and white ornaments to match the colour scheme of the room.[67] Though Adam's 'Great (silver) Table Service' of 1773–5, distinguished as 'the largest architect-designed silver service of the eighteenth century' (part of which

is now in the National Museum and Gallery of Wales),[68] would not have been displayed on the sideboard, his silver-gilt punch bowl (pl. 400), commissioned by Sir Watkin in 1771 to celebrate the success of his horse in the Chester Races in the two previous years and made by Thomas Heming, is likely to have been placed there, along with other gilt display plate not designed by him, including Heming's Hollywell Hunt and Wynnstay Hunt race cups.[69] Four silver tripod candelabra (pl. 401) were designed for the room in 1773 and made by John Carter in the following year (they now belong to Lloyds of London).[70] Two of these may have been placed on the pair of Adam torchères now in the V&A (pl. 402). The latter are composed of two stages: the lower part, resting on sphinxes, is a concave pedestal with ram's-head corners, lion's feet and Wynn eagles on each front, all of carved Honduras mahogany; the upper part is of pine and consists of a bowl supported on a central baluster and four outer legs capped with satyr's masks. The remarkably realistic carving suggests the same maker as the chimney-glass, Sefferin Alken. The closest design is uninscribed and undated; however, 1773 is more likely than 1777, the date of Adam's other designs for candlestands, which were almost certainly intended for different rooms.[71] In the nineteenth century, the eating-room became an informal drawing-room and the adjacent music-room was used for dining. The similar, but by no means identical, pair of torchères now in the Melbourne Art Gallery, Australia and the unpainted mahogany sideboard in the National Gallery of Scotland were most likely made for the new dining-room.

The music-room (pl. 403), though not quite so grand as the second drawing-room, was undoubtedly the most important room in the house. Music was what Sir Watkin knew and loved best. His annual expenditure on lessons, instruments, musicians and singers, averaging about £300, was large enough to merit a

404 The music-room chimney-piece designed by Robert Adam in 1772; with a tablet of Apollo and the nine muses executed from a drawing by Antonio Zucchi When this photograph was taken, c.1918, the fireplace contained the grate designed by Adam and made for the eating-room. It has since vanished

405 Design for a more ornate grate for the music-room, by Robert Adam, 1774 (Sir John Soane's Museum: Adam drawings, vol. 17:126, detail)

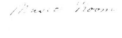

separate 'Music Accompt'. He was an influential member of the Catch Club and the Concert of Antient Music founded in 1776 to perpetuate the great works of early composers, notably Handel. It was Sir Watkin and two other members of the Concert of Antient Music who organized the Handel Commemoration in 1784 held at Westminster Abbey and at the Pantheon in Oxford Street 'on so grand and magnificent a scale as no other part of the world could equal'.[72]

A carefully worked out programme of musical themes, directed by Sir Watkin with Adam at hand, runs through every part of the decoration of the music-room. In the frieze of the chimney-piece is a large tablet, designed by Zucchi, depicting *Apollo and a musical party of nine muses* (five muses playing instruments and four singing), and in the blocks over the simplified Corinthian columns are dancing muses (pl. 404).[73] The name of the carver is not recorded.

Zucchi was also responsible for the oblong panel over the door to the eating-room, which, he said, represented 'Shepherds & Nymphs doing honour to the Ashes of Corelli or Handel'[74] and the five painted roundels in the ceiling (the central one, a chiaroscuro painting of *The dispute between Menalcas and Damoetas in poetry and music* from Virgil's *Eclogues*, has disappeared; the four smaller ones of dancing nymphs remain *in situ*). Adam's wall elevation dated August 1773 shows the spaces over the smaller doors leading to the staircase hall and Sir Watkin's library with inset portraits of famous musicians (pl. 406). In the event, however, mythological paintings of pairs of figures playing musical instruments were provided by Nathaniel Dance and are still in the room.[75]

Flanking the chimney-piece were two larger paintings, approximately 8 feet (2.4 metres) tall, by Dance and Reynolds. Dance's picture, which he exhibited at the Royal Academy in 1774, was of *Orpheus lamenting the loss of Eurydice*, his song taming the tigers and leading the oaks. Apart from its subject, all that is known about this lost picture is that its colour was 'cold and stoney' and that Orpheus, the master of pagan music, was depicted nude much to the distaste of Reynolds's sister.[76] The nude Orpheus in a woodland would have matched the very pale pink and green ceiling.

Reynolds's subject was *Saint Cecilia*, the patron saint of Christian music, playing a harp, the national instrument of Wales, and dressed in pale purple and green, the predominant colours of the walls.[77] Though ultimately indebted to Domenichino, the immediate source for the painting is the more humble and pertinent title-page to Handel's opera *Tamerlaine*, first produced in 1724 and published in the same year by John Cluer, '*truly translated* into English Verse . . . never done before in any OPERA'.[78] The title-page was used for most of Handel's operas published by Cluer and must therefore have been well known to Sir Watkin, one of Handel's most devoted and active admirers in England.

Adam's 1773 elevation of the chimney-piece wall has a sketch of Saint Cecilia playing an organ, which was her original Renaissance attribute, on the right and an empty picture frame inscribed 'St Cecilia' on the left. Could Sir Watkin have wanted two Saint Cecilias – one Welsh, the other Italian? One may never know, for in the event Dance's *Orpheus* filled the empty frame on the left and Reynolds's *Saint Cecilia*, the harpist, was on the right.

406 Wall elevation showing the organ flanked by doors to the staircase with paintings by Nathaniel Dance above them, by Robert Adam, 1773 (Sir John Soane's Museum: Adam drawings, vol. 40:71, detail)

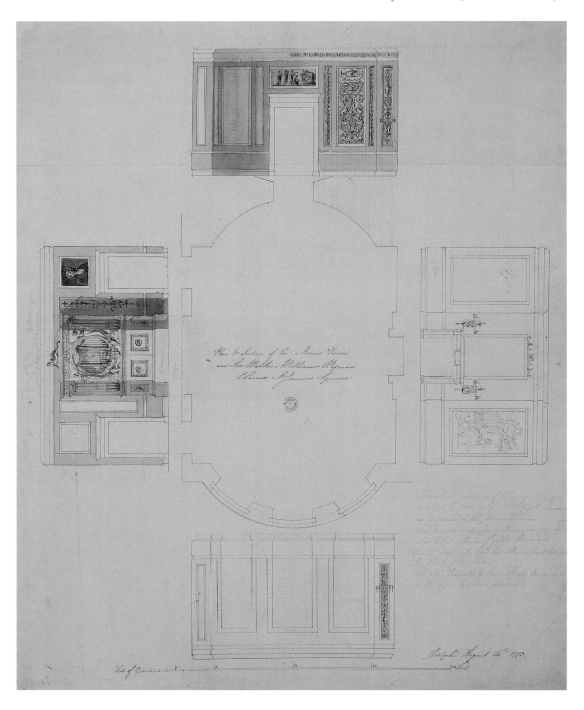

The paintings were well lit by a pair of four-branch lyre girandoles which formed part of the central element of the stucco wall decorations incorporating musical trophies, putti and heads of Apollo on either side of the chimney breast. There were six more lyre girandoles, each with two branches, in the slender stucco panels flanking the organ recess, the apse and the bow window.[79] They have all been removed, along with the great canvases which were recorded at Wynnstay in 1840, and replaced by panels of stucco arabesques copied from those in the apse.[80]

Reynolds's *Saint Cecilia* and Dance's *Orpheus* served to counterbalance Adam's spectacular organ. These three important objects – together with the original colour scheme of pale-green walls, purple panels with white mouldings and arabesques, a purple and white frieze, a white dado, and purple skirting – gave the 'great spirit, beauty and effect to the composition' that was vital to Adam. With them gone and the walls repainted pale green and grey, the room is bland and static, which may suit its present corporate use better than Adam's gaiety.

Little is known about the furnishing of the music-room and nothing survives apart from the organ and the chimney-glass minus the wreathed head of Apollo flanked by lyres in the crest.[81] An Adam grate with matching fender and fire-irons supplied by William Hopkins in March 1774 was still in the fireplace when Bolton published his book in 1922 (pl. 405).[82] The 141$\frac{1}{2}$ yards (129.3 metres) of fashionable striped satin supplied by the upholders, King and Padget, in 1776 were presumably used to make draw curtains for the three windows in the bow and cushions for chairs.[83] There were music desks and music stands for which William Kinman made a total of sixteen candle-branches in May 1775. He also made '2 lamps with gilt feet to stand' that may have been placed on the mantelshelf.[84]

Adam's finished design for the organ does not survive. In all probability, it was sent to the engraver, Domenico Cunego, in Rome to make the plate for the second volume of the *Works* (1779) and never returned. His 'Plan & Section of the Music Room', dated 'August 24^h 1773', contains the earliest known drawing of the organ (pl. 406); it resembles the engraving and is painted with watercolour washes as it was intended to be executed.[85]

408 Detail of the frieze of the Williams-Wynn organ showing alternating Apollo heads and rosettes in interlaced laurel wreaths

The composition owes much to the elaborate organ case designed in 1762 for Lord Scarsdale at Kedleston with two winged female figures on shaped pedestals lifting a curtain to reveal the pipes in a large circular opening (pl. 407, see pl. 26). Owing to lack of space, this was reduced in size and stripped of almost all ornaments. The skeletal outcome must have been a great disappointment to Adam, making the opportunity provided by Sir Watkin's munificence and music mania all the more gratifying. This is not to say that the design approved by Sir Watkin and engraved by Adam was executed without any alterations whatsoever. There is, for example, no evidence, either in the surviving accounts or on the case itself, that the recumbent figure of Apollo with his lyre intended to crown the organ and the coat of arms flanked by kneeling putti in front of the pipes were ever executed. The frieze, meant to have string and wind instruments in laurel wreaths, has alternating Apollo heads and rosettes instead (pl. 408).

Handel, of course, is the hero of the organ. Adam's engraved design shows the central medallion with a head-and-shoulders portrait of him in a full-bottom wig. This bears some similarity to the portrait by the German artist, Balthasar Denner, that

407 The organ from 20 St James's Square now in the National Museum of Wales, Cardiff

Handel gave to the younger John Christopher Smith, son of his principal copyist and treasurer, who was a composer and organist at the Foundling Hospital.[86] Whether a copy of this portrait or some other was used on Sir Watkin's organ is not known. Whatever it was that first filled the circular frame was subsequently replaced by a profile medallion closely modelled on the medal struck in 1784 for the Handel Commemoration, of which Sir Watkin was a director.[87]

The muses, Euterpe with a pipe (pl. 409) and Terpsichore with a lyre, were carved in 1777 by Richard Collins. According to his bill for £42.0.6, they 'replace those made by Mr. Ansell'.[88] Robert Ansell, carver and gilder of Edward Street, Cavendish Square, began supplying frames for Sir Watkin's ever-growing picture collection in 1769 and also made two large, richly carved and gilt candelabra for Ruabon church in 1771. Why Ansell's fig-

409 Figure of the muse Euterpe with her horn on the right side of the organ

ures should have needed replacing only two or three years after they were put up remains a mystery.

There are no accounts for the making of the rest of the case. From what we know of the Kedleston organ, the work was almost certainly done by carvers and joiners already employed at the house, rather than a specialist cabinet-maker. Collins, who executed Adam's cabinet-bookcases for Lady Wynn's dressing-room in 1776, was perfectly capable of making the organ-case. Ansell may have been responsible for carving the frieze, the Corinthian capitals to the fluted pilasters, the draped curtains above the pipes, the swags of berried laurel, and the trophies of musical instruments that originally ornamented the side panels of the base but are now lost.

The case was evidently finished by 10 December 1774, when the locksmith, Edward Gascoigne, supplied 'a Latch Lock for ye Orgin & 2 Keys'; '2 sides (of 'lacquerd festoon furniture') for the orgin' followed on 5 January 1775 (pl. 410).[89] The modelled gilt-brass knobs are still on the organ doors, but may have lost part of their festoons. They are identical to the knobs that Gascoigne supplied for all the principal doors on the ground floor, but without the oval escutcheons linked by festoons, for which there is not sufficient space on the organ case. The case was now ready to receive the precious organ made by John Snetzler. On 31 May

412 The barrel-vaulted end of the library

1775, Snetzler was paid 'Two hundred & fifty Pounds in full for the Organ Put up in S^t. James's Square house which (he) promise(d) to keep in tune for the remainder of this Year likewise to tune it for the future at four Guineas @ time.'[90]

Other external fittings for the organ – '2 (candle) Branches & Backs', '2 Brass Jappan'd plates', '2 (pipe) Shades fluted & with sphinxes & heads part japanned & part gilt' – were supplied by William Kinman in March, May and June 1775.[91] The sphinxes for the sides of the organ were returned, being unnecessary as the upper parts on the side pipes, like those in the projecting centre, are concealed by the carved curtains.

Sir Watkin could hardly be expected to wait for all these fin-

ishing touches before launching his spectacular organ in an appropriately grand manner. The first performance was given on 5 February 1775 by Benjamin Cooke, organist and Master of the Choristers of Westminster Abbey, conductor of the Academy of Ancient Music, a fellow member with Sir Watkin of the Catch Club and an assistant director of the 1784 Handel Commemoration.[92] The magnificent sound of the Snetzler organ, renowned for its purity of tone and brilliancy of chorus stops, must have filled the entire house. Parties gathered for organ concerts would not have been confined to the close quarters of the music-room. With the folding doors thrown open, the adjacent eating-room would have made a perfectly suitable

413   View of the library c.1910 showing the richly decorated end wall and the simpler chimney-piece wall with one of Adam's cabinet-bookcases still *in situ*

auditorium and no doubt the music could be appreciated in the principal reception rooms on the first floor.

The sixth Baronet, whose sporting activities kept him more in Wales than in London, had the organ removed from 20 St James's Square on 16 February 1864 and re-erected on a specially constructed gallery in the great hall at Wynnstay, which had been rebuilt by Benjamin Ferrey after a devastating fire in 1858. Alterations were made to the pipe works, and an 'Hydraulic Blowing Engine' was added by Gray and Davison, one of the foremost firms of organ builders in England at that time, makers of the Handel organ at the Great Exhibition of 1851 and the organ for Llandaff Cathedral in 1861.[93] The invigorated Snetzler organ made its début at the grand ball given by Sir Watkin and Lady Wynn in their new house in 1865 on the occasion of the first birthday of their daughter, heiress to the estate, whose god-parents included the Queen of Denmark and the Princess of Wales.[94]

Although the organ was not seen to advantage on the high-sided balcony close to the ceiling of the great hall at Wynnstay, it was at least safely out of the reach of over-zealous restorers and far too difficult for removal or disposal to be contemplated. So there it stood on its cramped balcony, undisturbed, for over a century. It is the only surviving organ case faithfully executed to Adam's design, without any of the drastic modifications suffered by the Kedleston organ. The fate of his designs for the Earl of Exeter at Burghley House, Hutchinson Mure at Great Saxham Hall, Suffolk and the Duke of Cumberland at Cumberland House on Pall Mall is unknown. While they may never have got beyond the drawing-board, the Countess of Home's organ at Home House is known to have been executed and has recently been reconstructed as a drinks cabinet.[95]

The space allotted to Sir Watkin's library (the first room in the rear wing, entered from the music-room) is twice as long as it is wide (15 by 30 feet, 4.5 by 9.1 metres): the same as Lady Wynn's dressing-room, but lower. By screening both ends with unfluted Corinthian columns, Adam succeeded in reducing the length and creating a well-proportioned room out of what might otherwise have looked like a passage. These end sections were treated quite differently from the rest of the room (pls 411, 412): their ceilings were groined in the centre and barrel-vaulted each side, and their walls articulated with shallow niches. Both screens were removed in the nineteenth century, the rear one being replaced by a pilastered partition to facilitate the conversion of Sir Watkin's dressing-room into a larger bedroom.

The library, which served primarily as a study rather than a repository for books, is comparatively simple and masculine; the richest decoration is on the end walls over the columns and consists of arched tympana ornamented with swags and tassels and a frieze of oxheads and rosettes (pl. 413). A similar frieze appears on the large Venetian window (fitted with sliding shutters like those in Lady Wynn's dressing-room) and was formerly on the chimney-piece as well.[96] No designs for a chimney-glass are known, which suggests that the space was occupied by a picture instead. Flanking the chimney-breast are round-headed niches containing a pair of projecting cabinet bookcases divided into two sections by the chair rail, the upper part framed by Corinthian pilasters supporting a frieze of classical heads and urns linked by festoons. These were almost certainly made to Adam's design and finished by 1774, when they were fitted with locks supplied by Blockley and altered by Gascoigne.[97] They may well have housed part of Sir Watkin's important collection of early music and were probably painted white or pale green to match the walls. The stucco decoration of the ceiling revolves around a large circle with five roundels containing chiaroscuro paintings of the classical poets by Zucchi.[98] The central one has been removed, but the others remain *in situ*.

En suite with the library was Sir Watkin's private dressing-room, an octagonal room with a coved ceiling, semicircular apses filled with cupboards on three walls and a matching door to his oval powdering-room on the remaining angle.[99] Between these were the door to the library, the chimney-piece and framed overmantel, the window and an oval mirror flanked by female terms like those proposed for Lady Wynn's toilet-glass.

17

DERBY HOUSE

On 31 March 1773 the *Morning Chronicle* published the following notice:

> This day Lord Stanley (Edward Smith Stanley, later twelfth Earl of Derby) is to give a grand Ball and Supper, at his house in Grosvenor-square, to those of the first rank, and most distinguished for beauty . . . In order that this entertainment shall cede to none in point of *elegance*, taste, and magnificence, he has given the direction of the arrangement of the ornamental part of the house to the celebrated brothers, Adams's, without restriction or limitation of expence! preparation has been making, and a display of taste going forward in his Lordship's house *these three weeks past*! There is to be a grand Quadrille, consisting of eight, habited in the dress of the four seasons.

Lord Stanley's extravaganza – carefully timed for the start of the London season – was to celebrate his coming-of-age in the following September. Its organization, like his pre-nuptial *fête champêtre* at The Oaks in Surrey in 1774, was managed by his uncle and mentor, General John Burgoyne, the fast-living 'Gentleman Johnny'.[1] And it was doubtless Burgoyne who brought Adam on to the scene. He and his wife, Lady Charlotte Stanley, had struck up a friendship with the dandy young architect in France and Italy some twenty years earlier, and in 1769–71 employed him to decorate their house, 10 Hertford Street.[2]

Adam's rôle on this occasion was that of a stage designer responsible for transforming the old-fashioned interiors of 23 (later 26) Grosvenor Square, London (pls 414, 415) into a sequence of varied settings as magnificent, glamorous and entertaining as Wyatt's Pantheon on Oxford Street, for just one night's performance. His expensive display of taste, though not recorded visually, is well documented in the letters and diaries of Horace Walpole and Elizabeth, Duchess of Northumberland.[3]

Guests were greeted by General Burgoyne's regimental band, dressed in Lord Stanley's blue livery with 'Red and silver Lace, & vast Scarlet Feathers in their Hats', standing in the hall, which was draped with gold-fringed crimson damask curtains. The

staircase, covered with a temporary dome and 'beautifully illuminated with coloured-glass lanthorns',[4] took them up to the ante-room where tea was served by a bevy of ladies dressed as vestals in white lutestring with blue ribbons and accompanied by an orchestra in matching white dominos.

From the ante-room they entered the front drawing-room which was draped with sarsenet (silk) 'that with a very funeral air crossed the chimney and depended in vast festoons over the sconces'.[5] A large square mirror and two large oval ones were borrowed for this room and oval frames were specially made, probably to a design by Adam.[6] In the 'third chamber' (the back drawing-room) the 'doors were heightened with candles in gilt vases'. The large room in the rear wing was made into a grand ball-room: Lord Strange's tapestries were taken down, and the room was 'formed into an oval with benches above each other, not unlike pews, and covered with red serge; above which were arbours of flowers, red and green pilasters, more sarcenet, and Lord March's glasses, which he had lent, as an upholster(er) asked Lord Stanley £300 for the loan of some'.[7] The wall overlooking the garden was 'burst open . . . to build an orchestra' in which were placed scarlet-robed musicians and a 'pendant mirror to reflect the dancers'.

The crowds prevented Walpole from reaching the next two rooms on the first floor, and he did not stay for the magnificent supper which was served to 300 guests in 'the six rooms below', presumably including the hall. The high point of the evening was a quadrille led by Lord Stanley dressed as Spring, in white 'spangl'd all over with little Tufts of real Violets'. Apart from being his début as one of the most profuse and ostentatious party-givers in London, this was also the genesis – the *fons et origo* – of Adam's recasting of his house.

The three-storey, five-bay house on the west side of Grosvenor Square was built around 1728 on land belonging to Sir Robert Grosvenor.[8] In 1750, James Smith Stanley, eldest son of the eleventh Earl of Derby, commonly, though erroneously, called Lord Strange, bought the remainder of the lease and lived there (when not at the family seat, Knowsley Hall in Lancashire) until his death in June 1771. Most of his time was spent alone: his wife died in 1759, his young children were brought up in Lancashire, and he devoted himself chiefly to politics and the turf rather than to entertaining. He evidently saw no need to make any significant alterations to the house; hence, the sequence of rooms

414   The front of Derby House, Grosvenor Square built *c*.1728 with a porch added by Robert Adam. Drawn for Sir John Soane's Royal Academy lectures (Sir John Soane's Museum: Soane lecture drawings, 18/2/10)

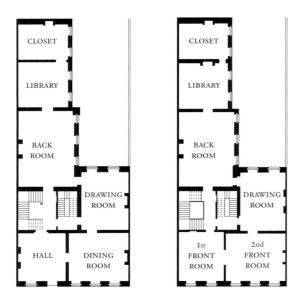

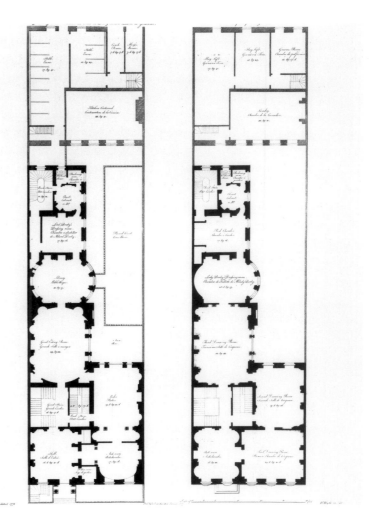

415 A reconstruction of the ground and first-floor plans of the early eighteenth-century house

416 Ground and first-floor plans of Derby House, by Robert Adam, 1773 (*The works in architecture of Robert and James Adam*, vol. II (1779), pt. I, pl. I)

described by Walpole in 1773 was much the same as that listed in the inventory of the previous owner, Sir Robert Sutton, MP in 1732.[9]

The ground floor had an entrance hall, a front dining-room with a drawing-room behind, a central staircase hall and a back room, library and closet in the rear wing (pl. 415). On the first floor were a first and second front room, a drawing-room, a back room, bedchamber and closet. The nursery rooms and *valet de chambre's* room were on the second floor, and the kitchen and other service rooms in the basement.

Lord Stanley's requirements were quite different from his father's. He and his young bride, Lady Elizabeth Hamilton (daughter of James, sixth Duke of Hamilton), whom he married in June 1774, were full of fun and vitality, and enormously extravagant. They wanted suites of the most dazzling reception rooms in town, fashionably got up for great assemblies, gaming, balls and suppers – a house that came to life at night, and reflected and enhanced the gaiety of their lives.

Adam responded – after the 'grand Ball' was over – with ingenious plans to reshape the 'Parlour and principal Stories' (pl. 416). These, he said, were 'an attempt to arrange the apartments in the French style, which . . . is best calculated for the convenience and elegance of life'.[10] Sequences of interconnecting rooms were skilfully fitted together in the French manner to form two different apartments on each floor. To begin with, each floor had an *appartement de parade* or public apartment, with rooms pro-

gressively increasing in size and importance. The ground floor apartment had a hall, ante-room, parlour and grand dining-room; the principal apartment on the *piano nobile* consisted of an ante-room, first and second drawing-room and a third or 'Great Withdrawing-room' – a noble suite 'well suited to every occasion of public parade'. An intermediary room of semi-public character – the earl's library–dressing-room on the ground floor and the countess's dressing-room above – separated the *appartement de parade* from the *appartement de commodité* or private apartment at the far end of the house. While 'the French in their great hôtels, with their usual attention to what is agreeable and commodious', would have placed both Lord and Lady Derby's private apartments on the principal floor, the narrowness of London houses required them to be on separate floors. To render their private apartments 'commodious', a small extension to the rear wing (not a large one, as Adam claimed) was built, containing closets, toilets, powdering-rooms and a private stair giving 'convenient access and communication to both stories'.

The dining-room, normally placed outside the main *enfilade* or excluded altogether in French houses, was considered an essential reception room in England. Derby House had two: a 'Great Eating Room' and a parlour which was used for informal meals as well as private business and other daytime activities. To cope with the multitude of elaborate late-night suppers given by Lord Derby, the kitchen was 'continued' in a large room in the stable block at the end of the garden.

A proper progression demanded that the large front room on the ground floor (the old dining-room) be reduced to an ante-room ancillary to the parlour. One of its three bays was therefore remodelled as an extension of the hall, containing a screened lobby flanked by a closet and porter's room to serve the increased number of visitors. The space was further contracted and its contour varied by the introduction of a broad apse on the window wall and the removal of about 5 feet (1.5 metres) from the opposite end of the room in order to create a vestibule set off by columns in the parlour, which enhanced the latter's size and antique spirit in preparation for the great dining-room. The only other rooms requiring structural alterations – walls moved and ceilings raised – were the first-floor back room, which became

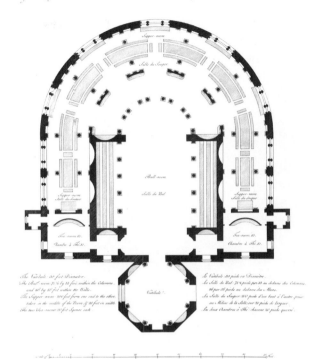

417   Plan of the pavilion for the Earl of Derby's *fête champêtre* at The Oaks, Surrey, designed by Robert Adam, 1774 (*The works in architecture of Robert and James Adam*, vol. III (1822), pl. xx)

418   Antonio Zucchi, the ball-room in the pavilion erected for the Earl of Derby's *fête champêtre* at The Oaks, Surrey, designed by Robert Adam, 1774. (Reproduced by kind permission of the Earl and Countess of Derby).

419 Antonio Zucchi, the supper-room in the pavilion erected for the Earl of Derby's *fête champêtre* at The Oaks, Surrey, designed by Robert Adam, 1774. (Reproduced by kind permission of the Earl and Countess of Derby).

the 'Great Withdrawing-room', with a heightened groin vault; the bedroom behind it; and the corresponding room on the ground floor, where semicircular bows were built for the countess's dressing-room and the earl's library respectively.

Every room had its walls modelled – or advanced and recessed, as Adam would say – with pilasters and columns, niches and apses of different sizes and shapes, some curved, others angular, but all symmetrically disposed. The results were a lively contrast of light and shadow and a diversity of contours, proportions and character expressly intended to please and entertain the observer. Entertainment was, of course, paramount in these parade rooms; the private apartments, with their square bedrooms and circular and octagonal closets, are dull by comparison. No other Adam house was as imaginatively planned as Derby House, but then none of his patrons was so devoted to the pleasures of society and so lavishly hospitable as the twelfth Earl and Countess of Derby and their advisor, 'Gentleman Johnny' Burgoyne, whose influence was considerable.

Adam's earliest surviving designs for Lord Stanley are dated 1773 and are for ceilings and chimney-pieces in the parade and private apartments on the principal floor. Wall elevations were

also made at this time for the 'Great Withdrawing-room' and no doubt for other first-floor rooms as well. Designs for the ground-floor rooms and for mirrors and other furnishings followed in 1774, except for a brief interval in May and June, when Adam's attention was focused on the *fête champêtre* at The Oaks on 9 June (pls 417–19).[11] His last designs for furniture were made in January 1775.

The execution of the work was supervised by Burgoyne, who was experienced in such matters, having organized the building in 1771–2 of the house designed by Sir Robert Taylor for Admiral Howe at 3 Grafton Street. By the beginning of September 1774, 'Mr Burgoyne (was) fully imploy'd hurrying the Work Men (of whom only the plasterer Joseph Rose and the carver, Thomas Carter, junior, are recorded) to get Ld Stanley's House finish'd for November as they are then expected in Town'.[12]

The Stanleys were evidently delighted with what they found and at the end of November Lady Betty 'had a party . . . of three tables to shew her fine house'.[13] However, it was not until the following spring, after their son and heir was born and all the important pieces of furniture were delivered, that their 'great' and 'abominably late' assemblies began in earnest.[14]

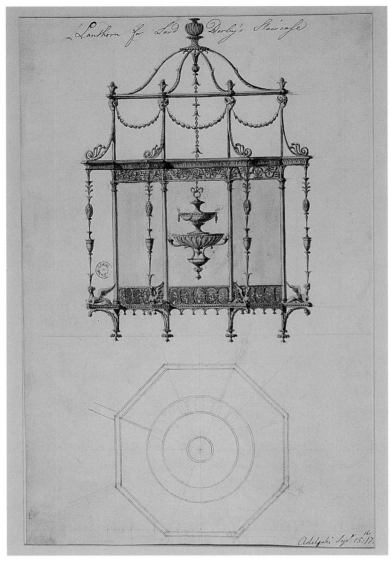

420 Design for a glass lantern, by Robert Adam, 1774 (Sir John Soane's Museum: Adam drawings, vol. 25:41)

Adam had good reason to congratulate himself on his achievement and was quick to do so in print. Derby House was the opening number of the second volume of his *Works*, published in 1779. One would have expected Sir Watkin Williams-Wynn's house at 20 St James's Square to have had priority, being slightly earlier and one of the few houses in town or country that was not only decorated but also built by Adam. However, it was the Countess of Derby's Etruscan dressing-room that decided the issue, for in 1777 an urgent need arose for Adam to stake his claim to have been the first (at Derby House) ever to adapt the colour and two-dimensional ornaments of Etruscan vase painting to the decoration of apartments.

In April of that year, Michelangelo Pergolesi announced the publication, in twelve numbers, beginning in May, of 'Original Designs . . . in the Etruscan and grotesque Style dedicated to the Duke of Northumberland'.[15] His proposals informed subscribers that he had 'long applied his Attention to the Ornaments of the Ancients' and 'had the Honour of designing and painting Rooms, Ceilings, Staircases and Ornaments for many of the Nobility and Gentry in England, and other Countries'. His collaboration with Adam at Syon in 1765–8 had won him the favour of the Duke of Northumberland and in 1774 he was employed by Chambers at Gower House in

Whitehall.[16] What troubled Adam was not that Pergolesi's plates offered anything new, but rather that they were imitations of his style.

Self-defence and bumptiousness were integral parts of Adam's character and it is not surprising that he should devote the whole of his preface to the second volume of the *Works* to asserting himself as the originator of the new Etruscan mode of decoration and parading his superior knowledge of the subject in lengthy footnotes. He was determined that 'judges in architecture . . . may know to whom the art is indebted for this improvement'. Mrs Child's Etruscan dressing-room at Osterley and the Countess of Home's at Home House, both finished by 1778, were more complete and would have served his purpose better. But it was too late; the plates for Derby House and 20 St James's Square had already been engraved in 1777.

Derby House was demolished in 1862 and the appearance of the ensemble of furniture and decoration is difficult to recreate. There are many reports of the night-life there, the constant balls and suppers, the games of commerce, tessier and quinze played till five in the morning, but not a word about the decor, except for Walpole's sideways snipe about it being 'filigreed into puerility'.[17] Nor have any building accounts survived apart from a few bills for furniture and one for steel grates.[18] The designs published by Adam in his *Works* are but a small selection, which he adjusted for 'picturesque' purposes. Those in the Soane Museum, though more numerous, are still not comprehensive and the presentation drawings made for Lord Stanley have vanished altogether.

The ground-floor rooms were not so richly decorated or so well recorded as those on the *piano nobile*. Nothing is known about the great dining-room except that it was all painted 'Blue of different tints'.[19] How its undulating walls were furnished is very hard to reconstruct. As there was no place for a single table, the sideboard must have been in two sections, either on the curved walls flanking the main entrance, or, for more striking effect, fitted into the semicircular niches on the opposite wall. Full-length statues were presumably placed in the two tall niches on either side of the chimney-piece. A jib door gave access through a triangular recess into the parlour or lesser eating-room. Here, a Venetian window was inserted to answer the columnar screen across the new vestibule added to the front of the room. The principal attraction must have been the two large paintings by Antonio Zucchi of *The Supper Room* and *The Ball Room* at the *fête champêtre* at The Oaks, which hung on the long wall between the two doors and over the chimney-piece respectively.[20]

The *beau monde* made its way straight from the front hall up the stairs, lit by Adam's gilt lantern filled with green glass (pl. 420),[21] to the *appartement de parade*. Judges of architecture and persons of taste who did not have entry were given a glimpse of each room in succession in Adam's *Works*. First, we are shown a 'Section of the Chimney-side of the Anti-room' (pl. 421), with three, arched recesses: a shallow one in the centre containing a statuary marble chimney-piece carved by Thomas Carter, Jr, with the Derby supporters (a wyvern and deer) in the frieze, flanked by semi-domed recesses.[22] It is clear from the plan that the opposite wall was similarly articulated, with the entrance to the first drawing-room in a deep, arched recess corresponding to

421 Section of the chimney side of the first-floor ante-room, designed by Robert Adam 1774 (*The works in architecture of Robert and James Adam*, vol. II (1779), pt. I, pl. II)

422 Design for a combined pier-glass and girandole for the ante-room, by Robert Adam, 1774 (Sir John Soane's Museum: Adam drawings, vol. 20:134)

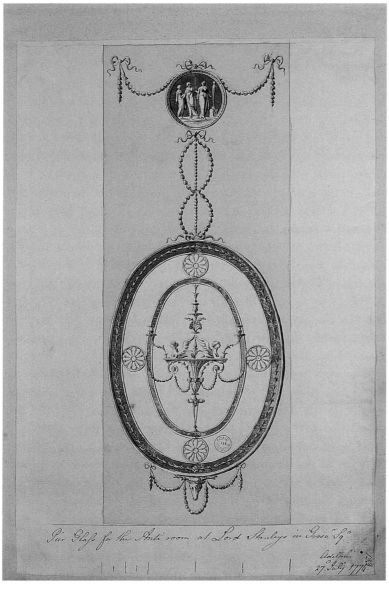

the chimney-piece. No doubt this was continued on the remaining walls, with two arches over the window embrasures and another over the door to the stair.

Bringing the walls forward to create these cavities was bound to make the space slightly narrower, but the recesses themselves gave a greater illusion of depth than the confinement of flat walls. Pinching-in the ante-room also served to make the first drawing-room seem somewhat larger than it was in reality. According to Adam, stucco ornaments and grounds 'both of the cieling (*sic*) and side-walls, (were) all picked in, with different tints of green, which (had) a simple and elegant effect'. His handling of the various ornaments was as harmonious and elegant as their colour: the medallions in the spandrels and the sphinx girandoles on the piers were united in the oval pier-glass between the windows (pl. 422), which, in turn, was echoed in the oval pattern of the ceiling. One can only speculate on the furniture: seats were probably placed in some, if not all, of the recesses; the pier-glass would have been accompanied by a table; and there may have been another mirror or a painting in the overmantel frame.

The first drawing-room was more colourful than the ante-room and much more ornate. Opposite the entrance was a statuary marble chimney-piece with Piranesian clawed-feet and a gilt tripartite mirror (pl. 423) – a refined version of the one designed in 1772 for the Earl of Bute at Luton – with a raised centre held aloft by seated female figures and topped by winged sphinxes flanking an oval medallion painted by Zucchi.[23] There were two pier-glasses with similar crests on the window wall and more medallions and cameos by Zucchi in the ceiling.[24] The two horizontal overdoors, depicting *The return of Telemachus* (from Homer's *Odyssey*) and *Andromache fainting at the unexpected sight of Aeneas on his arrival at Epirus* (Virgil's *Aeneid*), were painted by Angelica Kauffmann and exhibited at the Royal Academy in 1775 before being placed in frames specially designed for them by Adam. They are among her very few securely documented works.[25]

As this room had more unbroken wall-space than any other, it would have been the principal picture-room at Derby House and was probably hung with green damask to accord with the predominantly green and violet ceiling and curtain-cornices.[26] Though the bulk of the Derby collection was formed by the tenth earl, eight old masters were acquired by the twelfth earl, including four paintings by Borgognone on sheets of gilt leather purchased in 1776 at the Consul Smith sale, which would have added greatly to the glamour of the room.[27]

In the second drawing-room, the arcaded theme of the ante-room and the green-and-violet colouring of the first drawing-room were brought together to create an altogether different composition in the manner of the ancients (pl. 424). There were three slightly recessed, round arches on both sides of the room and single segmental arches – broad enough to embrace two doors (one to the first drawing-room, the other false) and two windows with a pier-glass and table between them – on the end walls.[28] Framing these arches were composite pilasters on pedestals, which were 'beautifully painted by Zucchi' with grotesque ornaments inspired by Raphael's Vatican logetta, as were the lunettes and door-panels. The four ovals in the ceiling can also be attributed to Zucchi.[29]

423 Chimney-piece and mirror for the first drawing-room (left), the chimney-piece and mirror frame in the second drawing-room (right), designed by Robert Adam, 1774 (*The works in architecture of Robert and James Adam*, vol. II (1779), pt. I, pl. III)

424 Section of one side of the second drawing-room (above), section of one end of the second drawing-room (below), designed by Robert Adam, 1774 (*The works in architecture of Robert and James Adam*, vol. II (1779), pt. I, pl. IV)

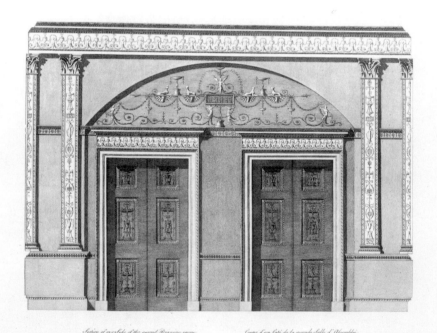

*Ceiling for the Second Drawing Room.
at Lord Stanley's in Grosvenor Square*

425 Design for the ceiling of the second drawing-room, by Robert Adam, 1774 (Sir John Soane's Museum: Adam drawings, vol. 12:143)

426 View of the great drawing-room looking through to the Countess of Derby's dressing-room, designed by Robert Adam, 1774; engraved by Bernadetto Pastorini (*The works in architecture of Robert and James Adam*, vol. II (1779), pt. I, pl. v)

Mirrors with identical semicircular fanlight-tops and pairs of female terms holding husk festoons were placed over the chimney-piece and in the arched recess on the opposite wall (pl. 423, 424).[30] Their design, having been published in the *Works*, became a favourite model for Adam revivalists: there was one in the drawing-room at 20 Mansfield Street in the early 1900s which A. T. Bolton thought was the original rescued from Derby House, and there are now two at Basildon House, Berkshire. Adam's first design for the chimney-piece (dated 1773) was

rejected and used instead in a somewhat altered form for the first drawing-room.[31] The accepted design (dated '28 Febry 1774') is related to one made in October 1772 for the drawing-room at 20 St James's Square and ultimately inspired by Piranesi. It was evidently executed by Thomas Carter, Jr.[32]

The second drawing-room was conceived as a frontispiece, prefiguring the third or great drawing-room, above all in its ceiling decoration. It has been suggested that the large circle with radiating ornaments occupying the centre of Adam's design was

Ceiling for the Great Drawing Room at Lord Stanley's in Grosvenor Square

427   Design for the ceiling of the great drawing-room, by Robert Adam, 1773 (Sir John Soane's Museum: Adam drawings, vol. 12:144)

formed into a shallow dome (pl. 425).[33] If that was the case, then the narrow compartments on either side (towards the window and entrance) may also have been vaulted (and their ribs decorated with bell-flowers) in a manner similar to Lady Wynn's dressing-room and Sir Watkin's library at 20 St James's Square, designed just a year earlier and also like the great drawing-room next door.

With the 'Third and Great Withdrawing-room', the progression of the parade rooms at Derby House reached its climax (pl. 426). Adam, placing the room in a broader context, asserted that it was 'undoubtedly one of the most elegant in Europe, whether we consider the variety or the richness of its decoration'.[34] Though his boastfulness may be offensive and his engraved view of the room overdramatized, he had a point. There were very few domestic interiors of the period in which the spirit of Roman antiquity was so successfully introduced and so completely transfused with novelty, variety and gaiety: not only by surface decoration, but also by modelling the walls in relief, as it were, bringing them forward from the flat plane and raising the ceiling to create an impressive groin vault in the centre, with barrel vaults at either end.

The ornaments of the ceiling and entablature were, he said, 'chiefly of stucco gilt, with a mixture of paintings (pl. 427). The

grounds are coloured with various tints', predominantly pale green.[35] Giovanni da Udine's painted ceilings in the Vatican loggia and the Villa Madama were the inspiration for this and other important Adam ceilings of the late 1760s and early 1770s, notably those in the drawing-rooms at Lansdowne House (1767) and Northumberland House (1770). A carpet corresponding to the pattern of the ceiling was intended, but whether it was ever executed is unknown.[36]

Contrary to normal practice, two orders were employed in this room (pl. 428). The entablature, with metopes in the form of gilt stucco rosettes corresponding to those in the vault and lunettes, was Doric; and the pilasters, which support the vault and effectively divide the walls into three sections, can also be regarded as Doric. Engaged columns and half-columns of a fluted Ionic order with gilt fillets and capitals were used to divide the end walls and the large full-length window into three sections in a manner reminiscent of the Roman baths. The arched recesses and niches on the chimney-side not only contributed to the antique look, but also gave rise to a play of light and shadow that animated the room.

As in the library at Kenwood, the recesses were filled with mirrors in elaborate carved and gilt frames made by Sefferin Nelson, beneath which were Adam sofas (pl. 429).[37] In the niches were

428 Elevation of the window wall of the great drawing-room inscribed with colour notes, by Robert Adam, *c.*1773, detail (Sir John Soane's Museum: Adam drawings, vol. 50:80)

429 A detail of the engraved view of the great drawing-room showing one of the pair of gilded tripod pedestals and urns made by Ince and Mayhew in 1775 to Adam's design and one of the four gilt-wood girandoles made by Sefferin Nelson (*The works in architecture of Robert and James Adam*, vol. II (1779), pt. I, pl. v)

this furniture survives, and it is unlikely that the six semicircular commodes with apsidal lunettes shown in Adam's wall elevations were executed. They were apparently inspired by the extremely expensive Diana and Minerva commode made earlier in 1773 by Chippendale for the state dressing-room at Harewood.[40] A design dated 1774 for glasses 7 feet (2 metres) tall replaced those shown above the commodes.[41] If all six of these glasses were executed as originally planned, the room would have had a total of nine mirrors in gilt frames. The centre of the outer wall, which had been 'burst open . . . to build an orchestra' for the famous ball, was made into a vast window for which Adam designed a pink and gold curtain-cornice with gilded putti and a flaming antique urn (pl. 430).[42] To add to the lustre, the walls – what little of them remained unbroken – were hung with satin, which was the *dernier cri*, and the painted papier-maché door panels were 'so highly japanned as to appear like glass'.[43] The sparkle and gaiety of the candle-lit drawing-room, with its glossy, reflecting surfaces, its gilded furniture and gold enrichments on the vault, chimney-piece and columns, must have been magical and quite exhilarating to the numerous fashionable party-goers who gathered there.

All that survives of one of the most elegant rooms in Europe is the chimney-piece (pl. 431), now in the English Speaking Union in Charles Street, a little the worse for wear, but, as Adam described it, 'finely executed, in statuary marble, inlaid with various coloured *scagliola*, and brass ornaments, gilt in *or moulu*'.[44] An elaborate grate and fender with sphinxes and rams' heads answering those on the chimney-piece was designed in January 1775 and probably executed in gold-coloured paktong, like the one in the drawing-room at Osterley. Its maker has not been identified; presumably he was more of a specialist than William Hopkins, who supplied grates for all the other rooms at Derby House, none of which survive.[45] Sadly, the accompanying chimney-glass has also vanished. It had a crest of military trophies more appropriate to General Burgoyne than young Lord Stanley.[46]

two gilded tripod pedestals carved with 'antique Ornaments. The Tops supported by Hieroglipical Birds Medallions & Drapery etc^a' made in 1775 by Ince and Mayhew from a 'Design of Messrs Adams'.[38] And on the four pilasters were gilt girandoles, over 3^1/$_2$ feet (1 metre) tall, composed of classical vases, boys and other ornaments, also supplied by Nelson.[39] None of

430   Design for curtain cornices for the great drawing-room, by Robert Adam, 1774 (Sir John Soane's Museum: Adam drawings, vol. 17:III)

431   The inlaid scagliola chimney-piece with ormolu mounts from the great drawing-room at Derby House, now in The English Speaking Union, London

432   Furniture and furnishing for Derby House (great drawing-room, left, and Etruscan dressing-room, right and centre)) , designed by Robert Adam, 1774 (*The works in architecture of Robert and James Adam*, vol. II (1779), pt. I, pl. VIII; hand-coloured copy at Sir John Soane's Museum)

433 'Design of a Ceiling in the Etruscan taste in the Countess of
Derby's Dressing room', Robert Adam, 1773 (*The works in architecture of
Robert and James Adam*, vol. II (1779), pt. I, pl. VII; hand-coloured copy
at Sir John Soane's Museum)

Artistic license permitted Adam to have the back wall of the
great drawing-room removed in Benedetto Pastorini's engraving,
so as to give his admiring public a glimpse of the Countess of
Derby's bow dressing-room, which he considered to be the most
novel room in the house, or, indeed, anywhere in Europe. From
this view and the following plates of the chimney-piece, ceiling,
painted doors, girandoles, curtain cornice and commode, 'persons of taste' would, he claimed,

> no doubt observe, that a mode of Decoration has been here
> attempted, which differs from any thing hitherto practised in
> Europe: for although the style of the ornament, and the
> colouring . . . are both evidently imitated from vases and urns
> of the Etruscans . . . researches into antiquity, or in the works
> of modern artists, (failed to reveal) any idea of applying this
> taste to the decoration of apartments.[47]

Owners of the few hand-tinted copies of his *Works* were at a
distinct advantage, for what was most different about this style

was its black and terracotta colouring, inspired by the coloured
plates in P. F. D'Hancarville's catalogue of the *Collection of
Etruscan, Greek and Roman antiquities from the cabinet of the
Hon. William Hamilton*, published in four folio volumes from
1767 to 1776.[48] Most of the ornaments belong to the wider classical vocabulary and only a limited number can be identified as
having come from antique vases: complicated arcading, a styl-
ized laurel and berry motif, slanted running anthemian, flat isolated rosettes and the use of multiple frames around tablets and
medallions. Etruscan vases had little or nothing to do with the
omission of naturalistic rinceaux or the open compositions made
up of small motifs linked by delicate bell-flower chains, which
distinguish the Etruscan style from grotesques; a distinction
clearly demonstrated by the door panels of the great drawing-
room and the dressing-room depicted in the plate showing
Derby House furniture (pl. 432). The sources for these so-called
'Etruscan' features were, in fact, Roman and Renaissance: the
Domus Aurea and Giovanni da Udine's early sixteenth-century

434 Design for the chimney-piece and mirror for the glass drawing-room at Northumberland House, by Robert Adam, 1773 (Sir John Soane's Museum: Adam drawings, vol. 22:55)

435 'Chimney-piece for the Countess of Derby's Etruscan Dressing room of white Marble, inlaid with Ornaments of Scagliola in the Etruscan taste with the Glass frame over it', Robert Adam, 1774 (*The works in architecture of Robert and James Adam*, vol. II (1779), pt. I, pl. VI; hand-coloured copy at Sir John Soane's Museum)

decorations in the loggia of the Villa Madama. Piranesi has also been suggested as a source, though he is conspicuous by his absence from the list of authorities cited in Adam's preface.[49]

While there is no doubt that Adam was a pioneer of the Etruscan style, he was not the only one, and his professed failure to discover *any idea* of applying the style of vase decoration to the decoration of apartments is very surprising indeed.[50] Josiah Wedgwood, encouraged by his friend Sir Watkin Williams-Wynn, had perfected and patented a method of encaustic decoration in imitation of the Greek red-figure style by November 1769, and was also manufacturing 'antique' tablets, medallions and large cameos in 'black Basaltes with Etruscan red burnt-in Grounds, and in polished Biscuits, with brown and grey grounds'.[51] His first catalogue, published in 1773, recommended these Etruscan ornaments as 'fit either for inlaying, as Medallions, in the Pannels of Rooms, as Tablets for Chimney Pieces, or for hanging up, as Ornaments in Libraries, &c. . . . as Pictures in Dressing-Rooms, or for ornamenting Writing-Tables,

Book-Cases, Cabinets, and the Walls of Apartments, in the richest Manner, and at very moderate Expence'.[52] Tablets for chimney-pieces made in this way, with 'durable burnt-in Grounds', were guaranteed to be 'much harder and more durable than marble', and there were eighty-two classical subjects to choose from. There was, in addition, another class of 'Tablets for Chimney Pieces; and Pictures for Cabinets and inlaying upon Plates of artificial Basaltes, and upon a new kind of enamelled Plates. These Paintings . . . (had) already been applied to great Advantage in Chimney-Pieces and Cabinets'.[53]

Wedgwood's furniture-mounts, chimney-tablets, medallions and cameos were certainly known to Adam. In August 1772 he designed a chimney-piece for Lady Williams-Wynn's dressing-room to receive three of the new 'antique' tablets (see pl. 396), and Wedgwood, for his part, was well aware of 'Mr. Adams's power to introduce (their) things into use & (was) glad to find he seems so well disposed to do it'.[54] Indeed, in 1773 Adam did propose 'to introduce some of Messrs Wedgwood and Bentley's

la Commode for Lord Stanley

Adelphi October 24. 1774

work into (a) Chimney' at Lord Ashburnham's house in Dover Street (no. 19, later 30) or to have it 'done colour'd in Scagliola by Richter & Bartoli if Lord Ashburnham chuses it'.[55] However, it was not Etruscan; and when it came to choosing, Adam and his clients were evidently more disposed to imitate Wedgwood's encaustic and basalt plaques in paint, scagliola, plaster and even inlaid wood than to use the pottery itself, which was comparatively costly and prone to shrinkage.[56] Etruscan colours – black and terracotta – were used as early as 1768 on the French-grey dining-room (now the library) ceiling at Newby.[57] Though black-and-red-painted cameos were introduced in 1772 in his revised design for the ceiling of Mrs Child's dressing-room at Osterley,[58] the decision to execute this ceiling may not have been taken by Robert Child until 1775, when the chimney-piece and Etruscan wall decorations for the room were designed and when Lady Derby's dressing-room was finished.

Lady Derby was offered the choice in 1773 of having the 'antique' Renaissance ornaments on her ceiling – winged sphinxes with tails of rinceaux – painted in shades of pink on a dark green ground, or fawn on a dark brown ground, which Adam described as 'the colouring of the Etruscans' (pl. 433).[59] Her preference for the latter, the more novel of the two schemes, determined the Etruscan taste not only of the rest of her dressing-room, but of the rest of her private apartment as well, distinguishing it *en bloc* from the preceding public apartment.

As luck would have it, Adam had just (in June 1773) made full-size coloured drawings for an inlaid scagliola chimney-piece in the Etruscan style for the glass drawing-room at Northumberland House (pl. 434), which he was able to persuade the Duke of Northumberland to release for more appropriate use at Derby House (pl. 435).[60] The statuary marble surround was

436   Design for the commode in the Countess of Derby's dressing-room, by Robert Adam, 1774 (Sir John Soane's Museum: Adam drawings, vol. 17:27)

437   Commode from the Countess of Derby's dressing room by Ince and Mayhew, 1775 (The Earl of Derby)

438 Elevation of General Fitzroy's circular dressing-room in Fitzroy House, Highgate, by Robert Adam, 1774 (Sir John Soane's Museum: Adam drawings, vol. 50:89)

executed in 1774 by Thomas Carter, Jr; Bartoli and Richter were presumably responsible for the inlaid brown and fawn and red and black scagliola ornaments.[61] An 'extreame Curious steel grate very highly polished & neatly finished to a Design of Mess.rs Adams' and a matching fender were made by William Hopkins on 19 December 1774, at a total cost of £56.4.3.[62] The chimney-piece and grate are both lost, but the chimney-glass, with a black and gold Etruscan-style frame flanked by carved and gilt female terms, now hangs in Heaton Hall in Manchester.[63] Though Adam is not known to have designed any other mirrors for the room, there would almost certainly have been one over the countess's Etruscan commode, which must have stood in the inner bow, opposite the large bow window.

This superb piece (pls 436, 437) was designed by Adam in 1774 and made in 1775 by Ince and Mayhew 'of fine and curious Woods very Finely inlaid with Etruscan Ornaments enriched with rich wrought brass Mouldings Antique Heads and Drapery Ovals for Gems and large Pannels in Front and Top . . . the whole engraved and finished in the best Manner'.[64] The three painted roundels on the front, depicting Diana with her hounds and dancing nymphs on either side, and the painted rectangular

tablet of Venus and Cupid on the top, are attributed to Zucchi and were probably derived from engraved sources.

Adam's earliest designs for neo-classical bow-fronted commodes were made in January 1773 for the Duke of Bolton's drawing-room at Russell Square and Robert Child's at Osterley. Only the latter is known to survive. The pale blue, pink, terracotta and black washes used in all these designs and in the hand-tinted copies of Pastorini's engraving of the Derby House commode were translated into colour-stained marquetry which must have had a more showy effect than the faded survivors suggest. Even without the application of Etruscan colours to the Derby House commode, the vase-painting style was immediately recognizable by the sharp contrast of light and dark woods, the black or nearly black frames and the painted panels, and above all by the flatness, the absence of modelling, the abstraction and isolation of the figures. This was Adam's most comprehensive adaption of the Etruscan manner of decorating vases to contemporary furniture. Its success may owe something to the elliptical shape of the piece.

Wall decorations like those designed for General Fitzroy's (first Baron Southampton) circular dressing-room in Fitzroy House,

439   Design for a bed for the Earl of Derby, by Robert Adam, 1774 (Sir John Soane's Museum: Adam drawings, vol. 17:154)

440   Design for curtain-cornices for the Countess of Derby's dressing-room (top) and bedroom (bottom), by Robert Adam, 1774 (Sir John Soane's Museum: Adam drawings, vol. 17:112)

441   Design for an Etruscan-style arm-chair for the Earl of Derby's bedroom on the ground floor of Derby House, by Robert Adam, 1775 (Sir John Soane's Museum: Adam drawings, vol. 17:94)

Highgate, in December 1774 (pl. 438) and for Apsley House, Osterley and Home House in 1775 were evidently not yet contemplated in 1773, when Lady Derby's Etruscan-style dressing-room was conceived.[65] However, much the same effect would have been achieved by the combination of two different sorts of girandoles incorporating *faux* Wedgwood black and terracotta medallions hung in pairs or possibly in groups of three (see pl. 432), and by the painted doors spotted with black and terracotta medallions. In this respect, Adam's claims for the originality of the Countess of Derby's dressing-room were not unjustified.

Nor was the Etruscan taste confined to that room alone. It spread and gathered force in the countess's bedroom next door, where there was a coved ceiling with an unmistakably Etruscan black and terracotta oval border, cameos of amorini in shades of

brown, and a central medallion of *The figure of Night sowing Poppies*, whose sleep-inducing pods were repeated in black and red on the curtain-cornice (pl. 440).[66] But the *coup de théâtre* was the extraordinary matrimonial bed consisting of twin beds under one great domed canopy supported by palm-tree columns and upholstered in a hybrid Etruscan style with terracotta ornaments on a fawn-coloured ground (pl. 439). Presumably, this theatrical prodigy, designed in September 1774, was not intended for everyday use, but rather as a raree-show to be seen on special occasions when the whole house was thrown open to assembled guests. Whether it was executed is not known. Nothing else like it was ever attempted by Adam. It was 'an odd fancy', as Mrs Agneta Yorke said of the twin beds under one tester with 'curtains (that) let down in the Middle to part those

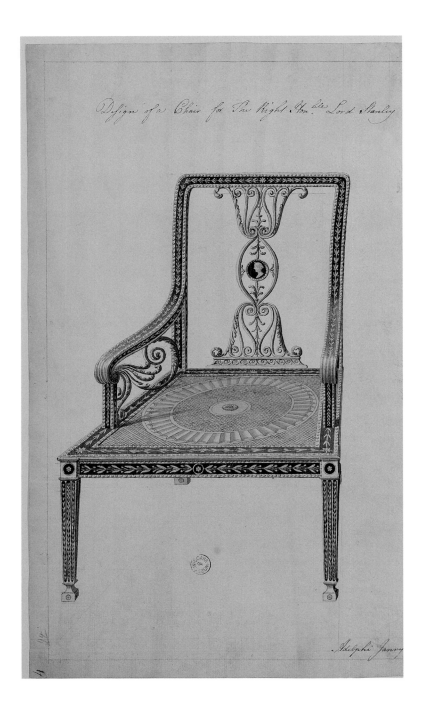

Design of a Chair for The Right Honble Lord Stanley

Adelphi Janry

who lie in them' which she saw in 1764 at Blickling.[67] The odd Etruscan armchair designed in January 1775 for Lord Stanley's bedroom on the floor below, regardless of whether it was executed or not, spawned the Etruscan seat furniture at Osterley (pl. 441).[68]

Adam's design work for Derby House was finished early in 1775, in time for the birth of the Stanleys' first child, a son and heir, on 21 April, an event that was celebrated in June by a gondola race on the Thames.[69] On 22 February 1776, Lord Stanley succeeded his grandfather as twelfth Earl of Derby and owner of the ancestral estate at Knowsley in Lancashire; the death of his aunt, Lady Charlotte Burgoyne, a few months later, brought him The Oaks as well. Exciting new building projects were now in the offing for Adam: first to transform the old-fashioned house at Knowsley into a great castle, and then, around 1777, to do much the same at The Oaks.[70] But sadly they came to very little. The partial recasting of The Oaks and a new dairy at Knowsley were all that was accomplished when suddenly everything was brought to a complete halt by Lady Derby's affair with 'the vicious' Duke of Dorset. In December 1778, the earl and countess separated; the countess went into exile abroad and the earl, when not entertaining at Derby House, devoted himself to the turf – founding the Oaks in 1779 and the Derby in 1780 – cockfighting, amateur theatricals and the noted actress, Elizabeth Farren, whom he married in May 1797, a week after the countess died.

The last member of the Derby family to occupy the house in Grosvenor Square was the thirteenth earl, a noted naturalist. His son, who succeeded in 1851, sold the lease to the Dowager Duchess of Cleveland and moved to a larger house in Stratford Place, taking with him at least two chimney-pieces, a mirror and two overdoors by Angelica Kauffmann.[71] After the Dowager Duchess of Cleveland's death in 1861, the property was bought by a builder–developer, (Sir) Charles Freake, who demolished the old house and built a new one which was eventually pulled down to make way for the American Embassy.

442   The front of Home House, 20 Portman Square, London

18

HOME HOUSE

The interiors of 20 Portman Square, London, built for Elizabeth, Dowager Countess of Home, are rightly regarded as among Adam's masterpieces. However, until recently it has passed unnoticed that the first architect of the building, from 1772 to 1775, was not Adam, but his chief competitor, James Wyatt, the star of the Oxford Street Pantheon, and that at least three of Wyatt's ceilings still survive: the first-floor ante-room, the back parlour and the library.[1] That Adam should have been called upon to transform Wyatt's architecture was a triumph of tremendous significance. He could not have wished for a more appropriate place to display his superior genius than Home House, and he made the most of the opportunity.

The countess first took up residence in Portman Square in a house on the south side, which she rented in 1771 from the builder–developer, Samuel Adams.[2] She was then sixty-seven years old, twice widowed, childless and very rich. In addition to what she had inherited from her father, William Gibbons, a West India merchant of Vere in Jamaica, she had a large fortune from her first husband, the Hon. James Lawes, son of Sir Nicholas Lawes, Governor of Jamaica, who had died in 1734. Her second husband, William, eighth Earl of Home, was a dissipated spendthrift who married her for her money in December 1742 and deserted her in February 1744, a few months before the birth of their child, who did not survive. He himself died in 1761, leaving her only his name and title.[3]

Instead of returning to Jamaica, the deserted heiress stayed in England and made a life for herself in somewhat dubious circles with West Indian connections, at the centre of which were members of the Lawes family – notably her sister-in-law, Judith Maria Lawes and her husband, Simon Luttrell (created Baron Irnham in 1768 and Earl of Carhampton in 1785), 'known to all the Town by the emphatic title of the King of Hell'.[4] The notoriously disreputable Luttrells were evidently favourites of the countess – who was herself dubbed 'Queen of Hell' by 'all the Irish chairmen and riff-raff of the metropolis';[5] and it has been suggested that the marriage of the Luttrells' widowed daughter, Ann Horton, to HRH Henry Frederick, Duke of Cumberland in October 1771 prompted her move to Portman Square in the same year.[6]

The house on the south side of the square was no more than a temporary expedient. Following the lead of her neighbours, William Lock of Norbury, William Attwick and William Baker,

she decided after a year to build a larger and more permanent residence on the north side, which was only just beginning to be developed.[7] On 24 June 1772 she took a ninety-year lease from William Baker on 'a parcel of ground' 60 by 184 feet (18.2 by 56 metres) on which she was permitted to erect a brick house and offices.[8] Exactly when she began building is not known, but it cannot have been long after this: the house was rated in 1774, and must by then have been roofed and well on the way to completion (pls 442, 443).[9] The builder was Richard Norris, who was paid £627.12.0 on 7 November 1775, presumably for work com-

443   Plan of first floor of 20 Portman Square

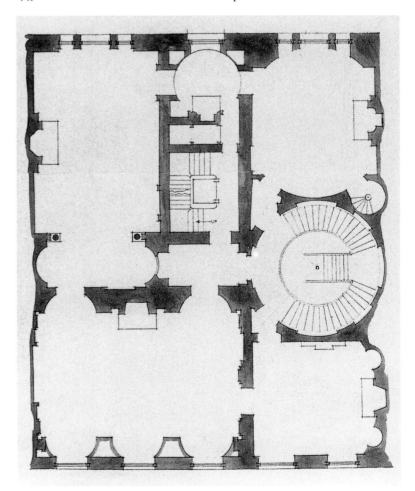

Lady Home's Staircase

444   Design for 'Lady Home's Staircase', by Robert Adam, *c*.1775 (Sir John Soane's Museum: Adam drawings, vol. 14:116)

445   The staircase showing the ram's-head bannisters which were originally painted grey and white. The marbling of the walls is later, replacing the original dead-stone and buff colours

pleted in the previous year.[10] As her architect, she chose James Wyatt, who had been rocketed to fame on the grand opening of the Pantheon in January 1772 when he was only twenty-six years old. In so doing, she was again following the lead of William Lock, who selected Wyatt to build the corner house next door to hers in preference to James Adam, whom he had employed in 1765–6 for his house on the opposite side of the square.[11] The similarity between the exteriors of the two buildings can now be explained.

Proof of Wyatt's employment at Home House rests in five ceiling designs by him in the National Library of Ireland, inscribed as being for Lady Home's 'Ante Chamber, Vestibule, Dining Parlour, Front Parl(our) and Library', and a payment to him of £520 is recorded in the countess's bank account on 8 November 1775.[12] On the same day, the stuccoist Joseph Rose (who incidentally was an original shareholder in the Pantheon) was paid £603.10.0, which must have been for the execution of at least three of the five ceiling designs, if not more.[13]

However, all was not well. Wyatt's dilatory manner – which had been brought to William Lock's attention two years earlier – had evidently become so intolerable to Lady Home that in January 1775 she dismissed him and brought Adam in to finish the job.[14] Robert and James must have derived enormous satisfaction from ousting their principal competitor; the pressure for them to make the most of the opportunity to show themselves to very best advantage was correspondingly intense. This competitive urgency elicited the highest degree of Adam's artistic imagination. He was at his best when confronted with such a challenge, and his confidence was bolstered by having just revolutionized Derby House. The creative energy generated there was released at full force on Lady Home's staircase and principal reception rooms. Once he had gained control, he did not stop at completing the unfinished rooms, but immediately went on to alter and embellish those begun by Wyatt, making them so much his own that the presence of an earlier hand has never been noticed.

Of all the changes Adam made, the most radical, dramatic and extravagant was the staircase. The space he inherited from Wyatt was nearly square and top-lit, with doors north and south to the library and entrance hall and a large arch flanked by pilasters in the centre of the west wall, leading to a vestibule giving access to the front and back parlours and the secondary stairs from the basement to the attic.[15] How Wyatt arranged the principal staircase is uncertain: one can only assume that it rose to the first floor in three stages set against the walls. Despite the fact that it had only been in place for a short time – two years at most – the countess evidently agreed to its demolition so as to enable Adam to trumpet a fanfare for himself and for her by constructing an extraordinary circular staircase hall and imperial stairs within the confines of Wyatt's shell.

It was a tight fit, with no room for manoeuvre (pls 444, 445). The only type of staircase that would allow a uniform architectural treatment of the cylinder was a symmetrical imperial one and the only place this could be put was at right angles to the entrance. An axial approach from the hall would have given a more complete and striking view of the double flights, but for that the circular compartment would have had to be in the centre of the house, as it was in Chambers's unexecuted design of 1759 for York House, Pall Mall.[16]

Adam's predicament was similar to that of William Kent at 44 Berkeley Square and the brilliant success of the imperial staircase there must have encouraged him to turn the awkward situation at Home House to advantage. His alignment of the projecting first flight with the vestibule to the ground-floor reception rooms defines the important cross axis and helps to direct the circuit. Visitors, unable to go straight up, were drawn further into and around the circle, and thus given a greater variety of views and a more extended experience of the astonishing *coup de théâtre.*

There is no hint in the restrained entrance hall of the drama to come.[17] Three of its four doors conceal cupboards; leaving only one opening through which visitors are funnelled into a dark, cramped space before emerging into the tower-like stairwell that rises the whole height of the house to a dome and skylight.[18] Adam's design for the grand staircase rings subtle changes on the rhythms of the three floors. Round the walls at ground and first-floor levels are tall arches flanked by lower rectangles in the manner of a triumphal arch. This arrangement is reversed on the top floor, where there are large rectangular loggia and smaller round-headed niches. Ionic columns in the upper loggias answer the Doric screen in the arched opening fronting the foot of the stairs, which was needed to conceal Wyatt's unsatisfactory vestibule. The north and south sides of the stairs were meant to have matching blind arches with Doric screens, but in the event these would not fit under the stairs and were omitted.

What Adam created here was a concentrated entity of architectural elements, better integrated than his staircase at 20 St James's Square, firmly disciplined, but by no means dull. Everything – Rose's stucco trophies and medallions, Zucchi's grisaille paintings of fictive bas-reliefs and scenes from the *Aeneid,* even the form of the stair itself – is subordinate to its container. The *trompe-l'œil* statues of Minerva and Juno in fictive niches at first-floor level (which presumably replaced the square recesses holding tripod pedestals and lamps shown in Adam's design) were added in the early twentieth century and are totally inappropriate to the architecture.[19] The marbling is also later. Originally the walls were painted dead white, grey and fawn to look like stone; even the '360 Enrich'd Bannisters (were painted) Grey & White'.[20] Dead white and brown were also the principal colours of the hall, with the frieze picked in in blue and some grey in the niche.

The south arm of the staircase takes the visitor right to the door of the ante-room, where the parade begins. Ironically, the more important arched entrance in the centre of the landing leads to a modest vestibule for private and service use. There was very little for Adam to do in the ante-room, for Wyatt had provided the ceiling and the elegantly curved east wall with two niches above the dado.[21] Adam's first design, dated 1 February 1775, was for a chimney-piece with a frieze of husk arcades and rosettes related to the ones he introduced over the doors.[22] The latter remain *in situ,* but the chimney-piece has vanished and been replaced by one from Piercefield Park, Monmouthshire, inserted by Samuel Courtauld. Its overmantel mirror was also removed. At the time of the 1796 restorations, there was a mirror with 'Gold Ornaments to top of Glass Pickd White', which was probably Adam's five-pane chimney-glass with flower-basket

446 View of the music-room. The door to the right leads to the ante-room; the other door is false

447 Design for the chimney side of the music room (Sir John Soane's Museum: Adam drawings, vol. 50:34)

Section of the Musick Room at Lady Homes

crests over the centre and end panels. Two drawings were made for this mirror, both dated 11 October 1777: one includes pencil sketches for alternative girandoles at either side; the other proposes alterations to enrich the chimney-piece.[23] That there were thoughts, at this late stage, of making Wyatt's ante-room more interesting is hardly surprising, for the distinction between it and Adam's music-room next door had become too great.

The music-room (pl. 446) is a brilliantly orchestrated display of Adam's genius in the manipulation of space. 'Movement' is the pervasive spirit, present not only in the five large apses that embrace the windows and doors, but also in the flat ceiling of large contiguous circles cut off at the edges as if stopped in motion. With the addition of tall panels of mirror glass round

the walls, creating a paradoxical system of arches seemingly supported on glass, the effect becomes kaleidoscopic, but not restless. Every element is tightly controlled and totally integrated. The room repays close scrutiny and indeed gains an extra dimension when considered in relation to the inherited shell.

It is not clear whether it was the countess or her architect who had the idea to treat the first drawing-room as a music-room, in keeping with the current fashion for musical parties.[24] Whatever the case, the focus of the room was to be an organ (pl. 447), for which the best place was undoubtedly the end wall facing the main entrance, where it would not only be seen to advantage but would also serve to balance the two closely spaced doors opposite (one of them false). This, however, displaced the existing

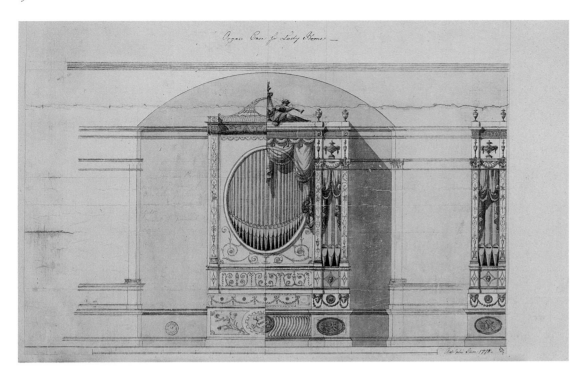

448   Design of the 'Organ Case for Lady Home (and) Plan of the Organ', by Robert Adam, 1775 (Sir John Soane's Museum: Adam drawings, vol. 25:15)

449   The second drawing-room showing the late nineteenth-century alterations to the screened area at the far end

flue, requiring the construction of a new one opposite the windows and ultimately determining Adam's designs for the entire room – walls and ceiling alike.[25]

Simply to erect a projecting chimney-breast in the centre of the north wall would have been far too easy and dull for Adam, who knew from recent experience at Derby House that he could create something far more original and impressive by adding an inner shell. His transformation of the chimney side of the ante-room on the principal floor of Derby House was the model for the new chimney wall in the music-room at Home House (pl. 448): he brought the wall forward about three feet and divided it into three arches: a blind one in the centre for the chimney-piece, flanked by two large apses containing doors to the second drawing-room and the vestibule. This, of course, demanded symmetrical treatment of the window side and it is the three apses there that make the music-room unique.

The semi-domes, in turn, control the circular pattern of the ceiling: each one (plus the chimney-piece arch) being matched by a half-roundel containing a semicircular painting by Zucchi of a musical subject. On the main east–west axis are three full circles with Zucchi roundels, and contiguous to them are circles containing simpler rosettes. Similar circular patterns had been used by Adam in 1763 in the great drawing-room at Bowood (which contemporary visitors associated with Palmyra) and in 1767 on the coved ceilings of the dressing-room at Harewood and the saloon at Nostell.[26]

Another room at Derby House, the second drawing-room, was the model for the articulation of the east wall with two doors under one broad segmental arch (pl. 424). The similarity to Derby House would have been more apparent had the lunette over the paired doors not been altered to match the lunette on the west wall, which was added after the organ was removed. In its original form, it had two pairs of winged sphinxes separated by two trumpeting tritons on the central pier, answering the trumpeting figures above the organ.[27] Other departures from Adam's designs can be noted, but whether they were made by him in the course of execution, or in the nineteenth and early twentieth centuries is difficult to determine. Although the new owners of Home House have made every effort to replace original decorations shown in the designs and recorded in the 1796 accounts, an accurate recreation of the lunette over the two doors and the chimney-piece with its accompanying mirror was not possible.

Given the character and evolution of the room, it seems quite likely that the chimney-piece was executed as shown in Adam's design of February 1775, with musical instruments, popinjays (the heraldic charge of the Earl of Home) and music-making muses.[28] The three-part mirror brought up in the middle with concave sides was a new form, first introduced in January 1775 and adapted a few months later for the pier-glass in the Etruscan room at Osterley.[29] Its side panels were treated like pilaster strips, richly embellished; and the concave centre like a classical pedestal, raised above the entablature and topped with a vase and more popinjays. References in the 1796 accounts to putting '2 New Plates of Glass Silver'd' in the chimney-glass and 'Gilding a Rich glass frame in Burnished Gold' suggest that Adam's design was in fact executed. When it was removed in the nineteenth century, the frieze, which Adam had left plain, as it would have

been obscured by the mirror, was embellished with swags and paterae to conform to the main frieze. The same was done in the organ recess, making the room more homogeneous and less varied than Adam intended it to be.

Adam's design for the organ, dated June 1775 (pl. 448), shows the central section containing the mechanism and pipework partly recessed in the unused flue, with additional display pipes in two projecting side units of coupled pilasters matching those round the room.[30] Unlike the organs at Kedleston and 20 St James's Square, this was literally a fixture whose painted cladding (renewed in 1796) was an integral part of the wall decoration. The instrument itself was removed some time in the nineteenth century and its cladding dismantled in the process. Mirrors were put into the organ recess and divided into three bays by pilasters that probably came from the organ case. At the same time, the rest of the room was 'mutilated':[31] the apses holding the windows were cut away to widen the room, the pilasters were stripped of their decorative, individual pedestals and carried straight down to the base, and all the mirrors between them were removed, along with their applied ormolu embellishments and attached candle-branches.

Although most of these elements were carefully reconstructed for Samuel Courtauld, who took the house in 1926, there were omissions, like the canted mirrors in the apses, and notable additions to the ornaments in the restored mirrors, which were gilded and much more elaborate than Adam's green and white paterae and swags.[32] Apart from the overmantel-mirror, there was hardly any decorative gilding in this essentially glass room – gold was reserved for the grander, more important second drawing-room. The ceiling was grey and the walls green; most of the ornaments were picked out in white, with green, pink and lilac in the richer semi-domes and curtain cornices.

The music-room is altogether unparalleled; even in Adam's own work there is nothing quite like it. It aimed to outshine Wyatt's Pantheon on a small compass, and it succeeded. This was a scintillating venue for high-spirited musical parties like the hilarious 'charivari' given in honour of William Beckford in 1782. Beckford's account, though no doubt exaggerated, gives some idea of the countess's life-style.

> But what is this honour compared with that I accepted yesterday from another neighbour, a much more extraordinary lady than Madame Montagu, no less a person in short than the Countess of Home, known among all the Irish chairmen and riff-raff of the metropolis by the name, style and title of Queen of Hell. As her infernal majesty happens to have immense possessions not only, as of course, in the realms below, but in the island of Jamaica, which some think next door to them, she took it into her extremely eccentric head that as a West Indian potentate I ought to receive distinguished homage.
>
> Aware of my musical propensities she determined to celebrate my accession to Portman Square by a sumptuous dinner and a concert of equal magnificence. Last evening it took place and you never beheld so splendidly heterogeneous a repast as the dinner nor ever heard such a confounded jumble of good and bad music – such a charivari in fact – as the concert. Poor old Giardini[33] who, for the punishment of his youthful sins, I presume, is become her Maestro di Capella,

Ceiling of the Drawing room at Lady Stones in Portman Square.

450 Design (executed) for the ceiling of the second drawing-room, by Robert Adam, 1775 (Sir John Soane's Museum: Adam drawings, vol. 12:167)

went fairly distracted. Not without cause, as you shall hear, for during her morning round she happened to meet with a brace of tall, athletic negros in flaming laced jackets, tooting away on the French Horn as loud as their lungs permitted. 'By God,' exclaimed her majesty (she swears like a trooper), 'you play delightfully. Get up behind the carriage and come home with me. You shall perform to-night at my concert.' 'Here,' said she to the hapless Maestro who was waiting at the street door to hand her in, 'Here, my fine fiddler, I have brought you a great acquisition. These glorious fellows have quite enchanted me. I never heard horns blown with so capital a gusto in all the days of my life.'

'My lady,' answered the Maestro, casting a very suspicious glance on the sable pair, 'I doubt whether they play in score; persons of their sort seldom do.' 'Never mind that,' replied the despotic Countess. 'Put them into the orchestra; they shall chime in.' Happily for us all, having been made extremely welcome below stairs, they slept most of the time, nodding and bobbing their woolly pates about in so ludicrous a manner that I was convulsed with laughter. However, the moment her ladyship approached, I was just able to assume a civilized expression of countenance and praised these charming examples of original talent as warmly as their patroness could pos-

sibly desire. 'There,' said the Countess, turning round triumphantly to the rueful Maestro, 'did I not tell you so? Mr Beckford is a real judge.'[34]

In the proper progress of the parade apartment, the music-room or first drawing-room was but a prelude to the most important room in the house, the second or great drawing-room (pl. 449). Considerable significance was placed on the relationship between the two and they were conceived together. A preliminary sketch-plan and elevation of the south end of the drawing-room shows it screened off by a broad segmental arch and flat impost resting on two Corinthian columns, reminiscent of the library at Kenwood.[35] This was radically altered in the second half of the nineteenth century: the arch, the impost and the figures it supported were all removed, and the columns were raised on pedestals as tall as the dado and brought closer to the pilaster responds, thereby enlarging the opening and weakening the clear distinction that Adam had made between the two parts of the room. The Adam-revival wall decorations also date from this period, but the dado of inlaid zebra wood (Coromandel ebony with light-colour strips) mounted with ormolu heads, the mahogany grained skirting and inlaid satinwood doors are all original.[36] The use of inlaid wood in English architectural decoration is quite exceptional. It occurs on the staircase at Claydon House and in some rooms in West Wycombe Park, both of the late 1760s, but is not recorded in any other Adam house.

The drawing-room, also known as the 'Sattin Room', was the only room hung with fabric – not the usual damask, but glossy satin, the *dernier cri*, to be seen at Derby House, and probably not familiar green, but one of the newer colours then in fashion, white or lilac, which would not only have had a more striking effect against the zebra-wood dado, but would also have been in keeping with the extraordinary character of the rest of the interiors.[37] White, gold and lilac were the colours of the 'Very Rich Ornamented frieze' with laurel arches springing from baskets of anthemia and standing nymphs supporting tazze draped with husk chains (pl. 451).[38] Fortunately, it was left in place when the hangings were removed.

Two alternative schemes were prepared for the ceiling in March 1775: one 'not executed', with a large square compartment

451 Record drawing of the friezes in some of the principal rooms at Home House, Adam office, *c*.1775 (Sir John Soane's Museum: Adam drawings, vol. 5:83). The design for the drawing-room screen (third from the top) was not executed; the design second from the top was used instead

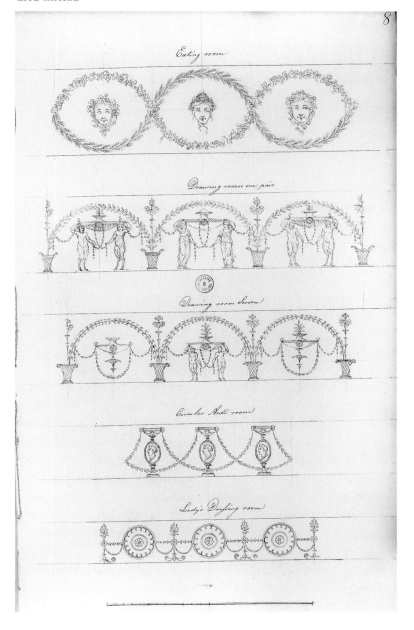

452 Design of a 'Frame for the Duke of Cumberland's Picture for the Countess of Home', by Robert Adam, 1777 (Sir John Soane's Museum: Adam drawings, vol. 20:162)

in the centre and two narrow panels at either end, designed to emphasize the width of the room, and the preferred one (pl. 451), with a full border of alternating medallions of putti and flowers and a longer, narrower, more elaborate inner part subdivided into three compartments.[39] The middle one is more or less aligned on the chimney-breast and incorporates five paintings by Zucchi: a central roundel depicting Venus reading the *Aeneid* to Augustus and Octavia, and four ovals with individual figures of Victory, Peace, Clemency and Generosity.

The chimney-piece, designed in February 1775, is an ornate one of white marble inlaid with coloured scagliola and mounted with ormolu.[40] Above it was a gilt tripartite mirror with coupled female terms on either side and a raised foliate frieze overlaid with an oval medallion surmounted by half-boys supporting a basket of flowers.[41] A taller and more elaborate variant of the chimney-glass, with recumbent lions from the Home arms, occupied the centre of the opposite wall and was presumably accompanied by a suitably grand console-table or sofa.

Exactly contemporary with the two mirrors is a design for picture frames (pl. 452) that are like canopied thrones, replete with independent pelmets adorned with ducal coronets, royal supporters and military trophies.[42] These were to receive Gainsborough's full-length portraits of the Duke and Duchess of

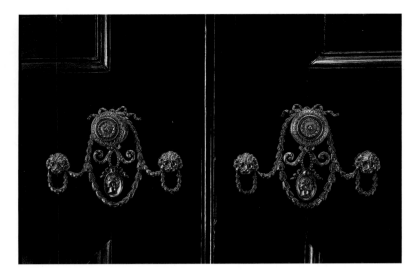

453   Door furniture in the principal rooms at Home House

Cumberland, which were presented to the countess by the sitters after exhibition at the Royal Academy in 1777, possibly in gratitude for her loyal support of their marriage, so fiercely opposed by George III. The portraits were her most treasured possessions, given pride of place on either side of the chimney-piece in her 'Capital Room' and bequeathed by her to the Lord Mayor, Aldermen and commonality of the City of London to hang in the Mansion House.[43] Evidently the Cumberlands, who had the last say, disapproved of her bequest and the pictures were taken into the Royal Collection, where they remain.

In addition to the main door from the music-room and a symmetrical false door, the second drawing-room had two doors on the east wall (pl. 453): one communicating with the principal and secondary stairs and the other (or rather half the other, as they were all folding doors)[44] opening to the small circular ante-room that is linked both to the service stairs and the Etruscan dressing-room.

As conceived by Wyatt, this little room was Lady Home's 'Principal Dressing Room', the larger room next door being her bedroom. Its ceiling, executed to Wyatt's design, had a shallow fan-pleated dome ringed by eight contiguous circles defining an octagonal umbrella in the centre.[45] Only the scalloped outline and small paterae in the circles were retained by Adam in his simplified design dated January 1775; the rest was removed and replaced by more delicate ornaments.[46] Whether Wyatt was also responsible for the circular shape of the room is uncertain and somewhat doubtful, though the semicircular Ionic porch on the garden front can be accepted as his.[47] The circular form was not chosen for the sake of variety and maximum contrast – important as those qualities were – but rather for its relation to the semicircular porch on the garden front. In fact, there was more to the relationship than similarity of form. Contemporary reference to the room as the 'Belvedere'[48] suggests that it opened on to the flat roof of the porch, from which the garden and the open fields of Marylebone could be viewed. Despite the cupboards concealed in the curves of the walls, it is most unlikely that Adam intended this room off the principal drawing-room to serve as a closet for the Etruscan room which Dr Whinney thought was used by Lady Home as her bedroom in accordance with Wyatt's plan.[49] In addition to his revised ceiling, Adam

made designs for the curved chimney-piece in February 1775 and for a curved overmantel mirror of five panes surmounted by coronets in 1777.[50]

The Etruscan room, also referred to as the '3ᵈ Drawing Room' and 'Lady's Dressing Room', completes the circuit of the *appartement de parade*. Like the first ante-room, where the circuit began, this was in the process of being decorated by Wyatt when Adam took over. Its ceiling poses a problem, for there are no known designs by either architect. However, Wyatt's design for the library ceiling at Hams Hall, Warwickshire can be regarded as a square version of the circular pattern that was executed in the Etruscan room before Adam's modifications.[51] The four painted tablets by Zucchi, the four medallions of nymphs also by Zucchi and the central roundel depicting *Iris entreating Helen to watch the combat between Paris and Menelaeus*, which is the main theme of the decoration, may also have been part of Wyatt's design. Adam eliminated Wyatt's narrow panels flanking the central square compartment and used the space to construct two semi-domed apses: one containing the large window overlooking the garden (pl. 454) and the other, on the opposite wall, embracing two separate doors to the main staircase and a small winding stair rising to the second or bedroom floor, which he fitted into a corner left over from Wyatt's staircase hall. The added apses make the shape of the room resemble the Countess of Derby's bow dressing-room in Grosvenor Square.

For the space under the semi-dome between the two doors Adam designed a *lit à la polonaise* with an oval canopy similar to the dome he designed in October 1775 for the state bed at Osterley (pl. 455).[52] The presence of a bed here is no indication that the room was used by the countess as her main bedroom. Had that been the case, the social parade – the prime function of such London houses – would have ended in the second drawing-room, requiring guests either to exit from the jib door into the service vestibule or to retrace their steps through the music-room and ante-room. It is inconceivable that Adam, the great showman, would have secreted his novel Etruscan decorations, which, he boasted, 'differ from any thing hitherto practised in Europe',[53] in a private room without public access and in a house that was meant to outstrip Wyatt. He had only applied the style to wall decoration three times before: first in 1774 or 1775 in a design for a circular 'Toilet Room' at General Fitzroy's house at Highgate, which is not known to have been executed, then at Apsley House in June 1775 and at Osterley in October the same year.[54]

Adam's undated coloured elevations of the north and south walls of Lady Home's Etruscan dressing-room may not have been made much before February 1777, the date of his design for the chimney-piece (pl. 456).[55] The latter, executed in white marble with black and red scagliola roundels, red figured vases and tripods, survives along with the painted and stucco decorations of the ceiling, half-domes and friezes. Unfortunately, the walls have been stripped of their Etruscan decorations, which were presumably painted on paper laid on canvas as at Osterley and may also have been by the same ornament painter, Pietro Maria Borgnis, but certainly not by Zucchi. They have been recreated from Adam's designs by Royston Jones.

Though many of the same motifs are to be found in Osterley and Home House, with the same open composition and distinctive colours, their ordering is quite different. Instead of the

454 Design for the window wall of the Etruscan room, by Robert Adam, *c.*1777 (Sir John Soane's Museum: Adam drawings, vol. 14:134)

455 Design for the south wall of the Etuscan room and the 'lit à polonaise', by Robert Adam, *c.*1777 (Sir John Soane's Museum: Adam drawings, vol. 14:132)

repeated pergola-like arcading around the walls of Osterley, Home House had separate, framed units of ornament, some quite complex, others simple, arranged in a formal and architectonic manner. Over the doors and on either side of the window were heavily framed compartments filled with elaborate grotesques incorporating painted ovals and tablets. The door panels were also decorated with grotesques and probably japanned, but the framed panel behind the bed was left plain, to show off the canopy. Flanking these compartments were tall vertical units defined by delicate bell-flower chains with Home

popinjays on top and pairs of winged sphinxes below. Though there are no surviving elevations for the east and west walls, we can be quite certain that the overdoors and alternating panels continued there; but it is impossible to reconstruct how the central compartments above the chimney-piece and between the doors on the opposite wall were treated. The whole was bound together by a broad band painted with interlaced circles containing cameo heads above the chair rail and a moulded string course of more cameos at the springing of the arches.

In the upper register defined by the string course are four

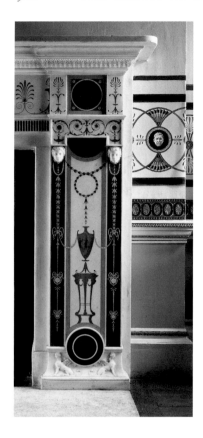

456 Detail of the inlaid scagliola chimney-piece in the Etruscan room, designed by Robert Adam 1777

457 James Wyatt, 'Scetch of Cieling of Lady Homes Dining Parlour', 1773 (National Library of Ireland, Penrose-Wyatt Collection)

458 View of the dining-room or back parlour

459 Plan and laid-out wall elevations of the dining-room or back parlouor, by Robert Adam, c.1776 (Sir John Soane's Museum: Adam drawings, vol. 14:119)

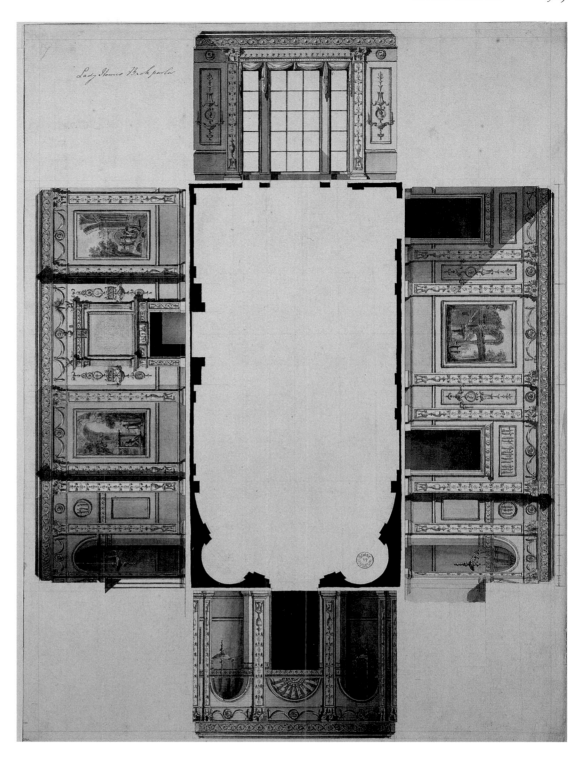

roundels of the continents flanking the apses, and on the straight east and west walls six long paintings of subjects drawn from the *Iliad* and *Odyssey*, including *Ulysses finding, and discovering himself to his father Laertes who was planting a garden*, appropriately placed on the garden end of the east wall, and *Telemachus accompanied by Minerva under the figure of Mentor, in the Island of Calypso*, which may refer to Lady Home's Jamaican origins.

The subordinate ground-floor apartment consists of a front parlour, a back parlour or dining-room and a library. Wyatt's work in this suite of rooms was somewhat further advanced than it was on the floor above: designs had been made for all the ceilings and those for the dining-room and library were executed (pls 457, 458). The plan, as a result, was fairly fixed, leaving Adam little scope for dramatic transformations like those he performed on the *piano nobile*. Not that show was called for on the ground floor: his prime concern there was to enliven Wyatt's

static arrangement, to imbue it with 'the variety and gracefulness of form, so particularly courted by the ancients'.[56]

The largest and most important room was the dining-room, which Wyatt planned as a 40 foot (12 metre)-long rectangular space partitioned at the south end by a screen of columns. On the ceiling of the main section was a large, concave diamond with a single pair of scrolled leaves on the east and west points and two pairs of leaves on the north and south.[57] Adam removed one of the latter pairs so as to create a square central compartment, which he enlivened with four oval paintings by Zucchi, and filled the vacant spaces on the north and south ends with narrow panels each containing round and oblong paintings of pastoral subjects.

The columnar screen was eliminated (probably before it was erected) and the end of the room formed into a large, semicircular apse, with an arched door in the centre leading to the front

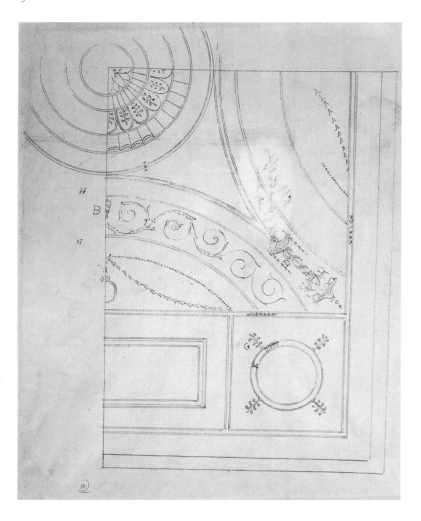

parlour. The tall niches on either side may originally have held sideboard tables for the display of plate, but the present built-in mahogany cupboards are a later addition. The omission of the five oval paintings in the ceiling of the apse from the printed description of the pictures painted by Zucchi raises the possibility of later alterations here too.

Height was a priority in this long room, just as it was in the second drawing-room; to gain it, the entablature was reduced to a frieze of wreathed heads and the walls articulated by extra-tall Corinthian pilasters going right down to the floor, with vertical stems of honeysuckle issuing from vases in low relief on their face. An upper register, the height of the capitals, was needed to fill the added wall space and tie the whole together. Its ribbon-tied swags and paterae are echoed in smaller scale on the frieze of the Corinthian overmantel. This was presumably executed in wood and stucco and later removed, leaving only the statuary marble chimney-piece carved with appropriate dining-room subjects: grape vines, baskets of fruit held aloft by boys and seated female figures holding wheat sheaves.[58]

Adam's coloured elevations of the four walls show the square space above the chimney-piece painted light blue (pl. 459), suggesting that it was to contain a mirror by way of contrast to Zucchi's three large paintings of 'Ruins and Cottages' flanking the chimney-breast and in the centre of the opposite wall. Two smaller blue panels in the apse were also to contain mirrors, but the treatment of the identically coloured tall strips on either side of the window and between the pilasters on the east wall is inde-

460 James Wyatt, 'Scetch of Front Parl (our) Cieling Lady Home', c.1773 (National Library of Ireland, Penrose-Wyatt Collection)

461 View of the front parlour around 1914, before the house was occupied by Samuel Courtauld

462 Plan and laid-out wall elevations
of the front parlour, by Robert Adam,
c.1775 (Sir John Soane's Museum: Adam
drawings, vol. 14:117)

terminable. Glass piers would be unusual in a dining-room; they were probably either painted flat blue or 'highly japanned so as to appear like glass' and to reflect the candlelight from the girandoles. Equipped with another pair of candle-branches fitted to the drops of stucco decoration flanking the chimney-piece and hanging lamps in the niches, the north-facing room – which was primarily intended for evening use – must have been quite spectacular, far more diversified and entertaining than hitherto imagined. Paint tests found pink, buff and white tints differing from the terracotta and straw colours on Adam's elevations, but similar to the shades of pink on his design for a carpet related to the ceiling.[59]

The back parlour or dining-room inherited from Wyatt had three doors: one at the north end, opening to the garden vestibule; a matching one at the south end, opening to the service vestibule off the main staircase; and the main door on the east

side of the south wall, with a matching false door to the west. Adam's replacement of the rectangular screened area with a semi-circular apse resulted in the main door being moved to the centre of the wall, and that, in turn, affected the position of the two doors in the front parlour, bringing them closer together. Though their alignment with the windows was unavoidably sacrificed in the process, the balance was improved by the division of the north wall into three units, the central one twice the width of the sides. In fact, every effort was made to divert attention away from the window wall to the end walls.

Wyatt's centralized ceiling design for the front parlour (pl. 460) (presumably corresponding to his arrangement of the walls) was replaced in 1775 by a large, independent oval pattern accompanied by concave triangles drawing the eye to the corners (pl. 461).[60] Here, Adam introduced four Corinthian columns of porphyry scagliola and brought the entablature forward above them

463 Detail of the Corinthian capital and frieze in the front parlour

464 Design for the chimney-piece in the front parlour, by Robert Adam, 1775 (Sir John Soane's Museum: Adam drawings, vol. 23:63)

465 'Scetch of Cieling for Library Lady Home', by James Wyatt, c.1773 (National Library of Ireland, Penrose-Wyatt Collection)

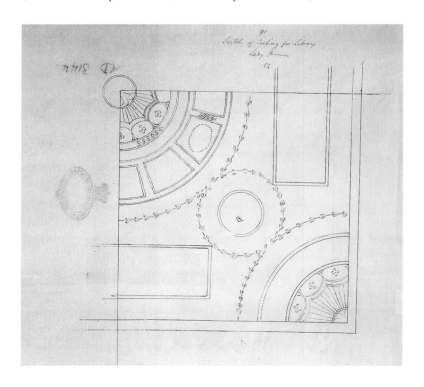

(pilaster responds are shown in his design but seem not to have been executed; pls 462, 463). This unusual feature, apart from reducing the length of the room and varying its shape, is effectively used to frame the end walls and make them appear to recede. The prominence of the columns is much enhanced by their dark red colour against the grey walls.[61]

Zucchi's grisaille of *Queen Dido receiving the Trojans, and treating them with the greatest hospitality* had pride of place in the centre of the east wall, near the entrance to this first reception room. Under it, Adam intended a console-table with pendant half-paterae and bell-flower chains, one of the few pieces of furniture included in his Home House elevations. Whether it was executed is not known. The chimney-piece (pl. 464) on the opposite wall was made to a design dated 13 May 1775 and has a tablet and colonettes derived from chimney-pieces of 1773 and 1774 in the ante-room and eating-room at Derby House.[62] Bacchic heads and vases echo the theme of hospitality announced in Zucchi's *Dido* and are repeated in the overmantel-surround, where the vases are fitted with candle-branches. The centrepiece here was a 'circular picture, shewing a muse inspiring Virgil to write the Aeneid, the Georgics and Eclogues', which survived *in situ* until about 1924, when the room was redecorated for Lord Islington. By then, the 'architecture picture' had already been removed, along with nine panels of stucco decoration, three of which (one between the doors and two on the window

466 Design for the ceiling of the library or 'Sanctuary' representing the triumph of wisdom with twelve cameos of the most celebrated poets and philosophers including Robert Adam, by Robert Adam, c.1775 (Sir John Soane's Museum: Adam drawings, vol. 12:163)

piers) incorporated oval mirrors surrounded by female figures holding chains of husks and winged sphinxes. The recent restoration of these decorative elements has brought the room to life, displaying the simple elegance of Adam's design.

The library, or 'Asylum' as it was called, was Lady Home's private sanctuary overlooking the garden. It could be entered directly from the staircase hall without passing through any other rooms and was not part of the ground-floor apartment. Adam did not have a great deal to do with this room. Wyatt designed the square ceiling with its central circle, corner quadrants, oblong panels and paterae (pls 465, 466),[63] and presumably also the round-headed niches on either side of the chimney-piece (pl. 467) and the deep recess flanked by the door to the staircase and a matching cupboard door. Whether the

shallow recess on the west wall and the arched tops of these two bays were his or Adam's is uncertain, but there can be no doubt that the unified architectural composition is by Adam. It was he who added the surface arch framing the chimney-piece, the string-course linking the units and the six square paintings by Zucchi that complete three triumphal-arch motifs formed by the arches, doors and niches.

The most distinctive feature of this room is not its architecture, but the iconography of its carved and painted decorations. Family and related nautical attributes are concentrated on the chimney-piece. The tablet carries the Home arms, with the ironic motto 'True to the end', perhaps referring to the countess but certainly not to her errant husband. Covering the frieze and stiles is a profusion of navigational instruments alluding to

467 The statuary marble chimney-piece with the Home arms and motto in the tablet and maritime trophies on the frieze and stiles. The overmantel painting depicts *Britannia attended by Faith and Justice being presented by Fame* with portraits of King Alfred and Queen Elizabeth

British sea power, the maritime trading activities of the countess's Jamaican ancestors and the naval careers of the Duke of Cumberland (Vice Admiral 1770, Admiral 1778, Admiral of the White 1778) and her youngest Luttrell nephew, the Hon. James Luttrell, RN. Though there are no known drawings for the chimney-piece, it is shown on Adam's wall elevation and was presumably designed by him. Its sculptor is unknown. Adam's wall elevation shows the navigational theme extended into the niches, where there are terrestrial and celestial globes on pedestals.[64] On the oblong overmantel is a painting signed by Zucchi and dated 1776, showing *Britannia attended by Faith and Justice being presented by Fame with portraits of King Alfred* (lawmaker, liberator and founder of the English navy) *and Queen Elizabeth*, (the countess's namesake: defender of the Protestant faith, whose reign was noted for its maritime exploits, including the founding of the East India Company).[65]

The triumph of wisdom is the overall theme of the room,

summed up in the centre of the ceiling in a painting of *Youth fleeing from Vice, and embracing Virtue, under the figure of Minerva*. This is ringed by 'Twelve small Circles, with heads in imitation of cameos, representing some of the most celebrated Poets and Philosophers, whose names are in the medals': Dr Edward Young, author of *Night Thoughts*, Sir Isaac Newton, Sir William Temple, Bishop Thomas Secker, Lord Lyttelton, Francis Bacon, Lord Verulam, Robert Adam, Sir Francis Drake, Joseph Addison, David Hume, John Locke and John Milton. The four oblong panels at the sides depict the *Vision of Mirza*, a moral allegory set in the East which was published by Addison in the *Spectator* in 1711 and became one of its most popular essays.[66] Flanking these are eight small panels, each with a figure of Theology, Philosophy, Mathematics, Justice, History, Astronomy and Geography.

Another *Spectator* essay, the 'Vision of the Poet conducted by Contemplation on the difficult path to Mount Parnassus where he encounters Fancy, Judgement, Wit and finally Apollo', published by Steele in 1712, is the subject of the six panels on the walls on either side of the arches.[67] In addition there were eight pictures of religious subjects – the *Nativity*, the *Institution of the Sacraments*, the *Crucifixion*, the *Resurrection*, the *Ascension*, the *Martyrdom of St Stephen*, the *Conversion of St Paul* and the *Four Evangelists* – in the panels of a bookcase that presumably stood in the large recess. This is not shown in Adam's elevation and there are no drawings that can be identified with it.[68] Nor is his rôle in the planning of the iconographic programme known. The subjects may have been proposed by Zucchi, who is said to have been assisted in such matters by the celebrated revolutionary, Marat, 'a man of extensive classical reading'.[69]

As a finishing touch for the library, Adam made designs in February 1777 for small tripod vase-candlesticks and green-and-white brackets to support them. These were probably placed on either side of the chimney-piece and the recess on the opposite wall.[70] There are very few furniture designs at all for Home House and these are the only ones for a specific room. The others, which are all undated, are for a fire screen and a tripod pedestal like the one designed in 1774 for Sir Watkin Williams-Wynn.[71]

Adam's exquisite work is all too often taken at face value, and for that reason misunderstood. Home House is a prime example. It is particularly ironic that the ingenious planning of the interior should in the past have been credited to the freedom afforded by the unusual width of the site. It was the constraints imposed by the house already built and partly decorated by Wyatt, and the unique challenge of giving a star performance on his rival's stage, that galvanized Adam's creative genius and brought it to an even higher peak than it would have reached had he designed the house from scratch.

468   Alexander Nasmyth, view of the north front of Culzean Castle,
painted for the 12th Earl of Cassillis in 1812 (National Trust for
Scotland, Culzean Collection)

19

CULZEAN CASTLE

In the early 1770s, it became increasingly apparent to Adam that his supremacy in the field of interior design was under threat from a host of successful imitators and competitors: Chambers, Paine, Taylor, 'Capability' Brown and the young Henry Holland. The public acclaim that greeted the opening of Wyatt's Pantheon in January 1772 stung his pride, and this was followed by the crash of the Scottish banks five months later. Financial disaster was only averted by the highly criticized lottery in 1774. Adam must have been frantic to discover ways to regain his declining prestige.

One answer lay in Scotland, where his father's architectural practice, which had been carried on by his elder brother John, was finally wound up in about 1770. His commissions in 1770 and 1771 for Mellerstain and Wedderburn Castle, both in Berwickshire, and Caldwell House, Ayrshire, in 1773 mark a significant change both in the quantity and manner of his work in Scotland. Unlike John's conventional Palladian houses, these are all in a simple and undemonstrative castle style, a style he first employed in the early 1760s at Ugbrooke in Devon.[1]

By prudently combining this traditional Scottish idiom with elements of ancient Roman military architecture, Italian medieval fortifications, classical, Renaissance and Georgian details, he managed, in Piranesi's words, 'to open himself a road to the finding out of new ornaments and new manners'.[2] His picturesque castle style – with its bold massing of exterior forms of different geometrical shapes and sizes, rising and falling, replete with battlements, bartizans and arrow slits – is every bit as original, distinctive and full of novelty and variety as the refined neo-classical decoration that had brought him fame.

Whereas his work in England was largely confined to redesigning the interiors of earlier houses, Scotland gave him the longed-for opportunity to display 'the richness and fertility of his invention'[3] on the 'outside compositions' of entire buildings: new ones like Mellerstain and Wedderburn, as well as old tower houses like Culzean Castle, Ayrshire (pl. 468), and Oxenfoord Castle, Midlothian, which he made larger, more imposing and 'much older'.[4] However, he was not given anything like as much freedom in his interior compositions. The plans of his Scottish villas and castles are, as Alistair Rowan has demonstrated, invariably symmetrical and for the most part 'clearly linked to normal country house and villa prototypes', though there are also some remarkably complex and inventive configurations: a V-shaped

house proposed for Bewley, Inverness-shire, in 1777, the D-shaped Airthry Castle, Stirlingshire, in 1790, or the triangular Walkinshaw, Renfrewshire, in 1791.[5]

His interiors are best described by the words he used for his ceiling designs for Mellerstain: 'plain and elegant and not expensive'.[6] Articulation by means of pilasters, niches or columnar screens was rarely attempted and surface decoration, if admitted at all, was confined to the ceilings. The exception is Archerfield, East Lothian, a 1740s house which Adam recast in the fashionable neo-classical style for William Nisbet in 1789.[7] On the whole, there were not the resources in Scotland that there were in England, nor was it easy to find native craftsmen of the calibre of Joseph Rose, Sefferin Nelson, Thomas and Benjamin Carter, capable of executing elaborate designs from the Adelphi office. One solution, employed by the Adams at Mellerstain, was to have some of the stucco-work modelled in London and plaster casts sent up.[8]

The diverse facets of Adam's castle style are all embodied in Culzean, a late sixteenth-century fortified tower house strategically situated on a rocky cliff commanding the Firth of Clyde, which he transformed into a comfortable and impressively modern castle for David Kennedy (c.1730–1792), tenth Earl of Cassillis. This was accomplished in two separate phases over a period of fifteen years, beginning in 1777 – a little over a year after David Kennedy succeeded to the title on the death of his unmarried brother, Sir Thomas – and finishing (or to be precise, ending unfinished) in 1792, the year Adam and his patron died.[9]

Adam could not have wished for a more congenial patron than the tenth Earl of Cassillis: enthusiastic and encouraging about the project; willing to spend money (even though encumbered by debts) and prompt about settling accounts; fairly decisive about what he wanted, yet completely trusting in the judgment of his architect and never interfering with his designs. James Boswell, his friend and fellow advocate, described him as a 'joker . . . and nothing more . . . a good honest merry fellow indeed, but one so totally incapable of the business of the legislation and so devoid of the talents which distinguish a man in public life'.[10] For all we know, Adam may have enjoyed his humour as much as Boswell did. Whether the fact that the two men were bachelors of similar age and sat in the same Parliament from 1768 to 1774 – Kennedy representing Ayrshire and Adam Kinross-shire – had any significant effect upon the outcome of

469 View of Culzean Castle from the south-west showing the existing tower house and out-buildings, by Robert Adam, c.1776 (Sir John Soane's Museum: Adam drawings, vol. 21:6)

470 James Adam, design for a villa for Sir Thomas Kennedy of Culzean, 1755 (The National Trust for Scotland)

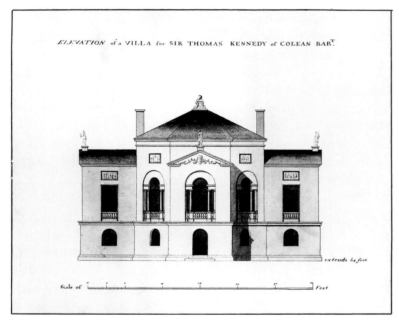

Culzean is, in my opinion, doubtful; though admittedly a wife, especially a rich one, might have had considerable influence upon the interiors.

Adam was called to Culzean in August 1776 to survey the situation and discuss improvements.[11] His sketch of the cliff-top site (pl. 469), taken from the south-west, which was the approach from the sea, shows the old, four-storey tower house rising above a jumble of offices to the north-east and, standing apart from the rest on the line of the escarpment overlooking the sea, a two-storey block 100 feet (30 metres) long, erected in 1766–7 by Sir Thomas Kennedy.[12] This plain, seven-bay, ancillary building of barrack-like appearance known as the 'Office House' determined the protracted building-history of Adam's castle.

In the background of Adam's view, rising above some trees to the south-east of the house, is the pediment of the Tower Gate built by Sir Thomas in c.1750–3.[13] Here, in contrast to the other buildings depicted, the hand of an architect is clearly apparent, though his identity remains a mystery. John or James Adam are

possible candidates. Tower Gate, the triumphal classical entrance to the medieval castle complex (subsequently modified – Romanized, one might say – by Robert Adam), belonged to Sir Thomas Kennedy's initial scheme of improvements which included the formation of a ground-floor, south-facing 'dyning room' (where the so-called Old Eating Room is now) with two large windows and 'big' double doors opening onto the terraces which he went on to plant with flowers in 1760.[14]

Whilst these improvements were in progress, Sir Thomas was in Rome, in the lively and cultivated circle of Lord Charlemont, which included George Brodrick, third Viscount Midleton, who showed him the sites; Lord Bruce, with whom he went to Tivoli, Palestrina and Naples; the Hon. John Ward with whom he was caricatured as a cellist by P. L. Ghezzi, and several others, all of whom appear in Reynolds's *Parody of the School of Athens* painted in Rome in 1751.[15] Through these antique-mad milords – and also as a subscriber to Charlemont's Academy for British artists in Rome – Kennedy evidently met William Chambers and Gavin Hamilton, and probably Piranesi, whose *Views of Rome* were one of the first of his many purchases which included 'ten cases of statuary' as well as the proverbial old-master paintings and prints.[16] He continued to employ Gavin Hamilton to buy works of art and books on his behalf after his return to Scotland early in 1755.[17]

Before leaving Italy in the winter of 1753 Kennedy must have heard of Lord Charlemont's plans to erect a small neo-classical pleasure pavilion on his estate in Ireland and was evidently inspired to do something similar at Culzean. His first idea was to build 'a small house betwixt the old one and the window looks to the Sea'. This, however, was promptly quashed by his overseer, Archibald Kennedy, who wrote on 11 January 1754 pointing out that his scheme was 'Impossible for from the inside of the wall towards the Sea there is Scarce two feet from the precipice ... nothing Can be built in the place you mention.'[18] Though the position initially envisaged by Sir Thomas probably had to be abandoned, that did not diminish his determination to have a banqueting room overlooking the sea.

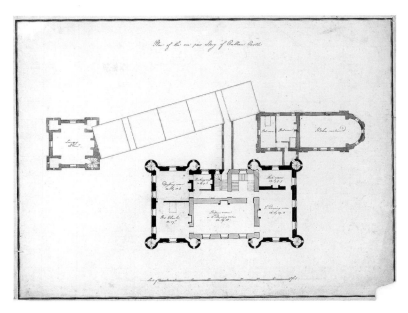

473   Plan of the first-floor of Culzean Castle showing the original L-shaped tower house in grey and Adam's additions, including the laundry tower (left) and kitchen block (right), in black, by Robert Adam, 1777 (The National Trust for Scotland)

471   William Chambers, plan and elevation of a design for a 'Casine' for Sir Thomas Kennedy of Culzean, c.1755 (W. Chambers, *Treatise on civil architecture* (1759), pl. (10))

472   William Chambers, first-floor plan of a 'Casine for Sir Thomas Kennedy Bar', near Glasgow in Scotland. The Situation commands four fine Views for which reason (I) have made the dining room open to all sides', c.1755 (Sir John Soane's Museum: Chambers drawings, 43/4/2)

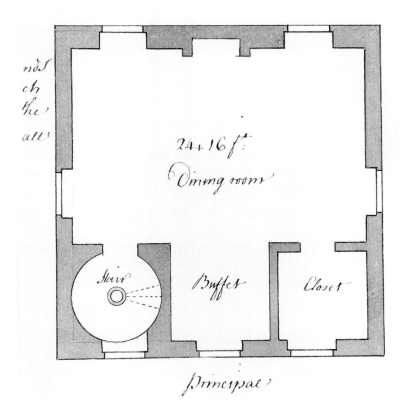

In 1755, James Adam provided him with designs for a 'Villa' (pl. 470) 54 feet (16.4 metres) in extent, with an octagonal dining-room of 30 feet (9 metres), an ante chamber and three small bedrooms in four projecting wings, and eight Venetian windows affording views in every direction.[19] Exactly where this was meant to be sited is not known, nor is there any firm evidence that it was executed. The likelihood is that Kennedy considered the scheme too decorative and expensive for his purposes and rejected it.

He then approached Chambers, Lord Charlemont's architect, who designed him a chaste Doric casino (pl. 471) which, though it had four porticos, was half the size of James Adam's fancy villa. This sophisticated design was published in Chambers's *Treatise on civil architecture* in 1759 with a dedication to Sir Thomas Kennedy who presumably paid for the plate.[20] Chambers also designed a very simple 'casine' (pl. 472), 24 feet (7.3 metres) square with windows 'commanding four fine views' unimpeded by porticos. All we have of this modest alternative are undated ground and first-floor plans of which there are versions in the Soane Museum and the National Monuments Record of Scotland.[21] The plan of the first-floor dining-room with a fireplace between two windows is virtually identical to the plan of the room at the east end of the oblique offices built by Sir Thomas in 1766 (see pl. 475). Whether Chambers's casino preceded the larger building or was an integral part of it may never be known. However, it seems quite likely, as Ian Gow has suggested, that the slant of the whole was determined not so much by the line and proximity of the precipice as by Sir Thomas's persistent demand for a clear view from his banqueting-belvedere of the terraces to the south, uninterrupted by the castle.

In 1762, Thomas Kennedy succeeded to the title of his kinsman, John, eighth Earl of Cassillis, who had died without issue three years earlier. While the sought-after title brought Kennedy Cassillis House, Maybole, Ayrshire and its estates (albeit somewhat diminished), it gave him less political influence than perhaps he had hoped for and, far worse, it loaded him with the

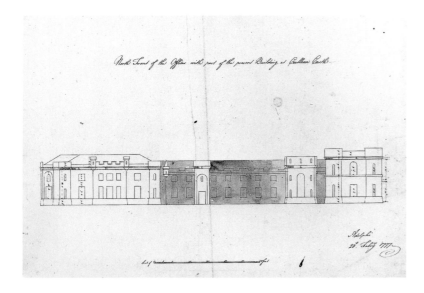

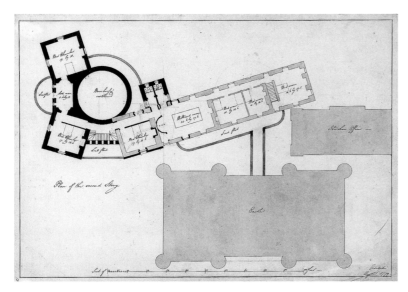

474   Design for refacing the north front of the offices including the slant-block, the laundry tower (left) and kitchen (right), by Robert Adam, 1777 (The National Trust for Scotland)

475   Plan of a circular brew-house probably incorporating the laundry tower and the first-floor of the slant-block, by Robert Adam, 1777

unwanted debts of the eighth earl. Regardless of financial pressures and ill-health which took him back to Italy in 1764 and frequently to Bath, Thomas, now ninth Earl of Cassillis, not only continued making improvements to Culzean, raising the walls of the old castle and altering the roof and top-floor bedrooms in 1766,[22] but he also bought Newark Castle, 'a little old shell of a house' in a 1,000 acre estate near Ayr which he gave to his advocate brother, David, who refurbished it and made it his principal residence.[23] These expenditures are reflected in the £30,000 debt left by Thomas at the time of his death in November 1775. The heavy liabilities inherited by David Kennedy did not prevent him from investing more than his cultivated brother had done and much more than he could afford in the aggrandizement of Culzean and, *ipso facto*, himself.[24]

Less than a year after Thomas died, David, tenth Earl of Cassillis and a representative peer of Scotland, commissioned

Robert Adam to design a new castle complex incorporating the cliff-side building as well as the old tower house (pl. 473). This decision, added to the immutable constraints imposed by the fall of the land to the west and south, left Adam hardly any room for manoeuvre and effectively determined his entire scheme. To begin with, he could only extend the L-shaped tower on its east and west sides to form a moderate-sized rectangular house 80 feet (24 metres) in extent. By making these extensions one story lower than the pre-existing core and giving them each four round turrets, he transfused the otherwise static block with a lively castle spirit and a little movement.

Paradoxically, the internal arrangement of the house was far more seriously affected by the constraints of the site than its outer shape and silhouette. Lack of space for carriages to turn prevented the principal entrance from being placed in the normal position in the centre of the long south front between the two turreted wings and left Adam no alternative but to treat the castle like a town house and keep the main front where he found it – on the short east end. One unavoidable deviation led to another: the suite of reception rooms could not be accommodated on a single floor in accordance with standard, country-house practice and had to be split between two floors in town-house fashion, with the eating-room (normally on the *piano nobile* in Scotland) on the ground-floor and the ante-room, first drawing-room and second drawing-room on the first-floor. The main staircase, rising to the second-floor bedrooms was located in the square space in the north wing of the L-shaped tower, and next to it Adam added a narrow secondary stair serving the whole tower from top to bottom. It should be noted that the north, or sea, front was deliberately reserved for staircases, dressing-rooms, powdering-rooms, a butler's pantry and waiting-room – rooms that would not be embarrassed by a view of offices and kitchen courts.[25] Whilst the ninth earl's plain 'Office House' looked out over the sea, the tenth earl's castle was forced by the walled terrace-gardens to turn its back on it.

Fire prevention often demanded the kitchen should be separated from the house. In this case, there was never any possibility of including it within the main block anyway, and the only place outside which was at all convenient to the eating-room was a small square just north of the east wing, which needed to be almost doubled in size to serve the purpose.[26] Confronted by the unavoidable asymmetry of an extension on the east front, Adam, in his inimitable way, made the most of it, turning it to advantage by erecting a long two-storey block (the same height as the ninth earl's 'Office House') ending in a large, semicircular bow, which, in its castle-style garb, looked more like a chapel than a kitchen. It was the model for Bewley,[27] the castle-style house designed for Simon Frazer, Master Lovat, later in 1777 and the castellated tea-house of 1778 at Auchencruive House, Ayreshire.[28]

Culzean as first planned was an accumulation of four separate parts: the enlarged tower house, the plain slant-block appropriately refaced in the castle style, the kitchen to the east and a square laundry tower to the west, making in all a continuous two-storey zigzag front to the sea (pl. 474).[29] Only after the enlargements to the house and the new kitchen were erected did the tedium of the proposed north front become apparent. In August 1779, Adam made a new plan, replacing the laundry tower with a bold, circular brew-house with a conical roof, surrounded by a cluster of radiating offices of various shapes and sizes (pl. 475) which literally enveloped the end of the 1760s block and were so arranged as to provide three symmetrical but different fronts.[30]

Building started on 28 February 1777 and continued until 28 February 1781 under the supervision of the master mason, Hugh Cairncross, as clerk of works.[31] Meanwhile, Adam made designs for chimney-pieces for all the principal rooms in April 1778 and for the ceilings of the eating-room, the first and second drawing-rooms and the main staircase in 1778 and 1780.[32] The ceilings of the other rooms, for which there are no known drawings, may have been plain. His final designs in March 1782 were for mirror frames: chimney-glasses for all the ground-floor rooms except the hall, pier-glasses and girandoles for the eating-room and an oval mirror for the dressing-room.[33] By summer 1782 the rectangular castle-style house was finished, furnished and ready for occupation. However, the bachelor earl continued to live at Newark Castle (where he had recently enlarged his estate) and it is doubtful that he spent more than the summer months at Culzean.[34]

It was during this first stage in the evolution of Culzean as we know it that the anonymous author of *A Tour of the Western Highlands*, visited in 1787. He found

> What rooms are finished in the castle are very elegant, and the whole upon a scale best adapted for use and enjoyment. But (he) was informed his Lordship, not content with the present extensive pile, intends adding a similar front to the sea ... At present it does great credit to Adam, the architect, and will, when complete, stand unrivalled in its way.[35]

The tenth earl first began to think of adding a new front to the sea in November 1784 when, presumably at his request, Adam drew a picturesque view of the cliff, showing the castle-like pile with an imposing three-storey rotunda in the centre, flanked by the crenellated kitchen and the billiard-room retained from slant-block (pl. 476).[36] What it was that finally made Cassillis realize at this late date that his brother's office block was the main cause of the north front not being as coherent, focused and elegant as the south front is hard to say.

The fact that it was no longer needed once the stable block was finished in 1781 may have been a contributory factor. The plans afoot for Dalquharran Castle, Dailly, Ayrshire, about ten miles south-east of Culzean and the seat of Thomas Kennedy of Dunure, who came from a junior branch of the family of the Earls of Cassillis and was married to Adam's niece, Jean, are certainly relevant. They were developed in 1782 (pl. 477) and could easily have been shown to both the earl and Hugh Cairncross (who was clerk of works there, as well as at Culzean) in November 1784 before they were finalized in the spring of 1785. Dalquharran was a symmetrical rectangular house with square angle turrets and round turrets framing the principal entrance, not unlike Culzean. What Dalquharran had, however, that Culzean lacked was a bold front on the opposite side with a large drum tower projecting from the centre. It cannot be sheer coincidence that this striking feature appeared in 1784 in Adam's picturesque design for the sea front of Culzean.[37] And it can be no accident that the greater projection of the Culzean rotunda, with six win-

dows as opposed to three at Dalquharran, closely resembles Paine's designs of 1759 for the garden front at Kedleston. The publication of this unusual plan in 1783 in the second volume of Paine's *Plans, elevations and sections, of noblemen and gentlemen's houses* must have refreshed Adam's earlier knowledge of it.[38]

Cassillis did not enter into this second building phase without long and careful deliberation. Eight months elapsed before Adam made a plan of the ground storey, dated 29 July 1785, showing the house as built, but with its stairs rearranged and the proposed additions and alterations to the north front (pl. 478).[39] It is a muddled affair, so unworthy of an architect of Adam's calibre that one can only conclude that, as in the first instance, Cassillis had once again imposed onerous conditions, probably (and understandably) restricting new building to an absolute minimum: to the drum tower replacing the ninth earl's building, and the link with the brew-house, which was to be in line with the kitchen and of the same height.

The kitchen block was to remain unaltered and detached from the house, which was only to be joined to the western half of the northern addition. By bringing the three-storey addition much closer to the house than the ninth earl's two-storey building set at a slant, the stairs constructed in 1777 would have been plunged into semi-darkness. Adam's solution was to replace his two existing staircases with a larger rectangular one lit by an ample Venetian window and to relocate the secondary stair in what was a powdering-room with nothing but borrowed light. Presumably the earlier service stair was to be retained between the second floor and the top of the tower. As the two parts of the house were effectively separated, the north side had to have a staircase of its own, rising from the ground to the first-floor of the drum tower. This awkwardly oriented, quarter-turn stair was located in a rectangular lobby that was retained in the final scheme of 1787. How the top floor was to be reached is unclear.

For Adam to have devised such a flawed plan of his own free will is inconceivable. It was clearly a compromise which he did not bother to work out fully and for which he evidently did not hold high hopes.[40] Predictably, it came to nothing, but the need to improve the sea front had been registered and was not abandoned. At last, after a lapse of two more years, the earl decided to take the plunge and 'without control, encouraged (Adam) to indulge to the utmost his romantic and fruitful genius'.[41]

A complete set of plans, sections and elevations of the north and east (sea and entrance) fronts was submitted to him in May 1787 (pls 479–82) and accepted more or less *in toto* despite the cost and inconvenience of the extensive demolition and new building involved.[42] Not only did the long cliff-side building that had been erected twenty years earlier have to be sacrificed for the drum tower, but his own house, only finished about six years ago, was to have the entire centre of its north front removed, including staircases, bedrooms, a powdering-room, two external turrets and part of the roof. Into this pivotal opening at the heart of the house Adam inserted a spectacular, top-lit, oval staircase which at one stroke pulled the whole design together and gave it the focus and diversity of form that he had been unable to provide in the first place. What had perforce been a static double-pile was now a fluid plan based on antiquity rather than conventional Palladian sources.

476 Design in perspective of the north front of Culzean Castle showing a new rotunda added to the north front of the enlarged tower house rising in the back, with the castellated kitchen block to the left and part of the slant-block and the brew-house to the right, by Robert Adam, 1784 (Sir John Soane's Museum: Adam drawings, vol. 37:9)

477 Plan and elevation of Dalquharran Castle, Dailly, Ayrshire, by Robert Adam, 1782 (Sir John Soane's Museum: Adam drawings, vol. 46:147)

478 'Plan of the ground Story of Culzean Castle The parts shaded red are the additions & alterations for the Earl of Cassilis', by Robert Adam, 1785 (Sir John Soane's Museum: Adam drawings, vol. 37:8)

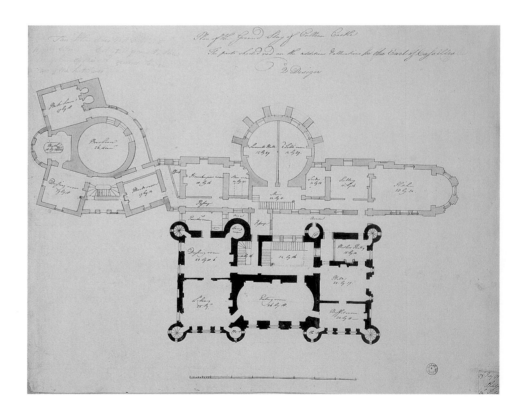

The culmination of this belated, classical enhancement of the interior of Culzean is the staircase (pl. 483) which has the look, and to some extent the function, of a Renaissance *cortile* (like the circular one at Caprarola)[43] ringed with continuous galleries on each floor: a Doric arcaded one at ground-floor level and Corinthian and Ionic colonnades above. Instead of placing the Ionic below the Corinthian, in accordance with the accepted rules for superimposed orders based on laws of solidity, Adam reversed the sequence, presumably on the basis that the richest, most delicate order was a more appropriate ornament to the

piano nobile than to the bedroom storey; the particular circumstances and the visual appearance of the whole being more important to him than rational considerations.[44] He did the same on the columnar screens fronting the staircases at Lansdowne House, Osterley and Apsley House.

The superimposed oval colonnades are the distinctive feature that sets the Culzean staircase apart from all others. They represent the consummation of an idea taken from Chambers's unexecuted design for York House (1759) (pl. 484) which Adam doubtlessly saw when it was exhibited at the Society of Artists in

479 New design for the north front, by Robert Adam, 1787 (Sir John Soane's Museum: Adam drawings, vol. 37:1)

480 Elevation of the east front showing from left to right: the principal entrance, the kitchen block, and the profile of the new rotunda, by Robert Adam, c.1787 (Sir John Soane's Museum: Adam drawings, vol. 37:2)

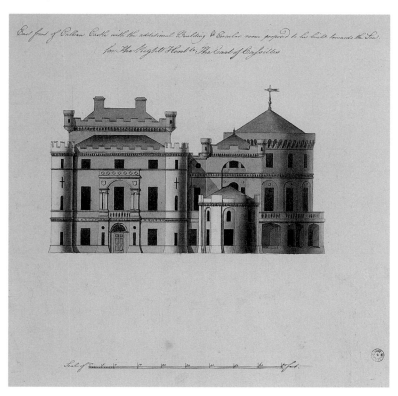

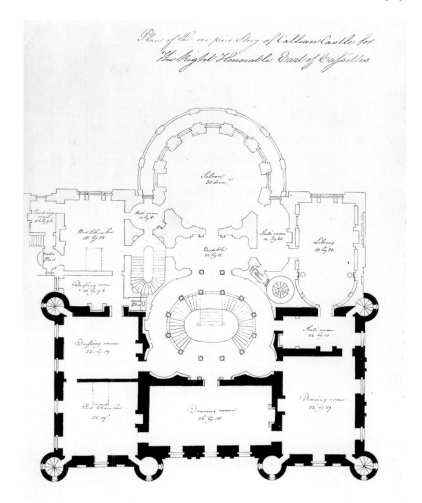

481 Plan of the first floor of Culzean Castle, by Robert Adam, 1787 (Sir John Soane's Museum: Adam drawings, vol. 37:6)

482 'Section through Culzean Castle from north to south', by Robert Adam, 1787 (Sir John Soane's Museum: Adam drawings, vol. 37:3)

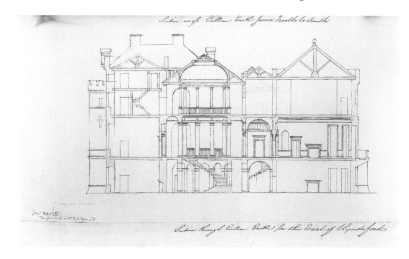

1761[45] and adapted on several occasions, the first being early in 1763 in a design for a new house at Great Saxham, Suffolk for Hutcheson Mure, nephew of William Mure, Baron of the Scots Exchequer, for whom Adam later built Caldwell House, Ayrshire (1773).[46] Though nothing came of this early scheme, the central oval staircase hall with a colonnade had evidently struck a chord and was reintroduced on the ground floor in two later sets of designs for Great Saxham made in 1779, one of which – an unusual D-shaped plan – was in fact begun and then abandoned at an early stage. At about the same date (1778), he designed an

octagonal colonnaded staircase containing an imperial stair located in the centre of a new octagonal house for John Robinson, MP at Wyke Manor, Isleworth. This remained a paper fantasy, just like his design of 1789 for an oval staircase closely modelled on Culzean's in a vast castle in Banffshire for the Earl of Findlater.[47]

Whether Adam's choice of an imperial stair for Culzean was influenced by Chambers's York House design, Paine's stair at Wardour Castle executed from 1770, or his own spectacular achievement at Home House in 1773 is a moot point. What mat-

483   View of the oval staircase with Corinthian columns on the principal floor and Ionic ones above

484   William Chambers, section of York House, Pall Mall, 1759 (RIBA, Drawings Collection). Not executed

ters is the perceptible contribution this stair makes to the dramatic effect – the *coup de théâtre* – of the whole composition. Also important, though not so immediately apparent, is the definition of a north–south axis provided by the central flight and reinforced by the screen of Corinthian columns on the *piano nobile*, marking the entrance, via an apsed vestibule, to the circular saloon. Though compromised on the south side, the direction is clear enough and in that respect is a great improvement upon the 1777 plan. The imperial stair was designed in the normal way, to serve only the *piano nobile*; there is a secondary oval stair on the north-west side which rises to the second storey and a short straight stair in the centre of the south front, leading to the top of the tower.

As at Home House, a non-axial approach to the staircase was unavoidable. However, it is more gradual here, being moderated by a large apse generous enough to contain the door from the entrance hall as well as one from the 'Old Eating Room'. A corresponding apse in the opposite corner opens to the rooms on the south-west side of the house, where the private apartments were. These doors were all part of the existing house; the only new one needed on the ground floor was on the east wall of the staircase, providing a link to the kitchen.

The staircase at Culzean ranks with the gallery and vestibule at Syon and the library at Kenwood as one of Adam's masterpieces, despite the fact that some of the details – the Corinthian capitals in particular – are not up to his standard and were almost certainly executed after his death. Of all the rooms in the castle, this was the least affected by the extensive Adam-revival additions and alterations carried out in 1877 for the third Marquess of Ailsa by the Edinburgh architects James Maitland Wardrop and Charles Reid. Early twentieth-century photographs show it filled with a clutter of arms and armour, stags horns, potted palms and a stuffed monkey climbing on a gasolier

hanging from the skylight, which though entertaining was at odds with the architecture. All this has since been removed and in 1981 the National Trust for Scotland restored Adam's balustrade and colour scheme, only to spoil it with yards and yards of harsh red carpet on the stone stairs and galleries which in the eighteenth century would have been left bare.

From the modest entrance hall (now the armoury, with an 1877 screen of columns in place of the original wall between it and the adjacent buffet-room), visitors went straight to the staircase and up to the *piano nobile*, emerging in the centre of the south side, near the entrance to the second drawing-room. Their route through the Adam rooms is undefined. It is a fair assumption, however, that it was determined by the spectacular view of the sea. On fine days, guests were bound to be drawn first to the circular saloon before taking dinner, which the Scots normally took in the afternoon; in foul weather, when visibility was nil or the temperature low, the ill-heated saloon would not have been so enticing and their visit was probably confined to the suite of reception rooms. Regardless of how this unconventional house was viewed in the past, the logical way to examine it here is to take Adam's first interiors first.

After the excitement of the staircase, the suite of two rectangular reception rooms is a sober, prosaic experience, offering no surprises, none of the variety, novelty or picturesque relief found in Adam interiors outside Scotland. Only the initiated may detect the unusual Jacobean spirit that relates the ceiling in the second drawing-room (originally the high hall of the seventeenth-century tower house) to the ceilings in the gallery at Syon and the great drawing-room at Audley End, early houses of a similar period (pls 485, 486).[48] Serlio is the common source, possibly via Wolsey's Closet at Hampton Court.[49] This was the nearest Adam came to bringing Culzean's medieval, castle-style architecture to bear on its interior decoration.

485 Design for the ceiling of the second drawing-room (later known as the Picture Room) at Culzean Castle, by Robert Adam, 1778 (Sir John Soane's Museum: Adam drawings, vol. 14:60)

486 The Great Drawing Room at Audley End, Essex, showing the ceiling designed by Robert Adam c.1763–65. The three-coloured silk damask hangings are related to those in the red drawing-room at Syon

Of all the rooms in the first Adam house, the second drawing-room was the most affected by the building of the new north front. Its chimney-piece, which was faithfully executed from Adam's design of 1778 (pl. 487),[50] was moved from the north to the east wall so as to accommodate a central doorway to the staircase; the redundant door to the old staircase (further along to the east) and its symmetrical false door (to the west) were removed altogether. Only the window wall remained untouched; all the others required repairs to the existing dado and wall covering, which was either of canvas-backed paper or damask. In the course of rehabilitation in the 1970s, a batten signed by the Edinburgh upholsterer, Charles Boyd, and dated 1795 was discovered on the north wall. It presumably marked the completion of the repairs caused by the 1787 alterations and the rehanging of the entire room by the twelfth earl (created first Marquess of Ailsa in 1831), who succeeded his father in December 1794.

Sir Thomas Kennedy's Grand Tour pictures must have been the glory of the second drawing-room and the principal reason for its being called, right from the beginning, the 'Picture Room'. Being a picture-room, one would expect it to have had a painting over the chimney-piece (possibly Batoni's portrait of Sir Thomas Kennedy);[51] hence the absence of any Adam designs for a chimney-glass. The chimney-glass now in the room was designed in 1782 for the tenth earl's dressing-room, the ground-floor room that served as an office or study off the library, with which it was later united to form the dining-room. It originally had the Kennedy swan supporters on top, but these vanished and were replaced by the present addorsed griffons which were removed from the mirror in the buffet-room when it was amalgamated with the hall in 1877.[52] Kennedy swan supporters were the unifying theme of the earl's dressing-room: they also featured in the unusual circular tablet on the chimney-piece (now lost).[53]

The 'dressing-room' referred to on Adam's design for an oval pier-glass surmounted by seated female figures was presumably the first-floor dressing-room adjoining the 'best' bedroom, where the restored mirror has recently been placed. In the 1870s, this room was made into Lady Ailsa's boudoir and became the incongruous home for Adam's displaced library chimney-piece.

Seeing that no direct link could be forged between his new circular saloon and the existing sequence of reception rooms, Adam created a special apartment for it, less formal than the parade apartment and primarily for daytime use, which included a large apsidal library leading to the ante-room to the first drawing-room. The smaller, existing library was to become a study. Though the new library might have suited the bachelor tenth earl, it was not at all what was wanted by the pleasure-loving twelfth earl and his rich wife, Margaret, second daughter of John Erskine of Dun, a man of considerable wealth with no sons to pass it on to. They were accustomed to a glamorous London life, spent in the racy circle of Queen Charlotte, William, Duke of Clarence and Mrs Jordan.

Little work was done at Culzean until after 1824 when Margaret inherited her father's fortune. Improvements were stepped up with a certain urgency in 1832 when Cassillis, created first Marquess of Ailsa the previous year, lost his eldest son and daughter-in-law and was left with twelve orphaned grandchildren to maintain in the House of Dun in the winter months and Culzean in the summer. The space which Adam proposed to

487 The chimney-piece and mirror in the second drawing-room, designed by Robert Adam 1778. The original crest of swans was replaced by the griffon crest from the mirror formerly in the Buffet Room

make into an apsidal library was fitted up as a special guest apartment called the Royal Suite and presumably intended to receive King William IV, Cassillis's friend, to whom he owed his English peerage. There was a corresponding bedroom suite on the opposite (private) side of the house for the marquess and marchioness, where the Eisenhower gallery is now.

The isolation of the saloon from the other Adam rooms had the knock-on effect of giving greater emphasis to the differences in the character of its decoration (notably the design and modelling of its stucco ceiling; pl. 488) than might have been the case had the accompanying library been executed. Some disparity between the north and south sides of the house was inevitable given the gap of ten years between them, but the apparent inequality in the standard of workmanship must stem from the fact that the room was not finished until after both Adam and his patron were dead, possibly as late as the 1830s. The friezes over the doors, for example, were evidently left undone and have been painted by the National Trust for Scotland in *trompe-l'oeil* to match the wall frieze which, though more crowded and fussy than usual, is comparable to the frieze in the dining-room (now the music-room) at Mellerstain.[54] The original carpet has also been copied, but there is no evidence that it was designed by Adam, despite claims to the contrary. It was probably made for the room by the first Marquess of Ailsa, as was the chimney-

490 Initial design for the ceiling of the eating-room, by Robert Adam, 1779 (Sir John Soane's Museum: Adam drawings, vol. 14:62). A simplified version of this was executed

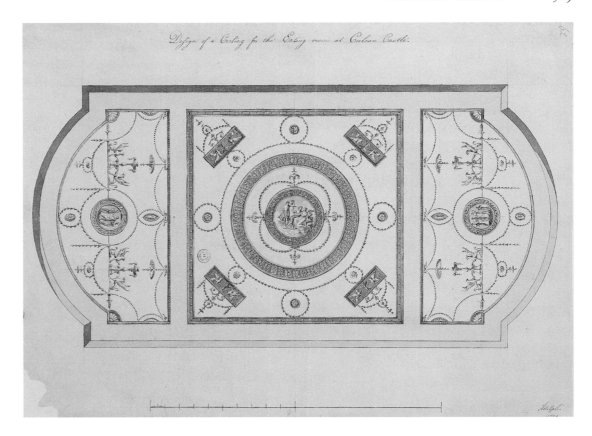

piece. Even allowing for provincial workmanship, both are too coarse for Adam (pl. 489).[55]

In any case, decorative details are of minor importance here. The excitement of the saloon arises from the circular space as a whole and its spectacular panoramic view. The key to the arrangement of the various wall elements is the twelve alternating pedestals and sphinxes – like a clock-face – in the central band of the ceiling. Seven of these – from 9 o'clock to 3 o'clock – point to the chimney-piece and the six full-length windows; the remaining five are aligned on two niches and three doors. Having french windows opening on to a balcony makes the room literally a belvedere for use in daylight and in mild weather, there being only one fireplace here, as opposed to two in the constantly used steward's room below.[56]

In Scotland – as in England – the dining-room normally formed part of the principal suite of reception rooms or state apartment located on the *piano nobile*.[57] Culzean was exceptional in having its dining-room on the ground floor – townhouse fashion – under the second drawing-room rather than adjacent to it. What motivated this break with convention, no one knows. Most likely it was a matter of making the best use of one of the finest and largest spaces in the house before the rotunda was built; a more informal room, like a library, would have been inappropriate in this situation. As a result, the sexes were separated after dinner on two floors: the men had the dining-room, library and dressing-room to themselves on the ground floor; the ladies withdrew to the drawing-rooms upstairs. In Adam's first house, the dining-room was the showplace of the tenth earl's discriminating taste in architecture, just as the second drawing-room was the show-place of his brother's pictures. Its two apsidal ends made it the only room with any modelling; its ceiling, incorporating three painted roundels attributed to Zucchi, was the most elaborate and no doubt the most expensive in the house (pl. 490); and it boasted more fur-

491 Design for the eating-room pier-glass, by Robert Adam, 1782 (Sir John Soane's Museum: Adam drawings, vol. 20:228)

492 Design for the girandoles for the eating-room, by Robert Adam, 1782 (Sir John Soane's Museum: Adam drawings, vol. 20:236)

493 Design for the glass frame over the chimney-piece in the Buffet Room, by Robert Adam, 1782 (Sir John Soane's Museum: Adam drawings, vol. 20:231)

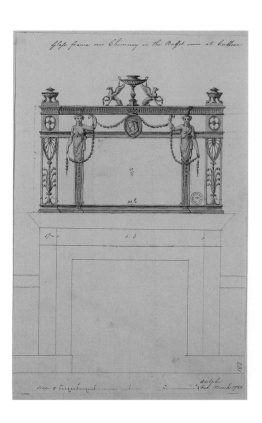

niture designed by Adam than any other room: a pair of pier-glasses (pl. 491) and girandoles (pl. 492), both with painted roundels.[58] Though its pier-tables and curtain-cornices enriched with baskets of fruit echoing those on the pier-glasses are said to be by Adam, there are no known designs for them.[59] Nor are there any designs for a chimney-glass. The one now in the room was brought from the adjacent library when it was converted to a dining-room in 1877 and this room, in turn, became the library. Presumably the original eating-room had a

painting over the chimney-piece flanked by the two girandoles which are now in the apses. The asymmetry of the current arrangement of the apses (accentuated by the centralized girandoles) is uncharacteristic of Adam (pl. 494), who would either have maintained the integrity of the curved walls with jibs (in which case the present doors must date from the nineteenth century), or, if he had proper doors, would have balanced them with false ones, as he did on the north wall, or at least with vertical panels of stucco arabesques.

494 View of the west end of the eating-room

495 View of the library (later the dining-room) looking south. The window wall is the only wall to retain its original Adam decorations

496 Two bookcases from the library, now installed in the entrance hall

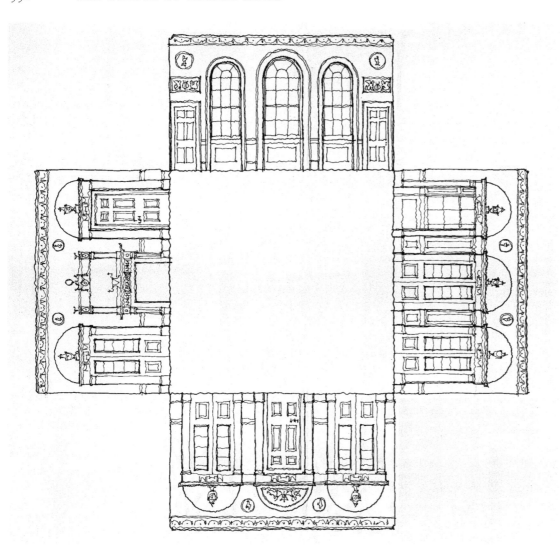

497 A conjectural reconstruction of the library at Culzean by Ian Gow, drawn by Ptolemy Dean

The principal entrance to the eating-room was from the staircase rather than the buffet-room to the east. Although the buffet-room was quite small, it was evidently a show-place of sufficient importance to warrant a Doric chimney-piece with the head of Bacchus in its tablet and a fashionable gilt chimney-glass enriched with draped female terms, a medallion surmounted by an earl's coronet and a crest of winged griffons (pl. 493).[60] However, its precise function in relation to the eating-room is unclear: was it an informal dining- or breakfast-room, or an ante-room where china and plate were laid-out? It is unlikely to have been on the route from the kitchen to the principal eating-room, which went behind the arcade on one side of the main staircase.

On the west side of the house was the tenth earl's library (pl. 495) and dressing-room or study, which were thrown together by Wardrop and Reid in 1877 to form a grand dining-room for the third Marquess of Ailsa. The only original Adam decorations remaining in what was once the library are the buchranium frieze and the stucco medallions and tablets on the south wall. Two complete bookcases were rescued and re-erected in the third Marquess of Ailsa's 'Ship-building Room', now part of the entrance hall (pl. 496). They have unusual hinged pilasters which open to narrow spaces convenient for the storage of large maps and drawings. The same idea was proposed in 1790 for the bookcases in the circular library at Dahquaharran.[61] The chimney-piece, as previously noted, is now in the best bedroom and its mirror is in the old eating-room. All the rest is Adam-revival

of about 1880: reproducing some of what was already there, and adding a new chimney-piece and consoled doorcases cleverly copied from the old eating-room and a papier-mâché ceiling copied from the apsidal music-room at 20 St James's Square as published in Adam's *Works*, with its semicircular ends turned inwards to suit the rectangular shape of the ceiling.[62] A great deal of careful thought went into the creation of this new Adam-style room; sadly this was not the case in 1975 when the National Trust for Scotland, in an effort to be authentic, repainted the Victorian dining-room in the putative eighteenth-century colour scheme of Adam's library. There is clearly a close relationship between Wardrop and Reid's dining-room at Culzean, described by Ian Gow as one of the very first Adam-revival rooms in a real Adam house, and their extensive Adam-revival work of about the same date for the seventh Earl and Countess of Aberdeen at Haddo Hall, Aberdeenshire, a William Adam house. It is tempting to think that Wright and Mansfield, who were responsible for the high quality, Adam-style furniture and decoration at Haddo, were involved here as well.[63]

A plausible, albeit tentative, reconstruction of the original library can be made by collating the several decorative elements preserved in the house with Adam's plans and James Donaldson's survey of 1818 (pl. 497).[64] The south wall remains unchanged: with three arched windows flanked by doors to the round turrets, stucco tablets of classical subjects and medallions in the upper register. Its fenestration seems to have provided the pattern of articulation for the rest of the room (except the chimney-piece) with shallow arched recesses containing doors to the dressing-room and eating-room on the north and east walls respectively, a window on the west wall, and five bookcases. On the west wall were the two surviving cases in the entrance hall which were constructed as one piece and used to fill the space of a blocked window that would have made that wall asymmetrical in relation to the chimney side. Also in the entrance hall are three arches (the central one containing a semi-circular tablet) which are thought to have come from the north wall. The remaining semi-circular recesses over the bookcases and the door to the eating-room probably contained plaster versions of classical vases some of which have survived. The chimney-piece, as previously noted, was the only element that was neither arched nor recessed. As for the ceiling of this comprehensive scheme of wall decoration, there is nothing to suggest that was anything but plain. The ornamental ceilings that were *de rigueur* in Adam's English interiors did not accord with Scottish taste and economy.

Culzean's early interiors were lavish by Scottish standards and the demolition of the core of the six-year-old house to build the north front was by any standards sheer extravagance. If this was the whim of a self-indulgent bachelor, it was a whim with a purpose – to establish his right 'to the honour and dignity of Earl of Cassillis', which was under dispute from 1759 to 1762 and finally judged in his brother Thomas's favour.[65] Ancestral considerations led him to preserve Sir Thomas's utilitarian 'Office House' at the expense of his own castle. Without that impediment, Culzean would have been quite different, perhaps like Bewley or The Oaks in Surrey, better integrated and more economical.

In February 1790 the beleaguered tenth earl, crippled by illness and debts of over £60,000, entailed the estate of Cassilis and Culzean on a distant cousin in America, Captain Archibald Kennedy, and made a will placing the management of all his properties (except for Culzean) in the hands of trustees. A month later, he wrote to his banker in Ayr, John Balantyne, 'I am really wearied of Building and wish to be at rest'.[66]

ABBREVIATIONS

BL	British Library, London
BM MS	British Museum Manuscripts, British Library, London
LMA	London Metropolitan Archives, London
NLI	National Library of Ireland, Dublin
NLW	National Library of Wales, Aberystwyth
NH	Newby Hall Architectural Drawings, MS catalogue by J. Low
NMRS	National Monuments Record of Scotland, Edinburgh
PRO	Public Record Office, Kew
RIBA	Royal Institute of British Architects, London
SM	Sir John Soane's Museum, London
SRO	Scottish Record Office, Edinburgh
V&A	Victoria and Albert Museum, London
WYAS	West Yorkshire Archive Services, Leeds
—— HAR	Harewood Papers
—— NH	Newby Hall Papers
—— NP	Nostell Papers
—— VR	Vyner Papers

NOTES

INTRODUCTION

1. Robert to Nelly Adam, 12 July 1755, J. Fleming, *Robert Adam and his circle*, London, 1962, pp. 351–2. Henceforth referred to as Fleming.
2. Robert to James Adam, 18 June 1755, ibid., pp. 168–9.
3. Ibid., p. 165.
4. Ibid., p. 168.
5. Ibid., p. 354.
6. Ibid., p. 167.
7. E. Harris and N. Savage, *British architectural books and writers, 1560–1780*, Cambridge, 1990, pp. 72–6.
8. Fleming, p. 217.
9. Ibid., pp. 228, 251, 362. He evidently began his collection shortly after he arrived in Rome.
10. Ibid., p. 247.
11. Robert Adam to his mother, Rome, November 1756, Clerk of Penicuik MSS, SRO, Edinburgh, quoted by Fleming, p. 363. Harris and Savage, op. cit. at note 7 above, p. 71.
12. Robert Adam to his sister Nelly, Rome, July 1755. Fleming, p. 352.
13. A. A. Tait, *Robert Adam drawings and imagination*, Cambridge 1993, pp. 88–9.
14. E. Croft Murray, *Decorative painting in England 1537–1837*, London, 1970, II, pp. 296–300.
15. Tait, op. cit. at note 13 above, pp. 94, 97, 98, 100. D. Stillman, *The decorative work of Robert Adam*, London, 1966, pp. 42–3. Henceforth referred to as Stillman.
16. P. Meadows, *Joseph Bonomi Architect*, RIBA, London, 1988, p. 4.
17. Fleming, p. 369.
18. G. Richardson, *Book of ceilings*, London, 1776, preface.
19. Robert Adam to the Earl of Coventry, 3 April 1764. Croome Archives.
20. A. T. Bolton, *The works of Robert and James Adam*, London, 1922, II, p. 345. Henceforth referred to as Bolton.
21. Ibid., II, p. 346 and appendix D. See also A. Rowan, *Robert Adam, Catalogues of architectural drawings in the V&A*, London, 1988, p. 19.
22. Fleming, p. 249.
23. His designs for remodeling the interior of Castle Ashby for Charles Compton, seventh Earl of Northampton, whom he met in Padua in 1755, were not executed and may not have been formally commissioned, though Compton had promised him 'his employment' four years earlier. Fleming, p. 260; Stillman, p. 62, pl. 9.
24. He also designed a monument for General Wolfe but this commission went to Joseph Wilton instead. See Harris and Savage, op. cit. at note 7 above, p. 91, n. 91.
25. Robert Adam to Lord Scarsdale, 15 June 1763, Kedleston Archives.
26. Robert Clerk to the Earl of Shelburne, 1 November 1765; quoted Bolton, II, p. 5.
27. R. and J. Adam, *The works in architecture of Robert and James Adam*, London, 1778, I, p. 3. Henceforth referred to as Adam, *Works*.
28. D. Watkin, *Sir John Soane, Enlightenment though and the Royal Academy lectures*, Cambridge 1996, p. 642.
29. Adam, *Works*, I, i, p. 4.
30. Fleming, pp. 258–60. I. Bristow, *Architectural colour in British interiors 1615–1840*, London, 1996, p. 79. On the subject of grotesque ornament see F. Piel, *Die ornament-grotteske in der italischer Renaissance*, Berlin, 1962 and N. Dacos, *La découverte de la Domus Aurea et la formation des grotesques à la Renaissance*, London–Leiden, 1971.
31. Robert to James Adam 1762, 'Antique ceilings at Windsor are not in the Castle as you imagine it is a drawing of them at Eton college which is exceedingly fine', SRO GD 18/ 4952. 'Acct Book of Thomas Butler, Steward' to the Duke of Northumberland at Syon, 5 July 1765, 'Paid for post chaises for Mr. Cipriani and myself going to Eaton to examine the Antique paintings there . . .'. Alnwick archives, U I/41.
32. Robert to James Adam, 8 February 1760 (i.e. 1761), asking if he 'picked up any sketches of any painted cielings (*sic*) at Herculaneum or had any ancient painting copied by Zucchi. I should think this is usefull as any thing work as he could be employed about, as we are much at a loss for their colouring and much we shall want of it about a palace and other places as ye see that taste must come in and will be a good hunch for two or three clever heads.' SRO GD 18/ 4926.
33. C. Hussey, *Mid Georgian 1760–1800*, London, 1956, pp. 12–13.
34. April 1756, Fleming, p. 160.
35. Adam, *Works*, I. The concept was expressed ten years earlier, in 1762, by James in an unfinished draft of an essay on architectural theory and was almost certainly the result of discussions with Robert in 1758. The essay, dated 27 November 1762, was published by Fleming, pp. 315–16.
36. Fleming, p. 315.
37. Adam, *Works*, I, i, p. 9.
38. Letter from James Adam to the Earl of Shelburne, 6 November 1765, Bolton, II, p. 11.
39. Adam, *Works*, I, i, p. 10.
40. R. Adam, *The ruins of the palace of Diocletian at Spalatro*, London, 1764, p. 9. *Works*, I, i, p. 10.
41. Adam, *Works*, I, i, p. 10.
42. H. Home, Lord Kames, *Elements of Criticism*, London, 1762, III, p. 341–2 and ch. XVIII. Adam's appreciation of climax in planning is noted by R. Middleton in his essay on *The ruins of the palace of the Emperor Diocletian at Spalatro* in the catalogue of *The Mark Millard Architectural Collection. British Books*, National Gallery, Washington, 1998, p. 6. Other elements of picturesque planning are discussed by Middleton in 'Soane's Space and the Matter of Fragmentation', *John Soane Architect*, London, 1999, p. 32.
43. Robert Adam to his mother, 13 November 1756. Clerk of Penicuik MSS., SRO, Edinburgh, quoted by Fleming, p. 363.
44. Adam, *Works*, I, v.
45. Adam, *Works*, I, i, p. 11.
46. There is a design of *c*.1747 by Daniel Garrett for a library–gallery at Kirtlington Park, Oxon.
47. B. FitzGerald, ed., *The correspondence of Emily, Duchess of Leinster*, 1957, III, p. 2.
48. J. Plumptre, *James Plumptre's Britain, the journal of a tourist in the 1790s*, London, 1992, p. 103.
49. J. Cornforth, 'Saltram, Devon – III', *Country Life*, 11 May 1967, pp. 1161–2.
50. L. Simond, *Journal of a tour and residence in Great Britain during the year 1810 and 1811*, Edinburgh, 1817, II, p. 285.
51. R. Blunt, ed., *Mrs Montagu 'Queen of the Blues'*, London, 1923, I, pp. 152–3. See K. Bristol, 'The Painted Rooms of 'Athenian' Stuart', *The Georgian Group Journal*, London, 2000, X, pp. 168–9 and n. 35.
52. Adam, *Works*, II, i.
53. Fleming, p. 319.
54. A list of his rare repeats is given by Stillman, p. 27.
55. J. Adam, 'Journal of a Tour in Italy. By Robert (i.e. James) Adam, Esq.', *Library of the fine arts*, London, October 1831, II, no. 9, p. 173.
56. SM 22: 227, 228., H. Walpole, *A description of the villa of Mr Horace Walpole, . . . at Strawberry Hill near Twickenham*, Strawberry Hill, 1784, p. 53.
57. C. O'Neill, 'In search of Bossi', Irish architectural and decorative studies, I, *Journal of the Irish Georgian Society*, I, 1998, p. 152.
58. SM 23:13, the ivy swags and fluted Ionic column are drawn in pencil and not coloured. The central tablet and side blocks are shown by Adam as green which was one of the encaustic colours patented by Wedgwood in 1769, A. Kelley, *Decorative Wedgwood*, London, 1965, p. 35.
59. Adam, *Works*, II, i, preface.
60. K. Bristol, loc.cit. at note 51 above, pp. 170–1. Bristol makes the sweeping assumption that Stuart's painted tea-room in the 'park' building at Wimpole Hall, Cambs. was the earliest example of Etruscan-style decoration, predating Adam's work at Derby House (1773) and Wyatt's in the island temple at Fawley Court, Bucks., which I was mistaken in dating 1771 (E. Harris and J. M. Robinson, 'New Light on Wyatt at Fawley', *Architectural History*, London, 1984, XXVII, p. 264). It is somewhat later, as convincingly demonstrated by D. Stillman, *English neo-classical architecture*, London, 1988, pp. 319, 572

n. 145. See my chapter here on Derby House, note 50. The precise date of the Wimpole 'park' building is uncertain; though contemplated in 1766, it seems unlikely to have been completed before c.1775 at the earliest; see D. Adshead, 'A Modern Italian Loggia at Wimpole Hall', *The Georgian Group Journal*, London, 2000, X, pp. 150, 152 and n. 8. We know absolutely nothing about Stuart's tea-room apart from an 1800 description of it as 'a rare specimen of painting; of Etruscan figures in Colours'. The indiscriminate use of the term 'Etruscan' to describe Raphael grotesques as well as Greek vases is well noted by J. Wilton-Ely, 'Pompeian and Etruscan Tastes in the Neo-Classical Country-House', in G. Jackson-Stops, ed., *The fashioning and functioning of the British Country House*, Washington, 1989, p. 60.

61. E. Meteyard, *The life of Josiah Wedgwood*, London, 1866, I, p. 132; R. Reilly, *Wedgwood*, London, 1989, I, pp. 409, 715 n. 18; A. Kelley, op. cit. at note 58 above, p. 36.

62. J. Wedgwood, *A catalogue of cameos, intaglios, medals, and bas-reliefs; with a general account of Vases and other ornaments after the antique, made by Wedgwood and Bentley and sold at their rooms in Great Newport Street*, London, 1773, p. 17.

63. H. Walpole to W. Mason, 16 July 1778, *The correspondence of Horace Walpole*, ed. W. S. Lewis, New Haven, XXVIII, p. 414. (Henceforth Walpole, *Correspondence*.)

64. Stillman, p. 76, pl. 47 was the first to note the similarity between the Etruscan wall-decorations at Osterley and engraved designs in Piranesi's *Diverse maniere*. See also J. Wilton-Ely, loc.cit. at note 60 above, p. 61; and 'Antiquity for the Designer: the British Neoclassical Interior', *Rassegna*, 55, Bologna, September 1993, p. 22.

65. J. Wedgwood to T. Bentley, 31 March 1768; quoted Meteyard, op. cit. at note 61 above, I, p. 212. Two months later, Bentley was complaining about Voyers's work. Voyers was also employed by Chambers c.1762 to make the wax model of his state coach. J. T. Smith, *Nollekens and his times*, London, 1949, p. 12.

66. Letter from Wedgwood to Bentley, 30 August 1772; quoted in Reilly, op. cit. at note 61 above, I, p. 578.

67. Wedgwood to Bentley, 7 September 1771. *Letters of Josiah Wedgwood*, Manchester, 1973, II, p. 40.

68. Cumberland dining-room, SM 17:57, 118, 119; 49:23; Byram ceiling, SM 14:93.

69. Subjects which have been painstakingly analysed by I. Bristow, op. cit. at note 30 above.

70. Letter from Robert Adam to Sir Edward Knatchbull, 10 February 1772, regarding Mersham-le-Hatch. Kent Record Office, U 951 A. 18.

71. I. Bristow, op. cit. at note 30 above, I, pp. 91ff.

72. Adam, *Works*, I, iii, p. 4.

73. Adam, *Works*, II, i, preface.

74. J. Summerson, *Georgian London*, London, 1962, p. 143.

75. Many other permutations of paint colours on walls are cited and codified by Ian Bristow, *op. cit.* at note 30 above.

76. Document cited at note 70 above. The design for the ceiling at the Soane Museum, SM 11:182, is dated 1766. Either this date is incorrect, or there was an intermediary design about which nothing is known. The ceiling was executed in 1772 in accordance with the Soane design.

77. Bristow, op. cit. at note 30 above, I, p. 151.

78. Lady Shelburne's diary, 22 August 1768, Bowood Archives; quoted Bolton II, p. 8.

79. Lady Knatchbull to Robert Adam, 17 November 1774, National Art Library, V&A, 86QQ, box I(a)-XX.

80. C. Gilbert, 'New Light on the Furnishing of Nostell Priory', *Furniture History*, XXVI, 1990, pp. 58–60. Sefferin Nelson executed Adam's designs for curtain cornices and four pedestals and vases for Paine's rococo dining-room, but no

work in Adam's rooms.

81. C. Gilbert, *The life and work of Thomas Chippendale*, London, 1978, I, p. 97. (Henceforth Gilbert.)

82. He is unlikely to have had access to Stuart's designs of c.1758–9 for Georgiana (later Countess) Spencer's closet at Wimbledon House, Surrey, which included a neo-classical sofa and bookcase-cabinet, RIBA Drawings Collection, reproduced by Bristol, loc. cit. at note 51 above, p. 165. Bristol's suggestion (p. 166) that Adam, unlike Stuart, did not 'design and provide everything from furniture to chimneypieces . . . until the early 1770s and then only for extraordinary clients . . .' is unwarranted, viz. Kedleston and Croome Court both 1760.

83. J. Peacock (pseudo J. MacPacke), *Oikida, or Nutshells*, London, 1785, p. 80.

84. Letter from Chippendale to Edwin Knatchbull, 23 June 1778. Gilbert, I, p. 226.

85. Summerson, op. cit. at note 73 above, p. 143.

86. George Baillie to Robert Adam, quoted in M. H. B. Sanderson, *Robert Adam and Scotland*, Edinburgh, 1992, p. 85, n. 2.

87. There are designs for tables and mirrors for the Earl of Findlater at Cullen, Banffshire, 1781; mirrors for the Earl of Kinnoull at Dupplin House, Perth., 1768–9; a chair for Lord Chief Baron Orde at 8 Queen Street, Edinburgh; and mirrors for John Adam's house in Edinburgh, 1771. How many of these designs were executed is not known.

88. Adam, *Works*, I, i, preface.

89. J. Farington, *The diary of Joseph Farington*, ed. Kenneth Garlick and Angus Macintyre, New Haven and London, 1979, VI, p. 2214.

90. R. Shanhagan, *The Exhibition or a second anticipation*, London, 1779, p. 8.

91. Ibid., pp. 10, 11, 92.

92. J. Soane, *An appeal to the public occasioned by the suspension of the architectural lectures in the Royal Academy*, (printed, not published), London, 1812, p. 24n.

93. Walpole to H. Mann, 17 April 1775, *Correspondence*, XXIV, p. 93.

94. W. Chambers, *Treatise on the decorative part of civil architecture*, London, 1791, p. 132.

95. J. Soane, *Lectures*, ed. D. Watkin, op. cit. at note 28 above, p. 642.

96. Ibid., p. 650.

97. Soane, op. cit. at note 90 above, p. 30n.

98. R. Middleton, loc. cit. at note 42 above, p. 30.

99. R. Stuart, *Dictionary of architecture*, London, 1832, I , n.p.

100. A. Cunningham, 'Lives of the Most Eminent British Architects', *Library of fine arts*, London (March 1831); W. H. Leeds, *Biographical dictionary of the Society for the Diffusion of Useful Knowledge*, London, 1862, p. 292. For a summary of nineteenth-century opinions, see J. Swarbrick, *The life, work and influence of Robert Adam and his brothers. Being the AA prize essay for 1903*, London, 1903, pp. 19–20.

101. J. Gwilt, *Encyclopedia of architecture*, London, 1842, p. 226.

102. 'The Art-Journal Catalogue of the International Exhibition; Part I', *The Art-Journal*, London, 1862, p. 12.

103. *The decorative work of Robert and James Adam*, ed. Batsford, London, 1901.

I. KEDLESTON HALL, DERBYSHIRE

1. Robert Adam to James Adam, 11 December 1758. SRO Clerk MS 4854.

2. The Curzons were a Tory family with extensive coal-mining estates in Derbyshire. According to a report sent by a Jacobite to the King of France in 1743, Sir Nathaniel's father had 'a yearly income of £12,000 p.a. and 10,000 miners in his employ'. His wealth was further increased by the large fortune left to him in 1749 by his brother, William. This accumulated fortune was inherited

by Sir Nathaniel after his father's death on 18 November 1758. R. Sedgwick, *The House of Commons 1715-1754*, London, 1970, I, p. 599.

3. Document cited at note 1 above.

4. Among Adam's drawings at the Soane is a rapid sketch of details in Stuart's abortive Kedleston scheme: SM 54, i:59.

5. Stuart's designs for a room 15 metres (50 feet) long are at Kedleston and are published in L. Harris, *Robert Adam and Kedleston*, exh. cat., The National Trust, London (1987), nos. 11–14.

6. L. Harris, 'The Picture Collection at Kedleston Hall', *Connoisseur*, (July 1978), pp. 208–17; F. Russell, 'Securing the Future', *Country Life*, CLXXXI (23 July 1987), pp. 96–9; J. Kenworthy-Browne, 'Designing around the Statues. Matthew Brettingham's Casts at Kedleston', *Apollo*, ns 137 (April, 1993), pp. 248–52. One of the designs for an entrance hall is unconvincingly attributed to Gibbs, c.1726, L. Harris, op. cit. at note 5 above, no. 3.

7. *Architectural drawings from Lowther Castle*, ed. H. Colvin, J. Mordaunt Crook, T. Friedman, Architectural History Monographs: no. 2, Society of Architectural Historians of Great Britain, 1980, nos. 39–73.

8. The precise date of this change-over has not been determined. A payment of £200 was made to Paine in January 1760 for work done in 1759 on the north-west pavilion. Kedleston Archive.

9. R. Castell, *Villas of the ancients*, London (1728), vignette of elevation, plan.

10. J. Paine, *Plans, elevations and sections, of noblemen and gentlemen's houses*, pt. II, London (1783), p. 14, pls 42–52. The north elevation with two alternative porticos on flaps is at Kedleston; see L. Harris, op. cit. at note 5 above, no. 6. Harris states (p. 23) that the idea of the projecting rotunda almost certainly came from Curzon himself.

11. C. Webster, 'Architectural Illustration as Revenge: James Paine's designs for Kedleston', *The image of the building. Papers from the annual symposium of the Society of Architectural Historians of Great Britain. 1995*, ed. M. Howard, London, 1996, pp. 83–92. This was refuted by P. Leach, 'James Paine's Design for the South Front of Kedleston Hall: Dating and Sources', *Architectural History*, XL, London, 1997, pp. 159–70; and by E. Harris, 'Don't Wag the Dog: a Brief Defence of the Status Quo of James Paine's Designs for Kedleston', *Architectural History*, XLII, 1999, pp. 344–8.

12. Adam's plan can be fairly precisely dated by a letter of 10 May 1760 to Curzon regarding a door on the east wall of the music-room 'which had been drawn by mistake in the first copy of your plans & overlooked in the clean Design Though I had marked it with pencil lines to be shut up'. Kedleston Archive. The plan at the Soane, SM 40:6, has the door hatched in pencil and is evidently the 'first copy'.

13. Paine received his last payment of £300 on 3 June 1761. In response to questions about his final account, he wrote to Lord Scarsdale on 1 March 1762, 'I beg leave to assure your Lordship, that whatever petty light Mr Wyatt may see in, I have no such views, nor any but to behave with that becoming Respect, & Duty that is required from me to you.' His final account was settled in February 1763. Kedleston Archive.

14. Kedleston Archive.

15. *A catalogue of the pictures, sculptures, models, drawings, prints, &c. exhibited by the Society of Artists of Great Britain . . . May the 9th, 1761*, no. 206.

16. Robert to James Adam, 24 July 1760, SRO GD 18/4866.

17. Document cited at note 16 above. His coloured wall elevations and ceiling design were sent to Kedleston in August 1760 and are still there. L. Harris, op. cit. at note 5 above, no. 37–9.

18. B. de Montfaucon, *Supplement au livre de*

l'antiquité expliquée, Paris (1724), III, pl. XLI of which there is a copy at Kedleston. The design at the Soane, SM 11:44, dated 1760 is closer to the engraved model than the simplified coloured design at Kedleston is. See L. Harris, op. cit. at note 5 above, no. 37.
Catalogue of the pictures, statues, etc. with some account of the architecture at Kedleston, privately printed, (1769). This catalogue was updated in 1770, 1778, and 1796.

19. Robinson's bills for the table frames are dated 7 December 1761, 22 March 1762 and 10 May 1762. There is a small Adam sketch, SM 54, i:93 (see pl. 23), for a table with similar legs but a different frieze and notes concerning Kedleston on the verso dated May 1763. His bill for the stools is dated 22 Feb. 1762. For Adam's sketch from Stuart's design, see SM 54, i:59. The stools appear in Adam's sketch of the window wall, SM 54, i:48, and his finished elevation at Kedleston; see J. Hardy, 'Robert Adam and the furnishing of Kedleston Hall', *Connoisseur*, CXCVIII, July 1978, pp. 200–1, figs. 5, 6.

20. L. Harris, op. cit. at note 5 above, p. 14.

21. Receipt for £450 from John Snetzler, 5 February 1759. Kedleston Archive, KL 7/1. Preparations were made for its temporary accommodation in Scarsdale's town house in June 1758 and in December 1758 it was boarded up by Jason Harris. L. Harris, op. cit. at note 5 above, p. 28. A. Barnes, 'The eighteenth-century chamber organ in Kedleston Hall, Derbyshire', Warwickshire, 1990.

22. Elevation of the west side of the music-room dated 1760 at Kedleston, L. Harris. op. cit. at note 5 above, no. 21; SM 40:17 undated. Mentioned in Robert's letter to James Adam, 24 July 1760, document cited at note 16 above. Sir Watkin Williams-Wynn had a similar but considerably smaller organ 4.2 × 3 × 1.3 metres (14 × 10 × 4½ feet) in a larger room, 12.1 × 7.7 metres (40 × 25½ feet), at 20 St James's Square.

23. Adam to Curzon, 10 May 1760, explaining that it 'would pinch (the west) End of the Music room to put a Closet in it for Musical Books' and that it was also necessary to avoid 'thinning the wall opposite to a Niche in the Hall'. Kedleston Archive.

24. Curzon to Bute, cited by F. Russell, *John 3rd Earl of Bute (1713–1792): Patron and Collector*, London (forthcoming). Curzon's undated, alphabetically arranged notebook in the Kedleston Archive, under G, 'Gallery in chappell in the South East Pavillion contains the great organ'; under M, Music Room, 'the organ may be put in this room'.

25. Snetzler bought the organ back for £300 on 4 March 1766. It is thought to have been sold on to the Pantheon in Oxford Street. Adam's c.1764–5 plan, showing the organ gallery, was presumably given to Woolfe to engrave for *Vitruvius Britannicus* prior to the sale of the organ.

26. SM 25:2, 3; Kedleston drawing see L. Harris, op. cit. at note 5 above, no. 22. Adam to Scarsdale, 14 July 1762. Kedleston Archive.

27. In 1765 the misattributed Rembrandt was hung over the organ where, as Samuel Wyatt predicted, Scarsdale found it too high. Wyatt to Scarsdale, 29 May 1765, Kedleston Archive. It was replaced by Viviano's *Temple of Flora*; see 1769 *Catalogue*, op. cit. at note 18 above.

28. The craftsmen involved were James Gravenor, Mr Gamble, William Johnson and Thomas Bedson, whose bills are at Kedleston. S. Wyatt to Scarsdale, 23 December 1765, informing him that the case was fixed on to the organ. Information regarding missing ornaments supplied by Dominic Gwynn, one of the restorers of the organ. Lack of funds does not seem to have had anything to do with the outcome as I previously suggested, E. Harris, *The Williams Wynn Chamber Organ*, Phillips Sale Cat., London, 21

April 1995, p. 31.

29. R. Adam to Curzon, 27 August 1760, Kedleston Archive. Ceiling design at Kedleston dated 1760; unfinished design at the Soane, SM 11:57, dated 1761.

30. P. S. Bartoli, *Admiranda Romanarum antiquitatum*, Rome, 1693, pl. 60. The subject and source of the tablet are given in Curzon's notebook. Document cited at note 24 above.

31. L. Harris, op. cit. at note 5 above, p. 38.

32. J. Hardy and H. Hayward,' Kedleston Hall, Derbyshire – III', *Country Life*, 9 February 1978, pp. 322–33.

33. These features are attributed to Paine by N. Antram and G. Jackson-Stops, *Kedleston Hall*, National Trust Guidebook, 1998, p. 23. An alabaster cornice was being pieced and cramped by Joseph Hall on 14 May 1760, Kedleston Archive, K C/3.

34. Chimney-piece, SM 22:15 dated 1760; SM 22:18 inscribed *Chimney Piece for Kedleston* and dated 1760 has an open pediment but is otherwise quite close to the 1777 chimney-pieces designs for Harewood, SM 22:203, 204.

35. The finished coloured design for the ceiling that was sent to Curzon and is still at Kedleston is dated 1759; the uncoloured office copy at the Soane, SM 11:43, is dated 1760. In a letter to Curzon dated 27 August 1760, Adam said that he had sent a copy of his design for the drawing-room ceiling to Rose to estimate. The Hatchlands ceiling design, SM 11:43.

36. L. Harris, op. cit., at note 5 above, no. 23.

37. SM 17:164 for which there is a rough sketch SM 54, i, 37 and SM 17:165. SM 17:164 has a central oval with trompe coffering similar to the dining-room ceiling at Hatchlands, Stillman, no. 151, p. 106. Curzon's carpets were among the designs considered for possible publication in July 1760, document cited above at note 16.

38. The 1804 inventory in the Kedleston Archive lists a drawing-room carpet 26 feet 4 inches by 16 feet (8 by 4.8 metres), which is still in the room. The Duchess of Northumberland noted 'a very expensive Derbyshire carpet' in the drawing-room when she visited in 1766.

39. L. Namier and J. Brooke, *The House of Commons 1754–1790*, II London, 1964, pp. 287–8.

40. H. Walpole, 'Journals of Visits to Country Seats', *The Walpole Society*, XVI, 1928, p. 64. J. Harris, *Sir William Chambers*, London, 1970, pp. 219–20.

41. Letter from James Adam to his mother, 12 Jan. 1761, 'Jenny also writes to me of a coach which Bob was asked to do and Ch__rs is doing'. SRO GD 18/4890.

42. J. Summerson, *Architecture in Britain 1530–1830*, London, 1970, p. 432.

43. SM 17:69. The fish-tailed caryatids in this design are comparable to those illustrated in Chambers's *Treatise on civil architecture*, London, 1759, pl. opp. p. 36. There is another related sofa design (SM 20:106) which is not in Adam's hand but may be by William or John Linnell. This design was executed, possibly for Mrs Elizabeth Montagu, who was one of Linnell's early patrons, and is now in the Philadelphia Museum of Art. To complicate matters, there are two similar sofas: one a modern version sold by Francis Lenygon to the V&A in 1946 and said to be based on an original in the collection of Viscount Massereene at Antrim Castle, Ireland, and another which came up for sale at Sotheby's in London on 7 July 1995, but was withdrawn.

44. Drawings by Linnell for the sofa as executed are at the V&A, P&D, E. 119, 124, 129, 131, 140 – 1929, and at Kedleston. See H. Hayward and P. Kirkham. *William and John Linnell*, London, 1980, p. 111, figs. 64, 236–40, 243; L. Harris, op. cit at note 5 above, no. 27.

45. Hayward and Kirkham, ibid., pp. 106, 111, figs. 276–7, 281–4.

46. Kedleston Archive.

47. Adam to Scarsdale, 1 September 1761. Kedleston Archive.

48. SM 20:8. A similar pier-glass design, SM 20:8, was made in 1765 for the Duke of Manchester for Kimbolton Castle, but was not executed.

49. Wyatt to Scarsdale, 5 January 1766. Kedleston Archive.

50. SM 20:9 and Kedleston, L. Harris, op. cit. at note 5 above, no. 25.

51. There was also a pair of rococo torchères which probably came from the earlier house or from London and were sold in 1930. L. Harris, op. cit. at note 5 above, p. 40.

52. *Ceiling for the Library at Shardeloes 1761*, SM 11:70; L. Harris, op. cit. at note 5 above, no. 28.

53. Adam, *Works*, I, ii, p. 10.

54. SM 40:11; L. Harris, op. cit. at note 5 above, no. 30.

55. Plan, SM 40:9.

56. The plan, SM 40:9, shows the bookcase at the southern end of the wall recessed in the opening made for the door. None of the other bookcases is recessed.

57. SM 40:10.

58. L. Harris, op. cit. at note 5 above, no. 29.

59. SM 40:12; L. Harris, ibid., no. 32. Note Adam's strictures on the use of heavy tabernacle frames in interiors, *Works*, I, i, preface, p. 5.

60. Kedleston Archive, Richardson drawings.

61. Adam to Curzon, 5 August 1760, wanting to know whether Lady Caroline 'would have (her bookcase) to hold Books to the Bottom or Drawers for Cloathes, etc below'. Kedleston Archive. The piece was made in London, probably by William Linnell, and delivered to Kedleston in June 1761. Hayward and Kirkman, op. cit. at note 44 above, p. 110. It is the only piece of furniture apart from the hall stools listed in the 1778 *Catalogue*, op. cit. at note 18 above.

62. L. Harris, op. cit. at note 5 above, no. 40. See also SM 11:46–8; 14:122–3; 40:14–16.

63. This is inscribed in pencil on Adam's c.1764–5 plan, with a flap showing his revised scheme for the south front. L. Harris, ibid., detail no. 9.

64. Ceiling, SM 11:48, dated March 1768; wall elevations, SM 14: 124, 125. See also L. Harris, ibid., nos. 41–2.

65. Ceiling, SM 11:148, 149, dated 1767; wall elevations and pier-glasses, SM 14:121; 20:71, 72, dated 1769.

66. J. Hardy and H. Hayward, op. cit. at note 32 above, p. 324.

67. A set of chairs with palm motifs was made in about 1740, probably by William Bradshaw, for Curzon's father. Though it was appropriate that these should have been used in the 'Principal Apartment', it seems unlikely that they were the source of inspiration for the exotic palm furniture of the mid-1760s as suggested by L. Harris, op. cit. at note 5 above, p. 12.

68. At Kedleston there are elevations of the window wall and the chimney-side, both dated 1762, and a finished design for the ceiling dated 1763. L. Harris, ibid., nos. 33–4, pp. 48–9. The cove in ceiling design does not correspond to that shown in the wall elevations. Normally, ceilings were designed before or at the same date as wall elevations; at the Soane, SM 11:52, there is a partly finished version of the ceiling design dated 1761, which may be its correct date.

69. Adam to Scarsdale, 22 September 1764. Kedleston Archive.

70. Adam to Scarsdale, 1 September 1763, 'I shall make a Design for the Bed Chamber ceiling which I would not put any painting in', Kedleston Archive; the finished drawing at Kedleston is dated 1763, but the unfinished version at the Soane is dated 1761, SM 11:56. The star pattern comes from P. S. Bartoli's *Gli antichi sepolchri*, Rome (1697), pl. 16; see also W. Chambers, *Kew*, London, 1763, pl. 20. The ceiling for the new state bedchamber was designed in 1767, SM 11:50. James Adam to Lord

Scarsdale, 29 October 1767, 'I have got all the working Drawings for the apartment for Estimating by Rose', Kedleston Archive.

71. The cistern probably arrived late in 1757; Hayward's bill for it and a cast of Lord Bateman's *Mercury* then in the Duke of Richmond's gallery is dated 23 January 1758. Kedleston Archive.

72. Adam's plan and elevation of the sideboard dated 1762 are at Kedleston; see E. Harris, no. 3, pp. 63–4. The design was executed in 1764 with minor alterations and at little cost by local craftsmen. Kedleston Archive.

73. Record drawings of these pieces, which were stored in Scarsdale's London house, were made by Adam around 1760, after the fountains were altered in November 1759: SM 25:80, 83, 89, 91. For the silver, see M. Snodin, 'Adam Silver reassessed', *Burlington Magazine*, CXXXIX, January 1997, pp. 17–25; for the fountains, one of which is now in the J. Paul Getty Museum, see G. Wilson 'The Kedleston Fountain', *Journal of the J. Paul Getty Museum*, II, 1983, pp. 1–12; for the tripod, see N. Goodison, 'Mr Stuart's Tripod', *Burlington Magazine*, CXIV, October 1972, pp. 695–704.

74. L. Harris, op. cit. at note 5 above, no. 18.; also SM 25:15 which is a record drawing.

75. George Montagu to Horace Walpole, 12 October 1766. *Correspondence*, X, p. 230.

76. L. Harris, op. cit. at note 5 above, no. 15. Evidently Scarsdale did not decide to have the niche 'raised in stucco' until June 1764. Adam to Scarsdale, 27 June 1764. Kedleston Archive.

77. The tables and cistern were 'all fix'd compleat' in the dining room niche on 17 July 1765, but Smith, the gilder, had not finished gilding the ornaments on 23 December 1765. Kedleston Archive.

78. The plinth was removed by William Johnson who was then paid for moving and fixing the cistern on 6 July 1766. Kedleston Archive.

79. The pier-tables were finished by June 1765 and their marble slabs were requested to be sent from London. Wyatt to Scarsdale, 23 June 1765. Kedleston Archive.

80. SM 20:10 inscribed 'for the front Drawing Room at Lord Scarsdale's in Mansfield Street' and dated 'October 1772'.

81. Adam to Scarsdale, 23 April 1761. Wyatt to Scarsdale, 25 May 1765, reporting that the pictures had all been fitted in their places, Smith had 'made out' the Snyders and Zuccarelli's *Porsenna* 'to their proper size' and was gilding the picture frames. Kedleston Archive. F. Russell, op. cit. at note 6 above, p. 99. SM 40:2–23.

82. SM 22:16, 17. Wyatt to Scarsdale, May 1765, reporting that John Devall's man had put up the chimney-piece in the dining-room. Kedleston Archive.

83. The finished, coloured design at Kedleston is dated 1762, L. Harris, op. cit. at note 5 above, no. 17; a partly finished version at the Soane is dated 1761, SM 11:53. There is a coloured drawing of an antique ceiling in the Palace of Augustus amongst the Adam drawings at the Soane, SM 26:129; see I. C. Bristow, *Architectural colour in British interiors 1615–1840*, London, 1996, p. 83, fig. 85. The ceiling was later published in Charles Cameron's *Baths of the Romans*, London, 1772, pl. 54

84. Duchess of Northumberland's journal. Northumberland MS. Alnwick.

85. N. Goodison, *Ormolu: the work of Matthew Boulton*, London, 1974, p. 129 pls 45–7.

86. Adam, *Works* II, iv, pl. VIII.

87. Adam to Scarsdale, 31 July 1760. This was evidently a veneered, panelled door; presumably the ones executed for the principal rooms.

88. Walpole, op. cit. at note 40 above, p. 64.

89. The columns were erected around 1763 and the pavement laid shortly afterwards. L. Harris, op. cit. at note 5 above, no. 44.

90. *Catalogue* (1769), op. cit. at note 18 above.

91. A. Palladio, *Four Books of Architecture*, trs. I. Ware, London (1735), bk IV, ch. XVIII, p. 98, pl. 48. At Kedleston there is a working drawing of the capital and letters referring to its design from Adam to Lord Scarsdale, dated April and May 1761. L. Harris, op. cit. at note 5 above, no. 48.

92. Ibid., bk IV, ch. XV, pl. XL. The paintings were attributed to William Hamilton by George Richardson in the second edition of his *Book of ceilings*, London (1793), p. 12, but this attribution is questionable.

93. SM 54, pt. i:33, inscribed 'This sketch it is imagined will answer for the flatt part of the Ceiling of Sr Nathl Cursons Hall of which the Cove to be done with Pannellings also'.

94. Letter from Adam to Scarsdale, 15 September 1763, assuring him that 'the three skielights (sic) will throw in more Light than if the End of the Hall was all one Window'. There are two unfinished outline drawings at the Soane, SM 11:45 and 40:8, which L. Harris dates around 1761, L. Harris, op. cit. at note 5 above, no. 45. J. Boswell, *Life of Johnson*, ed. G. B. Hill and L. F. Powell, London (1950), III, p. 161.

95. Kedleston Archive.

96. G. Richardson, *Book of Ceilings*, London (1776), pl. 48. Robert and James Adam are conspicuously absent from the list of subscribers which includes all the major architects of the time. L. Harris, op. cit. at note 5 above, nos. 45, 46.

97. (W. Mitford), *Principles of design in architecture*, London, 1809, p. 248.

98. Richardson, op. cit. at note 92 above. The plate (pl. 48) in this edition is coloured.

99. The earlier chimney-piece tablets are described in the 1769 and 1770 editions of the *Catalogue*; the new one is first described in the 1778 edition, op. cit. at note 18 above.

100. Letters to George Nathaniel, Earl Scarsdale from Francis Lenygon, 16 March 1912 and Percy Macquoid, 31 July 1914. Kedleston Archive.

101. Hayward and Kirkham, op. cit. at note 44 above, p. 113, fig. 259.

102. Ibid., p. 113, fig. 96.

103. J. Boswell, op. cit. at note 94 above, V, p. 431.

104. Ibid., III, p. 161.

105. Palladio, op. cit. at note 91 above, bk IV, ch. VI, pl. III; ch. X, pl. XXIII.

106. Adam to Scarsdale, 14 July 1761, reporting that he had made a section of the saloon; the section at the Soane, SM 40:15 is presumably of that date. Regarding the statues see Kenworthy-Browne, op. cit. at note 6 above, p. 252.

107. Ibid. Kenworthy-Browne suggests that Scarsdale intended filling the eight hall niches with antique marble statues of which he acquired two in 1759. Presumably their high cost prevented him from buying more.

108. Walpole, op. cit. at note 40 above.

2. CROOME COURT

1. Robert Adam to James Adam, 24 July 1760. SRO GD 18/4866.

2. Adam's accounts, Croome Archives. See G. Beard, 'Decorators and Furniture Makers at Croome Court', *Furniture History*, 1993, XXIX, appendix A, p. 91.

3. R. Sedgwick, *The House of Commons 1715–1754*, London, 1970 I, p. 588.

4. Walpole to Horace Mann, 28 October 1752, *Correspondence*, XX, p. 338.

5. Quoted by Bolton, II, Index of Clients, p. 67. However, 'The very best thing in petticoats I ever saw in my life' does not refer to the earl, as Bolton implies, but to his second wife; see Gilly Williams to George Selwyn, 28 October 1765, J. J. Jesse, *George Selwyn and his contemporaries*, London, 1901, I, p. 47.

6. Walpole to Mann, 28 October 1752, op.cit. at note 4 above.

7. Jesse, op.cit. at note 5 above, I, p. 396. According

to *Town and Country Magazine*, 1775, VII, p. 65, he not only spent his money in Paris on furniture, but also supported an 'opera girl' mistress and her 'cher ami', a 'black musquetter'.

8. Ibid, II, p. 25.

9. There is an anonymous view of the north front dated 1750 in the Croome Estate Office; a view from the south signed by Henry Beighton and dated 1714 is in the Prattinton Collection, I (18) in the Society of Antiquaries, London.

10. Lord Guernsey to Sanderson Miller, 25 August 1750, 'I am glad of your surprize at what Deerhurst has done at Croombe . . .', L. Dickens and M. Stanton (eds.), *An Eighteenth Century Correspondence*, London, 1910, p. 173; Lord Deerhurst to Sanderson Miller, February 1750/51, pp. 162–3.

11. Coventry to Miller, undated, ibid., p. 214.

12. Work on the park had evidently begun in 1748 when Sir Edward Turner wrote to Miller, 'Deerhurst conducts his River well', ibid., p. 138. See also D. Stroud, *Capability Brown*, London, 1975, pp. 57–60.

13. The retention of the earlier house is not only evident in the plans of the house, but also confirmed by contemporary reports. See H. Colvin, 'Croome Church and Its Architect', *Georgian Group Journal*, VIII 1998, p. 29.

14. Beard, loc.cit. at note 2 above, pp. 88–110; H. Hayward, 'Splendour at Croome Court: new light on Vile and Cobb', *Apollo*, May 1974, pp. 350–2.

15. Croome Archives, Croome Estate Office, Worcestershire, henceforth Croome Archives.

16. Beard, loc.cit. at note 2 above, p. 88.

17. Adam's bill for designs in the Croome Archives includes a plan and elevation of the bridge in 1761; and two different designs for an alcove bed and one for a chimney-piece for Grosvenor Square in September 1761. Carvers' work, including the alcove bed, was done by Sefferin Alken (Croome Archives). Sir Edward Turner was Coventry's next-door neighbour in Grosvenor Square. For the completion of the church see Colvin, loc.cit. at note 13 above.

18. The 'Sections of the Inside finishings of the Gothic Church' and 'Different designs of Ceilings for D°' listed in Adam's account can be related to drawings at the Soane: a section and ceiling on one sheet, SM 50:18; another section, SM 50:16; and a ceiling design SM 50:19.

19. The 'Design of a painted window for the Chancel of the church' for which Adam charged £10.10.0 in 1762 is in the Croome Archives; other window designs are in the Soane, SM 50:16, and the V&A A3436–5, see A. Rowan, *Robert Adam, catalogue of the drawings at the V&A*, London 1988, nos. 55–57.

20. France and Bradburn's account, Croome Archives. See N. Pevsner's appreciation of its exterior, *Buildings of England. Worcestershire*, London, 1968, pp. 125–6.

21. Sefferin Alken's bill for carving the font in January 1763, Croome Archives. See Beard, loc.cit. at note 2 above, p. 94. Design for the pulpit SM 25:209.

22. SM 50:21.

23. Croome Archives.

24. SM 11:34.

25. SM 11:36. A.Palladio, *The four books on architecture*, trans. R. Tavenor and R. Schofield, Cambridge, Mass., 1997, bk IV, ch. VI, p. 221.

26. SM 50:9,10. The chimney-piece is only shown in outline in this design.

27. Early design for the gallery at Syon, SM 43:95. In Adam's first plans for Osterley in 1761 the existing gallery was to be divided into a large library flanked by two small rooms, SM 43:97.

28. SM 11:37.

29. Croome Archives: the bookcase designs listed in Adam's account do not survive; Cobb acknowledged receipt of payment of £260 on 16 January 1765; Alken's bill for £107.8.11 was paid

on 4 February 1765. J. Hardy, 'The Croome Court Library', *Connoisseur*, January 1976, CXCI, p. 30–1.

30. The Choragic Monument of Lysicrates was engraved in 1755 as a specimen for subscribers. The book, though dated 1762, was not published until January 1763. See E. Harris and N. Savage, *British architectural books and writers 1556–1785*, Cambridge, 1990, pp. 441, 443. Coventry's copy of vol. I, which was sold at Sotheby's on 25 October 1948, had a red morocco, gilt-tooled binding probably designed by Stuart.

31. Croome Archives, Vile and Cobb's bill. The bookcases were rescued from Croome Court in 1973 by the V&A.

32. Croome Archives, Bradburn's bill.

33. The earl's continued book purchases, for which the accounts survive (Croome Archives) required additional shelving by June 1772 when Ince and Mayhew supplied a 'case to fit into the recess of window in Library of Fine Mahogany neatly carved'. Part of the library was sold at Sotheby's on 25 October 1948. It included a copy of Adam's *Spalatro* in a red morocco binding decorated with tools designed by him; Brettingham's *Holkham*; Paine's *Plans*, vol. I only; Chambers's *Treatise*; Leoni's edition of Palladio; Palladio's *Fabbriche Antiche* and several other architectural books.

34. 'Gilly' Williams to George Selwyn, 4 August 1763. Jesse, op.cit. at note 5 above, I, p. 265.

35. M. Fenaille, *État général des tapisseries de la Manufacture de Gobelins, periode du dix-huitième siecle*, deuxieme partie, Paris, 1907, IV, pp. 228, 229, 246. E. A. Standen, 'Croome Court – The Tapestries', *Metropolitan Museum of Art Bulletin*, November, 1959, p. 49.

36. Ibid. The tapestry room mock-up has not been traced. See E. Harris, 'Robert Adam and the Gobelins', *Apollo*, April 1962, pp. 100–6.

37. Standen, loc.cit. at note 35 above, pp. 51–2. E. Harris, 'The Moor Park Tapestries', *Apollo*, September 1967, pp. 180–9. Adam made a ceiling design (SM 14:18) in 1775 for the tapestry room at Weston, Shropshire for Sir Henry Bridgeman, not Sir Anthony as given by Bolton. Sir Henry succeeded to the Weston estate of his uncle, Thomas, 4th Earl of Bradford in 1764; he succeeded his father, Sir Orlando Bridgeman, as 5th Baronet in July 1764. Bridgeman's tapestries were made from 1766 to 1771.

38. In the Croome Archives there is a French design for the vase and border above the chimney-piece which is close but not identical to the executed tapestry.

39. SM 50:12. When the Duke of Portland's medallion tapestries were rehung at Welbeck Abbey, Adam's design for Croome at the Soane was consulted and an almost identical foliate border was executed. See *Country Life*, 21 April 1906, p. 559.

40. The borders were designed by Maurice Jacques in July 1764. In December 1764 Jacques submitted a bill for designs for borders related to the Croome tapestries. Further designs for the borders were billed in 1765 and 1766. Fenaille, op.cit. at note 35 above, IV, p. 230, 247–9; Standen, loc.cit. at note 35 above, pp. 49–50.

41. Ince and Mayhew bills, Croome Archives. The tapestries were provided with protective 'Paper Case' hangings made of linen. The chairs and sofas had two sets of protective coverings: one of 'Calico and White Shammy skin', the other of red and white checked material, as well as 'Stockings' for the legs. Ince and Mayhew's bill dated 5 October 1769 for making the seat furniture includes 'the patterns', meaning their own designs. Standen, loc.cit. at note 35 above, p. 38.

42. Fiske Kimball, 'Les influences anglaises dans la formation du style Louis XVI', *Gazette des Beaux-Arts*, 6ᵐ ser., V, 1931, pp. 231–55. Two earlier examples of chairs with oval backs were

published by S. Eriksen, *Early neo-classicism in France*, London, 1974, pp. 86–7, 389, pl. 389.

43. Ince and Mayhew's bill for a 'very neat carved Stand for Bason & Ewer of Redwood and Varnish'd (£)14.17.-', Croome Archives. The Sèvres basin bears the date 1767 and the mark of the painter, Mereand. See A. Coleridge, 'English furniture supplied for Coome Court Robert Adam and the 6th Earl of Coventry' *Apollo*, February 2000, pp. 8–19.

44. SM 6:177. Adam, *Works*, I, i, p. 12.

45. The design for a candelabra for Dundas is included in Adam's bill published by Bolton, II, p. 345. Samuel Norman's bill for 'new Gilding 6 large Brass Lamps', dated 20 June 1763, is believed to refer in part to the set of four candelabra. A. Coleridge, 'Sir Lawrence Dundas and Chippendale', *Apollo*, September 1967, pp. 194–5, fig. 9. The Duke of Bolton's candelabra was presumably made for his house on Russell Square which Adam began remodelling in 1770. How many there were now are now is not known. E. Harris, 'Robert Adam on Park Avenue: the interiors for Bolton House', *Burlington Magazine*, February 1995, pp. 68–75.

46. The pair of gilt torcheres sold at Sotheby's by the Countess of Coventry and the Trustees of the Croome Estate on 25 June 1948, lot 140, and bought by the Philadelphia Museum of Art, may be related to Adam's bill of 10 October 1767 for a design for a 'Term to stand in the angles of the room'. Which room is not specified, but the carved wheatsheaf and grapevine ornaments suggest the eating-room at Croome. They are almost identical to a design at the Soane, SM 54:53, inscribed 'pedestal for the Bust in the Temple of Bacchus for Mr Hamilton', undated, but after 1761, the year of Adam's ceiling design for the temple at Paineshill, Cobham, Surrey. On 7 December 1948 a 'Very fine Adam Plinth with festoon decorations, griffon supports and medallion centre' was sold from the Green Drawing Room, formerly the tapestry room, at Croome. This was a favourite Adam model. Bentley, Hobbs, & Myton, Sale of the contents of Croome Court, Worcestershire, 7 December 1948, lot 200.

47. Croome Archives, 9th Earl's notes.

48. The Veronese marble chimney-piece was made in June 1760 by John Wildsmith and incorporates a lapis lazuli tablet by Joseph Wilton, Croome Archives. The drawing at the Soane, SM 22:59, is a record of what was executed rather than an original design.

49. Croome Archives, France and Bradburn accounts. On 31 May 1763 William France was appointed Royal cabinet-maker 'in the room and place of William Vile and John Cobb' who were 'discharged'. In 1764 France went into partnership with John Bradburn, who had been employed by Vile and Cobb and held the Royal Warrant of 'Upholsterer to his Majesty and Cabinet-Maker to the Great Wardrobe'.

50. Adam's design for the bed, listed in his accounts for December 1763, corresponds to an undated drawing at the Soane, SM 17:152, inscribed for the Earl of Coventry. The alcove, shown on a plan inscribed '*Lord Coventry's Bedroom*', SM 50:11, still survives.

51. The design for the gallery at the Soane, SM 50:9, is an office copy of the finished design in the Croome Archives. For the definition of a Horreum see R. Adam, *Ruins of the Palace of the Emperor Diocletian at Spalatro*, London, 1764, p. 13.

52. The frieze is the same as one used on the exterior of Lansdowne House, which Adam said was taken from the Temple of Concord. *Works*, II, i, pl. 3. Palladio, op. cit. at note 25 above, bk IV, ch. XXX, p. 337. See Stillman, pp. 81–2, pls 70, 71. Charles Aylmer was paid £2 on 8 March 1768 for painting the glass frames '4 times Dead Stone Colour' and £1.16 for painting the sideboard

tables to match, Croome Archives. See J. Parker, 'Patrons of Robert Adam at the Metropolitan Museum of Art', *Metropolitan Museum of Art Journal*, 1960, I, p. 117.

53. Hatchlands chimney-piece, SM 22:11, 12; Kedleston SM 22:15, 18; Harewood, SM 22:203, 204.

54. Croome Archives. The grate is shown *in situ* in the illustration of the chimney-piece in Bolton, I, p. 182. Stillman, p. 109.

55. Alken's bill for a picture frame over the chimney-piece in the gallery, August 1765, Croome Archives. The grisaille painting has been mistakenly identified with Adam's bill of January 1766 for '2 large Ornamental Paintings in Chiaroscuro'. There was, in fact, no place in the room for another painting similar to the *trompe-l'œil* overmantel. Furthermore, the description in the bill makes it clear that they were not figurative but arabesque ornaments.

56. The two tables were bought by Philadelphia in 1945; in 1950 the Metropolitan bought the pier-glasses; and in 1965 an exchange was effected whereby each museum has a pier-glass and table.

57. Alken's bill, Croome Archives. Lord Coventry was said to be planning a trip to Paris 'to talk of . . . glasses' amongst other things in July 1763. He was there again in 1764. Jesse, op. cit. at note 5 above, I, p. 255.

58. SM 54, pt. i:93 is a sketch design of two pier-glasses and tables with notes dated May 1763 on the verso (see pl. 23). The left-hand sketch shows the pier-glass more or less as executed and the rejected table-frame; the one on the right shows a table of the same design with added pendant festoons, and an oval mirror in a square frame with front-facing female terms. For the commission to James Adam, see Fleming, p. 376.

59. SM 17:4. Syon Library Case.

60. W. Dean, *An historical and descriptive account of Croome D'Abitot*, Worcester, 1824, p. 51. Lady Maria Coventry remembers it being used in her time as a summer sitting-room; personal communication, 1995.

61. Croome Archives, Bradburn's bill. Alken carved '44 legs with Pateras a top . . . 90 raffld leaves; 20 elbows enrichd, bead close berries & Guthroon to Rail . . .' for which he charged £35.6.3. The stools were lent to the 1847 Exhibition. Five stools were sold by the Countess of Coventry at Sotheby's on 25 June 1948, lots 114–16. The measurements given in the sale catalogue do not exactly tally with those given in Bradburn's bill. Three stools, one formerly in the W. P. Chrysler collection, are now at Kenwood. Adam's accounts also include designs and drawings at large for a scroll stool for the greenhouse. Neither the stool nor the designs have been traced.

62. SM 17:73. Adam's bill for work done at Moor Park in 1766, including a 'Design of Scroll Stools for Salon £3.3.0', is reprinted by Bolton, II, p. 345.

63. The chairs are closely related to an undated drawing, SM 6:162, of which there is a variant, SM 6:160, inscribed 'Lord Coventry'. These may be preliminary drawings for the finished design supplied in February 1765. Croome Archives: Cobb's bill; Alken's bill for £19.16.0 for eight chairs.

3 · COVENTRY HOUSE

1. Croome Archives, Adam's account; bill for the execution of the alcove. *Survey of London*, The Grosvenor Estate, 1980, XL, p. 119.

2. Bolton, II, p. 340.

3. Adam accounts, Croome Archives.

4. G. Williams to G. Selwyn, Christmas Day, 1764, stating that he paid £10,000 guineas for the house. J. J. Jesse, *George Selwyn and his contemporaries*, London, 1901, I, p. 339. An excellent unpublished history of the house was written for the GLC by Neil Burton in 1976.

5. Croome Archives.

6. SM 7:144.

7. SM 11:40. The 'great room' was also equated with the dining-room in Sefferin Alken's bill for the drawing-room tables, dated 18 November 1768, Croome Archives. There is a variant design for the ceiling, SM 11:39, which is unfinished and uncoloured. It is correctly inscribed for the 'Drawing room' and dated June 1765, but is inexplicably omitted from Adam's accounts. The absence of the Coventry heraldic eagles on the inner ring of medallions, which are shown as executed in SM 11:40, militates against the association of this design with the 'Alterations on the Design for the painted Ceiling of the great Room' for which Adam charged the small sum of £1.1.0 later in 1765.

8. Zucchi's bill, Croome Archives.

9. SM 17:172.

10. On 24 November 1767, John Hobcraft drew a plan of the room for a carpet; Adam's full-size coloured detail of the border and ogee pattern, SM 18:57; Zucchi's bill for his 'Model', Croome Archives.

11. Lady M. Coke, The letters and Journals of Lady Mary Coke, London, 1970, II, p. 242. Moore was paid £112.1.0 on 29 October 1768 for 'A fine Persia Carpet to your own plan 83 ells (105 yards)', Croome Archives.

12. Croome Archives. Moore was paid £18.14.0 for the circular pattern carpet. SM 17:169, is a large scale pattern with variant colour schemes; SM 8:105 and SM 49:53 are record drawings showing the ogee and circle-pattern carpets together, the latter in colour.

13. J. Summerson, Georgian London, London, 1962, p. 143.

14. Adam's 'Design of a Table Frame for the Earl of Coventry', dated August 1767, SM 17:10. Sefferin Alken's bill, 19 November 1768, Croome Archives. It has been suggested that the joiner of the tables was the firm of Ince and Mayhew, whose workshops were next door to Alken's. Christie's, sale catalogue, London, 20 November 1986, lot 194.

15. Adam's full-size partly coloured design of the slab, SM 5:78, was entered in his accounts for 8 February 1768 as 'Part of a slab at full size & Part of another design of a slab at large', Croome Archives. The Soane drawing is inscribed in pencil: 'Centre of the Table in Length and Breadth. Lord Coventry'; and at the base, 'Mr Adam had not time to fix the Colours of the Border but thinks that need not stop the Estimate from being made. When that fixt if the drawing is return'd to Mr. Adam he will settle the other Parts of the Colouring.' This drawing has been mistakenly linked with his designs for the ante-room carpet of the same pattern, SM 8:105,106; 17:169; 49:53, Stillman, p. 107. Bartoli and Richter's bill for £134.5.0, 1 October and 8 December 1768, Croome Archives.

16. Christie's, 20 November 1986, lot 194.

17. Sefferin Alken's account 18 July 1769 for '2 Glass frames alike over the Tables In the Clear 9ft by 4,6 . . .' £68.16.7½, Croome Archives.
Adam's Coventry account includes a design for the mirror frame made around March 1768 and a drawing of the top and bottom at large on 14 November 1768. The undated design at the Soane (SM 20:64) is for a mirror 9 × 4½ feet (2.7 × 1.3 metres).
The pair of mirrors from Coventry House recently sold at Christie's (Christie's, London, 6 July 2000, lot 24) were 10 inches wider than those designed by Adam and made by Alken and had quite different ornaments on top and bottom, though the frames themselves were similar to Adam's design.

18. The design for Lansdowne House, SM 20:24, though dated 1768, is probably associated with the glass and table frame included in Adam's estimate of work at Lansdowne House made in February 1767.

19. Croome Archives, John Touzey.

20. Croome Archives, Gordon and Taitt.

21. Croome Archives. Devall was paid £240.0.0 on 1 July 1767. There are two undated drawings related to the chimney-piece at the Soane, SM 20:67, 68. While the tablet is the same in both, the frieze in SM 20:68 is closer to the executed one as described in Devall's account.

22. Croome Archives, Hartley & Cooper. Adam's account for 29 November 1767 includes a 'Design of a Grate for the Great Room 3.3.0 (and) . . . part of ditto at large 1.1.0'. This may be related to SM 17:122, which is undated.

23. Croome Archives, Adam's account, 20 December 1769, 'To a Concave Glass frame & Girandoles for the Antiroom & taking dimentions of pictures 3.3.0'; 30 June (1770) 'To a rich moulding for the Concave Glass at large – 5.0'. There are two related Adam drawings at the Soane: SM 20:59, which is dated 1768, and SM 20:60, which is undated.

24. Croome Archives, Robert Adam to Lord Coventry, 19 September 1766, 'The Bed Chamber is the only room that is yet finished & I hope the Ceiling will please you . . .'.

25. Croome Archives, Adam's account 1765. His charge of 7 guineas is significantly less than the 10 guineas charged for the design of the ante-room ceiling which is smaller and no more ornate. There is a bill from Joseph Rose for taking down the ornaments in August 1765. Adam's design for the ceiling at the Soane is dated May 1765, SM 11:38.

26. Sotheby's, 8 October 1965, lot 138.

27. Adam's design for the pier-glass, SM 20:65, is dated 1768. Chippendale's invoice, 3 July 1768, 'To a Looking Glass 46 × 46 Inches £167', Gilbert, I, p. 163. Alken's bill, Croome Archives.

28. Croome Archives, Adam accounts: 31 December 1766 – 31 January 1767.

29. Croome Archives, Adam's bill includes 'Sections in the antique stile of the eighth sides & Ceiling . . . 25.0.0'. There are coloured offices copies of these drawings in the Soane, SM 14:141–148.

30. Croome Archives, John Touzey.

31. Croome Archives, Rose's bill for ornaments over the chimney-piece and door, November 1767. Adam's design, SM 14:145.

32. Croome Archives, Adam's bill for the design and Alken's bill for the mirror. (See also John Touzey's bill for gilding the frame in January 1768.)

33. Adam's design, SM 22:70, is dated January 1766; it has a variant tablet. Croome Archives, payment of £136.6.9 for work done in 1767 was received 'for Self & Cº' by 'John Devall Jun' on 21 May 1768. The chimney-piece is not mentioned in R. Gunnis, Dictionary of British sculptors, London, 1978, p. 129. Adam made a design for a grate for the octagon room and a drawing of part of it at large on 29 November 1767; however, these designs have not been identified and the grate does not survive.

34. The alterations were carried out by the architect, C. R. Robson. See The Builder, 20 October 1888, p. 294, cited by N. Burton, document cited at note 4 above, p. 6, n. 14.

35. Croome Archives, Adam's bill 20 March and 6 May 1767 for a 'Design of a Carpet for the Octagon Room £5.5' and 'part of ditto at large £4.4.0'. There are related drawings at the Soane, SM 17:170, 54:65. Zucchi was paid £16.0.0 for his 'Model' in June 1768. The carpet was sold at Sotheby's , 17 June 1983, lot 14 and is now in the De Young Museum, San Francisco, California. The '2 New Trusses for my Lady's work frame' made by John Hobcraft in November 1767 may confirm Bolton's suggestion that the carpet was made by Lady Coventry, Bolton, I, p. 184.

36. Croome Archives.

37. SM 20:61, inscribed 'For The Earl of Coventry',

a shaped oval with a coronet crest and swags of husks over the glass. SM 20:62, 'Glass frame for Lady Coventry', corresponding to Alken's bill (Croome Archives) except for the swags of husks which are absent. Adam's account includes a design for a dressing glass on 16 October 1768, a drawing of the top and bottom at large early in 1769, '2 Designs of two Dressing Glasses' on 27 March 1769, and a 'Drawing of one of Glasses at large' in August.

38. SM 17:16.

39. Croome Archives, Ince and Mayhew's bill for £7.7.0. The less expensive wainscot toilet-table supplied by Hobcraft in February 1768 was presumably for another room. Which of the two octagon rooms received the three cupboards fitted up by Hobcraft in December 1767 is uncertain.

40. SM 54:69, one end of a stool; hall-chair, SM 17:92, 6:157.

41. Croome Archives, John Bradburn accounts.

42. Hobcraft's account (Croome Archives) includes a charge for easing a jib door in the bedroom, but whether that refers to the first-floor room is uncertain. Nor has it been determined whether the present service space entered from a jib door in the bedroom ever communicated with the dressing-room.

43. Croome Archives, Bradburn account.

44. The idea that the dining-room was to be decorated in the antique style stems from the incorrectly labelled office copy of Adam's design for the drawing-room ceiling at the Soane. See note 7 above.

45. SM 20:66; SM 20:67 is a half elevation of the design. The oval frame measures 5 × 3¾ feet (1.5 × 1.1 metres) and the hanging device 6 feet (1.8 metres).

46. The first annual fine arts exposition sponsored by The Antique and Decorative League, Inc., New York, 1934, p. 33.

47. The Benjamin Sonnenberg Collection. Sale catalogue, Sotheby's Park Bernet, New York, 5 September 1979, lot 1628.

48. Coventry Archives. As in the case of the pier-glass which Alken made for the drawing-room, the 'demands' of the gilder and joiner were included in his total bill and added considerably to it. The firm of Tatham, Bailey and Sanders submitted bills in December 1810 for 'repairing and Gilding the frames of two large Oval Glasses 7.10.' and for '. . . carving new Ornaments where deficient and new gilding 18.15.'. These almost certainly refer to the dining-room mirrors. However, I am less certain than Ince and Mayhew's charge in July 1771 for '2 Mens time fixing the 2 Ovals & Ornaments, to the Gilt frames, screws, etc.' refers to these mirrors.

4. SYON HOUSE

1. H. Walpole to Lord Hertford, 27 August 1764. Walpole Correspondence, XXXVIII, p. 429.

2. Adam, Works, I, i, p. 9.

3. Walpole reported in October 1762 that the earl and countess were 'building at Northumberland House, at Sion, at Stanwick, at Alnwick and Warkworth Castles! they live by the etiquette of the old peerage, have Swiss porters, the Countess has her pipers – in short, they will very soon have no estate'. Walpole, Correspondence, XX, p. 341.

4. Syon House, guidebook, Derby, 1987, p. 27. For the history of the early house, see Malcolm Starr, 'England's lost renaissance?', unpublished thesis, Architectural Association, London, June 1991; G. R. Batho, 'Syon House: The first two hundred years', Transactions of the London and Middlesex Archaeological Society, 1956, XIX, pt. 1.

5. R. Dodsley, London and its environs, London, 1761, VI, p. 14. There are bills from the carver, James Whittle for gilding ceilings and chimney-pieces here and for supplying five gilt lanterns for

the staircase in 1752–4; and from George Evans for painting a coat of arms over the door to of the 'Grand Salon'. Alnwick MS. U/I/25/ak/4; U/I/25/o/1. Adam's engraved plan shows the existing dining-room to the west of his proposed 'Grand Stair'. The drawing-room on the opposite side he intended to make into a dressing-room or boudoir for the duchess, behind the gallery. None of this was realized and at present the north front contains a large private dining-room and drawing-room.

6. Ibid., pp. 12, 13; P. Leach, *James Paine*, London, 1988, p. 190.

7. A letter from Robert to James Adam at Rome, July 1760, discussing a proposed publication of his works suggested by Nathaniel Curzon, mentions the possibility of including what he had done for Lord Northumberland. SRO GD 18/4866.

8. Alnwick archives, architectural drawings.

9. SM 39:3.

10. Mention of steps as a source of movement in a long room in James Adam's draft essay on architectural theory dated 27 November 1762 suggests that the square recess in the hall had been decided upon before that date (Fleming, p. 315). The *Dying Gladiator* was set up in the hall by the mason Thomas Hardwick in the summer of 1769, Alnwick MS U/I/27/1-71. A bronze cast of the Belvedere *Antinous* was brought into the hall and fixed on a pedestal in summer 1771, U/I/28/ G1-70. It is shown paired with the *Apollo Belvedere*, flanking the door to the central courtyard, *Works*, II, iv, pl. I. In spring 1773 Hardwick unloaded a 'Bardge of Figures . . . (carried) Do to the House' and got 'old Marble Figures into the Hall' and hoisted them on to their pedestals, U/I/2/W1-71. The 1847 inventory (Alnwick Archives) lists the Dying Gaul, the life-size copy of Apollo, Mark Anthony, Cicero and two female figures.

11. The first plan (drawing cited at note 8 above) shows a fireplace in the apse. To the left (west), concealed in a cupboard, is a stranded door above floor level belonging to the earlier house.

12. Adam, *Works*, I, i, pl. VI, engraving of the apse. The pedestal itself was engraved in the *Works*, II, iv, pl. II. For Sir Robert Walpole's bronze cast of *Laocoön*, see F. Haskell and N. Penny, *Taste and the antique*, London, 1981, p. 244.

13. 'Extracts of letters to and from James Adam concerning My Lord Northumberland's Commission of Marbles, Statues, Plaster Casts and painted Bas Reliefs, 1761', Alnwick Archives, G/I/3. 1761. James was advised that a cast of a consular figure would cost £100, which evidently was considered too much. In the 'Duchess of Northumberland's Syon House Book', 1769 (Alnwick Archives U/I/121-93), the cost of the *Dying Gladiator* is given as £300. I am grateful to Ruth Guilding for information regarding James Adam's correspondence.

14. Adam, Works, I, i, p. 10.

15. I am indebted to Robin Middleton for drawing this to my attention.

16. The Duke of Northumberland's annotation in his copy of Dodsley, op. cit. at note 5 above. Alnwick archives, Duke of Northumberland's MSS 93A/14.

17. Chambers' design for the pavilion is in the Soane, SM Chambers 43/4/29. D. Stillman, *English neo-classical architecture*, London, 1988, II, pp. 476–6, pl. 342.

18. Adam, Works, I, i, p. 12.

19. Letter from Robert Adam to Lord Kames, 31 March 1763, describing the enriched Doric order as 'very proper in Halls'. SRO, Abercairny MS GD 24/1/564.

20. The 'Carv'd Trusses under the Hall windows' costing £100 were included in the duchess's list of prices, document cited at note 13 above.

21. The hall was described by Lady Shelburne after a visit she and the Earl made to Syon in March

1765. Lady Shelburne's diary, Bowood Archives. The present picking out in grey was done by John Fowler in 1972.

22. Mary Anderson (1726–1816), daughter of Edmund Anderson, 5th Bt., was under-housekeeper at Hampton Court. Lincolnshire Archives Office/AND/8/2/32. Adam's pavement design, SM 39:4.

23. Haskell and Penny, op. cit. at note 12 above, p. 88.

24. Alnwick MS U/I/41. Evidently some of the columns were already at Syon where they were seen by Lady Shelburne in March 1765, document cited at note 21 above.

25. Adam, Works, II, iv.

26. G. B. Piranesi, *Della magnificenza ed architettura de' Romani*, Rome, 1761, pl. XX. J.-D. Le Roy, *Ruines des plus beaux monumens de la Grèce*, Paris, 1758, pl. XXXI.

27. Adam, *Works*, II, iv, pl. V.

28. There are renderings of the Campidoglio trophies in the Adam collection at the Soane, SM 26:89–92. They were also published in Piranesi's *Trofei di Ottaviano Augusto*, Rome, 1753, pl. 6.
See Stillman, pp. 64–5, pl. 16, 17.

29. Adam made five designs for the chimney-piece: three in 1762 without the rams' heads and with alternate friezes related to the wall decorations SM 22:36–38; and two in 1764 with the ram's heads and alternate stiles, SM 22:39–41. SM 22:39 was the executed design.

30. Bill from Thomas Ponsonby, Lady Day 1832. Alnwick MS U/III/8/M.

31. Anderson, document cited at note 22 above, was not sure whether the *Dying Gladiator* and the *Antinous* were 'brass or painted green'.

32. A. T. Bolton, 'Syon House – I', *Country Life*, 6 December 1919, p. 735.

33. Adam's design, c.1761, SM 18:60, may have been executed by Bartoli and Richter, who were the leading makers of scagliola in England at that date. The replacement was supplied by William Croggan who managed Mrs Coade's artificial stone works in Lambeth. He received £300 as the first instalment on 11 June 1831, Alnwick MS U/III/L. His final bill, 'Jan. 31 1832 To a rich inlaid Scagliola Floor executed in Hard Materials and various Colors, the Whole laid complete in the Vestibule at Syon House – including all expences of Drawings, patterns, Carriage, fixing &c. – as per estimate £900', U/III/8/M. Reprinted in C. Gilbert, J. Lomax, A. Wells-Cole, *Country House Floors 1660–1850*, Leeds, 1981, p. 26, which also quotes (p. 25) the explanation given by Isaac Ware in his *Complete Body of Architecture*, London, 1756, for the poor quality of the scagliola floors in England. The Syon floor had protective coverings of India hemp and red baize supplied on 8 June 1833 by Henry Watson, Carpet Manufacturers. U/III/8/N-V(O).

34. The French Empire seat furniture in the vestibule came from Northumberland House and before that from the Tuileries.

35. SM 17:3, 'Design for a Table frame for the Dining Room at Sion' dated 1765. Ponsonby bills 1826–27, Alnwick MS U/III/8/h.

36. The sections of the room engraved by Piranesi for the *Works*, II, iv. pl. IV, inscribed as designed by Adam 1761. The table shown under the niche on the south wall corresponds to a 'Design of a Table frame for the Vestibule at Sion House' dated 1765, SM 17:1,2, and to the engraving published after Adam's death in the *Works*, III, pl. XI. No table of this description has been traced.
Anderson, document cited at note 22 above.
1847 Inventory, document cited at note 10 above.

37. The design which is at Alnwick is described in a list of 'Prints in Library North Ho' as a 'Design for a Vauze to be executed in Silver Mr Adam',

Alnwick archives.

38. Adam, *Works*, I, i, p. 11. James Adam described the uses of ante-rooms in a letter to Lord Shelburne, 6 November 1765: 'upper servants do wait there . . . in a suite of Levee rooms it is infinitely better to go first into the antiroom and from thence directly into the room for Company before dinner, without any Passage or back stairs intervening'. Bolton, II, p. 11.

39. Documents cited at notes 21 and 22 above.

40. Ware, op. cit. at note 32 above, p. 335.

41. The quadrant spaces behind the apses were put to practical uses: a water-closet entered from the vestibule, a store for the leaves of the dining-table and cupboards for other equipment.

42. Adam, *Works*, I, i, p. 11.

43. The design for the dining-room at Syon is dated December 1761, SM 11:16,18. Shardeloes library ceiling design, SM 11:172.

44. Chimney-piece design, SM 22:42,43. Letter from James to Helen Adam mentioning Breton's work, 7 March 1762. S.R.O., Clerk of Penicuik Papers 4929. A cost of £70 for the 'Bas Relief of Graces' is given by the duchess, document cited at note 13 above.

45. Bill, 10 July 1761, Alnwick MS U/I/46/3. Mary Anderson reported seeing a 'most elegant statue of Bacchus, as large as life, full length white Marble' in the apse in the hall when she visited the house in 1770. Document cited at note 22 above.

46. Section of the dining-room, SM 27:64. Laid-out elevation of the 4 walls of the dining-room, SM 5,i:160,161; Alnwick archives, architectural drawings 03444.

47. Casali was paid £200 in 1769, 'Lord Northumberland's Memorandum Book', Alnwick MS U/I/59. The subjects, as identified by Croft-Murray, are not what one would expect to find in a convivial dining-room: 'a widow being consoled, based on the composition of the *Aldobrandini Marriage*; a death-bed scene; and entombment; and a procession of female figures with lachrymatories'. E. Croft-Murray, *Decorative Painting in England*, London, 1970, II, p. 183.

48. Design for a table frame, SM 17:3; design for a pier-glass, 1765, 20:14. Designs for an almost identical pier-glass were prepared for Sir Lawrence Dundas at Arlington Street in 1765, SM 20:13, and for John Luke Niccol in 1766, 20:29. The Syon table and pier-glass were published in *Works*, III, pl. XI.

49. The pier-glass frames were also repaired and regilded in 1831. Alnwick MS U/III/8/M. 'Extra to measured Acc' Syon House.'

50. Document cited at note 47 above.

51. 1847 Inventory, document cited at note 10 above.

52. Adam, *Works*, I, i, p. 10.

53. Lady Holland wrote to her sister, Lady Kildare, on her return from Paris in 1764, 'I have three immense looking glasses to put in ye drawing room and propose hanging it with a damask or brocatelle of two or three colours'. J. Cornforth 'Audley End, Essex I', *Country Life*, 27 December 1990, p. 31. The large drawing-room at Holderness (later Londonderry) House, built for the fourth Earl of Holderness by 'Athenian' Stuart from 1760–65, was hung with four-colour damask in 1767. The Holdernesses were neighbours of the Northumberlands at Syon Hill and the countess, like the duchess, was a Lady of the Bed Chamber.
     The Northumberlands also used crimson, green and white damask to cover furniture in the drawing-room at Alnwick in 1768 (Walle & Reilly bills, Alnwick MS. U/I/27/R1-4) and for festoon curtains, &c. in the glass drawing-room at Northumberland House in 1778 (King & Padget bills, Alnwick MS. U/I/46/34).

54. Dodsley, op. cit. at note 16 above. A bill for a 'Coach to Mr. Triquets in Spittel Fields' on 10 September 1766 may be related to the three-coloured damask. Small Account Book, Alnwick

Ms U/I/44.

55. There are three designs for the ceiling at the Soane, none as executed: SM 11:19 dated 'Decr 1761' and inscribed 'not executed'; 11:21 dated '1761' inscribed 'not executed'; 11:20 dated '1762' with the letters 'No' of a cut inscription below.

56. The drawing-room ceiling is discussed at some length in a letter from Northumberland to Adam written on 4 November 1763 from Ireland, where he was Lord lieutenant, Alnwick MS 94:44–5.

57. Document cited at note 13 above.

58. Chambers, without mentioning Adam by name, castigated against gaudy ceilings, 'which, composed as they are of little rounds, squares, octagons, hexagons and ovals; excite no other idea, than that of a desert: upon the plates of which are dished out, bad copies of indifferent antiques', *Treatise on Civil Architecture*, London, 1791, p. 135. This was rephrased as 'skied dinner plates' and applied to the drawing-room at Syon by James Lees Milne, *The Age of Adam*, London, 1947, p. 111.

59. Documented cited at note 22 above. Lady Shelburne also thought the ceiling 'beautifully collor'd & painted', but the walls were not yet hung when she visited in March 1765, document cited at note 21 above.

60. Bill from Robert Hughes, upholsterer & cabinet maker, Alnwick MS U/III/8/L. The old hangings were sent to Alnwick but do not survive.

61. The curtain cornices are illustrated in Adam's *Works*, III, pl. XI. His design for the overmantel-mirror, dated 1765, is in the Soane, SM 20:16. It calls for elaborate pendant and two-branch candelabra on either side. There is another design (SM 20:15) for a frame 5 feet high and 6 feet wide, which was presumably intended for a picture over the chimney-piece.

62. Walpole to Montagu, 8 June 1762, Walpole, *Correspondence*, X, p. 34.

63. 23 December 1763 'Mr Selwyn Glasses Syon 421–9–8', Alnwick MS. U/IV/2a. 24 October 1766, bill for 8 guineas porterage for a case of looking glasses from Paris, Alnwick MS U/I/44.

Selwyn was also involved in Northumberland's purchase of tapestries from the Gobelins in 1764 or 1765. 12 December 1764, Letter from 'Gilly' Williams to George Selwyn in Paris, 'Lord Northumberland wants to hear from you on a tapestry commission, I think it was'. J. J. Jesse, *George Selwyn and his contemporaries*, London, 1901, I, p. 330. On 17 July 1767, Jacques Neilson, *entrepreneur* at the Gobelins wrote to the French ambassador, '*Il reste quelques pieces de Tapisseries a faire passer a Londres pour completer celles qui j'y ay envoye a M. le Duc de Northumberland, a Mgr a Mgr Fife et a M. Weddell*', M. Fenaille, *Etat general des tapisseries de la manufacture des Gobelins periode du dix-huitieme siecle*, Paris, 1907, IV, pp. 263, 264.

64. Dodsley, op. cit. at note 16 above. They measure (9 ft.3½ in. × 5 ft.5¼ in.) 3.69 m. × 1.65 m.

65. The frames correspond to a rejected design made in 1765 for Sir Laurence Dundas, SM 20:12.

Guichard was paid £123, which may have included gilding, Alnwick MS U/IV/2a. Guichard is also mentioned in a short list of 'Ebenistes' compiled by the duchess before 1767 and in a longer list of 'Ebenistes Cabt Makers Inlayers Uphold'rs' thought to have been compiled around 1776, Alnwick MS 121/60, p. 344 and Alnwick MS 121/63. See Gilbert, I, pp. 153–4. Jean Bruno Guichard was presumably related to Joseph-Nicolas Guichard who was registered in Paris as a *maître sculpteur* in 1765 and whose only recorded work is for Madame du Barry at Louveciennes in 1770. S. Eriksen, *Early neo-classicism in France*, London, 1974, p. 190.

Mary Anderson noted that the narrowness of the frames 'has this effect to show the place to greater advantage', op. cit. at note 22 above.

66. Dodsley, op. cit. at note 16 above. Fleming, p. 371. The mosaic tables arrived at London on 4

January 1764 and were taken first to Northumberland House (Alnwick MS U/I/41). The duchess gave the price of the tables as £200, document cited at note 13 above.

67. Typed hand list, Alnwick Archives U/I/121-93.

68. Though no drawings survive, the design was published in 1822 in the *Works*, III, pl. XI. The husk festoons beneath the bat's wing pendants were probably executed but are now lacking.

69. On 8 February 1760 (i.e. 1761), Robert Adam wrote to his brother James in Rome, informing him that the Duke of Northumberland was wanting an 'ancient mosaic paving to be found at Rome that would answer for making a hearth as he thinks one of that kind cleverly composed could be pretty for the Drawing Room', SRO 4926.

70. A. T. Bolton, 'Syon House – III', *Country Life*, 20 December 1919, p. 841.

71. Alnwick Archives, Syon D/18. The ornaments were fixed to the chimney-piece on 13–14 May 1766, Alnwick MS U/I/41.

72. N. Goodison, *Ormolu: The work of Matthew Boulton*, London, 1974, p. 102. Bermingham (or Brimingham) was paid £2.2.0 for 'Gilt ornaments for the Drawing Room Doors at Syon' on 7 January 1766 and £30 for the gilt metal ornaments for the drawing-room shutters on 7 January 1767. On 24 June 1765 the doors were measured 'for the Ornamts with Mr Davis', the gilder. Anderson was paid £10 on 24 January 1767 for 'Brass edging gilt to the Mosaic Tables & Medals for the Drawing Room Doors at Syon'. His widow was paid the remaining £7.11.6 owed him on 24 November 1767, Alnwick MS U/I/41.

G. Collett of the firm of Jack and Collett, who supplied most of the cast lead mouldings for the Northumberland House glass drawing-room, also supplied 64 ft 6 in. of cast lead mouldings and 820 roses for Syon, possibly for the drawing-room, in October 1773, Alnwick MS U/III/6/1.

73. Document cited at note 47 above.

74. G. Jackson-Stops, 'Syon Park, Middlesex', *Country Life*, 16 April 1992, p. 97.

75. 'Carpet drawing room 34.6 × 13. 9¼', 'carpet dining Room 31.5 long 14.8 broad', document cited at note 47 above. The narrower drawing-room carpet would have allowed for the large mosaic tables.

76. Design for the carpet, dated 1768, SM 17:172. Anderson, document cited at note 22 above. At the time of the 1847 inventory, the 'State Drawing Room' had an Axminster Carpet planned to room and an Axminster hearth rug, document cited at note 51 above, p. 34. Where Moore's carpet was is not known. A carpet almost identical to the Syon drawing-room carpet was on the London market (C. John) in 1977. It was said to have come from Ingestre Hall, Staffs., *Burlington Magazine*, December 1977.

77. Adam made very few designs for dining-room carpets, all of them fairly late: the back parlour or dining-room at Home House, 20 Portman Square, 1776, SM 17:195; the eating-room at Sir Abraham Hume's house at Wormleybury, Herts., 1778, SM 17:197; the private dining-room at Cumberland House, 1780, SM 17:203,204 and the 'Great Dining Room' at Cumberland House, 1780, SM 17:207.

78. J. Summerson, *Georgian London*, London, 1962, p. 143.

79. Letter from H. Walpole to Lord Hertford, 27 August 1764, Walpole, *Correspondence*, XXXVIII, p. 429. Richard Bentley made designs for a 'Gothic Columbarium' for Walpole at Strawberry Hill and for John Chute at The Vyne, Hampshire, neither of which was executed.

80. Adam, *Works*, III, pl. II.

81. Alnwick Archives, draft letter from Lord Northumberland to Adam, 4 November 1763: 'I

wish the Gallery may be proceeded upon with all possible Expedition, so as to be finished again at my Return. I intirely approve of having folding doors shut into the Recesses after the manner of those at Northumberland House. I do not apprehend you will find in Execution the difficulty you mention about the Bases and Caps of the Pilasters to the Book Cases as the Books might be placed behind them like those in the Library at Northd House'. The folding doors would have had panels either of wire mesh or of glass; the latter would have reflected some of the light from the opposite wall.

82. Dodsley, op. cit. at note 16 above.

83. 1828, Thomas Ponsonby bill for sundry works including mouldings on the edges of bookshelves, Alnwick MS U/III/8/l.

84. Document cited at note 47 above. Northumberland also wrote to Sir William Hamilton at Naples on 7 June 1765, asking him to purchase on his behalf 'Statues, Vases, Tripods or other Pieces of Vertu' fit to stand in the ten niches in the gallery and 'flat Vases or Sepulchral Urns' for the four circular recesses. He was also after 'coloured Drawings of any Paintings Mosaick Pavements or Stucco Ornaments found in the Antient Sepulchre at Cuma or in any other Place near Naples', Alnwick MS G/I/4. Information communicated by Ruth Guilding.

85. Alnwick MS U/I/44, Zuccarelli went to Syon on 24 June 1766 to retouch his pictures. Mr Lindo the painter was paid £42 on 7 November 1766; on 27 June 1767 his widow was paid £65.2.0. He also painted a full-length portrait of the Duchess.

Duke's 'Memorandum Book', document cited at note 47 above, p. 11: '32 Circles Heads 1:4½ Diam./ 4 Oval "/6 Square pannels over Door 2:6½ by 1'7 high'. According to the duchess, document cited at note 13 above, the circular portraits cost £3.3.0 each, and the Zucarelli's over the chimney-pieces £126.

86. Dodsley, op. cit. at note 16 above.

87. Patent 844. Dennis Mc McCarthy, 6 March 1776.

On 1 May 1767 Northumberland had 'the King's Bust & other pieces of artificial stone' sent to Mr McCarthy's in Cold Bath Fields; on 5 May '2 medallions of His Grace's Bust' were obtained from Mr McCarthy's (Alnwick MS U/I/44).

Mary Anderson described the chimney-pieces as having 'whole Length figures done upon a Composition of Green Wax with a polish, but I rather think it is glass with a Foil behind it', Anderson, op. cit. at note 22 above.

88. The '6 semi-circulr Bas Reliefs in stucco Gallery 4 Circular Do at Ends at 6:6:0 25:4:0', Duchess' 'Syon House Book', document cited at note 13 above.

A. T. Bolton, 'Syon House – II', *Country Life*, 13 December 1919, p. 808.

89. Duchess's 'Syon House Book', document cited at note 13 above.

90. Thomas Ponsonby, 1828 bill for 'sundry works' including chimney-glasses and pier-glasses, Alnwick MS U/III/8/L. A. and J. Rykwert, *The brothers Adam*, London, 1985, p. 80.

91. Duchess's 'Syon House Book', document cited at note 13 above. G. Wills, *English looking glasses*, London, 1965, p. 35. See also Adam's design for a concave glass frame for Coventry House, 1768, SM 20:59,60.

92. Anderson, document cited at note 22 above.

93. Pergolesi's bill for painting the pilasters includes '20 oz Flowers of Bismuth for a White Ground to all the Ornaments on the Pilasters'. The other colours listed in the bill are 12 oz smalt (blue), 10 oz Lake (crimson), 16 oz verdigo (green) (Alnwick MS U/I//42/C/5).

94. Pergolesi's account for 'painting 31 stucco pannels in different colours and gilding the ornaments on one of them and retouching & mending a few other parts. NB 20 of the pannels on the sides of the Gallery were painted 3 times over

because they had been first Gilt'.

The account also itemizes nine 'Different Designs made . . . for paintings for Frize over the Pilasters in the Gallery which were not executed the same being done in stucco'. These include 'Altering Mr Adam's original Design for the Frize & reducing it to a smaller Proportion different coloured Ornaments on a Pink Ground'; and making 'A New Design . . . for the like with different coloured Ornaments on a pink ground' (Alnwick MS U/I/42/C/5).

The first payment for Pergolesi's designs for the pilasters was made in July 1765. There were continuous payments for the pilasters throughout 1766 and 1767, the final one being on 16 April 1768 (Alnwick MS U/I/44).

95. SM 11:23 replacing an earlier design of August 1761, SM 11:22. According to the duchess, the 'Stucco work in Gallery' cost £825, document cited at note 13 above.

96. One set is 4 ft 3³/₄ in. (1.31 m.) long, the other 4 ft 4¹/₂ in. (1.33 m.). Their positions are given in the duke's 'Memorandum Book', document cited at note 47 above.

97. The only pieces of gallery furniture mentioned in the duchess's 'Syon House Book', document cited at note 16 above, are a pair of 'marble tables . . . one (£)43, 3 at (£)21 each (totalling) £105', and 'cane chairs'. Adam had nothing to do with the '12 cane chairs' supplied by Walle and Reilly on 13 May 1768 (Alnwick MS U/I/27, Walle & Reilly bills).

98. The distinctive apron also occurs on the Osterley dining-room sideboard table, designed in 1767 and published in the *Works*, III, pl. IX. Designs at Osterley and Soane, SM 17:7. The square tapered legs with lion masks and paw feet are reminiscent of the tables in 'Athenian' Stuart's drawing of 1759 for the painted room at Spencer House.

99. SM 17:172. Stillman, p. 108 found the source of Adam's ogee pattern in mosaic pavements of the second and third centuries AD. However, the Soane drawings (SM 8:105 and 49:53) with two patterns (ogee and circular) which he thought were partly for the gallery at Syon and partly for Coventry House were in fact for the ante-room and drawing-room at Coventry House, not for Syon. See note 101 below.

100. 'Oyl cloth to be 24:10¹/₂ long' and 'Carpet Chimney 21:3¹/₂ long 13:9¹/₂ broad', duke's 'Memorandum Book', document cited at note 43 above.

101. SM 18:57. The ogee pattern can by process of elimination be linked with the carpet for the drawing-room at Coventry House designed by Adam on 8 July 1767 and made by Thomas Moore who described it as a 'Persia Carpet'; the smaller ante-room carpet was described by Moore as a 'circle pattern'. See SM 8:106 and 17:169. Thus the record drawings of carpets combining ogee and circular patterns (SM 8:105 and 49:53) are not for two different houses, Syon and Coventry House, but for two rooms in the latter house. See W. Hefford, 'Thomas Moore of Moorfields', *Burlington Magazine*, December 1977, p. 847, n. 32.

102. John Farnell, carpenter, October–December 1770, 'to cutting Doors for Carpetts in Long Gallery' (Alnwick, MS U/I/28/D 1–46). 5 October 1767 'Pd Mr Chilton for 40 Pieces of Indian Matting for the Gallery at Syon 15.10.0' (Alnwick MS U/I/44).

103. 'Account Book of Thomas Butler, Steward June 1759 – '. 30 Dec. 1765 'Paid Mr Pergolesi in full for his Designs for the Carpet & Tapestry at Syon House £25-5-0' (Alnwick MS U/I/41).

104. Ibid., 13 September 1765.

105. Duke's 'Memorandum Book', document cited at note 43 above, p. 13.

106. Adam, *Works*, I, i, p. 11. Dodsley, op. cit. at note 5 above, p. 14.

107. Mary Anderson, document cited at note 22

above. Its frieze was painted green and gold by Pergolesi in July 1768, but this evidently was not liked and in November he was paid for 'new painting the frize & repainting the other paintings in the Turret' (Alnwick MS U/I/44). The present pale pink and blue are John Fowler's colours.

108. J. Summerson, *Architecture in Britain*, London, 1970, p. 434.

109. Duke's annotations to Dodsley, op. cit. at note 16 above. Between July and September 1761 there were '3 windows clean'd in the Painted Turrett' by 'Mr Rhodes Glazier' and unspecified work was done in the 'Painted Room in the Turret' by Edward Palmer, Carpenter (Alnwick MS U/I/26/G 1–105).

110. SM 27:74,75; 54:i,48.

5. ALNWICK CASTLE

1. John Adam, 'Jaint in to England', spring 1759. Blair Adam MS.

2. W. Hutchinson, *A view of Northumberland . . . 1776*, Newcastle-upon-Tyne, 1778, II, p. 194.

3. SM 11:29. G. Worsley, 'Alnwick Castle, Northumberland – II', *Country Life*, 8 December 1988, p. 76, fig. 7, suggests that the 'survey drawing' may be by Henry Keene. Hutchinson, ibid., p. 206; Alnwick MS (P. Waddell), 'Alnwick Castle described and illustrated with drawings by P. W. 1785'.

4. SM 22:51. J. Macaulay, *The Gothic revival 1745–1845*, London, 1975, p. 71.

5. Macaulay, ibid., pp. 72, 353 n.80, quoting A. C. S. Dixon, 'The Restoration of Alnwick Castle 1750–86', BArch Dissertation, University of Newcastle-upon-Tyne, 1960, p. 7, claiming that the breakfast-room was still intact in 1887. However, in the paper read to the RIBA in November 1856 by T. L. Donaldson it is mentioned in the past tense, though the semi-octagonal turrets off it, which were 'traditionally appropriated to the Duke and Duchess', were still there and in use. T. L. Donaldson, 'Some Description of Alnwick Castle, Northumberland', *RIBA Papers Session 1856–7*, p. 14.

6. Messrs Hoare Bank, pass books of the Duke of Somerset's and the Duke of Northumberland's accounts with Messrs Hoare 1748–62.

7. G. Worsley, loc. cit. at note 3 above, p. 77. Hoare's Bank. Vincent Shepherd (c.1750–1812), who was apprenticed to the Alnwick carpenter, George Thompson in 1764, later acted as resident architect at Alnwick and is thought by Colvin to have been responsible for the execution of Adam's designs.

8. F. Grose, *The antiquities of England and Wales*, London, 1775, III. Grose's descriptions were quoted in full by Hutchinson, op. cit. at note 2 above. P. Leach, *James Paine*, London, 1988, p. 143.

9. Waddell, op. cit. at note 3 above. A copy of the note, reading 'This castle was built by Matthew and Thomas Mills, master masons in the Year 1764', was discovered by Salvin and is among his drawings for Alnwick at the RIBA Drawings Collection, W8/17(38). A commemorative medal by John Kirk was also struck in that year. Leach, op. cit. at note 8 above, p. 172.

10. Alnwick MS U/I/27.

11. Alnwick MS U/I/44. According to Waddell, there were 110 escutions, though Grose and others reported 120.

12. Grose, op. cit. at note 8 above, Leach, op. cit. at note 8 above, p. 172, and Worsley, loc. cit. at note 3 above confused the saloon with the original, 'Gothic' drawing-room (renamed the breakfast-room) in which Rose worked in 1755–7.

13. Waddell, op. cit. at note 3 above. H. Hayward and P. Kirkham, *William and John Linnell*, London, 1980, I, p. 122.

14. Waddell, op. cit. at note 3 above. SM 22:50.

15. Waddell, op. cit. at note 3 above.

16. Repairs to the pink, green and white dado were carried out by John Wateridge of London in 1780. Alnwick MS U/I/46, 47.

17. SM 22:52, 53. The chimney-piece survives in a housekeeper's room at the castle.

18. In October 1778, Thomas King and Joseph Padget, Mercers to His Majesty at the Wheatsheaf, King's Street, Covent Garden, supplied nearly 285 yards of three-coloured damask costing approximately £225. Alnwick MS U/I/46. When the Syon hangings were rewoven in 1810, the original three-coloured damask put up around 1765 was sent to Alnwick, where it was easily accommodated. C. R. Cockerell, who visited Alnwick on 5 September 1822 and was quite critical of the interiors, thought the 'Silk hangings in drawing ro: quite thrown away', J. Harris, 'C. R. Cockerell's "Ichnographica Domestica"', *Architectural History*, 1971, XIV, p. 7.

There was also a suite of 'ten matted chairs, the Seats of which are White, Pink and Green in conformity to the other Furniture, and the Backs and Frames painted with Trophies'.

19. Hayward and Kirkham op. cit. at note 13 above, p. 122, suggest that the card-tables were delivered to Alnwick early in 1765, which would make them predate not only the Kedleston pair, but also Adam's arrival at Alnwick. If they had been delivered to the castle at that early date, they could not have been placed in Adam's 'great' drawing-room but in its predecessor, the Gothic drawing-room, later called the breakfast-room. It seems more likely that they were supplied with the other furniture for Alnwick for which Linnell was paid £217 on 17 January 1771 and £33 on 22 December 1772, Alnwick MS.

20. Alnwick MS 121/63, p. 22.

21. Alnwick MS 121/31A p. 279. She married Sir Hugh Smithson on 16 July 1740.

22. Waddell, op. cit. at note 3 above. SM 11:29 and 39:13. This was the 'Blue Room' decorated in 1780 by the painter and gilder John Wateridge, of St Martin's in the Fields, London. Alnwick MS U/I/46.

23. On 2 September 1770, Revd Theophilus Lindsey, in a letter to the Earl of Huntingdon, reported that 100–200 hands were daily employed at Alnwick 'on widening the river and finishing the new-made chapel etc' which was linked to the library. Historical Manuscripts Commission, Report on the manuscripts of the late Reginal Rawdon Hastings, Esq., London, 1934, III, pp. 149–50.

24. Waddell, op. cit. at note 3 above. SM 22:54 is a design for the chimney-piece with a clock in the centre, SM 39:11 an unfinished version. SM 22:214 and 39:12 are earlier designs for the chimney-piece wall in the library with variant chimney-pieces. The inscription on the verso of SM 39:12 *Circular Room* is misleading.

25. Waddell; Grose, op. cit. at note 8 above.

26. Hayward and Kirkham, op. cit. at note 13 above, pp. 122–3. These tables are almost identical to Linnell's writing tables at Osterley, made c.1768–9.

27. J. Plumptre, *James Plumptre's Britain, the journal of a tourist in the 1790s*, London, 1992, p. 103.

28. Waddell, op. cit. at note 3 above; SM 39:17, inscribed 'Section of one side of the Chapel at Alnwick Castle, from A to B on the Plan. Only 5 recesses besides the large one done in the original which were slightly shaded and not coloured' and dated '5 Dec. 1780'. The 'original' referred to here is probably the design included in Adam's account, 11 August 1780, 'To a Section of part of the side of the Chapel, with Shields, Trophies, &c. introduc'd in the pannels £11.19', Alnwick MS U/I/46/42.

29. Waddell, op. cit. at note 3 above; SM 39:19; 27:33. On 19 August 1777, Adam billed the duke for a 'coloured drawing of the manner of

finishing the pannels in the Chapel by introducing the pedigree of the Family £5.5.0.', Alnwick MS U/I/46.

30. Grose, op. cit. at note 8 above.

31. The Percys seem to have had a tradition of building Gothic chapels. In June 1749, the 7th Duchess of Somerset wrote to Lady Luxborough that her husband, Algernon Seymour, who succeeded as 7th Duke in 1748 and was president of the Society of Antiquaries, had thrown two rooms together at Northumberland House in the Strand 'to make a chapel, with a Gothic wainscot, ceiling, and painted windows; there is to be a Dutch stove in it, which is so contrived as to represent a tomb with an urn upon it'.

32. Grose, op. cit. at note 8 above. Adam's bill, 22 December 1773, 'To Two Different Designs for Painting the Chapel Window £10.10.0', Alnwick MS U/I/46. SM 39:18. On 9 March 1779, 'Proposals for painting & Staining on Glass Three Windows in the Chapel of Alnwick' were submitted by James Pearson. The painted glass and iron framing was completed in March 1780 at a cost of £345.13.0, Alnwick MS U/I/46/48.

33. Waddell, op. cit. at note 3 above. Alnwick MS U/I/46/1 and 46/48.

34. C. L. Eastlake, *A history of the Gothic revival*, ed. J. M. Crook, London, 1970, p. 108.

35. Adam's bill, 11 August 1780, 'To a design of a Carpet for the Chapel at Alnwick Castle in two different ways', Alnwick MS U/I/46/16, 21, 43. SM 17:202 inscribed 'Design of a Carpet for the Chapel at Alnwick Castle in two different ways. One full half of the Original finished. 5 Dec. 1780.'

36. Waddell, op. cit. at note 3 above. The 1786 inventory of Alnwick, includes '1 figured oil cloth & green cover' in the chapel, Alnwick MS H/IV/2/d.

37. Adam's bill, 11 August 1780, 'To a design for a Carpet for the Circular Recess of Pew in the Chapel', Alnwick MS/U/I/46/16, 21, 43; SM 17:201 is dated 5 December 1780 and is probably an office copy.

38. Waddell's description brings to mind the circular closet at Syon. Could it also have caused the Syon design at the Soane (SM 39:15) to be mislabelled 'Alnwick', or is that mere coincidence? The error was compounded by James Macaulay, who attempted to link the miscaptioned Soane design to the 'apse' of the saloon. Macaulay, op. cit., p. 71.

39. Waddell, op. cit. at note 3 above. The 1786 inventory (Alnwick MS H IV 2.d.) is more specific in its description of the chairs in the family pew as wheel-back. These and the stools survive at Alnwick. There is no evidence that they were designed by Adam.

40. SM 50:2. There is a drawing of a larger reading desk at Alnwick which is unrelated to the surviving piece. This has lost some finishing ornaments at the top of the front. An identical chair and lectern were designed by John Hobcraft for the Gothic chapel at Audley End and executed by Sefferin Alken. Hobcraft executed Adam's Gothic chair for Croome Church. M. Sutherill, 'John Hobcraft and James Essex at Audley End House', *The Georgian Group Journal*, 1999, IX, pp. 23–4, fig. 10.

The gilt tripod at Alnwick with rams' heads at the top and sphinxes at the base was made for the drawing-room at 20 St James's Square in 1773, SM 17:60.

41. Wateridge agreed to gild the mouldings and ornaments in the chapel on 11 January 1780. On 6 February 1782, his widow Susanna was paid £691.8.6 for his work. Alnwick MS /U/I/46/1; folders 47–94 contain itemized bills for the chapel, including that for 1480 books of gold leaf. Pearson was paid on 7 March 1780, Alnwick MS U/I/46/1 and U/I/46/48. R. Warner, *A tour through the northern counties of England*, Bath, 1802, II, p. 14; (S. Shaw), *A tour, in 1787 from London, to the western highlands of Scotland*, London, 1788, p. 216.

42. J. Farington, *Diary*, ed. K. Garlick and A. Macintyre, London, 1979, V, p. 1621. Warner, op. cit. at note 41 above, p. 20.

43. Plumptre, op. cit. at note 27 above.

44. Warner, op. cit. at note 41 above.

45. Read's agreement 'to execute a sarcophagus agreeable to Mr Adam's design', 28 February 1778. On 18 March 1779 he received 'payment for Gothic sarcophagus to be put up in the chapel at Alnwick £240'. On 4 July 1782 he was paid 90 guineas 'for Executing the top of a Sarcophagus to be placed at Alnwick Castle', Alnwick MS U/I/46/59, 60. Read also executed the duchess's monument at Westminster Abbey.

46. SM 11:30; 52:36 is a pencil sketch related to the banqueting-room ceiling. There is also a finished watercolour drawing at Alnwick.

47. SM 39:10.

48. SM 27:39 inscribed 'Impost for the Circular Room'.

49. Designs for a chimney-piece, 1767:SM 22:228, 229; large-scale partly coloured details of chimney-piece, SM 18:59, 61; design for a ceiling, 1766, SM 11:234.

Walpole wrote to William Hamilton on 22 September 1768 that he had 'been projecting (that year) a chimney in imitation of the tomb of Edward the Confessor, and had partly given it up, on finding how enormously expensive it would be. Mr Adam had drawn me a design a little in that style, prettier it is true, and at half the price.' *Correspondence*, XXXV, pp. 406–7. In an undated letter to Adam, Walpole wrote 'Mr Walpole has sent Mr Adam the two books, and hopes at his leisure he will think of the ceiling and chimney-piece. The ceiling is to be taken from the plate 165 of St Paul's, the circular window The Chimney from the shrine of Edward the Confessor At Westminster.' Printed in *The Builder*, 6 January 1866, p. 6.

50. Design for a 'Cieling for the Drawing room at Northumberland House not executed', SM 11:32, 102.

51. Grose, op. cit. at note 8 above. The gothic decoration of the interior of the garden house at Hulne Priory, previously credited to Adam, is now convincingly attributed to the architect, John Bell. A. Rowan, 'The Duke of Northumberland's Garden House at Hulne Priory', *Architectural History*, XLI, 1998, pp. 265–73.

52. T. Pennant, *A tour in Scotland MDCCLXIX*, Chester, 1771, p. 31. Joseph Farington, who visited Alnwick on 15 September 1801, thought the decoration 'to be in a very bad taste, loaded & crowded without the least simplicity.' op. cit. at note 42 above, p. 1621.

53. J. Harris, loc. cit. at note 18 above, p. 6.

54. Donaldson, op. cit. at note 5 above, pp. 14–15.

55. Ibid., p. 16.

56. Ibid., p. 24.

6. NORTHUMBERLAND HOUSE

1. Letter from the Duchess of Somerset to Lady Luxborough, June 1749, quoted in *Survey of London, The Strand*, 1937, XVIII, p. 13. D. Owsley and W. Rieder, *The glass drawing room from Northumberland House*, London, Victoria and Albert Museum, 1974 is the seminal work on the subject.

2. The opening of the gallery was reported by Walpole in a letter to Horace Mann on 5 May 1757, *Correspondence*, XXI, p. 88. 'It is a sumptuous chamber', Walpole wrote, 'but might have been in a better taste.'

According to Thomas Williams's 'Description of Northumberland House written in 1875', Alnwick MS, the tapestries were made in 1758 from drawings by Zuccarelli of scenes of Eastern travel. Three of these panels are at Alnwick Castle, the rest are at Albury Park, Surrey. The 1786 inventory of Northumberland House notes two festoon window curtains of three coloured damask to match the seat furniture, Alnwick MS H/IV/2d.

3. SM 11:31, inscribed 'Ceiling for the Dining room at Northumberland House/not executed June 1770'; SM 11:32, inscribed 'Ceiling for the Drawing room at Northumberland House/not executed June 1770'; SM 8:102 a pencil sketch of rejected drawing room ceiling; SM 11:33 is a large watercolour design of the ceiling as executed, also dated June 1770.

4. Sir William Chambers surveyed Tinmouth (or Tynemouth) Park, Northumberland in 1769–70. Mr Rhodes made a survey and plans of Syon. Mr Armstrong made two maps of Northumberland on 20 March 1770. A rough drawing of the plan of Northumberland House was copied by a Mr Halfpenny on 28 June, another plan of Northumberland House was made by Mr Billingham, a third plan and survey was made by the painter, George Lambert, and a copy of his survey was made by Mr Bentley in December 1771. Alnwick MS U/I/44.

5. The bill for £2.2.0 for work done by 'Plasterers, and Carpenters' Men at Northumberland House', paid on 1 July 1773, 'by order, sent by Mr Corner when his Grace was out of town' (Alnwick MS U/I/44) cannot definitely be linked with the new drawing-room and is too small to indicate significant new work. Owsley and Rieder, op. cit. at note 1 above, p. 1.

6. Alnwick MS U/I/46/15–46. The ceiling design, SM 11:33 or a version of it, having been accepted 'for the Execution' was included in the bill for 9 June 1773. So too were the three 'sections' or wall elevations 'for the Execution'. The related drawings at the Soane, SM 39:6,7,8 are not dated. The possibility that, like the ceiling design, they were made in 1770 and only billed when their execution was decided upon cannot be ruled out.

7. W. Rieder, 'Furniture-Smuggling for a Duke', *Apollo*, September 1970, p. 206.

8. Alnwick MS I/I/42.

9. Ibid.; Rieder, loc.cit. at note 7 above, pp. 207, 209 n. 16.

10. *Gazetteer*, 10 April 1770. Three days earlier, Thomas Butler, the Duke's steward, 'Paid for 3 Advertisements in the Daily Advertiser and 3 in the Gazeteer for the establishment of a Plate Glass Manufactory £1.10.0', Alnwick MS/U/I/44.

11. G. Wills, *English looking glasses*, London, 1965, Appendix I, 'Parliamentary Proceedings Relating to the Cast Glass Company'.

12. Neither Garrick nor the duke were named in the petition to parliament, though the latter is known to have had an early interest in the venture. Owsley and Rieder, op. cit. at note 1 above, p. 14. See W. H. Bowles, *History of the Vauxhall and Ratcliff glass houses and their owners, 1670–1800*, London, 1926.

13. It is interesting to note that Lord Coventry's French tapestry-room at Croome Court was put up in June 1771 and Adam's designs for the ceiling of the Osterley tapestry-room date from 1772. Although the duke purchased large quantities of French furniture, glasses and tapestry, he gave active support to the Society for the Encouragement of Arts, Manufactures and Commerce.

14. *Survey of London, The Theatre Royal, Drury Lane, and the Royal Opera House, Covent Garden*, 1970, XXXV, pp. 46–7. *Public Advertiser* 30 September 1775. Owsley and Rieder, op. cit. at note 1 above, p. 14. Adam's designs for the theatre dated 1775, SM 14:16,17; 27:85; Adam, *Works*, II.

15. For the duke's purchases of tapestry from the Gobelins in 1764 or 1765, see chapter 4 on Syon, n. 63.

16. J. Ralph, *A critical review of the public buildings . . . in and about London*, London, 1783, p. 76. See

E. Harris and N. Savage, *British architectural books and writers 1556–1785*, Cambridge, 1991, no. 729 for the identification of the editor as William Nicholson.

17. D. Watkin, *Sir John Soane Enlightenment thought and the Royal Academy lectures*, Cambridge, 1996, p. 87.

18. Charlotte Boyle, Lady Henry Fitzgerald (1769–1831) impressed Walpole in 1787 with her 'genius . . . painting panels in grotesque for the library, with pilasters of glass in black and gold' at her mother, Mrs Walsingham's, house at Thames Ditton. Walpole, *Correspondence*, XXXV, pp. 251, 390.

19. Alnwick MS U/I/42. Rieder, loc.cit. at note 7 above, p. 207.

20. Bills for baize supplied by Thomas Thomas in November and December 1774 and January 1775, Bills for drilling by Richard Sedgley and Charles Dologal (or Delegal) 6 August and December 1774, 10 January 1775, Alnwick MS U/III/6/1. Owsley and Rieder, op. cit. at note 1 above, p. 15.

21. SM 20:17.

22. L. Harris and G. Jackson-Stops, *Robert Adam and Kedleston*, London, 1987, p. 55, pl. 40. Lloyd's Coffee House designs, SM 30:59.

23. Luton Hoo, SM 20:116; Bolton House, SM 20:82–84.

24. Adam's sections, SM 39:6–8, show the green pilasters painted with red ornament. His bills include alternative designs supplied on 4 August 1774 'to a pilaster for the drawing room to be painted'; 'to another ornament for the Pilasters to be done in Metal', Alnwick MS U/I/46/15–46.

25. Alnwick MS U/III/6/1, '1773–4. Jack & Collett Founders Work Done for His Grace Duke of Northumberland'. The firm supplied in all 757 feet, 2 inches of lead moulding in different lengths at 8d per foot. In 1774 they supplied '247 small lead Patres with Mask faces cast in lead & repaired 4 sett copper ornaments with Honey Surcles and Husks at 18s0 per sett', Alnwick MS U/III/6/1. Dominique Jean's bills for gilding are dated January and February 1775. Owsley and Rieder, op. cit. at note 1 above, pp. 15, 30 n. 64–7.

26. Those on the pilasters were figures of Minerva, only one of which survives; the three displayed in the former V&A installation were photocopies. The small medallion from the overmantel also survives.

Alnwick MS 121/63 Duchess of Northumberland's notebook, 'London Prices', p. 24. 'Angelica 4 pictures over ye Doors 125/Zucchi painting Dº 220'. The subjects of the paintings are Nymphs adorning Pan, Juno Cestum a Venera Postulat, Nymphs awakening Cupid, Venus and Adonis. The first two became very well known through engravings by W. W. Ryland, 1776/7.

27. The surviving frieze from the door surrounds has gilt ornaments. The doors themselves are lost. There is a separate drawing for the decoration of their six panels, SM 52:62, but whether this ornament was applied or painted is not known. A surviving fragment of the wall entablature was copied for the V&A installation.

28. At Syon there is a watercolour drawing of the room, made after it had been altered in 1820 but before 1874, when it was dismantled and the ceiling destroyed, which shows the colouring to have been more or less the same as that indicated in Adam's ceiling design, SM 11:33.

29. Stillman, p. 104. Owsley and Rieder, op. cit. at note 1 above, p. 6.

30. Stillman, pls 41, 134, 135, 142.

31. The 1788 edition of Hepplewhite's *Cabinet-maker and upholsterer's guide* contains the following description of the *confidente*. 'This piece of furniture is of French origin and is in pretty general request for large and spacious suites of apartments. An elegant drawing-room, with modern furniture, is scarce complete without a confidente: the extent of which may be 9 feet . . .'

32. Owsley and Rieder, op. cit. at note 1 above, pp. 23–5. The 1786 inventory of the room also includes twelve cabriole chairs with carved and gilt frames and needlework upholstery, Alnwick MS H/IV/2/d p. 60. Owsley and Rieder suggest that this was an extra set, probably kept in the waiting-room behind the drawing-room and brought in when the occasion demanded.

33. King and Padget's bill, Alnwick MS U/I/46/34. Inventory Alnwick MS H/IV/2/d. p. 60.

34. SM 38:8. This corresponds with Adam's bill of 6 May 1774 for a 'design of a table slab coloured at full size', Alnwick MS U/I/46/15–46. See Owsley and Rieder, op. cit. at note 1 above, p. 31, n. 76 regarding the nineteenth-century restoration of the tables.

Sir Rowland Winn was supplied with a similar design in August 1775 for a pair of tables in the saloon at Nostell: SM 17:28 table and SM 49:42 table top.

35. Adam's bills for drawings, Alnwick MS U/I/46 cited by Stillman, no. 109, p. 94, include: 26 June, chimney-glass; 29 June 1773, chimney-piece full-size and coloured 5.5.0; 15 July, another drawing of the chimney-piece at full size with various alterations, 3.3.0; another design of chimney-piece and glass, probably corresponding to SM 22:55; 15 March 1774, another design for chimney-piece and mirror, 8.8.0; 21 March 1774, another design of the chimney-piece, 3.3.0; 26 March 1774, a large scale drawing of chimney-piece, corresponding to SM 18:33; 11 April 1774, a full-size drawing of the chimney-glass, 2.2.0; 10 May 1774, alterations to the design for the chimney-glass.

36. The Etruscan-style chimney-piece designed in 1773, SM 20:55, was adapted for the Countess of Derby's Etruscan dressing-room, Adam, *Works*, II, i, pl. VI. The plate is signed and dated 1773, though the design at the Soane, SM 23:51, is dated 1774.

37. Designs for the slab for the chimney-piece were made on 17 June, 7 July and 9 July 1774, the last 'drawn to scale'; SM 17:51–3.

38. One vase appears on the chimney-piece in the nineteenth-century watercolour of the room. Owsley and Rieder, op. cit. at note 1 above, p. 25 and fig. 24. The vases cannot be linked with the 2 vases bought from Boulton and Fothergill in January 1772, N. Goodison, *Ormolu: the work of Matthew Boulton*, London, 1974, pp. 37, 179, n. 186. Their maker remains unknown.

39. SM 17:173, now Drawer 72, dated June 25 1774.

40. There are bills for a drawing of the girandoles and ornament between the pilasters in full size made in July 1773, and for making alterations to the chimney-glass girandole, 10 May 1774. These drawings do not survive. Sixteen gilt metal branches were recorded in 1822. Alnwick MS U.III. 8d (5).

41. These are all included in the 1786 inventory, Alnwick MS H/IV/2/d. Dominique Jean's bill of 25 February 1775 for 'Gilding 6 Branch & nozal and pans 1.12.0' might refer to the chimney-piece branches, Alnwick MS U/III/6/1.

The duchess's list of 'London Prices' (Alnwick MS 121/63 p. 24) includes a lustre costing £150. This must have been considerably larger than the 18-branch lustre in the 'great' drawing room at Alnwick which cost £126. The chandelier in the 1874 photographs of the glass drawing room is said to date from the 1821 refitting of the room. It now hangs in the green drawing-room at Syon. Owsley and Rieder, op. cit. at note 1 above, pp. 18, 31 n. 72.

The lighting of the drawing-room can perhaps be judged by Count Frederick Kielmansegge's report of the lighting of the picture gallery in 1762 'Four large crystal chandeliers, each with twenty-five candles, light up the room even more brilliantly than is necessary'. *Diary of a journey to England in the years 1761–1762*, London, 1902, pp. 146–7.

42. Alnwick MS 121/59, p. 398.

43. *Northumberland House: its saloon and picture gallery, with a description of its magnificent staircase*, London, 1851. Quoted by Owsley and Rieder, op. cit. at note 1 above, pp. 28, 31 n. 100.

44. J. Summerson, *Georgian London*, London, 1962, p. 143.

7 · BOWOOD HOUSE

1. This description was given by Richard Sutton, who had served in the army under Shelburne from 1766 to 1768. Quoted by L. Namier and J. Brooke, *The House of Commons 1754–1790*, London, 1964, p. 272.

2. Earl of Kerry, 'Kings Bowood, III', *Wiltshire Archaeological and Natural History Magazine*, 1924, XLII, p. 33.

3. Letter from Henry Fox (later Lord Holland) to Shelburne, 29 June 1761. Quoted by Bolton I, p. 196.

4. Kerry, 'Kings Bowood, II', loc. cit. at note 2 above, XLI, p. 512.

5. Ibid., pp. 516–17. Revd Joseph Townsend (1739–1816), a noted geologist, brother of 'Alderman' Townsend MP for Calne, was employed by Shelburne to report on the possibility of restarting the iron mines in Co. Kerry which had been successfully worked in the seventeenth century by Sir William Petty. Townshend's report is dated April 1762.

6. Keene's accounts for work 'From Sept 1st 1755 to Feby 1760' were presented soon after the 1st earl's death. Bowood Archives, papers of the 1st Marquess of Lansdowne. Quoted by Kerry, loc. cit., at note 2 above, XLI, p. 511.

7. Ceiling design, SM 11:75, dated December 1761. The 'Section' of the four sides, SM 39:69, is undated but was presumably made at about the same time or early in 1762.

8. Fleming, pp. 376–7. The hall was painted stone-colour by John Spinnage. Bowood Archives. There is a watercolour drawing of the hall by C. J. Richardson at the V&A, 93.H. 17.

9. The antique vessel was found in the Baths of Agrippa and thought by Desgodetz to be Agrippa's tomb. It was given a prominent place in one of the niches in the portico of the Pantheon. A. Desgodetz, *Les edifices antiques de Rome*, Paris, 1682, pl. V, p. 19. According to Piranesi, it was not a sarcophagus but a bathing vessel. It was removed from the Pantheon and used as the receptacle for the ashes of Clement XII in his monument in the basilica of S. Giovanni Laterano. It had already been illustrated by Piranesi in his *Opere Varie*, Rome, 1750, pl. 6.

In July and November 1768, Linnell made eight more stools 'like them at Bowood' for Lansdowne House. There is a pencil sketch for the stool, SM 54:69; and a design, SM 17:76, which is inscribed 'Stool for the Hall at Shelburne House' and dated 1768. The 1764 design used by Linnell does not survive. Linnell's bills are in the Bowood Archives, papers of the 1st Marquess of Lansdowne. See H. Hayward and P. Kirkham, *William and John Linnell*, London, 1980, I, p. 124. Two stools found their way to Sainthill, Surrey and were sold by Wooley and Wallis, Salisbury, Wiltshire in 1984. These are now at Kenwood; one is a later eighteenth-century copy. Linnell was also responsible for carving the balustrades on the balconies, the doors and doorcases. The central doorway under the screen is now in the Birmingham Museum of Art, Alabama, USA. Hayward and Kirkham, II, fig. 34.

10. J. Britton, *Beauties of England and Wales. Wiltshire*, London, 1814, XV, p. 542. Quoted by Bolton, I, p. 204. The uses of the 'Cube Room' and 'King's Room' are not known.

11. Laid-out elevation of all four walls. SM 39:68. This shows the cove of the ceiling decorated with octagons and rectangles similar to the library at Shardeloes, SM 11:70, rather than the circular coffers in the executed ceiling design of 1763 in the V&A, A. Rowan, *Robert Adam*, Catalogues of Architectural Drawings in the Victoria and Albert Museum, London, 1988, no. 52, p. 48. There is an alternative version with more coffers (15 as opposed to 9) in the Soane, SM 11:79.
R. Wood, *Ruins of Palmyra*, London, 1753, pl. XXXVII. Somewhat heavier and more stilted grotesque panels were proposed in 1759 for the Earl of Northampton's hall at Castle Ashby, Northants. SM 54: pt. i, 56 and 29:21 (Stillman, p. 62, no. 9) and for the dining-room at Hatchlands, SM 35:83 (Stillman, p. 62, no. 12), but neither was executed. The Shardeloes dining-room panels must date from before February 1763, when the plaster-work in the house was completed by Rose. It was the hall, SM 31:102, not the dining-room, that was originally intended to be decorated in this manner (Stillman, p. 63, no. 13).

12. One of the two doors on the south wall was false, the other opened to the hall; one door on the east wall opened to the cube room, the other to a cupboard; one door on the west wall opened to a waiting(?) room, the other was false. The Van Dyck, listed in an 'Inventory of Pictures' at Bowood which must have been made in 1767 at the same time as the accompanying dated inventory of china (Bowood Archives), was evidently a copy. There is a design for the panel over the chimney-piece, SM 3:74.

13. An estimate was made by Carter on 18 November 1763 for £276.2.6 each, Bowood Archives. Adam made alternative designs with Ionic columns, SM 22:94,95, which were rejected. The Corinthian one, SM 22:96, was executed with modifications. The chimney-piece and the ceiling taken from Palmyra were noted by Mrs Montagu, who visited the house in 1765. Letter to Mr Montagu. R. Blunt, ed., *Mrs Montagu 'Queen of the Blues'*, London, 1923, I, p. 127.

14. Carter's accounts: on 22 May 1762 'part of the two Column chimney pieces' were sent to Bowood; on 18 September 'setting up & cleaning one of the Column chy pieces in Drawing Room at Bowood'. This was sold in 1955. *A sale by public auction of the valuable antique fixtures, fittings and indoor and outdoor architectural features of that part of this celebrated mansion which is shortly to be demolished . . . to be held at Bowood, . . . Auctioneer E. Clifford Smith*, 30 June 1955, lot 165.

15. 'Inventory of Pictures', presumably the same date as the accompanying 'Inventory of China at Bowood taken 1767'. Bowood Archives.

16. I. Bristow, 'The Great Drawing Room From Bowood' *ASCHB Transactions*, 1986, X, p. 33. The room was purchased by Lloyds at the 1955 auction prior to the demolition of the house and was reconstructed in their previous headquarters under the direction of Terence Heysham FRIBA.

17. Elevation of window wall, SM 39:68. Design for pier-glass for the drawing-room, SM 20:19; Glass frame for the Earl of Thanet, SM 20:5. On 28 February 1766 Lady Shelburne 'saw Lord Thanet's House which Mr Adam's is decorating & has made very pretty.' Lady Shelburne's diary, Bowood Archives.

18. 1805 sale catalogue at Bowood. No. LXIII Drawing Room, lots 73–5. One mirror sold for £73.10, the other two for £84 each. To complicate matters, the original drawing-room, which was then the dining-room, had three 'large oval pier glass(es)' (No. XXXVII, Dining Room, lots 2–4) which fetched only 4 guineas each and must have been smaller and much less elaborate.

19. Lady Shelburne's diary, document cited at note 17 above.

20. Letter from John Bull of Calne to Shelburne 4 August 1766. Quoted by J. Cornforth, 'Bowood, Wiltshire Revisited I', *Country Life*, 8 June 1972, p. 1450.

21. The ceiling design is described in Adam's Bowood accounts, Bowood Archives, but has not been traced. Lady Shelburne's diary, document cited at note 17 above, refers to the plans for the additional apartment.

22. Adam's Bowood accounts, Bowood Archives. Adam's bill of £154.11.0 for drawings made between 1766 and June 1770 is reprinted by the Earl of Kerry, 'Kings Bowood Park', loc. cit. at note 2 above, XLI, pp. 519–22.

23. The 'Lords Protest' was published on 10 May 1771 in *The Gazetteer and New Daily Advertiser* and reprinted in the *Gentlemans Magazine* for that month, pp. 211–13.

24. Holland's dismissal is thought to have been caused by his dealings in connection with Shelburne's purchase of a site at Hyde Park Corner in 1765, Kerry, loc. cit. at note 2 above, XLI, p. 518.

25. SM 39:72–4.

26. Dance's plans are in the Soane Museum D 3/4/9,10. Cipriani paintings now at Bowood were probably removed from the new drawing-room ceiling in 1833, when it was replaced by Barry's 'rather uninteresting 'barrel ceiling', Kerry, loc. cit. at note 2 above, XLII, p. 35.

27. Kerry, ibid., p. 34.

8. LANSDOWNE HOUSE

1. 'Lansdowne House: A great London House Reconstructed', *Country Life*, 11 May 1935, pp. 490–5.

2. Letter from Henry Fox, later Lord Holland, to Shelburne, 29 June 1761. Quoted by Bolton, I, p. 196.

3. Ibid.

4. M. Brettingham, *Holkham*, London, 1761, preface. Brettingham's plans went to Thomas Worsley, probably through Bute, and are now in the RIBA Drawings Collection J 3/16/9–18.

5. Earl of Kerry, 'Kings Bowood II', *Wiltshire Archaeological Magazine*, 1924, XLI, pp. 512, 516–17.

6. Letter from Thomas Worsley to Bute, February 1760. 'If my dear Lord thinks of the piece of ground by Berkeley Square he will please to say his pleasure.' Bute Archives.

7. Middlesex Deeds Register 4/356, 3 December 1761. Agreements were made between the Earl of Leicester's executors, Sir Matthew Lamb of Brocket Hall, Hertfordshire and Ralph Cauldwell of Holkham, assigning to Bute for 1,000 years two tenements fronting south on Curzon Street, one measuring 51 feet, 2 inches (16 m.) the other 21 feet (6.4 m.), and several stables, coach houses and other erections and buildings on the said pieces of ground.
Adam's surveys and variant plans are in the Bute Archives. See F. Russell, 'The House That Became A Hostage', *Country Life*, 18 October 1998, pp. 64–7.

8. RIBA Drawings Collection: J 3/16/1–18 are plans and elevations for a house on Berkeley Square. J3/16/1–6 are designs by Adam for a 7- or 13-bay house for Bute; J3/16/7 is for a 7-bay house facing north; J3/16/8 is a plan for Bute by another hand, possibly Stiff Leadbetter. J3/16/9–18 are plans and elevations by Brettingham for the Earl of Leicester. This whole group of drawings came from Thomas Worsley of Hovingham via Bute.
In addition, there are five related Adam plans for Bute House, K12/3/1–5. Of these, K12/3/1–3 are c.1761; K12/3/4,5 are dated 1764 and show the library extension on the north-west corner in a more developed form. J3/16/3/1,3 are the earliest plans with the library in this position, c.1762–3.

Other Adam designs for Bute House are at the Soane Museum, SM 21:82, 220; 39:49.

9. Letter from Thomas Worsley to Bute, undated: 'I neglect not however your plans, & shall bring them with me, together with some calculations, as far as related to the carcassing.' Bute Archives.

10. Letter from Sir Thomas Robinson of Rokeby to Bute, 15 August 1762. Bute Archives.

11. Sir Thomas Robinson, ibid., recommended two alternative sites: one belonging to Lord Bath at Green Park, the other owned by Hamilton, MP at Hyde Park Corner, which was bought by Shelburne in 1765. In October, Wyndham offered to sell him his house in Pall Mall for £11,000, but that was too expensive. In December, Adam suggested Lord Robert Manners's house at 22 (later 25) Grosvenor Square.

12. British Museum, Department of Prints and Drawings, F. G. Stephens, *Catalogue of Prints and Drawings in the British Museum. Division I. Political and personal satires*, London, 1877, IV, no. 4043, p. 269.

13. RIBA Drawings Collection, K16/3/4,5 plans of the basement and principal storey, signed by Adam and dated 1764. The plan of the first floor is in the Bute library.

14. General Robert Clerk to the Earl of Shelburne, 1 November 1765. Bolton, II, p. 5.

15. Lady Shelburne's diary, Bowood Archives. Adam's accounts for designs for Shelburne's London house began in 1764, before the site was purchased, with 'Plans, Elevations and Sections of a new Design for his Lordship's House at Hyde Park Corner (£)50.0.0'. An 'Estimate of this Design', for which he charged £12, was sent on 2 October 1765. Adam Accounts, Bowood Archives, reprinted by Bolton, II, p. 340. Several plans are at Bowood and it was from these that Bolton's drawings, II, p. 2, were made.

16. Clerk to Shelburne, Paris, 14 May 1765. Bolton, II, pp. 3–4.

17. Lady Shelburne's diary, document cited at note 15 above. Middlesex Deeds Register 7/345, 28–9 July 1768. There was a 'quadripartite release between Alexander Wedderburn of the 1st part, John, Earl of Bute, 2nd part, Wm. Petty, Earl of Shelburne, 3rd part, and Rt. Hon. Stuart Mackenzie PC, Bute's brother, 4th part'.

18. Bowood Archives.

19. Clerk to Shelburne, 1 November 1765. Bolton, II, p. 5. The security Bute planned to give Shelburne for the money he needed to borrow was thought by Clerk to be 'the house . . . with the ground . . . at least for one half, and insured at that value the house and stables alone. Your (Shelburne's) ground at Hyde Park for the rest.'

20. Adam is reported by Clerk to have said that 'when he undertook the house these stairs were fixed.' According to Clerk, 'Lord Bute's notions of stairs are very particular and . . . in his way of thinking, at least at that time, this alteration would not have been to his mind. The Back stairs upon the right were to be for himself alone, and no other person was to come down that way.' Clerk to Shelburne, 1 November 1765. Bolton, II, p. 5.
Shelburne paid Adam £3,578.12.5½ 'for removing the Staircase from the place intended by Bute to the South east corner', 'Observations on Mr Adams Accots. delivered in 21st April 1769', Bowood Archives; reprinted by Bolton, II, p. 341, where the date is given as '8/21 Aug. 1769'.

21. James Adam to Lord Shelburne, 6 November 1765, Bolton, II, p. 11. This was in reply to letters written by Lord Shelburne on 28 and 30 October, after he had received Adam's 'Plans & Estimates of Shelburne House . . . with all the alterations made from Lord Bute's Design (£)20' and a 'Design of an additional Stair and retiring rooms &c with an estimate thereof (£)18', both included in Adam's accounts, Bowood Archives; reprinted by Bolton, II, p. 340.

Shelburne evidently thought the columns on Adam's design for the façade were pilasters and objected, citing Laugier. Although Laugier's objection to pilasters was that they were irrational, Adam replied 'The French Author Your Lordship mentions is in the right, when he prefers Columns in outside decoration, for as they are more projecting they have greater effect, and round bodies are for the most part, more agreeable to the eye than Square ones.'

22. Lady Shelburne's diary, document cited at note 15 above, January 1766, 'Lord Shelburne consulting Mr Adams about the chain of my watch, and also desired me to ask him at the same time the names of the busts now placed on the stairs'. Most of the surviving building accounts are at Bowood. Those relating to Adam were published by Bolton, II, pt. VII, appendix D, p. 340. Joseph Rose's account for plasterwork is at the Soane Museum among the papers of Henry Holland whose father was employed at Bowood (Soane Archives Priv.Corr.IV.W.9c,13). It too was published by Bolton, II, pp. 342–3. These building accounts relate primarily to works ordered and paid for by Shelburne, not by Bute. Shelburne's 'Observations on Mr Adam's Acc^ts. . . . 1769', document cited at note 20 above, demonstrate his concern to separate the two, which was not always easily done.

23. Lady Shelburne's diary, document cited at note 15 above, 20 August 1768; quoted by Bolton, II, p. 8.

24. Ibid., 10 August 1768.

25. See chapter 7, on Bowood, n. 23.

26. Adam, *Works*, II, no. iii, pl. VIII. The hall chimney-piece was also engraved in the *Works*, pl. VIII. Adam's design for it, SM 22:116, was carved in Portland stone by James Hill for £22 in April 1768.

27. SM 17:112, dated 1768. Gilbert's bills for work done between March 1767 and December 1768: 'To carving a table frame gilt enrich'd for Hall £13.10.0'. The 'Enrich'd carv'd frame for Slab' was '3 times done finished dead White' by the painter, Francis Pitsala, Bowood Archives.

28. Adam's design, SM 17:76, is inscribed 'Stool for the Hall at Shelburne House' and dated 1768. Linnell's bills: 'July 28th 1768. To making and carving 5 hall stools like them at Bowood and painting same £21.5.0'; and November 1768, '3 hall stools to match the above'. H. Hayward and P. Kirkham, *William and John Linnell*, London, 1980, I, p. 124.

29. Peter Cox Burrell & Foster, London. *Lansdowne House. A catalogue of all the handsome household furniture. Sold by Peter Cox Burrell & Foster.* 21 March and 7 following days, 1806. 3 April, XXXIII, lots 2 and 8. One of the stools is now at Kenwood, see chapter 7, on Bowood, n. 9.

30. Columnar screen, SM 27:62. Shelburne's 'Observations on Mr Adams' Acc^ts . . . 1769', document cited at note 20 above.

31. Design for the ceiling composed of octagons, circles, diamonds and rectangles, SM 11:80. Chimney-piece, SM 22:117.

32. Francis Pitsala accounts, Bowood Archives.

33. On 18 March 1769, Lord and Lady Shelburne visited Zucchi's studio, where they saw 'a large Architecture Picture painting for ye Antechamber with wch however my Lord is not particularly pleas'd'. Lady Shelburne's diary, document cited at note 15 above.
The painting measuring 3.07 by 2.03 metres (10 feet 1 inches by 6 feet 8 inches) was exhibited at the Royal Academy in 1770, no. 216. It was sold at Christie's, 7 March 1930, lot 80.
On 2 April 1773 Zucchi was paid £120 for '*Un grand Tableau d'architecture, qui represente les ruines de quelque grand monument de la ville de Cibaris, ou l'on voit Platon qu'on admire la magnificence de si beau monument et en pleurent le sort*'. Fiske Kimball, 'Lansdowne House Redivivus', *Philadelphia Museum of Art Bulletin*,

November 1943, XXXIX, n.p.
Adam's accounts include a 'Design of a section of 4 sides for the ante room (£)12 12.0', August 1766. The design at the Soane, SM 39:58, is incorrectly labelled 'Anti Room to Library', i.e. the second ante-room on the first-floor, which it is not.

34. According to 'A General Estimate of the Apartment to be finished This year in Shelburne House', dated 28 February 1767, the ante-room was to have 'Gilt frames to pictures (£)110.0.0'. Bowood Archives, published in 'Drawing Room from Lansdowne House', *Philadelphia Museum of Art Bulletin*, 1986, LXXXII, p. 54. See also H. Potterton, 'Neo Classical Decorative Scheme: G. B. Cipriani at Lansdowne House', *Apollo*, October 1972, pp. 332–5. Two of the paintings feature Ciron, the centaur that is part of the Shelburne crest. These were sold at Christie's, London on 7 March 1930, lot 38, and were bought by the Philadelphia Museum of Art in 1972 under the mistaken belief that they came from the drawing-room. J. Rishel, 'The Painted Decoration', *Philadelphia Museum of Art Bulletin*, ibid., pp. 28, 29 n. 3.

35. 'Memorandum by Lord Shelburne on his collection of Sculpture', February 1777, published in A. H. Smith, ed., *A catalogue of the ancient marbles at Lansdowne House*, London, 1889, p. 82.

36. On 17 December 1768, Lady Shelburne saw 'some more pictures put into the pannels of ye Antechamber', Lady Shelburne's diary, document cited at note 15 above. These must have been the bacchanals. Zucchi's bills were published by Fiske Kimball, loc. cit. at note 33 above.

37. SM 17:174, 175, the latter partly coloured. Sale catalogue, 1806, op. cit. at note 29 above, Front Drawing Room, lot 13.

38. SM 20:26, inscribed 'Glass & Table frame for the Anteroom at Shelburne House' and dated 1768; see E. Harris, pl. 18. Gilbert's bill for work done at Shelburne House 1767–8 includes 'Ante room To making carving and gilding in Burnish'd Gold a large Glass frame with ornaments at top and bottom £33. To making carving and gilding in Burnish'd Gold a Circular table frame under ditto, full enriched £30.' Bowood Archives, reprinted by Bolton, II, p. 345. Lord Shelburne complained in 1769 that 'The Glass frame in the Anti-Room is very ill executed & wants Gilding again.' 'Observations on Mr Adams' Acco^ts . . . 1769', document cited at note 20 above.

39. The mirror and table frame designed in 1768 for Lord Coventry's Piccadilly house, SM 20:63. The table for Dundas, SM 17:5, described in Adam's bill as 'a Table frame for Long Room next the Eating Parlour £5.5s', Bolton, II, p. 345.

40. Lady Shelburne's diary, document cited at note 15 above.

41. Sale catalogue, op. cit. at note 29 above, XXXIII. Front Drawing Room (i.e., the ante-room) lot 4, 'a varigated marble slab on a gilt frame with green baize cover'; and lot 8, 'French plate of glass 108 inches by 48 inches (2.7 m by 1.2 m) with head plate 48 inches by 27 inches (1.2 m by 68 cm) in a gilt frame and brass rod.'

42. On 7 November 1767, Joseph Rose billed for 'cutting ground for panel over chimney'. On 4 March 1768, Oliver Alken carved the mouldings of the frame which Rose repaired on 21 May 1768. The chimney-glass frame was painted white by Francis Pitsala whose work was measured and settled in 1768 and 1769. The mirror was described in the 1806 sale catalogue, op. cit., lot 9 as '73 inches by 56 inches in a white frame.' Alken also carved the chimney-piece to an Adam design dated 1768, SM 22:118, the mahogany doors and the Corinthian pilasters framing the door in the apse. Bowood Archives.

43. Lady Shelburne's diary, document cited at note 15 above, 22 August 1768; Bolton, II, p. 8. On 24 August, she 'bespoke a hundred Yards of the

spotted Satin for furniture of Buck & Swann which (she was) to have in three weeks'.

44. Sale catalogue, op. cit. at note 29 above, XXIV. Back Drawing Room, lots 3–6 consisting of a gilt cabriole sofa, 18 gilt cabriole chairs, 4 large gilt cabriole chairs and 2 stools.

45. Ibid., XXXIII. Front drawing-Room, lots 3 and 11.

46. The designs for needlework chair backs are at Bowood. Adam made similar designs for chair backs for Mrs Montagu at Hill Street, c.1766, SM 49:51, and Chief Baron Orde at Queen Street, Edinburgh, SM 49:50.

47. This appears on the final plan for Bute House in the Bute Archives and on the revised plan eliminating one of the back stairs, which was drawn for the Earl of Shelburne in October 1765, SM 39:53.

48. M. I. Wilson, 'Lord Bute's Barrel Organ', *Musical Opinion*, February 1966, LXXXIX, pp. 289–91. For a fuller account of the organ, see chapter 15 on Luton.

49. SM 25:4, inscribed 'Organ Case for the Earl of Bute' and dated 1763; SM 25:5 is similarly inscribed but undated. See chapter 15 on Luton.

50. A partly coloured ceiling design survives, SM 11:83, but no wall elevations. 'A General Estimate of the Apartments to be finish'd This Year in Shelburne House', document cited at note 34 above.

51. Documents 'that specifically mention or incontrovertibly refer to the Lansdowne House drawing room' were published in the *Philadelphia Museum of Art Bulletin*, loc. cit. at note 34 above, pp. 52–8. Other bills are in the Bowood Archives. Joseph Rose's bill for ornamental plastering, published by Bolton, II, p. 343, is among the papers of Henry Holland in the Soane Museum.

52. Chimney-piece design, SM 22:96. Carter's bills are among the papers pertaining to Bowood House in the Bowood Archives.

53. Pitsala's bills for painting were measured and settled in 1768 and 1769, Bowood Archives. *Philadelphia Museum of Art Bulletin*, loc. cit. at note 34 above, p. 56. In 1776 Shelburne asked Gavin Hamilton to find a painting to go over the chimney-piece. Gavin Hamilton to Lord Shelburne, Rome, 8 August 1776, Bowood Archives. Smith, loc. cit. at note 35 above, p. 58.

54. Designs for caryatid table and mirror: SM 20:24 and 3:87. The pierced border of the mirror is comparable to the border of the pier-glasses made for the picture gallery at Corsham Court in 1767 and those in the gallery at Osterley which were made from a design of 1768 originally submitted to Shelburne, SM 20:23, dated 1768. See E. Harris, nos. 55, 56. The crest of the mirror is identical to one on a design of 1768 for the mirror frame for the drawing-room at Coventry House, Piccadilly, SM 20:64, which was executed in 1769 by Sefferin Alken.

55. Pier-glass and caryatid table for the Duke of Cumberland, SM 49:24. There is a pair of caryatid tables, possibly designed by 'Athenian' Stuart, at Basildon House, Berkshire. See E. Harris, 'Imposing puzzles at Basildon House', *Apollo*, April 1997, pp. 33–6.

56. SM 20:27, inscribed 'Glass frame for Drawing room at Shelburne House 1769'.

57. Sale catalogue, op. cit. at note 29 above, XXIV. Back Drawing Room, lot 9, 'French plate of glass 106 inches by 62 inches in a gilt frame'; lot 8, the oriental granite table.

58. M. Butler and D. de Florio, Jr, 'The Restoration', loc. cit. at note 34 above, p. 31. Cipriani's bill, p. 56; Zucchi's bill, p. 57.

59. Perfetti's bill. Bowood Archives, ibid., p. 58.

60. E. Harris, 'The Lansdowne House drawing room: reconstructing Adam properly', *Apollo*, August 1992, pp. 83–6.

61. Rishel, loc. cit. at note 34 above, p. 21.

62. 'Memoire de M. Zucchi . . . 1773', ibid., p. 57.

'Sofa for the Earl of Shelburne', SM 17:75. Sale catalogue, op. cit. at note 29 above, XXIV, lot 3, 'A gilt cabriole sofa, covered with green satin, with bordered feather cushions, 5 hair bolsters, 2 feather pillows, a set of serge cases, a set of manchester ditto, and a drapery curtain to alcove.'

63. The mirror shown in photographs of the room taken early this century was almost certainly a later, nineteenth-century addition. It has been inadequately improved upon in the Philadelphia installation, without any apparent reference to the exactly contemporary alcove mirrors in Adam's library at Kenwood, which are overlaid with more elaborate gilded ornament.

64. SM 50:54. E. Harris, pl. 113.

65. Gavin Hamilton to Lord Shelburne, Rome, 8 August 1776, Bowood Archives, loc. cit. at note 34 above, p. 58.

66. Bowood Archives.

67. K. F. Schinkel, *'The English Journey' Journal of a visit to France and Britain in 1826*, ed. D. Bindman and G. Riehmann, Yale, 1993, p. 116.

68. Letter from Fiske Kimball to Graeme Lorimer, Philadelphia, 29 September 1949, cited by K. B. Hiesinger, 'The Drawing Room: A Documentary Study', loc. cit. at note 34 above, p. 10.

69. M. Butler and D. de Florio, Jr, loc. cit. at note 34 above, p. 32.

70. Carpet design, SM 17:177.

71. The order was illustrated in the *Works* II, iii, pl. VII. See Adam's definition of movement and variety, *Works*, I, preface.

72. Linnell's bill, dated 4 February 1769, is in the Bowood Archives. He was paid £19 for the table and £29 for the '2 coopers', See Hayward and Kirkham, op. cit. at note 28 above, I, p. 125, and W. Rieder, 'John Linnell's Furniture For The Dining Room Of Lansdowne House', *Furniture History*, 1993, pp. 66–7. The round pedestals were identical to those made by Linnell in 1767 for the dining-room at Osterley.

73. Adam, *Works*, I, p. 11.

74. John Gilbert's accounts in the Bowood Archives are quoted by Bolton, II, 344. Denys Sutton, not being familiar with the building accounts, naturally assumed that most of the figures were bought after 1771 in Italy, D. Sutton, 'The lure of the antique', *Apollo*, May 1984, pp. 317–19. The Metropolitan has only two of the original statues – Tyche and Hermes; the others are dispersed in other museums and collections. The Greek figure of Dionysus, stripped of extensive later additions, is now in a private collection in California. The sculptures were sold at Christie's in 1810 but bought back by the 3rd Marquess and remained in place until 1930. See J. Parker, 'Patrons of Robert Adam at the Metropolitan Museum', *Metropolitan Museum of Art Journal*, I, 1968, p. 123, and W. Rieder, loc. cit. at note 72 above, pp. 66–71.

75. Ceiling design, SM Drawer 68/3/3, and *Section of the Great Eating Room*, SM 39:56, both made in August 1766. Adam's account also includes a 'Design at large of 4 panels representing the Seasons' for the ceiling, Bolton, II, 340. This has not been located.

76. Bolton II, p. 12.

77. For Linnell's accounts, see Rieder, loc. cit. at note 72 above; for Chippendale's accounts, see Gilbert, I, p. 253.

78. Sale catalogue, op. cit. at note 29 above, XXII. Dining Room, lots 17–19.

79. Lady Shelburne's diary, document cited at note 15 above, 27 August 1768.

80. Bowood Archives, quoted by Bolton, II, p. 341.

81. Bolton, II, p. 12. Adam, *Works*, II, iii, pl. VI. Devall accounts, Bowood Archives.

82. Bolton, II, p. 8.

83. Sale catalogue, op. cit. at note 29 above, Dining Room, lots 3–7.

84. A 'Section of Great stairs' and a 'Design of a Ceiling' are listed in Adam's accounts, Bowood

Archives, quoted by Bolton, II, p. 340. The section, SM 39:63, and the ceiling design, SM 39:67, are both dated 1766. According to Lord Shelburne's 'Observations on Mr Adams' Acco^ts. . . . 1769, document cited at note 20 above, Adam's 'first design . . . was almost entirely laid aside'. The ruinscapes in his section were evidently replaced by busts; how these were displayed is not known.

85. Most of the chimney-pieces in the upper rooms were executed by Oliver Alken in 1767–8. Bowood Archives.

86. Ceiling design, SM 11:84, dated 1767 but listed in Adam's accounts for August 1766, Bolton, II, p. 140.

87. 'To a design of a section of four sides of the Library (£)6.6.0', related to SM 39:61; 'To a design of a ceiling for ditto (£)4.4.0', sketch SM 8:104, finished design, SM 11:84. This is dated 1767, though it is listed in Adam's accounts for August 1766, Bolton, II, p. 340. Sefferin Nelson's account, 18 October 1768, Bowood Archives. Adam's section shows no ornament on the pilasters.

88. Accounts of Joseph Rose, 3 October 1766, 6 February 1768. The carpenter, George Shakespeare, was responsible for the bookcases and picture frames, accounts 1767. Bowood Archives.

89. Accounts of Francis Pitsala for painting, Bowood Archives. The bookcases, chimney-piece (SM 22:109), window and door frames were white; the walls above the bookcases were stone-colour, which was also the ground colour of the ceiling, with the ornaments picked out in dead white.

90. Cabinets, SM 17:216.

91. F. Pitsala bills for painting pilasters and '2 Ionic capitals to Ditto' dead white, 1768–9, Bowood Archives. For the Lansdowne porcelain, see sale catalogue, op. cit. at note 29 above, X, Centre Room, lots 8–12, 19.

92. Glass and table frame, SM 20:25, provides alternative legs and apron and must precede the executed design for the table frame, SM 17:15. The latter is inscribed 'for the room between Anti Room and Library in the 1 pair of stairs at Shelburne House'.

93. 1806 sale catalogue, op. cit. at note 29 above, X, Centre Room, lots 1–3.

94. Mirror, SM 20:25; and a sketch, SM 3:88, inscribed 'The pier in the 3 front Rooms is 5.2 the two back rooms about 5.11'.

95. Mirror designs: SM 3:40 rectangular mirror with rounded corners and table frame; SM 20:20, 21, mirror alone, dated 1768. SM 3:59, oval mirror and table frame; SM 20:22, oval mirror inscribed 'Doing by Mr Royle in __?'. Table frame dated July 1768, SM 17:13.

96. Gavin Hamilton to Lord Shelburne, 15 December 1771: 'the drawing of the room with the bow window is finished', Smith, op. cit. at note 35 above, p. 52.

97. Accounts of William Evans for Painting, 5 November 1776: 'To a Man 21 Days Putting up Pictures and Assisting Mr Chipero and Mr Bagne in painting ye Sky in ye Ceiling &c £ 5.13.6 Measured Jany 13 1777', Bowood Archives. Memorandum by Lord Shelburne of his collection of Sculpture (February 1777), Smith, op. cit. at note 35 above, p. 81.

98. Accounts of William Evans for Painting, 5 November 1776, Bowood Archives.

99. Smith, op. cit. at note 35 above, pp. 81–2.

100. RIBA J 3/16/1/3.

101. The great or west library of Buckingham House was built between 1762 and 1766; the south library and octagon between 1766 and 1768, after Adam's designs for Bute House. J. Harris, *Sir William Chambers*, London, 1970, pp. 217–18.

102. The first sections made for Bute are in the Bute archives, see F. Russell, loc. cit. at note 7 above. The copy for Shelburne is at the Soane, SM 30:59–62.

103. Adam, *Works*, I, preface.

104. See R. Wood, *Ruins of Palmyra*, London, 1753, pl. 42.

105. Smith, op. cit. at note 35 above, pp. 54–5. D. Stillman, 'The Gallery for Lansdowne House: International Neoclassical Architecture and Decoration in Microcosm', *Art Bulletin*, New York, 1970, LIII, pp. 75–80.

9. HAREWOOD HOUSE

1. The new house was built on a rise above the Old Hall at Gawthorpe which was demolished in 1771. The fullest history of the house is M. Mauchline, *Harewood House*, London, 1992.

2. Lady Lindores was the wife of the Scottish peer, Alexander, 6th Lord Lindores, who died in 1765. Her father, Colin Campbell, son of Sir Colin Campbell of Aberuchill, was Commissioner of the Customs and would have known the Lascelles family and their West Indian firm of sugar factors. Fleming, p. 246. R. Pares, 'A London West-India Merchant House 1740–1769', *Essays presented to Sir Lewis Namier*, London, 1956. R. Sedgwick, *The House of Commons 1715–54*, London, 1970, pp. 198–200.

3. J. Carr to Samuel Popplewell, Lascelles's steward, 1755. West Yorkshire Archive Service (WYAS), Leeds, Har/SC 1.

4. Chambers's drawings are kept at Harewood House. Mauchline, pp. 34–6. D. Stroud, *Capability Brown*, London, 1957, p. 147.

5. Robert to James Adam, 17 June 1758. SRO, GD 18/4848. Mauchline, op. cit. at note 1 above, pp. 38–9.

6. SM 35:5–9, north and south elevations; basement, principal storey and bedchamber storey plans.

7. The drawings sent by Carr to Popplewell on 4 October 1758 were most likely related to the alterations proposed by Adam. Evidently the circular room was included in the plan before 22 January 1759, when Carr wrote to Popplewell, 'I have made a Circular room 30 feet in Diam^r more than we had before without either enlarging the house or altering the size of any room but one which room is large enough to the full for its use'. The altered room was probably the library, which was made smaller than the corresponding room on the west side. WYAS, HAR/SC2.

8. Robert Adam to James Adam, 24 July 1760. SRO, GD 18/4866.

9. Robert Adam to James Adam, 5 September 1758. SRO, GD 18/4852. Mauchline, op. cit. at note 1 above, p. 39.

10. Carr's signed version of the compromise plan is illustrated by Mauchline, ibid., p. 35, fig. 4. An 'intermediate plan' was published by Bolton, I, p. 161. There is a plan in the Harewood archives, WYAS HAR/Buildings 9, with a different arrangement at the ends of the gallery, which is related to a detailed Adam design for the windows, SM 50:88.

11. Bolton, I, p. 161. The original has not been located.

12. WYAS, HAR/Buildings 9; SM 50:88.

13. Harewood church: SM 21:148, dated '23^d April 1759'.

14. WYAS, Har/Buildings 9. This has marginal chimney-piece measurements inscribed with Carr's name and the date '8 Octob^re: 1762'.

15. Edwin Lascelles to Samuel Popplewell, 15 June 1762. WYAS, Har/SC 3.

16. Lascelles to Popplewell, 5 June 1762, ibid.

17. The gallery, being entered at either end, could no longer have apses to reduce its length, and columnar screens were difficult to adjust to the position of the windows. It is little wonder, therefore, that Lascelles thought of using the space to form a varied state apartment consisting of a state bedchamber with oval dressing-rooms on either side. This was suggested in writing,

which is said to be in Lascelles's hand, on the revised plan of the west side, HAR\Buildings 9. Mauchline, op. cit. at note 1 above, p. 53.

18. Popplewell to Lascelles, 12 June 1765 and 22 June 1765. WYAS, HAR/SC 5

19. A letter from Gilly Williams to George Selwyn on 22 August 1765 reported Lascelles's return from France with 'the prettiest watch for Lady Coventry (he) ever saw' and some manuscripts dealing with the longitude to be delivered to Selwyn who was expected 'to explain them properly to the Commissioners appointed by Parliament for issuing the reward'. Reprinted by Bolton, I, pp. 169–70.

20. Gilbert, I, pp. 195–211. I. Hall, 'Newly discovered Chippendale drawings relating to Harewood', *Leeds Arts Calendar*, no. 69, 1971, pp. 5–71; A. Stevenson, 'Chippendale Furniture at Harewood', *Furniture History*, 1968, IV, pp. 62–80.

21. J. Woolfe and J. Gandon, *Vitruvius Britannicus*, London, 1771, V. p. 4, pls. 23–8; E. Hargrove, *History of Knaresborough*, 5th ed., Knaresborough, 1798, pp. 152–5 goes counter-clockwise; but J. Jewell, *The tourist's companion or the history and antiquities of Harewood in Yorkshire*, Leeds, 1819 begins with the library and goes clockwise, ending with the music-room, which is the route taken at present.

22. Carr's plan cited at note 10 above; Adam's last plan, dated 8 October 1762, cited at note 14 above, gives the measurements of the hall and shows it with semicircular niches and engaged columns.

23. SM 35:8; Bolton, I, p. 160.

24. SM 35:13, 'Design for finishing the Hall at Gawthorp'; SM 11:130, '1st Design of a Ceiling for Gawthorp Hall not executed 1765'; SM 11:131, 'Design of a Ceiling for the Hall at Gawthorp 41 long by 31'3" wide 1765'; SM 49:35, 'design for a vase to put on the chimney-pieces', dated 11 March 1778. Four vases were made and put up on 15 August 1778.

25. Lascelles to Adam, 19 November 1766, WYAS, HAR/ACC 4111.

26. The hall was painted in September 1769 by Thomas Sunderland. Mauchline, op. cit. at note 1 above, p. 70.

27. Hargrove, op. cit., at note 21 above, p. 152.; Jewell, op. cit. at note 21 above, p. 21. Gilbert, I, p. 199, pl. 260.

28. SM 35:14 'Design for finishing the Saloon at Gawthorp', n.d.; SM 11:152, ceiling design dated 1767.

29. SM 22:192, chimney-piece design dated 1768. G. Worsley, *Classical architecture in Britain*, London, 1995, p. 283.

30. WYAS, HAR/Building Accounts 492. 23, 30 September 1769, Muschamp extra work, 'assisting Mr. Devals Man with 2 Marble Chimneys in the Saloon'.

31. Jewell, op. cit. at note 21 above, pp. 25–6.; *Harewood Yorkshire, a guide*, 1995, p. 29.

32. J. Farington, *The diary of Joseph Farington*, ed. K. Garlick and A. Macintyre, London, 1979, V, p. 1599.

33. SM 11:159, dated 1765.

34. P. S. Bartoli, *Gli antichi sepolchri, ovvero mausolei Romani ed Etruschi trovati in Roma ed in altri luoghi celebri*, Rome, 1768, pl. XVI 'Botte del Sepolchro dell Villa Corsina'.

35. SM 8:158, rough sketch; SM 11:160, 'Ceiling for the 1st Drawing room at Harewood House' dated 1768, without the oval cameos in the points of the star and calix framing the central rosette; partly coloured pink and green. SM 11:161 finished coloured design with colour key. SM 11:162, 'Ceiling for the 1st Drawing Room at Harewood A Duplicate' dated 1768, partly coloured.

36. Bolton, I, p. 173 and 'Harewood House, Yorkshire', *Country Life*, 4 July 1914, p. 24.

37. SM 11:194, dated 1770 with pilasters and a frieze

repeating that on the wall. SM 22:196, 'Design of a Chimney Piece for the first Drawing Room', dated 1771, with a diamond pattern frieze filled with rosettes, a tablet and ram's head consoles but no pilasters. SM 22:197, 'Chimney Piece for the first' (crossed out and '2d' added) 'Drawing room', dated 1771, with a frieze of candelabra joined by festoons and rosettes, and ram's head consoles. SM 22:198, 'Chimney Piece for the 2d' (crossed and corrected to '1st') 'Drawing room 2d Design', dated 1771, with a frieze of five putti roundels and candelabra, inscribed in pencil 'Nolekens'. SM 22:195, 'Chimney Piece for the first Drawing room', dated 1771, as executed with three putti roundels. Evidently the inscriptions identifying the rooms were added later and there was some confusion.

38. Gilbert, I, pp. 209–10.

39. (Stebbing Shaw), *A tour, in 1787 from London, to the Western Highlands of Scotland*, London, 1788, p. 250.

40. SM 11: 163, 'Design of a Ceiling for the Room in the South West Corridore at Gawthorp House 39.0 by 21.10 17.6 high', dated 1765; SM 11:164 a duplicate. These are uncoloured and possibly intended to be white to give height to the ceiling. They are related to the Shardeloes and Osterley ceilings. SM 11:165, 'Ceiling for the second Drawing room at Gawthorp House not executed' dated 1765, coloured. SM 11:166 'Ceiling for the second Drawing room not executed', dated 1765, coloured. The inscriptions for the second drawing-room are later.

41. WYAS, HAR\Building Accounts 492. Muschamp extra work June 1769.

42. SM 11:167, design for a coved ceiling, coloured with alternative decorations of the cove, dated 1767. SM 35:11 incorrectly inscribed 'Library at Gawthorp', laid-out elevations, coloured, undated. This shows the chosen cove decoration.

43. WYAS. HAR\Building Accounts 491, 15 September 1770, Christopher Theakstone for a marble chimney-piece for 2nd drawing room and putting up ditto. Theakstone's bill for a piece of marble astragal for the chimney-piece on 17 June 1773 suggests imperfect execution. HAR\Bills 513.

44. WYAS, HAR\Bills and Vouchers 388. 4 November 1784 bill for total of £106.17.0.

45. (S. Shaw), op. cit. at note 39 above, p. 250. There would have been two mirrors on the window piers, one over the chimney-piece and two on the end walls, making a total of five mirrors, not six as given by Hargrove, op. cit. at note 21 above, p. 153.

46. SM 35:8, first plan of 1758 showing square recesses with columnar screens across them and an oval stair and closet on the south and square stairs and closet on the north. WYAS, HAR/Buildings 9, a c.1759 plan showing semicircular apses with engaged columns framing the windows; the northern apse has additional pairs of columns corresponding to Adam's design of a 'Chapel & Window', SM 50:88.

47. Mauchline, op. cit. at note 1 above, p. 121. Designs were made in 1820 for installing two chimney-pieces on the east wall and filling the space between with bookcases. There are designs by Atkinson and Sharpe for the bookcases in the Harewood archives, WYAS HAR\Buildings 4.

48. SM 35:10.

49. SM 11:168, 169.

50. SM 11:170, dated 1769, coloured; SM 11:171 a duplicate. Mauchline, op. cit. at note 1 above, p. 103.

51. SM 22:199, '1st. Design', dated '1774'. SM 22:200, '2d. design', coloured, dated '22 June 1776'. SM 22:201, '3d Design', dated '11 June 1777'. SM 22:202, '3d Design', dated '11 June 1777'. SM 22:203, '4th Design', dated '13th June 1777', coloured. SM 22:204, '4th Design', dated '13th June 1777', outline.

52. Gilbert, I, p. 210.

53. SM 22:199, 'Chimney Piece for the Gallery at

Harewood House 1st Design', 1774; SM 22:200; SM 22:201, '3d Design of a Chimney Piece for the Gallery at Harewood Adelphi 11 June 1777'; SM 22:202 similarly inscribed and dated; SM 22:203 '4th Design . . . 13th June 1777', coloured; SM 22:203 uncoloured outline, similarly inscribed and dated. There is a finished presentation drawing at the Metropolitan Museum of Art, New York (34, 78.2.(7)) with a different tablet and cameos as executed. A. Rowan, Robert Adam, Catalogue of architectural drawings in the V&A, London, 1988, p. 102, pl. 72.

54. Hargrove, op. cit. at note 21 above, p. 52. Shaw, op. cit. at note 39 above, p. 249.

55. SM 35:12, laid-out elevations, undated but probably contemporary with the ceiling design dated 1765, SM 11:134; SM 22:181 chimney-piece design, dated 1766. Regarding Devall see Mauchline, op. cit. at note 1 above, pp. 75–6. Jewell, op. cit. at note 21 above, p. 29, notes four paintings, presumably overdoors, by Zucchi: the *Four seasons*, a *Grecian dance*, the *Binding of Bacchus with ivy bands*, the *Rape of Helena*, and a *Festival of Bacchus*.

56. SM 14:118 laid-out elevations, undated, c.1765. The panels of grotesques are shown particoloured; Joseph Rose charged £35.5.0 for 'extra work in the first Estimate; Viz. Ornament'd Panels over two doors & two ditto next Picture frame'. Stillman, p. 71.

57. B. de Montfaucon, *Supplement au livre de l'antiquité expliquée*, Paris, 1724, pp. 159–61, pl. LVIII.

58. SM 11:132, 133, 'Design of a Ceiling for the Musick Room', dated 1765. The subjects of the roundels are given by Hargrove, op. cit. at note 21 above, p. 152. The ring of circles, particularly on the carpet, is comparable to an unexecuted ceiling design for the gallery at Syon, SM 11:23 dated 'August 1763'; to a chinoiserie ceiling for Mrs Montagu's house in Hill Street, dated 1766, SM 11:200; and to the ceiling design dated 1769 for the back room on the first floor of General Burgoyne's house in Hertford Street, SM 13:144.

59. SM 22:177, dated 1766 with pencil modifications; SM 22:178, 179, two copies of the modified version incorrectly dated 1769, the year after the chimney-piece was put up. WYAS, HAR/ Building Accounts 492. Mauchline, op. cit. at note 1 above, p. 75.

60. SM 22:180.

61. WYAS, HAR/Building Accounts 492, p. 109, 29 May 1772, 'Mr. Devall Fixing the chimney piece in the Music room'. Mauchline, ibid., p. 76. William Burland, one of Muschamp's masons, assisted with fixing the chimney-piece in the music-room, 1–13 June 1772.

62. Farington, op. cit. at note 32 above, V, p. 1599. John Scarlett Davis's watercolour showing the gallery around 1827 is reproduced in the *Harewood House guide*, 1995, p. 39.

63. Hargrove, op. cit. at note 21 above, p. 158. The girandoles were supplied on 26 August 1774. Gilbert, I, p. 208.

64. Laid-out elevations SM 35:15, undated but showing the coved ceiling as designed in 1765, SM 11:35, 36. The revised, executed design, SM 11:37, is dated 1766. The chimney-piece design, SM 22:182, dated 1766, was executed by Devall in 1768 with a different tablet containing half-boys flanking an orrery, like the ones in the library at Osterley. Jewell, op. cit. at note 21 above, p. 22 gives the subjects of the eight paintings as: *Triumph of Homer, Minerva and various emblematical figures*, the *Education of Pliny's daughter* (four subjects) and two historical subjects. See also T. Borenius, *Catalogue of the pictures and drawings at Harewood House*, London, 1936, p. 165. Chippendale's celebrated marquetry library writing-table made for the room in 1772 was sold in 1965. Gilbert, I, p. 210.

65. A photograph of the library boarded up was

published by A. T. Bolton, 'Harewood House, Yorkshire', *Country Life*, 4 July 1914, p. 24.

66. SM 11:138, ceiling dated 1766. See King, p. 240, pls. 334, 335. SM 35:18, laid-out elevation. SM 22:183, chimney-piece design dated 1768, executed with modifications.

67. SM 11:150, 'Room on the left hand side of the Saloon', dated 1767. SM 11:151, ceiling coloured. At Harewood there is a quarter detail coloured and with colour notes. SM 22:191, chimney-piece dated 1767 with a tablet flanked by winged griffons. The tablet was omitted and the frieze simplified in execution.

68. Gilbert, I, pp. 197, 207. The girandoles were later moved to make way for Reynolds's portraits of Edwin Lascelles's step-daughters, Lady Harrington and Lady Worsley. Hargrove, op. cit. at note 21 above, p. 154, noted them in the room in 1798.

69. Gilbert, I, pp. 196, 206–7.

70. Mauchline, op. cit. at note 1 above, p. 128.

71. A. Westman, 'A Bed in Burnished Gold', *Country Life*, 4 May 2000, pp. 28–9.

72. WYAS, HAR/Building Accts 492.

73. SM 22:188, dated 1767; SM 22:189, the same, partial outline with measurements, dated 1767; SM 22:190, 'for the Bed Chamber', dated 1768. The ceiling design, SM 11:147, dated 1767 coloured pink and light green. There is another design, WYAS, HAR/Buildings 5, dated 'Octr 8 1767' with colour notes for the ceiling and other parts of the room 'Frieze Straw Colour/Columns green flutes & white fillets/Dado Straw Colour Plinth Dark Green/Mouldings White/Shutters Green Mouldings White'.

74. Carr's signed but undated plan published by Mauchline, op. cit. at note 1 above, p. 35, fig. 6. One of Adam's wall elevations, SM 50:87, is incorrectly inscribed for the chapel.

75. SM 11:148, 149, ceiling designs; SM 14:120, 121 and SM 50:87, wall elevations.

76. SM 14:124, 125. L. Harris, *Robert Adam and Kedleston*, The National Trust, London, 1987, p. 25, n. 10, pp. 56–7, n. 41–2.

77. Jewell, op. cit. at note 21 above.

78. Hargrove, op. cit. at note 21 above, p. 154. This was exaggerated by Jewell into 'seven representations'. There is a bill for cutting a recess for a glass frame on 24 June 1769, WYAS, HAR/Building Accounts 492.

79. WYAS, HAR/Buildings 5.

10. OSTERLEY PARK

1. H. Walpole to Lady Ossory, 21 June 1773, *Correspondence*, XXXII, p. 127. The basis of this chapter is my National Trust guidebook, E. Harris, *Osterley Park, Middlesex*, London, 1994.

2. The survey belongs to the Duke of Northumberland and is at Syon House. Its accuracy is attested to by the depiction of Syon. Alterations to Osterley may have been made by its subsequent owners, Sir Edward Coke (1552–1634) or the Earl of Desmond (1614–66) who in 1630 married Bridget, daughter of Sir Michael Stanhope by Anne, daughter of Sir William Reade of Osterley. For the early history of the house see *Victoria County History, Middlesex*, London, 1962, pp. 108–10; J. Yorke, 'Osterley Before Adam', *Country Life*, 14 September 1989, pp. 220–2.

3. PRO/PROB.5/2019. M. Reed, 'Osterley Park in 1668: The Probate Inventory of Sir William Waller', *London and Middlesex Archaeological Society Transactions*, 1994, XLII, pp. 115–20.

4. F. Kelsall, 'Osterley from Gresham to Barbon', *Aspects of Osterley*, The National Trust, London, 2000, pp. 6–12.

5. Barbon raised a £12,000 mortgage on the house in 1684, £3,000 of which was provided by a trustee of Francis Child's, Christopher Cratford. Yorke, loc. cit. at note 2 above, p. 222.

6. F. G. Hilton Price, *Marygold by Temple Bar*,

London (1902). R. Sedgwick, *The House of Commons 1715–1754*, London, 1970, I, p. 549–50; *The House of Commons 1754–1790*, London, 1964, II, p. 212; C. J. Feret, *Fulham old and new*, London, 1900, II, pp. 90–7.

7. A bill addressed to Sir Robert Child from Edward Stanton & Brown for masons work at Lincoln's Inn Fields and Osterley. March 9 (1721) 'Vein'd Marble in a Chimney piece . . . to Osterly to Sett up ye S^d Chimney piece. 1721 April 21 Rec'd.'. London Metropolitan Archives (LMA), Jersey papers, box 12/3.

8. E. Harris, 'The Childs in London', *Aspects of Osterley*, London, 2000, pp. 35–44.

9. J. Rocque, *A new and accurate survey of the Cities of London and Westminster, the borough of Southwark, with the country about it for nineteen miles in Length and thirteen miles in depth . . . Begun in 1741, and finished in 1745, and published in 1746*, London, 1747. Pl. XIV, containing Osterley, is undated but is presumably of the same date or slightly earlier than pl. XIII, which is dated 28 December 1744. Both Sir Francis Child the younger and Samuel Child were subscribers.

The undated survey of the south front, SM 43:94; Adam's section dated 1761, SM 43:95.

10. E. Gibbon, *The history of the decline and fall of the Roman empire*, ed. D. Womersley, London, 1994, I, 253.

11. I. Ware, *Designs of Inigo Jones and others*, London, 1731, p. 53.

12. This corrects the earlier date given in my guidebook, E. Harris, op. cit. at note 1 above, p. 20.

13. Matthew Hillyard's bill for work done from 19 April 1756 to 28 June 1759, examined by Boulton Manwaring and paid on 1 April 1760, includes 'making centres for the bricklayers over stone steps', LMA, Jersey papers, box 3, 53, p. 11. This may have been on the garden front where there was other work being done at this date. The puzzling curved walls under the present portico may relate to the front stairs.

14. A. Rowan, 'The Evolution of Osterley in the Eighteenth Century', *Aspects of Osterley*, London, 2000, pp. 19, 22, asserts that this system of vaulting was built specifically to support the floor of the courtyard (i.e. portico) when Robert Child first agreed to open up the courtyard into a U-shaped plan. He misquotes me in his note 10 as suggesting that the hall was at ground level and the library above. See E. Harris, op. cit. at note 1 above, pp. 20–1. The first floor hall was evidently finished by June 1749, when Hillyard attended 'masons at fixing a Pedestal in the Hall', documented cited at note 13 above.

15. According to Rowan, ibid., p. 22, it was raised by approximately three feet and the difference in level can be seen clearly from the north corridor. Adam's 1761 section, SM 43:95, also shows the forecourt raised above the ground level of the west range. The accounts of Richard Norris, bricklayer, for May 1764 include 'footing to new front', which I take to mean the new courtyard front of the west block. The courtyard was presumably raised at that time. LMA Jersey Acc., p. 11.

16. T. F. Dibdin, *The bibliographical decameron*, London, 1817, III, pp. 306–12; J. Nichols, *Literary Anecdotes*, London, 1812, V, p. 327. The Childs's library was catalogued in 1771 by Thomas Morell of Eton, curate at Kew and Twickenham, who probably added books for Robert Child. Robert Trevor Hampden, who had been commissioned to buy rare books in Holland for Sir Richard Ellys and Sir Francis Dashwood in the 1740s, and whose daughter was engaged to marry Francis Child, may also have been instrumental in the formation of the library. A copy of Morell's catalogue was purchased by Gough and is in the Bodleian Library.

17. Bryan Fairfax was the son of Brian Fairfax who was equerry to Charles II, brother of Sir Thomas Fairfax of Cameron and cousin to the Duke of Buckingham. His brother, Charles Fairfax (d. 1723) was a Christ Church colleague of Henry Aldrich who persuaded him to make a Latin translation of Palladio's *Antichita de Roma*, published in 1709.

Sir Francis Child's niece, Martha Collins (d. 1743), married Robert, Lord Fairfax of Cameron. On a visit to the Low Countries in 1697, Sir Francis Child bought Rubens's large portrait of the Duke of Buckingham and the *Glorification of the Duke of Buckingham* painted for York House.

18. Matthew Hillyard's account for work done in April 1756 includes 'taking down old press at the end of the library & removing some wainscott'. Document cited at note 13 above, pp. 1, 2, 12. Norris's bill for bricklaying, 30 May 1764, includes 'D^r stopt up attic into library', document cited at note 15 above, p. 20.

19. Rowan, loc. cit. at note 14 above, p. 27, n. 15, suggests that the library was located 'in the three rooms above the hall on the west side of the courtyard'. However, we know from Hillyard's bill that the library was in a single large space of 1,167 square feet and not divided into three rooms. The three rooms, as Rowan goes on to explain, were only thrown together into one large space when the new hall was formed around 1764. The logical reason for making a new library *and* hall was the demolition of the earlier rooms.

20. There are bills from Matthew Hillyard for framing at least one of the Venetian windows in 1756 and for 'cutting Out the Timbers . . . & Attending the Mason' in February 1759, document cited at note 13 above. Richard Norris's bill for brickwork includes filling in the Venetian window at the north end in May 1764, document cited at note 15 above.

21. Mainwaring was a JP for the county of Middlesex as well as one of its surveyors from 1750–64. He was also surveyor to London Hospital, Whitechapel Road, of which an engraving was made in 1753 describing him as architect. He was still acting as clerk of the works at Osterley in May 1774 when John Gilbert submitted a bill for making pedestals for the hall 'By order of Bolton Mainwaring'. LMA, Jersey papers, box 1/270.

22. Wilton's copy of Chambers's drawing, SM 22:201.

23. Numerous speculative attributions to Chambers were made in the V&A's 1977 guide to Osterley Park by M. Tomlin and P. K. Thornton; these multiplied in the museum's 1985 guide to the house by J. Hardy and M. Tomlin, and in M. Tomlin's *Catalogue of Adam period furniture*, London, 1982.

24. The design is in the Avery Library, Columbia University, New York (IC/2 1–4, 8, 10–26); J. Harris, *Catalogue of British drawings for architecture, decoration, sculpture and landscape gardening 1500–1900 in American collections*, London, 1971, p. 62; J. Harris, *Sir William Chambers*, London, 1970, p. 240, pl. 185, 186. Norris, document cited at note 15 above, p. 21.

25. SM 43:92, 93, 95–8. Number 92, elevation of the east front 'Extends 149 Feet', signed and dated 1761; 93, elevation of north front, not signed or dated; 95, section west to east not signed or dated; 96, plan of ground floor, not signed or dated; 97, 'Plan of the principal Story of Osterley House . . . Robert Adam Architect 1761. The Faint Shadowing Shows what is already Built & the Dark Colour the proposed addition'; 98, plan of the bedchamber story, not signed or dated. The elevation of the south front is at Osterley, where there are versions of SM 43:92, 93, 95, 96.

26. There is nothing to suggest that this was Robert Child's decision as Rowan states, loc. cit. at note

14 above, p. 19, and no reason for Francis to delay taking the decision immediately, in 1762.

27. Rowan, ibid.

28. Undated design for the open portico, OPH 412–1949, A. Rowan, *Catalogues of Architectural Drawings in the Victoria and Albert Museum: Robert Adam*, London, 1988, no. 81, p. 64, pl. 35. Mrs Agneta Yorke, extract from a letter dated 1772 to her sister, Lady Beauchamp Proctor. MS volume in the possession of Gerald Yorke of Forthampton Court, Gloucestershire.

29. Payments in 1762 for work done in 1761 include: £50.3.0 to the carpenter, Matthew Hillyard; £42.18.0 to the painter, Christopher Speed; £59.18.0 to Richard Norris, bricklayer; £58.17.0 to an unnamed mason. In 1762, Grace Weston was paid £69.15.0 for whitewashing and plastering done that year. In 1763, there were the following payments for work done in 1762: £28.5.0 to William Canfield for glazing; £138.15.0 to Christopher Speed for exterior painting; £114.1.0 to Richard Norris, bricklayer, £125.12.0 to Hillyard, carpenter; £26.12.0 to Payce the plumber. LMA, Jersey papers, box 6/8, 11. The design for the orangery is undated but inscribed for Francis Child, SM 43:99, 100.

30. George Montagu to Horace Walpole, 27 September 1763; Walpole to Montagu, 3 October 1763, Walpole, *Correspondence*, X, 103, 104.

31. For Robert Trevor (afterwards Hampden) 4th Baron Trevor, as an architect and collector of drawings see Colvin. Sir Francis Child the elder bought 42 Lincoln's Inn Fields from Sir Thomas Trevor, Robert's father, in 1702, and was no doubt acquainted with the family before that. Like the Trevors, the Childs were Jacobites.

32. Norris's bill for bricklaying, document cited at note 15 above.

33. There is an uninscribed sketch for the urn signed and dated 1766 in a private collection. Linnell's bill is among the Drake papers in Buckinghamshire County Record Office. See E. Harris, nos. 132, 133 and H. Hayward and P. Kirkham, *William and John Linnell*, London, 1980, p. 101.

34. Designs for the sideboard are at Osterley, OPH 400–1949, Rowan, op. cit. at note 28 above, no. 92 and the Soane, SM 17:7; design for the pier-glass SM 20:33. An engraving of the sideboard composition was published in the *Works*, III in 1822 mislabelled 'furniture at Sion-house'. The ruin-paintings are in the style of Charles Louis Clérisseau, who came to London in 1766, shortly after painting a ruin room in S. Trinità dei Monte, Rome. 1766 was also the year that Zucchi arrived in England. The Osterley paintings are his first datable works for Adam. See Stillman, p. 69.

35. The wall elevations are at Osterley, OPH 398–1949. Rowan, ibid., p. 91, pl. 43.

36. Design for the Shardeloes ceiling, SM 11:69. The ceiling is included in Joseph Rose's bill for stucco-work between 10 October 1761 and 19 February 1763 in the Buckinghamshire Country Record Office. Stillman, pp. 97–8, pl. 122, 123.

37. Ceiling design for Harewood, SM 11:163, 164.

38. The plaster-work may have been done by George Bacon who repaired the plaster frame over the chimney-piece in the dining-room in 1779, LMA, Jersey papers, box 1/23. No other works by him are recorded.

39. Agneta Yorke, document cited at note 28 above.

40. Coventry House table, SM 17:10. See also the console table designed in 1768 for 'the Room between Anti Room and Library in the 1 pair of Stairs at Shelburne House', SM 17:15.

41. LMA, Jersey papers, box 10/54.

42. Pier-glass design, SM 20:33.

43. Walpole to Lady Ossory, 26 June 1773. *Correspondence*, XXXII, p. 126, According to M. Tomlin, 'Osterley in the Eighteenth Century: Furniture Re-arranged to the Original Designs – I', *Country Life*, 18 June 1970, pp. 1164, 1167, the

chairs were intended to stand against the walls: three each side of the chimney-piece, one each side of the sideboard; four on the opposite wall under the painting and the two *en suite* armchairs with upholstered backs in the two end windows.

44. S. Eriksen, *Early neo-classicism in France*, London, 1974, p. 346.

45. SM 20:35.

46. OPH 420–1949, Rowan, op. cit. at note 28 above, p. 93; SM 11:204.

47. R. Wood, *Ruins of Palmyra*, London, 1753, pl. XIX, B.

48. The nave ceiling was attributed by Croft-Murray to Giovanni's father, Giuseppe Mattia Borgnis (1701–61), who was evidently brought to England in the early 1750s by Dashwood especially to work at West Wycombe. E. Croft-Murray, *Decorative Painting in England*, London, 1971, II, pp. 173–4. However, as the church was only begun in 1760, its ceiling is unlikely to have been painted by Giuseppi before his death in October 1761. G. Jackson-Stops, *West Wycombe Park*, National Trust guidebook, 1973, p. 19. R. Hewlings, 'A Palmyra ceiling in Lincoln', *Architectural History*, 1988, XXXI, p. 167–8.

49. Bolton, I, pp. 55–60. Portico for West Wycombe Park, SM 44:144; Hanover Square, designs for a library extension and library ceiling and chimney-piece, SM 50:72; 8:97; 11:199; 22:233.

50. Robert Trevor (1706–83) inherited the large Buckinghamshire estates of the famous John Hampden of Great Hampden, Buckinghamshire in 1754 and took the name Hampden. He was Secretary of Embassy at the Hague 1734–6; Envoy Extra. (and Minister Plenipotentiary from 1741) to the Hague 1739–46, Commissioner of Revenue in Ireland 1746–59, joint postmaster-general in the Grenville Administration, 1763–5 and after that remained politically connected with Grenville. Namier and Brooke, *The House of Commons 1754–1790*, op. cit. at note 6 above, II, pp. 212, 576; III, p. 591. See also J. R. G. Tomlinson, *Additional Grenville Papers 1763–1765*, London, 1962, pp. 41, 44, 78, 79.

51. Drawing-room wall elevations, OPH 420–1949. Rowan, op. cit. at note 28 above, p. 93.

52. Chimney-piece design, OPH 406–1949. Rowan, ibid., p. 94.

53. Daniel Adamson's bill, LMA, Jersey papers, box 3/30.

54. Walpole, Correspondence, XXXIV, p. 237.

55. As the room was probably not hung until after the ceiling was painted in 1772, the furniture, which is covered in matching pea-green damask, is unlikely to have been supplied much before 1770. The model was clearly a popular and often repeated one, considered suitable for drawing-rooms in the neo-classical style. Tomlin, op. cit. at note 23 above, pp. 51–2; Hayward and Kirkham, op. cit. at note 33 above, I, p. 119. Adam's design for the carpet, OPH 418–1949, Rowan, op. cit. at note 28 above, p. 97, is not dated but was probably made in 1768, shortly after his unexecuted design for a pier-glass dated 1767.

56. Hayward and Kirkham, op. cit. at note 33 above, I, pp. 118–9.

57. H. Roberts, 'The Derby House Commode', *Burlington Magazine*, May 1985, pp. 276–7.

58. Design for the top of the commode dated 30 January 1773, SM 18:63; details of the decoration of the case, SM 18:58, 67–76, 80, 97, 98; 5:20, 21; 24:238; 25:56, 210.

59. Design of a commode for the Duke of Bolton, SM 17:18. E. Harris, p. 74, pl. 44.

60. SM 20:41. See E. Harris, loc. cit. at note 8 above.

61. LMA, Jersey papers, box 3/2.

62. The executed grate design, OPH 415–1949, Rowan, op. cit. at note 28 above, p. 95, pl. 45. SM 17:124, inscribed 'Grate for Robert Child Esqr' and dated '22d April 1773' is much more elaborate than the executed design, with pairs of

griffons in place of the end legs and standing putti flanking pedestals and urns above them.

63. Undated plan and wall elevations, OPH 419–1949. Rowan, op. cit. at note 34 above, p. 84. The ceiling designs, OPH 399–1949, 417–1949, and SM 11:202 are dated 1766.

64. There is a bill from the jobbing carpenter, Thomas Cordery, dated 3 March 1777 for work 'to the Book Cease in ye passage by ye Library'. LMA, Jersey papers box 10/24.

65. The subjects are given by E. Croft-Murray, op. cit. at note 48 above, p. 198. See also E. Harris, op. cit. at note 1 above.

66. LMA, Jersey papers, 'An inventory of all the household goods . . . at Osterley House . . . 1782'. Reprinted by M. Tomlin in *Furniture History*, XXII, 1986, pp. 120–1. See also box 10/53. Bill from Ravald and Morland, April 1787 for repairing and painting green Venetian blinds for the library and dining-room.

67. OPH 399–1949 and SM 11:202 are differently coloured; OPH 417–1949 is uncoloured.

68. Adam, *Works*, I, iii, p. 4.

69. Hayward and Kirkham, op. cit. at note 33 above, pp. 83, 117–18. Linnell had doubtlessly seen the Earl of Coventry's *bureau à la grec* purchased from Poirier in Paris in 1765, before Fürlohg arrived in London. Adam's design for a table frame for two porphyry slabs for Sir Charles Farnaby, dated 1765, is also similar and may have been inspired by the same French model, SM 17:6; E. Harris, p. 65, pl. 7. The Osterley library table is almost identical to one supplied by Linnell for Alnwick c.1770.

70. Tomlin, loc. cit. at note 43 above, p. 1168. The 1782 inventory also lists a small satinwood table with a drawer, two fire screens, a small mahogany Pembroke table and a small mahogany cabinet with folding doors. The latter was not the marquetry medal cabinet, which was probably made for Child's house in Berkeley Square by Linnell and Haupt and is now at Radier, Jersey.

71. Sarah, Lady Lyttelton to Mrs Hugh Wyndham, 8 July 1809, *Correspondence of Sarah Spencer, Lady Lyttelton*, ed. Hon. Mrs Hugh Wyndham, London, 1912, p. 75.

72. 'Design for finishing the Great Hall at Osterly', signed and dated 'Robt Adam Architect 1767'. OPH 397–1949. Rowan, op. cit. at note 28 above, p. 88, pl. 41. The ceiling designs, OPH 396–1949, Rowan, p. 89, pl. 42 and SM 11:203, are also dated 1767.

73. Agneta Yorke, document cited at note 28 above.

74. Most of the hall must have been painted before Agneta Yorke's visit in 1772. David Adamson's bill for painter's work done at Osterley in 1772, 73 and 74 lists only eleven items in the 'Great Hall', all to do with the window wall and the door friezes. Jersey papers, box 3/30. The room was repainted by Adamson in the spring 1787, box 3/31. It was probably in the 1907 redecoration of the hall that the grey grounds were replaced by different shades of light blue.

75. James Kerr's receipted bills for repairing the pavement on 31 October 1778 and 16 January 1779, LMA, Jersey papers, box 1/20, 21.

76. Design for the bracket and vase, SM 6:33. Sketch of scroll stool, SM 54:66.

77. Two stools, two settees and two chairs from the Moor Park suite are now at Kenwood, together with two reproduction chairs. James Lawson invoiced Sir Lawrence Dundas in 1764 for '2 Carved & gilt Sophas', '2 Carved & gilt scroll stools' and '6 Carved & gilt Chairs' all 'covered with blue Turkey leather'. The Osterley hall stools were also covered with blue leather.

78. The four pedestals ornamented with heavy swags predate Adam's arrival at Osterley. The carpenter Matthew Hillyard's bill for 'Attending the Masons at fixing a Pedestal in the Hall' in May 1758 may relate to one of these pedestals. LMA, Jersey papers, box 3/83. In May 1774 John

Gilbert, by order of Bolton Mainwaring, made two smaller pedestals 'Inrichd with Oak Leaves and Rafled Leaves &c' to match the four larger ones. LMA, Jersey papers, box 1/270. The four urns and pedestals are thought to have been placed at the corners of the central rectangle of the pavement, flanking the statues of the *Reclining Magdalen* and *Sleeping Jesus* that stood in front of the alcoves.

79. Design of a ceiling for the staircase, SM 11:205.

80. Design for the hanging lanterns, SM 6:60. For the sake of symmetry, the standing lamp was depicted as a hanging lantern in the plate of Osterley furniture engraved for the *Works* but incorrectly labelled 'furniture at Sion-house' and not published until 1822 in volume III, pl. 8.

81. 1782 inventory, LMA, Jersey papers.

82. The design for the glass frame inscribed for the Earl and Shelburne and dated 1768 also has a faint pencil inscription *A Glass frame like this for Osterley*. SM 20:23, box 1. The mirrors were described by Agneta Yorke, document cited at note 28 above.

83. Designs for glass frames for Coventry House, SM 20:61, 62, and 66. The latter is for the dining room mirror now at the V&A. For the oval mirrors in the gallery at Syon, see Adam, *Works*, III, pl. III.

84. Hayward and Kirkham, op. cit. at note 33 above, p. 115; Tomlin, op. cit. at note 23 above, pp. 34–6, D/3–5. The two largest settees have different arms from the other four in the suite but are otherwise identical. An uninscribed Adam design for a settee with similar arms but with a different back, seat-rail and legs, SM 17:102, has led Tomlin to suggest that Adam added the two largest pieces to the set. This seems extremely unlikely, not least because it would have been unnecessary to employ Adam just to adjust the arms of the additional settees.

85. L. Simond, *Journal of a tour and residence in Great Britain during the year 1810 and 1811*, Edinburgh, 1817, p. 285.

See also Sarah, Lady Lyttelton's description of the gallery as a drawing-room, op. cit. at note 71 above, p. 76.

86. H. James, *The Lesson of the Master*, first published in *The Universal Review*, July–August 1888. Somersoft, the house in the story, was identified with Osterley by Lady Jersey.

87. Design for the tapestry-room ceiling, SM 11:206, 207. The painted roundels were fixed in the stucco surrounds after the ceiling itself was painted in July 1775.

Design for the ceiling of the Duchess of Bolton's dressing-room at Bolton House, 26 Southampton Row, 1770, SM 12:35. See Stillman, p. 104, pl. 142.

88. Although Neilson's son was in London in 1767–8, it is most unlikely that Child would have ordered his set of tapestries then and waited four years before commissioning a ceiling design from Adam. See E. A. Standen, 'The Croome Court Tapestries', *Metropolitan Museum of Art Bulletin*, New York, November 1959, pp. 9, 51. In a letter to Soufflot on 30 July 1776, Neilson proposed that the tapestries, finished in March 1776, should be considered as having been made for the king, '*afin d'employer les fonds du budget des Gobelins et de diminuer, par la vente de cette tenture à un particulier* (Robert Child), *une partie de la dette des Batiments à l'atelier Neilson.*' M. Fenaille, *Etat général des tapisseries de la manufacture des Gobelins*, Paris, 1907, IV, pp. 280–4.

89. The others were the Earl of Coventry, 1764; Sir Lawrence Dundas for Moor Park, Herts. 1766–9; William Weddell of Newby, 1766–71, Sir Henry Bridgeman of Weston Park, Staffordshire, 1771.

90. Tomlin, op. cit. at note 23 above, pp. 55–6, G/1, 2.

91. Receipted bill from Thomas Cordery, jobbing

carpenter, July 1775 for 'taking down scaffolding in ye new rooms after painters and Refixing some scaffolding again for Dº./Making blinds to screen the Sun and making some blinds for ye windows in ye new Tapestry room.' LMA, Jersey papers, box 10/123. The undated design for the chimney-piece is at Osterley, OPH 407–1949, Rowan, op. cit. at note 28 above, p. 98.

92. Walpole to Mason, 16 July 1778, *Correspondence*, XXVIII, p. 413.

93. Design for the 'Table frame and slab for the Tapestry room at Osterly', dated 18 March 1775, SM 17:8; undated design for chimney-piece, OPH 407–1949, Rowan, op. cit. at note 28 above, p. 98.

94. 'Design of a Glass frame for the Tapestry room at Osterly', dated 28 November 1775, SM 20:43.

95. The present whereabouts of the Gobelins design, formerly in the possession of Lord Jersey, is not known. There is, however, a photograph in the archives of the Department of Furniture and Woodwork at the V&A.

Designs for the carpet, SM 17:187, dated 8 July 1775; SM 17:88 as executed.

96. Design for the Osterley tripod stands, dated 13 November 1776, SM 17:62. See E. Harris, pl. 138. For the 20 St James's Square tripods, made to a design of 1773, see E. Harris, pl. 137.

97. H. Avray Tipping, 'Osterley Park – III', *Country Life*, 4 December 1926, p. 859.

98. C. Lybbe Powys, *Passages from the diary of Mrs Lybbe Powys*, London, 1899, p. 231.

99. First design for the ceiling dated 1772, SM 11:208; executed design dated 1773, SM 11:209.

100. The first design dated 1775, SM 20:47; the slightly modified executed design, dated 15 May 1775, SM 20:46.

101. Design for the chimney-glass dated 24 April 1777, SM 20:48. The plate, 8ft × 5ft (2.4 m × 1.5 m), was described in the 1782 inventory, document cited at note 81 above, as the '1st plate made in England'.

102. 'Design of a Bed for Robert Child Esqr', SM 17:157.

103. Design for a bed dated 11 October 1775, SM 17:156.

104. Tomlin, op. cit. at note 23 above, p. 64, H/1a, 1b.

105. First design for the bed-carpet dated 8 November 1778, SM 17:191; the executed design, SM 17:192, is dated 16 February 1778 (i.e. 1779?) and inscribed with a note 'The Green the colour of the Velvet. No 13 Mr Child thinks this should be made of the thin sort of carpetting. The border is much approved of.' The colour of the velvet was described by Walpole as 'light plain green', Walpole to Revd Wm. Mason, 16 July 1778, *Correspondence*, XXVIII, p. 413–4. The Vitruvian scroll borders in the first design are replaced by a lozenge border related to the counterpane.

106. Ibid., p. 414.

107. Design for the Osterley chairs, dated 24 April 1777, SM 17:97. Design of a chair for Sir Abraham Hume, 3 April 1779, SM 17:86, box 2; SM 6:160, 162. E. Harris, p. 97, pls. 121, 122.

108. Design for the counterpane, dated 19 August 1776, SM 17:159; design for the interior of the dome, dated 18 October 1777, SM 17:158.

'Design of a bed for Derby House', 7 September 17(74), SM 17:154; design of the Etruscan bedroom for Lady Home, c.1776, SM 14:132, box 1.

109. Walpole to Mason, 16 July 1778, *Correspondence*, XXVIII, p. 414.

110. SM 27:83.

111. SM 11:210.

112. The final design, SM 11:212, for a quarter of the ceiling has a pale-blue ground as executed. The intermediary revision, SM 11:211, is coloured pale pink and green like the first design. The medallions at this intermediary stage were intended to contain 'A picture'.

113. The design dated 1768 for the dining-room

ceiling at Newby (Newby House 1/7/6) seems to be the first to have so-called Etruscan colouring, i.e. black and terracotta ornaments on a French grey ground. The ceiling designs for the second drawing room at Ashburnham House, 1773 (SM 12:131) and Lady Fitzroy's circular dressing room at Fitzroy House, Highgate, December 1774 (SM 12:156) also have Etruscan colours as do the wall elevations of General Fitzroy's circular toilet room, presumably also made in December 1774 (SM 50:89) and a room in Apsley House in June 1775 (SM 14:115; 32:104).

114. Adam, *Works*, I, i, preface.

115. 1766 is the date given on the title-page; for the actual date of publication, i.e. 1767, see N. Ramage, 'Publication dates of Sir William Hamilton's four volumes', *Ars Ceramica*, 8, 1991, p. 35 and P. Griener, *La antichità Etrusche Greche e Romane 1766–1776 di Pierre Hugues d'Hancarville*, Rome, 1992.

116. Wedgwood and Bentley, *A catalogue of cameos, intaglios, medals and bas reliefs*, London, 1773.

117. Walpole to Mason, 16 July 1778, *Correspondence*, XXVIII, p. 414.

118. Stillman, p. 76, pls. 46, 47; and Stillman, *English neo-classical architecture*, London, 1988, II, p. 320.

119. SM 22:55.

120. I. Bristow, *Architectural Colour in British Interiors 1615–1850*, London, I, pp. 143–6.

121. Adam, *Works*, II, i, explanation to pl. VIII.

122. Walpole to Mason, 16 July 1778, *Correspondence*, XXVIII, p. 414.

123. SM 14:54 inscribed 'Ceiling for the Vestibule under the Steps at Osterly' and dated September 1779. SM 14:55 is similarly dated but incorrectly inscribed 'for the Vestibule under the front steps'. It is in fact the same design as SM 14:54, with blue and pink instead of black and terracotta colouring. The Etruscan colouring was executed.

124. SM 14:128, 130, 131; SM 50:71; friezes SM 53:23. There is a preliminary design for the decoration of the walls in the V&A Dept. of Prints and Drawings, 3436.41. Rowan, op. cit. at note 28 above, p. 101, pl. 49.

125. 31 August 1782, Borgnis was paid for cleaning the pictures. He was referred to in a letter from Adam to Paul Sandby, 9 March 1783, as 'Mr Peter Bornis' who 'paints ornaments & figures'. Croft-Murray, op. cit. at note 48 above, p. 174. In 1793 he was paid a total of £63.17.0 for painting and putting up a frieze containing 57 figures including ornaments for Lord Ducie, husband of the widowed Sarah Child. LMA, Jersey papers, box 10/22A. The frieze may have been for 38 Berkeley Square.

126. SM 17:137.

127. Carpet design dated 11 October 1775, SM 17:189, 190.

128. SM 17:96.

129. SM 17:95.

130. Design for a needlework panel dated 14 April 1777, SM 17:140, 24:234; another design for a firescreen 'to be in grey silk . . . in the same style as Lord Derby's & about the Same Size', SM 24:233. 'Copy of ornaments upon the edge of Mrs. Child's fire-screen', SM 17:149. Unexecuted alternative designs, SM 17:141–143, dated November and December 1776, and 17:155, 156, dated 4 November 1779. The design for the tripod stand is dated 14 April 1779, SM 17:148. Tomlin, op. cit. at note 23 above, p. 83, J/4. Adam also designed a chimney-board for this room, SM 17:137. SM 24:221 is an unexecuted alternative. Tomlin, pp. 80–1, J/2, 21, 2b.

131. E. Balch, *Glimpses of English Homes*, London, 1890, p. 221.

132. Design for the glass and table frame for the breakfasting-room, dated 24 April 1777, SM 20:49. See E. Harris, pp. 71–2, 84, pls. 32, 74. Tomlin, op. cit. at note 23 above, pp. 86–7, K/1, K/1a, K/2. 'Design of a Bed for Robert Child Esqr.' dated 10 April 1779, SM 17:163. Tomlin, p. 92, L/1, L/1a.

11. KENWOOD HOUSE

1. The principal sources of historical information are the guide book by J. Bryant, *Kenwood*, London, 1990, ch. II, III. *Survey of London*, St Pancras I (Highgate), London, 1936, XVII, pp. 121–31.

2. Lord E. Fitzmaurice, *Life of William, Earl of Shelburne*, London, 1875, I, p. 87. See also *Complete Peerage*, VIII, p. 389.

3. R. Sedgwick, *The House of Commons 1715–1754*, London, 1970, II, p. 286.

4. From about 1739 to 1754, Murray occupied 56 Lincoln's Inn Fields. He then moved to Bloomsbury Square, where he remained until the destruction of his house and its contents by the Gordon rioters in 1780. In 1781 he took up residence in Thanet House in Great Russell Street and remained there until 1785, when he moved to 57 Lincoln's Inn Fields. *Survey of London*, Parish of St Giles-in-the-Fields (part II), London, 1914, V, p. 149.

5. Bryant, op. cit. at note 1 above, pp. 58–9.

6. In April 1757, Thomas Bromwich and Leonard Leigh supplied Lady Mansfield with 'painted Chinese Rail Borders 18 in. wide put round the blue room' and '23 Doz/Painted rail Borders put round 3 Indian Rooms'. They also charged for 'repairing India paper'. Mansfield MS. SRO EXTD 79/104 bundle 1400.

7. 17 June 1758, Robert to James mentioning meeting Lord Mansfield; 24 July 1760, Robert to James mentioning a visit to Lord Mansfield 'out of politeness'; James to Peggy Adam, 13 December 1760, from Florence, looking for porphyry for Lord Mansfield; 14 January 1762, James to Jenny Adam, from Rome, regarding sculpture for Mansfield, SRO GD 18/4858, 4866, 4878, 4923.

8. Elevation of the north wall of the library and ante-room, signed and dated 'James Adam Archt 1764', SM 43:3; design for the west apse, similarly signed and dated, SM 43:4; designs for the ceiling similarly signed and dated, SM 11:110, 111. Elevation of the south front, signed and dated 'Robt Adam Archt 1764', SM 43:2. Plan, SM 43:5. Elevation of the south front, SM 43:2.

9. This is described by Adam in his *Works*, I, ii, p. 9.

10. Bryant, op. cit. at note 1 above, p. 14. Hoskins was 'moulder and caster in plaster' to the Royal Academy and was responsible for the only recorded bust of Robert Adam.

11. The undated ceiling design, SM 11:115, is for the executed room with a large cove and must therefore date from 1767. It is not related to the 1764 scheme, as Bryant states, op. cit. at note 1 above, p. 14, as that called for a flat ceiling.

12. Joseph Rose's bill for '1768 & 1769 Stucco & Plaisterers Work'; John Minshull's bill for carvers work, examined by Robert Adam, 9 August 1769. Mansfield MS, SRO EXTD 79/104, box 121, bundle 8.

13. 'An Account of Work done for the Rt Honble the Earl of Mansfield at Kenwood' (1815–17). Mansfield MS., SRO EXTD 79/104, bundle 975.

14. In the inventory taken by William France on 13 October 1796 following the death of the second earl (Mansfield MS, Scone Palace, Perthshire), the four 'long' stools were described as painted white with loose seats in blue leather.

15. Bryant, op. cit., pp. 9, 10, 14. The stools were not in the hall when inventories were made in 1796, 1831 and 1840. Bryant's conclusion that they were there is based on a photograph of the hall published by A. T. Bolton, 'Kenwood, Hampstead', *Country Life*, 22 November 1913, p. 715 and the catalogue of the sale of the contents of the house by C. B. King Ltd at Kenwood, London, 6–9 November 1922, lots 874, 875.

16. Adam, *Works*, I, ii, p. 8.

17. Robert Adam's designs for the library: ceiling as executed SM 11:112; sections SM 14:113–4.

18. Ibid., pp. 9–10.

19. Plan of the principal story of Witham House for William Beckford, signed and dated 1762, SM 43:29. J. Woolfe and J. Gandon, *Vitruvius Britannicus*, London, 1771, V, pl. 38.

20. T. Ruddock, *Arch bridges and their builders*, Cambridge, 1979, p. 116.

21. Rose's bill submitted 29 December 1769 and paid 3 February 1770, document cited at note 12 above.

22. Zucchi's bill for £152.3.0 was examined by Robert Adam on 22 June 1769. Mansfield MS, Scone Palace, Perths.

23. I. Bristow, *Architectural colour in British interiors 1615–1840*, London, 1996, pp. 100–1.

24. The ceiling designs, SM 11:112 with pencil notes and SM 11: 113, a 'Duplicate'. There is a copy of the *Works* at the Soane with a hand-coloured plate of the ceiling.

25. Bryant, op. cit. at note 1 above, p. 15.

26. William France's account and the bricklayer Thomas Melton's bill for cutting away the way for the pier-glasses, 8 April 1769, Mansfield MS, Scone Palace, Perths.

27. The mirrors were described by Samuel Curwen in April 1776 as 'the largest . . . I ever saw being seven and a half feet high by three and a half feet in breadth.' A. Oliver, ed., *The journal of Samuel Curwen, loyalist*, Cambridge, Massachussets, 1972, p. 142. Though they were included in 1922 sale, op. cit. at note 15 above, lots 905, 906, they were evidently found too large to remove.

28. William France's bill includes unpacking and cleaning the slabs and making 2 leather covers lined with flannel to 'preserve them from dust £4.2.0' in December 1769. On 16 June 1769 the mason, John Devall, was paid £5.18.0 for 'Repairing, peicing & new polishing the broken Verde Antique Marble Table'. It had a gilt brass moulding that was also repaired. France's and Devall's bills, documents cited at notes 26 and 12 above. Is it possible that the 'very fine 6 ft. "Adam" Side Table, richly carved frieze and legs, on 12 stretchers and a variegated marble top' in the hall, lot 884 in the 1922 sale, was made up from the two pier-tables?

29. John Devall's bill for mason's work. 1769, document cited at note 12 above

30. Mansfield MS, bundle 1400. The agreement is quoted in full and discussed by Gilbert, I, pp. 256–7.

31. Adam's sketch, SM 6:151, is related to the executed sofas shown in the left-hand recess in his design for finishing the north wall, SM 14:114. There is also a sketch, SM 3:31, for the unexecuted, straight-backed sofa shown in the right-hand recess. The suite was sold in 1922, document cited at note 15 above, lots 900–902, 907. Unlike the pier-tables, its appearance is at least known from photographs taken in 1913, Bolton, loc. cit. at note 15 above. The battered remains of one of the window stools, shown above heating vents in the *Country Life* photographs, is still at Kenwood.

32. Bill from William France, 4 December 1770, document cited at note 26 above.

33. Inventories of 1796, document cited at note 14 above; and 1831 inventory, Mansfield MS, Scone Palace, Perthshire, cited by J. Bryant, 'The Adam Library Carpet Recreated at Kenwood', *English Heritage Conservation Bulletin*, February 1991, p. 5. Also listed in the 1841 inventory, SRO GD 79/104, vol. 268.

34. Bryant, ibid.

35. Porphyry marbling was applied to the columns in 1950 when Kenwood re-opened after the war. Christopher Hussey was led to believe that this was the original colouring and thought it an improvement upon the white that it replaced, 'The Re-opening of Kenwood', *Country Life*, 26 May 1950, CVII, p. 1552, figs 4, 5. Proper scientific colour tests have not yet been done on the columns in the library. The grey wash on Adam's elevation, being used on the mahogany

doors as well as the columns, cannot be indicative of the colour as executed. See I. Bristow, op. cit. at note 23 above, p. 132.

36. Staircase ceiling, SM 11:114.

37. The balusters were made by the smith, William Yates, who also supplied ironwork for the back stairs in May 1769. Joseph Rose was responsible for the stucco-work: see document cited at note 12 above.

38. Document cited at note 13 above.

39. SM 6:69.

40. Bolton, loc. cit. at note 15 above.

41. Adam's design for the parlour frieze, SM 53:26, is labelled 'Dining room'. The carver, George Burns, described this room as the dining-parlour and the hall as the dining-room. The carpenter, John Phillips, retained the name 'hall' and referred to the parlour as both the dining-room and dining-parlour. Mansfield MS, document cited at note 12 above, bundle 9.

42. SM 11:116.

43. Zucchi's account, document cited at note 12 above, bundle 9. Rose charged £84.19.10 for 'finishing the Hall as pr Estimate'. His bill was examined by Robert Adam on 10 August 1773.

44. SM 3:29.

45. Nelson's account, document cited at note 12 above, bundle 9.

46. Nelson's bill for £59.13.0 is dated 16 December 1773. The brass rail was supplied by William Kinman & Co., who submitted a bill for £10 in October 1773. Document cited at note 12 above, bundle 9. The sideboard and pedestals are quite close to the designs for 20 St James's Square, dated 14 September 1773, SM 17:21.

47. The table that is now in the George III dining-room in the Legion of Honor Museum, San Francisco is presumably the one illustrated in R. Edwards, *Dictionary of English furniture*, London, 1954, III, fig. 13, p. 128. The information given here corrects the errors in my book, E. Harris, p. 68.

48. Document cited at note 13 above.

49. 1922 sale catalogue, op. cit. at note 15 above, lots 873, 880, 883. The urns, lot 883, are described as mahogany.

50. Curwen, op. cit. at note 27 above, p. 142.

51. *National Art Collections Fund Review*, 1994, p. 132. 1796 inventory, document cited at note 14 above. 1922 sale catalogue, op. cit. at note 15 above, lots 1038, 1039; illustrated p. 45. The attribution to France is Bryant's, op. cit. at note 1 above, p. 38.

52. Document cited at note 14 above.

53. Curwen, op. cit. at note 27 above. Chinoiserie papers may have been introduced at Kenwood by Lady Bute.

54. Bill for painters work at Kenwood in 1773 and 1774 by George Steuart, document cited at note 12 above, bundle 9.

55. D. Lysons, *Environs of London*, London, 1795, III, p. 349. 1796 inventory, document cited at note 14 above.

56. Document cited at note 14 above, lot 886. The absence of any ram's-head pedestals from the 1796 inventory raises the possibility that the '3 ft. 7 in. (1 metre) Square Tapered "Adam" Carved Pedestal with animal corners' sold in 1922 was made from the painting.

57. John Phillips's account for carpenters' work and George Burns's account for carving, 1772. Document cited at note 12 above, bundle 9. Phillips used the word 'gib', meaning blank, and this was repeated and made more confusing by Bryant, op. cit. at note 1 above.

58. 30 Curzon Street is now a club. It has a circular room on the ground floor of the rear wing, which Bolton described as a dining-room. Bolton, II, index, p. 36. D. King, pp. 315–6. Joseph Rose's sketchbook contains a 'Domed ceiling at Mr Thyn's in Curzon Street Octb.26 1772', G. Beard, *Decorative Plasterwork in Great Britain*, London, 1975, p. 242. Adam designed

another oval mirror with lateral shelves in 1772 for George Keate's house at 8 Charlotte Street, now 10 Bloomsbury Street, SM 20:104.

59. George Burns account, 1772. Document cited at note 12 above, bundle 9.

60. Sale catalogue, document cited at note 15 above, lot 505. J. Swarbrick, *Robert Adam and his brothers*, London, 1915, fig. 127, p. 176. The 1796 inventory, document cited at note 14 above, lists the semicircular table in the 'Reading Room', the room with the Venetian window to the west of what had been Lady Mansfield's boudoir.

61. Carpenters' work done by John Phillips in 1772, document cited at note 12 above, bundle 14.

62. SM 24:182, verso. 1796 inventory, document cited at note 14 above.

63. The frieze, SM 53:41; the chimney-piece, SM 23:131, 234.

64. 1796 inventory, document cited at note 14 above; account of work done 1815–17, document cited at note 13 above. According to the latter, the partition in Lady Mansfield's sitting-room was taken down and a new trussed partition put up. The only partition wall in that room is the one that divides it from the middle room. This is above the partition wall that divided the dining-parlour and the drawing-room.

65. This room was described by Bolton as the Earl of Mansfield's bedroom, on what evidence is not known. Bolton, I, p. 315.

66. Designs for the 'Painted Chimney': SM 23:164, SM 24:180, SM 49:31, 32.

67. Adam's sketch for the chimney-piece, SM 23:243. Nelson's bill, document cited at note 12 above, bundle 9.

68. SM 49:29, 30. The coloured elevation (SM 49:29) is inscribed on the verso 'Lord Mansfields Epergne'. SM 49:30 is inscribed 'Plateau for Lord Mansfiel'. SM 5:79, 83, 84 are related coloured drawings for the plateau. Amidst them in volume 5 (SM 5:80–82) is a set of designs for a smaller and quite different plateau which is not related to the elevation of the epergne. SM 5:81 and 82 are dated 1781; the latter is inscribed in pencil 'drawings for Lord Mansfield' which is probably later and incorrect.

69. E. Maxtone Graham, *The beautiful Mrs Graham*, London, 1927, pp. 88–89. Viscount Stormont commissioned several mirror designs from Adam in 1778 and 1779, SM 20:185–92. These are thought to be for 37 Portland Place, which he occupied in 1779. However, Adam is not known to have participated in the interior alterations to Scone Palace, Perthshire in c.1780–3.
Stormont was one of his pall-bearers.

12. NOSTELL PRIORY

1. Moyser is named as architect in a list of houses in a copy of *The Builder's Dictionary*, London, 1734 at the Metropolitan Museum of Art, New York, and in a note in a book of plans of Kirtlington Park, Oxon. which states that the idea of that house 'is taken from Sᵗ Rowland Winn's which was originally planned by Col. Moyser of Beverley'. Oxfordshire County Record Office. Dash. III/xlix/1.

2. West Yorkshire Archive Service (WYAS), Nostell Papers (NP) C3/1/1/2. The block plan is also shown in an undated, contemporary 'Plan of new intended House, Offices, Gardens & c. drawn by Stephen Switzer Redrawn by Jean Godwin'.

3. J. Harris, *Catalogue of the Drawings Collection of the RIBA. Colen Campbell*, London, 1973, no. (40) p. 17, fig. 137. Susannah Henshaw was one of three daughters of Edward Henshaw of Hampshire and Elizabeth Roper, daughter and sole heir of Edward Roper of Well Hall, Eltham, Kent. Her sisters, Katherine and Elizabeth, married William Strickland, MP of Beverley and Sir Edward Dering, Bt of Kent respectively.

4. James Moyser's mother, Catherine, daughter of John Heron, was the widow of Sir John Hotham, 3rd Bt, who died in 1691, whereupon the title reverted to his cousin, Sir Charles Hotham. His father, John Moyser, was MP for Beverley with Hotham. In 1752, James Moyser's daughter married (as his second wife) William Strickland, whose first wife, Katherine, daughter of Edward Charles Henshaw, was Winn's sister-in-law.

5. J. Paine, *Plans, elevations and sections of noblemen and gentlemen's houses*, London, 1767, I, p. i. P. Leach, *James Paine*, London, 1988, pp. 18, 19, 21–2, 203–4. Paine was probably recommended by the Hon. Richard Arundell, Surveyor General of the King's Works from 1726 to 1737, whose brother, William Monkton Arundell, 2nd Lord Galway, had control over twice as many burgages in Pontefract as Winn.

6. R. Pococke, 'The travels through England of Dr. Richard Pococke', ed. J. J. Cartwright. Camden Society, N.S., 1888, I, p. 63.

7. Isaac Dulon to Sir Rowland Winn, 4th Bt, August 1757. WYAS, NP A1/4/15.

8. Dulon to Sir Rowland Winn, 4th Bt, February 1758. WYAS NP A1/4/15.

9. Ibid.

10. Winn, 4th Bt to Baron d'Hewart, 12 January 1762. WYAS NP A1/5B/11.

11. Rose to Winn, 7 November 1765, WYAS NP C3/1/5/4/9. This is printed in full in M. N. Brockwell, *Catalogue of the pictures and other works of art in the collection of Lord St Oswald at Nostell Priory*, London, 1915, p. 14. In March 1761, Paine wrote to Winn, saying that he had finished a large set of 'Plans, Elevations & Sections of yr House' which (he) delivered to the Duke of Northumberland who promised to show them to the king, but he had heard no more; pp. 12–13.

12. Gilbert, I, pp. 166–7. R. W. Symonds, 'Chippendale Furniture at Nostell Priory', *Country Life*, 3 October 1952, p. 1028. Winn also spent £604.15.6 at the sale of the late Earl of Macclesfield's household goods, furniture and pictures on 7 May 1766.

13. Adam to Winn, 26 August 1766, WYAS NP 1562/27. 'Memorandum of Drawings Mʳ. Ware takes with him', NP 1528/61. This is preceded on the same sheet by 'Memorandum of Mouldings left at Sir Rowland Winn's at Nostille' which Adam must have made prior to Ware's appointment in August. All are for the library and include 'A Drawing of the Library Ceiling'.

14. In Paine's plan published by Woolfe and Gandon in *Vitruvius Britannicus*, London, 1767, IV, pl. 71, this room is loosely described as part of 'an Apartment'. In Adam's plan of 1776 it is called 'Gentleman's Dressing Room' and is paired with 'Lady Wynn's Toilet Room' on the right side of the hall, SM 41:45. It was entirely redecorated for Charles Winn between 1819 and 1821 by Thomas Ward of Frith Street who introduced a chimney-piece with a frieze of putti in place of the earlier one. This was destroyed by fire in April 1980 and replaced in the National Trust's restoration by a rococo chimney-piece from an upper room. See Bolton, II, p. 130 and J. Cornforth, 'Restoration at Nostell Priory', *Country Life*, 11 April 1985, pp. 947–8, figs 4, 5.
There are only three known chimney-piece designs for Nostell dated 1766: two are for the library, the third, SM 22:224, is most likely for the 'Anti Chamber'. The latter is very closely related to the chimney-piece now in the vestibule/billiard room and virtually identical to a chimney-piece design of 1765 for the ante-room at Coventry House, Piccadilly, SM 22:66.

15. Paine's engraved plan shows the room with a semicircular bed alcove screened by columns as the main, central feature of a three-room 'Apartment'. There are two designs for a library, one attributed to Chippendale, the other to Paine. G. Jackson-Stops, 'Pre-Adam Furniture

Designs at Nostell Priory', *Furniture History*, 1974, X, p. 29, pls 21, 22.

16. The room is first mentioned in a letter from Adam to Winn, 26 August 1766, WYAS NP 1562/27. Drawings for it are listed in 'Memorandum of Drawings', NP 1528/61. Ceiling design, Nostell NT folder 42B. Instructions for the colour are given in a letter from James Adam to Ware, undated, c.September 1767, Nostell, Hon. C. Winn, folder 92.

17. Adam to Winn, 26 August 1766, WYAS NP 1562/27. Some of the floors in the Earl of Thanet's house at 19 (formerly 18) Grosvenor Square had polished plaster floors, *Survey of London*, The Grosvenor Estate, XL, p. 136. Adam was working for the Earl of Thanet in 1766. Lansdowne House also had plaster floors.

18. Full-size drawings of the pediment decoration with a central roundel containing the Winn arms. Nostell, Hon. C. Winn, folder 55. These designs have been attributed on stylistic grounds and paper watermarks to Thomas Ward, the London upholsterer and decorator employed by Charles Winn in the 1820s.

19. Adam to Ware, 14 October 1766. Adam's known designs for the Earl of Thanet's house at 18 (later 19) Grosvenor Square are dated 1764 and 1765 but do not include pilasters of the description given here. The letter also implies that Ware had worked for Adam at that house before being sent to Nostell. See note 17 above.

20. Chippendale's bill, dated 30 June 1767. Gilbert, I, pp. 181–5. The finishing and hanging of the door evidently caused some problems which required the advice of William Belwood of York 'who (had) done things of that kind before at Sion' and was then working at Newby and Harewood, Adam to Ware, 23 May 1767, WYAS NP 1525/33. See also NP 1525/28, 2 December 1766; NP 1525/27, 11 April 1767; NP 1525/26, 18 April 1767.

21. The medal cabinet was designed by Chippendale, 30 June 1767. Gilbert, I, p. 185.

22. Adam to Ware, 2 December 1766, WYAS NP 1525/28; 11 April 1767, informing Ware that Winn was determined not to have shelves over the chimney, NP 1525/27. Lansdowne House library, domed octagons, SM 39:61; see chapter 8, on Lansdowne House.

23. Adam to Winn 18 August, 15 September, 27 September 1767. Winn was not entirely pleased with Zucchi's oval, which he found 'not High enough finishd as it is so near the eye therefore would not fix it up for good till I had your opinion about it'. James Adam replied to Winn on 6 October 1767, relaying Zucchi's explanation 'that a newly painted picture never looks so highly finished as an old one, as the Colours seem raw & unmellowed . . . if you should choose to have him retouch the oval one, with more care, he will chearfully do it & begs you would return it for that purpose by first safe opportunity . . .'. Zucchi charged 27 guineas for 'Les neuf Tableaux & oval', WYAS NP 1570/3. On 23 May 1767 Adam sent a design for the oval picture frame, NP 1525/33. Adam to Ware, 13 and 18 June 1767, sending a drawing for the mirror frames with instructions, NP 1525/20 and /16.

24. Chimney-piece design, SM 22:222. Adam's design for the library chimney-piece at Harewood also dated 1766, SM 22:182, has a similar gadrooned frieze and a figured tablet. There is a variant design with a simple urn and no sphinxes at Nostell, Hon. C. Winn, folder 66.

25. Adam to Ware, 18 April 1767 informing him that the tablet was to be of wood carved in London; the wood surround of the chimney-piece was to be made in the country, WYAS NP 1525/26. The inner marble surround was made in London by John Devall, whose bill for £41.14.6 is dated 23 July 1767, NP C3/1/5/4/17.
Adam to Winn, 18 August, 15 September 1767, regarding the bas-relief; Winn to Adam, 27

September 1767; James Adam to Winn, 6 October, 28 November 1767.

26. John Austin, Adam's London clerk to Ware, 19 December 1770, WYAS NP 1525/38. 'Memorandum of Drawings for Mr. Ware' including cornice for the library chimney, NP 1528/60 undated, c.1772.

27. These colours were discovered by recent paint investigations undertaken for the National Trust by Jane Waddington. The paintwork on the skirting is lost, but the dark-green colour is indicated on a drawing by James Adam enclosed in a letter to Ware, undated, c.September 1767. Nostell, Hon. C. Winn, folder 92.

28. Design for the Nostell library ceiling dated 1766, SM 11:226 with colour notes. The same colours are somewhat differently distributed in the contemporary portrait of Sir Rowland and Lady Winn in the library. Design for the tapestry-room ceiling at Croome Court incorrectly inscribed for the library, SM 11:37; design for the 'old library' ceiling at Harewood, SM 11:135.

29. Recent paint analysis of the Nostell library carried out for the National Trust revealed a second scheme of decoration between the several layers of graining and the initial painting of 1767. (John Austin to Ware, 25 June 1767, saying that a painter from Mr Adamson was sent to Nostell, WYAS NP 1525/44.) The second layer of paint was only marginally different from the first one, but had more surface dirt, indicating longer exposure. Its date is unknown but could conceivably be connected with the creation in 1777–80 of a vestibule on the north front between the library and a new private apartment.

30. Gilbert, I, pp. 169, 175, 185, 186.

31. Ibid. p. 182, an unheaded list of work to be done which Gilbert dates c.1770.

32. WYAS NP 1562/32, a bill for several paintings made for Winn by Hamilton and for the bust.

33. Ceiling design dated 1767, SM 11:225. Adam to Ware, 11 April 1767, reporting that he is getting drawings ready for the drawing-room which will be sent to Nostell as soon as possible, WYAS NP 1525/27. Adam to Ware, 18 April 1767, list of drawings sent, NP 1525/26. The list does not include designs for the chimney-piece, but the two in the Soane are dated 1767, SM 22:224, 225.
    Adam to Winn, 18 August and 15 September 1767, reporting on Zucchi's progress in the drawing-room. James Adam to Ware, 14 October 1767 asking for patterns of the ceiling panel, NP 1525/7.

34. Adam to Winn, 27 September 1771, WYAS NP C3/1/5/2/9.

35. Ware's notes for Sir Rowland, datable April 1772 from references to the hall floor, WYAS NP C3/1/5/4. Reference to the chimney-piece marble, 21 June 1772, NP C3/1/5/16.

36. Henry Gill to Ware, WYAS NP 1525/36. Devall proposed to come to Nostell and then go on to Newby. The Soane designs, SM 22:224, 225, are dated 1767. SM 22:225 has a fluted inner surround and is inscribed in pencil 'Lord Mansfield's Room'. The design for Kenwood dated 1767, SM 22:234, also has a different tablet. This and other chimney-piece designs for Nostell were presumably kept in London where they were made, and therefore do not appear on the lists of drawings sent to Ware.

37. M. W. Brockwell, op. cit. at note 11 above, p. 17, reports that the pilasters were stored in an outbuilding and later destroyed by fire.

38. Work done at Nostell by Thomas Ward, 1819–38. WYAS NP C3/1/6.

39. Adam to Ware, 18 April 1767 mentioning damask hangings, WYAS NP 1525/26. The large mirrors are all shown on Adam's 'Section of the Great Drawing Room at Nostille', Nostell, folder 29, and are described along with the girandoles and other furniture in a letter from Haig & Chippendale to Winn, 30 June 1781, and in a 'List of Sundries now in hand' sent to Winn on

6 April 1785, both reprinted by C. Gilbert, 'New Light on the Furnishing of Nostell Priory', Furniture History, 1990, XXVI, pp. 60, 192–3.

40. Gilbert, ibid., p. 59. Chippendale's section is lost.

41. Ibid., pp. 60–1. After Sir Rowland's death, the firm sent another account of the furniture in hand to Lady Winn.

42. Adam to Winn, 18 August 1767, busy with designs for hall and saloon; 18 November 1767, sent a figured section of the saloon and other drawings, 'These Drawings will be sufficient for you at present to get the Room battened and prepared for the Plaisterers . . . The Design for the Ceiling and Section of the Salon are not quite finished . . .', WYAC NP 1525/34. Finished section of the saloon, c.December 1767, Nostell, folder 28.

43. John Austin to Ware, 2 May 1770, WYAS NP 1525/4. Austin to Ware, 3 July 1771, NP 1525/18. 'Design of Nich Head', SM 41:46. The classical figures in the medallions were rejected and crossed sacrificial urns and axes executed instead.

44. Austin to Ware, 19 December 1769, WYAS NP 1525/48. A 'figured section' of the saloon had been sent by James Adam in November 1768, NP 1525/34. Austin to Ware, 31 January 1770, NP 1525/2. Ware to Winn, 13 May 1770, reporting on the progress of work in the saloon.

45. Austin to Ware, 2 May 1770, listing drawings sent, including 'a drawing of the flat part of the Saloon Ceiling, centre part of Ceiling at large, another part of do. at large', WYAS NP 1525/4. SM 8:77, sketch; SM 11:228, diagrammatic design dated 1770. Finished design, Hon. C. Winn, folder 53.

46. Finished, coloured ceiling design dated 1767, Hon. C. Winn, folder 54. 'Flat of Saloon' with colour notes, Nostell, folder 21. Quarter design coloured, dated 1767, SM 11:227. Harewood, principal dressing-room ceiling, 1767. SM 11:150, 151.

47. Bowood great room ceiling, SM 11:78. Home House music-room ceiling, 1775, SM 12:164. R. Wood, Ruins of Palmyra, London, 1753, pl. 37b. Harewood study ceiling, SM 11:138.

48. Nostell, folder 21. This may have been sent in response to a memo dated 11 April 1773, 'write to Adam about colouring of Salon Seeling & Sides', WYAS NP C3/1/5/2/19/1.

49. Zucchi to Winn, 16 August 1776, WYAS NP C3/1/5/3A/5. Ware's 'Memorandum for Mr Adam Augst 1776 Sept ye 3rd 1776' includes a note 'To write to Mr Zucchi for to send the picture for the Saloon', WYAS NP C3/1/5/2/19/2.

50. SM 22:267 dated 1772. There is no bill from Devall for the pair of chimney-pieces, and the letter of December 1773, WYAS NP 1525/36, refers to a single chimney-piece having 'come down' to Yorkshire. See note 36 above.

51. A 'Sketch of Glass frame' for a glass 7ft × 4ft (2 m × 1.2 m) was sent on 19 December 1770. Austin to Ware, WYAS NP 1525/38. The finished coloured design (Hon. C. Winn, folder 52) calls for a glass which measured by the scale would be 9ft × 5ft (2.7 m × 1.5 m). It is undated.
    Rose accounts, NP C3/1/5/4/2, in which the medallions in the crest are credited to Mr Rose, Jr.
    Nelson's bill for the curtain cornices reprinted by Gilbert in loc. cit. at note 39 above, p. 58.

52. Ibid., pp. 59–60.

53. Table design dated 10 June 1775, SM 17:27, 28. Sideboard for Sir Watkin Williams-Wynn, dated 21 August 1773, SM 17:20.

54. Richter and Bartoli charged 75 guineas per table. WYAS NP C3/1/5/4/5.

55. Haig & Chippendale to Mr Leadbeater at Nostell, 16 April 1785. Reprinted by Gilbert, loc. cit. at note 39 above, p. 61. The suite of seat furniture consisted of 8 open back armchairs and 2 sofas which were waiting to be japanned and covered with green taberay to match the window curtains.

56. Adam to Winn, 27 September 1771, document cited at note 34 above.

57. By the time Sir Rowland succeeded in 1765, sections had been made and were ready to be finished by Rose. See above, note 11.

58. The basic plan was made on 18 August 1767, when Adam wrote to Winn, 'I am just now busy with the Designs of your Hall & Saloon'. Finished plan and elevations of three sides of the hall, Hon. C. Winn, folder 52. This is probably the 'section' referred to in a letter of 27 September 1771, document cited at note 34 above. It shows irregular shaped lobbies suggesting that the ovals were an after thought.

59. 2 September 1776, 'Memorandum for Mr Adam'. Gilbert, loc. cit. at note 39 above, pp. 59, 60.

60. Austin to Ware, 22 April 1772, WYAS NP 1525/43. The chimney-pieces were executed in white freestone by Christopher Theakston of Doncaster in May 1773, NP C3/1/5/4/12.

61. Nostell, folders 5, 11, 12, 13; SM 11:230. Austin to Ware, 7 July 1772, WYAS NP 1525/41 and 'A list of Drawings Sent to Nostel by the Carrier', NP 1528/60, undated but all for the hall and of the same date as the letter, i.e. 1772.

62. Zucchi to Winn, 16 August 1776.

63. SM 41:47, dated 1 August 1776. There is no pavement design in the Nostell collection.

64. Document cited at note 38 above.

65. SM 17:28, inscribed 'Design of two Tables for the Hall to have Statuary Slabs at Nostel Adelphi 10 June 1775'. Their maker is not recorded. R. W. Symonds, op. cit. at note 12 above, p. 1030, attributed them to Chippendale but Gilbert, I, p. 172., does not. T. Chippendale, The gentleman and cabinet-maker's director, London, 1762, pl. CXXII. The relationship between Chippendale's published design and Adam's Nostell tables was noted by Ivan Hall, 'Neo-classical elements in Chippendale's designs for the 'Director' of 1762, Leeds Arts Calendar, 65, 1969, pp. 14–19.

66. Design for an iron-work balustrade for Home House, undated, c.1775, SM 52:3.

67. Adam to Ware, 1 June 1768, WYAS NP 1525/23. The inner marble surround for the chimney-piece was reported to have been finished by Mr Jackson on 13 May 1770. Jackson was probably responsible for carving the outer wooden surround as well.

68. Austin to Ware, 12 May 1772, WYAS NP 1525/5. Rose's account, 23 May–June 1777, NP C3/1/5/4/2.

69. 11 April 1773, 'To write to Mr Adam about as under . . . The two brass rails for sideboard in Ding. Rm. The two vases with pedstls. for do. & branches for candles', WYAS NP C3/1/5/2/19/1. Nelson's bill is quoted in full by Gilbert, loc. cit. at note 39 above, p. 58. Though Adam's name is not mentioned, the pedestals and vases are comparable to those published in the Works, III, pl. IX and executed by Linnell for Osterley and Shardeloes in 1767. See chapter 10 on Osterley.

70. Winn to Adam, 7 March 1776, WYAS NP C3/1/5/2/13.

71. SM 41:44, 45, undated plans; finished versions dated 1776, Hon. C. Winn, folder 59. The elevation of the new north front dated 1 August 1776. Adam's list of drawings made between September 1776 and 1785, WYAS NP 1551/2 includes figured plans, elevations and a section sent to Nostell on 1 October 1776.

72. SM 41:43, 'North end of Nostel', dated 'August 1st 1776' and a finished elevation dated, Hon. C. Winn, folder 62. Measured plans of the court and stairs on the ground, principal and attic storey, dated 24 September 1778, Nostell, folder 43.

73. Rose to Winn, 1777, complaining about deductions to his bill, WYAS NP C3/1/5/4/11; Adam to Andrew Adams, carpenter at Nostell, 27 March 1779, re. Winn's complaints about prices which Adam thought were low, WYAS NP C3/1/5/2/18; 10 July 1778, Adam to Winn,

commiserating about his gout being so bad that
he could not hold a pen, WYAS C3/1/5/2/17;
Zucchi to Winn, 7 November 1781 regarding
money owing to Zucchi which Winn had said he
could not pay because of his 'difficulty in
receiving rents', WYAS NP 1575/13.

74. List of drawings, June and September 1783,
WYAS NP 1551/2. A ceiling design for the new
vestibule dated 26 September 1783 is at the
Soane, SM 14:87; other designs are at Nostell,
folders 14A, 19, 42A, 43.

75. Charles Winn, 1846. See G. Worsley, 'Thornton
Hall, Lincs.', *Country Life*, 2 January 1986, p. 21.

76. Adam to Winn, 18 August 1767, WYAS NP
C3/1/5/2/1.

77. Adam to Winn, 25 July, 22 August 1772, WYAS
NP C3/1/5/2/6, 7.

13. NEWBY HALL

1. J. Low, 'The Art and Architectural Patronage of
William Weddell (1736–92) of Newby Hall and
his Circle', unpublished Ph.D. thesis,
Department of Fine Arts, University of Leeds,
1981. Henceforth cited as Low, thesis.
   J. Low, 'Newby Hall: Two Late Eighteenth-
Century Inventories', *Furniture History*, 1986,
XXII, pp. 135–65. Henceforth cited as Low,
inventories. There are surprisingly few drawings
for Newby in the Soane collection, which is
difficult to explain.

2. J. Low, 'William Belwood: Architect and
Surveyor', *The Yorkshire Archaeological Journal*,
1984, LVI, pp. 131–54. For Belwood's work at
Nostell and Syon not noted by Low see letter
from Robert Adam to Mr Ware at Nostell, 23
May 1767, West Yorkshire Archive Service Leeds
(WYAS) NPA 4/1525/33.

3. Chambers's designs for a boudoir, said to be for
Newby Hall, do not correspond to the
measurements of any room in Earl de Grey's plan
of the first floor of that house, and are more
likely to be for Newby Park. See 'Architectural
Drawings at Newby Hall', MS catalogue
prepared by J. Low (cited henceforth as NH),
NH I/3/5. Similarly, his beautiful coloured
designs for an entablature, NH I/13/7–10, have
no inscriptions that firmly connect them with
Newby Hall, nor do his designs for a pheasantry.
More work is need on the cataloguing of the
large collection of drawings at Newby Hall.

4. Survey, drawn 21 March 1682, Northumberland
County Record Office, ZBL 269/2. See J.
Cornforth, 'Designs for Newby',
'Correspondence', *Country Life*, 19 July 1979, p.
173.

5. C. Fiennes, *The journeys of Celia Fiennes*, ed. C.
Morris, London, 1947, p. 85.

6. J. Kip, and L. Knyff, *Britannia illustrata*,
London, 1707, I. See *Early printed books
1478–1840 catalogue of the British Architectural
Library early imprints collection*, 1994, no. 384.

7. WYAS NH 2200. Garrett's employment by Sir
Walter Blackett at Wallington Hall,
Northumberland from *c.*1735 until his death in
1753 may be significant. His practice, in any case,
was largely in the north of England.

8. WYAS VR 13633.

9. Plan *c.*1758, NH/I/3/2. My suggested date,
between 1758 and 1762, is based on a letter from
Richard Weddell to his agent Mr Bewlay, 9
March 1758, enquiring about alterations to the
kitchen and iron doors and windows in his 'new
rooms', probably the wine cellars or safe in the
basement. He wrote again on 9 April 1758
expressing his pleasure that 'the kitchen is
finished', WYAS NH 2034. Richard Weddell
died in December 1762.

10. His eldest son, Thomas, died, aged 22, in
December 1756 and a second son, Richard, died
in infancy.

11. WYAS VR 13796.

12. WYAS NH 2839/39.

13. Robinsons's friend, James Grant, wrote to Abbé
Peter Grant in Rome on behalf of Weddell and
Palgrave. The Abbé replied on 3 October 1764
that he had sent letters to meet them at Turin
and arranged for others for Genoa and Bologna,
SRO Seafield MS. GD 248/99/3. Low, thesis, p.
246. Palgrave wrote to James Grant from Rome
on 31 March 1765, 'Your letters to Jenkins and
Hamilton were not in vain, for Weddell is
buying such a quantity of pictures, marbles, etc.
as will astonish the West Riding of Yorkshire', Sir
W. Frazer, *The chiefs of Grant*, 1883, II, pp.
445–6. Robinson also recommended Thomas
Jenkins to Weddell. On 5 June 1765, Jenkins
wrote to Robinson thanking him for
recommending Weddell who, he said, 'purchased
the greater part of the Paintings and Sculpture
that I had', G. Beard, 'On Patronage', *Leeds Art
Calendar*, 1961, no. 46–7, p. 10. Gray to Palgrave,
March 1765, P. Toynbee and L. Whibley,
Correspondence of Thomas Gray, Oxford, 1935,
letter 400, pp. 866–8.

14. William Palgrave to James Grant, Rome, 31
March 1765, Frazer, op. cit. at note 13 above.
Letter from Thomas Jenkins to the Society of
Antiquaries, 5 June 1765, telling them that 'it is
now some weeks since Mr Weddell & Mr
Palgrave left Rome', SRO Seafield MS. GD
248/49/3/24.

15. See note 12 above. Sir B. Ford, 'Thomas Jenkins,
Banker, Dealer and Unofficial English Agent',
Apollo, 1974, XCIX, pp. 416–25. A. Michaelis,
Ancient marbles in Great Britain, Cambridge,
1882, pp. 522–35. This remains the fullest account
of Weddell's collection.

16. Letter of 19 September 1765, reporting that 'the
house looks much better in being lowered',
WYAS 2839/22. Letter of 23 September
1765, WYAS 2839/23.

17. The idea of a Palladian pavilion with two-storey
pedimented ends was also considered, it is shown
in pencil on the left of NH I/5/2, but was
rejected. This drawing and the survey drawing of
the south front, NH I/5/1, to which it is related,
are dated 'before 1757' in Mrs Low's catalogue,
but are after 1765 as are all the other designs for
the gallery.

18. NH I/5/3. There is no evidence for the date 1757
given to this design by Mrs Low. Nor is it
possible to accept her idea that the new south
wing was an orangery; its windows are not only
too small but those in the centre would have
been cast in shadow by the portico. Low,
inventory, p. 236.

19. NH I 6/2, 3.

20. R. Middleton, 'The Sculpture Gallery at Newby
Hall', *AA Files*, 1986, XIII, p. 51. This offers the
best analysis of the plan in relation to other
sculpture galleries, though the dating of the
designs is unfortunately flawed owing to the
incorrect cataloguing of the drawings at Newby
Hall.

21. Inventory of furniture at Newby Park, 5
November 1787, WYAS NH 2798A. See Jenkins
letter to Robinson, 5 June 1765, cited in note 13
above. Michaelis, op. cit. at note 15 above, pp.
527–9.

22. NH I/6/2. The date given in the drawings
catalogue, 'before 1764', is incorrect. Other notes
by Chambers on the plan: 'Cast of Venus at
Wiltons/Brutus dover Street & V' (?). The large
sarcophagus is also shown opposite the front
door in the laid-out elevation of the four walls
probably drawn by Weddell, NH I/6/9. This and
a drawing by the same hand, NH I/6/8, show
the canted bow with three windows rather than
an apse. The sarcophagus, described by
Michaelis, op. cit. at note 15 above, p. 534, as a
'large tub, of pavonazzetto marble, with fluted
(modern?) cover . . . Probably a bath', was only
found in May 1765, just about the time Weddell
left Rome. S. R. Pierce, 'Thomas Jenkins in
Rome', *The Antiquaries Journal*, 1965, XLV, pt.

II, p. 220.

23. NH I/6/3. This plan was almost certainly drawn
after Weddell's plan, NH I/6/4. There is a
finished version in the Soane, SM 41:76, which is
clearly not the final one as it does not include
the niches in the passages between the rooms or
the apse of the dining-room. There are two
versions of the final plan at Newby Hall, NH
I/6/5 and NH I/6/6.

24. NH I/6/4. Whether this rough plan is in Adam's
hand or Weddell's, as Low maintains, or both, is
uncertain. The concept is certainly Adam's.

25. Middleton, op. cit. at note 20 above, pp. 51–2.

26. D. Stroud, *George Dance, architect, 1741–1825*,
London, 1971, pp. 70–1, pl. 14. Fleming, pp.
302–3.

27. The sequence of apse-ended, domed and
rectangular drawing-rooms which Adam planned
around 1772 for Weddell's newly acquired house,
6 Upper Brook Street, has been compared to 20
St James's Square, but was probably inspired by
the gallery and dining-room at Newby. The
London interiors were not executed. J. Low,
'French Taste in London. William Weddell's
Town House', *Country Life*, 27 December 1979,
pp. 2470–72. *The Survey of London*, The
Grosvenor Estate in Mayfair, London, 1980, XL,
pt. II, pp. 202–3, pls 56a, 56b.

28. SM 11:236, quarter design for the 'Ceiling for
Gallery Dome at Newby 1767'. SM 11:237,
'Ceiling of one of the end rooms of the Gallery
at Newby 1767', full outline but only one quarter
in detail and that partly coloured with a pink
ground and darker rose ornaments; the general
ground colour is not indicated. The finished
presentation drawing at Newby, NH I/17/4, is
not coloured or dated or indeed catalogued as
the gallery ceiling. The corner trapezoids with
parabolic sides, though often used by Adam for
the central element of ceilings, are rarely found
as a secondary ornament. Apart from Newby, it
occurs in an exactly contemporary ceiling design
for Lady Holland's bedroom at Kingsgate, Isle of
Thanet, SM 11:236. It is interesting to note that
this house, built by Henry Fox, 1st Baron
Holland, contained a large number of antiquities
that he had purchased.

29. SM 41:74. See note 22 above.

30. 'Section of a Room for the Reception of
Antiquities, Statues Busts and Sarcophagi &c.',
presentation drawing showing the elevation of
the north wall, NH I/6/13. 'Section of the End
next the Dining Room', NH I/6/13. Part
elevation of the south wall, NH I/6/16. Outline
sections showing north, south, east and west
walls, NH I/6/10 (north), I/6/11 (south), I/6/14
(east and west).

31. R. Warner, *A tour through the northern counties of
England, and the borders of Scotland*, Bath, 1802,
II, p. 254.

32. BM, TY7/387. At Jenkins's request, Towneley
sent him a first-hand account of the contents of
the gallery in 1774, BM TY7/336, 339. On
another visit in 1779, he made a plan of the
layout of the statues, BM TY15/1/4. I am
indebted to Jonathan Scott for this information.

33. NH I/6/25.

34. SM 41:79, 'Pavement for the Room of
Antiquities at Newby', partial design, pencil, pen
and ink with pink and grey washes. NH I/6/23
finished presentation drawing similarly coloured.
There are not many designs for pavements of
this sort amongst the Adam drawings. One, SM
7: 228, was made for the brothers' octagonal
sculpture gallery at the rear of their house in 75
(later 76) Lower Grosvenor Street, where they
lived from 1758 to 1772. There is no evidence
that the gallery was built. *Survey of London*, op.
cit. at note 27 above, p. 56. pl. 15 b & c.
Another, SM 7: 8, was for the principal circular
court in James Adam's scheme for a new
Parliament House. See A. A. Tait, *Robert Adam
Drawings and Imagination*, Cambridge, 1993, pp.

57–67.

35. SM 41:77, 'Pavement of the Room for Antiquities Adelphi. April 10[h] 1772', partial drawing coloured red, yellow and green. NH I/6/24, half drawing similarly coloured.

36. Low, inventory, p. 155.

37. Ceiling designs: NH I/7/5, finished presentation drawing, pen and ink and grey wash, signed and dated 1767. NH I/7/6, quarter design coloured. It is unusual that there are no record drawings or sketches for this ceiling at the Soane. The compartmented composition is not one Adam repeated. Wall elevations: SM 41:75, undated. NH I/7/1, finished presentation drawing, undated. Chimney-piece: SM 22:254, dated 1769, SM 22:255, outline drawing of the above, dated 1769.

38. NH I/7/3, drawing by Belwood for timber construction of the ends of the dining-room. There are similar drawings by Belwood for the ends and the dome of the gallery, NH I/6/17, 18, 19, 21. The drawing at large of the Corinthian capital, NH I/7/4, appears to be in Adam's hand.

39. NH I/7/7, a large-scale working drawing of the bell-flower and rosette border round the ceiling, dated 'Febry 4 1768' and attributed to Rose. Joseph Rose's sketchbook at Harewood contains two drawings for Newby: p. 7, 'Dineing room at Wm Weddles Esqr. Newby York'; and p. 29, 'Hall ceiling Mr Weddles at Newby Yorkshire'. NH I/7/8, a large-scale working drawing by Belwood of the guilloche moulding in the ceiling.

40. For Zucchi, see Low, inventory, p. 164. E. Croft-Murray, Decorative painting in England 1537–1837, London, 1970, II, p. 299b. For Devall, see M. Mauchline, Harewood House, London, 1974, p. 83.

41. G. B. Piranesi, Diverse maniere d'adornare i cammini, Rome, 1769, pl. 2. J. Wilton-Ely, Piranesi as architect and designer, New York, 1993, pls 124, 125. Hope's chimney-piece, composed of antique fragments put together by Piranesi, is now in the Rijksmuseum. Apart from the fact that it was executed before 1769, Wilton-Ely gives no date. Adam designed a chimney-piece almost identical to the Newby one in the same year for General Burgoyne's house at 10 Hertford Street, SM 22:265. Whether it was executed is not known. It is not discussed in T. Draper, 'No 10 Hertford Street', Georgian Group Journal, 1999, IX, pp. 116–38. See note 62 below for the relationship between the Newby ante-room chimney-piece and one for General Burgoyne. There is also a relationship between Piranesi's chimney-piece for Hope and the bacchic term designed by Chambers for the eating-room at Gower House which is thought to date from 1767. See J. Harris and M. Snodin, eds, Sir William Chambers architect to George III, London, 1997, pp. 140–1, fig. 201.

42. SM 14:93, drawing-room ceiling, Byram, 1780.

43. Uncoloured presentation drawing of the whole ceiling, dated 1767, NH I/7/5; undated large scale drawing of one quarter of the dining-room ceiling coloured, NH I/7/6; large-scale drawing of bell-flower and rosette border dated 'Febry 4. 1768', NH I/7/7. R. Reilly, Wedgwood, London, 1989, I, p. 409. See chapters 17, on Derby House, and 10, on Osterley.

44. SM 17:32. Slab, SM 49:40. The farm house at Newby had a parlour furnished in the Etruscan style. Low, inventory, p. 161. There are some designs attributed to Mrs Weddell and Belwood for wall decorations for this room, NH I/21/2–5. Low, loc. cit. at note 2 above, p. 139.

45. SM 49:41.

46. The perfume burner was purchased on 30 March 1776. N. Goodison, Ormolu: the work of Matthew Boulton, London, 1974, pp. 157–8, 238, pl. 90. Low, inventory, p. 140.

47. Low, inventory, p. 154.

48. Sideboard: SM 60:140, dated 11 April 1783; 6:115,

49. SM 6:48.

50. NH I/7/1c, design for the vase and pedestal showing the griffons gilded and the vase with ormolu mounts of drapery suspended from lions' masks. SM: 6:56, a preliminary design. Warner, op. cit. at note 31 above, II, p. 254.

51. Low, inventory, p. 139.

52. Information supplied by Dr Ruth Guilding.

53. J. Cornforth, 'Newby in the 19th Century', Country Life, 25 December 1980, p. 2407.

54. Low, inventory, p. 155.

55. NH I/7/9, finished presentation drawing, pen and ink and coloured washes. SM 25:138, a design for 4 plate warmers. The one on the bottom left is identical to the Newby Hall finished drawing, the one on the right, though different, has the rams' heads and lions' feet described in the 1792 inventory.

56. SM 24:230, 'Design of a Commode Table for the Piers in the Dining room at Newby', coloured.

57. Low, inventory, p. 154.

58. SM 20:79. The design published by Low (SM 20:77, also dated 1770) is for a more intricate gilded mirror. Low, inventory, p. 139, fig. 7. See also SM 20:27.

59. Gilbert, I, p. 266.

60. Warner, op. cit. at note 31 above, II, pp. 253–4.

61. Low, inventory, pp. 155, 164.

62. NH I/11/1, laid-out wall elevations. SM 23:267, chimney-piece for General Burgoyne. SM 23:169 is similar but uninscribed. See above, note 41, for the relationship between the dining-room chimney-piece and one designed in 1769 for Burgoyne.

63. This use is suggested by the two rosewood card-tables listed in the 1792 inventory. Low, inventory, p. 155.

64. NH I/11/3; SM 22:262. Low, inventory, p. 164.

65. Low, inventory, p. 164.

66. Warner, op. cit. at note 31 above, II, p. 254.

67. NH/I/11/2. SM 8:18.

68. NH/I/8/1, laid-out wall elevations of the hall. There are no sketches or record copies of this design at the Soane. NH I/8/2, 'Section of Mr Weddles Hall', a working drawing with measurements, is attributed to Joseph Rose. NH I/8/3 is an outline drawing of the four sides as executed with a large painting (i.e. the Rosa de Tivoli rather than a ruinscape) on the west wall. Ceiling design, SM 11:238. There is no copy at Newby.

69. J. Cornforth, 'Newby Hall, Yorkshire – I', Country Life, 7 June 1979, p. 1804. RIBA Drawings Collection, CC 4/50. D. Watkin, James Stuart, London, 1982, p. 41, figs 43, 44. Weddell's great friend and political patron, the Marquess of Rockingham, employed Stuart at Wentworth Woodhouse, Yorks. from c.1755. Weddell would also have known Stuart through the Society of Dilettanti, to which he was elected in 1766. An abortive meeting between Weddell and Stuart was mentioned in a letter from Thomas Gray to William Mason on 23 May 1767, op. cit. at note 13 above, letter 440, p. 957.

70. G. B. Piranesi, Vasi, Candelabri, Cippi, Sarcophagi, Rome, 1778, pl. 128a. G. B. Piranesi, The Complete Etchings, ed. J. Wilton-Ely, San Francisco, 1994, p. 1059, no. 980.

71. E. Hargrove, History of the castle, town, and forest of Knaresborough with Harrowgate, 4th ed., York, 1789, p. 261. However, the figure is not mentioned in the 1792 inventory, Low, p. 154.

72. J. Nollekens, 'Inventory of all the Statues Busts Vases Pedestals and other Marbles in the Mansion . . .', no. 42. Low, inventory, p. 164.

73. Weddell's marriage took place on 14 February 1771. Evidently it had been planned since August 1770. WYAS VR 6013/14557, 14558.

74. SM 41:78.

75. Evidently the late seventeenth-century house had two drawing-rooms; one, which later became the hall, had a marble floor and this may have been

76. SM 22:260, dated 1772 and a related sketch 23:236 are for the chimney-piece shown in the laid-out wall elevation of 1769, NH I/8/1. The revised design, also dated 1772, SM 22:262. The frieze of the hall doors, SM 53:45 and the Doric wall frieze, SM 53:44.

77. A voucher reading 'Mr Carr 1768' was found in 1789 amongst the accounts at the house. WYAS VR 5571. Low, thesis, p. 346. Carr seems to have been principally concerned with the stables, but his designs were rejected in favour of Belwood's. They are in Cumbria Record Office (Carlyle) D/Penn/Yorks. houses. Low, loc. cit. at note 2 above, p. 139.

78. 17 July 1767, letter from Jacques Neilson to the Comte du Chastelet Lomont: 'Il reste quelque pièces de Tapisseries à faire passer à Londres pour compléter celles que j'y ay envoyé à M. le Duc de Northumberland, à Mgr Coventry, à Mgr Fife et à M. Weddell.' M. Fenaille, État général des tapisseries de la manufacture des Gobelins, Paris, 1907, IV, pp. 263, 264. Weddell was one of the four patrons named in Neilson's list of tapestries made in 1768, Fenaille, p. 265.

79. 3 July 1769, letter from Jacques Neilson to Thomas Dundas. Zetland archives.

80. SM 8: 103, sketch dated 21 July 1769. SM 11:240, revised quarter design, coloured. NH I/9/2, revised quarter design, coloured, folded and probably sent to Weddell. Another copy, Cumbria Record Office (Carlyle), D/Penn/Yorkshire.

81. Low, inventory, p. 164.

82. SM 17:194. Low, inventory, p. 155.

83. J. Cornforth, 'Newby Hall, Yorkshire – II', Country Life, 14 June 1979, p. 1920. The '2 Large French Plates of Glass in Carv'd Burnish'd Gold frames' were valued at £300, the glasses being the principal cost, and the '2 Large fine Veined Antique Slabs vaneer'd on Rich Carv'd & Gilt frames' valued at £36'. Low, inventory, p. 155.

84. Gilbert, I, pp. 264–7.

85. SM 22:180.

86. SM 22:258. This is dated 20 June 1770. The ornaments on the pilaster are sketched in pencil.

87. SM 22:257. This is dated 1770.

88. SM 22:259.

89. SM 23:140. NH I/17/2, a modification of Adam's design attributed to Belwood. The yellow and white chimney-piece listed in the inventory of fixtures conforms to the notes on the Soane drawing. Two bookcases were also listed as fixtures; two others in recesses and a 'Mahogany Library Bookcase Pediment top' were in the inventory of furniture. Low, inventory, pp. 155, 164. In Adam's 'Plan of the Alterations', c.1766–7, this was to be a powdering-room.

90. Ceiling design coloured pink and green, dated 1769, SM 11: 239. The ceiling is all that survives. Chimney-piece, partial design dated 1769, SM 22:257; finished presentation drawing, NH I/10/9. The inventory of fixtures lists a white marble chimney-piece. Low, inventory, p. 164. Adam originally planned this as Mr Weddell's dressing-room, with a powdering-room where Mrs Compton's boudoir is now and a water-closet behind a secondary stair.

91. NH/I/10/2.

92. SM 22:78. The inventory lists 'A Peir Glass in a Stucco frame Gilt in Burnish'd Gold' and 'A Serpentine Marble Table with Rich Mosaic Border on a Carv'd frame Gilt in Burnish'd Gold – Valued £20'. The room also contained a backgammon table and four other tables, a piano forte, and two 'block' (fire?) screens which suggests that like most libraries it was used as an everyday family room.

93. NH/I/10/2.

94. NH I/10/4, 5, 6, 8.

95. Low, inventory, p. 156.

96. R. Adam to Mr Ware at Nostell, 23 May 1767, WYAS, NP A4/1525/33.

97. NH I/12/5 design for the strings, attributed to Joseph Rose.

98. The antique sculptures are noted in the laid out elevation attributed to Rose, NH I/12/4. See also Low, inventory, p. 164.

99. NH I/12/1, laid-out wall elevations showing arcades; I/12/2, section of the staircase and upper landing; I/12/3, section of the first floor.

100. J. Harris, *Sir William Chambers*, London, 1970, pp. 233–4 (100), pl. 98.

101. NH I/3/8, finished presentation drawing. SM 41:73, outline drawing dated 'Novr 9^h 1776'. The plan of the portico is faintly added in pencil to Adam's earlier 'Plan of Alterations', SM 41:74.

14. SALTRAM

1. J. Cornforth, 'Saltram, Devon – I', *Country Life*, 27 April 1967, p. 1001.

2. Thomas Carter's bill for chimney-piece, 1768, J. Parker's Cash Book.

3. L. Namier and J. Brooke, *The House of Commons 1754–1790*, London, 1964, III, pp. 249–50.

4. Ibid., p. 367. According to the marriage agreement, John Parker received £6,000 from the 1st Lord Grantham immediately, and another £6,000 on Lord Grantham's death. West Yorkshire Archive Service (WYAS), Newby Hall papers, 2750.

5. Notice of Therese Robinson's death by Sir Joshua Reynolds, BM Add. Ms. 4825 f.15.
   The Parker–Robinson correspondence is divided between the Parker papers in the Devon Record Office, the Morley Papers in the British Museum (BM Add. Ms. 48218), the Grantham letters among the Vyner papers in West Yorkshire Archive Service, and those among the Lucas papers (the 2nd Lord Grantham married Mary Jemima, daughter of Philip Yorke, 2nd Earl of Hardwicke and Jemima, Marchioness Grey) in the Bedfordshire Record Office.

6. Therese Parker to Lord Grantham, 23 August 1771, BM Add. Ms. 48218, f.107–8.

7. SM 11:257. The ceiling survives. Frederick Robinson was looking for a house for the Parkers in September 1769, Therese Parker to Frederick Robinson, WYAS, Vyner Papers 6160/6013/14476. The house on Sackville Street was being done up in August 1770 when Therese asked Frederick to 'go over (it) & give us a very exact account of the state it is in at present . . . but chiefly if all the Blue Paper is up, & those three Rooms (one of which was presumably the drawing-room with the Adam ceiling) ready to receive the pictures & furniture . . .', Vyner papers, 6160/6013/14481.

8. Wall elevations, SM 50:67, 68; ceilings SM 11:253–6; chimney-pieces SM 22:247–50.

9. Chimney-piece design, SM 22:249.

10. First ceiling design, not executed, dated 1768, SM 11:253. Second design as executed, SM 11:254, 255.

11. Thomas Robinson to Lord Pelham, Saltram, 1 September 1769, BM Add. Ms. 3099.

12. John Parker's cash book, Saltram. September 1770 and 31 January 1772.

13. *Catalogue of the pictures, casts and busts belonging to the Earl of Morley at Saltram*, Plymouth, 1819.

14. SM 17:178.

15. B. Jacobs, *Axminster carpets (hand-made) 1755–1957*, London, 1970, pp. 24–9.

16. Thomas Robinson to his brother, Frederick, 22 August 1769, WYAS Vyner Papers 6160/6013/14539.

17. Frederick Robinson to Lord Grantham, Bedfordshire Record Office. L 30/14/333/63. John Parker's cash book, Saltram. 2 October 1770 'Pd Whitty for an Axminster Carpet for the Great Room £126.0.0'.

18. SM 12:73, 74.

19. SM 50:68.

20. SM 20:69.

21. Mirror frame for Paul Methuen, SM 20:56, 57; for General Burgoyne, SM 20:84.

22. Therese Parker to Lord Grantham, 2 April 1772, BM Add. Ms. 48218, f.112. The Parkers also received advice about pictures for the saloon from Sir Joshua Reynolds, whose opinion that the room 'should admit none but good & original' ones was shared by Lord Grantham. Lord Grantham to Therese Parker, 16 September 1770, WYAS Vyner papers 6160/6013/14561.

23. Gilbert I, pp. 257–8.

24. John Parker's cash book, Saltram. E. Harris, p. 69, pl. 21; the notes to the illustrations are misnumbered: 21 refers to the saloon table and 22 to the Velvet Drawing Room.

25. SM 17:11, 'Design of a Table Frame for his Grace the Archbishop of York May 1768'. Robert Hay Drummond was the son of Henry, 8th Earl of Kinnoull.

26. Thomas to Frederick Robinson, 1 June 1766, referring to a two day stay at Brodsworth, WYAS Vyner papers 6160/6013/14496. Though this predates Adam's design for the Archbishop, it is unlikely to have been Robinson's last visit to Brodsworth. Robert Hay Drummond lived at Brodsworth from 1758 until his death in 1777, during which time he is said to have made many improvements, probably employing the York architect, Thomas Atkinson. See J. Hunter, *South Yorkshire. The history and topography of the Deanery of Doncaster*, London, 1828, I, p. 316.

27. 13 September 1771, Therese Parker to Frederick Robinson, concerning one of Thomas's drawings of the lodges at Stanmer, BM Add. MS. 48218, f.172.

28. N. Goodison, *Ormolu: the work of Matthew Boulton*, London, 1974, pp. 160–1, 204 n.487, 205 n.488, 489, 490. There was a payment of £34.14.0 to Mr Draper for a vase from Mr Boulton on 18 June 1772, John Parker's cash book.

29. SM 20:116. The engraving of this design was not published until 1822 in Adam's *Works*, III. E. Harris, p. 81, pl. 62.

30. Therese Parker to Frederick Robinson, 17 September 1769, WYAS Vyner papers 6160/6013/14476. John Parker's cash book, 8 September 1770, 'Mr Parker left with Mr Robinson to pay for ye Genoa Damask £300'. On 24 March 1772, Vansommer was paid £26.14.0 for curtains at Saltram.

31. Frederick Robinson to Lord Grantham, 11 September 1770, Bedfordshire Record Office, L30/14/333/61.

32. SM 20:70.

33. Perfetti was paid £41 for the two tables on 31 March 1772, John Parker's cash book. The maker of the mirror frames is not known.

34. 'Plan of a House and Offices for John Parker Esqr near Saltram 1779', SM 50:66.

35. Frederick Robinson to Lord Grantham, 11 September 1770, Bedfordshire Record Office. L/30/14/333/61.

36. Ibid.

37. A. Rowan, 'Ugbrooke Park, Devon – II', *Country Life*, 22 July 1967, p. 207.

38. *Plato and his pupils, Virgil reading the Aeneid, Alexander and Aristotle*, and *Anacreon sacrificing to the Graces*. John Parker's cash book, 27 June 1781, 'To Zucchi for the Paintings in the eating Room £150.0.0'.

39. Therese Parker to Frederick Robinson, 17 September 1769, WYAS Vyner papers 6160/6013/14476.

40. SM 11:138.

41. There is a carpet of the same design in different colours at the Rijksmuseum. B. Jacobs, op. cit. at note 15 above, pp. 44–5, pls 40, 41.

42. BM Add. MS. 48218, f.182.

43. Anne Robinson to Lord Grantham, 13 November 1778, BM Add. MS. 48218, f.53.

44. Ibid. Four members of the Stockman family are recorded in the Saltram accounts and wage books between 1770 and the early nineteenth century. The one referred to here is probably Mr Richard Stockman, the elder. The National Trust, *Saltram Devon*, 1981, p. 54.

45. SM 50:66.

46. J. Cornforth, 'Saltram, Devon – III', *Country Life*, 11 May 1967, p. 1160.

47. SM 25:128, uncoloured design of a pedestal and vase dated 22 November 1780; SM 25:159, coloured version dated 23 November 1780. The vases are lined with zinc for water and the pedestals fitted as pot cupboards. The figured medallions were probably painted by Zucchi or Angelica Kauffmann. E. Harris, p. 102, pl. 142.

48. SM 20:70.

15. LUTON HOO

1. As a mark of his commitment, Bute subscribed to ten copies of Adam's *Ruins of the palace of the Emperor Diocletian at Spalatro*, which was published in 1764. That was twice as many as any other subscriber. The Earl of Shelburne and Mrs Montagu had five copies each, and John Parker of Saltram, four copies.

2. An exception is Adam's '1st Design' of c.1773 for Ray Hall, Essex, seat of Sir James Wright, Bart., British Minister at Venice and a friend of Bute's, which has a long spinal corridor and large bow-windowed picture gallery with a columnar porch that were inspired by the plans for Luton. The bow window was not executed. J. King, 'An Ambassador's House in Essex', *The Georgian Group Journal*, London, 1997, VII, p. 121, fig. 6.

3. The Bute drawings were the basis of F. Russell's article, 'Luton Hoo, Bedfordshire – I', *Country Life*, 16 January 1992, pp. 44–7, which illustrates most of the elevations but none of the plans. See also F. Russell, *John, 3rd Earl of Bute (1713–1792): Patron and Collector*, London (forthcoming).

4. Thomas Worsley suggested an estate near Oxford on 18 May 1761 and Lord Harcourt recommended Wittenham, Berks. F. Russell, loc. cit. at note 3 above, p. 44.

5. Bute Collection. The northern bow contained a chapel. Walpole was told in April 1769 that this was going to be demolished and he might purchase the woodwork 'for a song'. Walpole to Lord Strafford, 3 July 1769. *Correspondence*, XXXV, pp. 332–3.

6. Bute Collection. SM 37:44–6. F. Russell, loc. cit. at note 3 above, p. 44, fig. 5.

7. The organ was constructed by Christopher Pinchbeck, builder of the *Theatre of the Muses* clockwork organ. Bute's separate account at Coutts Bank records a payment of £1,155 to Pinchbeck in April 1763; an additional payment of £312 on 31 May 1763 is recorded in his ordinary account. John Christopher Smith, Handel's amanuensis, is said to have supervised the construction and arranged the music for the barrels which were pinned by John Langshaw, organist and mechanic. John Snetzler was responsible for the pipework. See A. W. J. G. Ord-Hume, *Barrel Organ*, London, 1978, pp. 88–95; W. Malloch, 'The Earl of Bute's machine Organ', *Early Music Quarterly*, London, April 1983, pp. 172–5; M. I. Wilson, 'Lord Bute's Barrel Organ', *The Organ World: Musical Opinion* London, February 1966, pp. 289–91. Little attention has been paid to Bute's other musical interests. Evidently he was also a collector of printed and manuscript music. Walpole, *Correspondence*, XXIII, p. 96, n.12.

8. Quadrangular plan with one long wing, Bute Collection. R. Castell, *Villas of the ancients*, London, 1728, see pl. 363. Bute House plans: RIBA Drawings Collection; SM 21:82, 220; SM 39:49. See chapter 8 on Lansdowne House, n.8.

9. Bute Collection; SM 39:31–3.

10. See General R. Clerk's letter to the Earl of Shelburne, 1 November 1765, recounting Adam's

difficulties with Bute, Bolton, II, p. 5.

11. The rooms on the ground-floor plan at the Soane (SM 39:31) are not named, but must have included the hall, dining-room, an informal drawing-room and the library apartment.

12. Bute Collection. SM 39:27–30. The courtyard plan, SM 39:29, is very close to a drawing inscribed 'Plan for Stuart Mackenzie', possibly for Rosehaugh, Ross and Cromarty, SM 37:63. The Rt. Hon. James Stewart Mackenzie was the Earl of Bute's brother. F. Russell, loc. cit., at note 3 above, fig. 6.

13. J. Harris, *Sir William Chambers*, London, 1970, p. 78, fig. 12, pls 109, 110.

14. Bute Collection. SM 39:24–6. F. Russell, loc. cit. at note 3 above, fig. 3.

15. The plan was described as a 'double T' by L. Dutens, *Memoirs of a Traveller*, London, 1806, II, p. 113.

16. Long corridors are occasionally found in English baroque houses like Castle Howard and Blenheim. There is a survey plan of Mount Stuart made in 1769 by James Craig, National Monuments Record of Scotland, Wamerston Collection.

17. There is a rough double-sided sketch in the Bute Archives that establishes Bute's responsibility for the notion of the wing with a long corridor and a series of five rooms behind, ending in a library wing. F. Russell, loc. cit. at note 3 above, p. 46.

18. M. Coke, *The Letters and Journals of Lady Mary Coke*, London, 1970, III, p. 111.

19. Bute Collection. Bute's first trip to Italy was from August 1768 to July 1769; the second from November 1769 to May 1771. J. Ingamells, *A Dictionary of British and Irish Travellers in Italy 1701–1800 compiled from the Brinsley Ford Archive*, London, 1997, pp. 164–5.

20. Bute Collection.

21. These alterations were mainly to the north and south elevations. Adam, *Works*, I, iii, pl. V. Bute Collection. F. Russell, loc. cit. at note 3 above, figs 8, 9.

22. SM: Chambers 43/4/35. Unlike the engraved plan, the drawing in the Chambers collection does not include stairs or an entrance from the loggia into the vestibule.

23. J. Harris, op. cit. at note 13 above, pp. 209–20, pl. 45. A colonnaded tribune is also found in Paine's plan for Worksop, but it is not accompanied by open courts.

24. This is contrary to the statement in J. Summerson, *Architecture in Britain 1530 to 1830*, London, 1963, p. 263. See chapter 4, on Syon.

25. Adam, *Works*, I, iii, preface.

26. Bute Collection. *Plan proposed for completing the House at Luton Park . . . Robert Smirke 1825*. See also M. Hall, 'Luton Hoo – Bedfordshire – II', *Country Life*, 22 January 1992, pp. 50–3.
There is a plan of the house signed and dated 'C.R.C. (C. R. Cockerell) Aug 20. 1821' and headed 'Sketch of Luton Marquess of Bute's/ Bedfords:/ by Mr Adams 1770', giving measurements of the rooms and showing the north wing more or less as it appears in the penultimate plan and the colonnaded screen and courts of the final plan. It is uncertain whether this is a copy of an intermediate plan that was shown to Cockerell when he visited Luton in 1821 and mistakenly described as a sketch made by Adam in 1770, or Cockerell's own idea of how the house could be finished. J. Harris, 'C. R. Cockerell's "Ichnographica Domestica"', *Architectural History*, London, 1971, XIV, p. 23.

27. M. Coke, op. cit. at note 18 above, IV, p. 390.

28. M. Delany, *Autobiography and correspondence of Mary Granville, Mrs. Delany*, ed. Lady Llanover, London, 1862, ser. 2, II (= V), p. 35.

29. M. Coke, op. cit. at note 18 above, IV, pp. 390, 395. M. Delany, op. cit. at note 28 above, ser. 2, II (= V), p. 35. Adam's curtain cornices executed for the two ante-rooms, the drawing-room and saloon were published in his *Works*, I, iii, pl.

VIII, 'as an attempt to banish the absurd French compositions of this kind, heretofore so servilely imitated by the upholsterers of this country', i.e. rococo designs.

30. M. Coke, op. cit. at note 18 above, IV, p. 395. SM 8:145, a sketch for the ceiling; SM 12:24, coloured design dated 1770. It is possible that the outlines of the oval compartments and some of the decorations were executed in stucco.

31. SM 12:20, with paintings, inscribed 'not executed'; SM 12:21, without paintings; both dated 1769. The library ceiling at Mellerstain, dated 1770, SM 12:59.

32. The design for the saloon ceiling, SM 12:19, inscribed 'not executed', is more ornate than SM 12:18. Both are dated 1769. The rejected design for Lady Bute's dressing-room ceiling, SM 12:22, has several elements in common with the design chosen for the saloon. In the Bute collection there is an undated, coloured presentation drawing of the engraved design that was published in the *Works*, I, iii, pl. VII with the date 1769, but there are no drawings of this ceiling in the Soane collection. The stucco-work was executed by Joseph Rose and the paintings by Antonio Zucchi.

33. Adam, *Works*, II, i, pl. VII.

34. Chimney-piece designs: drawing-room dated 1770, SM 22:253; ante-room dated 6 April 1770, SM 22:252; Saloon, incorrectly labelled 'Anti Room' but inscribed in pencil 'Bow Window Room *Parlour Story 1769*', SM 22:251.

35. F. Russell, op. cit. at note 3 above. Lady Coke wrote that 'a great many of the Chimney pieces were done in Italy: the designs very pretty, but . . . they don't polish the Marble so highly as they do here.' M. Coke, op. cit. at note 18 above, IV, p. 390.

36. SM 22:251.

37. Adam, *Works*, I, iii, preface.

38. SM 17:19.

39. Adam, *Works*, I, iii, preface. and pl. VIII. C. Avery, 'Busy and picturesque – some rediscovered bronze firedogs cast by Andrea Baruzzi, Il Bresciano (1530–69), and the Earl of Bute's patronage of Robert Adam', *Christie's International Magazine*, London, July/August 1996, p. 24. One andiron with a figure of Hercules is in Sir Brinsley Ford's collection; its pair with Jupiter Tonens was sold at Christie's, London, 9 July 1996, lot 27. The second fragmentary pair was sold in the same sale, lot 28.

40. A 'Mosaic Table 5 ft 10$^1/_2$ in' is referred to and drawn in section on Adam's unexecuted design for the pier 'Glass frame for the Drawing room at Luton', SM 20:112. The first design for the table frame (SM 20:116), made on 27 October 1772, was long enough for the mosaics but too short for the 7-foot wide (2.13 metre) pier-glass. By setting the mosaics in marble surrounds the tables were made the same width as the pier-glasses. *Works*, III, pl. XI, incorrectly labelled 'Furniture at Sion House'.

41. One pair of torchères was sold by Pearl Assurance, High Holborn, Christie's house sale, 1 November 1990, lot 137, the other sold by the Executors of Lady Rhyl at Christie's, 9 July 1992, lot 40. It is possible that these were made from the engraving published in the *Works*, III, pl. XI.

42. The first designs for the mirror frames, dated 10 September 1772, had pilaster strips dividing the mirrors in three sections and medallions and sphinxes on the crest, SM 20:112, 113. SM 20:113 has term figures added in pencil. These were rejected and alternative designs with term figures were prepared on 29 September and 27 October 1772, SM 3:33 and SM 20:114–116.

43. M. Coke, op. cit. at note 18 above, IV, p. 390.

44. For the Company of British Cast Plate Manufacturers see G. Wills, *English looking glasses*, London, 1965, appendix I. *The Survey of London*, The Grosvenor Estate in Mayfair,

London, 1980, XL, pp. 312–37. A bill of 1773 from the carver Sefferin Nelson certified by Robert and James Adam refers to a chimney-piece 'for the Town House'. In October 1774 Bute bought part of Lord Milton's house and stabling and added it to his own. Substantial alterations were carried out in 1775–6 by Brown and Holland. The last recorded payment to Messrs Adam in Bute's Coutts account was for £350 on 14 July 1774. Wm. Adam & Co. were paid £400 on 25 October 1776.

45. Bolton, II, p. 58. The similarity between the chimney-glass in the drawing-room at 20 St James's Square and the rejected design for Luton's drawing-room, SM 20:112, is also worth noting.

46. M. Delany, op. cit. at note 28 above, p. 35.

47. 'Organ Case for The Earl of Bute', dated 1763, SM 25:4; a similarly inscribed, somewhat simpler, undated design, SM 25:5. The design is said by David King, p. 411, to be for Luton, but is too early and must be for Bute's London house. The organ itself was presumably destroyed in the 1843 fire.

48. Adam, *Works*, I, iii, preface; M. Delany, op. cit. at note 28 above, p. 34.

49. G. Teyssot, *Città e utopia nell'illuminismo inglese: George Dance il giovane*, Rome, 1974, pl. 22.

50. L. Dutens, op. cit. at note 15 above, p. 115. Letter from Lady Polwarth, 31 August 1780, Bedfordshire County Record Office, quoted by D. King, p. 123 and p. 154, n.17.

51. The maps and models were noted by C. R. Cockerell in 1821 on his plan of the house, see note 26 above. The contents of the rooms adjoining the library were described by M. Delany, op. cit. at note 28 above, p. 34 and L. Dutens, op. cit. at note 15 above, p. 114. Bute's collection of optical, mathematical, and philosophical instruments, etc. was sold at auction by Messrs Skinner and Dyke at Mr Hutchins's Rooms, King Street on 5 February 1793, and on 30 May 1793 the same auction house sold the contents of the laboratory at Luton.

52. Adam, *Works*, I, iii, pl. VIII and preface. 1764, the date given on the engraving, is evidently a mistake; even 1768 is early, given the fact that building work only began late in 1767 and the library ceiling was not designed until 1769. There is a sketch for a similar but not identical stove-grate in the Soane Museum, SM 24:60.

53. Cockerell's plan of Luton, see note 26 above. By contrast, Mrs Delany found the Library 'extreamly well lighted'. M. Delany, op. cit. at note 28 above, p. 34

54. L. Dutens, op. cit. at note 15 above, pp. 114–5.

55. L. Stuart, *The letters of Lady Louisa Stuart*, ed. R. B. Johnson, London, 1926, pp. 40, 47.

16. 20 ST JAMES'S SQUARE

1. T. W. Pritchard, *The Wynns of Wynnstay*, Caerwys, 1982. B. Ford, 'Sir Watkin Williams-Wynn. A Welsh Maecenas', *Apollo* June, 1974, pp. 435–9.

2. Pritchard, ibid., pp. 67 ff.

3. Ford, loc. cit. at note 1 above, pp. 436–7.

4. On his return to England he stopped in Paris where he purchased diamond jewellery for his bride and a china dinner service for her mother. Pritchard, op. cit. at note 1 above, p. 12.

5. P. Howell and T. W. Pritchard, 'Wynnstay, Denbighshire – II', *Country Life*, 30 March 1972, p. 782. National Library of Wales (NLW), Wynnstay MSS. 122, p. 7.

6. Pritchard, op. cit. at note 1 above, p. 100. NLW, Wynnstay MSS. 115/21/18, 17 October 1768, payment to Devall of £19.10.6 for a chimney-piece for Grosvenor Square; MSS. 115/21/11, March 1770–February 1771, Etruscan vases purchased from Wedgwood; MSS. 102, p. 25, 10 August 1767–7, April 1770 payment to Bradshaw for furnishing Grosvenor Square house and

articles sent to Wynnstay, £2,886; MSS. 115/7, Account book 1769, 1 March, Mr Dickens paid for plasterers' work at Grosvenor Square.

7. SM 22:240–241. The 5th Duke of Beaufort, born 1744, matric. Oriel College, Oxford 1760, married Elizabeth, youngest daughter of Admiral the Hon. Edward Boscowan, Adam's patron at Hatchlands.

8. NLW, Wynnstay MSS. 2258C. *Gentleman's Magazine*, May 1770, p. 233.

9. P. Howell and T. W. Pritchard, 'Wynnstay, Denbighshire – I', *Country Life*, 23 March 1972, p. 689. J. Ionides, *Thomas Farnolls Pritchard of Shrewsbury*, Ludlow, 1999, p. 144. Ceiling designs for Wynnstay, SM 12:41–3.

10. It is also possible that Gandon was introduced to Sir Watkin by Paul Sandby, his close friend and mentor. He made a design for Sir Watkin's theatre at Wynnstay on 5 February 1771. NLW, Wynnstay MSS. 115/25/26. See E. MacParland, *James Gandon*, London, 1985, pp. 15, 207, pl. 143.

11. *Survey of London*, St James's, Westminster. Pt. I, London, 1960, XXIX, p. 164. This is the fullest account of the house. See also J. Olley, '20 St James's Square', *Architectural Journal*, London, 21, 28 February 1990, pp. 34–57, 34–53.

12. The marriage took place on 21 December 1771, but preparations were afoot at least by May when he paid Heming & Co. £1,221.0.0 for plate including marriage plate. NLW Wynnstay MSS. 102, p. 19.

13. NLW Wynnstay MSS. 115/25/26.

14. RIBA Drawings Collection; SM 40:65, 66; Adam, *Works*, II, ii, pl. I.

15. Undated plan for Wynnstay, SM 40:63.

16. J. Harris, *Sir William Chambers*, London, 1970, p. 225, no. 84, p. 64, fig. 6. A. Palladio, *I quattro libri dell'architettura*, Venice, 1570, bk IV, ch. X.

17. William Kinman was paid £200 on 9 July 1774 for the copper stair-rail. In addition he supplied a copper pillar for the bottom and an iron rail to strengthen the copper costing £5 and £9.10 respectively. NLW Wynnstay MSS. 115/17/8.

18. The *Transfiguration* was then the altarpiece of S. Pietro in Montorio and is now in the Vatican Museum. The painting was one of the most admired in Rome and James Byres also had a copy in his house in Rome. Parry's copy was put up in June 1776. NLW Wynnstay MSS. 115/8, p. 13. Sir Watkin is reported to have paid the large sum of 400 guineas for it. Ford, loc. cit. at note 1 above, p. 436. The original copy having left the house, a new one was made for the Distillers Company by Theodore Ramos in 1978.
Roberts's landscapes were placed on the great stairs on 3 April 1775. They cost £52.10.0. NLW Wynnstay MSS. 115/7, p. 33. A. Crookshank and D. Fitzgerald, The Knight of Glin, *The watercolours of Ireland*, London, 1994, p. 186.

19. Adam, *Works*, II, ii, description of pl. III.

20. Ceiling design, SM 12:50, dated 3 September 1772.

21. Chimney-piece design, SM 23:9, dated 27 August 1772. Hinchcliff was paid £150 in 1773, NLW Wynnstay MSS. 115/17/12. The grate, fender, shovel and tongs were supplied on 19 December 1773 by William Hopkins & Co., whose bill does not mention a design by Adam, Wynnstay MSS. 115/17/13.

22. Chimney-glass design, SM 12:121.

23. G. B. Piranesi, *Diversi maniere d'adornare i cammini*, Rome, 1769, pl. 9A.

24. Design for the chimney-piece, SM 23:10, dated 1 October 1772. Zucchi's bill dated 26 September 1774, NLW Wynnstay MSS. 115/17/9.

25. William Hopkins' bill, NLW Wynnstay MSS. 115/17/13. Adam's design, SM 17:126, dated 25 March 1774, calls for an anthemion frieze and tripods on the sides.

26. SM 20:124, 'Glass frame over Chimney' with note in pencil 'The Top when (?) I am afraid will be heavy & expensive'. SM 20:125, a slightly simplified version of 20:124. SM 20:122, 'Pier Glass', 9 feet by 5 feet 1 inch (2.7 metres by 1.7 metres), dated 21 August 1773 and inscribed 'Glass too heavy too expensive (?) without beasts'. The crest consists of a medallion with an eagle on top, a sheath of arrows and winged putti at the base and winged horses on each side. SM 20:123, 'Pier Glass', dated 14 September 1773, a slightly simplified version.

27. The design for the pier glass, SM 20:122, is inscribed 'Should not there be a Scaliola Table here'. Bolton, II, pp. 59, 61. E. Harris, p. 70, pl. 24. Creswell's payment recorded in 1776 Account Book, NLW Wynnstay MSS. 115/8, p. 29.

28. Part of the suite of drawing-room furniture was sold at Sotheby's on 19 November 1993. Thomas Moore supplied a 'fine Brussels Carpet' in February 1775, NLW Wynnstay MSS. 115/17/11.

29. Ceiling design, SM 12:51. The design is inscribed with the subjects of the medallions: *The initiation of Bacchus, the mystical concert, Sacrifice and libation, Death of Meleagre, Aldobrandini Marriage*.

30. Zucchi's bill, NLW Wynnstay MSS. 115/17/9.

31. In Adam's initial plan, the apse in the first drawing-room was broader than that in the second drawing-room.

32. The earliest design, dated 10 August 1772, for a repeat pattern of painted roundels in shaped squares set in larger quatrefoils, SM 12:52. The executed design, dated 2 September 1772 and coloured, SM 12:53. There is a preliminary sketch for this with only three subdivisions consisting of a central oval flanked by lunettes to the three main sections, SM 8:126.

33. Sir Watkin presented Wedgwood with the first published volume of D'Hancarville's catalogue of Sir William Hamilton's collection of Etruscan vases. R. Reilly, *Wedgwood*, London, 1989, I, p. 414. He also lent Wedgwood 172 intaglios and 173 gems or cameos to copy. E. Meteyard, *The life of Josiah Wedgwood*, London, 1866, II, p. 357.

34. Zucchi's bill, Wynnstay MSS. 115/17/9, gives the subjects of the 6 long panels as 'The Triumph of Venus, The Triumph of Galatea, Diana going out to the chase, The judgment of Paris & the meeting of Bacchus & Ariadne'. These cost £25 each.

35. Carpet designs: SM 17:181, dated 24 August 1773; SM 17:182, also dated 24 August 1773; SM 17:183, uncoloured and dated 16 November 1773. The carpet was made by Thomas Moore on 29 December 1774 at a cost of £140.14.0, excluding £10 for Zucchi's painting, 12 guineas for his own large scale painting and £9 for a green baize cover. Moore's bill, NLW Wynnstay MSS. 115/17/11.

36. Account Book for 1777, 17 May, Messrs Walshand paid £25.14.6 for a Van Goyen landscape 'hung up in the best drawing room', NLW Wynnstay MSS. 115/9, p. 35. The ornaments and frames for the 'piers of the Bow in the 2^d Drawing room, and the girandoles' are referred to in a note dated 12 February 1775, SM 52:59.

37. 'Tripod for the Drawing room at Sir W. Wynn's in St James's Square', dated 24 August 1773, SM 17:60. The design includes both the 4-foot-tall tripod and the 2-foot-tall candelabra consisting of a tazza on a tripod base. E. Harris, p. 101, pl. 137. Zucchi supplied 'Drawings for 2 figures in wood for Trypods £2', NLW Wynnstay MSS. 115/17/9.

38. Another variant of Sir Watkin's torchères with different figures was formerly in the possession of Geoffrey Hobson and is illustrated in M. Jourdain's *English furniture of the later 18th century*, London, 1920, IV, fig. 291.
The design for Lady Home's torchere, SM 17:60.

39. Chimney-glass, SM 20:126 dated 21 August 1773 and 20:127. 'Glass Frame Fronting the Chimney in the Second Drawing Room 21 August 1773' measuring 8 feet 10 inches × 4 feet 2 inches (2.6 by 1.7 metres); inscribed *NB*. 'The two Glasses in the Nich to have the same Frame &c.', SM 20:128. SM 52:59, alternative crests for the 'Second Drawing Room' – griffons flanking a vase and sphinxes flanking a medallion.

40. Bolton House mirrors, SM 20:82–85. E. Harris, 'Robert Adam on Park Avenue; the interiors for Bolton House', *Burlington Magazine*, February 1995, CXXXVII, pp. 71–3.

41. Design for the chimney-glass, SM 20:126, dated 11 August 1773.

42. SM 23:11, 12. Zucchi's bill, NLW Wynnstay MSS. 115/17/9. On 5 November 1774 William Hopkins supplied an embossed steel grate with ram's heads and a matching fender lined on the bottom with green baize, Wynnstay MSS. 115/17/13. Adam's design for a grate with anthemion, lion's heads and vases, SM 17:126, was evidently not used.

43. SM 40:70.

44. When this alteration was made is not known. In 1910 there was a large mirror in the central arch at the far end and a small cabinet hanging in the opposite arch. J. M. W. Halley, 'Historical Town Houses, No. 20 St James's Square', *Architectural Review*, September 1910, p. 107.

45. SM 20:129, dated 21 August 1773, with a note: 'Medallion to be placed upon the moulding without the knot & honey suckle Scroll to remain'. SM 20:130, dated 14 September 1773, revised with a crest quite similar to that designed for the chimney-glass in the ante-room (SM 20:121).

46. SM 12:54, dated 18 January 1773, and SM 12:55, a duplicate of the same date, were 'not wanted'. SM 12:56, dated 22 May 1773, is the revised, definitive design.

47. SM 6:138, 'Sketch for Semicircles at Sir W. W.^{s} House The Sides flater & over ye window only the Border'.

48. Hinchcliff's bill: 'A Statuary Marble Inlaid Chimney Peice for Lady Wynnes Dressing Room, was Estimated for a Pillaster one at £128.0.0 2 Extra to the Above being a Column Chimney Peice £22.0.0', NLW Wynnstay MSS. 115/17/12. Adam's design, dated 27 August 1772, (SM 23:13) has a finished, coloured rendering of a pilaster stile (left) and a frieze ornamented with red cameos, a green and white tablet and blocks at either end and, on the right side, a sketchy pencil alternative with fluted Ionic columns and swags of ivy. The latter was executed, but with a Wedgwood tablet of several colours on a black ground and Etruscan red and black blocks. The green shown in Adam's design was one of the encaustic colours patented by Wedgwood in 1769, A. Kelley, *Decorative Wedgwood in architecture and furniture*, London, 1965, p. 35.
Bartoli's bill, 31 January 1775, Wynnstay MSS. Box 115/7 Account Book 1775, p. 33.

49. E.25–18398. Reilly, op. cit. at note 33 above, I, p. 415. Wedgwood & Bentley were paid £26.5.0 on 8 April 1775 for the tablet and two blocks. NLW Wynnstay MSS. 115/7 Account Book 1775, p. 33.

50. Wedgwood Catalogue, 1779. Introductory remarks to Class XIX, cited by Reilly, op. cit. at note 33 above, I, p. 415. See also A. Kelley, op. cit. at note 48 above, p. 37.

51. SM 23:22, 'Chimney piece for the Third Drawing Room at Ashburnham House 1773', with a note 'It is proposed to introduce some of Messrs. Wedgwood and Bentley's work into this Chimney or the ornaments may be done colour'd in Scagliola by Richter or Bartoli if Lord Ashburnham chuses it'. Kelley, op. cit. at note 48 above, p. 38. Other Adam patrons who had Wedgwood chimney-tablets were Sir John Hussey Delaval of Hanover Square; Sir John Hope Weir, 1777; and John Ramsden at Byram.

52. NLW Wynnstay MSS. 115/7 Account Book 1775, p. 34, 2 June, payment to Alwick & Hooper for Rose Mantua silk; 13 June, payment to Mr Bentley for lace and tassels for the toilet-table. Adam's wall elevation shows an oval toilet-glass

flanked by half-figures, which is reminiscent of the one designed in 1771 for the toilet-table in Lady Colebrooke's dressing-room in Arlington Street, SM 17:16, E. Harris, pl. 87. It is conceivable, however, that the spectacular silver-gilt toilet service (now in the National Museum and Gallery of Wales, Cardiff) made by Thomas Heming in 1768–9 for Sir Watkin's deceased first wife, Lady Henrietta Somerset, was displayed on the toilet-table. See O. Fairclough, 'Sir Watkin Williams-Wynn and Robert Adam: commissions for silver 1768–80', *Burlington Magazine*, CXXXVII, June 1995, p. 377.

53. October 1773, 'cutting away brickwork for sliding shutters to Venetian window in library & room over', NLW Wynnstay MSS. 115/17/3. Design for grotesque panel decoration, SM 52:60.

54. SM 6:35. Though the design itself is not dated, it is related to a memorandum dated 12 February 1775: 'A small Girandole for Lady W. Wynn Dressg Room to fix on pilasters', SM 52:59.

55. SM 17:222, dated 9 February 1776. SM 23:239 is a preliminary sketch.
Collins was paid £15.18.7 and Zucchi £20. NLW Wynnstay MSS. 115/17/9, 10. The cabinets seem to have been executed quite quickly. Collins's work was measured in June and Zucchi's bill for painting is dated 8 June 1776. This may explain the latter's promise 'to retouch the 2 Book Cases & finish them to the Satisfaction of Mr. Adam'.

56. SM 17:220, 221, the later dated 7 February 1776. The open bookcases were to be subdivided by gilded female terms which would have matched those on the proposed chimney-glass.

57. Ceiling design, dated 24 August 1773, SM 12:57, 58. Chimney-piece, dated 25 January 1774, SM 20:14.

58. SM 25:57, undated but inscribed 'for Mr Blockley's Locks at Sir W: Wynn's'. Edward Gascoigne's bill, 5 January 1775, NLW Wynnstay MSS. 115/17/4.

59. The two early plans at the RIBA show the dining-room without a screen. The screen is also omitted from Adam's design for the ceiling dated 3 December 1772, SM 12:45.

60. SM 12:45, ceiling design dated 3 December 1772 not showing the screen of columns. The octagons are pale green with darker green centres, the remaining ground is very pale blue, the ornaments picked out in white. In the hand-coloured copy of *Works*, II, ii, pl. vi, various tones of blue were used, but no green.

61. A 'steel loose front Grate, 4 fluted term feet with rams read on Do Curiously emboss'd £36' was supplied by W. Hopkins on 5 November 1773, NLW Wynnstay MSS. 115/17/13. The bill does not mention an Adam design. There is a drawing of four grates at the Soane, SM 17:126, dated 25 March 1774. The one labelled 'Eating Room' has urn finials and a frieze of interlaced husk wreaths and rosettes to match the other friezes in the room. The grate shown in the photograph of the eating-room fireplace published by Bolton, II, p. 58 appears to be a simplified and reduced version of the drawing labelled 'Music Room'. See below note 82.

62. SM 23:5, design dated 11 August 1772. The carver is unknown.

63. SM 20:116. This was published in the posthumous third volume of the *Works*, pl. VIII, erroneously captioned as a design for Syon.

64. Bolton, II, p. 58.

65. SM 20:131, dated 21 August 1773. Other mirrors with seated female figures: Corsham Court (1771), SM 20:56, 57; Bolton House (1772), SM 20:84; Osterley (1773), SM:34, 35.

66. Bolton, II, p. 58.

67. SM 17:20, the first design for the table, is dated 21 August 1773 and offers alternative legs. The more complicated ones incorporating roundels were rejected by Sir Watkin and used in a modified form for the pier-table in the saloon at

Nostell designed in 1775, SM 17:27. The executed design, SM 17:21, is dated 14 September 1773. Though there is no design for the pedestals, they are quite like those for Kenwood, *Works*, I, ii, pl. VIII. The ormolu-mounted mahogany wine cooler with lion masks and ring handles and a Snowdonian eagle crest is closely related to Adam's design for a soup tureen and platter, SM 25:118.

68. O. Fairclough, loc. cit. at note 52 above, p. 377. The table service was supplied at a cost of £2,408.18s by a little known retailer, Joseph Creswell, and is thought by Oliver Fairclough to have been made by John Carter (p. 383).

69. Information kindly supplied by Oliver Fairclough who suggested that the display may also have included two late seventeenth-century silver-gilt claret flagons.

70. Design for candlesticks, SM 25:125, dated 18 January 1773. The candelabra now belong to Lloyds and are used in the Adam dining-room from Bowood. R. Edwards, 'Torchères and Candelabra. Designs by Robert Adam', *Country Life*, 23 May 1947, pp. 966–7.

71. SM 6:49, uninscribed and undated, is closest to the V&A torchères. E. Harris, no. 139; however, the date I gave in the caption to pl. 139, 1777, is probably incorrect. I now think is more likely to be 1773. M. Tomlin, *Catalogue of Adam period furniture*, London, 1982, N/5, p. 108. SM 6:53, 54 are both dated 26 April 1777. SM 6:53 was executed with modifications and is in a private collection. SM 6:174 for a torchère with female term supports has a crossed-out inscription, 'Stand for Candles in Sir W. W. W's Eating Room' and measurement '4 feet high' (1.2 metres).

72. Pritchard, op. cit. at note 1 above, pp. 33ff. S. McVeigh, *Concert Life in London*, Cambridge, 1993, pp. 7, 47. Grove, *Dictionary of music*, London, 1980, VI, pp. 193, 194, 208–10. Regular evening concerts at Sir Watkins house in Grosvenor Square continued while 20 St James's Square was being built. For Sir Watkin's musical interests, the music-room and organ at 20 St James's Square, see Phillips catalogue of the sale of the organ, London, 21 April 1995.

73. SM 23:6, dated 27 August 1772. Zucchi's bill for a drawing of the tablet, NLW Wynnstay MSS. 115/17/9.

74. Ceiling design dated 23 May 1773, SM 12:47; SM 12:46 is a rejected design also dated 1773. Zucchi's bill, NLW Wynnstay MSS. 115/17/9. A note on Adam's wall elevation calls for an overdoor of *The Muses that honour the Tomb of Orpheus*, not Corelli or Handel, SM 40:71.

75. These are included in the accounts of 19 April 1775 when Dance was paid a total of £210 for 'two antic Musical Pieces over the side Doors' and a painting of *Orpheus*. NLW Wynnstay MSS. 115/7, Account Book for 1775, p. 34.

76. C. R. Leslie and T. Taylor, *Life and times of Sir Joshua Reynolds*, London, 1865, II, p. 94. W. Hazlitt, *Conversations of James Northcote, RA*, London, 1894, pp. 222–3. Lady V. Manners, 'Fresh Light on Nathaniel Dance, RA (Sir Nathaniel Dance-Holland, Bart.)', *Connoisseur*, London, 1923, LXV, p. 23. According to Lady Manners, the painting was still in the collection of Sir Watkin Williams-Wynn's descendants in 1923. D. A. Goodreau, 'Nathaniel Dance, RA (1735–1811)', Ph.D. thesis, University of California, 1973, p. 163.

77. NLW Wynnstay MSS., Account Book for 1775, 19 April, p. 34. Reynolds received £157.10.0 for the *Saint Cecilia*. The painting was sold at Sotheby's on 5 February 1947, lot 77 and is now in the William Randolph Hearst Collection in the Los Angeles County Museum of Art, California. N. Penny, *Reynolds*, Royal Academy of Art exhibition catalogue, London, 1986, no. 95.

78. *Handel, a celebration of his life and times*, ed. J.

Simon, National Portrait Gallery exhibition catalogue, London, 1985, no. 103, p. 132.

79. SM 20:131, design for the chimney-glass dated 9 August 1773 showing the girandoles each side. They are also shown in Adam's wall elevation dated 24 August 1773, SM 40:71. Twenty branches for the music-room were supplied by William Kinman & Co on 9 July 1774, NLW Wynnstay Mss. 115/17/8. The drawing, SM 6:84, inscribed 'Branch for the Girandole in the Music Room at Sir W. W. W.' and dated 'Augt. 10h 1774' must be a record drawing of the branches delivered by Kinman in July. SM 6:85 is a related pencil sketch, possibly a design.

80. 'List of Paintings in Wynnstay Mansion in 1840 by Charles Bowen', NLW, Wynnstay MSS W/37.

81. SM 20:131.

82. In Hopkins' bill dated 5 November 1774, the music-room grate is described as having '4 round twisted feet very curiously emboss'd to Mr Adam's Design', NLW Wynnstay MSS. 115/17/13. The drawing, SM 17:126, labelled 'Eating Room' is the one shown in the photograph of the music-room fireplace published by Bolton, II, p. 61. It had been slightly reduced in width to fit into the curtailed opening. The grate labelled 'Music Room' is narrower but more elaborate. See above, note 61.

83. King and Padget were paid £43.19.0 for satin for the music-room on 16 March 1776. NLW Wynnstay MSS. 115/8 Account Book for 1776.

84. Kinman's bill, March–June 1775. NLW Wynnstay MSS. 115/17/8.

85. SM 40:71. Adam, *Works*, II, ii, pl. VIII.

86. W. Coxe, *Anecdotes of George Frederick Handel and John Christopher Smith*, London, 1799. Reprint with introduction by P. M. Young, New York, 1979, pp. xx–xxi.

87. *Handel, a celebration*, op. cit. at note 78 above, no. 239, p. 255. There is a profile medallion of Handel in plaster at the Soane Museum which may also be related. The maker of these Handel plaques is not known.

88. NLW Wynnstay MSS., Account Book for 1777, 26 June, p. 36.

89. NLW Wynnstay MSS. 115/17/4.

90. NLW Wynnstay MSS. 115/24/9 and Account Book for 1775, 31 May. For Snetzler, see Grove, op. cit. at note 71 above, VI, p. 427; M. Wilson, *The English chamber organ*, London, 1968, pp. 11–12.

91. NLW Wynnstay MSS. 115/17/8.

92. NLW Wynnstay MSS. 115/7, Account Book for 1775, 5 February.

93. P. Howell and T. W. Pritchard, loc. cit. at note 5 above, 30 March 1972, pp. 785–6.

94. Pritchard, op. cit. at note 1 above, pp. 126–8.

95. E. Harris, 'Adam Organizing Handel', *Country Life*, 30 March 1995, pp. 56–9. When writing this article I had no evidence that Adam's organ design for 20 Portman Square had been executed. I have since seen accounts of the repairs to 20 Portman Square undertaken by John Tasker in 1796–7 for John Tharpe which refer to an organ in the music room, Cambridge Record Office. R/55/7/101/1.

96. SM 23:7, dated 27 August 1772. The description of the chimney-piece as 'interesting' in 1910 suggests that its frieze was still in place at that date. See J. M. W. Halley, op. cit. at note 44 above, p. 107. The grate was supplied in 1773 by William Hopkins whose bill does not mention an Adam design. NLW Wynnstay MSS. 115/17/13.

97. Adam's design has not been traced. Gascoigne's bill for altering Blockley's locks, dated 3 October 1774, NLW Wynnstay MSS. 115/17/4. Gascoigne also altered a 'Round Library Table' on 5 January 1775.

98. SM 12:48, ceiling design dated 1773. Zucchi's bill erroneously describes the paintings as for Sir Watkin's dressing-room. NLW Wynnstay MSS. 115/17/9.

99. SM 12:49, uncoloured ceiling design. SM 40:69,

'Section of the Dressing Room of the Library', dated 10 February 1773 with colour notes calling for light-green walls, white dado and dark-green skirting which most likely repeated the colour scheme of the library.

17. DERBY HOUSE

1. In 1743 John Burgoyne (1723–92) married Lady Charlotte Stanley, sister of his long-standing friend, James Smith Stanley, against the wishes of their father, the 11th Earl of Derby. James Smith Stanley, known as Lord Strange, died a widower in 1 June 1771, leaving the eighty-two-year old earl as legal guardian of his sons, Edward (1752–1834) and Thomas (1753–79). Burgoyne promptly assumed the role of mentor and in the summer of 1772 took the boys abroad for two months. Among the Derby papers at Knowsley (NH Cpd 18B (187)) is an interesting letter from Burgoyne to Lord Derby's sister, Lady Mary Stanley, explaining the advantages of this journey for which the approval of Lord Derby was required. See also Lady Mary Coke, *Letters and Journals*, London, 1970, IV, p. 125.

2. Fleming, pp. 118, 132, 158, 352. Adam's designs for ceilings, dated 1769, SM 12:5, 6 and 13:143–5; chimney-pieces, 1769, 22:265–8; friezes, 53:15; girandole, 1771, 20:87; mirrors, 1771, 20:88–90. Some of the interiors at 10 Hertford Street survive. See T. Draper, 'No. 10 Hertford Street', *Georgian Group Journal*, IX, 1999, pp. 116–38.
   Evidently Burgoyne not only organized the ball but also lent furnishings from his house in Hertford Street. The upholsterers, Ravald and Morland billed Lord Stanley for 'a man going three times from Grosvenor Square to General Burgoyne'. Derby MS, Knowsley Hall NH Cpd B (184). On 6 April they returned and fixed up '2 neat brass Girandoles . . . in Lady Burgoyne's dressing room'. These may be related to Adam's design of 1771 for a girandole for General Burgoyne incorporating a ram's-head vase. The first recorded sale of ormolu girandoles made by Boulton and Fothergill was in December 1771 to Colonel Burgoyne, after whom the firm named their 'Burgoyne's' vase with ram's head mounts. N. Goodison, *Ormolu: the work of Matthew Boulton*, London, 1974, pp. 136, 137, 217, pl. 103. This raises the possibility that Adam was the designer of Boulton's 'Burgoyne's' vase.

3. Walpole to Lady Ossory, 3 April 1773, *Correspondence*, XXIII, p. 115–16. Elizabeth, Duchess of Northumberland, *Diaries of a duchess*, ed. James Grieg, London, 1926, pp. 300–203. Among the Derby papers at Knowsley are bills from Negri and Wetten Confectioners at the Pot and Pine Apple in Berkeley Square for ornaments as well as sweets; from the firm of Ravald and Morland, upholsterers, for moving and adjusting existing furnishings and for hiring and borrowing additional pieces for the event; and from Daniel Bunning for carpentry (NH Cpd (184)).

4. Daniel Bunning's bill includes: 22 to 31 March 'Making a Circular work & ribs for ye Doom of ye Stair Case & putting up and Altering for ye tin Man 20 days', and 23–4 April 'taking Down the tables. Shelves and the doom in the Stair Case'.
   SM 25:41, 'A Lanthorn for Lord Derby's Staircase Sep.ʳ 15ᵗʰ 1774' with green glass. This may be related to the 'coloured-glass lanthorns' noted by Walpole, or the 'bell lights wᵗʰ gilt chain ornaments' supplied by Ravald and Morland for the ball.

5. Walpole, *Correspondence*, XXIII, pp. 115–16. The drapes were in fact old 'crims.ⁿ damask hangings in the two angles in the front room' which were taken down by Ravald and Morland and 'slightly' tacked up again. Adam's design of 1760 for the chimney-piece wall in the painted breakfast-room in the family pavilion at Kedleston made similar use of drapery. See L.

Harris, *Robert Adam and Kedleston*, National Trust, London, 1987, p. 139.

6. Ravald and Morland's bill includes porterage of the three glasses from 'a house to Grosvenor Square', making two 'strong oval frames' and putting the glasses up. However, it is not clear whether the 2 oval glasses put up in the front room were those borrowed from a Mr Hancox for £6.6.0.

7. Walpole's account of glasses borrowed from Lord March (William Douglas, 3rd Earl of March, later 4th Duke of Queensberry) is probably exaggerated. Ravald and Morland hung two oval glasses in the ball-room, but their origin is not specified. The firm advertised for large plates of glass on 10 March; two large oval mirrors and one large square were brought from an unidentified house; two other ovals and a large plate 5ft 6in. by 3ft 5in. were borrowed from a Mr Hancox for 6 guineas and £70 respectively.
   Lord March shared Lord Stanley and General Burgoyne's love of racing and gambling. He was evidently prompted by Lord Stanley's ball to employ Adam in 1774 to design a drawing-room ceiling for his house in Piccadilly, SM 12:154; frieze, SM 53:28.

8. The fullest account of Derby House is in the *Survey of London*, XL. *The Grosvenor Estate in Mayfair*, (1980), II, pp. 142–4.

9. *The particular and inventory of . . . the lands . . . and personal estate whatsoever of . . . Sir Robert Sutton* (1732). (BL 172.k.1(4))

10. *Works*, II, i, preface.

11. For the fullest contemporary account of the *fête champêtre*, said to be 'the first of its kind in England', see *Gentleman's Magazine*, 1774, XLIV, pp. 263–4. See also M. Burden 'Robert Adam, De Loutherbourg and the Sets for *The Maid of The Oaks*' Adam in Context, Georgian Group Symposium, London, 1992, pp. 65–9. Adam designed the magnificent temporary structure in which the ball and supper were held and Burgoyne's comic opera, *The Maid of the Oaks*, was performed. It was a large U-shaped building with a projecting octagonal vestibule. The vaulted interior was divided by colonnades into a central ballroom ringed by a supper room. The *fête* is reputed to have cost Lord Stanley £12,000. Paintings of the ballroom and supperroom by Antonio Zucchi are at Knowsley Hall. They were engraved by James Caldwell in 1780 and published along with Adam's plan in the *Works*, III, pls XX–XXII.

12. Lady Mark Coke, op. cit. at note 1 above, IV, 395.

13. *Ibid*, p. 439.

14. George Selwyn to Lord Carlisle, 9, 14 and 19 December 1775. *Hist. Mss Comm., 15th Report, Appendix*, Pt VI, 'Mss of The Earl of Carlisle, preserved at Castle Howard', pp. 308, 312. See also Walpole, *Correspondence*, XXIV, p. 310.; Mrs Delany, *The life and correspondence*, ed. Lady Llandover, 2nd series London, 1862, II, pp. 340, 401, 451.

15. John Johnson Collection, Oxford: Prospectuses 1–310. See E. Harris and N. Savage, *British architectural books and writers 1556–1785*, London, 1990, no. 699, p. 368.

16. J. Harris, *Sir William Chambers*, London, 1970, p. 257 (100).

17. Walpole to Lady Ossory, 8 August 1777, *Correspondence*, XXXII, p. 371. He was comparing it unfavourably to Lord Villier's house in Grafton Street by Sir Robert Taylor, which he thought 'magnificently furnished, and in good taste . . . On the first floor an anteroom, and three more very large rooms, all four quintessenced with Adamitic mode, and yet not filigreed into puerility like l'Hotel de Derby'.

18. These bills are in the Derby archives at Knowsley Hall. Most of the furniture bills were published by Hugh Roberts 'The Derby House Commode', *Burlington Magazine*, CXXVII, May 1985, p. 281

and n. 35.

19. SM 12:136, ceiling design dated 12 April 1774 and inscribed with colour notes.

20. G. Scharf, *A descriptive and historical catalogue of the collection of pictures at Knowsley Hall*, London, 1875. *The Supper Room*, no. 334, pp. 171–4 is said to be dated 1773 but must be 1775 or 1778. It is an upright square 6ft × 5ft 4in.; *The Ball Room*, no. 338, p. 175, is dated 1777 and measures 4ft 5in. × 5ft 4¹/₂ in. The two pictures are said to have 'formed panels in the Dining-Room of the Earl's former residence, 23 Grosvenor Square'. Engravings of the two paintings were made by James Caldwell and published in 1780.

21. Lantern designs, SM 6:106 and 25:41; friezes for the staircase, SM 53:4.

22. Chimney-piece design dated 1773, inscribed in pencil 'Carter £59', SM 23:43. The slender colonnettes may have been inspired by Piranesi's chimney-piece for Lord Exeter at Burghley House, *Diverse maniere d'adornare i cammini*, Rome, 1769, pl. I; J. Wilton-Ely, *The mind and art of Giovanni Battista Piranesi*, London, 1978, pp. 105–6, pl. 192–3. Adam also made designs for Burghley from 1765 to 1779, see M. Richardson 'A 'fair' drawing A little-known Adam design for Burghley', *Apollo*, August 1992, pp. 87–8.

23. Chimney-piece design dated 'Feby 28, 1774' and inscribed 'Mr. Carter has this', SM 23:47. The chimney-glass is comparable to the mirror designed on 1 October 1772 for the drawing-room at Luton, SM 20:116, *Works*, III, pl. VIII.

24. SM 20:134, pier-glass designs dated 17 July 1774.

25. Royal Academy Exhibitions, 1775 (174). Frame design, SM 54:267. W. W. Roworth, ed., *Angelica Kauffman*, London, 1992, p. 64, figs 46 and 93. Scharf, op. cit. at note 20 above, p. 45, nos. 85, 88.

26. Ceiling dated 1773, SM 12:142; curtain cornice September 13, 1774 violet ground, dark green and white ornament, SM 17:109.

27. A list of pictures brought to Knowsley from Grosvenor Square in 1850 is given by Scharf, op. cit. at note 20 above. Other pictures were presumably taken to the 14th Earl's house in St James's Square. For the Borgognones see: Scharf nos. 202, 278, 451, 453; the catalogue of Consul Smith's sale at Christie's, 16–17 May 1776, lots 11, 67; and F. Vivian, *The Consul Smith Collection*, London, 1989, p. 37.

28. Design for a pier-glass, approximately 9ft 6in. tall, including the crest, and 3ft 9in. wide, SM 20:135. Design for a semicircular slab dated 29 August 1774, SM 17:26.

29. SM 12:143, ceiling design inscribed 'The oval with Boys and Sea Horses to be Painted'.

30. There is no known design for the mirror alone. It is with the chimney-piece in a design dated February 1774, SM 23:46. See below, note 33. The female terms with husk festoons are comparable to mirrors designed for Robert Child at Berkeley Square in 1770 and 1771, SM 20:38, 41; the Earl of Bute at Luton in 1772, SM 20:116; and the Duke of Bolton's house in Southampton Row in 1773, SM 20:82. A mirror with similar female terms and a raised centre can be seen in the engraving of Adam's ballroom for the *fête champêtre* at the Oaks in June 1774. The Derby House mirror was widely imitated from the engraving in the *Works*.

31. SM 23:45, 47, chimney-piece design.

32. SM 23:46, chimney-piece design inscribed 'Mr Car(ter) has th(is)'. Chimney-piece for 20 St James's Square, SM 23:10. Piranesi, op. cit. at note 22 above, pl. 9A. Stillman, p. 93, pls 107, 108.

33. King, fig. 421. Ceiling design for the second drawing-room coloured shades of green and violet, SM 12:143.

34. Adam, *Works*, II, i, pl. V.

35. Ibid. The laid-out 'Plan and section of the Great Drawing Room' (SM 50:80) is inscribed with

pencil notes of colours: 'Door side /Columns white flutes and gilt fillets/ Violet Green & Pink Door Drawing for this Room/ Caps white & gilt ornmt/ Columns white flutes & gilt fillets/ Door pilasters pink/ Soffits white Door frieze/ the same as the (room?)./ (skirting) Dark green (niches with pedestals and urns) light green'. Ceiling for the Great Drawing Room dated 1773, SM 12:144. There is also a preliminary sketch incorrectly inscribed for the first drawing-room, SM 52:145.

36. 'Sketch of a Carpet for Lord Stanleys Great Room 1775', SM 17:184.

37. Derby MS, Knowsley Hall NH CPD 18B (183). Though Nelson's bill for making the mirror frames does not survive, it is clear from his account, dated 30 April 1776, for mending and cleaning the mirrors that they were his in the first place and were probably executed late in 1774 or early 1775. Adam's mirror design SM 20:137 is dated 27 July 1774. His sofa design, SM 17:81, is dated 5 July 1774. They too may have been made by Nelson at the same time as the mirror frames. Their upholstery is pink in the design.

38. Derby MS. Knowsley Hall, NH Cpd 18B (183), published by Roberts, loc. cit. at note 18 above, p. 281. Neither the pedestals nor Adam's design for them has been traced.

39. Ibid. Nelsons bill for £75.12.0 is dated 30 April 1776. Design for girandoles, SM 6:41.

40. Gilbert, I, p. 197; II, pl. 236.

41. Mirror design, SM 20:136.

42. Design for curtain-cornice dated 13 September 1774, SM 17:111.

43. Adam, *Works*, II, i, pl. VIII. SM 49:51, design for 'Top Panels for doors, in the Great Drawing Room May 10, 1774', inscribed with a note 'A fair copy sent to Mr Clay at Birmingham'.

44. Adam's first design for the chimney-piece (SM 23:48) has a frieze of figures inspired by Piranesi and quite like the frieze on the chimney-piece in the first drawing-room at 20 St James's Square. The executed design (SM 23:49) is inscribed 'Design of a Chimney Piece for the Great Drawing Room at Lord Stanley's in Grosvenor Square. Statuary marble inlaid with Scagliola Ornaments & Figures. The Mouldings in Or Moulu 1773.'

45. Derby MS. Knowsley Hall, NH Cpd 18B (183). Hopkins' account dates from October 1774 to 20 March 1775 and was paid in May 1776.

46. Adam, *Works*, II, i, pl. VI.

47. Adam, *Works*, II, i, preface.

48. Though 1766 is the date given on the title page, 1767 was the actual date of publication. See N. Ramage, 'Publication dates of Sir William Hamilton's four volumes', *Ars Ceramica* 8 (1991), p. 35 and P. Griener, *La antichità Etrusche Greche e Romane 1766–1776 di Pierre Hugues d'Hancarville*, Rome (1992).

49. Stillman, p. 76, figs 46, 47.

50. D. Stillman, *English neo-classical architecture*, London, 1988, pp. 319, 572 n. 145, has quite rightly pointed out that Mrs Lybbe Powys's description of the Etruscan decoration by James Wyatt in Sambrooke Freeman's temple on the island in the Thames at Henley is a later addition to her first account of Freeman's improvements at Fawley Court, dated October 1771. How much later is not known. Although this casts doubt upon my statement that Wyatt's work pre-dated Adam's first essay in the Etruscan style, E. Harris and J. M. Robinson, 'New Light on Wyatt at Fawley', *Architectural History*, 27, 1984, p. 264, it does not alter the fact that Wedgwood's priority.

51. R. Reilly, *Wedgwood*, London, 1989, I, pp. 409, 715, n. 18. 'Patent No. 939 for The Purpose of ornamenting Earthen and Porcelain Ware with an Encaustic Gold Bronze, together with a peculiar Species of Encaustic Painting in various Colours, in imitation of the Antient Etruscan

and Roman Earthenware'. Copy sent with letter E25–18290, 19 February 1770. In addition to the normal red and black and occasional purple and white, there were a few examples of red figures on a white ground.

In September 1769, before the patent was taken out, Wedgwood told Bentley that 'the encaustic will be imitated as soon as seen, let us therefore when once we begin *push it with all our force*' and requested him 'rigidly to confine (himself) to the red shaded with black 'till that is mimick'd and then strike out into other colours'. A. Kelley, *Decorative Wedgwood*, London, 1965, p. 35.

52. J. Wedgwood, *A catalogue of cameos, intaglios, medals, and bas-reliefs; with a general account of vases and other ornaments after the antique, made by Wedgwood and Bentley; and sold at their rooms in Great Newport Street*, London, 1773, p. 17. The idea of decorating walls with medallions may have been inspired by Raphael's decorations of the Vatican loggie. It is interesting to note that engravings of these decorations were published in G. T. Volpato and P. Camporesi, *Loggie di Rafaele nel Vaticano*, Rome, 1772–7. Their work was begun in 1760 for Clement XIII, who died in 1769.

53. Ibid., Class XX, p. 56.

54. Reilly, op. cit. at note 50 above, I, p. 578. Wedgwood's letter, 30 August 1772, E 25–18394.

55. Design for a chimney-piece for Lord Ashburnham, SM 23:22.

56. Kelley, op. cit. at note 50 above, pp. 37, 38.

57. Designs at Newby Hall, Ripon, NH I/7/6, 7. See chapter 13, on Newby.

58. The executed design for the dressing-room ceiling at Osterley, SM 11:212. The first design (SM 11:210) did not have these cameos.

59. The rejected green and pink design dated 1773, SM 12:145. The brown and fawn colouring of the executed ceiling is known only from tinted copies of the plate in the *Works*, II, i, pl. VII. The pattern of the ceiling, but not the ornaments, is closely related to Lady Bute's dressing-room ceiling at Luton designed in 1769. See chapter 15, on Luton. Though fawn-coloured Wedgwood ware of this early date is now rare and was never as popular as red and black, it did exist. Medallions in polished biscuit with brown and grey grounds are lists in the firm's 1773 catalogue.

60. Design for the Northumberland House chimney-piece dated 1773, SM 22:55. See chapter 6, on Northumberland House.

61. SM 23:51, design for the chimney-piece and mirror, dated 1774 and inscribed 'Mr Carter has not got this yet the drawing at large being not quite finished'. See also pencil sketch SM 24:173. The plate in the *Works*, II, i, pl. VI is signed and dated 1773.

62. Derby MS. Knowsley Hall. NH Cpd. 183 (183).

63. It was removed from Derby House by the 5th Duke of Cleveland, heir to the last tenant, the Dowager Duchess of Cleveland, and taken to Battle Abbey, Sussex, from whence it was bought by Manchester City Art Gallery in 1980. J. Lomax, 'Lady Derby's Looking-Glass', *Furniture History*, XXI, 1985, 236–40.

64. Roberts, loc. cit. at note 18 above, p. 281. Adam's design for the commode, dated 21 October 1774, SM 17:27. His uninscribed design for the inlaid wood top of the commode (SM 17:27) is comparable to his slightly earlier design, dated 6 May 1774, for the inlaid scagliola slabs on the semicircular tables in the drawing-room at Northumberland House, SM 38:8, see chapter 6, on Northumberland House. For the Derby House commode, see also *Works*, II, i. pl. VIII.

65. General Fitzroy's circular toilet-room (SM 50:89) was presumably contemporary with the ceiling design (also Etruscan) dated December 1774 for Lady Fitzroy's circular dressing-room, SM 12:156. For the history of Fitzroy House see J

Richardson, *Highgate its history since the fifteenth century*, London, 1983, pp. 84–5. Apsley House: ceiling design for the circular dressing-room dated 21 June 1775, SM 14:15; wall elevation, SM 32:104. Osterley, finished wall elevations, 11 October 1775, SM 14:128, 130, 131. Home House: Etruscan bedroom *c.*1775, SM 14:132, 134; chimney-piece, SM 23:69.

66. Ceiling design for the Countess of Derby's bedroom, SM 12:146. Design for the curtain-cornice, SM 17:112.

67. Mrs Agneta Yorke, extract from a letter dated 1772 to her sister, Lady Beauchamp Proctor, MS volume in the possession of Gerald Yorke of Forthampton Court, Glos.

68. Design of a chair for Lord Stanley dated 19 January 1775, SM 17:94.

69. M. Cox, *Derby. The life and times of the 12th Earl of Derby*, London, 1974, p. 44.

70. A. Rowan, 'Lord Derby's reconstruction of The Oaks'. *Burlington Magazine*, October 1985, pp. 678–86. See also Rowan, *Designs for castles and country villas by Robert & James Adam*, London, 1985, pp. 102ff., pl. 40.

71. One chimney-piece was placed in Lady Derby's dressing-room in new Derby House. R. Churchill, *Lord Derby*, London, 1959, p. 100. If it is still there, it has not been identified. Another chimney-piece, a mirror and the overdoors are said to have gone to Knowsley.

18. HOME HOUSE

1. E. Harris, 'Home House: Adam versus Wyatt', *Burlington Magazine*, CXXXIX, May 1997, pp. 308–21. Since the publication of my article, Home House has been carefully restored as a private club. A. A. Tait seems to have been the first to question Adam's primacy at Home House, but without identifying Wyatt as his predecessor. A. A. Tait, 'Home House', *Apollo*, CXXVI, no. 306, August 1987, p. 80 n. 13. The importance the Adams attached to the threat posed by Wyatt may be measured by the fact that the Pantheon is the only building named in the *Works*, I, p. iii, expl. pl. VI as imitating their style.

As the original numbering of the houses in Portman Square has been changed twice, to avoid confusion the current numbering is used here throughout.

The major publication on the house is M. Whinney, *Home House*, London, 1969 (cited hereafter as Whinney), which illustrates all the Adam drawings and reprints an eighteenth-century pamphlet on the 'Subjects Of The Pictures Painted By Anthony Zucchi, for the different Apartments at the Countess Dowager of Homes's House, in Portman-Square'.

2. Samuel and Abraham Adams were responsible for several properties in the area, which they subleased from the developer, William Baker, who, in turn, leased them from the owner of the estate, Henry William Berkeley Portman of Orchard Portman and Bryanston. William Baker of Bromley, Salop and Wick House, Sion-Hill developed the Baker Street area from which he is said to have made a fortune.

3. L. Lewis, 'Elizabeth, Countess of Home, and her house in Portman Square', *Burlington Magazine*, CIX, 1967, pp. 443–53. Regarding the birth and naming of her child, the 8th Earl's debts, etc., see SRO, Douglas-Home Papers, 859, Box 25, folders 1, 2, 4 and 6; Box 26, folder 1; Box 6, bundle 7.

4. J. L. Clifford, *Hester Lynch Piozzi (Mrs Thrale)*, Oxford, 1987, p. xxiii. See also L. Namier and J. Brooke, *The House of Commons 1754–1790*, London, 1964, III, pp. 65 and 70; *Complete Peerage*, London, 1913, III, p. 24 n. 2.

5. J. W. Oliver, *The life of William Beckford*, London, 1932, pp. 106–7. Lewis, loc. cit. at note 3 above, p. 450. In *The modern characters from Shakespeare*, London, 1778, she is referred to as 'a

witch, a quean, an old cozening quean'. Simon Luttrell was 'pronounced the greatest reprobate in England', Namier and Brooke, op. cit. at note 4 above, III, p. 70. His daughters, Anne and Elizabeth, were 'vulgar, noisy, indelicate, and intrepid: utter strangers to good company'. The Duchess of Cumberland's language was so foul that Lady Margaret Fordice recommended one 'to go home and wash one's ears' after hearing her talk, M. Coke, *The letters and journals of Lady Mary Coke*, Bath, 1970, I, p. xcv. Lady Elizabeth Luttrell was described as a gambler and cheat, convicted of picking pockets in Augsburg and condemned to clean the streets chained to a wheelbarrow, *Complete Peerage*, III, p. 24 n.a. Henry Lawes Luttrell was 'the most unpopular man in the House of Commons; newspapers were full of abuse of him; scores of pamphlets appeared, vilifying his character and private life; and the most scandalous stories were circulated about him and his family after he was illegally given the seat for Middlesex in preference to Wilkes in 1769', Namier and Brooke, op. cit. at note 4 above, III, p. 65.

6. Lewis, loc. cit. at note 3 above, p. 448.

7. Lock went from number 41, a house designed for him in 1765–6 by James Adam and built by Samuel Adams (RIBA Drawings Collection) on the south side, to 21 on the northwest corner next to the Countess of Home. William Attwick and William Baker moved from the west side to numbers 19 and 18 respectively.

8. Middlesex Deeds Register 1777 3/563. The deed was registered on 3 June 1776 by the trustees of William Baker, who died in 1774.

9. Westminster City Archive, Paving Rates, St Marylebone, 1774; Whinney, p. 12, wrongly says the house was first rated in midsummer 1776.

10. Account of Elizabeth, Countess of Home. Hoare's Bank, vol. 95, f. 104. This was a special account for the building works. It was opened on 7 November 1775, when the countess took a £1,000 bond from Hoare's (Letter Book, 1778) and closed on 11 March 1779. A payment to William Sleigh of Hanworth, who witnessed her deeds, suggests that she may also have borrowed money from him. The payment to Norris and other craftsmen in 1775 covers work completed in 1774–5. Any earlier payments would have been made from the countess's normal bank account which has not been located.

For Richard Norris the elder (*c*.1719–79) see Colvin. It is interesting to note that Norris's designs for Shire Hall, Hertford were set aside in 1767 for those by James Adam. See A. T. Bolton 'The Shire Hall, Hertford', *Architectural Review*, XLIII, 1918, p. 72.

11. Three plans for number 41 signed *Jas. Adam* and dated 1765–66 are in the RIBA Drawings Collection, K12/27[1-3].

K12/28 is an unsigned plan for no. 21 which is accompanied by a letter to Lock dateable to 22 September 1772 telling him that the foundations of his 'new house or rather no house is going on, and that Wyatt whom I have seen about it says it is to be even with the ground this season and that it will be the better for having no more done to it this year and that he will proceed with the utmost expedition next spring . . . now that we are aware of Mr Wyatt's dilatory method, you may depend on our looking after him next spring'. Wyatt was paid £400 by Lock's banker at that time. There is a design dated 1766 for a ceiling for the 'Drawing Room for Wm Lock Esq' at the Soane, SM 11:172; two similarly dated chimney-piece designs, one for 'Mr Lock's Dressing Room', SM 22:230, the other for an unspecified room, SM 22:231.

James and Samuel Wyatt were acting as developers in Portman Square by agreement with the Baker family on 24 December 1772. In 1774, Wyatt was rated for vacant ground for six houses on the north side up to the corner of Baker Street. John Johnson was involved with the Wyatts in the building of number 12 leased to the Hon. Charles Greville on 23 July 1778 and 13 leased to Henry Willoughby, later 5th Earl Middleton on 1 May 1777. See N. Briggs, *John Johnson*, Chelmsford, 1991, p. 12.

12. Dublin, National Library of Ireland, Penrose-Wyatt Collection. These may be record drawings.

Quite likely there were earlier payments to Wyatt which are not recorded in the Hoare's Bank account, see above, note 10.

13. See note 10 above. The back parlour, the library, and the first ante-room.

14. 27 January 1775 is the earliest date on Adam's drawings. He received payments in January, March and May 1776 amounting to £3,500 which, as usual, must have included the bills of some of his principal craftsmen, such as Rose and Zucchi, as well as his own charges.

If the date of '1775' inscribed on his design (SM 22:232) for a chimney-piece for Lock is correct, then it would seem that Wyatt had also been ousted there. However, this isolated design, which is very similar to one dated 1766 (SM 22:231) for Lock's first Portman Square house, cannot be taken as evidence that Adam superseded Wyatt at number 21.

15. Evidence for the shape of the space and the arched opening on the west wall is provided by Wyatt's 'Plan & Ceiling of Vestibule on Parlour Story Lady Home'. Dublin, NLI, Penrose-Wyatt Collection AD 3145.

16. Chambers's design, exhibited at the Society of Artists in 1761, was the model for the circular imperial staircase in the centre of Adam's abortive plan of 1764 for a house for the Earl of Shelburne near Hyde Park Corner. See J. Harris, *Sir William Chambers*, London, 1970, p. 225 (84).

17. Adam made only three designs for the hall: one for the ceiling and semi-dome dated 1775 (SM 12:160; Whinney, no. 6, p. 107) and two alternative designs for a stove; a pen and ink sketch of a figured urn on a round pedestal with a Doric frieze inscribed 'Lady Homes' (SM 54:267; not included in Whinney) and a finished design with grey washes inscribed 'Stove for Lady Home's Hall in Portman Square 25th March 1776' (SM 17:129; Whinney, no. 2, p. 106). This was presumably executed.

18. 'Lady Home's Staircase', SM 14:116; Whinney, no. 7, p. 108. The design for an 'Iron Ballustrade for Lady Houme' (SM 52:3; Whinney, no. 5, p. 197) was probably intended for the staircase but was not executed. It can be related to the executed design dated 10 June 1775 for a table in the hall at Nostell, SM 17:28.

19. Whinney, pp. 32–3.

20. 'John Tharpe Esq. To John Tasker For Sundry Business's Done at his House Portman Sq. from May 1796 to Feby 1797', Cambridge Record Office, R 55. 7. 101. 1. The Tharpes, or Thorpes, of Chippenham Park, Cambridgeshire had large estates in Jamaica. Lady Susan Tharpe, widow of Joseph Tharpe and sister of Lady Augusta Murray, whose clandestine marriage to the Duke of Sussex, sixth son of George III, was never recognized, took 20 Portman Square in 1795. It passed later that year to her son, John Tharpe (1744–1804), who restored it before moving in 1797 to Portland Place.

21. Dublin, NLI, Penrose-Wyatt Collection, AD 3163 inscribed 'Scetch of Ceiling Anti Chamber Lady Home'. There is a finished version of this design in the Wyatt Album at The Metropolitan Museum of Art, New York (1958. 511), no. 32.

22. 'Chimney Piece for the Anti Room at Lady Home's in Portman Square Adelphi 1st Febry 1775', SM 23:65; Whinney, no. 19, p. 114.

23. SM 20:164 has sketches of girandoles; 20:163 has a variant chimney-piece; Whinney, nos. 20–1, p. 115.

24. James Wyatt, 'Design for an organ for Burton upon Trent 1770'. D. Linstrum, *The Wyatt Family*, RIBA Drawings Catalogue. London, 1973, p. 137.

Adam organ designs: Kedleston, 1760, 1762, SM 25:1–3; Luton Park, 1763, SM 25:4–5; Burghley House, 1770, SM 25:6; 20; St James's Square, 1772, SM 40:71; Great Saxham Hall, 1775, SM 25:14; Cumberland House, Pall Mall, 1781, SM 25:16–189.

25. Adam's designs for the music-room were completed on 27 January 1775 and are the earliest dated drawings for the house: SM 50:33–36 wall elevations; SM 12:164 ceiling; Whinney, nos. 22–27, pp. 115–17.

26. Bowood, SM 11:78. The Palmyrene connection was made by Mrs Montagu in a letter to her husband in 1765. R. Blunt. ed., *Mrs Montagu 'Queen of the Blues'*, London, 1923, I, p. 127. Harewood dressing-room, SM 11:150; Nostell saloon, SM 11:227.

27. Elevation of the east wall, SM 50:35; Whinney 23, p. 116. The Tharpe account for work in the music-room, document cited at note 20 above, includes '4 Figures flatted Dead White & picked in Laylock (lilac)', which I take to be the figures above the organ and the central pier between the doors.

28. SM 23:66, dated '1st Febry 1775'; Whinney, no. 31, p. 119.

29. The mirror is shown in Adam's elevation of the north wall, SM 50:34, Whinney no. 22, p. 115. There is no separate design for it. Osterley, Etruscan room pier-glass, SM 20:44, 45, dated 15 May 1775. E. Harris, no. 71.

30. 'Organ Case for Lady Home' including 'Plan of the Organ', dated June 1775, SM 25:15, Whinney, no. 26, p. 117; an earlier elevation of the whole wall with the organ, dated 27 January 1775, SM 50:33, Whinney, no. 24, p. 116. The design gives alternatives for the cresting (with or without seated figures) and the base (painted green and strigillated or pale blue with foliate ornament like the upper part); the apparent narrowness and different articulation of the left-hand alternative solution may be explained in a lengthy annotation to the drawing, which is unfortunately illegible.

31. The architect, Philip Tilden, who was employed by Lord and Lady Islington when they took the house in 1920 described the music-room as 'unfinished or mutilated, but every other room remained in tact'. P. Tilden, *True remembrances, the memoirs of an architect*, London, 1954, pp. 89, 90. Cited by Whinney, p. 44.

32. The colour of the paterae is given in the Tharpe accounts, document cited at note 20 above.

33. Felice de Giardini (1715–96), a violinist and composer of French origin; the 'greatest performer in Europe', according to Dr Burney. His employment by the Countess of Home is appropriate, for he was music master to the Duke of Cumberland and from 1774–9 often led the orchestra of the Pantheon concerts.

34. Oliver, op. cit. at note 5 above.

35. SM 6:110, Whinney, no. 36, p. 121. This rapid sketch must be read as a conflation of two designs and not as a proposal for a radical alteration to the plan making the two principal rooms the same width as suggested by Whinney, p. 47. The verso of the sheet contains a rapid sketch of Lady Home's Etruscan bed.

36. These elements are included in the Tharpe account, document cited at note 20 above.

37. J. Fowler and J. Cornforth, *English decoration in the 18th century*, London, 1974, p. 206.

38. Adam's design, SM 53:8, Whinney no. 49, calls for pairs of satyrs under the laurel arches in the frieze of the screened area and alternating pairs of nymphs and satyrs in the main body of the room; in the event, both parts were executed with pairs of nymphs. The frieze of nymphs and satyrs is included in the volume of 'Sketches Of Ornamented Friezes From Original Models In the Possession of Joseph Rose Many of the Models

were made from the designs of the most Eminent Architects, and the whole Executed in Stucco work by Joseph & Joseph Rose' compiled in 1782, possibly for publication. RIBA Drawings Collection, no. 244.

Its colours are given in the Tharpe account, document cited at note 20 above.

39. SM 12:165, Whinney, no. 29, dated 25 March 1775, is inscribed 'not executed'. SM 12:166, Whinney, no. 30, is similar but not identical though it is inscribed a Duplicate. SM 8:41 is a preliminary sketch. The unusual motif of a square with circular corners is reminiscent of ceilings for Mersham-le-Hatch 1766, SM 11:183–5, and the hall at Newby 1769, SM 11:238. SM 12:167, Whinney, no. 28, dated 25 March 1775, the executed design for the second drawing-room ceiling at Home House, has some features in common with the ceiling designed in 1770 for the drawing-room at Northumberland House, SM 11:33.

40. SM 23:67, dated '1st Febry 1775'; Whinney, no. 32, p. 119.

41. SM 20:165, dated May 1777; Whinney, no. 34, p. 120.

42. SM 20:162, dated May 1777; Whinney, no. 35, p. 120.

43. Elizabeth, Countess of Home's will, London, Public Record Office, Prob 11/1112, proved 24 January 1784. L. Lewis, loc. cit. at note 3 above, p. 448.

44. Five folding doors and three blank doors are mentioned in the Tharpe account, document cited at note 20 above.

45. Ceiling design inscribed 'Designd for Mrs. Knox Ld. Knaptons Sister & Executed in Ly. Homes Principal Dressing Room', Wyatt Album, document cited at note 21 above, no. 30. The discovery of this drawing somewhat alters what I wrote in my Burlington Magazine article, loc. cit. at note 1 above.

46. Ceiling designs: 'Circular Antiroom at Lady Homes, between the 2d & 3d Drawing Rooms', SM 3:106; sketch, SM 8:48; finished drawing dated 'Janry 27th 1775', SM 12:168; Whinney, nos. 37–9. The ceiling was painted green with fawn-coloured ornaments picked in white and pink, the frieze was white picked-in green and pink and the mirror was painted dead white, Tharpe account, document cited at note 20 above.

47. Information supplied by Dr J. M. Robinson.

48. Whinney, p. 77.

49. Ibid., p. 52.

50. Chimney-piece design, dated '1st Febry 1775', SM 23:68; Whinney, no. 40. Mirror dated 1777, SM 20:167; Whinney, no. 43.

51. Wyatt Album, document cited at note 21 above, no. 13. Wyatt used a somewhat similar configuration of circles for the Home House library ceiling, SM 12:163; Whinney, no. 16.

52. Sketch plan and elevation of the bed, inscribed in pencil 'Some s (?) as Mrs Childs', SM 6:110; Whinney, no. 44. Finished wall elevations, SM 14:132, 134; Whinney, nos 42 and 41, p. 123. Design for wall decorations, uninscribed but probably for Home House, SM 52:68; Whinney, no. 51. Designs for door panels, SM 5:4, 12, 74; Whinney, nos 44–7, p. 125. Chimney-piece dated 1 February 1777, SM 23:69; Whinney, no. 48, p. 176. Designs for the Osterley bed, dated 11 October 1775, SM 17:156, 157.

53. Adam, Works, II, i, preface.

54. SM 50:89, 'Section for General Fitzroy' (undated, but possibly December 1774, the date of the ceiling design (SM 12:156) for Lady Fitzroy's circular dressing-room); SM 32:104, 'Section of a Room in Apsley House for the Lord Chancellor Adelphi June 27 1775', with Etruscan decoration on pale green walls. As this is mentioned in Adam's Works, II, i, preface, it was presumably executed. The circular dressing-room had a ceiling with black and terracotta ornaments, SM

14:15, dated 21 June 1775. SM 14:128, 130, 131; 50:71 are finished designs for the Etruscan wall decorations on a pale blue ground at Osterley, dated 11 October 1775.

55. Wall elevations, SM 14:132, 134; Whinney, nos 42 and 41; a sketch of the wall decorations, uninscribed but probably for Home House, SM 52:68; Whinney no. 51, p. 127; door panels, SM 5:4, 12, 74; Whinney nos 44–7, p. 125; chimney-piece dated '1st Febry 1777', SM 23:69; Whinney, no. 48, p. 126.

56. Adam, Works, I, p. 10.

57. Dublin, NLI, Penrose-Wyatt Collection, AD 3158, inscribed 'Scetch of Ceiling Lady Homes dining Parlour'. A finished copy of the same design for Lord Conyingham's dining-room at Slane Castle, co. Meath, Ireland is in the Wyatt Album, document cited at note 21 above, no. 3.

58. SM 23:64, 'Chimney Piece for the back Parlour at Lady home's in Portman Square 13 May 1775'; Whinney, no. 12, p. 111.

59. Whinney, p. 36. SM 17:196, 'Carpet for the back Parlour at Lady Home's in Portman Square 9th Oct. 1776'. SM 17:195, identically inscribed and dated, is a quarter design washed in three shades of pink; the sort of design required by a carpet maker. Whinney, nos. 13–15, p. 112

60. Dublin, NLI, Penrose-Wyatt Collection AD 3161, inscribed 'Scetch of Front Parl Ceiling Lady Home'. Adam's design, SM 12:161 is inscribed and dated 1775; Whinney, no. 9, p 109. The colours of the ceiling were described in 1796 (Tharpe account, document cited at note 20 above) as grey fawn and straw with white ornaments.

61. The placement of the columns at the west end 6 1/2 inches (16 centimetres) further from the wall rectified the space taken from the east side by the party wall. This difference is also reflected in the ceiling decoration.

62. SM 23:63, 'Chimney Piece for the front Parlor at Lady Home's in Portman Square 13th May 1775'; Whinney, no. 10, p. 109. For the Derby House chimney-pieces, see SM 23:43, SM 23:38.

63. Dublin, NLI, Penrose-Wyatt Collection, AD 3144, inscribed 'Scetch of Ceiling for Library Lady Home'.

64. SM 50:37.

65. Whinney, p. 39 n. 4, 79.

66. Spectator, no. 159. D. F. Bond, ed., The Spectator, Oxford, 1965, II, p. 124, n. 4.

67. Spectator, no. 514, in ibid., IV, p. 324.

68. If Dr Whinney is correct in associating the payment of £50 to Zucchi in 1777 with the overmantel painting, then perhaps the payment of £100 to Sefferin Nelson in the same year may have covered the bookcase.

69. K. Garlick and A. Macintyre, eds, The Diary of Joseph Farington, London, 1978, I, 129.

70. SM 6:67, 'a Small Bracket Green & White for Lady Homes Library and The small tripod Candlestick to Stand on the Brackett is 3 Ins 3/4 over (?) at Bottome'. SM 25:27 (left and right) 'Bracket for Lady Home's Library Feby 1777'. Whinney nos 17 and 18, pp. 113–14.

71. 'Lady Home's Fire Screen', SM 54:257, 'Design of a Tripod for Lady Home', SM 17:73; Whinney, nos 52, p. 128 and 50, p. 126. The pedestal design for Sir Watkin Williams-Wynn is SM 17:60 (E. Harris, no. 137).

19 · CULZEAN CASTLE

1. A. Rowan, 'Ugbrooke Park, Devon – II', Country Life. 27 July 1967, pp. 203–7.

2. G. B. Piranesi, Diversi maniere, Rome, 1769, p. 34.

3. Adam, Works, I, no. IV, preface.

4. M. H. B. Sanderson, Robert Adam and Scotland, Edinburgh, 1992, p. 88. quoting a letter written by Sir John Dalyrymple in 1784 regarding Oxenfoord.

5. A. Rowan, Designs for castles and country villas by

Robert & James Adam, Oxford, 1985, p. 18.

6. Sanderson, op. cit, at note 4 above, p. 85 n. 2.

7. I. Gow, 'Archerfield, Dirleton, East Lothian', Times Past to Present in Gullane and Dirleton Historical Essays, ed. M. Cox, published by The Gullane Local History Society and the Dirleton Local History Group, 1994.

8. Letter from Robert Adam in London to the Hon. George Baillie at Mellerstain, 13 January 1778, regarding the possible expense of having the figures to go over the columns in the library modelled in London. Mellerstain Correspondence, January–March 1778, p. 34.

9. The last payment to Robert Adam was for £50 on 23 January 1792. Ailsa MSS, SRO, GC 25/9/10.

10. L. Namier and J. Brooke, The House of Commons 1754–1790, London, 1964, III, p. 5.

11. Letter from Adam at Edinburgh to Sir Rowland Winn at Nostell, 15 August 1776 stating that he is 'under an engagement to go . . . to visit the Earl of Cassillis who has an old Castle that he wished to have my advice about'. Nostell Papers, C/3/1/5/1/14, West Yorkshire Archive Service.

12. Adam's topographical drawing of Culzean, SM 21:6. Accounts for building this block, SRO GD 25/9/8. This information and much else pertaining to the finances and expenditures of the Kennedys of Culzean was kindly given me by Michael Moss of the Archives & Business Record Centre, University of Glasgow who is preparing a detailed publication on the subject.

13. SRO GD 25/9/14, financial papers 1750–4. Tower Gate is clearly shown in John Clerk of Edlin's etched view of Culzean before it was transformed by Adam. See M. H. B. Sanderson, Robert Adam in Ayrshire, Ayrshire Monographs No. 11, Ayrshire, April, 1993, p. 21.

14. SRO GD 25/9/7, financial papers 1750–4, accounts for mansion house reparis. On 15 February 1751 Archibald Kennedy wrote to Sir Thomas informing him that his dining-room was finished before Christmas. 'Mr Clyton' (Thomas Clayton, the English plasterer who had worked for William Adam and was responsible for the ceilings at Dumfries House) is named as the 'undertaker', SRO GD 25/9/40. The 'lobby' mentioned in the accounts was presumably in the short northern arm of the L-shaped castle, entered either from the east or the west. See Adam's earliest surviving plan of 1777 for enlarging the house, AYD/43/5.

15. SRO Ailsa papers GD 25/9/7 and J. Ingamells, ed., A dictionary of British and Irish travellers in Italy 1701–1800. Compiled from the Brinsley Ford Archive, London, 1997, p. 568. The Grand Tourist and the sitter of the Batoni portrait at Culzean was Sir Thomas, not David as hitherto assumed.

16. SRO GD 25/9/27, invoices 1744–65, no. 4. These arrived at Culzean in 1756.

17. SRO GD 25/9/7, account with Gavin Hamilton 1761.

18. SRO GD 25/9/40. Evidently Archibald Kennedy was not informed of the hedonistic purpose of this small building, 'If you designed it for a house of office I shall fitt up the old one So as it may answer...'.

19. James Adam sketch book at Penicuik House, Sketch Book 2/1 signed and dated 1755. There are similar, undated plans and elevations for a villa in the Ailsa MSS, Inventory 58, 59, 60.

20. Chambers's published design has four Doric porticos: Treatise on civil architecture, London, 1759, pl. 45.

21. Among Chambers drawings at the Soane are undated ground and first-floor plans for a 'Casine for Sr Thomas Kennedy Bart' a plain square banqueting house without porticos, SM 43/4/2. There is another version of the plan giving room dimensions among the NTS Culzean Drawings. The ground-floor had a kitchen, bedroom and vestibule with a circular

stair to the first floor where there was a large dining-room, 24 × 16 feet, with windows on three sides and a buffet and closet.

22. SRO GD 25/9/8 bundle Culzean buildings 1766–7 and GD 25/9/9 financial papers 1766. See Sanderson, op. cit. at note 13 above, p. 20.

23. W. Robertson, *Ayrshire 1st history and historic families*, Ayr, 1908, p. 12.

24. Accounts with John Hunter, partner in Sir William Forbes & Co., SRO GD 25/9/9.

25. The small room labelled 'Ante room' facing into the kitchen court had no direct access from the stairs and must have functioned as a waiting or withdrawing-room.

26. This was probably the site of one of the pre-existing offices shown in Adam's topographical sketch, SM 21:6. It was demolished and the cellars adapted. The north side of a house, being the coolest, was generally favoured for kitchens. In a letter of 15 October 1761 to Sir Wyndham Knatchbull regarding Mersham-le-Hatch, Kent, Adam stated his reasons for thinking that a kitchen was best placed outside the body of the house in an adjoining wing. Kent Record Office.

27. Rowan, op. cit. at note 5 above, pl. 49.

28. J. Macaulay, *The Gothic Revival 1745–1845*, Glasgow, 1975, p. 100.

29. 'Plan of the one pair Story of Cullean Castle', Ailsa MSS, Inventory 4; 'North Front of the Offices with part of the present Building at Cullean Castle', dated 'Adelphi 28 Febry 1777', Ailsa MSS.

30. 'Plan of the second Story' dated August 1779, Ailsa MSS, Inventory 9; 'South front of the new Offices with the Elevation of the old front of the passage', Ailsa MSS.

31. The accounts kept by Hugh Cairncross, Ailsa MSS, SRO, GD/25.

32. Chimney-piece designs, SM 23:106–15; ceilings, SM 14:59–66, 90. The chimney-piece designs were taken to Scotland, along with designs for Mellerstain, on 15 April 1778 by William Cairncross, a kinsman of Hugh Cairncross, Mellerstain Correspondence, January–March 1778, p. 35, letter from Robert Adam to George Baillie.

33. Designs for mirrors and girandoles, SM 20:228, 231–4, 236.

34. J. Paterson, *History of Ayr and Wigton*, II, *Carrick*. Edinburgh, 1864, p. 389.

35. *Tour of the Western Highlands*, 1788, p. 119. Cited by Bolton, II, p. 274.

36. SM 37:9, dated 22 November 1784.

37. Dalquharran's central circular stair may also have suggested the final solution to the staircase at Culzean. The idea of a projecting rotunda on the garden front, rising above the rest interested Adam at this time. It was first expressed as a 'separate round tower' in his fourth scheme for The Oaks, 1777, and as a round tower at the apex of the V-shaped plan for Bewley, 21 October 1777. See Rowan, op. cit. at note 5 above, pls 46, 47, 49.

38. J. Paine, *Plans, elevations and sections, of noblemen and gentlemen's houses*, London, 1783, II, pls 44, 45.

39. SM 37:8.

40. The drawing (SM 37:8) is inscribed in pencil 'This plan does not shew the upper stories but it is given to shew the plan of (?) round tower and the kitchens'.

41. J. Clerk of Eldin, An unpublished life of Robert Adam, 1794. Clerk of Penicuik Papers, SRO, GD/18/4981.

42. Plans dated 4 May 1787, SM 37:5, 6, 7; 46:143, 144. Elevations, SM 37:1, 2. Sections, dated 4 May 1787, SM 1:35; SM 37:3, 4.

43. Raphael's original plan for the Villa Madama had a circular court, so did Charles V's palace at Granada. Both of these were probably unknown to Adam.

44. For Adam's views on the uncertainties surrounding the proportions of columns, which 'can only be properly ascertained by the correct taste of the skilful and experienced artist' see *Works*, I, ii, p. 4.

45. J. Harris, *Sir William Chambers*, London, 1970, p. 225, no. 84.

46. J. Abel Smith,'Great Saxham Hall, Suffolk', *Country Life*, 27 November 1986, pp. 1698–1702. Adam's plan, SM 34:19; section SM 34:17. The 1773 date of the plan at the Soane, if correct, would diminish the presumed influence of Paine's colonnaded staircase hall at Wardour Castle. See Rowan, op. cit. at note 5 above, p. 130.

47. Rowan, op. cit. at note 5 above: Wyke Manor, Isleworth, p. 54, pl. 16; Findlater Castle, Banffshire, p. 138, pl. 58.

48. The first ceiling design for the second drawing-room, dated 1778 (SM 14:60) was slightly revised on 11 April 1780 (SM 12:61, 66). It was the revised version that was executed.

49. S. Serlio, *Regole generali di architettura*, Venice, 1537, bk IV. See S. Thurley, *The royal palaces of Tudor England*, London, 1993, pp. 96–7. For two other early houses, Whitehaven Castle, Cumbria and Oxenfoord Castle, Midlothian, Adam designed ceilings with diamond tracery and circular joints (SM 11:261 and SM 14:81 respectively) which may be regarded as a two-dimensional abstractions of medieval vaulting patterns.

50. Design for second drawing-room chimney-piece dated 1778, SM 23:113.

51. Ingamells, op. cit. at note 15 above. This portrait is frequently and mistakenly published as David Kennedy, 10th Earl of Cassillis.

52. 'Glass frame for the Earl of Cassillis's Dressing room', 1782 SM 20:233. Design for the chimney-glass for the buffet-room, dated March 1782, SM 20:231.

53. Design for the dressing-room chimney-piece dated 1778, SM 23:115; chimney-glass dated 1782, SM 20:233.

54. Mellerstain friezes, SM 53:50.

55. The room is included in the sections of the house dated May 1787 (SM 1:35 and 37:3, 4), but no detail is shown. On 23 April 1790, Adam wrote to Hugh Cairncross, telling him that the earl had asked him 'to make out Designs for his Saloon and Staircase and particularly the ornamental stucco which his Lordship said he intended should be done by Mr Coney though he knew he was given to drinking, yet he did not

like new people and was to employ him' and asking to be informed 'what resolutions are taken' and to be sent 'a list of what drawings you think will be necessary by return of post, SRO GD 25/7/327. The watercolour design for the ceiling dated 1790 at the house and a quarter-detail at the RIBA Drawings Collection must have been made shortly after this letter. Though a preliminary design for the chimney-piece had been sent to Cassillis, Adam was still waiting for his comments. This drawing has not been traced. The present chimney-piece cannot be identified with the one supplied in April 1791 by M. Van Gelder, which had a statuary marble mantel and jambs with carved wood dressings. Ailsa MSS, SRO, GD 25.

56. Adam's 1787 plan shows this ground-floor room partitioned into a servants hall and '2d Table room', each with two windows and a chimney-piece. The building accounts suggest that this partitioning was executed; however, an 1818 drainage plan and all later nineteenth-century plans show a single 'Steward's Room'. RCHMS, Ailsa MSS.

57. I. Gow, 'The Dining Room', in A. Carruther, ed., *The Scottish Home*, Edinburgh, 1996, ch. 6. The views on dining-rooms published in Adam's *Works*, I, i, repeat the contents of a letter written in 1761 by another member of the family to Sir James Clerk, SRO, GD 18/1758b, quoted and mistakenly attributed to Robert Adam by J. Macaulay, *The classical country house in Scotland 1660–1800*, London, 1987, p. 170.

58. Adam's undated ceiling design (SM 14:90) is the one that was executed. It is a simplified version of SM 14:62, 63 which are dated 1779. His design for the girandoles (SM 22:236) is dated 1782; the pier glass design (SM 22:228) is dated March 1782. The design for the pier-glass indicates that it was to be composed of seven small plates of glass, costing considerably less than a single large plate.

59. *Culzean Castle*, National Trust for Scotland, Guidebook, 1988, p. 10. When the eating-room was converted to a library, its Adam girandoles and Adamesque pier-tables were transferred to the saloon which had much more furniture than it does now, including a telescope and a circular Adam-style table in the centre of the floor.

60. Design for the buffet-room chimney-piece, dated 1778, SM 23:107; design for the mirror, dated March 1782, SM 22:231.

61. Plan of the library inscribed with instructions regarding the bookcases: 'The Pilasters should be hung to open in front for the conveniency of Maps &c.', SM 31:46. See Rowan, op. cit. at note 5 above, p. 124, pl. 51.

62. Adam, *Works*, II, ii, pl. VII.

63. E. Harris, 'Adams in the Family: Wright and Mansfield at Haddo, Guisachan, Brook House and Grosvenor Square', *Furniture History*, 1996, p. 146.

64. Two tablets and one roundel now in the vestibule and Ship Model Room probably came from the original library.

65. *The Complete Peerage*, III, p. 79.

66. Ailsa MSS, SRO, GD 25/9.

SELECTED BIBLIOGRAPHY

ADAM, JAMES, 'Journal of a Tour in Italy. By Robert [i.e. James] Adam, Esq., *Library of the fine arts*, II, London, October, 1831

ADAM, ROBERT, *The ruins of the palace of Emperor Diocletian at Spalatro*, London, 1764

ADAM, ROBERT and JAMES, *The works in architecture of Robert and James Adam*, London, 1778, 1779

BARNES, A., *The eighteenth-century chamber organ in Kedleston Hall, Derbyshire*, Warwickshire, 1990

BATHO, G. R. 'Syon House: The first two hundred years', *Transactions of the London and Middlesex Archaeological Society*, XIX, i, 1956

BEARD, G., 'On Patronage', *Leeds Art Calendar*, 1961

——, 'The Rose family of plasterers', *Apollo*, LXXXV, 1967

——, *Decorative Plasterwork in Great Britain*, London, 1975

——, *The work of Robert Adam*, London, 1987

——, 'Decorators and Furniture Makers at Croome Court', *Furniture History*, XXIX, 1993

BLUNT, R., ed., *Mrs Montagu 'Queen of the Blues'*, London, 1923

BOLTON, A. T., 'Kenwood, Hampstead', *Country Life*, 22 November 1913

——, 'Harewood House, Yorkshire', *Country Life*, 4 July 1914

——, 'The Shire Hall, Hertford', *Architectural Review*, XLIII, 1918

——, 'Syon House', *Country Life*, 6 December; 13 December; 20 December 1919

——, *The works of Robert and James Adam*, London, 1922

BORENIUS, T., *Catalogue of the pictures and drawings at Harewood House*, London, 1936

BOWLES, W. H., *History of the Vauxhall and Ratcliff glass houses and their owners, 1670–1800*, London, 1926

BOWOOD, Wiltshire, *A sale by public auction of the valuable antique fixtures, fittings and indoor and outdoor architectural features of that part of this celebrated mansion which is shortly to be demolished . . . to be held at Bowood, . . . Auctioneer E. Clifford Smith*, 30 June 1955

BRIGGS, N., *John Johnson*, Chelmsford, 1991

BRISTOL, K., 'The Painted Rooms of "Athenian" Stuart', *The Georgian Group Journal*, X, London, 2000

BRISTOW, I., 'The Great Drawing Room from Bowood', *ASCHB Transactions*, X, 1986

——, *Architectural colour in British interiors 1615–1840*, New Haven and London, 1996

BROCKWELL, M. N., *Catalogue of the pictures and other works of art in the collection of Lord St. Oswald at Nostell Priory*, London, 1915

BRYANT, J., *Kenwood*, London, 1990

——, 'The Adam Library Carpet Recreated at Kenwood', *English Heritage Conservation Bulletin*, February 1991

BURDEN, M., 'Robert Adam, De Loutherbourg and the Sets for *The Maid of The Oaks*,' *Adam in Context*, Georgian Group Symposium, London, 1992

CASTELL, R., *Villas of the ancients*, London, 1728

CHAMBERS, W., *Treatise on the decorative part of civil architecture*, London, 1759; 3rd ed., 1791

CHIPPENDALE, T., *The gentleman and cabinet-maker's director*, London, 3rd ed. 1762

COKE, M., *The letters and Journals of Lady Mary Coke*, London, 1970

COLERIDGE, A., 'English furniture supplied for Croome Court: Robert Adam and the 6th Earl of Coventry' *Apollo*, February 2000

——, 'Sir Lawrence Dundas and Chippendale', *Apollo*, September 1967

COLVIN, H., *Biographical dictionary of British architects*, New Haven and London, 1995

——, 'Croome Church and Its Architect', *Georgian Group Journal*, VIII, 1998

CORNFORTH, J., 'Saltram, Devon', *Country Life*, 27 April, 4 May; 11 May 1967

——, 'Bowood, Wiltshire Revisited I', *Country Life*, 8 June 1972

——, 'Newby Hall, Yorkshire', *Country Life*, 7 June 1979; 14 June 1979; 25 December 1980

——, 'Designs for Newby', 'Correspondence', *Country Life*, 19 July 1979

——, 'Newby in the 19th Century', *Country Life*, 25 December 1980

——, 'Restoration at Nostell Priory', *Country Life*, 11 April 1985

——, 'Audley End, Essex I', *Country Life*, 27 December 1990

COX, M., *Derby. The life and times of the 12th Earl of Derby*, London, 1974

CROFT MURRAY, E., *Decorative painting in England 1537–1837*, II, London, 1970

Croome Court, Worcestershire, Bentley, Hobbs, & Myton, Sale of the contents of Croome Court, Worcestershire, 7 December 1948

Culzean Castle, National Trust for Scotland, Guidebook, 1988

CUNNINGHAM, M., *The story of the Oaks and Oaks Park*, London, 1993

CURWEN, S., *The journal of Samuel Curwen, loyalist*, ed. A. Oliver, Cambridge, MA, 1972

DACOS, N., *La découverte de la Domus Aurea et la formation des grotesques à la Renaissance*, London–Leiden, 1971

DEAN, W., *An historical and descriptive account of Croome D'Abitot*, Worcester, 1824

DELANY, MRS, *The life and correspondence*, ed. Lady Llandover, 2nd series, London, 1862

DICKENS, L., and STANTON, M. (eds), *An Eighteenth Century Correspondence*, London, 1910

DODSLEY, R., *London and its environs*, VI, London, 1761

DONALDSON, T. L., 'Some Description of Alnwick Castle, Northumberland', *RIBA Papers* Session 1856–7

DRAPER, T., 'No. 10 Hertford Street', *Georgian Group Journal*, IX, 1999

DUTENS, L., *Memoirs of a Traveller*, London, 1806

EDWARDS, R., 'Torcheres and Candelabra. Designs by Robert Adam', *Country Life*, 23 May 1947

——, *Dictionary of English furniture*, London, 1954

ERIKSEN, S., *Early neo-classicism in France*, London, 1974

FAIRCLOUGH, O., 'Sir Watkin Williams-Wynn and Robert Adam: commissions for silver 1768–80', *Burlington Magazine*, CXXXVII June 1995

FARINGTON, J., *The diary of Joseph Farington*, ed. Kenneth Garlick and Angus Macintyre, New Haven and London, 1979ff.

FENAILLE, M., *Etat général des tapisseries de la manufacture des Gobelins*, IV, Paris, 1907

FITZMAURICE, LORD E., *Life of William, Earl of Shelburne*, London, 1875

FLEMING, J., *Robert Adam and his circle*, London, 1962

FORD, B., 'Thomas Jenkins, Banker, Dealer and Unofficial English Agent', *Apollo*, XCIX, 1974

———, 'Sir Watkin Williams-Wynn. A Welsh Maecenas', *Apollo*, June, 1974

FOWLER, J. and CORNFORTH, J., *English decoration in the 18th century*, London, 1974

GILBERT, C., *The life and work of Thomas Chippendale*, London, 1978

———, 'New Light on the Furnishing of Nostell Priory', *Furniture History*, XXVI, 1990

———, LOMAX, J., and WELLS-COLE, A., *Country House Floors 1660–1850*, Leeds, 1981

GOODISON, N., 'Mr Stuart's Tripod', *Burlington Magazine*, CXIV, October 1972

———, *Ormolu: the work of Matthew Boulton*, London, 1974

GOW, I., 'The Dining Room', in A. Carruther, ed., *The Scottish Home*, Edinburgh, 1996

GRIENER, P., *La antichità Etrusche, Greche e Romane 1766–1776 di Pierre Hugues d'Hancarville*, Rome, 1992

HALL, I., 'Neo-classical elements in Chippendale's designs for the "Director" of 1762, *Leeds Arts Calendar*, 65, 1969

———, 'Newly discovered Chippendale drawings relating to Harewood', *Leeds Arts Calendar*, no. 69, 1971

HALL, M., 'Luton Hoo – Bedfordshire – II', *Country Life*, 22 January 1992

HARDY, J., 'The Croome Court Library', *Connoisseur*, CXCI, January 1976

———, 'Robert Adam and the furnishing of Kedleston Hall', *Connoisseur*, CXCVI-II, July 1978

———, and HAYWARD, H., 'Kedleston Hall, Derbyshire – III', *Country Life*, 9 February 1978

HARGROVE, E., *History of the castle, town, and forest of Knaresborough with Harrowgate*, 4th ed., York, 1789; 5th ed., Knaresborough, 1798

HARRIS, E., 'Robert Adam and the Gobelins', *Apollo*, LXXVI, 1962

———, *The furniture of Robert Adam*, London, 1963

———, 'The Moor Park Tapestries', *Apollo*, September 1967

———, and ROBINSON, J. M., 'New Light on Wyatt at Fawley', *Architectural History*, XXVII, 1984

———, and SAVAGE, N., *British architectural books and writers, 1560–1780*, Cambridge, 1990

———, 'The Lansdowne House drawing room: reconstructing Adam properly', *Apollo*, August 1992

———, 'Robert Adam on Park Avenue: the interiors for Bolton House', *Burlington Magazine*, February 1995

———, 'Adam Organizing Handel', *Country Life*, 30 March 1995

———, *The Williams-Wynn Chamber Organ*, Phillips Sale Catalogue, London, 21 April 1995

———, 'Imposing puzzles at Basildon House', *Apollo*, April 1997

———, 'Home House: Adam versus Wyatt', *Burlington Magazine*, CXXXIX, May 1997

———, 'Don't Wag the Dog: a Brief Defence of the Status Quo of James Paine's Designs for Kedleston', *Architectural History*, XLII, 1999

———, 'The Childs in London', *Aspects of Osterley*, London, 2000

HARRIS, J., Sir William Chambers, London, 1970

———, *Catalogue of British drawings for architecture, decoration, sculpture and landscape gardening 1500–1900 in American collections*, London, 1971

———, 'C. R. Cockerell's Ichnographica Domestica', *Architectural History*, XIV, 1971

———, and SNODIN, M., eds, *Sir William Chambers architect to George III*, London, 1997

HARRIS, L., 'The Picture Collection at Kedleston Hall', *Connoisseur*, July 1978

———, *Robert Adam and Kedleston*, National Trust, London, 1987

HASKELL, F. and PENNY, N., *Taste and the Antique*, New Haven and London, 1981

HAYWARD, H., 'Splendour at Croome Court: new light on Vile and Cobb', *Apollo*, May 1974

———, and KIRKHAM, P., *William and John Linnell*, London, 1980

HEFFORD, W., 'Thomas Moore of Moorfields', *Burlington Magazine*, December 1977

HEWLINGS, R., 'A Palmyra ceiling in Lincoln', *Architectural History*, XXXI, 1988

HOWELL, P. and PRITCHARD, T. W., 'Wynnstay, Denbighshire', *Country Life*, 23 March; 30 March 1972

HUNTER, J., *South Yorkshire. The history and topography of the Deanery of Doncaster*, London, 1828

HUSSEY, C., 'The Re-opening of Kenwood', *Country Life*, 26 May 1950

———, *Mid Georgian 1760–1800*, London, 1956

HUTCHINSON, W., *A view of Northumberland . . . 1776*, Newcastle-upon-Tyne, 1778

INGAMELLS, J., ed., *A dictionary of British and Irish travellers in Italy 1701–1800. Compiled from the Brinsley Ford Archive*, London, 1997

IONIDES, J., *Thomas Farnolls Pritchard of Shrewsbury*, Ludlow, 1999

JACKSON-STOPS, G., 'Pre-Adam Furniture Designs at Nostell Priory', *Furniture History*, X, 1974

———, 'Syon Park, Middlesex', *Country Life*, 16 April 1992

JACOBS, B., *Axminster carpets (hand-made) 1755–1957*, London, 1970

JESSE, J. J., *George Selwyn and his contemporaries*, London, 1901

JEWELL, J., *The tourist's companion or the history and antiquities of Harewood in Yorkshire*, Leeds, 1819

JOURDAIN, M., *English furniture of the later 18th century*, London, 1920

Kedleston, Catalogue of the pictures, statues, etc. with some account of the architecture at Kedleston, privately printed, 1769, 1770, 1778, 1796

Kedleston Hall, National Trust Guidebook by N. Antram and G. Jackson-Stops, London, 1998

KELLEY, A., *Decorative Wedgwood*, London, 1965

KELSALL, F., 'Liardet versus Adam', *Architectural History*, XXVII, 1984

———, 'Osterley from Gresham to Barbon', *Aspects of Osterley*, The National Trust, London, 2000

Kenwood House, Sale of the contents of the house by C. B. King Ltd at Kenwood, London, 6–9 November 1922

KERRY, EARL OF, 'Kings Bowood, II, III', *Wiltshire Archaeological and Natural History Magazine*, XLI, XLII, 1924, 1927

KIELMANSEGGE, F., *Diary of a journey to England in the years 1761–1762*, London, 1902

KIMBALL, S. FISKE, 'Les influences anglaises dans la formation du style Louis XVI', *Gazette des Beaux-Arts*, 6ᵐ serie, v, 1931

———, 'Lansdowne House Redivivus', *Philadelphia Museum of Art Bulletin*, XXXIX, November 1943

KING, D., *The complete works of Robert and James Adam*, Oxford, 1991

KING, J., 'An Ambassador's House in Essex', *The Georgian Group Journal*, VII, London, 1997

Lansdowne House. A catalogue of all the handsome household furniture. Sold by Peter Cox Burrell & Foster. 21 March and 7 following days, 1806

Lansdowne House, 'Drawing Room from Lansdowne House', *Philadelphia Museum of Art Bulletin*, LXXXII, 1986

LEACH, P., *James Paine*, London, 1988

———, 'James Paine's Design for the South Front of Kedleston Hall: Dating and Sources', *Architectural History*, XL, London, 1997

LEES MILNE, J., *The Age of Adam*, London, 1947

LEWIS, L., 'Elizabeth, Countess of Home, and her house in Portman Square', *Burlington Magazine*, CIX, 1967

LINSTRUM, D., *The Wyatt Family*, RIBA Drawings Catalogue, London, 1973

LOW, J., 'French Taste in London. William Weddell's Town House', *Country Life*, 27 December 1979

———, 'The Art and Architectural Patronage of William Weddell (1736–92) of Newby Hall and his Circle', unpublished Ph.D. thesis, Dept. of Fine Arts, University of Leeds, 1981

———, 'William Belwood: Architect and Surveyor', *The Yorkshire Archaeological Journal*, LVI, 1984

———, 'Newby Hall: Two Late Eighteenth-Century Inventories', *Furniture History*, XXII, 1986

Lowther Castle, Westmoreland, *Architectural drawings from Lowther Castle*, ed. H. Colvin, J. Mordaunt Crook, T. Friedman, *Architectural History Monographs*. no. 2, Society of Architectural Historians of Great Britain, 1980

LYBBE POWYS, C., *Passages from the diary of Mrs Lybbe Powys*, London, 1899

LYSONS, D., *Environs of London*, London, 1795

MACAULAY, J., *The classical country house in Scotland 1660–1800*, London, 1987

———, *The Gothic Revival 1745–1845*, Glasgow, 1975

MALLOCH, W., 'The Earl of Bute's machine Organ', *Early Music Quarterly*, London, April 1983

MAUCHLINE, M., *Harewood House*, 2nd ed., London, 1992

McVEIGH, S., *Concert Life in London*, Cambridge, 1993

MEADOWS, P., *Joseph Bonomi Architect*, RIBA, London, 1988

METEYARD, E., *The life of Josiah Wedgwood*, London, 1866

MICHAELIS, A., *Ancient marbles in Great Britain*, Cambridge, 1882

MIDDLETON, R., 'The Sculpture Gallery at Newby Hall', *AA Files*, XIII, 1986

———, 'Soane's Space and the Matter of Fragmentation', *John Soane Architect*, London, 1999

MITFORD, W., *Principles of design in architecture*, London, 1809

NAMIER, L. and Brooke, J., *The House of Commons 1754–1790*, London, 1964

NORTHUMBERLAND, E., DUCHESS OF, *Diaries of a duchess*, ed. James Grieg, London, 1926

OLLEY, J., '20 St James's Square', *Architectural Journal*, London 21, 28 February 1990

O'NEILL, C., 'In search of Bossi', Irish architectural and decorative studies, I, *Journal of the Irish Georgian Society*, I, 1998

ORD-HUME, A. W. J. G., *Barrel Organ*, London, 1978

Osterley Park, V&A Guidebook by M. Tomlin and P. K. Thornton, London, 1977

———, *V&A Guidebook* by J. Hardy and M. Tomlin, London, 1985

———, 'An inventory of all the household goods . . . at Osterley House . . . 1782'. Reprinted by M. Tomlin in *Furniture History*, XXII, 1986

———, National Trust Guidebook by E. Harris, London, 1994

OWSLEY, D. and RIEDER, W., *The glass drawing room from Northumberland House*, London, Victoria and Albert Museum, 1974

PAINE, J., *Plans, elevations and sections, of noblemen and gentlemen's houses*, II, London, 1783

PARISSIEN, S., *Adam Style*, London, 1992

PARKER, J., 'Patrons of Robert Adam at the Metropolitan Museum of Art', *Metropolitan Museum of Art Journal*, I, 1960

PEACOCK J., (pseudo. J. MacPacke), *Oikidia, or, Nutshells*, London, 1785

PENNANT, J., *A tour in Scotland MDCCLXIX*, Chester, 1771

PENNY, N., *Reynolds*, Royal Academy of Art exhibition catalogue, London, 1986

PIEL, F., *Die ornament-grotteske in der italienischer Renaissance*, Berlin, 1962

PIERCE, S. R., 'Thomas Jenkins in Rome', *The Antiquaries Journal*, XLV, pt II, 1965

PIRANESI, G. B., *Opere Varie*, Rome, 1750

———, *Trofèi di Ottaviano Augusto*, Rome, 1753

———, *Della magnificenza ed architettura de' Romani*, Rome, 1761

———, *Diversi maniere d'adornare i cammini*, Rome, 1769

———, *Vasi, Candelabri, Cippi, Sarcophagi*, Rome, 1778

———, *The Complete Etchings*, ed. J. Wilton-Ely, San Francisco, 1994

PLUMPTRE, J., *James Plumptre's Britain, the journal of a tourist in the 1790s*, London, 1992

POCOCKE, R., 'The travels through England of Dr. Richard Pococke', ed. J. J. Cartwright, Camden Society, N.S., I, 1888

POTTERTON, H., 'Neo Classical Decorative Scheme: G. B. Cipriani at Lansdowne House', *Apollo*, October 1972

PRICE, F. G. HILTON, *Marygold by Temple Bar*, London, 1902

PRITCHARD, T. W., *The Wynns of Wynnstay*, Caerwys, 1982

RALPH, J., *A critical review of the public buildings . . . in and about London*, London, 1783

RAMAGE, N., 'Publication dates of Sir William Hamilton's four volumes', *Ars Ceramica* 8, 1991

RAPHAEL, *Loggie di Rafaele nel Vaticano*, engr. G. T. Volpato and P. Camporesi, Rome, 1772–7

REED, M., 'Osterley Park in 1668: The Probate Inventory of Sir William Waller', *London and Middlesex Archaeological Society Transactions*, XLII, 1994

REILLY, R., *Wedgwood*, London, 1989

RICHARDSON, G., *Book of Ceilings*, London, 1776; 2nd ed., London, 1793

RICHARDSON, M., 'A "fair" drawing. A little-known Adam design for Burghley', *Apollo*, August 1992

RIEDER, W., 'Furniture-Smuggling for a Duke', *Apollo*, September 1970

———, 'John Linnell's Furniture For The Dining Room Of Lansdowne House', *Furniture History*, 1993

ROBERTS, H., 'The Derby House Commode', *Burlington Magazine*, CXXVII, May 1985

ROWAN, A., *Designs for castles and country villas by Robert & James Adam*, Oxford, 1985

———, 'Lord Derby's reconstruction of The Oaks'. *Burlington Magazine*, CXXVII, October 1985

———, *Robert Adam, Catalogues of architectural drawings in the V&A*, London, 1988

———, 'The Duke of Northumberland's Garden House at Hulne Priory', *Architectural History*, XLI, 1998

———, 'The Evolution of Osterley in the Eighteenth Century', *Aspects of Osterley*, London, 2000

ROWE, R., *Adam silver*, London, 1965

ROWORTH, W. W., ed., *Angelica Kauffman*, London, 1992

RUSSELL, F., 'Securing the Future', *Country Life*, CLXXXI, 23 July 1987

———, 'Luton Hoo, Bedfordshire – I', *Country Life*, 16 January 1992

———, 'The House That Became A Hostage', *Country Life*, 18 October 1998

———, *John, 3rd Earl of Bute (1713–1792): Patron and Collector*, London, forthcoming

RYKWERT, A. and J., *The brothers Adam*, London, 1985

Saltram, Devon, Catalogue of the pictures, casts and busts belonging to the Earl of Morley at Saltram, Plymouth, 1819

Saltram, Devon, National Trust Guidebook, London, 1981

SANDERSON, M. H. B., *Robert Adam and Scotland*, Edinburgh, 1992

———, *Robert Adam in Ayrshire*, Ayrshire, 1993

SCHARF, G., *A descriptive and historical catalogue of the collection of pictures at Knowsley Hall*, London, 1875

SEDGWICK, R., *The House of Commons 1715–1754*, London, 1970

SHANHAGAN, R., *The Exhibition or a second anticipation*, London, 1779

[SHAW, S.], *A tour, in 1787 from London, to the western highlands of Scotland*, London, 1788

SHERRILL, S., *Carpets and rugs of Europe and America*, New York, 1996

SIMOND, L., *Journal of a tour and residence in Great Britain during the year 1810 and 1811*, Edinburgh, 1817

SMITH, A. H. ed., *A catalogue of the ancient marbles at Lansdowne House*, London, 1889

SNODIN, M., 'Adam Silver reassessed', *Burlington Magazine*, CXXXIX, January 1997

SOANE, J., *An appeal to the public occasioned by the suspension of the architectural lectures in the Royal Academy*, (printed, not published), London, 1812

STANDEN, E. A., 'Croome Court – The Tapestries', *Metropolitan Museum of Art Bulletin*, November, 1959

STARR, M., 'England's lost renaissance?', unpublished thesis, Architectural Association, London, June 1991

STEVENSON, A., 'Chippendale Furniture at Harewood', *Furniture History*, 1968

STILLMAN, D., *The decorative work of Robert Adam*, London, 1966

———, 'The Gallery for Lansdowne House: International Neoclassical Architecture and Decoration in Microcosm', *Art Bulletin*, LIII, New York, 1970

———, *English neo-classical architecture*, London, 1988

STROUD, D., *George Dance*, London, 1971

———, *Capability Brown*, London, 1975

SUMMERSON, J., *Georgian London*, London, 1962

———, *Architecture in Britain 1530 to 1830*, London, 1963

Survey of London, V, Parish of St Giles-in-the-Fields, part II, London, 1914

———, XVII, St Pancras I (Highgate), London, 1936

———, XVIII, The Strand, London, 1937

———, XXIX, St James's Westminster, part I, South of Piccadilly, London, 1960

———, XXXV, The Theatre Royal, Drury Lane, and the Royal Opera House, Covent Garden, London, 1970

———, XL, The Grosvenor Estate in Mayfair, part II, London, 1980

SUTHERILL, M., 'John Hobcraft and James Essex at Audley End House', *The Georgian Group Journal*, IX, 1999

SWARBRICK, J., *The life, work and influence of Robert Adam and his brothers*, London, 1903

SYMONDS, R. W., 'Chippendale Furniture at Nostell Priory', *Country Life*, 3 October 1952

Syon House, guidebook, Derby, 1987

TAIT, A. A., 'Home House', *Apollo*, CXXVI, no. 306, August 1987

———, *Robert Adam drawings and imagination*, Cambridge, 1993

TEYSSOT, G., *Città e utopia nell'illuminism inglese: George Dance il giovane*, Rome, 1974

TIPPING, H. AVRAY, 'Osterley Park – III', *Country Life*, 4 December 1926

TOMLIN, M., 'Osterley in the Eighteenth Century: Furniture Re-arranged to the Original Designs – I', *Country Life*, 18 June 1970

———, *Catalogue of Adam period furniture*, Victoria and Albert Museum, London, 1982

Victoria County History, Middlesex, London, 1962

WALPOLE, H., 'Journals of Visits to Country Seats', *The Walpole Society*, XVI, 1928

———, *The correspondence of Horace Walpole*, ed. W. S. Lewis, New Haven, and London

WARNER, R., *A tour through the northern counties of England, and the borders of Scotland*, Bath, 1802

WATKIN, D., *James Stuart*, London, 1982

————, *Sir John Soane. Enlightenment thought and the Royal Academy lectures*, Cambridge, 1996

WEBSTER, C., 'Architectural Illustration as Revenge: James Paine's designs for Kedleston', *The image of the building. Papers from the annual symposium of the Society of Architectural Historians of Great Britain. 1995*, ed. M. Howard, London, 1996

WEDGWOOD, J., *A catalogue of cameos, intaglios, medals, and bas-reliefs; with a general account of Vases and other ornaments after the antique, made by Wedgwood and Bentley and sold at their rooms in Great Newport Street*, London, 1773

————, *Letters of Josiah Wedgwood*, Manchester, 1973

West Wycombe Park, National Trust Guidebook by G. Jackson-Stops, London, 1973

WHINNEY, M., *Home House*, London, 1969

WILLS, G., *English looking glasses*, London, 1965

WILSON, M. I., 'Lord Bute's Barrel Organ', *The Organ World: Musical Opinion*, LXXXIX, London, February 1966

————, *The English chamber organ*, Oxford, 1968

WILTON-ELY, J., *The mind and art of Giovanni Battista Piranesi*, London, 1978

————, 'Pompeian and Etruscan Tastes in the Neo-Classical Country-House', in G. Jackson-Stops ed., *The fashioning and functioning of the British Country House*, Washington, 1989

————, *Piranesi as architect and designer*, New York, 1993

————, 'Antiquity for the Designer: the British Neoclassical Interior', *Rassegna*, 55, Bologna, September 1993

WOOD, R., *Ruins of Palmyra*, London, 1753

WOOLFE, J. and GANDON, J., *Vitruvius Britannicus*, V, London, 1771

WORSLEY, G., 'Alnwick Castle, Northumberland – II', *Country Life*, 8 December 1988

————, *Classical architecture in Britain*, London, 1995

YORKE, J., 'Osterley Before Adam', *Country Life*, 14 September 19890

INDEX

PHOTOGRAPHIC CREDITS

Section of the New Design for Sir Nathaniel Curzon Baronet, at Kedleston.
now Lord Scarsdale
From North to South.